Fodor's® 99

Switzerland

Nancy Coons

The complete guide, thoroughly up-to-date

Packed with details that will make your trip

The must-see sights, off and on the beaten path

What to see, what to skip

Mix-and-match vacation itineraries

City strolls, countryside adventures

Smart lodging and dining options

Essential local do's and taboos

Transportation tips, distances and directions

Key contacts, savvy travel tips

When to go, what to pack

Clear, accurate, easy-to-use maps

Books to read, videos to watch, background essay

Fodor's Travel Publications, Inc.
New York • Toronto • London • Sydney • Auckland
www.fodors.previewtravel.com

Fodor's Switzerland

EDITOR: Jennifer J. Paull

Editorial Contributors: David Brown, Nancy Coons, Debbie Ebanks, Christina Knight, Kara Misenheimer, Ian Plenderleith, Jennifer Quale, Helayne Schiff, M. T. Schwartzman (Gold Guide editor), Beverly Stearns-Peterson, Lito Tejada-Flores, Susan Tuttle-Laube
Editorial Production: Nicole Revere
Maps: David Lindroth, *cartographer*; Bob Blake, *map editor*
Design: Fabrizio La Rocca, *creative director*; Guido Caroti, *associate art director*; Jolie Novak, *photo editor*
Production/Manufacturing: Mike Costa
Cover Photograph: Peter Guttman

Copyright

Special Sales

Fodor's Travel Publications are available at special discounts for bulk purchases for sales promotions or premiums. Special editions, including personalized covers, excerpts of existing guides, and corporate imprints, can be created in large quantities for special needs. For more information, contact your local bookseller or write to Special Markets, Fodor's Travel Publications, 201 East 50th Street, New York, NY 10022. Inquiries from Canada should be directed to your local Canadian bookseller or sent to Random House of Canada, Ltd., Marketing Department, 2775 Matheson Boulevard East, Mississauga, Ontario L4W 4P7. Inquiries from the United Kingdom should be sent to Fodor's Travel Publications, 20 Vauxhall Bridge Road, London SW1V 2SA, England.

PRINTED IN THE UNITED STATES OF AMERICA

10 9 8 7 6 5 4 3 2 1

CONTENTS

Maps and Charts

ON THE ROAD WITH FODOR'S

WHEN I PLAN A VACATION, the first thing I do is cast around among my friends and colleagues to find someone who's just been where I'm going. That's because there's no substitute for a recommendation from a good friend who knows your tastes, your budget, and your circumstances, someone who's just been there. Unfortunately, such friends are few and far between. So it's nice to know that there's Fodor's *Switzerland '99*.

In the first place, this book won't stay home when you hit the road. It will accompany you every step of the way, steering you away from wrong turns and wrong choices and never expecting a thing in return. It includes a wonderful, full-color map from Rand McNally, the world's largest commercial mapmaker. Most important of all, it's written and assiduously updated by the kind of people you *would* hit up for travel tips if you knew them. They're as choosy as your pickiest friend, and they have a wealth of insider's knowledge. In these pages, they don't send you chasing down every town and sight in Switzerland but have instead selected the best ones, the ones that are worthy of your time and money. To make it easy for you to put it all together in the time you have, they've created short, medium, and long itineraries and, in cities, neighborhood walks that you can mix and match in a snap. Just tear out the map at the perforation, and join us on the road in Switzerland.

About Our Writers

Our success in helping to make your trip the best of all possible vacations is a credit to the hard work of our extraordinary writers.

Nancy Coons has been tracing ancestral trails in Switzerland since moving to Europe in 1987, when she also began covering Luxembourg, Belgium, and much of northeastern France for Fodor's. Based in her 300-year-old farmhouse in Lorraine, she has written on European culture and food for the *Wall Street Journal, European Travel & Life, Opera News,* and *National Geographic Traveler.*

Debbie Ebanks has been living in Switzerland since 1994. After completing her M.A. in International Relations at the Graduate Institute of International Studies in Geneva, she is taking time off to raise her one-year-old daughter. A nonskier in an Alpine country, Debbie prefers to enjoy the mountains with her family at a slower pace—by hiking or rock climbing.

The first flight **Kara Misenheimer** took *anywhere* was to Switzerland. In more than a decade of constant contact with the country, she has made goat cheese in a hut, motorcycled over perilous passes, and had ski lessons from someone named Hans. Her search for broader cultural viewpoints has contributed to her career as a writer/producer in international media and marketing. When not backlit by an Alpine sunset or the flickering glow of her computer screen, she can be found on stage, singing with the Basel Opera.

Freelance journalist and full-time child-care provider **Ian Plenderleith** lives in Zürich. His favorite subject is the death of soccer through commercialization. He hopes that one day his great works of fiction will be published, but realizes that everyone involved in publishing is too busy to read them.

In 1991 **Jennifer Quale** moved from Manhattan to Vaud; her adopted town has more cows than people, and they all seem to live next door. Her favorite discovery during her Fodor's research was Noël Coward's house in Les Avants. She is currently working on a novel.

Beverly Stearns-Peterson is an American freelance writer and editor who has lived in a village south of Basel since 1984, within easy walking distance of three castles. She writes on a variety of topics, including business and finance, science, and culture.

Susan Tuttle-Laube has been showing Switzerland to family and friends since moving there in 1981. As an "outsider living on the inside," she enjoys discovering the details that make the difference between a good trip and a great one. Her book *Inside Outlandish* (Bergli Books,

Basel, Switzerland 1997) recounts her mostly humorous experiences as a foreigner living abroad.

We'd also like to thank the staff of the Swiss regional tourist offices, as well as Erica Lieben and Evelyne Mock of the Swiss National Tourist Office in New York, for their help with questions big and small.

Connections

We're pleased that the American Society of Travel Agents continues to endorse Fodor's as its guidebook of choice. ASTA is the world's largest and most influential travel trade association, operating in more than 170 countries, with 27,000 members pledged to adhere to a strict code of ethics reflecting the Society's motto, "Integrity in Travel." ASTA shares Fodor's devotion to providing smart, honest travel information and advice to travelers, and we've long recommended that our readers—even those who have guidebooks and traveling friends—consult ASTA member agents for the experience and professionalism they bring to your vacation planning.

On Fodor's Web site (www.fodors.com), check out the new Resource Center, an online companion to the Gold Guide section of this book, complete with useful hot links to related sites. In our forums, you can also get lively advice from other travelers and more great tips from Fodor's experts worldwide.

How to Use This Book

Organization

Up front is the **Gold Guide,** an easy-to-use section arranged alphabetically by topic. Under each listing you'll find tips and information that will help you accomplish what you need to in Switzerland. You'll also find addresses and telephone numbers of organizations and companies that offer destination-related services and detailed information and publications.

The first chapter in the guide, Destination: Switzerland helps get you in the mood for your trip. New and Noteworthy cues you in on trends and happenings, What's Where gets you oriented, Pleasures and Pastimes describes the activities and sights that make Switzerland unique, Great Itineraries lays out a selection of complete trips, Fodor's Choice showcases our top picks,

and Festivals and Seasonal Events alerts you to special events you'll want to seek out.

Chapters in *Switzerland '99* are arranged roughly by canton, starting with Zürich and moving clockwise. Each city chapter begins with Exploring information, which is divided into neighborhood sections; each recommends a walking or driving tour and lists sights in alphabetical order. Each regional chapter is divided by geographical area; within each area, towns are covered in logical geographical order, and attractive stretches of road and minor points of interest between them are indicated by the designation *En Route*. And within town sections, all restaurants and lodgings are grouped.

To help you decide what to visit in the time you have, all chapters begin with our recommended itineraries. The A to Z section that ends all chapters covers getting there and getting around. It also provides helpful contacts and resources.

At the end of the book you'll find Portraits, a wonderful essay about skiing, followed by suggestions for pretrip research, from recommended reading to movies on tape that use Switzerland as a backdrop.

Icons and Symbols

★	Our special recommendations
✕	Restaurant
🏨	Lodging establishment
✕🏨	Lodging establishment whose restaurant warrants a special trip
⬘	Campgrounds
☺	Good for kids (rubber duck)
☞	Sends you to another section of the guide for more information
✉	Address
☎	Telephone number
☉	Opening and closing times
💰	Admission prices (those we give apply to adults; substantially reduced fees are almost always available for children, students, and senior citizens)

Numbers in white and black circles ③ ❸ that appear on the maps, in the margins, and within the tours correspond to one another.

Dining and Lodging

The restaurants and lodgings we list are the cream of the crop in each price range. In regional chapters, price charts appear in the Pleasures and Pastimes section that follows each chapter introduction. In chapters devoted to a single city, price charts appear in the introductions to the Dining and Lodging sections.

Hotel Facilities

We always list the facilities that are available—but we don't specify whether you'll be charged extra to use them: When pricing accommodations, always ask what's included. In addition, assume that all rooms have private baths unless noted otherwise. When you book a room, be sure to mention if you have a disability or are traveling with children, if you prefer a private bath or a certain type of bed, or if you have specific dietary needs or other concerns.

Assume that hotels operate on the **European Plan** (EP, with no meals) unless we specify that they use the **Continental Plan** (CP, with a Continental breakfast daily). Particularly in ski resorts or in hotels where you've opted to stay for three days or more, you may be quoted a room price per person including *demipension* (half board). This means you've opted for breakfast included and to eat either lunch or dinner in the hotel, selecting from a limited, fixed menu. Unless you're holding out for gastronomic adventure, your best bet is to take half board. Most hotels will be flexible if you come in from the slopes craving a steaming pot of fondue, and they will subtract the day's pension supplement from your room price, charging you à la carte instead.

Restaurant Reservations and Dress Codes

Reservations are always a good idea; we mention them only when they're essential or are not accepted. Book as far ahead as you can and reconfirm as soon as you arrive. Unless otherwise noted, the restaurants listed are open daily for lunch and dinner. We mention dress only when men

are required to wear a jacket or a jacket and tie. Look for an overview of local dining-out habits in the Pleasures and Pastimes section that follows each chapter introduction.

Credit Cards

The following abbreviations are used: **AE**, American Express; **DC**, Diners Club; **MC**, MasterCard; and **V**, Visa.

Don't Forget to Write

You can use this book in the confidence that all prices and opening times are based on information supplied to us at press time; Fodor's cannot accept responsibility for any errors. Time inevitably brings changes, so always confirm information when it matters—especially if you're making a detour to visit a specific place.

Were the restaurants we recommended as described? Did our hotel picks exceed your expectations? Did you find a museum we recommended a waste of time? Keeping a travel guide fresh and up-to-date is a big job, and we welcome your feedback, positive *and* negative. If you have complaints, we'll look into them and revise our entries when the facts warrant it. If you've discovered a special place that we haven't included, we'll pass the information along to our correspondents and have them check it out. So send us your thoughts via E-mail at editors@fodors.com (specifying the name of the book on the subject line) or on paper in care of the Switzerland editor at Fodor's, 201 East 50th Street, New York, New York 10022. In the meantime, have a wonderful trip!

Karen Cure
Editorial Director

Switzerland (Suisse, Schweiz, Svizzera)

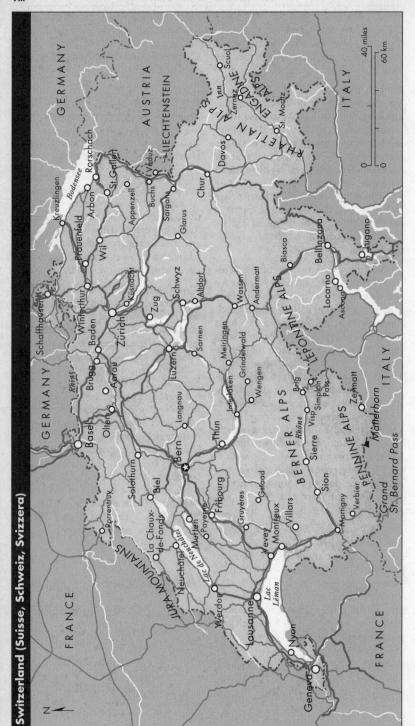

N

GERMANY

Kreuzlingen
Schaffhausen
Bodensee
Rorschach
Arbon
St. Gallen
Frauenfeld
Appenzell
Wil
Winterthur
Baden
Küsnacht
Zürich
Zug
Schwyz
Alldorf
Brugg
Aarau
Olten
Luzern
Sarnen
Langnau
Basel
Porrentruy
Solothurn
Biel
Bern
Thun
Interlaken
Meiringen
Grindelwald
Wengen
La Chaux-de-Fonds
Neuchâtel
Murten
Payerne
Fribourg
Gruyères
Gstaad
Yverdon
Lac de Neuchâtel
Vevey
Montreux
Villars
Lausanne
Lac Léman
Nyon
Geneva

JURA MOUNTAINS
FRANCE

Buchs
Vaduz
LIECHTENSTEIN
AUSTRIA
Sargans
Glarus
Chur
Davos
Scuol
Zernez
Ilanz
ENGADINE
RHAETIAN ALPS
St. Moritz
Inn

Wassen
Andermatt
Biasca
Bellinzona
Locarno
Ascona
Lugano
LEPONTINE ALPS

Brig
Visp
Simplon Pass
Sierre
Rhône
Sion
Zermatt
Matterhorn
Martigny
Verbier
PENNINE ALPS
Grand St. Bernard Pass

BERNER ALPS

Rhine

ITALY

FRANCE

40 miles
60 km

Cantons of Switzerland

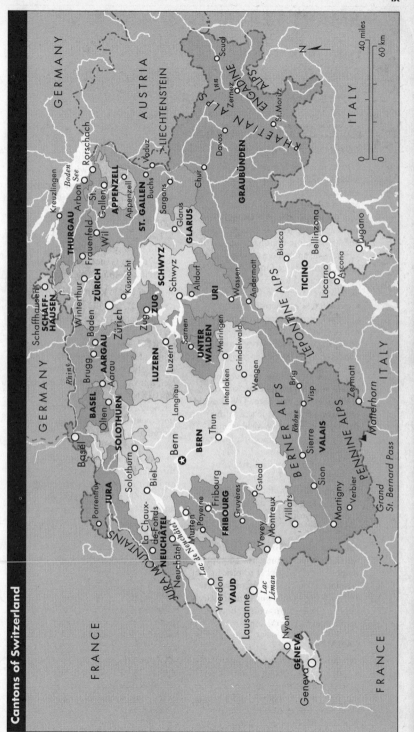

SMART TRAVEL TIPS A TO Z

Basic Information on Traveling in Switzerland, Savvy Tips to Make Your Trip a Breeze, and Companies and Organizations to Contact

AIR TRAVEL

BOOKING YOUR FLIGHT

Price is just one factor to consider when booking a flight: frequency of service and even a carrier's safety record are often just as important. Major airlines offer the greatest number of departures. Smaller airlines—including regional and no-frills airlines—usually have a limited number of flights daily. On the other hand, so-called low-cost airlines usually are cheaper, and their fares impose fewer restrictions, such as advance-purchase requirements. Safety-wise, low-cost carriers as a group have a good history—about equal to that of major carriers.

When you book, **look for nonstop flights** and **remember that "direct" flights stop at least once.** Try to **avoid connecting flights,** which require a change of plane. Two airlines may jointly operate a connecting flight, so ask if your airline operates every segment—you may find that your preferred carrier flies you only part of the way. International flights on a country's flag carrier are almost always nonstop; U.S. airlines often fly direct.

Ask your airline if it offers electronic ticketing, which eliminates all paperwork. There's no ticket to pick up or misplace. You go directly to the gate and give the agent your confirmation number. There's no worry about waiting on line at the airport.

CARRIERS

When flying internationally, you must usually choose among a domestic carrier, the national flag carrier of the country you are visiting, and a foreign carrier from a third country. National flag carriers have the greatest number of nonstops. Domestic carriers may have better connections to your hometown and serve a greater number of gateway cities. Third-party carriers may have a price advantage.

➤ MAJOR AIRLINES: **Air Canada** (☎ 800/776–3000) to Geneva, Zürich. **American Airlines** (☎ 800/433–7300) to Zürich. **Delta** (☎ 800/221–1212) to Zürich. **Swissair** (☎ 800/221–4750) to Geneva, Zürich. **Swiss World Airways** (☎ 011–800/11–767–767) to Geneva. **United Airlines** (☎ 800/241–6522) to Zürich.

➤ FROM THE U.K.: **British Airways** (☎ 0345/222–111) flies directly to Zürich from London's Heathrow or Gatwick airports, as does **Swissair** (☎ 0171/434–7300). There are nine flights daily. **Crossair** (☎ 0171/439–4144) offers direct service from London City, **Swissair** and **Aer Lingus** (☎ 0181/899–4747) from Manchester. Service to Geneva has greatly improved. There are now five nonstop flights daily by BA and four by Swissair from Heathrow. The flying time is 1 hour 35 minutes. There are three daily BA flights from Gatwick, and Crossair has three daily flights from London City Airport. Basel's airport (EuroAirport) has two British Airways flights from Heathrow daily, while Crossair offers three flights daily from Heathrow. Crossair also offers a weekly flight from Gatwick to Sion.

CHARTERS

Charters usually have the lowest fares but are the least dependable. Departures are infrequent and seldom on time; flights can be delayed for up to 48 hours or can be canceled for any reason up to 10 days before you're scheduled to leave. Itineraries and prices can change after you've booked your flight.

In the U.S., the Department of Transportation's Aviation Consumer Protection Division has jurisdiction over

THE GOLD GUIDE / SMART TRAVEL TIPS

charters and provides a certain degree of protection. The DOT requires that money paid to charter operators be held in escrow, so if you can't pay with a credit card, **always make your check payable to a charter carrier's escrow account.** The name of the bank should be in the charter contract. If you have any problems with a charter operator, contact the DOT (☞ Airline Complaints, *below*). If you buy a charter package that includes both air and land arrangements, remember that the escrow requirement applies only to the air component.

CONSOLIDATORS

Consolidators buy tickets for scheduled international flights at reduced rates from the airlines, then sell them at prices that beat the best fare available directly from the airlines, usually without restrictions. Sometimes you can even get your money back if you need to return the ticket. Carefully read the fine print detailing penalties for changes and cancellations, and **confirm your consolidator reservation with the airline.**

➤ CONSOLIDATORS: **Cheap Tickets** (☎ 800/377–1000). **Discount Travel Network** (☎ 800/576–1600). **Unitravel** (☎ 800/325–2222). **Up & Away Travel** (☎ 212/889–2345). **World Travel Network** (☎ 800/409–6753).

COURIERS

When you fly as a courier, you trade your checked-luggage space for a ticket deeply subsidized by a courier service. It's all perfectly legitimate, but there are restrictions: You can usually book your flight only a week or two in advance, your length of stay may be set for a certain number of days, and you probably won't be able to book a companion on the same flight.

Air Courier Association (✉ 15000 W. 6th Ave., Suite 203, Golden, CO 80401, ☎ 800/282–1202, www.air-courier.org).

International Association of Air Travel Couriers (✉ 220 S. Dixie Hwy. #3, P.O. Box 1349, Lake Worth, FL 33460, ☎ 561/582–8320, FAX 561/582–1581. www.courier.org).

Now Voyager Travel (✉ 74 Varick St., Suite 307, New York, NY 10013, ☎ 212/431–1616, FAX 212/219–1753 or 212/334–5243, www.nowvoyager-travel.com).

CUTTING COSTS

The least expensive airfares to Switzerland are priced for round-trip travel and usually must be purchased in advance. It's smart to **call a number of airlines, and when you are quoted a good price, book it on the spot**—the same fare may not be available the next day. Airlines generally allow you to change your return date for a fee. If you don't use your ticket, you can apply the cost toward the purchase of a new ticket, again for a small charge. However, most low-fare tickets are nonrefundable. To get the lowest airfare, **check different routings.** Compare prices of flights to and from different airports if your destination or home city has more than one gateway. Also price off-peak flights, which may be significantly less expensive.

Travel agents, especially those who specialize in finding the lowest fares (☞ Discounts & Deals, *below*), can be especially helpful when booking a plane ticket. When you're quoted a price, **ask your agent if the price is likely to get any lower.** Good agents know the seasonal fluctuations of airfares and can usually anticipate a sale or fare war. However, waiting can be risky: The fare could go *up* as seats become scarce, and you may wait so long that your preferred flight sells out. A wait-and-see strategy works best if your plans are flexible. If you must arrive and depart on certain dates, don't delay.

DOMESTIC FLIGHTS

The entire country of Switzerland is smaller in area than the state of West Virginia, so flying from one region to another is a luxury that, considering the efficiency of the trains, few travelers require—unless there's a convenient connection from your intercontinental arrival point (Geneva, Zürich) to a lesser airport (Basel, Bern, Lugano, Saint-Moritz). Crossair is Switzerland's domestic airline, servicing local airports and various Continental cities as well:

THE GOLD GUIDE / SMART TRAVEL TIPS

Brussels, Düsseldorf, Florence, Nice, Paris, London, and Venice.

For 20 SF per bag round-trip, air travelers on Swissair and partner airlines holding tickets or passes on Swiss Federal Railways can forward their luggage to their final destination, allowing them to make stops on the way unencumbered; the baggage is retrieved from the train station of the final destination. Baggage check-in and issuance of boarding passes is also possible at 116 train stations in Switzerland. A brochure "Fly–Rail Baggage" is available free of charge, in English, from the Swiss Federal Railways (☎ 157–2222; 1.19 SF/min).

CHECK IN & BOARDING

Airlines routinely overbook planes, assuming that not everyone with a ticket will show up, but sometimes everyone does. When that happens, airlines ask for volunteers to give up their seats. In return these volunteers usually get a certificate for a free flight and are rebooked on the next flight out. If there are not enough volunteers, the airline must choose who will be denied boarding. The first to get bumped are passengers who checked in late and those flying on discounted tickets, so **get to the gate and check in as early as possible,** especially during peak periods.

Although the trend on international flights is to drop reconfirmation requirements, many airlines still ask you to reconfirm each leg of your international itinerary. Failure to do so may result in your reservation being canceled.

Always **bring a government-issued photo ID to the airport.** You may be asked to show it before you are allowed to check in.

ENJOYING THE FLIGHT

For more legroom, **request an emergency-aisle seat.** Don't sit in the row in front of the emergency aisle or in front of a bulkhead, where seats may not recline.

If you don't like airline food, **ask for special meals when booking.** These can be vegetarian, low cholesterol, or kosher, for example.

When flying internationally try to maintain a normal routine to help fight jet lag. At night, **get some sleep.** By day, **eat light meals, drink water (not alcohol), and move around the cabin** to stretch your legs.

Many carriers have prohibited smoking on all their international flights; others allow smoking only on certain routes or certain departures, so **contact your carrier regarding its smoking policy.**

FLYING TIMES

Flying time is seven hours from New York, 10 hours from Chicago, and 14 hours from Los Angeles.

HOW TO COMPLAIN

If your baggage goes astray or your flight goes awry, complain right away. Most carriers require that you **file a claim immediately.**

➤ AIRLINE COMPLAINTS: U.S. Department of Transportation **Aviation Consumer Protection Division** (✉ C-75, Room 4107, Washington, DC 20590, ☎ 202/366–2220). **Federal Aviation Administration Consumer Hotline** (☎ 800/322–7873).

AIRPORTS

The major gateways are Zürich and Geneva.

➤ MAJOR AIRPORTS: Zürich: **Kloten Airport** (☎ 01/8162211). Geneva: **Cointrin International Airport** 022/7993111).

➤ OTHER AIRPORTS: Lugano: **Aeroporto Lugano-Agno** (☎ 091/6101212). **Upper Engadine:** (✉ CH-7503, Samedan, 081/8525433). Bern: **Belpmoos** (031/9602111). **Sion:** (✉ Rte. de Aeroport, CH-1950, ☎ 027/3222480).

BIKE TRAVEL

Bikes can be rented at all train stations and returned to any station. Rates for standard bikes are 17 SF per half day, 22 SF per day, and 88 SF per week. Mountain bikes are 24 SF per half day, 30 SF per day, or 120 SF per week. Groups get reductions according to the number of bikes. Individuals must make a reservation by 6 PM the day before they plan to use the bike, groups a week in advance. There is a daily charge of 6 SF to transport a bicycle on local trains and 12 SF on Inter-City trains. Local tourist offices are the best places to get cycling maps for specific areas; you can also contact **Cartes Cyclistes** (⊠ Case Postale, CH-3360 Herzogenbuchsee, ☎ 062/9615151, FAX 062/9616017).

BIKES IN FLIGHT

Most airlines will accommodate bikes as luggage, provided they are dismantled and put into a box. Call to see if your airline sells bike boxes (about $5; bike bags are at least $100) although you can often pick them up free at bike shops. International travelers can sometimes substitute a bike for a piece of checked luggage for free; otherwise, it will cost about $100. Domestic and Canadian airlines charge a $25–$50 fee.

BOAT & FERRY TRAVEL

All of Switzerland's larger lakes are crisscrossed by elegant steamers, some of them restored paddle steamers. Their café-restaurants serve drinks, snacks, and hot food at standard mealtimes; toilet facilities are provided. Service continues year-round but is very much reduced in winter. Unlimited travel is free to holders of the Swiss Pass. If you are not traveling by train, **consider the Swiss Boat Pass,** which for 35 SF allows half-fare travel on all lake steamers for the entire year (January 1–December 31). The Swiss Half–Fare Travel card (☞ Train Travel, *below*) may also be used for boat travel.

BUS TRAVEL

Switzerland's famous yellow postbuses, with their stentorian tritone horns, link main cities with villages off the beaten track and even crawl over the highest mountain passes. Both postbuses and city buses follow posted schedules to the minute: You can set your watch by them. Free timetables can be picked up in post offices, where the buses usually depart. Watch for the yellow sign with the picture of a hunting horn. The Swiss Pass (☞ Train Travel, *below*) gives unlimited travel on the postbuses. Postbuses cater especially to

hikers: Good walking itineraries are available at postbus stops.

BUSINESS HOURS

Businesses still close for lunch in Switzerland, generally from 12:30 to 2, but this is changing, especially in larger cities. All remain closed on Sunday, and many stay closed through Monday morning. Banks are open weekdays from 8:30 to 4:30. Museums generally close on Monday. There is, however, an increasing trend toward staying open until late evening hours, usually on Thursday or Friday evening. Stores in train stations often stay open until 9 PM; in Geneva and Zürich airports, shops are open on Sunday.

CAMERAS & COMPUTERS

EQUIPMENT PRECAUTIONS

Always **keep your film, tape, or computer disks out of the sun.** Carry an extra supply of batteries, and **be prepared to turn on your camera, camcorder, or laptop** to prove to security personnel that the device is real. Always **ask for hand inspection of film,** which becomes clouded after successive exposure to airport X-ray machines, and **keep videotapes and computer disks away from metal detectors.**

TRAVEL PHOTOGRAPHY

➤ PHOTO HELP: **Kodak Information Center** (☎ 800/242–2424). *Kodak Guide to Shooting Great Travel Pictures,* available in bookstores or from Fodor's Travel Publications (☎ 800/533–6478; $16.50 plus $4 shipping).

CAR RENTAL

If booked from overseas, rates in Zürich and Geneva begin at $45 a day and $178 a week for an economy car with air-conditioning, a manual transmission, and unlimited mileage. This does not include the 6.5% tax on car rentals. Try to arrange for a rental before you go; rentals booked in Switzerland are considerably more expensive.

➤ MAJOR AGENCIES: **Alamo** (☎ 800/522–9696, 0800/272–2000 in the U.K.). **Avis** (☎ 800/331–1084, 800/

879–2847 in Canada, 008/225–533 in Australia). **Budget** (☎ 800/527–0700, 0800/181181 in the U.K.). **Dollar** (☎ 800/800–4000; 0990/565656 in the U.K., where it is known as Eurodollar). **Hertz** (☎ 800/654–3001, 800/263–0600 in Canada, 0345/555888 in the U.K., 03/9222–2523 in Australia, 03/358–6777 in New Zealand). **National InterRent** (☎ 800/227–3876; 0345/222525 in the U.K., where it is known as Europcar InterRent).

CUTTING COSTS

To get the best deal, **book through a travel agent who is willing to shop around.**

Also **ask your travel agent about a company's customer-service record.** How has the company responded to late plane arrivals and vehicle mishaps? Are there often lines at the rental counter? If you're traveling during a holiday period, does a confirmed reservation guarantee you a car?

Be sure to **look into wholesalers,** companies that do not own fleets but rent in bulk from those that do and often offer better rates than traditional car-rental operations. Prices are best during off-peak periods. Rentals booked through wholesalers must be paid for before you leave the United States.

➤ RENTAL WHOLESALERS: **Auto Europe** (☎ 207/842–2000 or 800/223–5555, FAX 800–235–6321). **DER Travel Services** (✉ 9501 W. Devon Ave., Rosemont, IL 60018, ☎ 800/782–2424, FAX 800/282–7474 for information or 800/860–9944 for brochures). **Europe by Car** (☎ 212/581–3040 or 800/223–1516, FAX 212/246–1458). **Kemwel Holiday Autos** (☎ 914/835–5555 or 800/678–0678, FAX 914/835–5126).

INSURANCE

When driving a rented car, you are generally responsible for any damage to or loss of the vehicle. Before you rent, **see what coverage you already have** under the terms of your personal auto-insurance policy and credit cards.

Collision policies that car-rental companies sell for European rentals typically do not cover stolen vehicles. Before you buy additional coverage for theft, check with your credit-card company and personal auto insurance—you may already be covered.

REQUIREMENTS

In Switzerland your own driver's license is acceptable. An International Driver's Permit is a good idea; it's available from the American or Canadian automobile association, and, in the United Kingdom, from the Automobile Association or Royal Automobile Club. These international permits are universally recognized, and having one in your wallet may save you a problem with the local authorities.

SURCHARGES

Before you pick up a car in one city and leave it in another, **ask about drop-off charges or one-way service fees,** which can be substantial. Note, too, that some rental agencies charge extra if you return the car before the time specified in your contract. To avoid a hefty refueling fee, **fill the tank just before you turn in the car,** but be aware that gas stations near the rental outlet may overcharge.

CAR TRAVEL

AUTO CLUBS

➤ IN AUSTRALIA: **Australian Automobile Association** (☎ 06/247–7311).

➤ IN CANADA: **Canadian Automobile Association** (CAA, ☎ 613/247–0117).

➤ IN NEW ZEALAND: **New Zealand Automobile Association** (☎ 09/377–4660).

➤ IN THE U.K.: **Automobile Association** (AA, ☎ 0990/500–600), **Royal Automobile Club** (RAC, ☎ 0990/722–722 for membership, 0345/121–345 for insurance).

➤ IN THE U.S.: **American Automobile Association** (☎ 800/564–6222).

EMERGENCY SERVICES

All road **breakdowns** should be called in to the central Swiss-wide emergency number, 140. If you are on the autoroute, pull over to the shoulder and look for arrows pointing you to the nearest orange radio-telephone, called Bornes SOS; use these phones instead of your mobile phone, as police can locate you instantly and send help. There are SOS phones every kilometer (half mile), on alternate sides of the autoroute.

FROM THE U.K. BY FERRY

In addition to the relatively swift (and expensive) Channel Tunnel (Chunnel), on which cars piggyback trains to cross the channel from Dover to Boulogne, there are many drive-on/drive-off car ferry services across the Channel, but only a few are suitable as a means of getting to Switzerland. The situation is complicated by the different pricing systems operated by ferry companies and the many off-peak fares, and by the tolls charged by France on some of its motorways; these add up, particularly if you drive long distances. To avoid the tolls, **take a northerly route through Belgium or the Netherlands and Germany,** where motorways are free. The crossings for this route are Felixstowe or Dover to Zeebrugge; Sheerness to Vlissingen; and Ramsgate to Dunkirk. All these Continental ports have good road connections, and Switzerland can be reached in a day of hard driving.

GASOLINE

Unleaded (*sans plomb* or *bleifrei*) gas costs around 1.17 SF per liter, and super costs around 1.30 SF per liter. Leaded regular is no longer available. Prices are slightly higher in mountain areas. **Have some 10 SF and 20 SF notes available,** as many gas stations (especially in the mountains) offer vending-machine gas even when they're closed. Simply slide in a bill and fill your tank. Many of these machines also now accept major credit cards with precoded pin codes (☞ Money, *below*). You can get a receipt if you ask the machine for it.

PARKING

Parking areas are clearly marked. Parking in public lots normally costs 2 SF for the first hour, increasing by 1 SF every half hour thereafter.

ROAD CONDITIONS

Swiss roads are usually well surfaced but wind around considerably—especially in the mountains—so **don't plan on achieving high average speeds.** When estimating likely travel times, look carefully at the map: There may be only 32 km (20 mi) between one point and another—but there may be an Alpine pass in the way. There is a well-developed highway network, though some notable gaps still exist in the south along an east–west line, roughly between Lugano and Sion. A combination of steep or winding routes and hazardous weather means that some roads will be closed in winter. Signs are posted at the beginning of the climb.

To find out about road conditions, traffic jams, itineraries, etc., there are two places to turn: The **Swiss Automobile Club** has a number (☎ 031/3121515, ℻ 031/3110310) with operators standing by 24 hours a day to provide information in all languages. Dues-paying members of the **Touring Club of Switzerland** may call ☎ 022/7358000 for similar information. Note that neither of these numbers gets you breakdown service (☞ *below*). For frequent and precise information in Swiss languages, you can dial 163, or tune in to local radio stations.

RULES OF THE ROAD

Driving is on the right. In built-up areas, the speed limit is 50 kph (30 mph); on main highways, it's 80 kph (50 mph); on expressways, the limit is 120 kph (75 mph).

Children under 12 are not permitted to sit in the front seat. **Use headlights** in heavy rain or poor visibility and in road tunnels—they are compulsory. Always **carry your valid license and car-registration papers;** there are occasional roadblocks to check them. **Wear seat belts** in the front and back seats—they are required.

To use the main highways, you must display a sticker, or *vignette,* in the lower left-hand corner of the windshield. You can buy it at the border (cash only; neighboring foreign currencies can be changed). It costs 40 SF and can also be purchased from any post office and from most gas stations; it's valid to the end of the year.

Cars rented within Switzerland already have these stickers; if you rent a car elsewhere in Europe, **ask if the company will provide the vignette for you.**

Traffic going up a mountain has priority except for postbuses coming down. A sign with a yellow post horn on a blue background means that postbuses have priority.

In winter, **use snow chains,** compulsory in some areas and advisable in all. Snow-chain service stations have signs marked SERVICE DE CHAÎNES À NEIGE or SCHNEEKETTENDIENST; snow chains are available for rent.

If you have an accident, even a minor one, you must call the police.

CHILDREN & TRAVEL

CHILDREN IN SWITZERLAND

Be sure to plan ahead and **involve your youngsters** as you outline your trip. When packing, include things to keep them busy en route. On sightseeing days try to schedule activities of special interest to your children. If you are renting a car, don't forget to **arrange for a car seat** when you reserve.

➤ BABY-SITTING: Supervised playrooms are available in some of the better Swiss hotels, and many winter resorts also provide lists of reliable baby-sitters. For recommended local sitters, **check with your hotel desk.**

FLYING

If your children are two or older, **ask about children's airfares.** As a general rule, infants under two not occupying a seat fly at greatly reduced fares or even for free.

In general, the adult baggage allowance applies to children paying half or more of the adult fare. When booking, **ask about carry-on allowances for those traveling with infants.** In general, for babies charged 10% of the adult fare, you are allowed one carry-on bag and a collapsible stroller, which may have to be checked; you may be limited to less if the flight is full.

Experts agree that it's a good idea to use safety seats aloft for children weighing less than 40 pounds. Airlines, however, can set their own policies: U.S. carriers allow FAA-approved models but usually require that you buy a ticket, even if your child would otherwise ride free, since the seats must be strapped into regular seats. Airline rules vary, so it's important to **check your airline's policy about using safety seats during takeoff and landing.** Safety seats cannot obstruct the movement of other passengers in the row, so get an appropriate seat assignment as early as possible.

When making your reservation, **request children's meals or a free-standing bassinet** if you need them; the latter is available only to those seated at the bulkhead, where there's enough legroom. Remember, however, that bulkhead seats may not have their own overhead bins, and there's no storage space in front of you—a major inconvenience.

GETTING AROUND

Families traveling together in Switzerland should **buy a Family Card,** a special pass (20 SF if purchased in Switzerland or free with the purchase of a Swiss Pass or Europass) that allows children under 16 to travel free on trains, postbuses (☞ Bus Travel, *above*), and boats when accompanied by ticket-holding parents or guardians. The pass is valid for one year. Adults must hold a valid Swiss Pass, Swiss Card, Swiss Transfer Ticket, or Eurail tariff ticket to obtain the Family Card, available at any Swiss train station, for their children (☞ Train Travel, *below*).

GROUP TRAVEL

When planning to take your kids on a tour, look for companies that specialize in family travel.

➤ FAMILY-FRIENDLY TOUR OPERATORS: **Grandtravel** (✉ 6900 Wisconsin Ave., Suite 706, Chevy Chase, MD 20815, ☎ 301/986–0790 or 800/247–7651) for people traveling with grandchildren ages 7–17. **Families Welcome!** (✉ 92 N. Main St., Ashland, OR 97520, ☎ 541/482–6121 or 800/326–0724, FAX 541/482–0660).

LODGING

In many Swiss hotels, children six and under may stay in their parents' room at no extra charge; be sure to **ask about the cutoff age.** Some may charge extra for cribs, and cribs with sides are not always available. Children from 6 to 12 generally pay 50% of the adult rate; those 13–16 pay 70%. Apartments, with separate rooms and full hotel services, are also available.

Many hotels offer special facilities and services for families with children. Provisions range from supervised children's playrooms to special children's menus and organized family walks and visits.

➤ ORGANIZATIONS: For listings of family hotels throughout the country, contact the **Swiss Hotel Association** (✉ Monbijoustr. 130, Postfach, CH-3001 Bern, ☎ 031/3704111, FAX 031/3704444) or **Switzerland Tourism** (☞ Visitor Information, *below*).

CHILDREN'S CAMPS & HOLIDAY COURSES

Every summer, some 120 private schools in Switzerland offer leisurely language study and recreation courses for primary and secondary school age children from around the world. Summer camps similar to those in the United States are also available. Ask Switzerland Tourism (☞ Visitor Information, *below*) for a copy of "Holiday and Language Courses," a list of camps and summer programs in Switzerland.

CONSUMER PROTECTION

Whenever possible, **pay with a major credit card** so you can cancel payment or get reimbursed if there's a problem, provided that you can provide documentation. This is the best way to pay, whether you're buying travel arrangements before your trip or shopping at your destination.

If you're doing business with a particular company for the first time, **contact your local Better Business Bureau and the attorney general's offices** in your state and the company's home state, as well. Have any complaints been filed?

Finally, if you're buying a package or tour, always **consider travel insurance** that includes default coverage (☞ Insurance, *below*).

➤ LOCAL BBBs: **Council of Better Business Bureaus** (✉ 4200 Wilson Blvd., Suite 800, Arlington, VA 22203, ☎ 703/276–0100, FAX 703/525–8277).

CUSTOMS & DUTIES

When shopping, **keep receipts** for all of your purchases. Upon reentering the country, **be ready to show customs officials what you've bought.** If you feel a duty is incorrect, appeal the assessment. If you object to the way your clearance was handled, get the inspector's badge number. In either case, first ask to see a supervisor, then write to the appropriate authorities, beginning with the port director at your point of entry.

IN SWITZERLAND

Entering Switzerland, an overseas visitor 17 years or older may bring in 400 cigarettes or 100 cigars or 500 grams of tobacco; 2 liters of alcohol up to 15 proof; and a liter of alcohol over 15 proof. When entering from a European country, tobacco is restricted to 200 cigarettes or 50 cigars or 250 grams of tobacco. Medicine, such as insulin, is allowed for personal use only.

IN AUSTRALIA

Australia residents who are 18 or older may bring back A$400 worth of souvenirs and gifts (including jewelry), 250 cigarettes or 250 grams of tobacco, and 1,125 ml of alcohol (including wine, beer, and spirits). Residents under 18 may bring back A$200 worth of goods.

➤ INFORMATION: **Australian Customs Service** (Regional Director, ✉ Box 8, Sydney, NSW 2001, ☎ 02/9213–2000, FAX 02/9213–4000).

IN CANADA

Canadian residents who have been out of Canada for at least seven days may bring in C$500 worth of goods duty-free. If you've been away less than seven days but more than 48 hours, the duty-free allowance drops to C$200; if your trip lasts 24–48 hours, the allowance is C$50. You may not pool allowances with family members. Goods claimed under the C$500 exemption may follow you by mail; those claimed under the

THE GOLD GUIDE / SMART TRAVEL TIPS

lesser exemptions must accompany you. Alcohol and tobacco products may be included in the seven-day and 48-hour exemptions but not in the 24-hour exemption. If you meet the age requirements of the province or territory through which you reenter Canada, you may bring in, duty-free, 1.14 liters (40 imperial ounces) of wine or liquor *or* 24 12-ounce cans or bottles of beer or ale. If you are 16 or older, you may bring in, duty-free, 200 cigarettes and 50 cigars.

You may send an unlimited number of gifts worth up to C$60 each duty-free to Canada. Label the package UNSOLICITED GIFT—VALUE UNDER $60. Alcohol and tobacco are excluded.

➤ INFORMATION: **Revenue Canada** (✉ 2265 St. Laurent Blvd. S, Ottawa, Ontario K1G 4K3, ☎ 613/993–0534, 800/461–9999 in Canada).

IN NEW ZEALAND

Although greeted with a *"Haere Mai"* ("Welcome to New Zealand"), homeward-bound residents with goods to declare must present themselves for inspection. If you're 17 or older, you may bring back $700 worth of souvenirs and gifts. Your duty-free allowance also includes 4.5 liters of wine or beer; one 1,125-ml bottle of spirits; and either 200 cigarettes, 250 grams of tobacco, 50 cigars, or a combo of all three up to 250 grams.

➤ INFORMATION: **New Zealand Customs** (✉ Custom House, ✉ 50 Anzac Ave., Box 29, Auckland, ☎ 09/359–6655 or 09/309–2978).

IN THE U.K.

From countries outside the EU, including Switzerland, you may import, duty-free, 200 cigarettes or 50 cigars; 1 liter of spirits or 2 liters of fortified or sparkling wine or liqueurs; 2 liters of still table wine; 60 milliliters of perfume; 250 milliliters of toilet water; plus £136 worth of other goods, including gifts and souvenirs.

➤ INFORMATION: **HM Customs and Excise** (✉ Dorset House, ✉ Stamford St., London SE1 9NG, ☎ 0171/202–4227).

IN THE U.S.

U.S. residents may bring home $400 worth of foreign goods duty-free if they've been out of the country for at least 48 hours (and if they haven't used the $400 allowance or any part of it in the past 30 days).

U.S. residents 21 and older may bring back 1 liter of alcohol duty-free. In addition, regardless of your age, you are allowed 200 cigarettes and 100 non-Cuban cigars. Antiques, which the U.S. Customs Service defines as objects more than 100 years old, enter duty-free, as do original works of art done entirely by hand, including paintings, drawings, and sculptures.

You may also send packages home duty-free: up to $200 worth of goods for personal use, with a limit of one parcel per addressee per day (and no alcohol or tobacco products or perfume worth more than $5); label the package PERSONAL USE and attach a list of its contents and their retail value. Do not label the package UNSOLICITED GIFT, or your duty-free exemption will drop to $100. Mailed items do not affect your duty-free allowance on your return.

➤ INFORMATION: **U.S. Customs Service** (Inquiries, ✉ Box 7407, Washington, DC 20044, ☎ 202/927–6724; complaints, Office of Regulations and Rulings, ✉ 1301 Constitution Ave. NW, Washington, DC 20229; registration of equipment, Resource Management, ✉ 1301 Constitution Ave. NW, Washington, DC 20229, ☎ 202/927–0540).

DISABILITIES & ACCESSIBILITY

ACCESS IN SWITZERLAND

In Switzerland, most forms of public transportation offer special provisions, and accessible hotels are available in many areas of the country.

➤ LOCAL RESOURCES: **Mobility International Schweiz** (✉ Froburgstr. 4, CH-4601 Olten, ☎ 062/2068835, FAX 062/2068839) for information on special tours and travel. **Switzerland Tourism** (☞ Visitor Information, *below*) for a copy of "Swiss Hotel Guide for the Disabled," published by the Swiss Hotel Association in cooperation with the **Swiss Association for**

Disabled Persons (✉ Froburgstr. 4, CH-4601 Olten, ☎ 062/2068888, ℻ 062/2068889). This detailed guide to Swiss hotels offering facilities for guests with disabilities distinguishes between properties appropriate for visitors in wheelchairs and those suitable for visitors with walking impairments.

DRIVING

Foreign visitors with either the Disabled Badge of their country or the International Wheelchair Badge mounted inside the windshield of their car are entitled to use parking spaces reserved for people with disabilities throughout the country. Motorists who cannot walk unaided can obtain a special permit for parking privileges, as well as the international badge mentioned above, from the local police authority.

MAKING RESERVATIONS

When discussing accessibility with an operator or reservations agent, **ask hard questions.** Are there any stairs, inside *or* out? Are there grab bars next to the toilet *and* in the shower/tub? How wide is the doorway to the room? To the bathroom? For the most extensive facilities meeting the latest legal specifications, **opt for newer accommodations,** which are more likely to have been designed with access in mind. Older buildings or ships may have more limited facilities. Be sure to **discuss your needs before booking.**

TRAIN TRAVEL

Throughout the Swiss Federal Railways, wheelchairs are often available; inform the stations ahead of time that you will need one. In addition, ramps or lifts and wheelchair-accessible toilets have been installed in more than 100 stations. All InterCity and long-distance express trains and more than two-thirds of the country's regional shuttle trains now have wheelchair compartments. A brochure describing services for disabled travelers is available (in French, German and Italian) from the Swiss Federal Railways (☞ Train Travel, below).

TRANSPORTATION

➤ COMPLAINTS: **Disability Rights Section** (✉ U.S. Department of Justice, Civil Rights Division, ✉ Box 66738, Washington, DC 20035-6738, ☎ 202/514–0301 or 800/514–0301, TTY 202/514–0383 or 800/514–0383, ℻ 202/307–1198) for general complaints. **Aviation Consumer Protection Division** (☞ Air Travel, *above*) for airline-related problems. **Civil Rights Office** (✉ U.S. Department of Transportation, Departmental Office of Civil Rights, S-30, ✉ 400 7th St. SW, Room 10215, Washington, DC 20590, ☎ 202/366–4648, ℻ 202/366–9371) for problems with surface transportation.

TRAVEL AGENCIES & TOUR OPERATORS

As a whole, the travel industry has become more aware of the needs of travelers with disabilities. In the U.S., the Americans with Disabilities Act requires that travel firms serve the needs of all travelers. Note, though, that some agencies and operators specialize in making travel arrangements for individuals and groups with disabilities.

➤ TRAVELERS WITH MOBILITY PROBLEMS: **Access Adventures** (✉ 206 Chestnut Ridge Rd., Rochester, NY 14624, ☎ 716/889–9096), run by a former physical-rehabilitation counselor. **Accessible Journeys** (✉ 35 W. Sellers Ave., Ridley Park, PA 19078, ☎ 610/521–0339 or 800/846–4537, ℻ 610/521–6959) for escorted tours exclusively for travelers with mobility impairments. **Flying Wheels Travel** (✉ 143 W. Bridge St., Box 382, Owatonna, MN 55060, ☎ 507/451–5005 or 800/535–6790, ℻ 507/451–1685), a travel agency specializing in customized tours and itineraries worldwide. **Hinsdale Travel Service** (✉ 201 E. Ogden Ave., Suite 100, Hinsdale, IL 60521, ☎ 630/325–1335), a travel agency that benefits from the advice of wheelchair traveler Janice Perkins.

DISCOUNTS & DEALS

Be a smart shopper and **compare all your options** before making any choice. A plane ticket bought with a

THE GOLD GUIDE / SMART TRAVEL TIPS

promotional coupon may not be cheaper than the least expensive fare from a discount ticket agency. For high-price travel purchases, such as packages or tours, keep in mind that what you get is just as important as what you save. Just because something is cheap doesn't mean it's a bargain.

CLUBS & COUPONS

Many companies sell discounts in the form of travel clubs and coupon books, but these cost money. You must use participating advertisers to get a deal, and only after you recoup the initial membership cost or book price do you begin to save. If you plan to use the club or coupons frequently, you may save considerably. Before signing up, find out what discounts you get for free.

➤ DISCOUNT CLUBS: **Entertainment Travel Editions** (✉ 2125 Butterfield Rd., Troy, MI 48084, ☎ 800/445–4137; $20–$51, depending on destination). **Great American Traveler** (✉ Box 27965, Salt Lake City, UT 84127, ☎ 801/974–3033 or 800/548–2812; $49.95 per year). **Moment's Notice Discount Travel Club** (✉ 7301 New Utrecht Ave., Brooklyn, NY 11204, ☎ 718/234–6295; $25 per year, single or family). **Privilege Card International** (✉ 237 E. Front St., Youngstown, OH 44503, ☎ 330/746–5211 or 800/236–9732; $74.95 per year). **Sears's Mature Outlook** (✉ Box 9390, Des Moines, IA 50306, ☎ 800/336–6330; $19.95 per year). **Travelers Advantage** (✉ CUC Travel Service, ✉ 3033 S. Parker Rd., Suite 1000, Aurora, CO 80014, ☎ 800/548–1116 or 800/648–4037; $59.95 per year, single or family). **Worldwide Discount Travel Club** (✉ 1674 Meridian Ave., Miami Beach, FL 33139, ☎ 305/534–2082; $50 per year family, $40 single).

CREDIT-CARD BENEFITS

When you use your credit card to make travel purchases you may get free travel-accident insurance, collision-damage insurance, and medical or legal assistance, depending on the card and the bank that issued it. American Express, MasterCard, and Visa provide one or more of these services, so **get a copy of your credit card's travel-benefits policy.** If you are a member of an auto club, always **ask hotel and car-rental reservations agents about auto-club discounts.** Some clubs offer additional discounts on tours, cruises, and admission to attractions.

DISCOUNT RESERVATIONS

To save money, **look into discount-reservations services** with toll-free numbers, which use their buying power to get a better price on hotels, airline tickets, even car rentals. When booking a room, always **call the hotel's local toll-free number** (if one is available) rather than the central reservations number—you'll often get a better price. Always ask about special packages or corporate rates.

When shopping for the best deal on hotels and car rentals, **look for guaranteed exchange rates,** which protect you against a falling dollar. With your rate locked in, you won't pay more, even if the price goes up in the local currency.

➤ AIRLINE TICKETS: ☎ **800/FLY–4–LESS.**

➤ HOTEL ROOMS: **Hotels Plus** (☎ 800/235–0909). **International Marketing & Travel Concepts** (☎ 800/790–4682). **Steigenberger Reservation Service** (☎ 800/223–5652). **Travel Interlink** (☎ 800/888–5898).

PACKAGE DEALS

Packages and guided tours can save you money, but don't confuse the two. When you buy a package, your travel remains independent, just as though you had planned and booked the trip yourself. Fly/drive packages, which combine airfare and car rental, are often a good deal. If you **buy a rail/drive pass,** you'll save on train tickets and car rentals. All Eurailpass and Europass holders get a discount on Eurostar fares through the Channel Tunnel.

ELECTRICITY

To use your U.S.-purchased electric-powered equipment, **bring a converter and adapter.** The electrical current in Switzerland is 220 volts, 50 cycles alternating current (AC); wall outlets take Continental-type plugs, which have two round prongs.

If your appliances are dual-voltage, you'll need only an adapter. Don't use 110-volt outlets, marked FOR SHAVERS ONLY, for high-wattage appliances such as blow-dryers. Most laptops operate equally well on 110 and 220 volts and so require only an adapter.

EMERGENCIES

Anglo-Phone (☎ 1575014), a 24-hour English-language hot line, gives information on what to do in an emergency, besides many other topics. Calls cost 2.13 SF per minute.

➤ EMERGENCIES: Police (☎ 117). Ambulance (☎ 144).

GAY & LESBIAN TRAVEL

For resources in Switzerland, a good starting point is **Dialogai** (⊠ 11–13 rue de la Navigation, CH-1211 Geneva, ☎ 022/9064040, FAX 022/9064044), which has a bookstore and an English-speaking staff; it also hosts events. You can pick up a copy of "Coming In," a trilingual publication (including English) that gives more than a hundred gay-friendly contacts for Switzerland's French-speaking region.

➤ GAY- AND LESBIAN-FRIENDLY TRAVEL AGENCIES: **Corniche Travel** (⊠ 8721 Sunset Blvd., Suite 200, West Hollywood, CA 90069, ☎ 310/854–6000 or 800/429–8747, FAX 310/659–7441). **Islanders Kennedy Travel** (⊠ 183 W. 10th St., New York, NY 10014, ☎ 212/242–3222 or 800/988–1181, FAX 212/929–8530). **Now Voyager** (⊠ 4406 18th St., San Francisco, CA 94114, ☎ 415/626–1169 or 800/255–6951, FAX 415/626–8626). **Yellowbrick Road** (⊠ 1500 W. Balmoral Ave., Chicago, IL 60640, ☎ 773/561–1800 or 800/642–2488, FAX 773/561–4497). **Skylink Travel and Tour** (⊠ 3577 Moorland Ave., Santa Rosa, CA 95407, ☎ 707/585–8355 or 800/225–5759, FAX 707/584–5637), serving lesbian travelers.

HEALTH

Your trip to Switzerland is likely to be one of the most disease-free of any in your life: It's a country that has well earned its reputation for impeccable standards of cleanliness. But even at the foot of an icy-pure 2,000-m (6,560-ft) glacier, you'll find the locals drinking bottled mineral water; you'll have to wrangle with the waiter if you want tap water with your meal. This is as much a result of the tradition of expecting beverages in a café to be paid for as it is a response to health questions. If you're traveling with a child under two years old, you may be advised by locals not to carry him or her on excursions above 2,000 m (6,560 ft); check with your pediatrician before leaving home. Adults should limit strenuous excursions on the first day at extra-high-altitude resorts, those at 1,600 m (5,248 ft) and above. Adults with heart problems may want to avoid all excursions above 2,000 m (6,560 ft).

MEDICAL PLANS

No one plans to get sick while traveling, but it happens, so **consider signing up with a medical-assistance company.** Members get doctor referrals, emergency evacuation or repatriation, 24-hour telephone hot lines for medical consultation, cash for emergencies, and other personal and legal assistance. Coverage varies by plan, so **review the benefits of each carefully.**

➤ MEDICAL-ASSISTANCE COMPANIES: **International SOS Assistance** (⊠ 8 Neshaminy Interplex, Suite 207, Trevose, PA 19053, ☎ 215/245–4707 or 800/523–6586, FAX 215/244–9617; ⊠ 12 Chemin Riantbosson, 1217 Meyrin 1, Geneva, ☎ 4122/7856464, FAX 4122/7856424; ⊠ 10 Anson Rd., 14-07/08 International Plaza, Singapore 079903, ☎ 65/226–3936, FAX 65/226–3937).

INSURANCE

Travel insurance is the best way to **protect yourself against financial loss.** The most useful plan is a comprehensive policy that includes coverage for trip cancellation and interruption, default, trip delay, and medical expenses (with a waiver for preexisting conditions).

Without insurance, you will lose all or most of your money if you cancel your trip, regardless of the reason. Default insurance covers you if your tour operator, airline, or cruise line goes out of business. Trip-delay covers unforeseen expenses that you may incur due to bad weather or mechanical delays. It's important to compare the fine print regarding trip delay coverage when comparing policies.

For overseas travel, one of the most important components of travel insurance is its medical coverage. Supplemental health insurance will pick up the cost of your medical bills should you get sick or injured while traveling. U.S. residents should note that Medicare generally does not cover health-care costs outside the United States, nor do many privately issued policies. Residents of the United Kingdom can buy an annual travel-insurance policy valid for most vacations taken during the year in which the coverage is purchased. If you are pregnant or have a pre-existing condition, make sure you're covered. British citizens should buy extra medical coverage when traveling overseas, according to the Association of British Insurers. Australian travelers should buy travel insurance, including extra medical coverage, whenever they go abroad, according to the Insurance Council of Australia.

Always **buy travel insurance directly from the insurance company**; if you buy it from a cruise line, airline, or tour operator that goes out of business, you probably will not be covered for the agency's or operator's default, a major risk. Before you make any purchase, **review your existing health and home-owner's policies** to find out whether they cover expenses incurred while traveling.

➤ TRAVEL INSURERS: In the U.S., **Access America** (⊠ 6600 W. Broad St., Richmond, VA 23230, ☎ 804/285–3300 or 800/284–8300). **Travel Guard International** (⊠ 1145 Clark St., Stevens Point, WI 54481, ☎ 715/345–0505 or 800/826–1300). In Canada, **Mutual of Omaha** (⊠ Travel Division, ⊠ 500 University Ave., Toronto, Ontario M5G 1V8, ☎ 416/598–4083, 800/268–8825 in Canada).

➤ INSURANCE INFORMATION: In the U.K., **Association of British Insurers** (⊠ 51 Gresham St., London EC2V 7HQ, ☎ 0171/600–3333). In Australia, the **Insurance Council of Australia** (☎ 613/9614–1077, FAX 613/9614–7924).

LANGUAGE

Nearly 70% of the population of Switzerland speaks one dialect or another of German; Swiss German can be a far cry from high German, although standard German is generally understood. French is spoken in the southwest, around Lake Geneva, and in the cantons of Fribourg, Neuchâtel, Jura, Vaud, and most of the Valais. Italian is spoken in the Ticino. In the Upper and Lower Engadines, in the canton Graubünden, the last gasp of a Romance language called Romansh is still in daily use. There are several dialects of Romansh—five, in fact—so there's not much point in trying to pick up a few phrases. If you want to attempt communicating with the locals there, venture a little Italian. In the areas most frequented by English and American tourists—Zermatt, the Berner Oberland, Luzern—people in the tourist industry usually speak English. Elsewhere, you might not be as lucky. Ask before you plunge into your mother tongue—the person you're addressing may run to fetch the staff member who can converse with you on your own language terms.

LANGUAGES FOR TRAVELERS

A phrase book and language tape set can help get you started.

➤ PHRASE BOOKS AND LANGUAGE-TAPE SETS: Languages for Travelers phrase books and audio sets are available in French, German, and Italian ($16.95 for audio set, $7.00 for phrase book; to order call 800/533–6478).

LODGING

Switzerland is as famous for its hotels as it is for its mountains, knives, and chocolates, and its standards in hospitality are extremely high. Rooms are impeccably clean and well maintained, and they are furnished with comforts ranging from the simplest to the most deluxe. Prices are accordingly high: You will pay more for minimal comforts here than in any other European country. Americans accustomed to spacious motels with two double beds, a color TV, and a bath/shower combination may be disappointed in their first venture into the legendary Swiss hotel: Spaces are small, bathtubs cost extra, and single rooms may have single beds. What you're paying for is service, reliability, cleanliness, and a complex hierarchy of amenities you may not even know you need.

Where no address is provided in the hotel listings, none was necessary: In smaller towns and villages, a postal code is all you need. To find the hotel on arrival, watch for the official street signs pointing the way to every hotel that belongs to the local tourist association.

Some things to bear in mind when you check in: The standard double room in Switzerland has two prim beds built together with separate linens and, sometimes, sheets tucked firmly down the middle. If you prefer more sociable arrangements, ask for a "French bed," or *lit matrimoniale*— that will get you a single-mattress double. Some hotels may offer extra beds—for example, to expand a double room to a triple.

APARTMENT & VILLA RENTALS

If you want a home base that's roomy enough for a family and comes with cooking facilities, **consider a furnished rental.** These can save you money, especially if you're traveling with a large group of people. Home-exchange directories list rentals (often second homes owned by prospective house swappers), and some services search for a house or apartment for you (even a castle if that's your fancy) and handle the paperwork. Some send an illustrated catalog; others send photographs only of specific properties, sometimes at a charge. Up-front registration fees may apply.

➤ RENTAL AGENTS: **Drawbridge to Europe** (✉ 5456 Adams Rd., Talent, OR 97540, ☎ 541/512–8927 or 888/268–1148, FAX 541/512–0978). **Europa-Let/Tropical Inn-Let** (✉ 92 N. Main St., Ashland, OR 97520, ☎ 541/482–5806 or 800/462–4486, FAX 541/482–0660). **Hideaways International** (✉ 767 Islington St., Portsmouth, NH 03801, ☎ 603/430–4433 or 800/843–4433, FAX 603/430–4444; membership $99) is

a club for travelers who arrange rentals among themselves. **Hometours International** (✉ Box 11503, Knoxville, TN 37939, ☎ 423/690–8484 or 800/367–4668). **Interhome** (✉ 124 Little Falls Rd., Fairfield, NJ 07004, ☎ 973/882–6864 or 800/882–6864, FAX 973/808–1742). **Property Rentals International** (✉ 1008 Mansfield Crossing Rd., Richmond, VA 23236, ☎ 804/378–6054 or 800/220–3332, FAX 804/379–2073). **Rent-a-Home International** (✉ 7200 34th Ave. NW, Seattle, WA 98117, ☎ 206/789–9377 or 800/488–7368, FAX 206/789–9379). **Villas International** (✉ 605 Market St., San Francisco, CA 94105, ☎ 415/281–0910 or 800/221–2260, FAX 415/281–0919).

FARM STAYS

An unusual option for families seeking the local experience: Stay on a farm with a Swiss family, complete with children, animals, and the option to work in the fields. Participating farm families register with the Schweizerischer Bauernverband (Swiss Farmers Association), listing the birth dates of their children, rooms and facilities, and types of animals your children can see. Prices are often considerably lower than those of hotels and vacation flats; however, you should be reasonably fluent in French or German, depending on the region of your stay. Further information is available through Switzerland Tourism (☞ Visitor Information, *below*).

➤ ORGANIZATIONS: Contact the **Schweizerischer Bauernverband** (Swiss Farmers Association; ✉ CH-5200 Brugg, ☎ 056/4625111, FAX 056/4416348) or **Schweizer Reiserkasse** (Reka; ✉ Neueng. 15, CH-3100 Bern, ☎ 031/3296633, FAX 031/3296601) for listings.

HOME EXCHANGES

If you would like to exchange your home for someone else's, **join a home-exchange organization,** which will send you its updated listings of available exchanges for a year and will include your own listing in at least one of them. It's up to you to make specific arrangements.

➤ EXCHANGE CLUBS: **HomeLink International** (⊠ Box 650, Key West, FL 33041, ☎ 305/294–7766 or 800/638–3841, ℻ 305/294–1148; $83 per year).

HOSTELS

No matter what your age, you can **save on lodging costs by staying at hostels.** In some 5,000 locations in more than 70 countries around the world, Hostelling International (HI), the umbrella group for a number of national youth hostel associations, offers single-sex, dorm-style beds and, at many hostels, "couples" rooms and family accommodations. Membership in any HI national hostel association, open to travelers of all ages, allows you to stay in HI-affiliated hostels at member rates (one-year membership is about $25 for adults; hostels run about $10–$25 per night). Members also have priority if the hostel is full; they're eligible for discounts around the world, even on rail and bus travel in some countries.

➤ HOSTEL ORGANIZATIONS: **Hostelling International—American Youth Hostels** (⊠ 733 15th St. NW, Suite 840, Washington, DC 20005, ☎ 202/783–6161, ℻ 202/783–6171). **Hostelling International—Canada** (⊠ 400–205 Catherine St., Ottawa, Ontario K2P 1C3, ☎ 613/237–7884, ℻ 613/237–7868). **Youth Hostel Association of England and Wales** (⊠ Trevelyan House, ⊠ 8 St. Stephen's Hill, St. Albans, Hertfordshire AL1 2DY, ☎ 01727/855215 or 01727/845047, ℻ 01727/844126; membership in the U.S. $25, in Canada C$26.75, in the U.K. £9.30).

HOTELS

When selecting a place to stay, an important resource can be the Swiss Hotel Association (SHA), a rigorous and demanding organization that maintains a specific rating system for lodging standards. Eighty percent of Swiss hotels belong to this group and take their stars seriously. In contrast to more casual European countries, stars in Switzerland have precise meaning: A five-star hotel is required to have a specific staff-guest ratio, a daily change of bed linens, and extended-hour room service. A two-star hotel must have telephones, soap in

the room, and fabric tablecloths in the restaurant. But the SHA standards cannot control the quality of decor and the grace of service. Thus you may find a four-star hotel that meets these technical requirements but has shabby appointments, leaky plumbing, or a rude concierge; a good, family-run two-star may make you feel like royalty.

Some rules of thumb: If you are looking for American-style, chain-motel-level comfort—a big bed, color TV, minibar, safe—you will probably be happiest in four-star, business-class hotels, many of which cater to Americans through travel agents and tour organizers; Best Western owns a number of four-star hotels in Switzerland. If you are looking for regional atmosphere, family ownership (and the pride and care for details that implies), and moderate prices, but don't care about a TV or minibar, look for three stars: Nearly all of such rooms have showers and toilets. Two stars will get you tidy, minimal comfort with about a third of the rooms having baths. One-star properties are rare: They have no baths in rooms and no phone available in-house, and generally fall below the demanding Swiss national standard. Several hotels in the SHA are specially rated *Landgasthof* or *relais de campagne,* meaning "country inn." These generally are rustic-style lodgings typical of the region, but they may range from spare to luxurious and are rarely set apart in deep country, as Americans might expect; some are in the midst of small market towns or resorts. The SHA distinguishes them as offering especially high-quality service, personal attention, and parking.

INNS

Travelers on a budget can find help from the *Check-in E & G Hotels* guide (E & G stands for *einfach und gemütlich*: roughly, "simple and cozy"), available through Switzerland Tourism. These comfortable little hotels have banded together to dispel Switzerland's intimidating image as an elite, overpriced vacation spot and offer simple two-star standards in usually very atmospheric inns. To reach a wider public, they now have a Web site: http://www.rooms.ch.

Other organizations can help you find unusual properties: The Relais & Châteaux group seeks out manor houses, historic buildings, and generally atmospheric luxury, with most of its properties falling into the $$$ or $$$$ range. A similar group, Romantik Hotels and Restaurants, combines architectural interest, historic atmosphere, and fine regional food. Relais du Silence hotels are usually isolated in a peaceful, natural setting, with first-class comforts.

MAIL

POSTAL RATES

Mail rates are divided into first-class "A" (airmail) and second-class "B" (surface). Letters and postcards to the United States weighing up to 20 grams cost 1.80 SF first class, .90 SF second class; to the United Kingdom, 1 SF first class, .80 SF second class.

RECEIVING MAIL

If you're uncertain where you'll be staying, you can have your mail, marked POSTE RESTANTE or POSTLAGERND, sent to any post office in Switzerland. It needs the sender's name and address on the back, and you'll need proof of identity to collect it. You can also have your mail sent to American Express for a small fee; if you are a cardholder or have American Express traveler's checks, the service is free. Postal codes precede the names of cities and towns in Swiss addresses.

MONEY

COSTS

Despite increased competition across Europe, the recent decrease in the Swiss franc's value against other currencies, and the negligible inflation rate over the past several years, Switzerland remains one of the most expensive countries on the Continent for travelers, and you may find yourself shocked by the price of a light lunch or a generic hotel room. If you are traveling on a tight budget, avoid staying in well-known resorts and the most sophisticated cities; Geneva, Zürich, Zermatt, Gstaad, and Saint-Moritz are exceptionally expensive. If you are traveling by car, you have the luxury of seeking out small, family hotels in villages, where costs are relatively low. Unless you work hard at finding budget accommodations, you will average more than 150 SF a night for two—more if you stay in business-class hotels, with TV and direct-dial phone. Restaurant prices are standardized from region to region.

A cup of coffee or a beer costs about 3 SF in a simple restaurant; ordinary open wines, sold by the deciliter ("deci"), start at about 3 SF. All three beverages cost sometimes double that in resorts, city hotels, and fine restaurants. A plain, one-plate daily lunch special averages 14–18 SF. A city bus ride costs between 1.50 SF and 2.20 SF, a short cab ride 15 SF.

CREDIT & DEBIT CARDS

Should you use a credit card or a debit card when traveling? Both have benefits. A credit card allows you to delay payment and gives you certain rights as a consumer (☞ Consumer Protection, *above*). A debit card, also known as a check card, deducts funds directly from your checking account and helps you stay within your budget. When you want to rent a car, though, you may still need an old-fashioned credit card. Although you can always *pay* for your car with a debit card, some agencies will not allow you to *reserve* a car with a debit card.

Otherwise, the two types of plastic are virtually the same. Both will get you cash advances at ATMs worldwide if your card is properly programmed with your personal identification number (PIN). (For use in Switzerland, your PIN must be four digits long.) Both offer excellent, wholesale exchange rates. And both protect you against unauthorized use if the card is lost or stolen. Your liability is limited to $50, as long as you report the card missing.

➤ ATM LOCATIONS: **Cirrus** (☎ 800/424–7787). **Plus** (☎ 800/843–7587) for locations in the U.S. and Canada, or visit your local bank.

CURRENCY

The unit of currency in Switzerland is the Swiss franc (SF), available in notes of 10, 20, 50, 100, 200, and 1,000. Francs are divided into centimes (in Suisse Romande) or rappen (in Ger-

THE GOLD GUIDE / SMART TRAVEL TIPS

man Switzerland). There are coins for 5, 10, and 20 centimes. Larger coins are the ½-, 1-, 2-, and 5-franc pieces.

At press time (spring 1998), the Swiss franc stood at 1.44 to the U.S. dollar, 1.06 to the Canadian dollar, and 2.35 to the pound sterling.

EXCHANGING MONEY

For the most favorable rates, **change money through banks.** Although fees charged for ATM transactions may be higher abroad than at home, Cirrus and Plus exchange rates are excellent, because they are based on wholesale rates offered only by major banks. You won't do as well at exchange booths in airports or rail and bus stations, in hotels, in restaurants, or in stores, although you may find their hours more convenient. To avoid lines at airport exchange booths, **get a bit of local currency before you leave home.**

➤ EXCHANGE SERVICES: **Chase** *Currency To Go* (☎ 800/935–9935; 212/935–9935 in NY, NJ, and CT). **International Currency Express** (☎ 888/842–0880 on the East Coast, 888/278–6628 on the West Coast). **Thomas Cook Currency Services** (☎ 800/287–7362 for telephone orders and retail locations).

TRAVELER'S CHECKS

Do you need traveler's checks? It depends on where you're headed. If you're going to rural areas and small towns, go with cash; traveler's checks are best used in cities. Lost or stolen checks can usually be replaced within 24 hours. To ensure a speedy refund, buy your own traveler's checks—don't let someone else pay for them: irregularities like this can cause delays. The person who bought the checks should make the call to request a refund.

Note that there is a 300 SF limitation on the cashing of Eurocheques drawn on European banks.

OUTDOOR ACTIVITIES & SPORTS

BICYCLING

☞ Bike Travel, *above.*

BOATING

Holders of the Swiss Pass or Flexipass (☞ Train Travel, *below*) can go on boating excursions with Eurotrek's **Swiss Adventure program** (☎ 01/4620203, FAX 01/4631139).

CAMPING

Switzerland is ideal for campers, with approximately 450 sites throughout the country. All are classified with one to five stars according to amenities, location, and so on. The rates vary widely but average around 15 SF per night for a family of four, plus car or camper. For further details see the *Swiss Camping Guide*, published by the Swiss Camping Association, at bookshops for 15 SF or from the **Camping and Caravaning Association** (✉ Box 24, CH-6004 Luzern, ☎ 041/2104822, FAX 041/2104822). Listings are also available from the **Touring Club of Switzerland** (✉ Ch. de Blandonnet 4, CH-1214 Vernier, ☎ 022/4172727) and from the **Swiss Campsite Association** (✉ CH-3800 Interlaken, ☎ 033/8233523, FAX 033/8232991).

To stay in most European campsites, you must have an **International Camping Carnet** verifying your status as a bona fide camper. This is available from any national camping association within Europe or from the **National Campers and Hikers Association** (✉ 4804 Transit Rd., Bldg. 2, Depew, NY 14043, ☎ 716/668–6242).

GOLF

There are 52 golf courses throughout Switzerland where you can rent clubs and play on a daily greens fee basis. For more information, contact the **Swiss Association of Golf** (✉ pl. Croix-Blanche 19, 1066 Epalinges-Lausanne, ☎ 021/7843532, FAX 021/7843536), which has a directory of all courses. It can also provide specific information, such as course fees and conditions.

HIKING

The Swiss Alps, naturally, are riddled with hiking trails; hiking is an especially popular pastime in the German-speaking areas of the country, such as the Berner Oberland. For suggested hiking itineraries, contact regional tourist offices; many bookstores also carry detailed topographical maps with marked trails. You can also contact the **Association Suisse de Tourisme Pedestre** (☎ 061/6069340).

SKIING

A daily bulletin of ski conditions at 220 locations throughout Switzerland is available by calling 157/120120 (0.86 SF/min.); reports are in the local language. You can also check the Switzerland Tourism Web site (☞ Visitor Information, *below*). Applications to the **Swiss Alpine Club** should be addressed to the club at Sektion Zermatt, Mr. Edmond F. Krieger, Postfach 1, CH-3920 Zermatt (☎ FAX 027/9672610). For a directory of mountain-club huts (38 SF), contact the Swiss Alpine Club (✉ Brunng. 36, CH-3000 Bern 7, ☎ 031/3701818 FAX 031/3117980).

PACKING

LUGGAGE

How many carry-on bags you can bring with you is up to the airline. Most allow two, but the limit is often reduced to one on certain flights. Gate agents will take excess baggage—including bags they deem oversize—from you as you board and add it to checked luggage. To avoid this situation, make sure that everything you carry aboard will fit under your seat. Also, get to the gate early and request a seat at the back of the plane; you'll probably board first, while the overhead bins are still empty. Since big, bulky baggage attracts the attention of gate agents and flight attendants on a busy flight, make sure your carry-on is really a carry-on. Finally, a carry-on that's long and narrow is more likely to remain unnoticed than one that's wide and squarish.

If you are flying internationally, note that baggage allowances may be determined not by piece but by weight—generally 88 pounds (40 kilograms) in first class, 66 pounds (30 kilograms) in business class, and 44 pounds (20 kilograms) in economy.

Airline liability for baggage is limited to $1,250 per person on flights within the United States. On international flights it amounts to $9.07 per pound or $20 per kilogram for checked baggage (roughly $640 per 70-pound bag) and $400 per passenger for unchecked baggage. You can buy additional coverage at check-in for about $10 per $1,000 of coverage, but it excludes a rather extensive list of items, shown on your airline ticket.

Before departure, **itemize your bags' contents** and their worth and label the bags with your name, address, and phone number. (If you use your home address, cover it so that potential thieves can't see it readily.) Inside each bag, **pack a copy of your itinerary.** At check-in, **make sure that each bag is correctly tagged** with the destination airport's three-letter code. If your bags arrive damaged or fail to arrive at all, file a written report with the airline before leaving the airport.

PACKING LIST

Switzerland is essentially sportswear country. City dress is more formal. Men would be wise to pack a jacket and tie if dining in some of the great restaurants; otherwise, a tie and sweater is standard at night. Women wear skirts more frequently here than in America, especially women over 50, though anything fashionable goes. Except at the most chic hotels in international resorts, you won't need formal evening dress.

Even in July and August, the evening air grows chilly in the mountains, so **bring a warm sweater.** And **bring a hat or sunscreen,** as the atmosphere is thinner at high altitudes. Glaciers can be blinding in the sun, so **be sure to bring sunglasses, especially for high-altitude excursions.** Good walking shoes or hiking boots are a must, whether you're tackling medieval cobblestones or mountain trails.

To ensure comfort, **budget travelers should bring their own washcloth and soap,** not always standard equipment in one- and two-star-rated Swiss hotels. If you're planning on shopping and cooking, a tote bag will come in handy: Most groceries do not provide sacks, but sturdy, reusable plastic totes can be bought at checkout. Laundromats are rare, so laundry soap is useful for hand washing.

In your carry-on luggage **bring an extra pair of eyeglasses or contact lenses** and **enough of any medication you take** to last the entire trip. You may also want your doctor to write a spare prescription using the drug's generic name, since brand names may vary from country to country. **Never put prescription drugs or valuables in luggage to be checked.** To avoid customs delays, carry medications in their original packaging. And don't forget to copy down and carry addresses of offices that handle refunds of lost traveler's checks.

PASSPORTS & VISAS

When traveling internationally, **carry a passport even if you don't need one** (it's always the best form of ID), and make **two photocopies of the data page** (one for someone at home and another for you, carried separately from your passport). If you lose your passport, promptly call the nearest embassy or consulate and the local police.

ENTERING SWITZERLAND

All Australian, British, Canadian, New Zealand, and U.S. citizens need only a valid passport to enter Switzerland for stays of up to 90 days.

PASSPORT OFFICES

The best time to apply for a passport or to renew is during the fall and winter. Before any trip, be sure to check your passport's expiration date and, if necessary, renew it as soon as possible. (Some countries won't allow you to enter on a passport that's due to expire in six months or less.)

➤ AUSTRALIAN CITIZENS: **Australian Passport Office** (☎ 131–232).

➤ CANADIAN CITIZENS: **Passport Office** (☎ 819/994–3500 or 800/567–6868).

➤ NEW ZEALAND CITIZENS: **New Zealand Passport Office** (☎ 04/494–0700 for information on how to apply, 0800/727–776 for information on applications already submitted).

➤ U.K. CITIZENS: **London Passport Office** (☎ 0990/21010), for fees and documentation requirements and to request an emergency passport.

➤ U.S. CITIZENS: **National Passport Information Center** (☎ 900/225–5674; calls are charged at 35¢ per min for automated service, $1.05 per min for operator service).

SENIOR-CITIZEN TRAVEL

Women over 62 and men over 65 qualify for special seasonal (and in some cases year-round) discounts at a variety of Swiss hotels. With married couples, at least one spouse must fulfill these conditions. Prices include overnight lodging in a single or double room, breakfast, service charges, heating, and taxes. Arrangements can also be made for extended stays. Senior citizens are entitled to discounts on trains, buses, and boats, at all movie theaters in Switzerland, and, where posted, at museums and attractions.

To qualify for age-related discounts, **mention your senior-citizen status up front** when booking hotel reservations (not when checking out) and before you're seated in restaurants (not when paying the bill). Note that discounts may be limited to certain menus, days, or hours. When renting a car, **ask about promotional car-rental discounts**, which can be cheaper than senior-citizen rates.

➤ EDUCATIONAL PROGRAMS: **Elderhostel** (✉ 75 Federal St., 3rd floor, Boston, MA 02110, ☎ 617/426–8056). **Interhostel** (✉ University of New Hampshire, 6 Garrison Ave., Durham, NH 03824, ☎ 603/862–1147 or 800/733–9753, FAX 603/862–1113). **Folkways Institute** (✉ 14600 S.E. Aldridge Rd., Portland, or 97236–6518, ☎ 503/658–6600 or 800/225–4666, FAX 503/658–8672).

➤ LODGING: A special guide to hotels that offer senior discounts, "Season for Seniors", is available from the Swiss Hotel Association (✉ Monbijoustr. 130, CH-3001 Bern, ☎ 031/3704111) or from **Switzerland Tourism** (☞ Visitor Information, *below*).

STUDENT TRAVEL

TRAVEL AGENCIES

To save money, **look into deals available through student-oriented travel agencies.** To qualify you'll need a bona fide student ID card. Members of international student groups are also eligible.

➤ STUDENT IDs & SERVICES: **Council on International Educational Exchange** (CIEE, ✉ 205 E. 42nd St.,

14th floor, New York, NY 10017, ☎ 212/822–2600 or 888/268–6245, FAX 212/822–2699), for mail orders only, in the United States. **Travel Cuts** (✉ 187 College St., Toronto, Ontario M5T 1P7, ☎ 416/979–2406 or 800/667–2887) in Canada.

➤ STUDENT TOURS: **Contiki Holidays** (✉ 300 Plaza Alicante, Suite 900, Garden Grove, CA 92840, ☎ 714/740–0808 or 800/266–8454, FAX 714/740–2034). **AESU Travel** (✉ 2 Hamill Rd., Suite 248, Baltimore, MD 21210-1807, ☎ 410/323–4416 or 800/638–7640, FAX 410/323–4498).

TAXES

HOTEL

What you see is what you pay in Switzerland: Restaurant checks and hotel bills include all taxes.

VALUE-ADDED TAX (VAT)

On January 1, 1996, Switzerland introduced valued-added tax (VAT) of 6.5%, making it the 20th European country to adopt the measure. Although the rate is the lowest in Europe, it can add a significant amount to already pricey bills. Culture vultures are one of the only groups not to be affected by the VAT, with theater and cinema tickets exempt.

However, on any one purchase of 550 francs or more from one store, refunds are available to nonresidents for clothes, watches, and souvenirs, but not for meals or hotel rooms. To **get a VAT refund,** pay by credit card; at the time of purchase, the store clerk should fill out and give you a red form and keep a record of your credit card number. When leaving Switzerland, you must hand-deliver the red form to a customs officer at the customs office at the airport, or if leaving by car or train, at the border. Customs will process the form and return it to the store, which will refund the tax by crediting your card.

TELEPHONES

COUNTRY CODES

The country code for Switzerland is 41. When dialing a Swiss number from abroad, drop the initial 0 from the local area code.

DIRECTORY & OPERATOR INFORMATION

All telephone operators speak English, and instructions are printed in English in all telephone booths. Precede the area-code number with 0 when dialing long-distance within Switzerland. Omit the 0 when using the international code to dial Switzerland from another country. Remember, Switzerland's country code is 41.

Anglo-Phone (☎ 1575014) is a 24-hour English-language information line giving details on hotels, restaurants, museums, nightlife, skiing, what to do in an emergency, and more. Calls cost 2.13 SF per minute.

INTERNATIONAL CALLS

You can dial most international numbers direct from Switzerland, adding 00 before the country code. If you want a number that cannot be reached directly, dial 114 for a connection. Dial 191 for international numbers and information. It's cheapest to use the booths in train stations and post offices: Calls made from your hotel cost a great deal more. Rates are lower between 5 AM and 7 PM, after 9 PM, and on weekends. Calls to the United States cost about 1.80 SF a minute, to the United Kingdom about 1 SF a minute. If you're short on change and don't have a phone card, call from the phone cabins at the post office: Tell the clerk what country you want to call, then step in and dial. The cost is clocked behind the desk, and you may pay with a credit card. There's no difference in price between phone cabins and public phone booths.

AT&T, MCI, and Sprint international access codes make calling the United States relatively convenient, but you may find the local access number blocked in many hotel rooms. First ask the hotel operator to connect you. If the hotel operator balks, ask for an international operator or dial the international operator yourself. One way to improve your odds of getting connected to your long-distance carrier is to travel with more than one company's calling card (a hotel may block Sprint, for example, but not MCI). If all else fails, call from a pay phone in the hotel lobby.

➤ ACCESS CODES: **AT&T Direct** (☎ 800/435–0812 for other areas). **MCI WorldPhone** (☎ 800/444–4141 for other areas). **Sprint International Access** (☎ 800/877–4646 for other areas).

LONG-DISTANCE CALLS

On January 1, 1998, the state monopoly on telecommunications ended. Rates are expected to decrease following the entrance of new companies into the market to compete with the state-owned Swisscom. There is direct dialing to everywhere in Switzerland. For local and international codes, consult the pink pages at the front of the telephone book.

PUBLIC PHONES

To make a local call on a pay phone, pick up the receiver, put in a minimum of .60 SF, and dial the number. Digital readouts will tell you to add more as your time runs out. A useful alternative is the Swisscom phone card, available in 5 SF, 10 SF, or 20 SF units. You can buy them at the post office, train station, or kiosks, and you slip them into adapted public phones. The cost of the call will be counted against the card, with any remaining value still good for the next time you use it. If you drain the card and still need to talk, the readout will warn you: You can either pop in a new card or make up the difference with coins, although fewer and fewer phones still accept coins.

Cellular phones (*natels*) may be rented at either the Geneva (☎ 022/7178263) or Zürich (☎ 01/8165063) airports on a daily, weekly, or monthly basis.

TIPPING

Despite all protests to the contrary and menus marked SERVICE COMPRIS, the Swiss *do* tip at restaurant meals, giving quantities anywhere from the change from the nearest franc to 10 SF for a world-class meal exquisitely served. Unlike American-style tipping, calculated by a percentage, usually between 10% and 20%, a tip is still a tip here: a nod of approval for a job well done. If, in a café, the waitress settles the bill at the table, fishing the change from her leather purse, give

her the change on the spot—or calculate the total, including tip, and tell her the full sum before she counts it onto the tabletop. If you need to take more time to calculate, leave it on the table, though this isn't common practice in outdoor cafés. If you're paying for a meal with a credit card, try to tip with cash instead of filling in the tip slot on the slip: Not all managers are good about doling out the waiters' tips in cash. Tipping porters and doormen is easier: 2 SF per bag is adequate in good hotels, 1 SF per trip in humbler lodgings (unless you travel heavy). A fixed rate of 5 SF per bag applies to porter fees at the Geneva and Zürich airports.

TOUR OPERATORS

Buying a prepackaged tour or independent vacation can make your trip to Switzerland less expensive and more hassle-free. Because everything is prearranged, you'll spend less time planning.

Operators that handle several hundred thousand travelers per year can use their purchasing power to give you a good price. Their high volume may also indicate financial stability. But some small companies provide more personalized service; because they tend to specialize, they may also be more knowledgeable about a given area.

BOOKING WITH AN AGENT

Travel agents are excellent resources. In fact, large operators accept bookings made only through travel agents. But it's a good idea to **collect brochures from several agencies** because some agents' suggestions may be influenced by relationships with tour and package firms that reward them for volume sales. If you have a special interest, **find an agent with expertise in that area**; ASTA (☞ Travel Agencies, *below*) has a database of specialists worldwide.

Make sure your travel agent knows the accommodations and other services. Ask about the hotel's location, room size, and beds and whether it has a pool, room service, or programs for children, if you care about these. Has your agent been there in person or sent others you can contact?

Do some homework on your own, too: Local tourism boards can provide information about lesser-known and small-niche operators, some of which may sell only direct.

BUYER BEWARE

Each year consumers are stranded or lose their money when tour operators—even very large ones with excellent reputations—go out of business. So **check out the operator.** Find out how long the company has been in business and ask several travel agents about its reputation. If the package or tour you are considering is priced lower than in your wildest dreams, **be skeptical.** Try to **book with a company that has a consumer-protection program.** If the operator has such a program, you'll find information about it in the company's brochure. If the operator you are considering does not offer some kind of consumer protection, then ask for references from satisfied customers.

In the U.S., members of the National Tour Association and United States Tour Operators Association are required to set aside funds to cover your payments and travel arrangements in case the company defaults. It's also a good idea to choose a company that participates in the American Society of Travel Agent's Tour Operator Program (TOP). This gives you a forum if there are any disputes between you and your tour operator; ASTA will act as mediator.

➤ TOUR-OPERATOR RECOMMENDATIONS: **American Society of Travel Agents** (☞ Travel Agencies, *below*). **National Tour Association** (NTA; ✉ 546 E. Main St., Lexington, KY 40508, ☎ 606/226–4444 or 800/755–8687). **United States Tour Operators Association** (USTOA; ✉ 342 Madison Ave., Suite 1522, New York, NY 10173, ☎ 212/599–6599 or 800/468–7862, ℻ 212/599–6744).

COSTS

The more your package or tour includes, the better you can predict the ultimate cost of your vacation. Make sure you know exactly what is covered and **beware of hidden costs.** Are taxes, tips, and service charges

included? Transfers and baggage handling? Entertainment and excursions? These can add up.

Prices for packages and tours are usually quoted per person, based on two sharing a room. If traveling solo, you may be required to pay the full double-occupancy rate. Some operators eliminate this surcharge if you agree to be matched with a roommate of the same sex, even if one is not found by departure time.

GROUP TOURS

Among companies that sell tours to Switzerland, the following are nationally known, have a proven reputation, and offer plenty of options. The classifications used below represent different price categories, and you'll probably encounter these terms when talking to a travel agent or tour operator. The key difference is usually in accommodations, which run from budget to better, and better-yet to best.

➤ SUPER-DELUXE: **Abercrombie & Kent** (✉ 1520 Kensington Rd., Oak Brook, IL 60521-2141, ☎ 630/954–2944 or 800/323–7308, ℻ 630/954–3324). **Travcoa** (✉ Box 2630, 2350 S.E. Bristol St., Newport Beach, CA 92660, ☎ 714/476–2800 or 800/992–2003, ℻ 714/476–2538).

➤ DELUXE: **Globus** (✉ 5301 S. Federal Circle, Littleton, CO 80123-2980, ☎ 303/797–2800 or 800/221–0090, ℻ 303/347–2080). **Maupintour** (✉ 1515 St. Andrews Dr., Lawrence, KS 66047, ☎ 913/843–1211 or 800/255–4266, ℻ 913/843–8351). **Tauck Tours** (✉ Box 5027, 276 Post Rd. W, Westport, CT 06881-5027, ☎ 203/226–6911 or 800/468–2825, ℻ 203/221–6866).

➤ FIRST-CLASS: **Brendan Tours** (✉ 15137 Califa St., Van Nuys, CA 91411, ☎ 818/785–9696 or 800/421–8446, ℻ 818/902–9876). **Caravan Tours** (✉ 401 N. Michigan Ave., Chicago, IL 60611, ☎ 312/321–9800 or 800/227–2826, ℻ 312/321–9845). **Collette Tours** (✉ 162 Middle St., Pawtucket, RI 02860, ☎ 401/728–3805 or 800/340–5158, ℻ 401/728–4745). **DER Tours** (✉ 9501 W. Devon St., Rosemont, IL 60018, ☎ 800/937–1235, ℻ 847/692–4141 or 800/282–

7474, 800/860–9944 for brochures). **Gadabout Tours** (⌧ 700 E. Tahquitz Canyon Way, Palm Springs, CA 92262-6767, ☎ 619/325–5556 or 800/952–5068). **Trafalgar Tours** (⌧ 11 E. 26th St., New York, NY 10010, ☎ 212/689–8977 or 800/854–0103, FAX 800/457–6644).

➤ BUDGET: **Cosmos** (☞ Globus, *above*). **Trafalgar Tours** (☞ *above*).

PACKAGES

Like group tours, independent vacation packages are available from major tour operators and airlines. The companies listed below offer vacation packages in a broad price range.

➤ AIR/HOTEL: **Delta Vacations** (☎ 800/872–7786). **Swissair's SwissPak** (☎ 800/872–7786). **TWA Getaway Vacations** (☎ 800/438–2929). **United Vacations** (☎ 800/328–6877).

➤ FLY/DRIVE: **Delta Vacations** (☞ *above*).

➤ FROM THE U.K.: **Eurobreak** (⌧ 10–18 Putney Hill, London SW15 6AX, ☎ 0181/780–7700). **Kuoni Travel** (⌧ Kuoni House, Dorking, Surrey RH5 4AZ, ☎ 01306/740-500). **Swiss Travel Service Ltd.** (⌧ Bridge House, 55–59 High Rd., Broxbourne, Hertfordshire EN10 7DT, ☎ 01992/456–123). **Time Off Ltd.** (⌧ Chester Close, Chester St., London SW1X 7BQ, ☎ 0171/235–8070). **Wallace Arnold Tours Ltd.** (⌧ Gelderd Rd., Leeds LS12 6DH, ☎ 0113/231–0739; ⌧ 62 George St., Croydon, CR9 1DN, ☎ 0181/686–9833).

THEME TRIPS

➤ ADVENTURE: **Himalayan Travel** (⌧ 110 Prospect St., Stamford, CT 06901, ☎ 203/359–3711 or 800/225–2380, FAX 203/359–3669). **Horizons—Adventures of a Lifetime** (⌧ Box 670565, Marietta, GA 30066, ☎ 800/246–3180, FAX 770/565–4233).

➤ BALLOONING: **Buddy Bombard European Balloon Adventures** (⌧ 333 Pershing Way, West Palm Beach, FL 33401, ☎ 561/837–6610 or 800/862–8537, FAX 561/837–6623).

➤ BARGE/RIVER CRUISES: **KD River Cruises of Europe** (⌧ 2500 Westchester Ave., Purchase, NY 10577, ☎ 914/696–3600 or 800/346–6525, FAX 914/696–0833).

➤ BICYCLING: **Backroads** (⌧ 801 Cedar St., Berkeley, CA 94710-1800, ☎ 510/527–1555 or 800/462–2848, FAX 510-527–1444). **Butterfield & Robinson** (⌧ 70 Bond St., Toronto, Ontario, Canada M5B 1X3, ☎ 416/864–1354 or 800/678–1147, FAX 416/864–0541). **Edelweiss Bike Travel** (⌧ 129 Hillside Ave., Williston Park, NY 11596, ☎ 516/746–6761 or 800/877–2784, FAX 516/746–6690). **Euro-Bike Tours** (⌧ Box 990, De Kalb, IL 60115, ☎ 800/321–6060, FAX 815/758–8851). **Uniquely Europe** (⌧ 2819 1st Ave., #280, Seattle, WA 98121-1113, ☎ 206/441–8682 or 800/426–3615, FAX 206/441–8862). **Vermont Bicycle Touring** (⌧ Box 711, Bristol, VT, 05443-0711, ☎ 802/453–4811 or 800/245–3868, FAX 802/453–4806).

➤ HIKING/WALKING: **Adventure Center** (⌧ 1311 63rd St., #200, Emeryville, CA 94608, ☎ 510/654–1879 or 800/227–8747, FAX 510/654–4200). **Alpine Adventure Trails Tours** (⌧ 322 Pio Nono Ave., Macon, GA 31204, ☎ 912/478–4007). **Abercrombie & Kent** (☞ Group Tours, *above*). **Backroads** (☞ Bicycling, *above*). **Country Walkers** (⌧ Box 180, Waterbury, VT 05676-0180, ☎ 802/244–1387 or 800/464–9255, FAX 802/244–5661). **Euro-Bike Tours** (☞ Bicycling *above*). **Europeds** (⌧ 761 Lighthouse Ave., Monterey, CA 93940, ☎ 800/321–9552, FAX 408/655–4501). **Himalayan Travel** (☞ Adventure, *above*). **Mountain Travel-Sobek** (⌧ 6420 Fairmount Ave., El Cerrito, CA 94530, ☎ 510/527–8100 or 800/227–2384, FAX 510/525–7710). **Walking the World** (⌧ Box 1186, Fort Collins, CO 80522, ☎ 970/498–0500 or 800/340–9255, FAX 970/498–9100) specializes in tours for ages 50 and older. **Wilderness Travel** (⌧ 1102 Ninth St., Berkeley, CA 94710, ☎ 510/558–2488 or 800/368–2794).

➤ LEARNING: **Naturequest** (⌧ 934 Acapulco St., Laguna Beach, CA

92651, ☎ 714/499–9561 or 800/
369–3033, FAX 714/499–0812).
Smithsonian Study Tours and Seminars (✉ 1100 Jefferson Dr. SW,
Room 3045, MRC 702, Washington,
DC 20560, ☎ 202/357–4700,
FAX 202/633–9250).

➤ MOTORCYCLING: **Beach's Motorcycle Adventures** (✉ 2763 W. River
Pkwy., Grand Island, NY 14072-
2053, ☎ 716/773–4960, FAX 716/
773–5227).

➤ SPAS: **Custom Spa Vacations**
(✉ 1318 Beacon St., Brookline, MA
02146, ☎ 617/566–5144 or 800/
443–7727, FAX 617/731–0599).
Great Spas of the World (✉ 55 John
St., New York, NY 10038, ☎ 212/
267–5500 or 800/772–8463,
FAX 212/571–0510). **Spa-Finders**
(✉ 91 5th Ave., #301, New York,
NY 10003-3039, ☎ 212/924–6800
or 800/255–7727). **Spa Trek Travel**
(✉ 475 Park Ave. S, New York, NY
10016, ☎ 212/779–3480 or 800/
272–3480, FAX 212/779–3471).

PACKAGES

Like group tours, independent vacation packages are available from
major tour operators and airlines.

TRAIN TRAVEL

The Swiss Federal Railways, or **CFF**
(☎ 1572222), has a very extensive
network; trains and stations are clean,
and as you'd expect, service is extremely prompt. The cleanliness
extends to the train station bathrooms—in most countries these are
grim affairs, but in Switzerland's large
city stations, look for "McClean"
restrooms. They have nothing to do
with the red-and-yellow hamburger
chain; instead, they're immaculate,
sleekly designed spaces with bathrooms, changing stations, showers,
and a toiletries kiosk. Entrance is just
under 2 SF.

Trains described as InterCity or
express are the fastest, stopping only
at principal towns. *Regionalzug/Train
Régional* means a local train. If you're
planning to use the trains extensively,
get the official timetable (*Kursbuch* or
Horaire) for 16 SF; the portable,

pocket version is called "Fribo" and
costs 12 SF.

**Consider a first-class ticket only if the
extra comfort is worth the price.** The
principal difference between first- and
second class is more space to yourself;
the first-class cars are less crowded.
Seat size is the same, upholstery
fancier, and you usually will be delivered to track position closest to the
station. **Make seat reservations** for
trips during rush hours and in high
season, especially on international
trains.

If your itinerary requires changing
trains, **bear in mind that the average
connection time is from six to eight
minutes.**

DISCOUNT PASSES

To save money, **look into rail passes.**
But be aware that if you don't plan to
cover many miles, you may come out
ahead by buying individual tickets.

If Switzerland is your only destination
in Europe, **there are numerous passes
available** for visitors. The **Swiss Pass**
is the best value, offering unlimited
travel on Swiss Federal Railways,
postal buses (☞ Bus Travel, *above*),
lake steamers, and the local bus and
tram services of 30 cities. It also gives
reductions on many privately owned
railways, cable cars, and funiculars.
Available from Switzerland Tourism
and from travel agents outside
Switzerland, the card is valid for four
days (210 SF second class; 316 SF
first class); eight days (264 second
class; 378 SF first class); 15 days (306
SF second class; 442 SF first class); or
one month (420 SF second class; 610
SF first class). There is also a three-
day **Flexipass** (210 SF second class;
316 SF first class), which offers the
same unlimited travel options as a
regular Swiss Pass for any three days
within a 15-day period. The cost of a
children's pass is half the cost of the
adult pass. For information on the
Swiss Boat Pass, *see* Boat Travel,
above; for information on the Family
Pass, *see* Children & Travel, *above.*

Within some popular tourist areas,
Regional Holiday Season Tickets,
usually issued for 15 days, give five
days of travel at no additional cost by

THE GOLD GUIDE / SMART TRAVEL TIPS

train, post buses, steamers, and mountain railways, with half fare for the rest of the validity of the card. Central Switzerland (Berner Oberland) offers a similar pass for seven days, with two days of free travel. Prices vary widely, depending upon the region and period of validity. Increasingly popular with tourists is **Swiss Half-Fare Travel Card,** which allows half-fare travel for 30 days (90 SF) or one year (150 SF).

The **Swiss Card,** which can be purchased in the United States through Rail Europe and at train stations in the Zürich and Geneva airports and in Basel, is valid for 30 days and grants full round-trip travel from your arrival point to any destination in the country, plus a half-price reduction on any further excursions during your stay (140 SF second class; 170 SF first class). For more information about train travel in Switzerland, get the free "Swiss Travel System" or "Discover Switzerland" brochures from Switzerland Tourism (☞ Visitor Information, *below*).

Switzerland is one of 17 countries in which you can **use EurailPasses,** which provide unlimited first-class rail travel, in all of the participating countries, for the duration of the pass. If you plan to rack up the miles, get a standard pass. These are available for 15 days ($538), 21 days ($698), one month ($864), two months ($1,224), and three months ($1,512). If your plans call for only limited train travel, **look into a Europass,** which costs less money than a EurailPass. Unlike with EurailPasses, however, you get a limited number of travel days, in a limited number of countries, during a specified time period. For example, a two-month pass ($326) allows between 5 and 15 days of rail travel but costs $200 less than the least expensive EurailPass. Keep in mind, however, that the Europass is good only in France, Germany, Italy, Spain, and Switzerland, and the number of countries you can visit is further limited by the type of pass you buy. For example, the basic two-month pass allows you to visit only three of the five participating countries.

In addition to standard EurailPasses, **ask about special rail-pass plans.** Among these are the Eurail Youthpass (for those under age 26), the Eurail Saverpass (which gives a discount for two or more people traveling together), a Eurail Flexipass (which allows a certain number of travel days within a set period), the Euraildrive Pass and the Europass Drive (which combine travel by train and rental car). Whichever pass you choose, remember that you must **purchase your pass before you leave** for Europe.

Many travelers assume that rail passes guarantee them seats on the trains they wish to ride. Not so. You need to **book seats ahead even if you are using a rail pass**; seat reservations are required on some European trains, particularly high-speed trains, and are a good idea on trains that may be crowded—particularly in summer on popular routes. You will also need a reservation if you purchase sleeping accommodations.

➤ INFORMATION AND PASSES: **Rail Europe** (✉ 500 Mamaroneck Ave., Harrison, NY 10528, ☎ 914/682–5172 or 800/438–7245, FAX 800/432–1329; ✉ 2087 Dundas E, Suite 106, Mississauga, Ontario L4X 1M2, ☎ 800/361–7245, FAX 905/602–4198). **DER Travel Services** (✉ 9501 W. Devon Ave., Rosemont, IL 60018, ☎ 800/782–2424, FAX 800/282–7474 for information or 800/860–9944 for brochures). **CIT Tours Corp.** (✉ 15 W. 44th St., 10th floor, New York, NY 10036, ☎ 212/730–2400 or 800/248–7245 in the U.S., 800/387–0711 or 800/361–7799 in Canada).

SCENIC ROUTES

Switzerland makes the most of its Alpine rail engineering, which cuts through the icy granite landscape above 2,000 m (6,560 ft), by offering **special trains** that run from one tourist destination to another, crossing over spectacular passes with panoramic cars. The *Glacier Express* connects the two glamourous resorts of Zermatt and Saint-Moritz, crawling over the Oberalp Pass and serving lunch in a burnished-wood period dining car; the *William Tell Express* combines a rail crossing of the Saint Gotthard Pass with a cruise down the length of Lake Luzern. The *Golden Pass/Panoramic Express* climbs from the balmy waterfront of Montreux into the Alpine terrain around Interlaken and rolls on to Luzern via the Brünig Pass. The *Bernina Express* ascends from Chur to Saint-Moritz, then climbs over the magnificent Bernina Pass into Italy, where visitors can connect by post bus to Lugano. The **Palm Express** route (summer only) combines all modes: You ride by bus from Saint-Moritz to Locarno in Ticino, then take a train into Italy. From Domodossola you cross the Simplon Pass into Brig and continue by rail to Zermatt or by bus to Saas-Fee. These sightseeing itineraries take from four to 11 hours of travel time. For more information, contact CFF (☞ *above*) or Railtour Suisse (✉ Chutzenstr. 24, CH-3000 Bern, ☎ 031/3780000, FAX 031/3780222).

FROM THE U.K.

With the Channel Tunnel completing a seamless route, you can leave London around noon on the Eurostar and (thanks to connections via Paris/Lyon on the superb French *train à grande vitesse,* TGV) have a late supper in Geneva.

The *Venice–Simplon–Orient Express* (✉ 20 Upper Ground, London SE1 9PD, ☎ 0171/928–6000) runs from London to Zürich. Information is also available from Abercrombie & Kent (☞ Tour Operators, *above*).

TRANSPORTATION

Switzerland offers perhaps the best transit network in Europe: impeccable autoroutes studded with emergency phones; trams and buses snaking through city streets; steamers crisscrossing blue lakes on schedules as tight as airlines; and, of course, the famous trains, whose wheels roll to a stop under the station clock just as the second hand sweeps 12.

It doesn't end there. Once on site, a web of tourist transportation gets you even closer to those spectacular views: Cogwheel trains grind up 45-degree slopes, lifts and gondolas sail silently

to vantage points, and tiny Alpine metros bore through granite up to green tundra above 8,000 ft.

Traveling by car is the surest way to penetrate the Swiss landscape, but if you invest in a rail pass (☞ Train Travel, *above*), you will not feel cut off. Most Swiss trains intersect with private excursion networks and allow for comfortable sightseeing itineraries without huge layovers. And there's always a sturdy yellow postbus following its appointed rounds with mountain-goat efficiency at minimal cost; connections to obscure villages and trails are free to holders of the Swiss Pass.

TRAVEL AGENCIES

A good travel agent puts your needs first. Look for an agency that has been in business at least five years, emphasizes customer service, and has someone on staff who specializes in your destination. In addition, **make sure the agency belongs to a professional trade organization,** such as ASTA in the United States. If your travel agency is also acting as your tour operator, *see* Buyer Beware in Tour Operators, *above*.

➤ LOCAL AGENT REFERRALS: **American Society of Travel Agents** (ASTA, ☎ 800/965–2782 24-hr hot line, FAX 703/684–8319). **Association of Canadian Travel Agents** (✉ Suite 201, 1729 Bank St., Ottawa, Ontario K1V 7Z5, ☎ 613/521–0474, FAX 613/521–0805). **Association of British Travel Agents** (✉ 55–57 Newman St., London W1P 4AH, ☎ 0171/637–2444, FAX 0171/637–0713). **Australian Federation of Travel Agents** (☎ 02/9264–3299). **Travel Agents' Association of New Zealand** (☎ 04/499–0104).

TRAVEL GEAR

Travel catalogs specialize in useful items, such as compact alarm clocks and travel irons, that can **save space when packing.** They also offer dual-voltage appliances, currency converters, and foreign-language phrase books.

➤ CATALOGS: **Magellan's** (☎ 800/962–4943, FAX 805/568–5406). **Orvis Travel** (☎ 800/541–3541, FAX 540/

THE GOLD GUIDE / SMART TRAVEL TIPS

343–7053). **TravelSmith** (☎ 800/950–1600, FAX 800/950–1656).

U.S. GOVERNMENT

Government agencies can be an excellent source of inexpensive travel information. When planning your trip, **find out what government materials are available.**

➤ ADVISORIES: **U.S. Department of State** (✉ Overseas Citizens Services Office, ✉ Room 4811 N.S., Washington, DC 20520; ☎ 202/647–5225 or FAX 202/647–3000 for interactive hot line; ☎ 301/946–4400 for computer bulletin board); enclose a self-addressed, stamped, business-size envelope.

➤ PAMPHLETS: **Consumer Information Center** (✉ Consumer Information Catalogue, Pueblo, CO 81009, ☎ 719/948–3334 or 888/878–3256) for a free catalog that includes travel titles.

VISITOR INFORMATION

For general information about Switzerland, contact the tourist offices before you go.

➤ SWISS NATIONAL TOURIST OFFICE: **U.S. (nationwide):** (✉ 608 5th Ave., New York, NY 10020, ☎ 212/757–5944, FAX 212/262–6116). **El Segundo, CA:** (✉ 222 N. Sepulveda Blvd., Suite 1570, 90245, ☎ 310/335–5980, FAX 310/335–5982). **Chicago:** (✉ 150 N. Michigan Ave., Suite 2930, 60601, ☎ 312/630–5840, FAX 312/630–5848). **Canada:** (✉ 926 The East Mall, Etobicoke, Ontario M9B 6KI, ☎ 416/695–2090 or ☎ 514/333–9526, FAX 416/695–2774). **U.K.:** (✉ Swiss Centre, 1 New Coventry St., London W1V 8EE, ☎ 0171/734–1921, FAX 0171/437–4577).

➤ WEB SITES: **Do check out the World Wide Web** when you're planning. You'll find everything from up-to-date weather forecasts to virtual tours of famous cities. Fodor's Web site, www.fodors.com, is a great place to start your on-line travels. For more information specifically on Switzerland, visit: **Switzerland Tourism** (www.switzerlandtourism.com), which allows travelers to customize a vacation in Switzerland, and even to book it through an interactive travel planner; **Swiss Online** (www.swissonline.ch) and **Travel.Org** (www.travel.org/switz.html) for links and information on a dozen cities, general travel tips, and more specialized topics like vegetarian restaurants; or **Swiss Federal Railways** (www.sbb.ch), which broadcasts train schedules and time tables. For information on outdoor activities, try **Trento Bike Pages** (www-math.science.unitn.it/Bike) and **Walking in Europe** (www.gorp.com/gorp/activity/europe/europe.html), which has a special page on walking in the Alps.

WHEN TO GO

In July and August, Switzerland's best weather coincides with the heaviest crowds. June and September are still pleasant, and hotel prices can be slightly lower, especially in resorts. In May and June the mountains are at their loveliest, with Alpine flowers blooming and the peaks capped with snow; however, as ski season is over and high summer hasn't begun, this is often considered low season, and many resort hotels close down. Those that remain open reduce their prices considerably. Another low-season disadvantage: Some cable-car and cogwheel train operations take a break between the midwinter and midsummer rushes; some must wait for snow to clear before reopening. The most prestigious ski resorts charge top prices during the Christmas–New Year holidays but reduce them slightly in early January. February through Easter is prime time again. Many of the family-run, traditional hotels fill up a year ahead, and you'll have to settle for less appealing lodgings. Also, check with the resort for exact dates of high seasons: They vary slightly from region to region. Late autumn—from mid-October through early December—is the least appealing season for visiting the Alps because there's usually little snow, no foliage, and a tendency toward dampness and fog. If you're sticking to the cities to shop and tour museums, you won't notice the doldrums that take over the resorts. The exception to the above rules of thumb: Ticino, the only portion of Switzerland south of the Alps, boasts a Mediterranean climate and declares high season from April through October. Many of its hotels close down altogether from November through March.

CLIMATE

What follow are average daily maximum and minimum temperatures for major cities in Switzerland.

GENEVA

Jan.	40F	4C	May	67F	19C	Sept.	70F	21C
	29	– 2		49	9		54	12
Feb.	43F	6C	June	74F	23C	Oct.	58F	14C
	31	– 1		56	13		45	7
Mar.	50F	10C	July	77F	25C	Nov.	47F	8C
	36	2		59	15		38	3
Apr.	59F	15C	Aug.	76F	24C	Dec.	40F	4C
	41	5		58	14		32	0

LUGANO

Jan.	43F	6C	May	70F	21C	Sept.	74F	23C
	29	– 2		50	10		56	13
Feb.	49F	9C	June	77F	25C	Oct.	61F	16C
	31	– 1		58	14		47	8
Mar.	56F	13C	July	81F	27C	Nov.	52F	11C
	38	3		61	16		38	3
Apr.	63F	17C	Aug.	81F	27C	Dec.	45F	7C
	45	7		59	15		32	0

SAINT-MORITZ

Jan.	29F	– 2C	May	50F	10C	Sept.	58F	14C
	11	–12		32	0		38	13
Feb.	34F	1C	June	59F	15C	Oct.	50F	10C
	13	–11		40	4		31	– 1
Mar.	38F	3C	July	63F	17C	Nov.	38F	3C
	18	– 8		41	5		22	– 6
Apr.	45F	7C	Aug.	61F	16C	Dec.	31F	– 1C
	25	– 4		41	5		14	10

ZÜRICH

Jan.	36F	2C	May	67F	19C	Sept.	68F	20C
	27	– 3		47	8		52	11
Feb.	41F	5C	June	74F	23C	Oct.	58F	14C
	29	– 2		54	12		43	6
Mar.	50F	10C	July	77F	25C	Nov.	45F	7C
	34	1		58	14		36	2
Apr.	59F	15C	Aug.	76F	24C	Dec.	38F	3C
	40	4		56	13		29	– 2

➤ FORECASTS: **Weather Channel Connection** (☎ 900/932–8437), 95¢ per minute from a Touch-Tone phone.

THE GOLD GUIDE / SMART TRAVEL TIPS

1 Destination: Switzerland

THE GOOD, THE BAD, AND THE TIDY

UP IN THE HOARY windswept heights and black fir forests of the Alps, an electric eye beams open a glistening all-glass door—and reveals the honey-gold glow of wood, the sheen of copper, the burnt-chocolate tones of ancient wooden rafters. Candles flicker; Sterno radiates blue-white flames under russet pots of bubbling fondue. The cheery *boomp-chick boomp-chick* of an accordion filters down from high-tech stereo speakers cleverly concealed behind oversize cowbells. Waitresses in starched black dirndls and waiters in bleached white ties scuttle briskly from kitchen to table, table to kitchen, while platters of gravy-laden veal, sizzling *Rösti* (hash brown potatoes), and rosy entrecôte simmer over steel trivets—preheated, electrically controlled—ready to be proudly, seamlessly served.

Coziness under strict control, anachronism versus state-of-the-art technology: strange bedfellows in a storybook land. Nowhere else in Europe can you find a combination as welcoming and as alien, as comfortable and as remote, as engaging and as disengaged as a glass cable car to the clouds. This is the paradox of the Swiss, whose primary national aesthetic pitches rustic Alpine homeyness against high-tech urban efficiency. Though they're proud, sober, self-contained, independent culturally and politically, disdainful of the shabby and the slipshod, painfully neat, rigorously prompt—the Swiss have a weakness for cuteness, and they indulge in incongruously coy diminutives: A German *Bierstube* becomes a *Stübli, Kuchen* (cake) becomes *Küchli, Wurst* becomes *Würstli, Pastete* (puff pastry) becomes *Pastetli,* and a *coupe* (glass) of champagne becomes a *Cüpli.*

It is lucky for tourists, this dichotomy of the folksy and the functional. It means your trains get you to your firelighted lodge on time. It means the shower in your room runs as hot as a Turkish bath. It means the cable car that sweeps you to a mountaintop has been subjected to grueling inspections. It means the handwoven curtains are boiled and starched, and the high-thread-count bed linens are turned back with a chocolate at night. It means the scarlet geraniums that cascade from window boxes on every carved balcony are tended like prize orchids. It means the pipe smoke that builds up in the Stübli (cozy little pubs) at night is aired out daily, as sparkling clean, double-glazed windows are thrown open on every floor, every morning, to let sharp, cool mountain air course through hallways, bedrooms, and fresh-bleached baths.

Yet there is a stinginess that peeks around the apron of that rosy-cheeked efficiency. Liquor here is measured with scientific precision into glasses marked for one centiliter or two, and the local wines come in carafes reminiscent of laboratory beakers. Despite the fine linens and puffs of down that adorn each bed, double beds have separate mattresses with sheets tucked primly down the middle, sometimes so tightly you have to lift the mattress to loosen the barrier. And if you wash out your socks and hang them loosely on the shower rod in the morning, you may return at night and find them straightened, spaced, toes pointing the same direction, as orderly as little lead soldiers.

Nevertheless there is an earthiness about these people, as at ease with the soil as they are appalled by dirt. A banker in Zürich may rent a postage-stamp parcel of land in a crowded patchwork outside town, sowing tight rows of cabbages and strawberries, weeding bright borders of marigolds, and on Sunday he may visit his miniature estate, pull a chair out from the tidy toolshed, and simply sit and smoke, like Heidi's Alm-Uncle surveying his Alpine realm. An elderly woman may don knickers and loden hat and board a PTT postbus to the mountains and climb steep, rocky trails at a brisk clip, cheeks glowing, eyes as icy bright as the glaciers above her. A family of farmers—grandparents, schoolgirls, married sons—unite for the hay cutting as if for Christmas dinner, standing shoulder to shoulder in the hip-high gold, swinging scythes from dawn to sunset.

There's a 21st century counterpoint to this: the high-tech, jet-set glamour that splashes vivid colors across the slopes at Saint-Moritz, Gstaad, Zermatt, Verbier. Step out of a bulbous steel-and-glass cable car onto a concrete platform at 2,000 m (6,560 ft) and see Switzerland transformed, its workers' blue overalls and good wool suits exchanged for Day-Glo ski suits—mango, chartreuse, swimming-pool blue. Wholesome, healthy faces disappear behind mirrored goggles and war-paint sunblock, and gaudy skis and poles bristle militarily, like the pikes and halberds in the Battle of Sempach.

The contradictions mount: While fur-clad socialites raise jeweled fingers to bid at Sotheby's on Geneva's quai de Mont-Blanc, the women of Appenzell stand beside their husbands on the Landsgemeindeplatz and raise their hands to vote—a right not won until 1991. While digital screens tick off beef futures in Zürich, the crude harmony of cowbells echoes in velvet mountain pastures. While a Mercedes roars down an expressway expertly blasted through solid rock, a horse-drawn plow peels back thin topsoil in an Alpine garden plot, impossibly steep, improbably high.

And on August 1, the Swiss national holiday, while spectacular displays of fireworks explode in sizzling colors over the cities and towns, the mountain folk build the bonfires that glow quietly, splendidly, on every hillside of every Alp, uniting Swiss citizens as they celebrate their proud independence, their cultural wealth, and above all their diversity. It's that diversity and those quirky contradictions that make Switzerland a tourist capital—the folksy, fiercely efficient innkeeper to the world.

— Nancy Coons

Girardet's protégé, and Gérard Rabaey lead the pack, with Bernard Ravet in Vufflens-le-Château close on their heels. Horst Petermann in Zürich, Roland Pierroz in Verbier, Roland Jöhri in Saint-Moritz, and Georges Wenger in Le Noirmont still vie for the top of the national heap. One of the best chefs of recent years, however, is sadly gone; Basel-based Hans Stucki died in the winter of 1998. His protégé Jean-Claude Wicky now heads the kitchen.

One of the heights of the Swiss traditional festival calendar is coming up: the **Fête des Vignerons** (Winegrowers' Festival) will be held from late July through early August of 1999. Based in Vevey, in the Vaud canton, the festival is held roughly every 25 years. Pageants and parades engulf the town—and on opening day there's a coronation for prize-winning wine growers followed by a tremendous banquet.

Skiers who annually converge on such Graubünden resorts as Saint-Moritz and Klosters will have their path considerably smoothed; the **Vereina Tunnel,** stretching from Klosters to Susch/Lavin, is slated for completion in late fall 1999. The railway will load cars and whisk away twice an hour from each terminal—an especially big blessing when the Flüela Pass is closed by snow.

Luzern's world-renowned **International Music Festival** has a new home—the 1998 festival inaugurated the Kultur- und Kongresszentrum, a modern lakeside venue.

Recent dips in the **Swiss franc's** clout have eased the pain for American visitors, and tourism has begun to pick up steam.

In fall 1998, new carrier **Swiss World Airways** began service with nonstop flights from Newark to Geneva.

NEW AND NOTEWORTHY

Despite the departure of Fredy Girardet from the pantheon of European chefs, the Lac Léman (Lake Geneva) region has been able to retain its status as the country's gastronomic mecca. **Philippe Rochat,**

WHAT'S WHERE

Zürich

Known as one of the leading financial centers of the world, Zürich at first sight may appear to be a modest, small-scale city, but the array of luxury shops along its Bahnhofstrasse and its renowned Opera reveal its cultural and material riches. Its Old Town, which straddles the River Limmat, has few high-rise buildings; Gothic guildhalls take the place of imperial palaces. In the distance, snow-clad peaks overlook the waters of the lake, dwarfing everything below.

Eastern Switzerland

Near Zürich, the cantons of Glarus, Schaffhausen, Thurgau, Saint-Gallen, and Appenzell, as well as the independent principality of Liechtenstein, are dominated by the Rhine River. With its obscure backcountry and thriving cities, the German-influenced region has everything from wood-shingle farmhouses to town houses adorned with oriel windows and frescoes. Still, the eastern cantons remain one of the most untouched regions of Switzerland.

Graubünden

Dominated by its trendy resorts—Saint-Moritz, Davos, Klosters, Arosa, Pontresina—Graubünden is nonetheless Switzerland's most culturally diverse and largest canton. German, Italian, and Romansh—the ancient dialect that is thought to date from 600 BC—are all spoken here, in a land where stalwart native farmers subsist alongside fur-clad tourists from abroad. This is also the site of Switzerland's only national park, probably the only place in the country where skiing is forbidden.

Ticino

Italian in language, culture, and spirit, Ticino is an irresistible combination of Mediterranean pleasures and Swiss efficiency. With its yacht-filled waterfront promenades of Locarno and Lugano and its constantly sunny climate, Ticino is a canton set apart, a happy harbor for Switzerland's Italian-speaking minority.

Luzern and Central Switzerland

Endowed with a sophisticated transportation system that makes it one of the easiest regions to visit, central Switzerland is full of neat little towns, accessible mountains, and modest resorts. Centered around the Vierwaldstättersee, "the lake of the four forest cantons," the region is steeped in history: It is where the Oath of Eternal Alliance is said to have been renewed, and it's also the birthplace of the legend of William Tell.

Basel

At the juncture of France and Germany, German-speaking Basel is a cultural capital with a sense of fun. Cultivated and yet down-home, it has more than 30 museums, Switzerland's oldest university, and some of the most diverse shopping in the country. All the same, beer and sausages are the snack of choice, and the annual Fasnacht (Carnival) is observed with a boisterousness that's unparalleled by other Swiss towns.

Fribourg, Neuchâtel, and the Jura

Unself-conscious and largely undiscovered, the cantons of Fribourg, Neuchâtel, and the Jura represent three very different worlds in western Switzerland. Fribourg, part German and part French, is full of medieval villages; Neuchâtel, French in language and culture, is beginning to shift its focus from watchmaking to tourism; and the isolated Jura Mountains, part German and part French, exist in a realm of their own.

Bern

Humble and down-to-earth, Bern is a city of broad medieval streets, farmers' markets, and friendly, slow-spoken people. It is also the federal capital of Switzerland and, more remarkably, a World Cultural Heritage city known for its sandstone arcades, fountains, flowers, and thick, sturdy towers.

Berner Oberland

The Bernese Alps concentrate the very best of rural Switzerland: panoramas of the Eiger, Mönch, and Jungfrau mountains; crystalline lakes, gorges, and waterfalls; and emerald slopes dotted with gingerbread chalets and cows with bells—not to mention world-class skiing. It's no secret, though: The Berner Oberland is among the most popular tourist destinations in Switzerland.

Valais

Alpine villages, famous peaks (the Matterhorn, most notably), world-class resorts (Zermatt, Saas-Fee, Crans, Verbier), and verdant vineyards are all reasons to

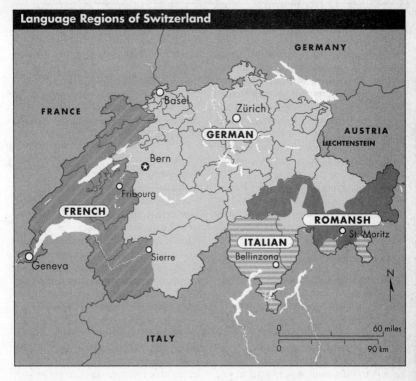

Language Regions of Switzerland

visit the valley of the Rhone. This is the Switzerland of tumbledown huts, raclette eaters, and yodelers. Separated from the modern world by mountains, it feels like a land apart.

Vaud

Lausanne, Montreux, and the Alpes Vaudoises comprise one of Switzerland's most diverse regions. Centered around Lac Léman (also known as Lake Geneva), this French-speaking canton harbors some of the country's most famous cathedrals and castles, as well as Alpine villages, balmy lake resorts, and above all, its most verdant vineyards.

Geneva

As the headquarters of the United Nations, the World Health Organization, and the International Red Cross; an international mecca for writers and thinkers of every stripe; and a stronghold of luxurious stores and extravagant restaurants, Geneva is Switzerland's most cosmopolitan city. This is a city of wealth and influence, where the rustic chalets of hilltop villages seem worlds away.

PLEASURES AND PASTIMES

Dining

If you're looking for diverse dining experiences, you can't do much better than Switzerland, where French, Italian, or German cuisine may dominate, depending on which cantons you visit. In French areas (roughly Vaud, Geneva, Jura, Neuchâtel, and western parts of Fribourg and Valais) the cuisine is clearly Gallic, and wine stews, organ meats, and subtle sausages appear alongside standard *cuisine bourgeoise:* thick, rare beef entrecôte with a choice of rich sauces and *truite meunière* (trout dredged in flour and sizzled in butter). In the Ticino, the Italian canton, Italian cuisine appears virtually unscathed, particularly the Alpine-forest specialties of Piedmont and Lombardy (risotto, gnocchi, polenta, porcini mushrooms). The German cantons serve more pork than their neighbors and favor another standard dish that represents Switzerland though it vanishes in French-speaking or Italian-speaking areas: Rösti, a broad patty of hash-brown potatoes crisped in a skillet and often flavored with bacon, herbs, or cheese, is as prevalent in the German regions as fondue in the French. Beyond the obvious cultural differences, Swiss cuisine is also influenced by the terrain: Mountain farmers have traditionally subsisted on such basic foods as raclette (cheese melted over boiled potatoes and garnished with pickled vegetables), while cities nurtured wealthy burghers and noblemen with the cream of the crops of outlying lands—milk-fed veal, fruits from low-lying orchards. Though fondue, Rösti, and veal are likely to be on any resort's menu these days, traces of these influences can still be found almost everywhere.

Hiking

When the snow melts and the mountain streams start to flow, Switzerland takes to the hills. That the Swiss Alps are the ultimate in hiking is no secret: On a sunny day in high season in the more popular vacation areas, footpaths can be almost as crowded as a line for World Series tickets. On narrow trails, hikers walk in single file, and the more aggressive pass on the left as if on the Autobahns of Germany. However, there is an almost infinite quantity of quiet, isolated routes to be explored; if you prefer to hike in peace, head for one of the less inhabited Alpine valleys—in the Valais or Graubünden there are several—and strike out on your own. Each of the regional tourist departments publishes suggested hiking itineraries, and major map publishers distribute excellent topographical maps of wilderness trails. In the German-speaking region especially, hiking is a deeply rooted tradition, and people of all ages and in all physical conditions head for well-beaten paths in jeans as often as knickers, woolen stockings, rucksacks, and hiking boots.

Regional Celebrations

Basel's extravagant pre-Lenten observance of Fasnacht (Carnival)—in which up to 20,000 costumed revelers fill the streets with the sounds of fifes and drums—is only one of the hundreds of festivals that the Swiss celebrate during the year. As if to prove that its spirit is vast despite its small size, almost every Swiss canton hosts its own popular celebration of one event or another. In Geneva, the Festival of the Escalade commemorates the heroic house-wife who repelled the Savoyards by dumping hot soup on their heads. Lesser-known festivals range from the frivolous—in the Schlitteda Engiadinaisa, young unmarried men and women ride decorated sleighs through the villages of the Engadine—to the symbolic—in the Landsgemeinde, the citizens of Appenzell pay homage to their country's democratic tradition by conducting a vote by public show of hands.

Shopping

Swiss Army knives, Swiss watches, Swiss chocolate—what could be more . . . Swiss? Though you won't find many bargains in Switzerland anytime soon, you will find some uniquely Swiss treasures. Some of the best souvenirs of this pragmatic country are typically practical, such as watches, clocks, and Swiss Army knives. Others are more luxurious, such as sweet milk chocolate: Lindt, Nestlé, and Tobler are major manufacturers. Marvelous music boxes from the watchmaking country around Lake Neuchâtel are sold in specialty shops all over the country. Linens and good cottons—dish and tea towels, aprons, sheets—are another Swiss specialty, as are pottery and ceramics—most of them dark-glazed and hand-painted with simple designs.

Skiing

Switzerland is Europe's winter playground, and its facilities are as technically advanced as its slopes are spectacular. As one recent skier put it, "There's just *more*"—more slopes; longer runs; more stunning, crisp scenery than you'll find in U.S. resorts. Any level of skier can find a resort to meet his or her needs, from a cozy family-oriented village with easy and moderate slopes to the world-class challenges at Verbier, Wengen, and Zermatt. Most of the resorts publish an area map showing their slopes and rating the trails for difficulty. Familiarize yourself with the resort's signs, including those warning of avalanche zones, before you set out. For an analysis of the best ski resorts, *see* Skiing Switzerland *in* Chapter 14.

Spectator Sports

If awards were given to countries with the most unusual sports competitions, Switzerland would win hands down. In the winter, the action centers around Saint-Moritz, where a frozen lake provides a novel setting for golf, polo, dogsled races, and horse races: In the Winter Golf Tournament, red balls on white "greens" are a festive sight; in the Racing Hounds Competition, a motley crew of canines races across 480 m (1,574 ft) of ice at an average speed of 90 kph (55 mph). Also in Saint-Moritz, the uniquely Swiss sport of *Skijöring* involves skiers being pulled by galloping horses. Cows are the players in another, nonwinter event: In April, small towns throughout the Valais hold a *combat de reines*, or cow fight. Female cows head-butt each other (though some contestants have been known to just placidly chew their cud); the winner, *la reine* (the queen), is decorated and awarded with the best grazing ground. Wrestling is a popular Swiss tradition: Men wear big baggy shorts of burlap and stand in sawdust rings; after the competition, costumed spectators sing and dance. Perhaps most unusual, stone-throwing competitions in Unspunnen (in the canton of Bern) take place every five years; 180-pound stones are used.

GREAT ITINERARIES

In a country as diverse as Switzerland, it makes sense to visit with a theme in mind. Below, we have outlined itineraries for culinary adventures and exploring historic castles. *Bon appétit* and happy exploring.

Swiss Gastronomy

This food-intensive itinerary offers aficionados an opportunity to travel from one great dining experience to another, sampling the very finest *haute gastronomie* at one stop, the most authentic regional classics—even the earthiest peasant cuisines—at another. Incidental pleasures—wandering in the Alps, for example, or strolling through medieval town centers in Switzerland's greatest cities—can be squeezed in between meals. We'll start in Geneva, sampling its Lyon-influenced cuisine, then head east toward Lausanne and Crissier, where Philippe Rochat attempts to replace the legendary (but retired) Fredy Girardet. Then it's northward to Basel, where his rival Jean-Claude Wicky at the restaurant Stucki competes for culinary stars. From Basel, it's an hour's journey

to Küsnacht near Zürich, where the third of the Swiss triumvirate—Horst Petermann—reigns. After that, take a dip south to Luzern for regional cuisine. Now it's time for a little exercise: crossing the Alps into the Valais (the Rhône Valley), resting at Saas-Fee for a mountain-inn getaway, and following the Rhône back toward Geneva, stopping at Verbier, another mountain resort, for a gastronomic feast to tide you over for the journey home.

DURATION➤ Depending on your capacity for stellar meals—one or two per day—you can concentrate the highlights of this trip into nine marathon days or stretch it out over two weeks or more. If you're planning to pack it all into a few days, check opening days carefully—and always book ahead. Many restaurants in Geneva close weekends, and many elsewhere close Monday or Tuesday.

GETTING AROUND➤ Each of the stopovers is accessible by train, though some of the restaurants may require cabs or tram rides; a rental car will give you more flexibility for reaching country inns.

THE MAIN ROUTE➤ **1 night: Geneva.** Your first night, indulge in a hearty Lyonnaise bistro meal at Le Boeuf Rouge. For lunch the next day, head for the elite country-club atmosphere in the suburb of Cologny to rub shoulders with jet-set diners over bouillabaisse at Le Lion d'Or. Back in Geneva, have a relatively light Ticinese supper at La Favola. Incidental distractions to fill time between meals: world-class museums (especially the International Red Cross Museum), Old Town antiques shops, or the early Christian diggings under the cathedral.

1 night: Lausanne. Testing Phillipe Rochat's mettle at Restaurant Rochat in nearby Crissier may be the triumph of the trip—but reserve judgment for after Basel and Zürich. At night, head down to the waterfront at Ouchy and have a chic, light supper at the Café Beau-Rivage.

1 night: Basel. Two hours north, compare Jean-Claude Wicky with Rochat at lunch. Then, after visiting, say, the Münster and the history museum, relax in the downstairs bistro at the Teufelhof: The light specialties are prepared by Michael Baader, who is chef for the top-notch restaurant upstairs as well.

2 nights: Zürich. Have lunch at Peter-mann's Kunststuben, in the suburb of Küsnacht, where the gastronomy vies for the title "best in Switzerland." Then, after a thorough walking tour of Zürich's Old Town, you can settle in for an atmospheric, old-world evening at the Kronenhalle or an outdoor meal of fresh lake fish on the terrace of the Fischstube.

1 night: Luzern. For a total contrast and perhaps the most authentically *Swiss* meal of your tour, head for Galliker and a lunch of real farm food. Having absorbed the Lion Monument, crossed the Kapell-brücke, and toured the history museum, you can think about the evening meal: A light, sophisticated river-fish meal at Des Balances affords waterfront views.

1 night: Saas-Fee. From Luzern, allow for a full day's scenic mountain drive south over the Brünigpass, then on over the Grimselpass and down the Rhône Valley to Brig and the spectacular little resort of Saas-Fee. Once there, retreat to the isolated Waldhotel Fletschhorn for a sophisticated dinner and a bare minimum of one night to take in the mountain air.

1 night: Verbier. Following the Rhône back west toward Geneva, take one more Alpine side trip up to this famous ski resort to feast and sleep at Rosalp, the popular rustic-chic inn in the village center.

INFORMATION➤ *See* Chapters 2, 6, 7, and 11–13.

Castles and Cathedrals

Romantics, history buffs, and architecture fans will enjoy a circle tour that takes in some of the best of western Switzerland's medieval and Gothic landmarks. Start at Geneva, where the cathedral covers Christian history from Gallo-Roman times through Calvin. At Montreux, you'll visit the famous waterfront Castle of Chillon, where Lord Byron signed the pillar where his "Prisoner of Chillon" was manacled. In the green Fribourg countryside, the Gruyères Castle perches at the top of a tiny preserved village. The bilingual capital Fribourg is the last Catholic stronghold of western Switzerland, rooted in its single-tower cathedral, and a stronghold for the dukes of Zähringen as well. A jog down to the Berner Oberland and Thun takes you to the mighty Zähringen Castle along the waters of the Thunersee. Then head

up to Bern, entirely fortified by the Zähringen dukes, with its spectacular *Münster,* and on to Basel, where its own Münster dominates the Old Town.

DURATION➤ Six days.

GETTING AROUND➤ All stops are easily accessible by expressway and connecting roads.

The complete itinerary works by rail, with most sites accessible on foot from the station; Gruyères has bus connections to the elevated castle and Old Town.

THE MAIN ROUTE➤ **1 night: Geneva.** The Cathédrale St-Pierre, begun during the 12th century, sinks roots into early Christianity: Immediately below its current structure, you'll find the *site archéologique,* where 3rd- and 5th-century ruins have been exposed.

1 night: Montreux. The Château de Chillon, partially surrounded by the waters of Lac Léman (Lake Geneva), may be the most completely and authentically furnished in Switzerland, with tapestries, carved fireplaces, ceramics, and painted wooden ceilings.

1 night: Gruyères. This craggy castle-village draws crowds to its ancient central street, souvenir shops, quaint inns, and frescoed castle, complete with dungeon and spectacular views.

1 night: Fribourg. The Last Judgment tympanum and Art Nouveau stained-glass windows of the Cathédrale St-Nicolas deserve attention—but leave time to explore the Old Town, with its multilevel fortifications constructed for the ubiquitous Zähringens.

1 night: Thun. If you're driving, cut across the rolling verdure of canton Fribourg toward Thun (by train, connect through Bern), where you'll see the Bernese Alps looming in all their splendor. Zähringen Castle, which dates from 1191, features a knight's hall, tapestries, local ceramics, and an intimidating collection of weapons.

1 night: Bern. The Zähringens fortified this gooseneck in the River Aare; its 14th-century Münster features an unusually restored (full-color, painted) main portal.

1 night: Basel. In this historic, cosmopolitan city is a Münster with a lovely Romanesque portal and the tomb of the great humanist Erasmus.

INFORMATION> *See* Chapters 8–10, 12, and 13.

FODOR'S CHOICE

No two people will agree on what makes a perfect vacation, but it's fun and helpful to know what others think. We hope you'll have a chance to experience some of Fodor's Choices yourself while visiting Switzerland.

Dining

★ The transfer is complete; the former Girardet, outside Lausanne, is now **Restaurant Rochat.** Philippe Rochat is no newcomer, though—having worked with Girardet for nearly 20 years, he maintains his mentor's standards with such dishes as preserved duckling in lemon and spices. *$$$$*

★ You'll have to go off the beaten track to find one of the best chefs in Switzerland; the **Hôtel-Restaurant de la Gare** is in the village of Le Noirmont, practically on the French border. It's well worth the trek, as chef Georges Wenger adapts local Jura ingredients to sophisticated, seasonal cuisine. *$$$$*

★ Inside what was once the Heuberg mansion in Basel, the **Teufelhof** has an excellent restaurant, a chic weinstübe, and a trendy bar—there are even medieval ruins in the basement. The menus are always intriguing. *$$–$$$$*

★ The 20th-century art collection is as plentiful as the food at Zürich's **Kronenhalle,** where robust cooking in hearty portions draws a genial crowd. *$$$*

★ At **Wirtschaft zum Frieden,** in Schaffhausen, you can opt for a daily plate lunch in an intimate stübli, a fancier meal in a tile-stove dining room, or selections from either menu in a private garden thick with wisteria. *$$–$$$*

★ Authentic Lyonnaise cuisine is the specialty at Geneva's **Boeuf Rouge,** where *boudin noir* (blood sausage) and *tarte Tatin* (caramelized apple tart) will make you think you've crossed the border. *$$*

★ In a 1677 inn at the hub of Chur, **Stern** carries on the age-old tradition of Graubündner culture, complete with local wine served in pewter pitchers and waitresses in folk costumes. *$–$$*

★ Under a giant boar's head and century-old murals at **Bierhalle Kropf,** businesspeople, workers, and shoppers share crowded tables to feast on hearty Zürich cuisine. *$–$$*

★ Tucked in a tiny basement in an alleyway off Lugano's Old Town, **La Tinera** draws crowds of locals and tourists for its hearty meats, pastas, and local wine served in ceramic bowls. *$*

Lodging

★ Lausanne's **Beau Rivage-Palace** stands apart in neoclassic grandeur, with manicured waterfront grounds and several first-class restaurants. *$$$$*

★ In Geneva's Old Town, **Les Armures** is an archaeological treasure with original stonework, frescoes, and stenciled beams. *$$$$*

★ Overlooking green waterfront grounds on the Murtensee, the turn-of-the-century **Le Vieux Manoir au Lac** offers sumptuously decorated rooms. *$$$$*

★ **Tamaro,** a Romantik property on the Ascona waterfront, has a grand Mediterranean air and excellent lake views. *$$$*

★ A 600-year-old structure on the banks of the Limmat, **Zum Storchen** is one of Zürich's most atmospheric hotels. *$$$*

★ In Château-d'Oex, the 18th-century **Bon Acceuil** has low wood-beam ceilings, creaking floors, antiques, and fresh flowers inside and out. *$$*

★ A demure little inn on a residential hillside between Chillon and Montreux, **Masson** has offered peace and quiet to weary travelers since 1829. *$$*

★ With lead-glass windows, homespun linen, and pewter pitchers, the all-wood chalet **Ruedihus** in Kandersteg re-creates the atmosphere of the 1753 original. *$$*

★ Basel's **Krafft am Rhein** is a rare find in Swiss cities—it's an elegant little inn sitting directly on the right-bank waterfront, with mosaic floors, elaborate moldings, and a sinuous atrium stairwell. Try for a Rhine-side room. *$–$$*

Perfect Moments

★ When the sound of fife-and-drum music drifts from upstairs windows of guild houses in **Basel's Old Town,** you'll think the Middle Ages have dawned once again.

★ Feeding swans and ducks by the **Kapellbrücke** in Luzern is a favorite pastime of locals and tourists alike.

★ Counting the waterfalls around the **Oeschinensee,** above Kandersteg, is a perfect way to celebrate spring.

★ A herd of male red deer, antlers silhouetted, in the **Parc Naziunal Svizzer** (Swiss National Park), is a memorable sight.

★ Drinking **steaming-fresh milk** in an Alpine barn, you'll understand why Heidi loved Switzerland.

★ Fireworks burst and mountain-farm bonfires smolder on the **Swiss National Holiday** (August 1).

★ For a festive, outdoorsy evening, rent a lap blanket for a summer night's outdoor performance of the **Tellspiel** at Interlaken.

Picturesque Villages and Towns

★ Clinging vertiginously to a hillside, its flower-filled balconies overlooking the sea, tiny **Gandria** retains the ambience of an ancient fishing village.

★ In the Lower Engadine, **Guarda** is a federally protected hamlet of architectural photo-ops, with cobblestone streets and flower boxes filled with red geraniums.

★ An eagle's-nest town set on a precarious 1,000-m (3,280-ft) slope in the Rhône Valley, **Isérables** is full of stone-shingled *mazots* (barns typical of the Valais) and narrow, winding streets.

★ **Morcote,** an old resort village below Lugano, has clay-color Lombard-style houses and arcades that look out on the waterfront.

★ In western Switzerland near Avenches, the ancient town of **Murten** (known in French as Morat) is a popular lake resort with a superbly preserved medieval center.

★ In the vineyard region of the Vaud, the cobblestone village of **St-Saphorin** is worth a stop, if only for a glass of the fruity local wine and a view of the lake from Café du Raisin.

★ On the Rhine River in eastern Switzerland, **Stein-am-Rhein** is a nearly perfectly preserved medieval village, replete with shingled, half-timber town houses boasting ornate oriels and flamboyant frescoes.

Views

★ The terrace café of the Disneyland-like **Château Gütsch** affords an idyllic view of Luzern and the Vierwaldstättersee.

★ In the **Emmental region** near Bern, the gentle hills begin to roll out village after beautiful village, dotted with many impressive examples of the classic Emmental farmstead.

★ From the summit station of **Gornergrat,** the snaggle-toothed Matterhorn steals the thunder from all surrounding peaks.

★ From the top of the 3,474-m (11,395-ft) **Jungfraujoch,** the Aletsch Glacier looks like a vast sea of ice.

★ With its mists, roaring water, jutting rocks, and bushy crags, the **Rheinfall,** from the Neuhausen side, appears truly Wagnerian.

★ Perched high above town, Bern's **Rose Garden** overlooks the entire Old Town.

★ The sunset from the south-facing hilltop resort of **Wengen** is a sublime way to end a day of skiing.

FESTIVALS AND SEASONAL EVENTS

Top seasonal events in Switzerland include Fasnacht (Carnival) celebrations in February and March, the Landsgemeinde open-air vote in Appenzell in April, the Montreux International Jazz Festival in July, the Menuhin Festival in Gstaad in August, the Knabenschiessen (Boys' Shooting Contest) in Zürich in September, and the Escalade festival in Geneva in December. Events are named below as publicized by the host region, usually in the local language.

WINTER

EARLY DEC.➤ **Geneva Escalade** commemorates the defeat of the Duke of Savoy, whose invading troops were repelled by a local woman dumping hot soup on their heads from atop the city walls.

MID-JAN.➤ **Vogel Gryff Volksfest** is a colorful Basel tradition, with a costumed Griffin, a Lion, and a Wild Man of the Woods floating down the Rhine and dancing on the Mittlere Rheinbrücke.

LATE JAN.➤ **Schlittedas Engiadinaisa** is a winter Engadine tradition in which young unmarried men and women ride decorated sleighs from village to village. **Châteaux-d'Oex Hot Air Balloon Week** showcases the Vaud resort's specialty.

EARLY FEB.➤ **Hom Strom** at Bad Scuol in the Lower Engadine observes the burning of Old Man Winter.

LATE FEB.–EARLY MAR.➤ **Fasnacht** is observed throughout Switzerland, but nowhere more festively than in Basel, where it begins at 4 AM on the Monday after Ash Wednesday, with a drum-roll and a costume parade. Luzern celebrates on the Thursday before Ash Wednesday, with a traditional **Fritschi** procession, distributing oranges to children. On the same day, Schwyz celebrates **Blätzli** with a mummers' procession of harlequins. Lugano celebrates Carnevale with a **Festa del Risotto,** with risotto and sausages served in the streets.

SPRING

EARLY MAR.➤ **Good Friday** (April 2) processions take place in several southern villages, including Mendrisio in the Ticino, where the procession derives from a medieval Passion Play that is performed on Maundy Thursday as well.

MID-MAR.➤ **Engadine Ski Marathon** covers the 42 km (26 mi) between Zuoz and Maloja.

MAR.–MAY➤ **Primavera Concertistica** music festival takes place in Lugano.

APR.➤ **Sechseläuten** in Zürich shows all its medieval guilds on parade and climaxes in the burning of the Böögg, a straw scarecrow representing winter.

APR.➤ **Landsgemeinde** takes place in the town of Appenzell on the last Sunday of the month punctually at noon, with all citizens voting by public show of hands. Women voted for the first time in 1991.

APR.➤ Small towns throughout the Valais hold a **Combat de Reines,** or cow fight, where female cows are pitted against each other in what amounts to a head-butting contest.

APR.–MAY➤ The **International Jazz Festival—Bern** lasts five days in the federal capital.

SUMMER

MID-JUNE➤ **Grindelwald Country-Festival** brings American country-and-western groups to this mountain resort.

LATE JUNE–MID-SEPT.➤ **Wilhelm Tell** outdoor theater production, in Interlaken, has an epic-scale cast of locals.

JULY➤ **Montreux International Jazz Festival** hosts world-class artists.

JULY–AUG.➤ **Engadiner Concert Weeks** bring outdoor classical music events to resorts throughout the region. **Festival International de l'Orgue Ancien** at Valère in Sion honors the 13th-century instrument within, the oldest functioning organ in the world.

LATE JULY–EARLY AUG.➤ Vevey's **Fête des Vignerons** (Wine Growers' Festival), which is held roughly every quarter century, sweeps through the town with pageants, music, parades, and the coronation of the best winegrowers.

AUG. 1➤ **Swiss National Holiday** celebrates the confederation's birth in 1291 with fireworks and bonfires.

EARLY AUG.➤ **Geneva Festival** celebrates with folk processions and fireworks.

AUG.➤ Locarno's **International Film Festival** unveils top new movies in the Piazza Grande.

MID-AUG.➤ **Grächen Country Festival** imports American C&W music to the Alps. Vevey **International Festival of Film Comedy** honors comic classics on the outdoor screen.

LATE AUG.➤ **International Folklore Festival** in Fribourg celebrates its 25th anniversary.

MID-AUG.–MID-SEPT.➤ **Internationale Musikfestwochen** in Luzern combines concerts, theater, and art exhibitions. Davos **Young Artists in Concert** features tomorrow's classical music stars.

AUG.–MID-SEPT.➤ **Yehudi Menuhin Festival** in Gstaad showcases world-class musicians. Lugano's **Blues to Bop Festival** brings authentic blues to the lakefront.

LATE AUG.➤ Zürich's **Theaterspektakel** showcases avant-garde and mainstream playwrights as well as theater troupes from around the world.

LATE AUG.–OCT.➤ **Vevey-Montreux Music Festival** invites important artists to these twin lake resorts.

AUTUMN

EARLY SEPT.➤ **Knabenschiessen** takes place in Zürich with a folk festival and fair.

MID-SEPT.➤ **Bénichon,** a traditional autumn Fribourg feast, is held during the second week of September; it celebrates not only the return of the cows from the high pastures to the plains, but also the season's final yield of hearty food.

LATE SEPT.➤ The **Neuchâtel Wine Festival** is the biggest in the country.

LATE SEPT.➤ **Etivaz Cheese Sharing** celebrates the division of spoils from the cheese cooperative with yodeling, wrestling, and other activities. **Fribourg Braderie** combines a citywide sidewalk sale, folk festival, and onion market.

LATE SEPT.–EARLY OCT.➤ The small Vaud town of St-Cergue has an annual **Fête Desalpe,** a ritual for the cows coming down from the mountains. It lasts all of a Saturday morning, allowing hundreds of cows to parade the streets in amazing floral headgear.

OCT.➤ In Lugano, a traditional **Wine Harvest Festival** is held at the Piazza della Riforma and on the lakeside.

LATE OCT.➤ **Olma Schweizer Messe für Land- und Milchwirtschaft** (agricultural and dairy fair) in Saint-Gallen gathers representatives of the farming industry from across Switzerland.

LATE NOV.➤ Bern's **Zwiebelemärit** (Onion Market) celebrates the open market established for area farmers in gratitude for aid they gave Bern after the great fire of 1405.

2 Zürich

*Known as one of the leading financial
centers of the world, Zürich is a
surprisingly modest, small-scale city.
Its Old Town, which straddles the
Limmat River, has just a handful
of high-rise buildings, and Gothic
guildhalls take the place of imperial
palaces. In the distance, snow-clad
peaks overlook the waters of the lake,
dwarfing everything below.*

Updated by
Nancy Coons

WHEN THE POUND STERLING sagged in the 1960s, the English coined the somewhat disparaging term "the gnomes of Zürich," which evoked images of sly little Swiss bankers rubbing their hands and manipulating world currencies behind closed doors. Yet the spirit that moves the Züricher doesn't come out of folkloric forests but rather from the pulpit of the Grossmünster, where the fiery Reformation leader Huldrych Zwingli preached sermons about idle hands and the devil's playgrounds. It's the Protestant work ethic that has made Zürich one of the world's leading financial centers and that keeps its workers on their toes. One Zwingli lesson stressed the transience of wealth, and Zürichers show native caution in enjoying their fabulous gains. Nor have they turned their backs on their humbler heritage: On a first visit, you might be surprised to see a graceful jumble of shuttered Gothic buildings instead of cold chrome-and-glass towers.

Zürich is, in fact, a beautiful city, sitting astride the Limmat River where it flows into the Zürichsee (Zürich Lake). Its charming Old Town, comprising a substantial part of the city center, is full of beautifully restored historic buildings and narrow, hilly alleys. In the distance, snowy mountains overlook the waters of the lake, and the shores are dominated by turn-of-the-century mansions. Only three high-rise buildings disturb the skyline, and even they are small by U.S. standards. There are not even any dominating castles to haunt the Züricher with memories of imperialism: In keeping with its solid bourgeois character, Zürich has always maintained a human scale.

The earliest known Zürichers lived around 4500 BC in small houses perched on stilts by the lakeside. The remains of 34 Stone Age and Bronze Age settlements are thought to be scattered around the lake. Underwater archaeologists have discovered a wealth of prehistoric artifacts dating back thousands of years, from Stone Age pottery and Bronze Age necklaces to charms made from boar fangs, bear teeth, and animal skulls; many relics are on display at the Schweizerisches Landesmuseum (Swiss National Museum) near the main train station.

During the 1st century BC the Romans, attracted by Zürich's central location, built a customs house on a hill overlooking the Limmat River. In time, the customs house became a fortress, the remains of which can be seen on the Lindenhof, a square in the city center. The Romans also were accommodating enough to provide Zürich with its patron saints. Legend has it that the Roman governor beheaded the Christian brother and sister Felix and Regula on a small island in the river. The martyrs then picked up their heads, waded through the water, and walked up a hill before collapsing where the Grossmünster now stands.

When the Germanic Alemanni, ancestors of the present-day Zürichers, drove out the Romans during the 5th century, the region gradually diminished in importance until the Carolingians built an imperial palace on the Limmat four centuries later. Louis the German, grandson of Charlemagne, then founded an abbey here, making his daughter the first abbess; it was built on the site of what is now the Fraumünster, near the Bahnhofstrasse.

By the 12th century, Zürich had already shown a knack for commerce, with its diligent merchants making fortunes in silk, wool, linen, and leather. By 1336 this merchant class had become too powerful for an up-and-coming band of tradesmen and laborers who, allied with a charismatic aristocrat named Rudolf Brun, overthrew the merchants' town council and established Zürich's famous guilds. Those 13 original guilds never really lost their power until the French Revolution—and have yet to lose their prestige: Every year prominent Zürich businessmen dress up in medieval costumes for the guilds' traditional march through the streets, heading for the magnificent guildhalls that still dominate the Old Town.

If the guilds defined Zürich's commerce, it was the Reformation that defined its soul. From his pulpit in the Grossmünster, Zwingli galvanized the region, and he ingrained in Zürichers their devotion to thrift and hard work—so successfully that it ultimately led them into temptation: the temptations of global influence and tremendous wealth. The Zürich stock exchange, fourth largest in the world, after those of New York, London, and Tokyo, turns over 13.6 billion Swiss francs in domestic shares a year. However, Zürich is far from a cold-hearted business center. In 1916 the avant-garde Dadaist movement started here, when a group of artists and writers, including Tristan Tzara, Jean Arp, and Hugo Ball, rebelled against traditional artistic expression. Zürich also drew in Irish author James Joyce, who spent years re-creating his native Dublin in writing *Ulysses* and *A Portrait of the Artist as a Young Man*. Now, the city's extraordinary museums and galleries and luxurious shops along the Bahnhofstrasse, Zürich's 5th Avenue, attest to its position as Switzerland's cultural—if not political—capital.

Pleasures and Pastimes

Dining

On German menus, the cuisine is called *nach Zürcher Art,* meaning cooked in the style of Zürich. What that means to Germans and to the rest of the world as well is meat, mushrooms, potatoes, butter, cream—and heartburn. Zürich's cuisine is one of the richest in the world, perfectly suited to the lead-glass and burnished-oak guild houses. The signature dish, and one you'll encounter throughout both French and German Switzerland, is *geschnetzeltes Kalbfleisch,* or in French *émincé de veau:* bite-size slices of milky veal (and sometimes veal kidneys) sautéed in butter and swimming in a rich brown sauce thick with cream, white wine, shallots, and mushrooms. Its closest cousin is *geschnetzeltes Kalbsleber* (calves' liver), in similar form. Both are served at the table from broad copper chafing dishes with hot, fresh plates standing by to be filled when you've cleaned the first one. The inevitable accompaniment is *Rösti* (hash brown potatoes), in portions of equal scale—often the full 8-inch-diameter patty is a serving for one. You may also find *Spätzli,* or "little sparrows": flour-egg dough fingers, either pressed through a sieve or snipped, gnocchi style, and served in butter. An even heartier tradition is the *Zouftschrübertopf* (sometimes known as the city councillor's platter), a straightforward spread of grilled meats: veal, calves' liver, beef, sweetbreads, kidneys, and thick smoked bacon.

The flip side of Zürich's penchant for rich meats and heavy sauces is its sweet tooth: Refined cafés draw crowds for afternoon pastries, and chocolate shops vie for the unofficial honor of making—and selling, by the thousands—the best chocolate truffles in town.

Guildhalls

In exploring the Old Town, you will want to enter at least one of the famous medieval union clubhouses scattered along the riverfront neighborhoods; the best way is to dine in one, as all but the Zunfthaus zur Meisen have been converted to public restaurants. Having consumed a traditionally meat-heavy meal, ask if you can have a peek into the other dining rooms—they are, for the most part, museum-perfect in their lead-glass and Gothic-wood detail.

Museums

The wealth of Zürich bankers and industrialists gave rise to private art collections that are now part of the public art scene. Among the best is the Kunsthaus, with one of the world's best collections of Swiss art; the Museum Rietberg is famous for its East Asian collections. Many local museums are devoted to design, since Zürich was one of the centers of the graphic design industry early in the 20th century.

Shopping

Though Zürichers as a whole are relatively discreet in displaying their wealth, shops along the famous Bahnhofstrasse testify to readily flowing liquid assets. Watches and jewelry glitter in dozens of shops, and high-end department stores radiate cachet. The Old Town, particularly between Paradeplatz, Weinplatz, and the Fraumünster, concentrates an impressive array of top-name designer boutiques—thus window-shopping is an intrinsic part of strolling among the medieval sights.

EXPLORING ZÜRICH

At the northern tip of the Zürichsee, where the Limmat River starts its brief journey to the Aare and, ultimately, to the Rhine, Zürich is neatly bisected by the river, which is crisscrossed with lovely low bridges. On the left bank are the Hauptbahnhof, the main train station, and the Bahnhofplatz, a major urban crossroads and the source of the world-famous luxury shopping street, Bahnhofstrasse. The right bank constitutes the younger, livelier section of the Old Town, known as Niederdorf. Most of the streets around the Rathausbrücke and Grossmünster are pedestrian zones.

Scattered throughout the town are 13 medieval guildhalls, or *Zunfthausen,* that once formed the backbone of Zürich's commercial society. Today most of these house atmospheric restaurants where high ceilings, lead-glass windows, and coats of arms evoke the mood of the merchants at their trade. Often these restaurants are one floor above street level; in the days before flood contol, the river would rise and inundate the ground floor.

Numbers in the text correspond to numbers in the margin and on the Zürich map.

Great Itineraries

IF YOU HAVE 1 DAY

Start in the small but luxuriously gentrified Old Town, including taking time for window-shopping along the Bahnhofstrasse. Catch a temporary exhibition of Swiss art at the Kunsthaus; admire the Asian art and beautiful grounds at the Museum Rietberg; learn about Swiss history and culture at the Swiss National Museum; or stroll along the pretty Limmat River. Then cross over to the bustling Niederdorf to see the Grossmünster, the Rathaus, and—farther west, uphill—the Kunsthaus.

IF YOU HAVE 3 DAYS

After exploring the city's churches and museums, consider opera or concert tickets. Or take a boat trip on the Zürichsee, followed by a trip to the outstanding Zürich Zoo. Consider a daylong side trip to well-preserved medieval Rapperswil, in the neighboring region of eastern Switzerland (☞ Chapter 3).

IF YOU HAVE 5 DAYS

For a taste of backcountry Switzerland, drive north through the scenic countryside up to Schaffhausen (☞ Chapter 3), passing the Rhine Falls and a slew of wood-shingle farmhouses. If art is more your calling, visit the Oskar Reinhart Collection Am Römerholz in the nearby reputed art town of Winterthur (☞ Off the Beaten Path, *below*).

Bahnhofstrasse and the Old Town

Zürich's Old Town is home to several of Zürich's most important landmarks—the Lindenhof, St. Peters Kirche, Fraumünster, and Stadthaus—as well as its luxury shopping street, the world-famous Bahnhofstrasse.

A Good Walk

Begin at the **Hauptbahnhof** ①, a massive 19th-century edifice, rejuvenated by a restoration. Directly behind the Hauptbahnhof is the **Schweizerisches Landesmuseum** ②, housed in an enormous 19th-century neo-Gothic mansion; behind that is a shady green park. Walk northward to the tip of the park, cross the left-hand side of the bridge, turn south a bit along Sihlquai, and head up Ausstellungsstrasse to the **Museum für Gestaltung** ③, which holds an impressive collection of 20th-century graphic art. Back at the train station, look across the Bahnhofplatz, and you'll see traffic careening around a statue of **Alfred Escher,** the man who brought Zürich into the modern age.

Don't attempt to cross the square; instead take the escalators down to a convenient underpass and emerge on the **Bahnhofstrasse,** Zürich's principal business and shopping boulevard. A quarter of the way up the street—about five blocks—veer left into the Rennweg and left again on Fortunagasse, an atmospheric medieval street well removed from the contemporary elegance of the Bahnhofstrasse. Climb up to the **Lindenhof** ④, a quiet grassless square with a view of the remains of the city's original Roman customs house and fortress. From here a maze of medieval alleys leads off to your right. Nestled among them, in one of the loveliest medieval squares in Switzerland, is **St. Peters Kirche** ⑤, whose tower has the largest clock face in Europe.

From St. Peters Kirche bear right on Schlüsselgasse and duck into a narrow alley, Thermengasse, which leads left; you'll walk directly over excavated ruins of **Roman baths.** At Weinplatz, turn right on Storchengasse, where some of the most elite boutiques are concentrated, and head toward the delicate spires of the **Fraumünster** ⑥. In the same square, you'll see two of Zürich's finest guildhalls, the **Zunfthaus zur Waag** ⑦ and **Zunfthaus zur Meisen** ⑧.

Wind left up Waaggasse past the Hotel Savoy to the **Paradeplatz** ⑨. Continue south on Bahnhofstrasse, which, as it nears the lake, opens onto a vista of bright-color boats, wide waters, and distant peaks. At the Bürkliplatz, look to your right: Those manicured parks are the front lawn of the **Hotel Baur au Lac,** the aristocrat of Swiss hotels. Beyond, you'll see the modern structure of the **Kongresshaus** and the **Tonhalle,** where the Zürich Tonhalle Orchestra holds forth. Across General-Guisan-Quai is one of the local swans' favorite hangouts: the boat dock, which is the base for trips around the Zürichsee.

Here you can take General-Guisan-Quai west to Seestrasse to the **Museum Rietberg** or turn left and cross the **Quai Brücke** (Quai Bridge), for one of the finest views in town, especially at night, when the floodlighted spires reflect in the inky river, whose surface is disturbed only by drifting, sleeping swans.

TIMING

This side of Zürich's Old Town is surprisingly compact; half a day is enough time for a cursory visit. The streets flood with businesspeople early and late, and lunch hour can be busy but never exceedingly so.

If you're planning on museum hopping, the Schweizerisches Landesmuseum and Rietberg merit at least two hours apiece.

Sights to See

Alfred Escher. Leave it to Zürich to have a statue that honors not a saint, not a poet or artist, but rather the financial wizard who single-handedly dragged Zürich into the modern age during the mid-19th century. Escher established the city as a major banking center, championed the development of the federal railways and the city's university, and pushed through the construction of the tunnel under the St. Gotthard Pass. ⊠ *In the middle of the Bahnhofpl.*

Bahnhofstrasse. Zürich's principal boulevard offers luxury shopping that grows more and more extravagant and proportionately more and more discreet as the street heads south toward the lake. Though you won't see particular evidence of it, much of the banking business takes place along this street, behind upstairs windows where the only clue to the activities within is a digital trail of market statistics. Below the Bahnhofstrasse, vaults house one of the world's great treasure troves: Zürich is a leading international precious-metals market, rivaled only by London, and much of the gold and silver lies heaped under this most glamorous boulevard. ⊠ *Runs north–south west of Limmat River.*

★ ⑥ **Fraumünster.** Of the church spires that are Zürich's signature, the Fraumünster's is the most delicate, a graceful sweep to a narrow spire; it was added to the Gothic structure in 1732. (The remains of Louis the German's original 9th-century abbey are below.) Its Romanesque, or pre-Gothic, choir has stained-glass windows by the Russian-born Marc Chagall, who loved Zürich. The Graubünden sculptor Alberto Giacometti's father, Augusto Giacometti, executed the fine painted window in the north transept. ⊠ *Stadthausquai.* ☉ *May–Sept., daily 9– noon and 2–6; Oct.–Apr., daily 10–noon and 2–5.*

OFF THE
BEATEN PATH

MUSEUM RIETBERG – A wonderful gathering of art from India, China, Africa, Japan, and Southeast Asia is displayed in the neoclassic Villa Wesendonck, once home to Richard Wagner (as in *Wesendonck Songs*). From the city center, follow Seestrasse south about 1¾ km (1 mi) until you see signs for the museum; or take Tram 7 to the Rietberg Museum stop. ⊠ *Gablerstr. 15,* ☎ *01/2024528.* ☜ *5 SF .* ☉ *Tues.–Sun. 10–5.*

① **Hauptbahnhof** (Main Railway Station). Buzzing with activity from morning till night, this immaculate 19th-century edifice arguably epitomizes Switzerland's obsession with order, cleanliness, and punctuality. Beneath it lies a better shopping mall than you'd find above ground in most cities, with everything from grocery stores to clothing boutiques and bookshops. ⊠ *Between Museumstr. and Bahnhofpl.*

④ **Lindenhof.** On this quiet square, overlooking the Old Town on both sides of the river, are the remains of the original Roman customs house and fortress and the imperial medieval residence. The fountain was erected in 1912, commemorating the day in 1292 when Zürich's women saved the city from the Hapsburgs. As the story goes, the town was on the brink of defeat as the imperial Hapsburg aggressors moved in. Determined to avoid this humiliation, the town's women donned armor and marched to the Lindenhof. On seeing them, the enemy thought they were faced with another army and promptly beat a strategic retreat. Today, the scene could hardly be less martial, as locals play boccie and chess under the trees. ⊠ *Bordered by Fortunag. to the west and intersected by Lindenhofstr.*

③ **Museum für Gestaltung.** Twentieth-century graphic arts, including typography and poster and advertising images, are explored at this museum devoted to design. ⊠ *Ausstellungstr. 60,* ☎ *01/4462211.* ⚐ *5 SF.* ⊙ *Tues., Thurs., and Fri. 10–6, Wed. 10–9, weekends 10–5.*

❾ Paradeplatz (Parade Place). The hub of the Bahnhofstrasse and a major tram crossroads, this square is ideal for people-watching. Always full of shoppers, it's one of the few spots in Zürich that doesn't hum with financial activity—even though the Union Bank of Switzerland and many other financial institutions are headquartered nearby. ⊠ *Intersection of Bahnhofstr. and Poststr.*

★ ❺ St. Peters Kirche. Dating from the early 13th century, Zürich's oldest parish church has the largest clock face in Europe. A church has been on this site since the 9th century. The existing building has, however, been considerably expanded over the years. The tower, for example, was extended in 1534, when the clock was added; the nave was rebuilt in 1705. Plays are often performed on the steps during summer. ⊠ *St. Peterhofstatt,* ☎ *no phone.* ⊙ *Daily 9–4.*

★ ❷ Schweizerisches Landesmuseum (Swiss National Museum). Housed in a gargantuan neo-Gothic building opened in 1889, the Swiss National Museum possesses an enormous collection of objects dating from the Stone Age to modern times. There are costumes, furniture, early watches, and a great deal of military history, including thousands of toy soldiers reenacting battle scenes. In the hall of arms there's a splendid mural, painted by the late-19th-century Bernese artist Ferdinand Hodler, *Retreat of the Swiss Confederates at Marignano*—depicting a defeat in 1515 by the French that set Zürich back considerably after generations of prosperity. ⊠ *Museumstr. 2,* ☎ *01/2186511.* ⚐ *Free.* ⊙ *Tues.–Sun. 10:30–5.*

❽ Zunfthaus zur Meisen. This aristocratic baroque edifice, erected for the city's wine merchants in the 18th century, today houses the Swiss National Museum's exquisite ceramics collection; the selection of 18th-century porcelain is particularly strong and includes works by Zürich and Nyon makers. Enter on the Fraumünster side. ⊠ *Münsterhof 20,* ☎ *01/2112144.* ⚐ *Free.* ⊙ *Tues.–Sun. 10:30–5.*

❼ Zunfthaus zur Waag. This circa-1637 guildhall was the meeting place for linen weavers and hat makers. Today it houses a lovely restaurant (☞ Dining, *below*). ⊠ *Münsterhof 8.*

Niederdorf

As soon as you step off the Quai Bridge on the right bank of the Limmat River, you'll notice a difference: The atmosphere is trendier and more casual. The area is also the center of Zürich's nightlife—both upscale and down, with the city's opera house and its historic theater, as well as plenty of bars and clubs.

Perusing the area along Münstergasse to Marktgasse parallel to the river, you'll notice a less Calvinistic bent. Each of the narrow streets and alleys that shoot east off Marktgasse (which quickly becomes Niederdorfstrasse) offers its own brand of entertainment. The latter eventually empties onto the Central tram intersection, opposite the main train station; from there it's easy to catch a tram down the Bahnhofstrasse or up the Limmatquai.

A Good Walk

Start at the Quai Bridge and head up Rämistrasse to Heimplatz, where you'll find the **Schauspielhaus** ⑩. Across Heimplatz is the important **Kunsthaus** ⑪ museum. Head back down Rämistrasse to Bellevueplatz—from where you can take a tram to the impressive private **Stiftung Sammlung E. G. Bührle** collection—and follow Limmatquai

Zürich

KEY

AE American Express Office

i Tourist Information

Tram Line

Museum Rietberg

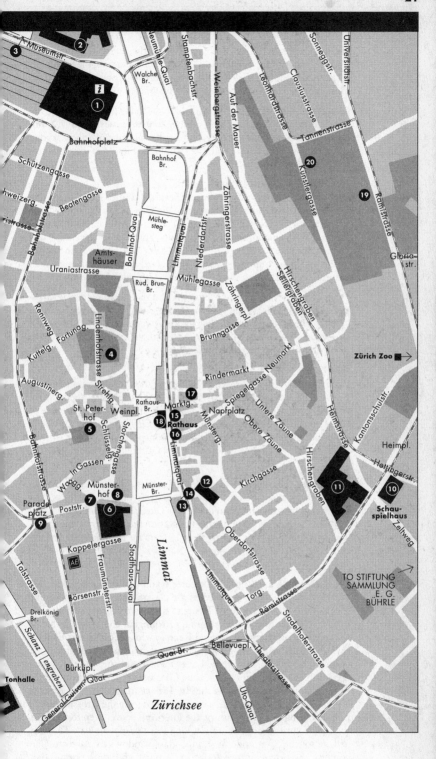

downstream to the gaunt, imposing **Grossmünster** ⑫, with its distinctive stout twin towers.

Head back down the steps to the banks of the Limmat, where you'll find the 18th-century **Helmhaus** ⑬. Now an art museum, the Helmhaus is attached to the late-15th-century **Wasserkirche** ⑭, one of Switzerland's most delicate late-Gothic structures, with stained glass by Giacometti.

Along the Limmatquai, a series of guildhalls today houses popular and atmospheric restaurants, the 13th-century **Zunfthaus zum Rüden** ⑮, **Zunfthaus zur Zimmerleuten** ⑯, and the **Zunfthaus zur Saffran** ⑰ among them. Across the Limmatquai, the striking Baroque **Rathaus** ⑱ seems to rise up from the river.

Head back across the Limmatquai and up into the Old Town streets, which meander past tiny houses, galleries, antiques shops, and neo-punk boutiques. Follow Marktgasse to **Rindermarkt**, site of the historic home of the Swiss poet and novelist Gottfried Keller. The Rindermarkt joins the picturesque Neumarkt and Spiegelgasse streets at a tiny medieval square where you'll see a fine early Gothic tower, the **Grimmenturm.** There's another Gothic tower farther down Spiegelgasse at **Napfplatz,** used during the 14th century by Zürich bankers.

From Napfplatz, take Obere Zäune up to the broad medieval **Kirchgasse,** packed with antiques shops, galleries, and bookstores. From here you can either return to the Grossmünster or venture north to see the **Graphische Sammlung** ⑲, with its woodcuts, etchings, and engravings; or head to the **Zoologisches Museum** ⑳.

TIMING

Exploring the Niederdorf won't take more than a half day, and pedestrian traffic is sparse in comparison with Bahnhofstrasse. Again, leave yourself extra time if you'd like to window-shop or invest a couple of hours in one of the galleries or museums, especially the Kunsthaus. Allow from four hours to a full day, including transportation, to visit the Am Römerholz collection in Winterthur (☞ Off the Beaten Path, *below*).

Sights to See

⑲ **Graphische Sammlung.** The impressive collection of the Federal Institute of Technology includes a vast library of woodcuts, etchings, and engravings by such European masters as Dürer, Rembrandt, Goya, and Picasso. Pieces from the permanent collection are often arranged in thematic exhibitions. Take Tram 6, 9, or 10 from the Bahnhofplatz or Central stops toward the ETH stop. ⊠ *Rämistr. 101,* ☎ *01/6324046.* ☜ *Free.* ⊙ *Mon., Tues., Thurs., and Fri. 10–5, Wed. 10–8.*

★ ⑫ **Grossmünster** (Large Church). Executed on the plump twin towers (circa 1781) of this impressive cathedral are classical caricatures of Gothic forms bordering on comical. The core of the structure was built during the 12th century on the site of a Carolingian church dedicated to the memory of martyrs Felix and Regula, who allegedly carried their severed heads to the spot. Charlemagne is said to have founded the church after his horse stumbled over their burial site. On the side of the south tower, an enormous stone Charlemagne sits enthroned; the original statue, carved during the late 15th century, is protected in the crypt. In keeping with what Zwingli preached from the Grossmünster's pulpits during the 16th century, the interior is spare, even forbidding, with all luxurious ornamentation long since stripped away. The only artistic touches are modern: stained-glass windows by Augusto Giacometti, and ornate bronze doors, in the north and south portals, dating from the late 1940s. ⊠ *Zwinglipl.,* ☎ *01/2526144.* ⊙ *Mar. 15–Oct., daily 9–6; Nov.–Mar. 14, daily 10–4.*

⓭ Helmhaus. The open court of this museum once served as a linen market. Inside, there are changing exhibitions of contemporary art, as well as a bookstore specializing in art, design, and photography. ⊠ *Limmatquai 31,* ☎ *01/2516177.* 🖾 *Free.* ☽ *Tues., Wed., and Fri.–Sun. 10–6, Thurs. 10–8.*

Kirchgasse. Antiques, art, and book enthusiasts will delight in the shops on this street. No. 13 was Zwingli's last home before he was killed in battle (1531) while defending the Reformation.

★ ⓫ Kunsthaus. With a varied and high-quality permanent collection of paintings—medieval, Dutch and Italian Baroque, and Impressionist, the Kunsthaus is Zürich's—and possibly Switzerland's—best art museum. The impressive Swiss collection includes nearly 100 works by Hodler, as well as pieces by Füssli, Böcklin, and Zürich masters from the 15th century to the present. There also are representative works from the origins of Dadaism, conceived in Zürich by French exile Hans Arp, who in the 1920s proclaimed the new movement one that could "heal mankind from the madness of the age." ⊠ *Heimpl. 1,* ☎ *01/2516765.* 🖾 *Varies with exhibition.* ☽ *Tues.–Thurs. 10–9, Fri.–Sun. 10–5.*

<table>
<tr><td>OFF THE
BEATEN PATH</td><td>STIFTUNG SAMMLUNG E. G. BÜHRLE – One of Switzerland's best private art collections is owned by the E. G. Bührle Foundation. Though it's known especially for its Impressionist and post-Impressionist paintings and sculptures, the collection also includes religious sculpture as well as Spanish and Italian paintings from the 16th to 18th centuries. Take Tram 11 from Bellevueplatz, then Bus 77 from Hegibachplatz. ⊠ Zollikerstr. 172, ☎ 01/4220086. 🖾 9 SF. ☽ Tues. and Fri. 2–5, Wed. 5–8.</td></tr>
</table>

★ ⓲ Rathaus (Town Hall). Zürich's striking Baroque town hall dates from 1694–98, and its interior remains as well preserved as its facade: There's a richly decorated stucco ceiling in the Banquet Hall and a fine ceramic stove in the government council room. ⊠ *Limmatquai 55,* ☎ *no phone.* ☽ *Closed to the public except for Mon.* AM *and Wed.* PM *cantonal and city parliament meetings.*

Rindermarkt. Fans of Gottfried Keller, commonly considered Switzerland's national poet and novelist, will want to visit this street. The 19th-century writer's former **home,** at No. 9, became famous in his novel *Der Grüne Heinrich* (*Green Henry*). Opposite is the restaurant, **Zur Oepfelchammer,** where Gottfried ate regularly. ⊠ *Street between Marktg. and Neumarkt.*

<table>
<tr><td>NEED A
BREAK?</td><td>Set back from the street in its own tiny courtyard is Cafe Schober (⊠ Napfg. 4, ☎ 01/2518060), a Victorian sweetshop with homemade hot chocolate, cakes, and sandwiches.</td></tr>
</table>

⓾ Schauspielhaus. During World War II this was the only German-language theater in Europe that wasn't muzzled by the Berlin regime, and it attracted some of the Continent's bravest and best artists. It's been presenting literary plays ever since it was built in 1884; today its productions aren't always so risky, but they are stunningly mounted and performed, in German of course. ⊠ *Rämistr. 34,* ☎ *01/2655858.*

⓮ Wasserkirche (Water Church). One of Switzerland's most delicate late-Gothic structures, this church displays stained glass by Giacometti. Both the church and the Helmhaus once stood on the island on which Felix and Regula supposedly lost their heads. ⊠ *Limmatquai 31,* ☎ *no phone.* ☽ *Daily 10–6.*

⑳ Zoologisches Museum. Engaging and high tech, the Zoological Museum allows you a close look in its accessible displays on Swiss insects, birds, and amphibians. You can examine butterflies and living water creatures through microscopes and listen to birdcalls as you compare avian markings. ⊠ *Karl Schmid-Str. 4,* ☎ *01/2573838.* ⊡ *Free.* ☉ *Tues.–Fri. 9–5, weekends 10–4.*

⑮ Zunfthaus zum Rüden. Now housing one of Zürich's finest restaurants (☞ Dining, *below*), this 13th-century structure was the noblemen's guildhall. Peek inside at the barrel-vaulted ceiling and 30-ft beams; or better yet, stay for a meal. ⊠ *Limmatquai 42.*

⑰ Zunfthaus zur Saffran. This guildhall for haberdashers dates in various forms from as early as 1389. It is now a highly acclaimed restaurant, with beautiful old rooms and a facade facing the river. ⊠ *Limmatquai 54.*

⑯ Zunfthaus zur Zimmerleuten. Dating from 1708, this was the carpenters' guild. Its main restaurant draws business groups to a number of lovely dark-wood halls; its former cave houses a cozy restaurant, too (☞ Dining, *below*). ⊠ *Limmatquai 40.*

OFF THE
BEATEN PATH

WINTERTHUR – A wealth of fine art was donated to textile town Winterthur by prosperous local merchants. One such denizen was Oskar Reinhart, whose splendid home now contains the huge **Am Römerholz** collection of paintings from five centuries, including works by Rembrandt, Manet, Renoir, and Cézanne. Winterthur is a half hour from Zürich by train, on the main rail route to Saint Gallen; fast trains depart daily from the main train station, about every half hour. By car, follow the Autobahn signs for Winterthur–Saint Gallen. ⊠ *Stadthausstr. 6, Winterthur,* ☎ *052/845172.* ☉ *Tues.–Sun. 10–5.*

ZÜRICH ZOO – This is one of Europe's outstanding zoos, with more than 1,500 animals and some 250 species, including Asian elephants, black rhinos, seals, and big cats. The naturalistic habitats must keep them happy: The Zürich Zoo enjoys an international reputation for successfully breeding wild animals. Set in a tree-filled park, it's just east of city center but easily reached by Trams 5 and 6. ⊠ *Zürichbergstr. 221,* ☎ *01/2527100.* ⊡ *12 SF.* ☉ *Daily 8–5.*

DINING

The price categories listed below are slightly higher than those applied in other regional chapters, except in Geneva, which shares Zürich's inflated cost of living. Though there's a shortage of truly budget options, you can always choose soup for a first course, which costs about 8 SF, and save by skipping dessert. It's important to note that daily fixed-price menus are considerably cheaper, and even the glossiest places have business-lunch menus at noon—your best bet for sampling Zürich's highest cuisine at cut rates. For tight-budget travel, watch posted daily *Tagesteller* listings: Cheap daily plates, with meat, potatoes, and possibly a hot vegetable, can still be found in the Niederdorf for under 15 SF; sometimes you even get soup to boot.

CATEGORY	COST*
$$$$	over 90 SF
$$$	50 SF–90 SF
$$	30 SF–50 SF
$	under 30 SF

Prices are per person for a three-course meal (two-course meal in $ category), including sales tax and 15% service charge

$$$$ ✕ **Baur au Lac Rive Gauche.** Though it's traded its self-important neo-Gothic decor for a light, Mediterranean look, businesspeople still flock to this traditional clubhouse-style institution. The cuisine is lighter and trendier now, with fresh seafood and salads, but the wine list still taps the Baur's impressive cave. ⊠ *Hotel Baur au Lac, Talstr. 1,* ☎ *01/ 2205060. Reservations essential. AE, DC, MC, V.*

$$$$ ✕ **La Rotonde.** Even when not illuminated by candlelight, the Dolder
★ Grand's haute-cuisine restaurant is one of Zürich's most romantic spots. Housed in a great arc of a room, La Rotonde provides sweeping park views that lure even the business crowd at lunchtime, even though the hotel is well out of the way of the business district. The atmosphere is formal, the staff attentive to a fault, the culinary style traditional French with a fashionably light touch—sweetbreads on a bed of gnocchi with asparagus and truffles, for instance. Those who love hors d'oeuvres will enjoy the Sunday lunch buffet. ⊠ *Kurhausstr. 65,* ☎ *01/2516231. AE, DC, MC, V.*

$$$$ ✕ **Petermann's Kunststuben.** Serious, chicly formal, and in a class of
★ its own now that rival chefs have retired, this is one of Switzerland's gastronomic meccas. Though it's south of city center, in Küssnacht on the lake's eastern shore, it's more than worth the investment of time, effort, and travel budget. Chef Horst Petermann, a German from Hamburg, never rests on his laurels: The ever-evolving menu may include lobster with artichoke and almond oil; grilled turbot with lemon sauce and capers; or Tuscan dove with pine nuts and herbs. ⊠ *Seestr. 160, Küssnacht,* ☎ *01/9100715. Reservations essential. AE, DC, MC, V. Closed Sun. and Mon.*

$$$–$$$$ ✕ **Kronenhalle.** From Stravinsky, Brecht, and Joyce to Nureyev,
★ Deneuve, and Saint-Laurent, this beloved landmark has always drawn a stellar crowd. The atmosphere is genial, the cooking hearty, and the collection of 20th-century art astonishing. Every panel of gleaming wood wainscoting frames works of Picasso, Braque, Miró, or Matisse, collected by patroness-hostess Hulda Zumsteg, who owned the restaurant from 1921 until her death in 1985. Her son, Gustav, carries on the tradition, serving robust cooking in hefty portions: herring in double cream, tournedos with truffle sauce, duck *à l'orange* with red cabbage and *Spätzli* (tiny dumplings). Despite linens and chafing-dish service, there's no shame in ordering the sausage and Rösti just to take in the animated scene. And be sure to have a cocktail in the small adjoining bar: *Le tout* Zürich drinks here. ⊠ *Rämistr. 4,* ☎ *01/2516669. AE, DC, MC, V.*

$$$ ✕ **Blaue Ente.** Part of a chic shopping gallery in a converted mill south
★ of the center, this modern bar-restaurant draws well-dressed crowds from the advertising and arts scene. In a setting of whitewashed brick and glass, with jazz filtering through from the adjoining bar, guests sample *zander* (pike-perch) roasted with bacon and sauerkraut, baked sea bass with basil cream sauce, or roast barbary duck with Spätzli. Take the No. 2 or 4 tram toward Wildbachstrasse. ⊠ *Seefeldstr. 223,* ☎ *01/ 4227706. AE, DC, MC, V.*

$$$ ✕ **Haus zum Rüden.** The most culinarily ambitious of Zürich's many Zunfthaus dining places, this fine restaurant is also the most architecturally spectacular, combining river views with a barrel-vaulted ceiling and 30-ft beams. Slick modern improvements—including a glassed-in elevator—manage to blend intelligently with the ancient decor, and by combining the upgraded ambience with chic graphics, damask, and sophisticated cuisine, its management keeps it a cut above its staid competitors. Specialties include lobster lasagna in saffron sauce, saddle of rabbit stuffed with cassis, and veal tenderloin in ginger sauce. It's especially impressive at night; ask for a window table. ⊠ *Limmatquai 42,* ☎ *01/2619566. AE, DC, MC, V.*

\$\$\$ ✕ **Hummer- und Austernbar.** In a fin de siècle setting of polished wood, candles, and rich scarlet, you can have your fill of impeccably fresh lobsters and oysters (*Hummer* means lobster; *Austern*, oysters), such as Brittany lobsters poached in champagne sauce. In August, the city's expatriate Swedes flock here for crayfish, a late-summer Nordic favorite. There's depth to the wine list, but champagne seems to be the beverage of choice. ⊠ *Hotel St. Gotthard, Bahnhofstr. 87,* ☎ *01/2118315. AE, DC, MC, V.*

\$\$\$ ✕ **Veltliner Keller.** Though its rich, carved-wood decor borrows from Graubündner Alpine culture, this dining spot is no tourist-trap transplant: The house, built in 1325 and functioning as a restaurant since 1551, has always stored Italian-Swiss Valtellina wines, which were carried over the Alps and imported to Zürich. There is a definite emphasis on the heavy and the meaty, but the kitchen is flexible and reasonably deft with more modern favorites as well: grilled salmon, veal steak with Gorgonzola, and dessert mousses. If you're not heading on to Graubünden, try the house version of *schoppa da giuotta,* the traditional barley soup. ⊠ *Schlüsselg. 8,* ☎ *01/2254040. AE, DC, MC, V.*

\$\$ ✕ **Bodega Española.** The dark paneled interior of this Niederdorf spot is encircled with the coats of arms of provinces of old Spain and strung with garlands of onions and garlic. In addition to being one of the only places in Zürich where you can get a big steak without paying through the nose, the Bodega also has good seafood, omelets, and paella. Be sure to sample the Bodega's excellent house Rioja (a Spanish-wine specialty shop adjoins, so the choice is extensive). The restaurant, like Niederdorf itself, is lively in the evenings and quiet at lunch. ⊠ *Münsterg. 15,* ☎ *01/2512310. AE, DC, MC, V.*

\$\$ ✕ **Oepfelchammer.** The oldest restaurant in Zürich, dating from 1801,
★ this was once the haunt of Zürich's beloved writer Gottfried Keller, and it still draws unpretentious literati. One section is a dark and heavily graffitied bar, with sagging timbers and slanting floors; there are also two welcoming little dining rooms, with coffered ceilings and plenty of carved oak and damask. Traditional meat dishes—calves' liver and *geschnetzeltes Kalbfleisch,* tripe in white wine sauce—come in generous portions; salads are fresh and seasonal. The place is always packed, and service can be slow, so stake out a table and plan to spend the evening. ⊠ *Rindermarkt 12,* ☎ *01/2512336. MC, V. Closed Sun.*

\$\$ ✕ **Opus.** In this warm, bookish decor, you can enjoy a chic supper of Italian-inspired specialties: olive risotto with shrimp, duck breast with orange and balsamic vinegar sauce. The three-course lunch menu is good value, especially the vegetarian version. On winter weekends, there's a hip salon/cabaret show between courses, with anything from Piaf to Gershwin to readings from Dorothy Parker (*auf Deutsch, natürlich*). ⊠ *Pfalzg. 1,* ☎ *01/2115917. AE, DC, MC, V.*

\$\$ ✕ **Zunfthaus zur Schmiden.** The sense of history and the decor alone— a magnificent mix of Gothic wood, lead glass, and tile stoves—justify a visit to this popular landmark, the guild house of blacksmiths and barbers since 1412. All the Zürich meat classics are available in enormous portions (steaming double portions of geschnetzeltes, whole skillets of crisp Rösti), and there's a considerable selection of alternatives—fish among them. The guild's own house-label wine is fine. ⊠ *Marktg. 20,* ☎ *01/2515287. AE, DC, MC, V.*

\$\$ ✕ **Zunfthaus zur Waag.** Another, airier guildhall, its woodwork whitewashed, its lead-glass windows looking out to the Fraumünster, this lovely dining spot offers generous portions of the local classics: richly sauced veal, butter-crisped salmon, and sizzling potatoes simmered in gleaming skillets and chafing dishes. ⊠ *Münsterhof 8,* ☎ *01/2110730. AE, DC, MC, V.*

$$ ✕ **Zunfthaus zur Zimmerleuten/Küferstube.** Although the pricier Zunft-
★ haus upstairs is often overwhelmed with large banquets and confer-
ence crowds, at substreet level a cozy, candlelighted haven dubbed
Coopers' Pub serves atmospheric meals in a dark-beam, old Zürich set-
ting. Standard dishes have enough novelty to stand apart: a first-course
salad with warm goose meat, roast hare with elderberry sauce, home-
made cinnamon ice cream with wine-poached pear. Service is friendly
but discreet, allowing for a romantic tête-à-tête. ⊠ *Limmatquai 40,*
☎ *01/2520834. AE, DC, MC, V.*

$–$$ ✕ **Bierhalle Kropf.** Under the giant boar's head and restored century-
★ old murals, businesspeople, workers, and shoppers share crowded ta-
bles to feast on generous hot dishes and a great selection of sausages.
The *Leberknödli* (liver dumplings) are tasty, the potato croquettes are
filled with farmer's cheese and garnished with a generous fresh salad,
and the *Apfelküchli* (fried apple slices) are tender and sweet. The bustle, clatter, and wisecracking waitresses provide a lively, sociable experience: You'll get to know your neighbor here, and most of them are
locals. ⊠ *In Gassen 16,* ☎ *01/2211805. AE, DC, MC, V.*

$–$$ ✕ **Zeughauskeller.** Built as an arsenal in 1487, this enormous stone-
★ and-beam hall offers hearty meat platters and a variety of beers and
wines in comfortable and friendly chaos. Waitresses are harried and
brisk, especially at lunchtime, when crowds are thick. Unlike the shabbier beer halls in Niederdorf, this is clean and bourgeois, and it reflects
its Paradeplatz location. They're not unaccustomed to tourists—menus
are posted in English, Japanese, and at least 10 other languages—but
locals consider this their home away from home. ⊠ *Bahnhofstr. 28,*
at Paradepl., ☎ *01/2112690. AE, DC, MC, V.*

$ ✕ **Adler's Swiss Chuchi.** A bit of an anomaly in a black-leather-and-
★ nose-ring neighborhood, this squeaky-clean, Swiss-kitsch restaurant has
an airy, modern decor, with Alpine-rustic chairs, Big Boy–style plastic menus, and good home-cooked national specialties. Excellent lunch
menus are rock-bottom cheap and served double quick; nights are reserved for fondue. ⊠ *Roseng. 10,* ☎ *01/2669696. AE, DC, MC, V.*

$ ✕ **Hiltl Vegi.** As the German world takes its cholesterol count, more
and more vegetarian restaurants are catching on, including this popular old landmark, founded in the late 19th century. The atmosphere
these days is all contemporary, with posted color photos of daily specials. By day there's a 50-variety salad bar; by night, an all-you-can-
eat Indian buffet. ⊠ *Sihlstr. 28,* ☎ *01/2213870. AE, DC, MC, V.*

$ ✕ **Mère Catherine.** This popular bistro with a Provençal veneer pre-
sents a dark and un-self-conscious old-style decor and blackboard specials. The chef turns out onion soup, duck liver terrine, seafood, and
a few meat dishes—even American-raised *steak de cheval* (horse steak).
The young, bohemian, and sociable clientele enjoys the ever-busy
Philosoph bar next door, a local favorite. On warm evenings, opt for
courtyard seating. ⊠ *Nägelihof 3,* ☎ *01/2622250. AE, MC, V.*

$ ✕ **Odéon.** This historic café-restaurant was once frequented by the pre-
★ revolutionary Lenin, who nursed a coffee and read the house's daily
papers. Now the crowd is just as intense, and a tonic air of counter-
cultural chic mixes with the nonfilter cigarette smoke. You can nurse
a coffee, too, or have a plate of pasta, a sandwich, or dessert from the
limited menu. The clientele is mixed by day, gay by night. ⊠ *Limmatquai*
2, ☎ *01/2511650. AE, DC, MC, V.*

$ ✕ **Reithalle.** In this hip downtown theater complex behind the Bahn-
★ hofstrasse, an old military horse barn has been converted into a popular restaurant, with candles perched on the mangers and beams and
heat ducts exposed. Young, street-smart locals share long tables arranged
mess-hall style to sample French and Italian specialties, many vegetarian,
and an excellent international blackboard list of open wines. Too bad

28

Zürich Dining and Lodging

KEY

ℹ Tourist Information

⌁ Tram Line

0   200 yards

0   200 meters

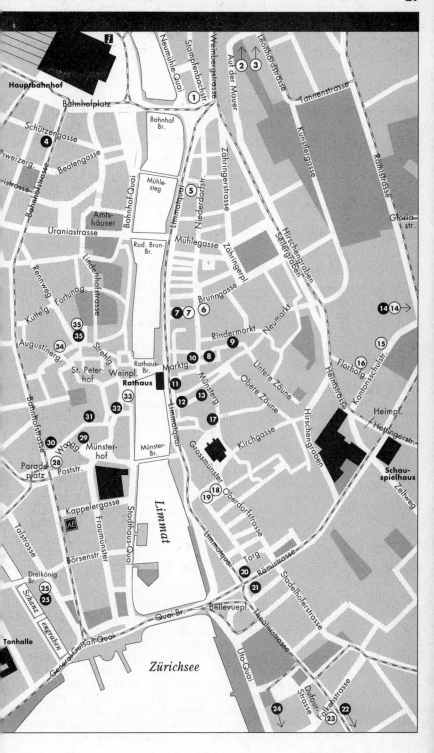

it's closed Saturday and Sunday nights. ⊠ *Gessnerallee 8,* ☎ *01/ 2120766. AE, MC, V.*

$ ✕ **Rheinfelder Bierhaus.** Dark and smoky, with every wooden table squeezing in mixed parties of workers, bikers, shoppers, and tourists, this solid old institution in the Niederdorf area serves a rich *Rindspfeffer* (preserved beef stew) with homemade Spätzli; sausage standbys; and the pride of the Spanish/Romansch owners: an incongruous but freshly homemade paella, served once a month. ⊠ *Marktg. 19,* ☎ *01/ 2512991. No credit cards.*

LODGING

Spending the night in Zürich is as expensive as eating out, though its options are no more outlandishly priced than those in the prestigious ski resorts. Deluxe hotels—the five-star landmarks—average between 450 SF and 600 SF per night for a double, and you'll be lucky to get a shower and toilet in your room for less than 140 SF. Yet a full (if top-heavy) range of choices is available in the city center, so even if you're flying into Zürich-Kloten on your way to a mountain retreat, don't shy away from a day or two stopover.

CATEGORY	COST*
$$$$	over 430 SF
$$$	300 SF–430 SF
$$	160 SF–300 SF
$	under 160 SF

Prices are for a standard double room, including breakfast, tax, and service charge.

$$$$ ☷ **Baur au Lac.** This highbrow patrician of Swiss hotels, its broad back
★   turned to the commercial center, its front rooms overlooking the lake, the canal, and the manicured lawns of its own private park, finished a sizable face-lift in 1997. Bathrooms have been brought up to the level of glitzier competitors, and the signature classic room decor gleams with new carpet, rich fabrics, and such ultramodern comforts as tripleglazed windows and CD players. Lakeside corner junior suites (priced as deluxe doubles) are a relatively good value. In summer, meals (including breakfast) are served in the glassed-in pavilion along the canal; in winter, in the glowing Restaurant Français. ⊠ *Talstr. 1, CH-8022,* ☎ *01/2205020,* ⻏ *01/2205044. 107 rooms, 18 suites. 2 restaurants, bar, café, beauty salon, dance club. AE, DC, MC, V.*

$$$$ ☷ **Dolder Grand.** A cross between Camp David and Maria Theresa's
★   summer palace, this sprawling Victorian fantasy-manse sits high on a hill over Zürich, quickly reached by funicular railway (free for guests) from Römerhof. A picturesque hodgepodge of turrets, cupolas, halftimbers, and mansards, it was opened in 1899 as a summer resort; the uncompromisingly modern wing was added in 1964, but from inside the connection is seamless. The garden and forest views from the rear rooms nearly match the beauty of those of the golf course, the park, and the city itself. Guest rooms, with Empire-cum-Euro-modern decor, are distinguished by their spaciousness and high ceilings. Restaurant La Rotonde (☞ Dining, *above*) serves excellent traditional French haute cuisine. Runners can tear around the park; swimmers can try out the pool's wave machine. ⊠ *Kurhausstr. 65, CH-8032,* ☎ *01/2516231,* ⻏ *01/2518829. 149 rooms, 34 suites. Restaurant, bar, café, pool, beauty salon, 9-hole golf course, tennis court, ice-skating, parking (fee). AE, DC, MC, V.*

$$$$ ☷ **Savoy Baur en Ville.** This luxurious downtown landmark is the city's oldest hotel (built in 1838), but you'll hardly be without running water—it was gutted in 1975 and solidly reconstructed as an urban

gem. It's directly on the Paradeplatz and thus at the hub of the banking, shopping, and sightseeing districts. Rooms have a warm, postmodern decor, with pear-wood cabinetry, brass, and chintz, and there are two fine restaurants—one French, one Italian—as well as a city-slick café-bar. ⊠ *Am Paradepl., Poststr. 12, CH-8022,* ☎ *01/2152525,* ℻ *01/2152500. 112 rooms, 8 suites. 2 restaurants, bar. AE, DC, MC, V.*

$$$$ 🖬 **Widder.** In this antithesis of a grande-dame hotel, there's not a
★ wingback in sight. Eight adjacent medieval houses were gutted to create the hotel; new and old were skillfully tumbled together, from the museum-perfect facade to the burnished cabinetry. And surprise: The new workmanship, in fruitwood and fir and semiprecious stones, carries it off. Inventive room decor may mix medieval frescoes with leather bedspreads, halogen bell jars, private faxes, and interactive television. Live top-drawer jazz and scotch sampling (there are 700 single malts) draw a posh local clientele to the glossy Widder Bar. ⊠ *Rennweg 7, CH-8001,* ☎ *01/2242526,* ℻ *01/2242424. 42 rooms, 7 suites. 2 restaurants, bar. AE, DC, MC, V.*

$$$ 🖬 **Central-Plaza.** Despite its landmark-quality exterior—it was built in 1883—this hotel aims to please a young and often American crowd, with slick, universally appreciated comforts and a fresh, if chain-style, decor: brass, bamboo, palms. The bars and theme restaurants all appear to have been contrived to appeal to habitués of shopping malls: The King's Cave, for instance, has faux Gothic stone and "medieval" goblets. It's directly on the Central tram crossroads on the Niederdorf side. ⊠ *Central 1, CH-8001,* ☎ *01/2515555,* ℻ *01/2518535. 100 rooms. 2 restaurants, 2 bars. AE, DC, MC, V.*

$$$ 🖬 **Florhof.** This is an anti-urban-hotel, a gentle antidote to the bustle
★ of downtown commerce. In a dreamily quiet residential area by the Kunsthaus and Schauspielhaus, this Romantik property pampers famous writers, theater directors, and visiting professors with its polished-wood, blue-willow fabric, and wisteria-sheltered garden. The restaurant serves light, fish-based cuisine, and meals on the terrace on a summer's night are positively otherworldly. ⊠ *Florhofsg. 4,* ☎ *01/2614470,* ℻ *01/2614611 33 rooms. Restaurant. AE, DC, MC, V.*

$$$ 🖬 **Neues Schloss.** Now managed by the German-owned Arabella chain, this small, intimate hotel in the business district, southeast of Paradeplatz, offers a warm welcome, good service, and a new, jewel-tone room decor. Its airy, floral restaurant, Le Jardin, is popular at lunch. ⊠ *Stockerstr. 17, CH-8022,* ☎ *01/2869400,* ℻ *01/2869445. 58 rooms. Restaurant. AE, DC, MC, V.*

$$$ 🖬 **Splügenschloss.** Constructed at the turn of the century as luxury apartments, this Relais & Châteaux property maintains its ornate, historic decor. Some rooms have been paneled completely in Graubünden-style pine; others are filled with fussy florals. The location—in a spare banking district—may be a little out of the way for sightseeing, but if you yearn for atmosphere, you'll find this worth the effort. No-smoking rooms are available. ⊠ *Splügenstr. 2, CH-8002,* ☎ *01/2899999,* ℻ *01/2899998. 50 rooms. Restaurant, bar. AE, DC, MC, V.*

$$$ 🖬 **Wellenberg.** This Niederdorf hotel makes a definite postmodern retro statement with its burled wood, black lacquer, Art Deco travel posters, and Hollywood photos. Guest rooms are relatively roomy, if occasionally garish, but the central location is superb. ⊠ *Niederdorfstr. 10, CH-8001,* ☎ *01/2624300,* ℻ *01/2513130. 45 rooms. Breakfast room. AE, DC, MC, V.*

$$$ 🖬 **Zum Storchen.** The central location of this airy 600-year-old struc-
★ ture—tucked between the Fraumünster and St. Peters Kirche on the gull-studded banks of the Limmat River—is stunning, the hotel itself modern, impeccable, and intimately scaled. It has warmly appointed rooms with pretty toile de Jouy fabrics, some with French windows

that open over the water. Both the lobby and the breakfast room have lovely river views; at press time, a lobby renovation was in the works. Deluxe corner rooms, with views toward both river and lake, are worth fighting for. ✉ *Weinpl. 2, CH-8001,* ☎ *01/2115510,* FAX *01/2116451. 73 rooms. Restaurant, bar. AE, DC, MC, V.*

$$–$$$ 🏨 **Europe.** Not quite centrally located, this lovely but small hotel lies south of Bahnhofstrasse in a quiet spot close to the southern Bellevue area (right behind the Opera House). Rooms are done in gaudy red trim and are spartan but comfortable. ✉ *Dufourstr. 4, CH-8008,* ☎ *01/2611030,* FAX *01/2510367. 40 rooms. Restaurant, bar. AE, DC, MC, V.*

$$ 🏨 **Adler.** This once-shabby place, smack in the middle of Niederdorf, has metamorphosed into an all-new, state-of-the-art hotel on a modest and affordable scale. From the gleaming lobby to the sleek, modular rooms, the ashwood-and-granite decor makes the most of tight spaces, and hand-painted murals of city landmarks remind you you're in Zürich. The restaurant off the lobby, Adler's Swiss Chuchi (☞ Dining, *above*), is known locally as a great place for fondue. ✉ *Roseng. 10, CH-8001,* ☎ *01/2669696,* FAX *01/2669669. 52 rooms. Restaurant. AE, DC, MC, V.*

$$ 🏨 **City.** Close to the Bahnhofstrasse, the main train station, and the Löwenstrasse shopping district, this is a hotel in miniature, with small furnishings and baths and a high proportion of single rooms. The whole place has a chic pastel polish. ✉ *Löwenstr. 34, CH-8021,* ☎ *01/2112055,* FAX *01/2120036. 73 rooms. AE, DC, MC, V.*

$$ 🏨 **Haus zum Kindli.** This charming little bijou hotel could pass for a 3-D Laura Ashley catalog, with every cushion and bibelot as artfully styled as a magazine ad. The result is welcoming, intimate, and a sight less contrived than many hotels' cookie-cutter decors. Even the Opus restaurant downstairs is filled with English bookcases and floral prints, and guests earn 20% off menu prices to vie with crowds of locals for a seat near the cabaret stage (☞ Dining, *above*). ✉ *Pfalzg. 1, CH-8001,* ☎ *01/2115917,* FAX *01/2116528. 21 rooms. AE, DC, MC, V.*

$$ 🏨 **Helmhaus.** In an assertively modernized 600-year-old building, this Old Town property softens its edges with bright florals, white furniture, and some lake views. The location—across the river from Paradeplatz in the Niederdorf area—is excellent, with access to young nightlife after dark. ✉ *Schiffländepl. 30, CH-8001,* ☎ *01/2518810,* FAX *01/2510430. 25 rooms. Breakfast room. AE, DC, MC, V.*

$$ 🏨 **Rex.** Its parking-garage architecture brightened up with assertive colors and jazz posters, this foursquare property has some business-people's necessaries (laptop jacks, desks big enough to spread your papers on), without the depth of service offered by more expensive hotels. Its restaurant, Blauer Apfel, draws a loyal, young-pro lunch clientele to its cool blue-halogen-lighted tables. It's two stops from the Central tram station. ✉ *Weinbergstr. 92, CH-8006,* ☎ *01/3602525,* FAX *01/3602552. 27 rooms. Restaurant. AE, DC, MC, V.*

$$ 🏨 **Rössli.** Limited staff and a laid-back attitude counter some of the conveniences built into this ultramodern small hotel, set in the heart of Oberdorf. The chic white-on-white decor mixes stone and wood textures with bold textiles and metallic-tile baths, and extras include safes and bathrobes—unusual in this price range. Some singles are tiny, but all have double beds. ✉ *Rösslig. 7, CH-8001,* ☎ *01/2522121,* FAX *01/2522131. 13 rooms, 1 suite. Breakfast room. AE, DC, MC, V.*

$$ 🏨 **Zürichberg.** This hotel is like the Dolder Grand's stepsister: Both hotels share the same view from atop the prestigious hill that gave its name to both the neighborhood and the hotel. However, where the Dolder is flashy and urbane, the Zürichberg is down-to-earth—especially the room rates. Decor is modern and airy; next door is an annex called the Schneckenhaus ("snail house"), where rooms radiate outward from a central, oval-shape atrium. Run by the Zürich Women's Association, the hotel is alcohol-free, but this restriction doesn't prevent the chef from concocting memorable meals in the popular restaurant. Tram 6 heads straight to the hotel from the Hauptbahnhof. ✉ *Orellistr. 21, CH-8044,* ☎ *01/2683535,* FAX *01/2683545. 67 rooms. Restaurant, café. AE, DC, MC, V.*

$ ☎ **Leoneck.** From the cowhide-covered front desk to the edelweiss-print curtains, this budget hotel wallows in its Swiss roots but balances this indulgence with no-nonsense conveniences: new tile baths (albeit with cow-print shower curtains), murals, and built-in pine furniture. The adjoining restaurant, Crazy Cow, slings out its own Swiss kitsch (Rösti-burgers) in an over-the-top decor of milk cans, miniature Matterhorns, and the ubiquitous black-and-white bovine. It's one stop from the Central tram stop, two from the Bahnhof. ✉ *Leonhardstr. 1, CH-8001,* ☎ *01/2616070,* FAX *01/2616492. 65 rooms. AE, DC, MC, V.*

$ ☎ **Limmathof.** This spare but welcoming hotel inhabits a handsome historic shell and is ideally placed on the Limmatquai, minutes from the Hauptbahnhof, and steps from the Limmatquai and Central tram stops. All rooms have tile bathrooms and plump down comforters. There's an old-fashioned wood-paneled weinstübe and a bright vegetarian restaurant that doubles as the breakfast room. ✉ *Limmatquai 142, CH-8023,* ☎ *01/2614220,* FAX *01/2620217. 62 rooms. Restaurant, weinstübe. AE, DC, MC, V.*

$ ☎ **St. Georges.** This simple former pension drenches its rooms in a milky, all-white look. Eleven rooms now offer full bathrooms; the rest, each under 100 square ft, have shower and toilet down the hall. Take Tram 3 or 14 from the station to Stauffacher; it's another five minutes on foot. ✉ *Weberstr. 11, CH-8004,* ☎ *01/2411144,* FAX *01/2411142. 40 rooms. Breakfast room. AE, MC, V.*

NIGHTLIFE AND THE ARTS

Nightlife

Of all the Swiss cities, Zürich has the liveliest nightlife, with bars, clubs, discos, and jazz. Niederdorf is Zürich's nightlife district, with cut-rate hotels, strip joints, and bars crowding along Marktgasse, which becomes Niederdorfstrasse. On Thursday and weekend nights, the streets flow with a rowdy crowd of club- and bar hoppers. But the bars close early here: Zwingli hasn't lost his hold altogether.

Bars and Lounges

Barrique (✉ Marktg. 17, ☎ 01/2525941) is a vino-theque featuring a world-renowned wine list. **Champagnertreff** in the Hotel Central (✉ Central 1, ☎ 01/2515555) is a popular neo–Art Deco piano bar with several champagnes available by the glass. The **James Joyce Pub** (✉ Pelikanstr. 8, off Bahnhofstr., ☎ 01/2211828) brims with bankers at happy hour, when whiskey and Guinness on tap flow freely. The **Jules Verne Panorama Bar** (✉ Uraniastr. 9, ☎ 01/2111155) serves up cocktails with a wraparound view of downtown. The narrow bar at the **Kronenhalle** (✉ Rämistr. 4, ☎ 01/2516669) draws mobs of well-heeled locals and internationals for its prize-winning cocktails. **Malatesta** (✉ Niederdorfstr. 15, ☎ 01/2514274) is a well-established bistro/hangout for locals 20–80; there are happy hour discounts from 5 to 7 (in Zürich this is a gimmick, not standard practice). Serving a young, arty set until 4 AM, **Odéon** (☞ Dining, *above*) is a cultural landmark—Mata Hari danced here—and a gay bar by night. **Zeughauskeller** (✉ Bahnhofstr. 28, ☎ 01/2112690) specializes in *Stangen* (steins of draft beers), with more than 70 brands to choose from.

Cabarets

Zwingli didn't get to everyone here: There are strip shows all over town. **Moulin Rouge** (⊠ Mühleg. 14, ☎ 01/2620730) presents nonstop strip shows. One of the most well known is at **Le Privé** (⊠ Stauffacherstr. 106, ☎ 01/2416487). **Terrasse** (⊠ Limmatquai 3, ☎ 01/2511074) puts on one of the more sophisticated shows, with "artistes" who actually sing and dance.

Dancing

The medieval-theme **Adagio** (⊠ Gotthardstr. 5, ☎ 01/2063666) books classic rock, jazz, and tango for well-dressed thirtysomethings. The most exclusive club is **Diagonal** (⊠ Talstr. 1, ☎ 01/2117396) at the Hotel Baur au Lac, where you must be a hotel guest—or the guest of one. **Kaufleuten** (⊠ Pelikanstr. 18, ☎ 01/2011098) is a landmark dance club that draws a hip, well-dressed crowd. Tuesday nights are free. **Mascotte** (⊠ Theaterstr. 10, ☎ 01/2524481), blasting funk and soul, is popular with all ages on weeknights, a young crowd on weekends. **Oxa Dance Hall** (⊠ Andreastr. 70, Oerlikon, ☎ 01/3116033) draws thousands of casual young Swiss who dance all night (and to noon Sunday) to techno. Take Tram 14 from the Hauptbahnhof. **Le Petit Prince** (⊠ Bleicherweg 21, ☎ 01/2011739) attracts a chichi set.

Jazz Clubs

Casa Bar (⊠ Münsterg. 30, ☎ 01/2612002), long the sole bastion of jazz here, now has excellent competition. **Moods** (⊠ Sihlamtstr. 5, ☎ 01/2018140), in an old train-station buffet, presents jazz groups Tuesday and Saturday in summer, more often in winter. There are also Sunday-afternoon jam sessions. The popular **Widder Bar** (⊠ Widderg. 6, ☎ 01/2242411), in the five-star Widder Hotel (☞ Lodging, *above*), attracts local celebrities with its 800-count "library of spirits" and top-name acts.

The Arts

Despite its small population, Zürich is a big city when it comes to the arts; it supports a top-rank orchestra, an opera company, and a theater. Check *Zürich News,* published weekly in English and German, or "Züri-tip," a German-language supplement to the Friday edition of the daily newspaper *Tages Anzeiger.* The city's first **Zürcher Festspiele**—a celebration of opera, ballet, concerts, theater, and art exhibitions from late June through mid-July—was held in 1997. You'll need to book well ahead for this—details are available from the tourist office or Info- und Ticketoffice (⊠ Postfach 6036, CH-8023, ☎ 01/2154030). For tickets to opera, concert, and theater events, contact **BiZZ** (⊠ Billettzentrale Zürich, Kulturpavillon, Werdmühlepl., ☎ 01/2212283). Depending on the event, **Musik Hug** (⊠ Limmatquai 28, ☎ 01/2611600) makes reservations. Also try **Jecklin** (⊠ Rämistr. 30, ☎ 01/2515900).

Film

Movies in Zürich are serious business, with films presented in the original language. Check *Zürich News* and watch for the initials *E/d/f,* which means an English-language version with German (Deutsch) and French subtitles.

Music

The Zürich Tonhalle Orchestra, named for its concert hall **Tonhalle** (⊠ Claridenstr. 7, ☎ 01/2063434), was inaugurated by Brahms in 1895 and enjoys international acclaim. There are also solo recitals and chamber programs here. Tickets sell out quickly, so book directly through the Tonhalle.

Opera

The permanent company at **Opernhaus** (⊠ Theaterpl., ☎ 01/2686666) is widely recognized and understandably difficult to drop in on if you haven't booked well ahead. Try anyway, at the ticket office.

Theater

The venerable **Schauspielhaus** (☞ Exploring Zürich, *above*) has a long history of cutting-edge performances with a strong inventive streak; during World War II this was the only German-language theater in Europe that remained independent. Nowadays its main stage presents finely tuned productions (in German), while experimental works are given in the Keller (cellar). ⊠ *Rämistr. 34,* ☎ *01/2655858.*

During late August and early September, the **Theaterspektakel** takes place, with circus tents housing avant-garde theater and experimental performances on the lawns by the lake at Mythenquai.

OUTDOOR ACTIVITIES AND SPORTS

Golf

The nine-hole **Dolder Golf Club** (☎ 01/2615045) is near the Dolder Grand Hotel (☞ Lodging, *above*). **Zumikon Golf Club** (☎ 01/9180050), with 18 holes, is near the city center in Zumikon, a suburb of Zürich.

Health and Fitness Clubs

Luxor (⊠ Glärnischstr. 35, ☎ 01/2023838) offers visitors four squash courts, StairMasters, saunas, and a steam bath, but no pool. At the Hotel Zürich's health club **Atmos** (⊠ Neumuehlequai 42, ☎ 01/3607070) you can use the large pool overlooking the park, as well as the steam bath, sauna, weight machines, and sundeck, for 35 SF per day.

Running

The Vita-Parcours track closest to the center is at **Allmend Sportplatz** (⊠ Take Tram 13 to the last stop). The **Dolder Grand** Hotel (☞ Lodging, *above*) has a running path that winds through the forest; it's open to nonguests.

SHOPPING

Stores are generally open weekdays 9–6:30, Saturday 8–4. On Thursday, most central shops stay open to 9. Some close Monday morning.

Department Stores

ABM (⊠ Bellevuepl., ☎ 01/2614484) is known for good value. **Globus** (⊠ Bahnhofstr. and Löwenpl., ☎ 01/2266060) is one of the city's best. **Jelmoli** (⊠ Bahnhofstr. and Seideng., ☎ 01/2204411) has top-notch merchandise. **Manor** (⊠ Bahnhofstr. 75, ☎ 01/2295111) has an affordable selection of department-store goods.

Markets

At **Bürkliplatz** (⊠ Lake end of Bahnhofstrasse), there's a fruit, vegetable, and flower market open Saturday from 6 to 3:30 from May to October. There's a curio market on the **Rosenhof** (⊠ At intersection of Niederdorfstr. and Marketg.) every Thursday 10–9 and Saturday 10–4 between April and Christmas.

Shopping Streets

The glittering **Bahnhofstrasse** concentrates much of Zürich's best shopping, with the most expensive and exclusive goods offered at the Paradeplatz end. There's another pocket of good stores around **Löwen-strasse,** southwest of the Hauptbahnhof. **Niederdorf** offers less expensive, younger fashions, as well as antiques and antiquarian bookshops. The west bank's **Old Town,** along Storchengasse near the Münsterhof, is a focal point for high-end designer goods.

Specialty Items

Auctions

The renowned auction house **Sotheby's** (⊠ Bleicherweg 20, ☎ 01/2020011), whose sales cover items from dazzling jewels to memorabilia, has a branch here.

Chocolate

Sprüngli (⊠ Paradepl., ☎ 01/2244646; ⊠ Hauptbahnhof, ☎ 01/2118483; ⊠ Löwenpl., ☎ 01/2119612), the landmark chocolatier and café for the wealthy Bahnhofstrasse habitués, concocts heavenly *truffes du jour* and *Luxembourgli,* small, cream-filled cookies that require immediate eating. Good, plain hot lunches and salads are also served. **Teuscher** (⊠ Storcheng. 9, ☎ 01/2266060; ⊠ Globus, Löwenpl., ☎ 01/2113311; ⊠ Cafe Schober, Napfg. 4, ☎ 01/2518060) specializes in champagne truffles.

Food

Even if you're not in the market for coffee beans, dried fruits, or nuts, visit **H. Schwarzenbach** (⊠ Münsterg. 19, ☎ 01/2611315); you'll find old-style open-bin shopping in an aromatic store with oak shelves.

Gifts and Souvenirs

Heimatwerk (⊠ Rennweg 14, Bahnhofstr. 2, ☎ 01/2115780) carries a broad range of good ceramics, linens, wood carvings, and toys, all handmade in Switzerland. There are additional branches on the Brun-Brücke and at the main train station; the main store normally has some discounted merchandise.

Leather Goods

Fendi (⊠ Paradepl., ☎ 01/2210234) has a central location and an appealing selection. **Leder Locher** (⊠ Bahnhofstr. 91, ☎ 01/2131020; ⊠ Münsterhof 18, ☎ 01/2111864) has a luxurious assortment.

Men's Clothes

The classic, elegant designs of **Giorgio Armani** (⊠ Zinneng. 6, ☎ 01/2212348) are found in the west bank's Old Town. **Trois Pommes** (⊠ Storcheng. 6/7, ☎ 01/2110239) is the central boutique of a series of designer shops scattered through the Storchengasse area; the racks are heavily stacked with such high-profile international designers as Jil Sander, Versace, Donna Karan, and Dolce & Gabbana.

Watches

It goes without saying that the shops of the finest watchmakers in Switzerland are worth visiting. However, there are fine jewelers on practically every street corner, and relatively inexpensive watches—ideal as souvenirs or gifts—can be found at department stores.

Beyer (⊠ Bahnhofstr. 31, ☎ 01/2211080) has one of Switzerland's finest selections. One of the broadest assortments in all price ranges is available at **Bucherer** (⊠ Bahnhofstr. 50, ☎ 01/2112635). **Gübelin** (⊠ Bahnhofstr. 36, ☎ 01/2213888) is a world-class watch purveyor.

Women's Clothes

Beatrice Dreher Presents (⊠ Gassen 14, ☎ 01/2111348) carries Chloë and Krizia. **En Soie** (⊠ Strehlg. 28, ☎ 01/2115902) carries gleaming, sometimes raw-textured silks, but although the fabrics are sophisticated, there's still an element of whimsy. Some cottons are printed with rabbits, flowers, and scrawled phrases in almost stream-of-consciousness designs. You can snag some of last season's fashions at deep discounts at Trois Pommes' bargain-basement **Lagerverkauf** (⊠ Weinpl. 10, ☎ 01/2128318), where DKNY, Calvin Klein, and Dolce & Gabbana are jumbled on the racks. For the absolute latest, go to the main **Trois Pommes** (⊠ Storcheng. 6/7) for Jil Sander, Alaïa, and Comme des Garçons.

ZÜRICH A TO Z

Arriving and Departing

By Car

The new **A2** expressway from Basel to Zürich leads directly into the city. **A1** continues east to Saint Gallen. Approaching from the south and the St. Gotthard route, take **A14** from Luzern (Lucerne); after a brief break of highway (**E41**) it feeds into **A3** and approaches the city along the lake's western shore. You can take **A3** all the way up from Chur in Graubünden.

By Plane

AIRPORTS AND AIRLINES

Zürich-Kloten (⊠ 11 km/7 mi north of Zürich, ☎ 1571060) is Switzerland's most important airport and the 10th busiest in the world. It is served by some 60 airlines, including **American, United,** and, of course, **Swissair.** You also can catch domestic and European flights out of Kloten on **Crossair** (☎ 084/8852000 for central reservations or ☎ 1553636 toll free within Switzerland), Switzerland's domestic airline.

BETWEEN THE AIRPORT AND THE CENTER

It's easy to take a **Swiss Federal Railways feeder train** directly from the airport to Zürich's **Hauptbahnhof** (main station; ☎ 01/1572222). Tickets cost 5.40 SF one way, and trains run every 10–15 minutes, arriving in 10 minutes. **Taxis** cost dearly in Zürich. A ride into the center costs 50 SF–60 SF and takes 20–40 minutes. **Airport Shuttle** (☎ 01/3001410) costs about 22 SF per person for a one-way trip and runs roughly every half hour to a series of downtown hotels.

By Train

There are straightforward connections and several express routes leading directly into Zürich from Basel, Geneva, Bern, and Lugano. All roads lead to the **Hauptbahnhof** (☞ *above*) in the city center.

Getting Around

By Bus and Tram

VBZ-Züri-Linie, the tram service in Zürich, is swift and timely. It runs from 5:30 AM to midnight, every six minutes at peak hours, every 12 minutes at other times. All-day passes cost 7.20 SF and can be purchased from the same vending machines at the stops that post legible maps and sell one-ride tickets; you must buy your ticket before you board. Free route plans are available from VBZ offices, located at major crossroads (Paradepl., Bellevue, Central, Kluspl.).

By Taxi

Taxis are very expensive, with an 8 SF minimum but no additional charge per passenger.

Contacts and Resources

Embassies and Consulates

Contact the **United States** embassy in Bern (⊠ Jubiläumsstr. 93, ☎ 031/3577011). Contact the **Canadian** embassy in Bern (⊠ Kirchenfeldstr. 88, ☎ 031/3526381). There is a consulate for the **United Kingdom** (⊠ Dufourstr. 56, ☎ 01/2611520) in Zürich.

Emergencies

Police (☎ 117). **Ambulance** (☎ 144). **Hospital** (⊠ Zürich Universitätsspital, Schmelzbergstr. 8, ☎ 01/2551111). **Doctors and dentists** can be referred in case of emergency by the English-speaking operators who man the *Notfalldienst* phones (☎ 01/2616100). Late-night pharmacy: **Bellevue Apotheke** (⊠ Theaterstr. 14, ☎ 01/2525600).

English-Language Bookstores

Payot (⊠ Bahnhofstr. 9, ☎ 01/2115452) carries a good stock of English fiction despite the store's French focus. **Stäheli** (⊠ Bahnhofstr. 70, ☎ 01/2013302) specializes in English publications and videos.

Guided Tours

ORIENTATION

Three introductory **bus tours** are offered by the tourist office. **Cityrama's** daily tour covers the main city sights and then goes on to Rapperswil to see the rose gardens and castle. The trip lasts 2½ hours, leaving at 11 AM; it costs 35 SF. The daily **Sights of Zürich** tour (29 SF) gives a good general idea of the city in two hours; it leaves at 2 PM. **In and Around Zürich** goes farther and includes an aerial cableway trip to Felsenegg. This is also a daily tour, starting at 9:30 AM; it takes 2½ hours and costs 39 SF for adults. All tours start from the Hauptbahnhof, the main train station.

WALKING

Daily from May to October, the tourist office offers two-hour walking tours (18 SF) that start at the Hauptbahnhof. You can join a group with English-language commentary, but the times vary, so call ahead. The tourist bureau also offers day trips by coach to Luzern, up the Rigi, Titlis, or Pilatus mountains and the Jungfrau. Ask the tourist service (☞ Visitor Information, *below*), or at your hotel, for information.

Travel Agencies

American Express (⊠ Bahnhofstr. 20, ☎ 01/2118370). **Kuoni Travel** (⊠ Bahnhofpl. 7, ☎ 01/2243333).

Visitor Information

Tourist service (⊠ Hauptbahnhof, CH-8023, ☎ 01/2154000). **Tourist office** (⊠ Bahnhofbrücke 1, ☎ ℻ 01/2154099). **Hotel reservations** (☎ 01/2154040, ℻ 01/2154044); on the Internet, go to www.zurichtourism.ch.

3 Eastern Switzerland

Appenzell, Liechtenstein, Schaffhausen, Saint Gallen

Near Zürich, the cantons of Glarus, Schaffhausen, Thurgau, Saint Gallen, and Appenzell, as well as Liechtenstein, are dominated by the Rhine River. With its obscure backcountry and thriving cities, the German-influenced region has everything from wood-shingle farmhouses to town houses adorned with oriel windows and frescoes. Still, the eastern cantons remain one of the most untouched regions of Switzerland.

DESPITE ITS PROXIMITY TO ZÜRICH, this Germanic region, bordered on the north by Germany and on the east by Austria, maintains a personality apart—

Updated by
Debbie Ebanks

a personality that often plays the wallflower when upstaged by more spectacular touristic regions. Lush with orchards and gardens, its north dominated by the romantic Rhine, with a generous share of mountains (including Mt. Säntis, at roughly 2,500 m/8,200 ft) and lovely hidden lakes, as well as the enormous Bodensee (Lake Constance), the region doesn't lack for variety—only tourists. Because the east draws fewer crowds, those who do venture in find a pleasant surprise: This is Switzerland sans kitsch, sans hard sell, where the people live out a natural, graceful combination of past and present. And although it's a prosperous region, with its famous textiles and fruit industry, its inns and restaurants cost noticeably less than those in regions nearby.

The region covers a broad sociological spectrum, from the thriving city of Saint Gallen, with its magnificent Baroque cathedral, to the very obscure, Ozarklike backcountry of Appenzell, where women couldn't vote in cantonal elections until the federal court in Lausanne intervened on their behalf in 1990 (federal law granted women the national vote in 1971). On alternating years in Glarus, Appenzell city, and Trogen/Hundwil, you still can witness the *Landsgemeinde,* an open-air election counted by a show of hands.

Architecture along the Rhine resembles that of old Germany and Austria, with half-timbers and rippling red-tile roofs. In cities like Schaffhausen, masterpieces of medieval frescoes decorate town houses, many of which have ornate first-floor bays called oriels. In the country, farmhouses are often covered with fine, feathery wooden shingles as narrow as Popsicle sticks and weathered to chinchilla gray. Appenzell has its own famous architecture: tidy narrow boxes painted cream, with repeated rows of windows and matching wood panels. The very countryside itself—conical green hills, fruit trees, belled cows, neat yellow cottages—resembles the naive art it inspires.

Pleasures and Pastimes

Dining

Your plate will feel the weight of German and Austrian influence in this most Teutonic of Swiss regions: Portions are on a Wagnerian scale, and pork appears often. A side of *Spätzli* (little sparrows), *Knöpfli* (little buttons), or *Hörnli* (little horns) adds further heft: These are flour-egg dough fingers, either pressed through a sieve or snipped, gnocchi style, and served in butter. You also can order a full-meal portion of *Käseknöpfli* (cheese dumplings), which come smothered in a pungent cheese sauce.

All across Switzerland you'll find the Saint Gallen bratwurst, called *Olmabratwurst* on its home turf (Olma is the name of an annual autumn agricultural exhibition here). In restaurants it's served with thick onion sauce and *Rösti* (hash brown potatoes), but in Saint Gallen itself the locals eat it on the hoof, lining up at lunchtime at one of two or three outdoor stands, then holding the thick white-veal sausage in a napkin with one hand and a round, chewy chunk of whole-grain *Bürli* bread in the other. They never add mustard.

In the quirky region of Appenzell, the famous Appenzeller cheese deserves its stardom, as among the fine hard cheeses of Switzerland it has the most complex, spicy flavor, with traces of nutmeg. Other Appenzeller treats include a variation of Graubünden's famous air-dried beef, here called *Mostbröckli* and steeped in sweet apple cider before drying. It is served in translucent slices, its moist, mildly sweet flavor countered with bits of pickled onion. *Bauernschublig* are dark dried-blood sausages. If you've got a sweet tooth, search out two regional specialties: Appenzeller *Biber* (honey cakes filled with almond and stamped with a design) and *Birnebrot* (thick dried-pear puree wrapped in glazed dough). *Chäsemagarone* is a rich, plain dish of large macaroni layered with butter, grated Appenzeller cheese, and butter-fried onions—it's often eaten with *Apfelmousse* (applesauce).

Eastern Switzerland is the country's orchard region, especially the Thurgau area. There are several fine fruit juices made here, as well as *Most* (sweet cider) and some good fruit schnapps. Among area wines, Berneck comes from the Rhine Valley, Hallau from near Schaffhausen, and crisp whites from Stein-am-Rhein.

CATEGORY	COST*
$$$$	over 70 SF
$$$	40 SF–70 SF
$$	20 SF–40 SF
$	under 20 SF

*Prices are per person for a three-course meal, including sales tax and 15% service charge

Hiking
Uncrowded hiking trails lead through all kinds of terrain, from rolling vineyards along the Rhine to isolated, rugged mountain wilderness above the Toggenburg Valley. This is a region of unspoiled nature, well-preserved villages, and breathtaking scenery.

Lodging
More and more hotels in this, one of Switzerland's least touristic regions, are throwing away their Formica and commissioning hand-painted furniture to complement the beams they've so carefully exposed. However, bargain renovations tend toward the crisp, if anonymous, look of light tongue-in-groove pine paneling and earth-tone ceramic baths. The prices are somewhat lower on average here, with only slight variations from high to low season. Half board is rarely included. Hotel rates are generally calculated on a per-person basis; be sure to clarify the prices when reserving.

CATEGORY	COST*
$$$$	over 250 SF
$$$	180 SF–250 SF
$$	120 SF–180 SF
$	under 120 SF

*Prices are for a standard double room, including breakfast, tax, and service charge.

Exploring Eastern Switzerland

With their obscure backcountry and thriving cities, the cantons of Glarus, Schaffhausen, Thurgau, Saint Gallen, and Appenzell are some of the most untouched in Switzerland. In the northern part of the region are the old Rhine city of Schaffhausen, the dramatic Rheinfall, and the preserved medieval town of Stein-am-Rhein. The Bodensee occupies the northeastern corner of Switzerland, just below Germany. Farther south are the textile center of Saint Gallen, the quirky Appenzell region, and the resort area of the Toggenburg Valley. The tiny principality of Liechtenstein lies just across the eastern border, within easy driving distance.

Numbers in the text correspond to numbers in the margin and on the Eastern Switzerland and Liechtenstein and Schaffhausen maps.

Great Itineraries

Although eastern Switzerland is topographically the country's lowest region, it's still fairly rugged. It will take only a short time to see the major sights, but they are spread throughout the region, so leave time each day to be in transit. Train travel here is more complicated than in neighboring areas, requiring more intercity changes, so plan your itinerary accordingly. If you want to get back into the Appenzell hills, though, you should rent a car. Saint Gallen is a good excursion center for visiting the Bodensee, Appenzell, Mt. Säntis, and the principality of Liechtenstein; farther west, Schaffhausen offers easy access to the magnificent Rheinfall, medieval Stein-am-Rhein, and the Bodensee, as well.

IF YOU HAVE 1 OR 2 DAYS

If you are coming from Zürich, enter the region at its northernmost tip and start with the old Rhine city of ⛰ **Schaffhausen** ①–⑩, known for its medieval frescoes and Baroque oriel windows. From there it's an easy excursion to the nearby **Neuhausen am Rheinfall** ⑪, the city known for its broad, dramatic series of falls. Just on the other side of Schaffhausen, spend your second day in ⛰ **Stein-am-Rhein** ⑫, a medieval gem situated on the river. Then dip south to old ⛰ **Saint Gallen** ⑰, a busy textile center with an active Old Town beside its grand Baroque cathedral. From Saint Gallen you can explore the picture-pretty, quirky ⛰ **Appenzell** ⑱.

IF YOU HAVE 3 OR 4 DAYS

With a little more time, you can spend your first two days in the northernmost areas, visiting ⛰ **Schaffhausen** ①–⑩, **Neuhausen am Rheinfall** ⑪, and ⛰ **Stein-am-Rhein** ⑫; then make your way south, starting below Germany's Konstanz and following the southern coast of the Bodensee, a popular spot for local resorters. See the twin cities of **Kreuzlingen** ⑮ and Konstanz (in Germany) and ⛰ **Gottlieben** ⑭. Visit ⛰ **Saint Gallen** ⑰ and ⛰ **Appenzell** ⑱, then trace the **Toggenburg Valley** ㉒, which runs in a great curve between Mt. Säntis and Wildhaus and draws Swiss tourists to its resorts and spas. Finally, head to the tiny principality of Liechtenstein to see the royal castle and explore its art and stamp museums and then go west to the isolated Walensee.

When to Tour Eastern Switzerland

Summers in eastern Switzerland provide the best weather and activities but also the greatest traffic, both on roads and in towns; spring and fall are good alternatives. Stein-am-Rhein alone receives enough coach tours to virtually paralyze the village with pedestrians during high season; if you go, arrive earlier in the day or come on a weekday when crowds are a bit thinner.

SCHAFFHAUSEN AND THE RHEIN

Known to many Swiss as Rheinfallstadt (Rhine Falls City), Schaffhausen is the seat of the country's northernmost canton, which also shares its name. To gaze upon the grand, mist-sprayed Rheinfalls, arguably the most famous waterfall in Europe, is to look straight into the romantic past of Switzerland. Goethe and Wordsworth were just two of the world's best-known wordsmiths to immortalize the Falls' powerful grandeur.

Schaffhausen

★ ❶–❿ *48 km (29 mi) northeast of Zürich, 20 km (12 mi) east of Stein-am-Rhein.*

A city of about 35,000, Schaffhausen was, from the early Middle Ages, an important depot for river cargoes, which—effectively stopped by the rapids and waterfall farther along—had to be unloaded there. The name *Schaffhausen* is probably derived from the skiff houses along the riverbank. The city has a small but beautiful *Altstadt* (Old Town), whose charm lies in its extraordinary preservation; examples of late Gothic, Baroque, and Rococo architecture line the streets. It doesn't feel like a museum, though; these buildings are very much in use, often as shops or restaurants, and lively crowds of shoppers and strollers throng the streets. Many streets (including Vorstadt, Fronwagplatz, Vordergasse, and Unterstadt) are pedestrians-only, and you can tell which ones are in this zone by the paving—the pedestrian streets are cobblestone.

A Good Walk

Upon entering the Old Town, it becomes obvious why Schaffhausen is also known as the Erkerstadt—the City of Oriel Windows. Begin your walk at the north end of the Old Town at **Schwabentorturm** ①, where one of the two remaining fortress towers houses the gates to the town. Continue along Vorstadt, glancing left and right at the oriel windows, many dating from the 17th century. If you cast your gaze up above the houses every now and then, you can see the other tower peek out above the rooftops. The brilliantly painted facade of **Zum Goldenen Ochsen** ② will be on your right—its oriel window is incredibly striking. Vorstadt then leads into **Fronwagplatz** ③, with its clock tower and the fountains **Mohrenbrunnen** and **Metzgerbrunnen** at its north and south ends. Then veer right for a quick glance at the second tower, **Obertorturm**, and retrace your steps.

Continue east along the Vordergasse, where on your right you will first admire the **Haus zum Ritter** ④, probably the most famous fresco in Schaffhausen, followed by the **Schmiedstube** ⑤. Farther up the street to your left is the imposing **St. Johannkirche.** To the right of the church lies the **Haus zum Sittich**, a bright yellow structure with Renaissance oriel windows and relief sculpture. Take a left at the fork in the road up ahead to see the duplex **zur Wasserquelle** and **zur Zieglerburg** ⑥. Across the duplex stands the **Tellenbrunnen** Fountain.

Double back to the fork in the road and stroll down the tail end of Vordergasse. As you wait at the pedestrian crossing at Bachstrasse, the gray-and-white **Gerberstube** ⑦ welcomes you to this quieter part of town. Farther along the Unterstadt looking north is a group of odd houses with crooked and sharp angles. This is the entrance to the **Munot** ⑧. The meandering steps that lead to the tower are flanked by vineyards. Having enjoyed the view from the tower, double back to the pedestrian crossing at Bachstrasse. Cross the street and take the first left. You will come upon a cluster of large buildings that house the city library and the **Münster zu Allerheiligen** ⑨. Head west on Münsterplatz. This leads you straight to the entrances of the Münster and the **Museum zu Allerheiligen** ⑩. Now head up the hill to the government buildings on your left. The **Alte Zeughaus** (Old Armory), built by Johannes Jacob Meyer, is regarded as a good example of Swiss Renaissance architecture. From here, take any of the streets heading north to get back to the pedestrian zone.

TIMING
The entire walk takes about two hours, including the hike up to the Munot. You may want to linger at the Munot if there is clear weather, when the view is particularly good. A visit at the Museum zu Allerheiligen will add another hour. Keep in mind that the museum and cathedral are closed on Monday, and from noon to 2 on weekdays.

Eastern Switzerland and Liechtenstein

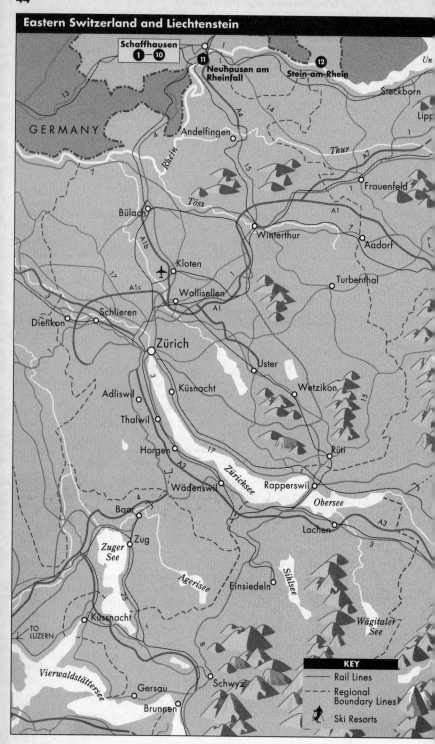

Schaffhausen

① — ⑩

⑪ Neuhausen am Rheinfall

⑫ Stein-am-Rhein

Steckborn

Lipp

Un

GERMANY

Andelfingen

Thur

Frauenfeld

Rhein

Töss

A4

A7

Bülach

A1b

Winterthur

A1

Aadorf

Kloten

Turbenthal

A1c

Wallisellen

A1

Schlieren

Diefikon

ZÜRICH

Uster

Wetzikon

Adliswil

Küsnacht

Thalwil

Horgen

Rüti

A3

Zürichsee

Wädenswil

Rapperswil

Obersee

Baar

Lachen

A3

Zug

Zuger See

Agerisee

Finsiedeln

Sihlsee

Küssnacht

TO LUZERN

Wägitaler See

Vierwaldstättersee

Gersau

Schwyz

Brunnen

KEY

—— Rail Lines

- - - Regional Boundary Lines

⛷ Ski Resorts

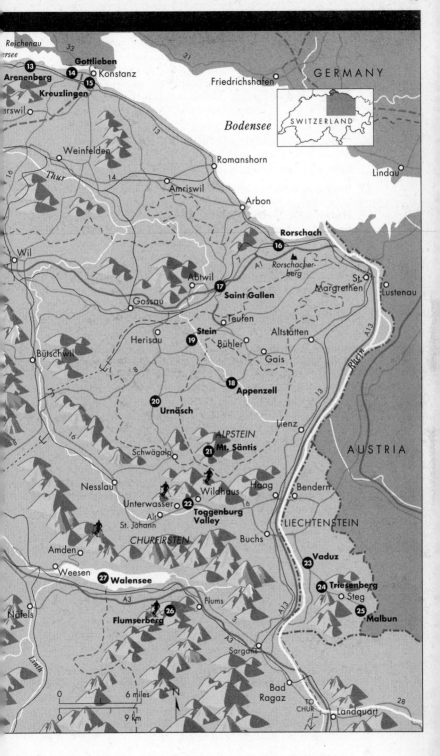

Sights to See

❸ **Fronwagplatz.** This marketplace is marked with the **Metzgerbrunnen,** a large 16th-century fountain-statue of a prosperous burgher. The large **clock tower** once held the market scales; its astronomical clock (1564) records not only the time but also eclipses, seasons, and the course of the moon through the zodiac. Across the square, a reproduction of the 1535 **Mohrenbrunnen** (Moor's Fountain) represents Kaspar of the Three Kings. The original fountain is stored in the Museum zu Allerheiligen (☞ *below*).

❼ **Gerberstube** (Tanners' Guild House). The Baroque building is known for its doorway framed by two lions stretching a two-handled tanner's knife. A restaurant is now here. ⊠ *Bachstr. 8.*

❹ **Haus zum Ritter** (Knight's House). The city's finest mansion dates from 1492. Its fresco facade was commissioned by the resident knight, Hans von Waldkirch. Tobias Stimmer painted all three stories in classical themes, which are now displayed in the Museum zu Allerheiligen (☞ *below*); the contemporary replacement was copied in the 1930s. ⊠ *Vorderg. 65.*

❽ **Munot.** Built between 1564 and 1589 in full circle form, the massive stone ramparts served as a fortress allowing the defense of the city from all sides. From its top are splendid Schaffhausen and Rhine Valley views. ⊠ *Munotstieg, Old Town.* ▣ *Free.* ◷ *May–Sept., daily 8–8; Oct.– Apr., daily 9–5.*

❾ **Münster zu Allerheiligen** (All Saints' Cathedral). This beautiful cathedral, along with its cloister and grounds, dominates the lower city. Founded in 1049, the original cathedral was dedicated in 1064, and the larger one that stands today was built in 1103. Its interior has been restored to Romanesque austerity with a modern aesthetic (hanging architect's lamps, Scandinavian-style pews). The **cloister,** begun in 1050, combines Romanesque and later Gothic elements. Memorial plates on the inside wall honor noblemen and civic leaders buried in the cloister's central garden. The enormous **Schiller Bell** in the courtyard beyond was cast in 1486 and hung in the cathedral tower until 1895. Its inscription, VIVOS—VOCO/MORTUOS—PLANGO/FULGURA—FRANGO ("I call the living, mourn the dead, stop the lightning"), supposedly inspired the German poet Friedrich von Schiller to write his *Lied von der Glocke* (*Song of the Bell*). You also will pass through the aromatic **herb garden;** it's re-created so effectively in the medieval style that you may feel you've stepped into a tapestry. ⊠ *Klosterpl. 1,* ☎ *052/6254377.* ▣ *Free.* ◷ *Tues.–Fri. 10–noon and 2–5, weekends 10–5.*

❿ **Museum zu Allerheiligen** (All Saints' Museum). This museum, on the cathedral grounds, houses an extensive collection of ancient and medieval historical artifacts, as well as displays on Schaffhausen industry. Temporary exhibitions on various themes reach international caliber as well. ⊠ *Klosterpl. 1,* ☎ *052/6254377.* ▣ *Free.* ◷ *Tues.– Sat. 10–noon and 2–5, weekends 10–5 (May–Oct. only).*

❺ **Schmiedstube** (Smith's Guild House). With its spectacular Renaissance portico and oriel dating from 1653, this building is an embodiment of Schaffhausen's state of suspended animation. Framed over the door are the symbols of the tongs and hammer for the smiths and that of a snake for doctors, who depended on smiths for their tools and thus belonged to the guild. ⊠ *Vorderg. 61.*

❶ **Schwabentorturm** (Swabian Gate Tower). Once a part of the city wall, the tower dates from 1370. Its counterpart, the **Obertorturm,** lies just off the Fronwagplatz (☞ *above*).

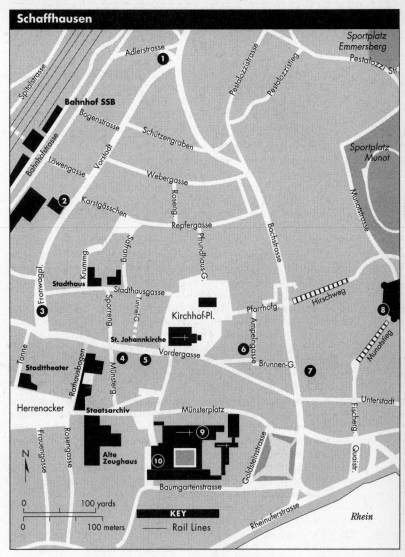

Schaffhausen

Fronwagplatz, **3**
Gerberstube, **7**
Haus zum Ritter, **4**
Munot, **8**
Münster zu
Allerheiligen, **9**
Museum zu
Allerheiligen, **10**

Schmiedstube, **5**
Schwabentorturm, **1**
Zum Goldenen
Ochsen, **2**
Zur Wasserquelle/
Zieglerburg, **6**

❷ **Zum Goldenen Ochsen** (At the Golden Ox). This building was remodeled in 1608 in the Renaissance style. Its exterior frescoes celebrate Greek and Babylonian history (you'll see the Hanging Gardens on the third level). ⊠ *Vorstadt 17.*

❻ **Zur Wasserquelle** and **Zur Zieglerburg.** The Rococo duplex dates from 1738; since they're private residences, you can only see them from the outside. Across the street are the **Tellenbrunnen,** a fountain-statue of William Tell copied from the 1522 original, and the **St. Johannkirche,** whose Gothic exterior dates from 1248. ⊠ *Pfarrhofg. 2.*

Dining and Lodging

$$–$$$ ✕ **Wirtschaft zum Frieden.** This unpretentious traditional restaurant
★ at the base of the theater square specializes in French cuisine. There's a variety of delightful settings: an intimate (read: tiny) stübli full of waxed and weathered wood; a graceful tile-stove dining room with antiques; and a small private garden thick with wisteria and luxuriant trees. You can have a cheap, generous *Tagesteller* (daily special) in the stübli, an ambitious meal upstairs, or choices from both menus in the garden, where the locals crowd to drink in a summer evening with their carafe of local wine. The menu includes home-smoked salmon, homemade Knöpfli, the very local *Kutteln* (tripe), and poached plums. ⊠ *Herrenacker 11,* ☎ *052/6254715. AE, DC, MC, V. Closed Sun.*

$ ✕ **Restaurant Falken.** This busy restaurant caters to crowds with a palate for simple, local fare—Rösti, *Geschnetzeltes* (stewed chopped meat, usually veal), and breaded fish. The *Tagesteller* (daily special) is an especially good deal at lunchtime. Though plain, the wooden facade and interior create gemütlichkeit without the clichés. It is an excellent choice for families; it even houses its own small bowling alley! ⊠ *Vorstadt 5,* ☎ *052/6253221. AE, DC, MC, V.*

$$$$ ✕🏨 **Rheinhotel Fischerzunft.** This modern Relais & Châteaux prop-
★ erty is a bit out of place in such a medieval city. Of its 10 rooms—some in fussy florals, others in sleek jewel-tone solids—six have river views, but everyone shares the lovely Rhine view at breakfast. Gault Millaut rates the restaurant among the country's five best. Its mixed nautical and Asian decor reflects the chef's Franco-Chinese leanings: He trained in Hong Kong and has created a brilliant, eclectic cuisine, with such dishes as crayfish wrapped in Thai noodles, deep fried and served with lentil sprouts. ⊠ *Rheinquai 8, CH-8200,* ☎ *052/6253281,* ℻ *052/6243285. 6 rooms, 4 suites. Restaurant. AE, DC, MC, V.*

$$$ 🏨 **Kronenhof.** This fine, quiet city hotel in the heart of Schaffhausen's
★ Old Town has a shutter- and flower-trimmed facade but an all-modern interior, with tidy, well-constructed rooms cheered by Asian prints and cherry-stained paneling. The American-cafeteria look in the restaurant seems at odds with the excellent, refined versions of local dishes, including trout, herring, and rich soups. This is a logical choice for families and business travelers. ⊠ *Kirchhofpl. 7, CH-8200,* ☎ *052/6256631,* ℻ *052/6244589. 38 rooms, 2 suites. Restaurant, bar. AE, DC, MC, V.*

$$–$$$ 🏨 **Park-Villa.** Despite the no-nonsense elevator tacked onto the exterior, this Belle Epoque–style mansion, built by a local industrialist, has been transformed into a small hotel with surprisingly little disruption to its grand but familial style. Many of the original furnishings—inlaid pieces, chandeliers, Persian rugs—remain. The upper floors are modern but retain their eccentric shapes, and some have Rhine or fortress views. The fine old garden room is luxurious and a steal (the toilet is down the hall); all the other rooms have full baths. The Park-Villa sits slightly apart, and uphill, from the Old Town. ⊠ *Parkstr. 18, CH-8200,* ☎ *052/6252737,* ℻ *052/6241253. 21 rooms, 2 suites. Restaurant, bar, tennis court. AE, DC, MC, V.*

$$ 🏨 **Promenade.** This solid, simple, Edwardian hotel, on the same res-
idential hill as the Park-Villa (☞ *above*) but with a pretty park walk
to the viaduct and the Old Town, offers spare Formica-and-beige
rooms, a garden restaurant, and modest fitness equipment. ⊠ *Fäsen-
staubstr. 43, CH-8200,* ☎ *052/6248004,* 🅵🅰🆇 *052/6241349. 37 rooms.
Restaurant, exercise room. AE, DC, MC, V.*

$ 🏨 **Löwen.** At the edge of suburban Herblingen, where the bedroom
community seems to melt back into its origins as a half-timber coun-
try town, this quintessential old guest house still draws the locals to
its pub and serves regional standards in its restaurant. Rooms, how-
ever, are all modern, with ceramic tile and modern pine paneling. ⊠
CH-8207 Herblingen, ☎ *052/6432208. 7 rooms. Restaurant, pub. No
credit cards.*

Outdoor Activities and Sports

Bicycles—a popular mode of transportation—can be rented at the
train station in Schaffhausen (☎ 051/2234500).

Neuhausen am Rheinfall

★ ⑪ *3 km (1¼ mi) south of Schaffhausen.*

Adjacent to Neuhausen, on the north bank of the Rhine, a series of
magnificent waterfalls powers the city's industry (arms, railroad cars,
aluminum). The **Rheinfalls** are 150 m (492 ft) wide, drop some 25 m
(82 ft) in a series of three dramatic leaps, and are split at the center by
a bushy crag straight out of a 19th-century landscape painting. The
effect—mists, roaring water, jutting rocks—is positively Wagnerian;
Goethe saw in the falls the "ocean's source." From Neuhausen there's
a good view toward the Schloss Laufen.

Stein-am-Rhein

★ ⑫ *20 km (13 mi) east of Schaffhausen.*

Stein-am-Rhein, a nearly perfectly preserved medieval village and one
of Switzerland's most picturesque towns, lies at the point where the
Rhein leaves the Bodensee. Crossing the bridge over the river, you see
the village spread along the waterfront, its foundations and docks ris-
ing directly out of the water. Here, restaurants, hotels, and souvenir
stands occupy 16th- and 17th-century buildings, and the Rhein appears
to be a narrow mountain stream—nothing like the sprawling indus-
trial trade route it becomes farther downstream.

The **Rathausplatz** and main street are flanked by tight rows of shin-
gled, half-timber town houses, each rivaling the next for the ornate-
ness of its oriels, the flamboyance of its frescoes. The elaborate decor
usually illustrates the name of the house: *Sonne* (Sun), *Ochsen* (Ox),
Weisser Adler (White Eagle), and so on. Most of the artwork dates from
the 16th century. The **Rathaus** (Town Hall) itself was built between
1539 and 1542, with the half-timber upper floors added in 1745; look
for its fantastical dragon waterspouts, typical of the region.

The Benedictine **Kloster St. Georgen** (Monastery of St. George), a cu-
rious half-timber structure built in 1005, houses a small museum of
woodwork and local paintings and also shelters a cloister. ⊠ *Edge of
Old Town, just upstream from the last bridge over the Rhine before
the Bodensee. Museum:* ⊙ *Weekdays 9–noon and 2–5, Sat. noon–4.*

Directly above the town atop vineyards and woods stands the 13th-
century hilltop castle of **Hohenklingen,** which now houses a restaurant
and offers broad views of the Rhine Valley and the lake beyond. ⊠
Above Schaffhausen.

Dining and Lodging

$$–$$$$ ✕ **Sonne.** Upstairs, you'll find a formal dining room (ceiling beams,
★ damask, and Biedermeier) where chef Philippe Combe's inventive,
contemporary cuisine—Rhine fish, crisp duck with cabbage—commands
top prices. Downstairs in the weinstübe, he offers a daily plate and sim-
ple light lunches, dished up in a spare, chic, gentrified pub: more
beams, stone, stucco, parquet—and exposed pipes painted maroon. The
weinstübe benefits from the kitchen upstairs; it offers homemade pas-
tas, simple but sophisticated stews, and selections from the fine wine
list. ⊠ *Rathauspl.,* ☎ *052/7412128. AE, DC, MC, V. Closed Wed.*

$$ ✕ **Roten Ochsen.** The beautiful frescoed facade invites its admirers into
this warm little *Weinstübli* (wine parlor), where dark antiques surround
a *Kachelofen* (tiled wood stove) and candles glow on the tables. The
simple menu is thick with hearty cuisine—a variety of sausages such
as *Bauernschübli* (farmer's sausage), local cheeses, but also delicious
homemade pastas. When they say the food is regional, they mean it:
all ingredients are obtained from the village and surrounding areas. Although no credit cards were accepted at press time, they did plan to
take Visa by summer 1998. ⊠ *Rathauspl. 129,* ☎ *052/7412328. No
credit cards. Closed Mon.*

$$$$ 🏨 **Chlosterhof.** Its brick-and-angled-glass exterior seems utterly mis-
placed in this medieval setting, but this hotel worked hard to face as
many rooms as possible toward the Rhine. Inside, the look is modern,
suburban, and business-class despite token vaulting in the lobby and
scattered antiques; indeed, the focus is on entertaining conference
groups and their spouses. The rooms feature sleek dark-pine cabinetry
and some four-poster beds, but the creamy pastels and carpets say upscale international chain. Suites claim the best Rhine views. ⊠ *Oehninger-
str. 201, CH-8260,* ☎ *052/7424242,* 🖷 *052/7411337. 44 rooms, 27
suites. 4 restaurants, bar, in-room VCRs, indoor pool, sauna, exercise
room, dance club. AE, DC, MC, V.*

$$ 🏨 **Rheinfels.** Even some of the bathrooms have ceiling beams in this
★ fine old waterfront landmark, which was built between 1508 and
1517. The public spaces have creaking pine plank floors and suits of
armor on display, and every room—modernized in beige and rose
tones, with all-tile baths—has a Rhine view. The restaurant specializes
in top-quality freshwater fish at reasonable prices. Both the hotel and
the restaurant are closed on Wednesday. ⊠ *Rhig. 8, CH-8260,* ☎ *052/
7412144,* 🖷 *052/7412522. 16 rooms. Restaurant. MC, V.*

$–$$ 🏨 **Adler.** With one of the most elaborately frescoed 15th-century fa-
★ cades on the Rathausplatz, this hotel has a split personality: Its inte-
rior is airy, slick, and immaculate, with gray industrial carpet, white
stucco, and blond wood throughout. The cabinetry is built-in, the
baths are tile, and the windows are double glazed. The young, local
family runs the hotel with pride; other families will fit right in. The
cheerful restaurant serves good regional cooking, along with some French
cuisine. ⊠ *Rathauspl. 15, CH-8260,* ☎ *052/7426161,* 🖷 *052/7414440.
25 rooms. Restaurant. AE, DC, MC, V.*

$ 🏨 **Bleiche.** This private farmhouse lodging, on a hill high over the Rhine
★ Valley, about a mile from the village center, offers a chance to sleep
under deep shingled eaves and wake to the sound of cowbells. The rooms
are rock-bottom simple (linoleum, a mix of dormitory and collectible
furniture), with showers down the hall, but the setting is surpassingly
beautiful. A friendly German-speaking woman runs it. ⊠ *Bleicherhof,
CH-8260,* ☎ *052/7412257. 5 rooms. No credit cards.*

$ 🏨 **Zur Rheingerbe.** Right on the busy waterfront promenade, this
small inn has wood-panel ceilings and big furniture reminiscent of Sears
(sculptured carpet, spindle beds). Some rooms overlook the Rhine. The
first-floor restaurant has a full-length bay window along the riverfront.

The hotel is closed on Wednesday. ⊠ *Schifflände 5, CH-8260,* ☎ *052/ 7412991,* ℻ *052/7412166. 7 rooms. Restaurant. AE, DC, MC, V.*

En Route Fourteen kilometers (9 miles) east of Stein-am-Rhein, the town of **Steck-born** has some fine old houses, including the Baronenhaus and the Gerichtshaus; it's also home to **Turmhof Steckborn,** a half-timber waterfront castle built in 1342 and now housing a small local museum containing artifacts from prehistoric times through the Roman and Alemannic settlements. ☎ *052/7611378.* ⊘ *May–Oct., Wed., Thurs., and Sat. 3–5.*

Arenenberg

⑬ *20 km (12 mi) east of Stein-am-Rhein, 40 km (25 mi) east of Schaffhausen.*

Just east of Stein-am-Rhein, the Rhine opens up into the Untersee, the lower branch of the Bodensee. In its center lies the German island of Reichenau. Charles the Fat, great-grandson of Charlemagne, was buried here.

The villages on either side of the Untersee are dominated by castles. On the Swiss side, behind the village of Mannenbach (nearly opposite Reichenau), the **castle at Arenenberg** was once home to the future Napoléon III and serves today as a museum with furnishings and artwork from the Second Empire. ⊠ *Behind Mannenbach,* ☎ *071/ 6641866.* 🎫 *5 SF.* ⊘ *Tues.–Sun. 10–5.*

Gottlieben

⑭ *5 km (3 mi) east of Arenenberg, 45 km (28 mi) east of Schaffhausen.*

As the Untersee narrows to the east, the village of Gottlieben has a Dominican monastery-castle, where the Protestant reformers Jan Hus and Jerome of Prague were imprisoned during the 15th century by order of Emperor Sigismund and Pope John XXII. Pope John was himself confined in the same castle a few years later. Today, though the castle can be viewed only from the outside, Gottlieben offers a romantic, half-timber waterfront promenade—and two fine old hotels—before you reach the urban complex of Kreuzlingen and Germany's Konstanz.

Lodging

$$$ 🏨 **Drachenburg und Waaghaus.** On the misty banks of the Rhine be-
★ tween the Bodensee and the Zellersee, this half-timber apparition of onion domes, shutters, and gilt gargoyles was first built in 1702. The original house, the Drachenburg, lies across a walk from the second building, the Waaghaus. A third house was added for overflow guests. The original Drachenburg has gleaming old staircases, four-poster beds, brocade, chaise lounges, and crystal sconces throughout the labyrinth of rooms and parlors; rooms in the other buildings follow this elegant lead. The scale is grand but cozy, and Rhine-view rooms are furnished like honeymoon suites. Three restaurants vary in ambience, the most sophisticated in the original house. ⊠ *CH-8274,* ☎ *071/ 6667474,* ℻ *071/6691709. 58 rooms, 2 suites. 3 restaurants, bar. AE, DC, MC, V.*

$$ 🏨 **Krone.** Immediately downstream from the Drachenburg und Waaghaus (☞ *above*), this member of the Romantik chain is smaller, cheaper, and a tad more generic than its flamboyant neighbor, though it dates from the same era. Standard doubles are done in mild, classic beiges; the suites are quite Baroque and have lake views. Breakfast is served in a beam-and-herringbone-ceiling hall overlooking the Rhine. The glowing dark-wood restaurant offers nouvelle-influenced seafood as well as lake fish. ⊠ *Seestr., CH-8274,* ☎ *071/6692323,* FAX *071/ 6668069. 22 rooms, 3 suites. Restaurant. AE, DC, MC, V.*

FROM THE BODENSEE TO SAINT GALLEN

Bodensee

Sometimes known as Lake Constance, the Bodensee is about 65 km (40 mi) long and 15 km (9 mi) wide, making it second in size in Switzerland only to Lac Léman (Lake Geneva). The strong German flavor of the towns on its Swiss edge is seasoned with a resort-village mellowness; sometimes palm trees fringe the waterfront. This isn't the Mediterranean, though; as the lake is not protected by mountains, it is turbulent in stormy weather and even on fine days is exposed to the wind. Compared with Switzerland's usual crystalline lakes, the Bodensee is gloomy and brooding; nonetheless, it draws European vacationers in summer for swimming, windsurfing, and fishing. Many Swiss have built tidy homes along the lakefront.

Outdoor Activities and Sports

HIKING

As a summer resort destination, the area around the Bodensee is usually thronged with hikers. For timed hiking itineraries, topographical maps, and suggestions on the areas best suited to your style of wandering, consult the **Tourismusverband Ostschweiz** (Tourist Association of Eastern Switzerland; ☞ Visitor Information *in* Eastern Switzerland A to Z, *below*).

SWIMMING

People do swim in the Bodensee; there are several **public beaches**, which are normally more grass than sand. Most have changing rooms and concession stands. **Arbon** (☎ 071/4461333) has a gravel beach—getting into the water can be a little rough on tender feet. **Kreuzlingen** (☎ 071/6881858) has some sand at the water's edge, though you'll be spreading your towel on the grass; **Romanshorn** (☎ 071/4631147) has a similar setup. **Rorschach** (☎ 071/8411684) is a pocket-size beach.

Kreuzlingen and Konstanz

⑮ *7 km (4 mi) east of Gottlieben, 46 km (28 mi) east of Schaffhausen.*

The big German city of Konstanz, with its Swiss twin of Kreuzlingen, dominates the straits that open into the Bodensee. Though Kreuzlingen itself offers little of interest to travelers, Konstanz has a lovely, concentrated *Altstadt* (Old Town) area. It's easily accessible from the Swiss side, though your passport may be checked even if you pass on foot. Konstanz belonged to Switzerland until 1805; today the two border towns share the dominant German influence.

En Route   About halfway between Kreuzlingen and Rorschach (follow Highway 13 east along the Bodensee), you'll come to the small town of **Romanshorn.** An industrial town and an important ferry port for Friedrichshafen in Germany, this is also a surprisingly enjoyable resort with fine views of the Swiss and Austrian mountains.

Between Romanshorn and Rorschach on Highway 13, **Arbon** (known to the Romans as Arbor Felix) lies on a little promontory jutting out into the Bodensee, surrounded by lovely meadows and orchards. It was a Celtic town before the Romans came in 60 BC and built military fortifications. Evidence of the Romans can be found in an interesting collection of relics in the late-Gothic St. Martinskirche.

Rorschach

⑯ *41 km (25 mi) southeast of Kreuzlingen, 80 km (49 mi) southeast of Schaffhausen.*

The lake resort of Rorschach, a port on the Bodensee, lies on a protected bay at the foot of the Rorschacherberg, an 883-m (2,896-ft) mountain covered with orchards, pine forests, and meadows. For generations, Rorschach has carried on a thriving grain trade with Germany, as the imposing Baroque **Kornhaus** (Granary), built in 1746, attests. There's a public beach here, too (☞ Bodensee, *above*).

Outdoor Activities and Sports

SAILING

There are several sailing schools in Goldach, including **Segelschule Rorschach** (☎ 071/8448989).

Saint Gallen

⑰ *14 km (9 mi) southwest of Rorschach, 94 km (59 mi) southeast of Schaffhausen.*

Switzerland's largest eastern city, Saint Gallen is a bustling city with students dominating its streets during the school year. The narrow streets of the *Altstadt* (Old Town) are flanked by a wonderful variety of boutiques and antiques shops. The city has been known for centuries as both an intellectual center and the source of some of the world's finest textiles. St. Gallus, an Irish missionary, came to the region in 612 to live in a hermit's cell in the Steinach Valley. In 720 an abbey was founded on the site where he died. Becoming a major cultural focus in medieval Europe, the abbey built a library of awesome proportions.

★ The abbey was largely destroyed in the Reformation and was closed down in 1805, but its magnificent Rococo **Stiftsbibliothek** (Abbey Library), built in 1758–67, still holds a collection of more than 100,000 books. The library hall itself is one of Switzerland's treasures. Visitors enter behind the cathedral. Large, gray carpet slippers are worn to protect the magnificently inlaid wooden flooring. The hall is a gorgeous explosion of gilt, frescoes, and undulating balconies, but the most striking aspect by far is the burnished woodwork, all luminous walnut and cherry. Its contents, including illuminated manuscripts that are more than 1,200 years old and incunabula, comprise one of the world's oldest and finest scholarly collections. ⊠ *Klosterhof 6d,* ☎ *071/ 2273415.* ☒ *5 SF.* ☉ *Apr.–Oct., Mon.–Sat. 9–noon and 1:30–5, Sun. 10–noon and 1:30–4; Nov.–Mar., Mon.–Sat. 9–noon and 1:30–4. Closed first 3 weeks in Nov.*

★ The **Kathedrale** (Cathedral) is impressive in its own right. Begun in 1755 and completed in 1766, it is the antithesis of the library, though the nave and rotunda are the work of the same architect, Peter Thumb: The scale is outsize and the decor light, bright, and open despite spectacular excesses of wedding-cake trim. ⊠ *Klosterhof,* ☎ *071/2273415.* ☉ *Weekdays 9–6:30, Sat. 9–5, Sun. noon–7.*

The grounds of the abbey and the cathedral border the **Old Town,** which demonstrates a healthy symbiosis between scrupulously preserved Renaissance and Baroque architecture and a thriving modern shopping scene. The best examples of oriel windows, timbers, and frescoes can be seen along Gallusstrasse, Schmiedgasse, Marktgasse, and Spisergasse, all pedestrian streets. A picnic-style diversion is the **Mühleggbahn,** a self-service funicular that runs up the hillside to a lovely view of Saint Gallen and the Bodensee. Once up top, take two immediate right turns to the wooden stairs leading to a paved path with park benches. ⊠ *Off the Abbey end of the Old Town,* ☎ *071/2439595.* 🎫 *1.40 SF.* ☉ *Daily 6 AM–11:30 PM.*

Saint Gallen's history as a textile capital dates from the Middle Ages, when convent workers wove linen toile of such exceptional quality that it was exported throughout Europe. The industry expanded into cotton and embroidery and today dominates the top of the market. To enjoy some marvelously ornate old embroidery, visit the **Textilmuseum** (Textile Museum). Its lighting is dim to protect the delicate fabrics and its captions are all in German, but the work speaks for itself. ⊠ *Vadianstr. 2,* ☎ *071/2221744.* 🎫 *5 SF.* ☉ *Nov.–Mar., weekdays 10–noon and 2–5; Apr.–Oct., weekdays 10–noon and 2–5, Sat. 10–noon and 2–5.*

Dining and Lodging

$$$$ ✕ **Am Gallusplatz.** This is the grandest restaurant Saint Gallen has to offer, serving contemporary cuisine (Norman pheasant with apple–brussels sprouts gnocchi) under deeply cross-vaulted ceilings and heavy chandeliers in a fine, old, half-timber building near the cathedral. Business travelers are often brought here to be impressed by the architecture, the formality, and the enormous wine list. A daily lunch menu offers fewer dishes, usually featuring cuisine *du marché* (based on the freshest ingredients possible). ⊠ *Gallusstr. 24,* ☎ *071/2233330. AE, MC, V. Closed Mon.*

$$–$$$ ✕ **Zum Goldenen Schäfli.** Of the first-floor (second-floor to Americans) restaurants that are Saint Gallen's trademark, this is the most popular, and its slanting floors groan under crowds of locals and tourists. The low ceiling and walls are all aged wood. The menu offers hearty regional standards with a special twist: sweetbreads in mushroom sauce, tripe in Calvados sauce, lake fish with almonds. ⊠ *Metzgerg. 5,* ☎ *071/2233737. AE, DC, MC, V. Closed Sun. No lunch Sat.*

$$
★   ✕ **Schlössli.** Tidy, bright, and modern despite its setting in a historic building, this first-floor landmark has a less woody atmosphere than its peers, the Bäumli and the Schäfli, but better cooking. The Käse Spätzli are homemade and the salads fresh and good, especially the maincourse salad with duck liver. Such classics as Rösti with *Geschnetzeltes* (veal bits in cream sauce) are dependable. The café draws casual families and locals playing a favorite card game, *Jass,* at lunch; businesspeople choose the only slightly more formal dining room that adjoins it. ⊠ *Am Spisertor, Zeughausg. 17,* ☎ *071/2221256. AE, DC, MC, V. Closed weekends.*

$–$$ ✕ **Weinstube zum Bäumli.** All dark, glossy wood and lead glass, this 500-year-old first-floor beauty serves classic local fare (veal, bratwurst, Rösti) to tourists, businesspeople, and workers, who share tables comfortably in the midst of the noisy bustle. ⊠ *Schmiedg. 18,* ☎ *071/ 2221174. MC, V. Closed Sun.–Mon.*

$$$$ 🛏 **Einstein.** Tucked back into a slope at the edge of the Old Town, this former embroidery factory is now a sleek, upscale business-class hotel, with Hilton-like interiors (polished cabinetry, lacquered rattan, subdued florals), a uniformed staff, and a five-star attitude. The generous breakfast buffet, laid out in the skylighted top-floor loft that serves as the à la carte restaurant by night, is not included in the room price. ⊠ *Berneggstr. 2, CH-9001,* ☎ *071/2200033,* 🖷 *071/2235474. 65 rooms, 3 suites. Restaurant, bar. AE, DC, MC, V.*

$$$ 🛏 **Gallo.** Now a relatively cheap business hotel, this graceful former apartment house is set beside a busy road but has double-glazed windows to shut out the roar. The location is not particularly convenient to the Old Town (Bus 3, named Heiligkreuz, stops at nearby Olma or carries you into the center), but interiors are fresh and attractive, with big tile baths and bright-color lacquer; two lovely attic doubles have beams and dormer windows. There is a great Italian restaurant on the ground floor. ⊠ *St. Jakobstr. 62, CH-9000,* ☎ *071/2452727,* F︀A︀X︀ *071/ 2454593. 24 rooms. Restaurant. AE, DC, MC, V.*

$$$ ⊡ **Im Portner & Pförtnerhof.** The original old Im Portner Hotel, in the
★ Old Town, is comfortable but undistinguished with its gold carpet, Naugahyde, and mix-and-match rooms. But across the street, the annexed Pförtnerhof stands apart: The big, bay-window, half-timber house has been restored and updated with style. The rooms combine antiquity (lead glass, painted woodwork, stone niches) with high tech (halogen, lithos, Euro-style baths). ⊠ *Bankg. 12, CH-9000,* ☎ *071/2229744,* F︀A︀X︀ *071/2229856. 17 rooms. Restaurant, café. AE, DC, MC, V.*

$$ ⊡ **Elite.** In the modern deco style of the 1950s, this Old Town spot has a functional air and a friendly staff. Half the rooms have baths; the others have sinks and cost less. The back rooms are quieter. ⊠ *Metzgerg. 9/11, CH-9004,* ☎ *071/2221236,* F︀A︀X︀ *071/2222177. 26 rooms. Breakfast room. AE, DC, MC, V.*

$–$$ ⊡ **Vadian.** A narrow town house tucked behind half-timber landmarks in the Old Town, this is a discreet and tidy little place with an alcohol-free policy. Most of its tiny rooms have been updated with beige stucco and knotty pine and new tile baths. Rooms without bath cost less. ⊠ *Gallusstr. 36, CH-9000,* ☎ *071/2236080,* F︀A︀X︀ *071/2224748. 13 rooms, 6 with bath. Breakfast room. AE, DC, MC, V.*

Outdoor Activities and Sports

Säntispark Just outside Saint Gallen lies this year-round, family-friendly sports and spa extravaganza. There is something to please (and exhaust) everyone—racquet sports, bowling, minigolf, billiards. Children can dive into the wave pool at the water park and enjoy the rides and playgrounds. For relaxing, there's a solarium, sauna, and massage center. Equipment can be rented; most activities cost under 20 SF. ⊠ *From the main train station in Saint Gallen, 15 mins by Bus 7 (Abtwil), or by car along Hwy. N1, exit Winkeln.* ☎ *071/3114433.* ▱ *Pay per activity.* ◯ *Daily 8 AM–10 PM.*

Shopping

ANTIQUE PRINTS
An outstanding assortment of antique prints of Swiss landscapes and costumes is sold at a broad range of prices at **Graphica Antiqua** (⊠ Oberer Graben 46, near the Einstein Hotel, ☎ 071/2235016). The pictures are cataloged alphabetically by canton for easy browsing.

TEXTILES AND EMBROIDERY
For a region world renowned for its textiles and embroidery, it's surprisingly difficult to find the real thing at a single store. The excellent exceptions: **Rocco Textil** (⊠ Spiserg. 41, ☎ 071/2222407) has a small but wonderful selection of Saint Gallen embroidery, linens, and lace; they're an especially good source for custom work. **Saphir** (⊠ Bleichestr. 9, ☎ 071/2236263 carries a high-quality collection of embroidered handkerchiefs, bed and table linens, and bolts of embroidered fabric and lace—all from the Saint Gallen region. **Sturzenegger** (⊠ St. Leonhardstr. 12, ☎ 071/2224576), the better-known embroidery firm, established in 1883, sells its own line of linens and lingerie, designed and manufactured in the factory a block away.

Appenzell

⑱ *20 km (12 mi) south of Saint Gallen, 98 km (60 mi) southeast of Schaffhausen.*

Isolated from Saint Gallen by a ridge of green hills, Appenzell is one of Switzerland's most eccentric regions. Fellow Swiss think of its people as hillbillies, citing their quirky sense of humor and old-fashioned costumes. The city of Saint Gallen melts away into undulating hills spotted with doe-skin cows, a steep-pastured, isolated verdure reminiscent of West Virginia or the Ozarks. Prim, symmetrical cottages inevitably show rows of windows facing the valley. Named Appenzell after the Latin *abbatis cella* (abbey cell), the region served as a sort of colony to the Saint Gallen abbey, and its tradition of fine embroidery dates from those early days. The perfect chance to see this embroidery is during a local festival, such as the Alpfahrten, when cows are herded down the mountains. Women wear tulle coifs and dresses with intricate embroidery and lace, often with an eidelweiss motif; men wear embroidered red vests and suspenders decorated with eidelweiss or cow figures. These traditional costumes are taken very seriously; they can cost thousands of francs, but in this case, pride supercedes economy. A small highway (No. 3) leads into the hills through Teufen; the quaint Appenzell–Teufen–Gais rail line also serves the region.

The town of Appenzell focuses some of the best and worst of the region, offering tourists a concentrated and somewhat self-conscious sampling of the culture. Its streets lined with bright-painted homes, bakeries full of *Birnebrot* (pear bread) and souvenir Biber, and shops full of embroidery (which, on close examination, often turns out to have been made in China), Appenzell seems to watch the tourists warily and get on with its life while profiting from the attention. Its **Landsgemeindeplatz** in the town center is the site of the famous open-air elections (until 1991, for men only), which take place the last Sunday in April. Embroidery has become big business here, but it's rare to find handmade examples of the local art; though women still do fine work at home, it's generally reserved for gifts or heirlooms. Instead, large factories have sprung up in Appenzell country, and famous fine-cotton handkerchiefs sold in specialty shops around the world are made by machine here at the Dörig, Alba, and Lehner plants.

The **Museum Appenzell** showcases handicrafts and local traditions, regional history, and an international embroidery collection. ✉ *Hauptg. 4,* ☎ *071/7889631.* 🎫 *5 SF.* 🕐 *Apr.–Oct., daily 10–noon and 2–5; Nov.–Mar., Tues.–Sun. 2–4.*

Dining and Lodging

$$ ✕ **Traube.** The understated traditional interior lacks personality, but in the summer months, it opens up onto a terrace overlooking a lovely landscaped garden hidden from major streets. The menu is heavy on pork and potatoes, but the selection is wide enough to please most palates. Fondue and Appenzeller *Chäshörnli* (cheese and potato gnocchi) round off the the mostly heavy offerings. The daily special is usually under 20 SF. ✉ *Marktg. 7,* ☎ *071/7871407. MC, V. Closed Mon.*

$$$ ✕🛏 **Appenzell.** This comfortable new lodging has all the gabled
★ gemütlichkeit of its neighbors, with rows of shuttered windows and a view over the Landsgemeindeplatz. Homey rooms, warmed with polished wood, owe their airiness to the traditional multiple windows. The fine woodwork and antiques in the breakfast room are remnants of the previous house on the property. The newly renovated restaurant offers fresh interpretations of regional fare, such as the *Hauptgass* steak (an Appenzeller cheese gratin with pork, prosciutto, and tomato). And, almost unheard of in these parts, the restaurant specializes in health and vegetarian dishes. ✉ *Landsgemeindepl., CH-9050,* ☎ *071/7874211,* FAX *071/7874284. 16 rooms. Restaurant, breakfast room, café, patisserie, no-smoking rooms. AE, DC, MC, V.*

$—$$ ✕⊞ **Hof.** One of Appenzell's most popular restaurants serves hearty re-
★ gional meats and cheese specialties, such as *Käseschnitte* (cheese toast)
and Käse Spätzli, to locals and tourists who crowd elbow to elbow
along shared tables and raise their voices to be heard over the clatter from
the service bar. The all-modern rustic-wood decor and ladder-back
chairs, the knotty pine, and the display of sports trophies add to the local
atmosphere. Upstairs, groups can rent up to 58 beds in cheap summer-
camp dormitory lodgings and play skittles after dinner. ⊠ *Engelg. 4, CH-
9050*, ☎ *071/7872210*, ℻ *071/7875883. 10 rooms. AE, DC, MC, V.*

$$$ ⊞ **Löwen.** Wising up to the tourists' quest for "typical" local decor, the
owners of this renovated 1780 guest house furnished several rooms in
authentic Appenzeller styles, with embroidered linens and built-in
woodwork (canopy beds, armoires) painted with bright designs and naive
local scenes—some actually reflecting the view from the window. Stan-
dard rooms in dormitory-style oak also are available for a slightly
lower price. ⊠ *Hauptg. 25, CH-9050,* ☎ *071/7872187,* ℻ *071/
7872579. 17 rooms, 9 suites. Restaurant, bar, sauna. AE, DC, MC, V.*

$$$ ⊞ **Säntis.** A member of the Romantik hotel group, Appenzell's pres-
tigious hotel has a somewhat new and formal ambience, though the
earliest wing has been a hotel-restaurant since 1835. Old-style touches—
inlaid wood furnishings, painted beams—mix comfortably with the jewel-
tone rooms and gleaming walnut cabinetry; some rooms have four-poster
or canopy beds. The main first-floor restaurant serves slightly Frenchi-
fied regional specialties in either of two wood-lined dining rooms, one
Biedermeier, the other a folksy Appenzeller style. A fresh cherry-wood
stübli at street level attracts locals. ⊠ *Landsgemeindepl., CH-9050,*
☎ *071/7881111,* ℻ *071/7881110. 31 rooms, 6 suites. Restaurant, bar,
sauna. AE, DC, MC, V.*

$$ ⊞ **Adler.** This lovely lodging, across the street from the roaring River
Sitter but at downtown's edge, offers a variety of decor, from the mod
avocado interiors of the café and restaurant to some of the nicest ver-
sions of regional style in town. The rooms in the main building, dat-
ing from 1895, are spacious and beige-Formica spare, with the public
areas trimmed in pseudo-Spanish ironwork. The older wing includes
four rooms in Appenzeller style, with the repeated square paneling and
colorful painted cabinetry loyally reproduced. Four no-shower rooms,
also in the old wing, are creaky but well priced. ⊠ *Adlerpl., CH-9050,*
☎ *071/7871389,* ℻ *071/7871365. 21 rooms. Restaurant, café, patis-
serie. AE, DC, MC, V.*

$ ⊞ **Freudenberg.** This is a cookie-cutter modern chalet, but its vantage
point on a velvety green hillside overlooking town is the most scenic and
tranquil you'll find here. Built in 1969, it still has dormlike rooms and
sculptured carpet in harvest gold, but some rooms have balconies, and
the broad, shaded terrace café—festive in the evening with strings of yel-
low lights—lets you take in the picture-pretty views. ⊠ *Behind the train
station, CH-9050,* ☎ ℻ *071/7871240. 7 rooms. Restaurant, café. AE.*

Shopping

CHEESES

Picnickers can sample the different grades of Appenzeller cheese and
its unsung mountain rivals at **Mösler** (⊠ Hauptg., ☎ 071/7871317).
Sutter (⊠ Marktstr. 8, ☎ 071/7871227) also has a good selection of
local cheeses.

EMBROIDERY

True locally made hand embroidery is rare in Appenzell. Many hand-
kerchiefs that beautifully reproduce the blindingly close work that lo-
cals no longer pursue have been hand-stitched in Portugal. Though an
odd souvenir, they capture the spirit of Appenzell handwork better than
much of the pretty, though broad, machine work available in the

stores. **Margreiter** (✉ Hauptg. 29, ☎ 071/7873313) carries a large stock of machine-made handkerchiefs from the local Dörig, Alba, and Lehner factories, many decorated with edelweiss or other Alpine flowers. **Trachtenstube** (✉ Hauptg. 23, ☎ 071/7871606) offers high-quality local handiwork—lace, embroidery, and crafts.

LIQUEURS

Butchers, bakers, and liquor shops up and down the streets offer souvenir bottles of **Appenzeller Bitter** (Alpenbitter), a very sweet aperitif made in town. A well-balanced **eau-de-vie** called Appenzeller Kräuter, made of blended herbs, is a specialty here.

Stein

⑲ *13 km (8 mi) northwest of Appenzell, 94 km (58 mi) southeast of Schaffhausen.*

At the **Schaukäserei** (showcase dairy) in Stein (not to be confused with Stein-am-Rhein), modern cheese-making methods are demonstrated. Note that cheese is made 9–2 only. ☎ 071/3685070. ▣ *Free.* ☉ *Mar.–Oct., daily 8–7; Nov.–Feb., daily 9–6.*

The **Appenzeller Volkskunde Museum** (Folklore Museum) demonstrates Appenzell arts and crafts, local costumes, and hand-painted furniture. ☎ 071/3685056. ▣ *7 SF.* ☉ *Nov.–Mar., Sun. 10–5; Apr.–Oct., Mon.–Sat. 10–noon and 1:30–5, Sun. 10–6.*

Urnäsch

⑳ *10 km (6 mi) west of Appenzell, 110 km (68 mi) southeast of Schaffhausen.*

In this modest countryside town, the **Museum für Appenzeller Brauchtum** (Museum of Appenzeller Traditions) displays costumes, cowbells, a cheese wagon, and examples of farmhouse living quarters. ☎ 071/3642322. ▣ *4 SF.* ☉ *May–Oct., daily 1:30–5; Apr., Wed. and weekends 1:30–5 and by appointment; Nov.–Mar., by appointment only.*

Mt. Säntis

㉑ *11 km (7 mi) south of Urnäsch, 121 km (75 mi) southeast of Schaffhausen.*

A pleasurable high-altitude excursion out of Appenzell takes you west to Urnäsch, then south to the hamlet of Schwägalp, where a cable car carries you up to the peak of Mt. Säntis, at 2,502 m (8,209 ft) the highest in the region and a source of fine views of the Bodensee as well as of the Graubünden and Bernese Alps. The very shape of the summit—an arc of jutting rock that swings up to the jagged peak housing the station—is spectacular. ☎ 071/3656565. ▣ *27 SF round-trip.* ☉ *July–Aug., daily 7:30–7; May, June, and Sept., daily 7:30–6:30; Oct.–Apr., 8:30–5; departures every 30 mins. Closed for 3 wks in Jan.*

Toggenburg Valley

㉒ *Entrance 11 km (7 mi) south of Mt. Säntis, 132 km (82 mi) southeast of Schaffhausen.*

A scenic pre-Alpine resort area popular with locals but relatively unexplored by outsiders, this is an ideal place for skiers and hikers who hate crowds. In the rugged Upper Toggenburg, weather-boarded dwellings surround the neighboring resorts of Wildhaus (birthplace of religious reformer Huldrych Zwingli), Unterwasser, and Alt–St. Johann—all of which draw Swiss families for winter skiing and summer hiking excursions into the Churfirsten and Alpstein mountains. As they lie within shouting distance of each other, the ski facilities can be shared, and the jagged teeth of the mountains behind provide a dramatic backdrop.

If you are fascinated by the Reformation, you may want to make a pilgrimage to Wildhaus's **Zwinglihaus,** the farmhouse where Huldrych Zwingli was born in 1484. His father was president of the village's political commune, and the house was used as a meeting place for its council. A small **museum** within displays some restored furniture from his time, though not from his family, and an impressive collection of period Bibles. The fire-and-brimstone preacher celebrated his first mass in the town's Protestant church and went on to lead the Protestant Reformation in Zürich. ⊠ *Schönenboden, Wildhaus/Lisighaus,* ☎ *071/9992178.* ⬛ *Free.* ☽ *Tues.–Sun. 2–4; closed mid-Apr.–May and mid-Nov.–Dec.*

Skiing

Equally popular with locals, the triplet ski resorts of Wildhaus, Unterwasser, and Alt–St. Johann combine forces to draw visitors into the Churfirsten "paradise" in the Toggenburg Valley. Here you'll find altitudes and drops to suit even jaded skiers, the most challenging starting on the 2,076-m-high (6,809-ft-high) Gamserrugg and winding down 1,000 m (3,280 ft) to Wildhaus itself; a medium-difficult rival winds from Chäserrugg (2,262 m/7,419 ft) all the way down to Unterwasser. A one-day pass for all three resorts costs 42 SF; a six-day pass costs 184 SF. There are ski schools in all three resorts. For more information and reservations, call ☎ 071/9999911, ℻ 071/9992929.

Alt–St. Johann, at 900 m (2,952 ft), has one chairlift and two T-bars. **Unterwasser,** at 910 m (2,985 ft), has one funicular railway, one cable car, four T-bars, 50 km (31 mi) of downhill runs, 45 km (28 mi) of cross-country trails, and 27 km (17 mi) of ski-hiking trails. At 1,098 m (3,601 ft), **Wildhaus** offers skiers four chairlifts, five T-bars, 50 km (31 mi) of downhill runs, 45 km (28 mi) of cross-country trails, and 27 km (17 mi) of ski-hiking trails. Besides skiing, you can go skating or curling.

Outdoor Activities and Sports

RACQUET SPORTS
Wildhaus (☎ 071/9991211) has two outdoor courts. **Unterwasser** has three outdoor tennis courts and a tennis-squash center (☎ 071/9993030).

LIECHTENSTEIN AND THE WALENSEE

When you cross the border from Switzerland into the principality of Liechtenstein, you will be surrounded by license plates marked FL: This stands for Fürstentum Liechtenstein (Principality of Liechtenstein). You are leaving the world's oldest democracy and entering a monarchy that is the last remnant of the Holy Roman Empire—all 157 square km (61 square mi) of it. If you blink, you may miss it entirely.

This postage-stamp principality was begun at the end of the 17th century, when a wealthy Austrian prince, Johann Adam von Liechtenstein, bought out two bankrupt counts in the Rhine Valley and united their lands. In 1719 he obtained an imperial deed from Kaiser Karl VI, creating the principality of Liechtenstein. The noble family poured generations of wealth into the new country, improving its standard of living, and in 1862 an heir named Prince Johann the Good helped Liechtenstein introduce its first constitution as a "democratic monarchy" in which the people and the prince share power equally.

Today the principality's 31,000 citizens enjoy one of the world's highest per-capita incomes and pay virtually no taxes. Its prosperous (though discreet) industries range from jam making to the molding of false teeth. Ironically, prosperity has built the lower reaches of Liechtenstein into a modern, comfortable, bourgeois community, full of big, new cream-color bungalows that hardly seem picturesque to tourists seeking traces of the Holy Roman Empire.

Vaduz (Liechtenstein)

㉓ *15 km (9 mi) southeast of the Toggenburg Valley, 159 km (98 mi) southeast of Schaffhausen.*

Arriving in downtown Vaduz (there are exits from the A13 expressway from both the north and the south), a visitor could make the mistake of thinking Liechtenstein's only attraction is its miniature scale. Liechtenstein's small **Briefmarkenmuseum** (Stamp Museum) demonstrates the principality's history as a maker of beautifully designed, limited-edition postage stamps. Have your passport stamped for 2 SF at the **Fremdenverkehrszentrale** (tourist office) (☞ Visitor Information, *below*) in the same building. ✉ *Städtle 37,* ☎ *075/2366105.* ✇ *Free.* ☉ *Apr.–Oct., daily 10–noon and 1:30–5:30; Nov.–Mar., daily 10–noon and 1:30–5.*

The **Liechtensteinische Staatliche Kunstsammlung** (Liechtenstein State Museum of Art) displays an ever-changing fraction of the country's extraordinary art collection, including graphic art, paintings, and works from the world-famous art collection of the prince. ✉ *Städtle 37,* ☎ *075/2322341.* ✇ *5 SF.* ☉ *Apr.–Oct., daily 10–noon and 1:30–5:30; Nov.–Mar., daily 10–noon and 1:30–5.*

Though at press time (summer 1998) it was closed temporarily for structural damage, the **Liechtensteinisches Landesmuseum** (National Museum), in a former tavern and customs house, covers the geology, Roman history, and folklore of the principality. ✉ *Städtle 43,* ☎ *075/2322310.* ✇ *2 SF.* ☉ *May–Sept., daily 10–noon and 1:30–5:30; Oct.–Apr., Tues.–Sun. 2–5:30.*

If you're a diehard museum enthusiast and skier, consider a short visit to the **Ski Museum Vaduz,** a small shrine to Switzerland's (and the Alps') preferred pastime. Here you'll find numerous variations on the theme, including skis, sleds, ski fashion, and literature. ✉ *Bangarten 10,* ☎ *075/2321502.* ✇ *5 SF.* ☉ *Weekdays 2–6.*

At the top of a well-marked hill road (you can climb the forest footpath behind the Hotel Engel) stands **Vaduz Castle.** Here, His Highness, Johannes Adam Pius, reigning prince of Liechtenstein, duke of Troppau and Jaegerndorf, reigns in a gratifyingly romantic fortress-home with striped medieval shutters, massive ramparts, and a broad perspective over the Rhine Valley. Originally built during the 12th century, the castle was burned down by troops of the Swiss Confederation in the Swabian Wars of 1499 and partly rebuilt during the following centuries, until a complete overhaul that started in 1905 gave it its present form. It is not open to the public, as Hans-Adam enjoys his privacy. He is the son of the late, beloved Franz Josef II, who died in November 1989 after a more than 50-year reign. Franz Josef's birthday, August 15, is still celebrated as the Liechtenstein national holiday; Hans-Adam—the last living heir to the Holy Roman Empire—has been known to join the crowds below to watch the fireworks while wearing jeans.

Dining and Lodging

$ ✕ **Wirthschaft zum Löwen.** Though there's plenty of French, Swiss, and
★   Austrian influence, Liechtenstein has a cuisine of its own, and this is
the place to try it. In a wood-shingle landmark farmhouse on the Austrian border, the friendly Biedermann family serves tender homemade
Schwartenmagen (the pressed-pork mold unfortunately known as
headcheese in English), pungent *Sauerkäse* (sour cheese), and
Käseknöpfli, plus lovely meats and the local crusty, chewy bread. Be
sure to try the region's wines. ⊠ *FL-9488 Schellenberg,* ☎ *075/
3731162. No credit cards.*

$$$–$$$$ ✕ ⊡ **Real.** Here you'll find rich, old-style Austrian-French cuisine in
★   this Relais & Châteaux establishment, prepared these days by Martin
Real, son of the unpretentious former chef, Felix Real—who, in his re-
tirement, presides over the 20,000-bottle cellar. There's an abundance
of game in season, richly sauced seafood, and soufflés. The extraor-
dinary wine list includes some rare (and excellent) local samplings, some
from the family vineyard. Downstairs, the more casual stübli atmo-
sphere is just right for *Geschnetzeltes mit Rösti* (veal bits in cream sauce
with hash brown potatoes); upstairs, the rooms are small but airily dec-
orated. ⊠ *Städtle 21, FL-9490,* ☎ *075/2322222,* ℻ *075/2320891. 11
rooms, 2 suites. Restaurant. AE, DC, MC, V.*

$$ ✕ ⊡ **Engel.** This elegant, centrally located hotel-restaurant has a comfortable local ambience despite the tour-bus crowds. The restaurant
downstairs dishes up home cooking, and there's a *biergarten* (beer garden) where Liechtensteiners meet. Upstairs, the more formal restaurant has a terrace and, surprisingly enough, Chinese cuisine. The guest
rooms are in fresh colors, with tile bathrooms. ⊠ *Städtle 13, FL-
9490,* ☎ *075/2320313,* ℻ *075/2331159. 20 rooms. Restaurant, pub.
AE, DC, MC, V.*

$$$$ ⊡ **Park-Hotel Sonnenhof.** A garden oasis—and Relais & Châteaux property—commanding a superb view over the valley and mountains beyond, this hillside retreat offers understated luxury minutes from
downtown Vaduz. Rooms are decorated in homey pastels; public areas
are full of antiques, rugs, woodwork, and familial touches. The excellent
French restaurant is exclusively for guests. ⊠ *Mareestr. 29, FL-9490,*
☎ *075/2321192,* ℻ *075/2320053. 17 rooms, 12 suites. Restaurant,
indoor pool, sauna. AE, DC, MC, V.*

Outdoor Activities and Sports

BICYCLES AND MOTORCYCLES

In Vaduz, bikes and small motorcycles can be rented from **Hans Mel-
liger** (☎ 075/2321606).

TENNIS

Vaduz (☎ 075/2327720) has public covered courts on Schaanerstrasse.
Covered courts are also accessible in nearby **Schaan** (☎ 075/2332343).

Shopping

POTTERY

Though shops on the main street of Vaduz carry samples of the local
dark-glaze pottery, painted with folksy flowers and figures, the central source is **Schaedler Keramik** (⊠ Nendeln, 8 km/5 mi north of Vaduz
on the main highway, ☎ 075/3731414). Simpler household pottery is
available for sale as well as the traditional and often ornate hand-painted
pieces. Pottery making is demonstrated daily; it's open weekdays 8–
noon and 1:30–6.

STAMPS

Liechtenstein is sometimes called the unofficial, per capita world cham-
pion of stamp collecting. To buy some of its famous stamps, whether
to send a postcard to a philatelist friend or to invest in limited issue

commemorative sheets, you must line up with the tour-bus crowds at the popular **post office** (⊠ Städtle).

Triesenberg

㉔ *3 km (2 mi) southeast of Vaduz, 162 km (100 mi) southeast of Schaffhausen.*

This cluster of pretty chalets clings to the mountainside, with panoramic views over the Rhine Valley. Triesenberg was settled during the 13th century by immigrants from the Valais in southwestern Switzerland. The **Walser Heimatmuseum** (Valais Heritage Museum) traces the culture of the people who emigrated from the Valais to Triesenberg during the 13th century. Furnishings and tools from farmers and craftsmen are displayed, and an entertaining 20-minute slide show illustrates their Alpine roots. ⊠ *Dorfenzentrum,* ☎ *075/2621926.* ⊡ *2 SF.* ☉ *Sept.– May, Tues.–Fri. 1:30–5:30, Sat. 1:30–5; June–Aug., Tues.–Fri. 1:30– 5:30, Sat. 1:30–5; Sun. 2–5.*

Malbun

㉕ *5 km (3 mi) southeast of Triesenberg, 167 km (103 mi) southeast of Schaffhausen.*

In winter, this 1,600-m (5,250-ft) high mountain resort near the border of Austria draws crowds of local families who come for the varied slopes, many of which are well suited to beginners. England's Prince Charles and Princess Anne learned to ski here while visiting the Liechtenstein royal family in Vaduz. In summer, Malbun becomes a quiet, unpretentious resort with reasonable prices.

Skiing

Malbun is a sunny, natural bowl with low, easy slopes and a couple of difficult runs; you can ride a chairlift to the top of the Sareiserjoch and experience the novelty of skiing from the Austrian border back into Liechtenstein. Facilities are concentrated at the center, including hotels and cafés overlooking the slopes. The resort also has a ski school (☎ 075/ 2639770). One-day lift tickets cost 32 SF; six-day passes cost 136 SF.

Lodging

$ 🏨 **Alpenhotel.** This 85-year-old chalet, well above the mists of the Rhine, has been remodeled and has added a modern wing. The old rooms are small, with creaky pine trim; the higher-priced new rooms are modern stucco. The Vögeli family's welcoming smiles and good food have made it a Liechtenstein institution. ⊠ *FL-9490,* ☎ *075/2631181,* FAX *075/ 2639646. 21 rooms. Restaurant, café, indoor pool. AE, DC, MC, V.*

Outdoor Activities and Sports

Liechtenstein has a 162-km (100-mi) network of Alpine hiking trails, and another 243 km (150 mi) of valley hiking. **Malbun** and **Steg** are ideal starting points for mountain hikes. You can get trail maps at the tourist office or at magazine kiosks.

Flumserberg

㉖ *25 km (15 mi) west of Malbun, 122 km (75 mi) southeast of Schaffhausen.*

On the windswept, timberless slopes overlooking the Walensee and the Churfirsten Mountains, this resort is the site of one of the world's longest cableways. Over a distance of about 3 km (1¾ mi), a procession of little four-seater cabins reaches up to the rocky summit at **Leist,** 2,056 m (6,743 ft) up.

Skiing

Flumserberg, spanning 1,200 m–2,222 m (3,936 ft–7,288 ft), has five cable cars, 10 chairlifts, four T-bars, 60 km (40 mi) of downhill runs, 21 km (13 mi) of cross-country trails, and 20 km (12 mi) of mountain trails. The runs are suitable for beginner to intermediate skiers. You can also endeavor to skate, skibob, and night ski, or snowboard in the newly constructed Funpark. A ski school (☎ 081/7333939) provides help for the less proficient. The German-only *Schneebericht* (☎ 081/7201510) gives current information on snow conditions. One-day lift tickets cost 45 SF; six-day passes, 188 SF.

Walensee

 5 km (3 mi) northwest of Flumserberg, 127 km (78 mi) southeast of Schaffhausen.

Between Liechtenstein and Zürich, the spectacular, mirrorlike lake called the Walensee is a deep emerald gash that stretches 16 km (10 mi) through the mountains, reflecting the jagged Churfirsten peaks. At the western end of the lake, **Weesen** is a quiet, shady resort noted for its mild climate and lovely lakeside walkway. Six kilometers (4 miles) north of Weesen on a winding mountain road lies **Amden,** perched 950 m (3,116 ft) above the Walensee in the relatively undiscovered region south of the Churfirsten Mountains. With its balance of up-to-date resources and traditional atmosphere, it is rarely penetrated by foreigners.

Skiing

Despite its small size, **Amden** is a major winter sports center, offering modest skiing in a ruggedly beautiful setting. Easy and medium slopes with unspectacular drops and quick, short-lift runs provide good weekend getaways for crowds of local Swiss families. The highest trails start at 1,700 m (5,576 ft); there are one chairlift, three T-bars, one children's lift, 25 km (16 mi) of downhill runs, and 8 km (5 mi) of cross-country trails. There are also a ski school, skating on a natural ice rink, and walking paths. One-day lift tickets cost 29 SF; six-day passes cost 110 SF.

Outdoor Activities and Sports

SKATING, SWIMMING, AND TENNIS

For sports enthusiasts, **Amden** also has a public skating rink (☎ 055/6111413), the heated indoor pool **Hallenbad Amden** (☎ 055/6111588), and an outdoor tennis court (☎ 055/6111413).

OFF THE BEATEN PATH

RAPPERSWIL – Between the Walensee and Zürich, this small town on Zürichsee (Lake Zürich) encourages pleasant views and summertime waterfront strolls. Three rose gardens in the town center, including one for people with disabilities, account for Rapperswil's claim as the "Swiss City of Roses." A forbidding 13th-century **castle** looks like part of a gothic novel, with a trio of grave towers. Inside is the small **Polenmuseum** (☎ 055/2101862; ☑ 4 SF) highlighting the history of Polish immigrants to Switzerland. The castle's walkway faces a small deer park and affords a view of Zürich; from the terrace you'll see the Glarus Alps. At the **Knie's Kinderzoo** (Children's Zoo), there are dolphin shows, 70 types of animals from around the world, elephant and pony rides, and plenty of creatures to feed and pet. (Elephant rides are not given on rainy days.) At press time there were plans to add an aquarium—and possibly to raise the entrance fee. Follow signs; it's near the train station. ☒ *About 36 km (22 mi) northwest of Weesen and 40 km (24 mi) southeast of Zürich. Children's Zoo:* ☎ *055/2206767.* ☑ *7 SF.* ☉ *Mid-Mar.–Oct., daily 9–6.*

EASTERN SWITZERLAND A TO Z

Arriving and Departing

By Car

The **A1** expressway from Zürich heads for Saint Gallen through Winterthur. To reach Schaffhausen from Zürich, take A1 to Winterthur, then head north on the cantonal highway **E41/15.** You also can leave Zürich by way of the **A4** expressway past Kloten Airport, crossing through Germany briefly and entering Schaffhausen through Neuhausen am Rheinfall. From the south, the **A13** expressway, shared with Austria, leads you from Chur along Liechtenstein to the east end of the Bodensee; from there, you take A1 into Saint Gallen.

By Plane

Zürich-Kloten Airport (☎ 1571060), the most important in Switzerland, lies in Zürich, about 48 km (30 mi) south of Schaffhausen, about 75 km (46 mi) west of Saint Gallen, and 130 km (81 mi) northwest of Liechtenstein.

By Train

A connection by train from the Zürich Hauptbahnhof into the **SBB Bahnhof Schaffhausen** (☎ 051/2234500) takes about 40 minutes; into **SBB Bahnhof Saint Gallen** (☎ 040/671040) and Sargans, about an hour. Connections from the south (Graubünden) are more complicated, as both Austria and the Alps intervene.

Getting Around

By Boat

Swiss Federal Railways provides regular year-round service on the Bodensee through **Schweizer Bodensee Schiffarht Gesellschaft** (Swiss Bodensee Cruiseline Co., ☎ 071/4633435), though fewer boats run in winter. There is also **Verkehrsverein Untersee am Rhein** (☎ 052/7612604), with a cruise-ship route on the Walensee and a Rhine cruise between Schaffhausen and Kreuzlingen-Konstanz. The Swiss Boat Pass allows half-fare travel (☞ Boat Travel *in* the Gold Guide).

By Bus

The famous yellow **postbuses** provide much of the public transport in areas not served by trains, particularly smaller towns and, of course, Liechtenstein, which has no rail service. The bus schedules are usually posted outside the town post office, but you can also obtain information from any train station.

By Cable Car

Although there are a few scattered across the region, the most popular and spectacular cable-car rides are up Mt. Säntis from Schwägalp and to the Ebenalp via Appenzell-Wasserauen.

By Car

Driving in eastern Switzerland allows you to see the best of this region, with its highway along the Bodensee and pretty back roads in Appenzell. Neither Saint Gallen nor Schaffhausen is a big enough city to warrant all-out panic, although you'll find it easiest to head directly for the center and abandon the car for the duration of your visit. Try to get into a parking lot, as finding a spot on the street can be difficult. In Schaffhausen, there's a big lot by the Stadttheater on Herrenacker.

By Train

Rail connections are somewhat complicated in this area, especially if you want to visit more of Appenzell than its major towns. Schaffhausen and Saint Gallen are the main hubs from which regional trains head into the countryside and along the Bodensee. The only railroads into the country are the narrow-gauge line between Saint Gallen and the town of Appenzell, which passes Teufen and Gais, and the Gossau–Appenzell–Wasserauen line. To see more of the territory, you may return to Saint Gallen on this same line by way of Herisau.

Although there is no regional rail pass available for eastern Switzerland, the general Swiss Pass (☞ Train Travel *in* the Gold Guide) includes Saint Gallen and Schaffhausen city transit as well as overall rail privileges. You cannot enter Liechtenstein by rail; the international express train that passes between Switzerland and Austria doesn't bother to stop. From the train stations at Buchs or Sargans, you can catch a postbus (☞ By Bus, *above*) into Vaduz.

Contacts and Resources

Emergencies

Police (☏ 117). **Ambulance** (☏ 144). **Doctor, dentist, late-night pharmacies** (☏ 111). **Medical assistance** in Saint Gallen (☏ 071/2261111).

Guided Tours

BOAT

The **Untersee und Rhein** ship company (✉ Freierpl. 7, CH-8202 Schaffhausen, ☏ 052/6254282, or contact the Schweizerische Bodenseeschiffahrtsgesellschaft AG at Romanshorn ☏ 071/4633435) offers a winning combination of a boat ride on the Rhine with romantic views of storybook castles, citadels, and monasteries gliding past. Boats run regularly up- and downstream, docking at Schaffhausen, Stein-am-Rhein, Gottlieben, Konstanz, and Kreuzlingen. Prices vary according to distance traveled. A one-way trip from Schaffhausen to Kreuzlingen takes about 4½ hours.

WALKING

The **Schaffhausen tourist office** (☞ Visitor Information, *below*) gives guided walking tours of the Old Town, the monastery, and the Munot.

Visitor Information

The tourist office for all of eastern Switzerland is based in Saint Gallen: **Tourismusverband Ostschweiz** (Tourist Association of Eastern Switzerland; ✉ Bahnhofpl. 1a, CH-9001, ☏ 071/2273737, ⅎⱯⅩ 071/2273767).

There are small regional visitor information offices throughout eastern Switzerland. **Appenzellerland** (✉ Hauptg. 4, CH-9050 Appenzell, ☏ 071/7889641; ✉ CH-9063 Stein, ☏ 071/3685050). **Schaffhausen** (✉ Fronwagturm 4, CH-8201 Schaffhausen, ☏ 052/6255141). **Liechtenstein** (✉ Städtle 37, FL-9490 Vaduz, ☏ 075/2321443). **Thurgau** (✉ Gemeindehaus, CH-8580 Amriswil, ☏ 071/4118181) services the Bodensee.

4 Graubünden

Arosa, Davos, Saint-Moritz

*Dominated by its trendy resorts—
Saint-Moritz, Davos, Klosters,
Arosa, Pontresina—Graubünden
is nonetheless Switzerland's most
culturally diverse and largest canton.
German, Italian, and Romansh—the
ancient dialect that is thought to date
from 600 BC—are all spoken here, in a
land where stalwart native farmers
subsist alongside the fur-clad jet set.*

Updated by
Kara
Misenheimer

THOUGH THE NAMES OF ITS RESORTS—Saint-Moritz, Davos, Klosters, Arosa, Pontresina—register almost automatic recognition, the region wrapped around them remains surprisingly unsung, untouched by the fur-clad poseurs who make stage sets out of its sports centers, aloof to the glamour trends—quirky, resilient, and decidedly apart. Nowhere in Switzerland will you find sharper contrasts than those between the bronze seven-day citizens who jet into Saint-Moritz and the stalwart native farmers who nurse their own archaic dialects and gather their crops by hand, as their Roman-Etruscan forefathers did.

Graubünden is the largest canton in Switzerland, covering more than one-sixth of the entire country. As it straddles the continental divide, its rains pour off north into the Rhine and Inn rivers and south into the Italian River Po. The land is thus riddled with bluff-lined valleys, and its southern half basks in crystalline light: Except for the Italian-speaking Ticino, it receives the most sunshine in the country. These valleys are flanked by dense blue-black wilderness and white peaks, among them Piz Buin (3,313 m/10,867 ft) in the north and Piz Bernina (4,050 m/13,284 ft) in the south.

Of all the Swiss cantons, Graubünden is the most culturally diverse. To the north it borders Austria and Liechtenstein, and in the east and south, it abuts Italy. Dialects of both German and Italian are widely spoken. But the obscure and ancient language called Romansh (literally, "Roman") is spoken by almost 20% of the population, harking back to its days during the 1st century BC, when it was a Roman province called Rhaetia Prima. Some say the tongue predates the Romans and trace its roots back as far as 600 BC, when an Etruscan prince named Rhaetus invaded the region.

Though anyone versed in a Latin language can follow Romansh's simpler signs (*camara da vacanza* is vacation apartment; *il büro da pulizia*, the police office), it is no easy matter to pick it up by ear. Nor do the Graubündners smooth the way: Rhaetian Romansh is fragmented into five subdialects beyond its codified form, so that people living in any of the isolated valleys of the region might call the same cup a *cuppina*, a *scadiola*, a *scariola*, a *cuppegn*, a *tazza*, or a *cupina*. The name *Graubünden*—Les Grisons (French), I Grigioni (Italian), and Il Grischun (Romansh)—means "gray confederation," referring to the 14th-century rebellion against Hapsburg rule. With these dialects and their derivatives cutting one valley culture neatly off from another, it's no wonder the back roads of the region seem as removed from the modern mainstream as the once-a-century world of Brigadoon.

Pleasures and Pastimes

Dining

In this relatively exotic region of Switzerland, with its myriad dialects and potent blend of Latin and German blood, the cuisine is as novel and unexpected as its culture. Though you hear of little but the ubiquitous *Bündnerfleisch* (air-dried beef pressed into rectangular loaves and shaved into chewy, translucent slices), you will find a much broader range of delights. Italian influence is strong here, but—unlike the Ticinese to the southwest, who borrow from Italy wholesale—the Graubündners have evolved their own versions and incorporate Germanic styles as well. Takeoffs on gnocchi (potato-based pasta) and *Spätzli* (tiny flour dumplings) coexist here, with relatives of *Rösti* (hash brown potatoes) and polenta asserting their own local flavor.

Originating in isolated rural areas, the cuisines of Graubünden are earthy and direct, with sausages, potatoes, cheese, and cabbage as staples and onions, garlic, bacon, and dried fruits providing the hearty flavors. You may feel you've stepped back to the Middle Ages when you sit down to *pizzoccheri neri* (little buckwheat Spätzli dumplings swimming in garlic) or to *maluns* (grated potatoes stirred in pools of butter until they form crisp balls) served with tart applesauce. *Capuns* or *krutka-puna* are bundles of Swiss chard smothered in butter and cheese and flavored with dried meat, and *hexenpolenta* is a harmless dish of cornmeal mush sweetened with raisins and apples.

In many kitchens, these down-to-earth treats are making a comeback in either traditional or more modern interpretations. On tourist menus, though, you're sure to see token regional specialities—robust *Gerstensuppe* (barley soup), *Engadiner Nusstorte* (a chewy walnut-and-honey cake found in every bake shop), and the inevitable (but wonderful) variety of cold local meats offered as a *Bündnerplatte*.

Watch for the annual winter Gourmet Festival in Saint-Moritz, when world-renowned chefs serve their specialties in host restaurants and hotels. The Grand Gourmet Finale is a gargantuan feast prepared by 30 chefs on the frozen Saint-Moritz Lake. For reservations call the Saint-Moritz tourist office (☞ Visitor Information, *below*).

CATEGORY	COST*
$$$$	over 80 SF
$$$	50 SF–80 SF
$$	20 SF–50 SF
$	under 20 SF

Prices are per person for a three-course meal (two-course meal in $ category), including sales tax and 15% service charge

Farmhouse Vacations

An unusual alternative to the typical resort experience can be found on more than 70 high- and low-altitude Bündner farms providing apartments or rooms for rent. Most have pastures full of cows and other domestic animals, sell farm products, and offer voluntary participation in daily chores. The booklet "Farm Holidays," available from the Verkehrsverein Graubünden (Graubünden Tourist Office; ☞ Graubünden A to Z, *below*), includes a list of participating families with descriptions of the various scenarios and available activities. Knowing some German is practically a prerequisite, as the host families usually don't speak English.

Lodging

Of all the regions in Switzerland—each trading on its homeyness, its quaintness, its own take on a storybook setting—Graubünden delivers the most, as its hoteliers invest fortunes in preserving Alpine coziness inside and out. Unlike other parts of Switzerland, where hotels radiate warmth and history from their shuttered facades but have interiors as stark as hospital rooms, Graubünden hotels are often softened from within with wood. The source is *Arvenholz,* the prized Alpine pine (*Pinus cembra*), thick with knots and rich in natural color—a color that deepens from buff to burnished toffee over the decades. You'll see this lovely wood in original installations, lovingly preserved, or in new but well-crafted beds, armoires, end tables, and even ceilings. Whether plain or elaborately carved, the effect is welcoming and unmistakably Swiss.

Prices in this popular region are comparably high—even if you leave exorbitant Saint-Moritz out of the curve—and they stay that way most of the year. Winter prices are highest, summer's close behind. Take note:

hotels publish tariffs in various ways; double check whether you're paying per person or per room, as well as whether you have *demipension* (half-board).

CATEGORY	COST*
$$$$	over 300 SF
$$$	200 SF–300 SF
$$	120 SF–200 SF
$	under 120 SF

Prices are for a standard double room, including breakfast, sales tax, and 15% service charge.

Skiing and Snow Sports

With Davos as the site of the first ski lift in history, Saint-Moritz as the world's ritziest resort, and a host of other justifiably famous winter wonderlands within its confines, Graubünden easily earns its reputation as the ultimate winter destination. You'll find downhill skiing at all levels, as well as cross-country and off-piste skiing, snowboarding, carving, and a multitude of other winter activities—from curling, skating, and tobogganing to more unusual spectator sports, such as dogsled racing, kite skiing, and ski *joering*, in which participants are pulled on skis by a horse. If it's played summers on green surfaces, it's done here winters on white turf: Silvaplana and other resorts have snow golf, and Saint-Moritz hosts polo and horse racing on its frozen lake. A phenomenon called the New Technology Center (☎ 081/9367900) has started up with branches in the Flims/Laax area; these centers equip you with a ski suit, skiing or snowboarding equipment, and a day ski pass, all for a flat fee of about 100 SF. The convenience even extends to location—the centers are based as close as possible to the lifts.

Trains

The bright red narrow-gauge trains of the Rhätische Bahn were designed with sightseeing in mind. Along with the legendary, panoramic *Glacier Express* to Zermatt, which takes you up and over the barren backbone of Switzerland near Andermatt, trains throughout the region traverse spectacular glacial terrain, crossing bridges built unbelievably high over mountain gorges, cutting through mountainsides by way of viaducts. Even as the most desolate landscapes pass by, signs of civilization are never far behind: the lofty little villages, serviced by tiny train stations, show once again the Swiss affinity for access and for making the impossible seem routine.

Wines

Graubünden has its own distinctive wines: red pinot noir, white Riesling Silvaner, and pinot gris from the Bündnerherrschaft, the sunny region around Maienfeld, Jenins, and Malans. The unique Veltliner, a hearty red Nebbiolo grown over the border in Valtellina, which was ceded to Italy in 1815 (and before then known as the Veltlin) also hails from the Graubünden. The wine has always been brought into Graubünden, where it is aged and bottled as a product that is, at least in spirit, Swiss.

Exploring Graubünden

The region is fairly neatly bisected, by a spine of 2,987-m (9,800-ft) peaks, into two very different sections connected only by the Julier Pass, the Albula Pass, and the Flüela Pass. In the northwest, the region's capital, Chur, is flanked by ancient villages and a few lesser-known ski resorts. Farther east is the wild and craggy Prättigau region, which includes the resorts of Klosters and Davos as well as the Flüela Pass. The other half of the canton is comprised of the famous Engadine region, home to mountain-ringed lakes and sophisticated resorts: Sils-

Maria, Pontresina, and Saint-Moritz—as well as the magnificent Parc Naziunal Svizzer.

Numbers in the text correspond to numbers in the margin and on the Graubünden map.

Great Itineraries

IF YOU HAVE 1 OR 2 DAYS

Concentrate on ⊞ **Saint-Moritz** ⑭, where you can indulge in some of the world's most varied sports activities as well as sophisticated cuisine and exclusive nightlife (expect to pay dearly for all). Wind down in ⊞ **Pontresina** ⑬, whose stately old hotels, sgraffitied buildings, and pine and larch forests form the ideal setting for those in search of a low-key resort.

IF YOU HAVE 3 OR 4 DAYS

Drive the mountain passes through "Heidi Country." Start at the region's capital ⊞ **Chur** ③, then continue to ⊞ **Klosters** ⑤, where the British royal family vacations. Alternatively, head from Chur to ⊞ **Arosa** ④— set apart by an isolated setting and old-village character.

IF YOU HAVE 5 OR MORE DAYS

From the bases in the three-day itinerary, above, visit the Upper and Lower Engadine valleys. Here, the superior **Parc Naziunal Svizzer** ⑩ is a magnificent federally protected preserve of virtually virgin wilderness. Climb the **Julier Pass** heading north to **Tiefencastel** ⑯ (if you're going that way, you can leave the region via the San Bernardino Pass into Lugano) or simply take in a spa at **Bad Ragaz** ①.

When to Tour Graubünden

Though the tourism industry breathlessly awaits winter, when Graubünden's resorts fill to capacity, summer is popular as well. Thanks to a plethora of such warm-weather sports as hiking, cycling, golfing, windsurfing, and even hot-air ballooning, the area is now pleasurably active year round. Avoid November, early December, and May, when most resorts close for preparations and annual renovations. From late September to late October, the weather is typically temperate, with clear skies and the gleaming yellow colors of its golden fall.

HEIDI COUNTRY, CHUR, AND AROSA

Though the gateway to Graubünden, this region has a catchier claim to fame: It was here that the legendary Heidi enjoyed the fresh air and rustic pleasures of the Alps.

Bad Ragaz

❶ *20 km (12 mi) north of Chur.*

The ambience in this old resort is more therapeutic than aesthetic, though the views of the mountains—including the Falknis (2,562 m/8,400 ft)— are lovely. When Heidi's crippled friend Clara needed to take a cure, she came first to Bad Ragaz, the renowned **thermal spa** in the Rhine Valley. Its warm (37°C/98°F), abundant springs have been tapped for a thousand years for the treatment of rheumatism, circulation problems, and—as in Clara's case—paralysis. Nowadays you can take the cure at either of two indoor **thermal pools,** open to the public, though preferably a public with more stringent medical needs than a good, hot soak. ✉ *Kurzentrum,* ☎ *081/3032741.* 🎫 *16 SF.* ☉ *Weekdays 7:30 AM–9 PM, weekends 7:30–7.*

Skiing and Golf

A cable car runs up to **Pardiel** (1,631 m/5,350 ft), with a lift to **Laufboden** (2,226 m/7,300 ft). This ski area spreads down two flanks of the 2,844-m (9,328 ft) Pizol. With a total of five lifts, it's a comparatively small resort, but the moderately difficult slopes offer plenty of challenges.

Maienfeld

2 *5 km (3 mi) east of Bad Ragaz, 17 km (11 mi) north of Chur.*

Above this graceful little village full of fountains, vineyards, and old stucco houses, the Zürich author Johanna Spyri set *Heidi,* the much-loved children's story of an orphan growing up with her grandfather on an isolated Alpine farm. Taken away to accompany the invalid Clara in murky Frankfurt, she languishes until returning to her mountain home. Spyri spent time in Maienfeld and hiked the mountains behind, but it's questionable whether actual people inspired her tale. Nonetheless, you can hike from the Heidihof Hotel across steep open meadows and up thick forest switchbacks to what have now been designated **Peter the Goatherd's Hut** and the **Alm-Uncle's Hut**—and take in awesome Rhine Valley views from flowered meadows that would have suited Heidi beautifully. When you've had enough of the high meadows, back in the village you can visit wine merchants or have a meal in the Knight's Hall of **Schloss Brandis** (☎ 081/3022423), a Toggenburger castle-tower with its earlier portions dating from the 10th century. It's closed on Monday and Tuesday.

Chur

3 *17 km (11 mi) south of Maienfeld.*

Now the region's capital and a small city of 33,000 with a bustling downtown and a busy rail crossroads, Chur is actually the oldest continuously settled site in Switzerland; there are traces of habitation from as far back as 3000 BC–2500 BC. The Romans founded Curia Raetorium on the rocky terrace south of the river; from here, they protected the Alpine routes that led to the Bodensee. By AD 284 it served as the capital of the flourishing Roman colony Rhaetia Prima. Its heyday, however, evident throughout the Old Town even now, was during the Middle Ages, when it was ruled by bishops and bishop-princes. Narrow streets, cobblestone alleys, hidden courtyards, and ancient shuttered buildings abound; towering over them all is the massive 12th-century Kathedrale (Cathedral) St. Maria Himmelfahrt.

A landmark of the Old Town is the **Rathaus** (Town Hall), built as two structures in 1464 and connected in 1540. Its striking deep roof, topped with a lantern tower, follows the odd form of the joined buildings—one end is narrower than the other. Inside, the **Grosser Ratsaal** has a timber ceiling dating from 1493 and an 18th-century ceramic stove. The **Bürgerratskammer** has Renaissance wall panels and another ceramic stove, this one from 1632. Embedded in the wall beside the **Reichsgasse** door of the Rathaus, there's a rod of iron about a foot long—the standard measure of a foot or shoe before the metric system was introduced. ⊠ *Old Town. Closed to the public; contact the tourist office* (☞ *Graubünden A to Z, below) to arrange visits.*

Though this unremarkable facade doesn't attract much notice, the early 18th-century **Altes Gebäude** (literally, Old Building) mansion was built for a Chur statesman who was one of the most important leaders in Graubünden at the time. This is also the site where Jürg Jenatsch, a 17th-century Graubünden dictator, was assassinated. ⊠ *Postsr. 14, Old Town.*

Graubünden

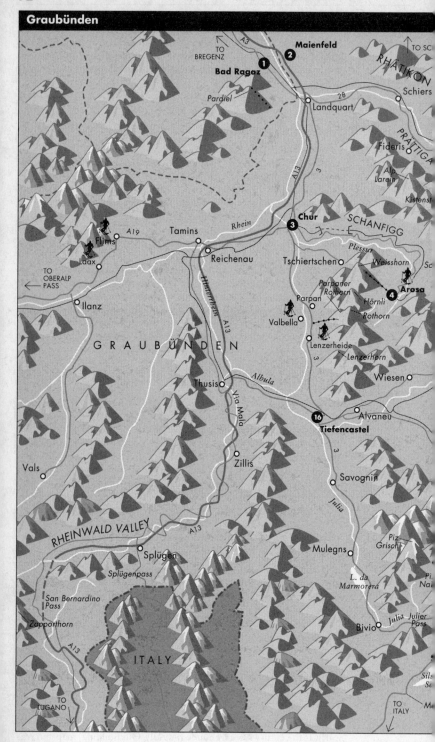

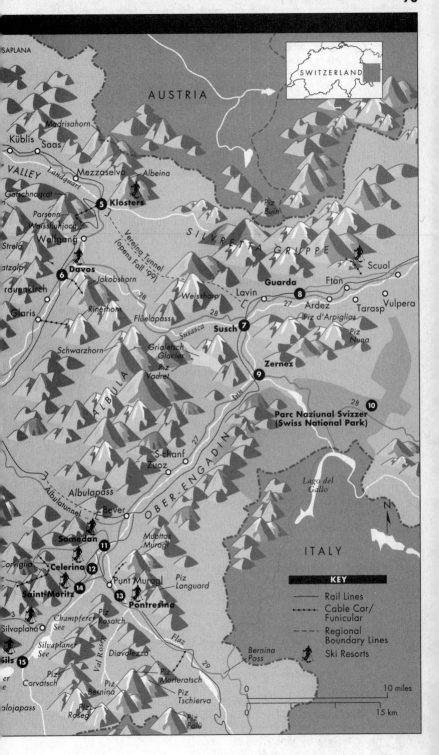

SWITZERLAND

SAPLANA

AUSTRIA

Madrisahorn

Küblis   Saas

VALLEY   Landquart   Mezzaselva   Albeina

Gotschnagrat

5 Klosters   SILVRETTA GRUPPE   Piz Buin

Parsenn
Weissfluhjoch

Wolfgang

Strela   Vereina Tunnel (opens Fall '99)   Scuol

atzalp

6 Davos   Guarda   **8**   Ftan

raugnkirch   Jakobshorn   Weissharn   Lavin   27   Ardez   Tarasp   Vulpera

Glaris   28   Flüelapass   28   Piz d'Arpiglias   Piz Nuna

Rinerhorn

Susasca

Schwarzhorn   Grialetsch Glacier   Susch   **7**

Piz Vadret   Zernez   **9**

ALBULA

Parc Naziunal Svizzer
(Swiss National Park)   28   **10**

S-chanf   27
Zuoz

Albulapass
Albulatunnel   Bever   OBER-ENGADIN   Lago del Gallo

ITALY

Samedan   **11**   Muottas Muragl

Corviglia   Celerina   **12**   Punt Muragl   Piz Languard

Saint-Moritz   **14**   **13** Pontresina

KEY

Silvaplana   Champfèrer See   Piz Rosatch

Silvaplaner See   Val Roseg   Flaz   Bernina Pass

ils **15**   Diavolezza

Piz Corvatsch   Piz Bernina   Piz Morteratsch   29

alojapass   Piz Roseg   Piz Tschierva

Piz Palü

	KEY
——	Rail Lines
····	Cable Car/Funicular
– – –	Regional Boundary Lines
⛷	Ski Resorts

0 ———— 10 miles

0 ———— 15 km

N

The slender, spired **Kirche St. Martin** (Church of St. Martin) was built in 1491 in the late-Gothic style after a fire destroyed the 8th-century original. Since 1526, it has been a Protestant church. Three stained-glass windows created in 1919 by the Graubünden sculptor Alberto Giacometti's father, Augusto Giacometti, are on your right as you enter. The steeple of the church dates from 1917; with permission from the sacristan, you can climb to the top to see the bells. ⊠ *Evangel. Kirchgemeinde, Kirchg. 12,* ☎ *081/2522292.*

The **Rätisches Museum** (Rhaetic Museum) is housed in the 1675 mansion of the wealthy von Buol family. Its collection includes not only furnishings and goods from the period, but also archaeological finds from the region, both Roman and prehistoric. ⊠ *Hofstr. 1,* ☎ *081/ 2572889.* ☜ *5 SF.* ☉ *Tues.–Sun. 10–noon and 2–5.*

The **Oberer Spaniöl,** another luxurious mansion from the 1640s, stands across from the Rätisches Museum (☞ *above*). There's a beautiful coat of arms signifying the owner's alliance with a Chur burgomaster. ⊠ *Kirchg. 16. Closed to the public.*

The stone archway under the **Hof-Torturm** (Court Entrance Tower) leads into the residence of the strong bishop-princes of Chur, once hosts to Holy Roman emperors who passed through on their way between Italy and Germany—sometimes with whole armies in tow. The bishops were repaid for their hospitality by imperial donations to the people. The thick fortifications of the residence demonstrate the disputed powers of the bishops; by the 15th century, irate inhabitants who rebelled again and again were rebuffed and punished with excommunication. By 1526 the Reformation broke the domination of the Church—although the city remains a Catholic bishopric today. The Hofkellerei restaurant is now at the site. ⊠ *Hof 1.*

The centerpiece of Chur is the **Kathedrale St. Maria Himmelfahrt** (Cathedral of the Ascension of the Virgin Mary), built between 1151 and 1272 in a mix of styles that spanned the century and drew on influences across Europe. The capitals of the columns are worked in a distinctly Romanesque style, carved with fantastical, evil beasts; at their base are clustered less threatening animals, many recognizable from the region—including sheep and the humble mountain marmot. In the choir, a magnificent three-side altar, elaborately carved in gilded wood, dates from the 15th century. The structure built on this site in prehistoric times was supplanted by a Roman castle, a bishop's house in 451, and a Carolingian cathedral during the 8th century. The marble panels under the altars of St. Laurentius and St. Fidelis have been preserved from this earliest church. ⊠ *Hof.* ☎ *081/2529250.* ☉ *Daily 8–7.*

Obere Gasse, once the main street through Chur and a major route between Germany and Italy, is now lined with small shops, cafés, and an open-air theater that draws local crowds. At the end stands the 16th-century **Obertor** (Upper Gate), guarding the bridge across the Plessur River. ⊠ *In Churer Alstadt, between the Obertor and Arcaspl.*

✑ At the **Kutschensammlung** (Coach Museum), a collection of turn-of-the-century carriages and sleighs, buffed to a picture-book high sheen, transports visitors back to the era of romance. One 1880 sleigh has a fur blanket and jingle bells straight out of Hans Christian Andersen's *The Ice Queen.* ⊠ *Hotel Stern, Reichg. 11,* ☎ *081/2523555.* ☜ *Free.* ☉ *Daily by appointment.*

Dining and Lodging

$–$$ ✕ **Controversa.** With a sleek, modern look to match its forward-looking menu—at last, a salad bar with everything from lamb's lettuce to beets—this lively, young restaurant offers a dose of nontradition in a very traditional town. In addition to salad, options range from superb carpaccio to such daring pasta dishes as tagliatelle with sliced chicken, mango, and hot curry sauce. Patrons frequent the bar into the wee hours. ⊠ *Steinbruchstr. 2,* ☎ *081/2529944. AE, DC, MC, V.*

$–$$$ ✕▣ **Stern.** This is a rare find: a historic inn in the hub of a city with
★ a restaurant that serves authentic regional cooking—moderately priced. Built in 1677, this Romantik hotel has modern, wood-warmed rooms, a fireplace lounge, and a lovely restaurant wrapped in seasoned Arvenholz. Unusual dishes range from *Kalbsleber dolce brusco* (breaded liver in sweet red wine sauce with raisin polenta and dried fruit compote) to air-dried beef with dried apples and pears; all are served with anise bread and local wine by waitresses in folk costume. ⊠ *Reichg. 11, CH-7000,* ☎ *081/2523555,* ℻ *081/2521915. 58 rooms. Restaurant, stübli. AE, DC, MC, V.*

$ ✕▣ **Zunfthaus zur Rebleuten.** This atmospheric wooden house in the middle of Old Town was the meeting place of wine producers back in 1483. Regional specialties and wines are the draw, plus a dozen affordable but quaint no-frills rooms. The restaurant's closed on Sunday and Monday. ⊠ *Pfisterpl. 1, CH-7000,* ☎ *081/2571357,* ℻ *081/2571358. 12 rooms. AE, DC, MC, V.*

$$–$$$ ▣ **ABC Terminus.** This newly renovated business hotel is merely yards
★ from the train station. Despite its sterile demeanor—the exterior a corporate metal-and-glass box—the amenities and rooms are state-of-the-art. Be sure to request a room that does not face the tracks. ⊠ *Bahnhofpl., CH-7000,* ☎ *081/2526033,* ℻ *081/2525524. 31 rooms. Sauna. AE, DC, MC, V.*

Nightlife

The futuristic **Giger Bar** (⊠ Comercialstr. 23, ☎ 081/2537506) is as close as you'll come to the flight deck of the *Starship Enterprise*. The strange space was created by 1980 visual effects Oscar winner H. R. Giger, a Chur native who designed the sets for the film *Alien*.

Outdoor Activities and Sports

Chur has an indoor **swimming pool** (⊠ Sportanlagen Obere Au, ☎ 081/2544288) for the aquatically inclined.

Arosa

★ ❹ *29 km (18 mi) east of Chur.*

The idyllic, high-altitude Arosa (1,830 m/6,000 ft) can be reached from Chur by rail or by car. Although it's one of the best known and most popular of Graubünden's winter and summer sports centers, its modest size, isolation, and natural beauty set it apart. There is none of the rush of Davos nor the pretensions of Saint-Moritz: This is a friendly, family-oriented spot staffed on all sides by upbeat, down-to-earth people. There are a few grand hotels with social ambitions, but their guests seem to keep a lid on it: Even the most well-heeled rarely dress for dinner.

The village lies at the end of a spectacular, winding 30-km (19-mi) road that cuts through a steep-walled valley and climbs through tiny steepled towns on grades of more than 12%. The town is gathered into two sections: one concentration is at the end of the valley (Inner-Arosa) and another around the lake and train station (Ausser-Arosa). The road empties into a sheltered, sunny mountain basin at the end of the Schanfigg, the valley source of the Plessur, a basin surrounded by white peaks and centered on two broad, accessible lakes. Cars should be left in the lakeside lots when possible, as a convenient free bus shuttles through the town, and traffic is forbidden between midnight and 6 AM.

Although the town has a slick, busy commercial center, it's strung along a narrow shelf with broad southern views, and within moments you can melt into the wilderness here on good mountain trails—they're even impeccably groomed for winter wandering. There are four skating rinks—one indoors—and the skiing at all levels of difficulty is among the best in Switzerland. The altitude ensures good snow, and pistes lead directly down into the village. A good network of well-located ski lifts and linking runs make the broad, high fields easily accessible. Arosa's branch of the Swiss Ski School is one of the largest.

From Arosa, you can take a cable car up to the Weisshorn (2,653 m/8,700 ft) for views over resorts, lakes, and a sweep of peaks. Gondola cars take you from Arosa to Hörnli (2,513 m/8,701 ft) for similar views from a different perspective.

Skiing

Open to ski tourism since 1877, Arosa is remote and humble in comparison to the worldly resorts of Gstaad and Saint-Moritz. Closely screened in by mountains, the 1,754-m-high (5,750-ft-high) resort is family oriented, with runs suitable for every level of skier. Arosa's 16 lifts have an hourly capacity of 21,000 people and cover 70 km (43 mi) of trails. Its facilities don't match those of Davos, the neighbor that an unbreachable rock barrier renders light years away, but they are sufficient for the 8,000 guests that the resort welcomes in high season, mostly in the end of December, February, and Easter. With the exception of one heavily trafficked strategic run, Arosa does not have snowmaking; nevertheless, it has often been possible to ski throughout an entire season despite poor snowfall. A one-day lift ticket costs 49 SF; a six-day pass costs 219 SF.

Beginners and children can enjoy the sunny and gentle slopes of **Pratschli.** Maniacs who want a battering will find on **Weisshorn** (2,654 m/8,700 ft) the black piste of their dreams. Most of the runs, however, are intermediate—even those of the **Hörnli** (2,460 m/8,200 ft), served by a cable car. These slopes are so broad and clear that moonlight and torchlight skiing is organized regularly, generally following fondue or raclette and wine in a restaurant high on the mountain—to the tunes of a *Ländlerkapelle,* a musical ensemble typical of German Switzerland. More than 150 instructors are staffed out of Arosa's official **Swiss Ski School** (☎ 081/3771150).

Dining and Lodging

$$$$ ✕ **Zum Wohl! Sein.** Eighteen hundred different wines await in the cellar of this restaurant, and chef Beat Caduff can recommend and retrieve a bottle in mere minutes. He's also a mastermind of modern Swiss-European cuisine with a traditional twist—somewhat fanatical in finding the freshest ingredients and insisting on serving seven-course meals only. His specialties include *Wildessenz,* a precious quantity of steaming bouillon obtained by simmering pounds of vegetables, choice meats, and plenty of red wine for hours. Reserve a week in advance and prepare to stay several hours—it's an eating event. ✉ *Hohe Promenade, in Hotel Anita,* ☎ *081/3771109. Reservations essential. AE, DC, MC, V. Closed Mon. No lunch.*

$$ ✕ **Grischuna.** Although most of the best food can be found in hotels in this accommodating resort, the Grischuna merits a stop for its comfortable ambience and regional decor—wood, ceramics, farm tools, game trophies. Its simple menu includes local cold meat and cheese dishes, as well as trout and plain bourgeois meats, including horse steak. ✉ *Poststr.,* ☎ *081/3771701. No credit cards.*

$$ ✕🏨 **Arve Central.** Although it's set back slightly from the main street, Central lives up to its name, with neither the elevation nor the isolation of its competitors. Yet it's solid and slickly done, with pristine stucco and knotty pine, and good views on the south side. (The back rooms have neither balcony nor view.) The restaurant, all richly detailed knotty pine, offers some of the best food in town: The changing menu updates French classics, with a focus on fish and game prepared with herbs. ✉ *Off Poststr., CH-7050,* ☎ *081/3770252,* 🅵🅰🆇 *081/3774271. 48 rooms. 2 restaurants, bar, hot tub, sauna. AE, DC, MC, V.*

$$ ✕🏨 **Hold.** This busy, happy family place—full of books and toys and
★ hikers—is just across the road from the luxurious Kulm and sits literally at the foot of the slopes. The rooms are simple and bright, with blond wood; the back rooms are larger, with big tile baths. The restaurant serves skiers'–appetite standards—fried fish, entrecôtes, and fondues. Keen supporters of folk culture, the owners host Alphorn and yodeling weeks on the premises during Arosa's summer music festival. Even beginners can enroll. ✉ *Poststr., CH-7050 Inner-Arosa,* ☎ *081/3771408,* 🅵🅰🆇 *081/ 3774927. 18 rooms. Restaurant, café. AE, DC, MC, V.*

$$$$ 🏨 **Kulm.** For a luxury hotel with roots in 1882, this is refreshingly young
★ and sporty. Now completely renovated, it combines international trends to an almost confusing degree. You wonder: Is this Vail? Santa Fe? Mykonos? Oslo? There are miles of curving stucco and glass, heavy beams and high-tech fixtures, chintz and primitive prints. The wraparound windows take in acres of green hills or snowy slopes. Indeed, the hotel's position is its biggest draw, as it stands on the farthest edge of town at the base of the slopes: You can ski home at the end of the day. ✉ *Poststr., CH-7050 Inner-Arosa,* ☎ *081/3770131,* 🅵🅰🆇 *081/3774090. 137 rooms. 3 restaurants, 2 cafés, tennis court, bowling, health club, dance club, baby-sitting. AE, DC, MC, V.*

$$$$ 🏨 **Waldhotel National.** First a health retreat, then a military hospital, this member of the Relais du Silence group became a hotel in 1965 and is consistently upgraded and refined. Northern rooms look over the forest and southern ones have the spectacular Arosa view; all are done in shades of rose and blue, with those in the Arven wing glowing with golden Swiss pine. Above the town and set on its own expansive, wooded park, it offers a peaceful retreat. The Kachelofastübli is a local favorite and alternative to the formal dining room. Rates are demipension only. ✉ *Prätschlistr., CH-7050 Ausser-Arosa,* ☎ *081/3771351,* 🅵🅰🆇 *081/3773210. 94 rooms. Restaurant, bar, indoor pool, massage, sauna. AE, DC, MC, V.*

$$ 🏨 **Alpina.** This hotel just above the main street, with views over the Untersee and the mountains, strikes an appealing balance between old and new. Built in 1908, it also has a more modern wing added in 1983, which has rustic furnishings, farm implements, and kitchen-equipped apartment units. The rooms in the higher, original building combine dark wood with newer Euro-style furnishings and superior views. The common rooms are comfortable, the dining areas bright and spacious, and the friendly management eager to please. ✉ *Off Poststr., CH-7050,* ☎ *081/3771658,* 🅵🅰🆇 *081/3773752. 35 rooms. Restaurant, bar, café, stübli, sauna. AE, DC, MC, V.*

$$ 🏨 **Panorama Raetia.** Among the bank of hotels on the shelf over the main street, this has the broadest sweep of view from both its original wing, which dates from the 1890s, and its new wing, built during the 1950s. As if they knew they couldn't top the beauty of its Bündnerstübli, with its original Arvenholz aged to burnished gold, its owners have left the newer portions untouched; perhaps the '70s-style avocado-and-shocking-orange decor will a acquire similar patina in years to come.

⊠ *Poststr., CH-7050 Ausser-Arosa,* ☎ *081/3770241,* FAX *081/3772279. 40 rooms. Restaurant, stübli. AE, DC, MC, V.*

$–$$ ⌺ **Sonnenhalde.** The automatic Arvenholz door that welcomes you to
★ this chaletlike *garni* (without a restaurant) hotel is your first sign of
its happy marriage between charm and modern comfort. There are no
tired furnishings here—rooms are bright and large, with wall-to-wall
wood and tasteful, minimalist decor. Admire the hand-detailed wooden
armoires as you head down the hall to the steam bath, or come back
from the ski lifts just behind the house. With rooms that easily accommodate extra beds (for an additional fee), this good-value gem sur-
passes the standards within its class and some of the those in the
category above. ⊠ *Sonnenbergstr. and Poststr., CH-7050 Inner-Arosa,*
☎ *081/3771531,* FAX *081/3774455. 23 rooms. Sauna, steam room. No
credit cards.*

Nightlife and the Arts

To find out what's happening in Arosa, check the *Wochenbulletin,* published every two weeks.

BARS

The Casino's **Espreso Bar** (☎ 081/3773940) is a trendy *Treffpunkt* (meeting point). There's a popular piano bar at **Hotel Carmenna** (☎ 081/
3771766).

CASINOS

Arosa's **Kursaal** (Casino; ⊠ Poststr., ☎ 081/3775051) has a roulette
wheel with the usual 5 SF gambling limit—but the casino's 75 slot machines, set up after their ban was withdrawn in 1994, are its prized
novelty.

DANCING

For dancing and discos, **Gada** (☎ 081/3771766) has a Wild West
theme and live music. The **Kitchen Club** (⊠ Hotel Eden, ☎ 081/
3770261) is a disco inside an original 1907 kitchen, where a young
crowd dances among old pots and pans while the disc jockey perches
above antique aluminum refrigerators. The après-ski crowd here is decidedly city chic—you should change out of your ski bibs first. **Nuts**
(☎ 081/3773940) is open until 3 AM. The tiny **Tschuetta Dancing-Bar**
(☎ 081/3771949) manages to squeeze a live band in front of a '70s-
style, rainbow-color backdrop.

MUSIC

There are **organ concerts** in Arosa's mountain chapel from Christmas
through mid-April, Tuesday at 5.

Outdoor Activities and Sports

CROSS-COUNTRY AND SNOWSHOEING

Langlaufschule Geeser (☎ 081/3775152) gives lessons and leads excursions. If you opt for snowshoeing, the rental equipment is included
with your excursion fee.

HIKING

The tourist office offers an unusual hiking package—it will not only
book your hotel ahead of time, but it will also deliver your luggage to
your destination so you're free of heavy bags on your trip (☞ Hiking
in Davos, *below;* Guided Tours *in* Graubünden A to Z, *below*).

HORSEBACK RIDING

Call **L. Messner** (☎ 081/3774196), which leads guided horseback
tours. It also has horse-drawn carriage rides in summer and sleigh rides
in winter.

PARAGLIDING
Contact **Flying School Arosa** (☎ 079/4361788).

SKATING
Arosa has no fewer than four skating rinks: the indoor **Eissporthalle** (☎ 081/3771745), **Offene Kunsteisbahn Obersee** (☎ 081/3771745), **Natureisbahn Hof Maran** (☎ 081/3770185), and **Natureisbahn Inner-Arosa** (☎ 081/3772930); the last three are outdoors.

SWIMMING
There's a free bathing **beach** on the Untersee.

TENNIS
There are three public courts at the **Hof Maran** (☎ 081/3770185).

PRÄTTIGAU

The name means "meadow valley," and it's just that—a lush landscape of alternating orchards, pastures, and pine-covered mountains. Here are the renowned ski resorts of Davos and Klosters, which attract skiers from all over the world. The predominant language is German, though most towns still have Romansh names that date from ancient times.

Klosters

⑤ *26 km (19 mi) southeast of Landquart.*

Once a group of hamlets, Klosters has become a small but chic resort town, framed between striking peaks. There's an aesthetic scattering of weathered-wood and white-stucco chalets and a clock-tower church, the only remnant of the medieval cloister that gave the town its name. Klosters is famed for its **skiing**—British royal family members are faithful visitors—and makes the most of its access to the slopes of the Parsenn, which afford some of the finest skiing anywhere.

The starting point for the best of the Klosters-Parsenn runs is the **Weissfluhjoch,** reached by a cable-car ride from town to the Gotschnagrat, a short ski run, and then a second cable car. The run back to Klosters, almost 10 km (6 mi), drops around 1,495 m (4,900 ft). The variety of runs from the Weissfluhjoch and the Gotschnagrat is almost unlimited, but the best known are those that lead north all the way to **Küblis** or south to **Wolfgang.** The **Madrisa** slopes, reached by the Albeina gondolas, are popular with both skiers and sunbathers.

A brief outing to the folk museum **Nutli-Hüschi** will illustrate how far this resort has evolved from its mountain roots: A pretty wood-and-stone chalet, built in 1565, has been restored and fitted with the spare furnishings of its day, including kitchen tools and a children's bed that lengthens as the child grows. ⊠ *Monbielerstr. at Talstr.,* ☎ *081/4102020.* ⌷ *3 SF.* ⊙ *Jan.–mid-Apr. and end of June–mid Oct., Wed. and Fri. 4–6.*

Skiing

Along with its twin resort Davos (☞ *below*), Klosters is known for its vast range of trails and facilities, with their hundreds of kilometers of downhill runs divided nearly equally among easy, moderate, and difficult pistes. More rural than Davos, Klosters is favored by the British royal family for its 315 km (196 mi) of maintained runs and 55 lifts in a half-dozen ski areas. **Küblis,** a red (moderately difficult) run leads toward Landquart, and you can return to Klosters or Davos on a short train ride, free with your ski pass. **Wolfgang** is a very difficult descent that takes you over near Davos's lake. The sunny **Madrisa** slopes, on the other hand, are quite easy; you'll see lots of parents teaching their children to ski. There's a snowboard park here as well. Lift tickets to the combined Davos/Klosters areas cost 52 SF for one day, 259 SF for six days.

Dining and Lodging

$$$ ✕ **Alte Post.** In this warm, woody local favorite, pleasantly cluttered with ceramics and game trophies, you can enjoy the straightforward cooking of John Ehrat, a Klosters native who specializes in game and salmon. There are token French classics and a few Swiss standards, but the old-style dishes are his forte: rabbit in thyme, *tête de veau* (veal head) vinaigrette, beef with marsala and risotto, and lots of trout and lamb. If you like salmon, go for the *Lachsmenu* (fixed-price salmon menu), with salmon in every dish but the sorbet. The restaurant is slightly apart from the town center but worth the trip. ✉ *Doggilochstr. 136, Klosters-Aeuja,* ☎ *081/4221716. DC, MC, V. Closed Mon. and Tues.*

$$ ✕ **Höhwald.** This is a friendly, touristy restaurant up the hill from Klosters in Monbiel, with a large, open terrace that takes in valley and mountain views and a wood-panel café and restaurant that draw festive crowds. There are hearty soups, cheese specialties (such as *Chäsgatschäder,* bread soaked in milk with grated cheese, all fried like a big pancake), Bündner meats, and a local mix of Italian and country cooking, stressing game. The fruit tarts are fresh and homemade. The interior restaurant is a little more starched; here game is elaborately prepared and served. ✉ *Monbiel,* ☎ *081/4223045. AE, MC, V. Closed Tues. in summer.*

$$ ✕ **Wynegg.** The English—including a few crowned heads—come here
★ to drink pints après-ski, eat enormous platters of local cold meats, and enjoy the cozy, slightly kitschy surroundings, with all the checkered tablecloths and cuckoo clocks. ✉ *Landstr. 205, CH-7250,* ☎ *081/4221340. AE, MC, V. Closed in summer.*

$$$ ✕🏠 **Walserhof.** Of the high-end hotels in Klosters, this is the most so-
★ phisticated, having struck a smart balance between old and new. It was built in 1981 with the weathered materials from an old farmhouse. Its restaurant and café are paneled with ancient carved wood; stone, stucco, and quarry tile are used elsewhere. The only drawback is its location, on the main road through town; the best views take in either the street or fairly well-developed fields behind. The superb restaurant specializes in upscale international and regional fare, and dishes from Prättigau, the Davos-Klosters region, are available every day, including such specialties as trout in cider, cabbage dumplings with wild mushrooms, game terrines, or lamb stew with polenta. ✉ *Landstr. 141, CH-7250,* ☎ *081/4224242,* 🆂 *081/4221437. 10 rooms, 3 suites. Restaurant, stübli. AE, DC, MC, V.*

$$$–$$$$ 🏠 **Chesa Grischuna.** Although it's directly in the town center at the main thoroughfare and crossroads, this creaky 1890 mountain farmhouse qualifies as a country inn—as well as one of the most popular places. Every room is full of old carved wood, and some have balconies to take in the sun. There are antiques and regional knickknacks throughout, and plenty of public spaces, as this is a sociable place: Whether you bowl in the vaulted cave, play cards, or dance to the piano music at happy hour, you'll be surrounded by Klosters regulars. Prices are high for the limited facilities (no elevator, a couple of rooms without bath), but you pay for the coveted social mix. ✉ *Bahnhofstr. 12, CH-7250,* ☎ *081/4222222,* 🆂 *081/4222225. 25 rooms, 23 with bath. Restaurant, bar, bowling. AE, MC, V.*

$$–$$$ 🏠 **Albeina.** This large and luxurious chalet-style resort complex lies in the lower valley of Klosters-Dorf, with easy access to skiing—but it provides its own activities regardless of season or weather. Rooms are tastefully decorated, with duvets and floral detail. The recently redone Dörfyi Bar draws regulars, sometimes royals. ✉ *CH-7252 Iltisweg,* ☎

081/4232100, FAX 081/4232121. 80 rooms. Restaurant, bar, indoor pool, 2 tennis courts, boccie, Ping-Pong, playground. AE, DC, MC, V.

$$ ★ **Rätia.** Set in Klosters-Dorf, in the broad, quiet valley west of the center, this Relais du Silence hotel lives up to the chain's name. It's a classic vacation lodge, with logs in the fireplace, a beam-timber dining hall, and balconies facing up toward the slopes. In summer, you can have tea on the broad porch under hanging geraniums; in winter, a schnapps by the fire after skiing to the doorstep from the Gotschnagrat. As a farmhouse, it started taking in guests and expanded to a neighboring home; in the 1970s a new wing was added. Most rooms have natural-tone decor with wood accents; some have tile baths. ⊠ CH-7252 Gäuggeliweg, ☎ 081/4224747, FAX 081/4224749. 24 rooms. Restaurant, bar. AE, DC, MC, V.

$$ ★ **Silvapina.** This delightful hotel, which enjoys the same valley position as the Rätia, places emphasis on family, as the owners have three children of their own and the father was born under the very roof he now repairs. The weathered-wood Victorian-style chalet was built in 1931, with a new wing added in 1960. Rooms in the new wing are spare white with pine touches; older rooms have lovely burnished wood everywhere. The sitting rooms and dining area are fresh and tidy. There's even a private tennis court. ⊠ Silvapena-Weg 6, CH-7252, ☎ 081/4221468, FAX 081/4224078. 15 rooms. Restaurant, stübli, sauna, tennis court. AE, MC, V.

Nightlife and the Arts

Revelers dance at **Casa Antica** (☎ 081/4221621), a 300-year-old converted barn, late into the night. **Chesa Grischuna** (☞ Dining and Lodging, *above*) is a popular after-dinner spot, with piano music and several intimate bars.

Outdoor Activities and Sports

PARAGLIDING

Contact **Flugschulcenter Grischa** (☎ 081/4132567).

SKATING

Kloster's **Sportszentrum** (⊠ Doggilochstr. 11, ☎ 081/4102141) offers rinks for skating, hockey, and curling in season.

SWIMMING

The local municipal heated outdoor **swimming pool** (⊠ Doggilochstr., ☎ 081/4221524) also has a restaurant and table tennis.

TENNIS

There are seven sand courts (five of which are floodlighted) to reserve at the **Sportszentrum** (☞ *above*).

TREKKING

Snowshoe treks are led by day to the Garfiun Alphut, or during evenings to Restaurant Höhwald by **Trek Out** (☎ 081/4223800). You can also get info on summer trekking routes from pamphlets in the tourist office (☞ Visitor Information *in* Graubünden A to Z, *below*).

Davos

❻ *11 km (7 mi) south of Klosters, 42 km (26 mi) south of Landquart.*

With a reputation nearly as far-flung as those of Saint-Moritz and Gstaad, Davos is one of Switzerland's most esteemed winter resorts—famed for its ice sports as well as its skiing. At 1,560 m (5,117 ft) this highest "city" in Europe is good for cold-weather sports even in the soggiest of winters.

Davos lies at the end of the Davos Valley, which runs parallel to the Upper Engadine though they're separated by the vast Albula chain, at some points more than 3,000 m (9,840 ft) high. On the opposite side of the valley stands the Strela chain, dominated by the **Weissfluh**. The open, sunbathed slopes of the Strela Range provide magnificent skiing. The Parsenn funicular railway runs from Davos up to Weissfluhgipfel, 2,844 m (9,328 ft) high, and the upper end of the **Parsenn** run. From there you can ski down over vast, open snowfields to the town, a drop of around 1,000 m (3,280 ft). Or, striking off to the northeast, you come to Davos's neighboring resort: Klosters (☞ *above*). Another funicular, combined with a chairlift, goes to **Strela.** There are a lift to **Rinerhorn** (2,046 m/6,708 ft) and a couple of dozen other mountain railways, cable cars, and assorted lifts. On the opposite side of the valley is the Jakobshorn, flanked by the Disma and Sertig valleys; you have direct access to the well-equipped **Brämabüel-Jakobshorn** ski area, reached by cable car and lift from Davos-Platz. In addition, there are more than 75 km (47 mi) of prepared cross-country ski trails.

Take note: This is a capital for action-oriented sports enthusiasts and not necessarily for anyone seeking a peaceful, rustic mountain retreat. Davos-Dorf and its twin, Davos-Platz, are strung along the valley in one noisier-than-average urban strip, with traffic, timed parking, department stores, and trendy bars. But except for a few token historic structures, most of Davos consists of awkward concrete-balcony hotels and apartment buildings. In town, the bracing mountain air that drew Davos's first visitors, tuberculosis sufferers taking medical cures, can be offset by the exhaust of city traffic. Yet this Alpine metropolis is surrounded by dramatic mountain passes, green hillsides, and farms punctuated by weathered sheds and outbuildings. And no matter how densely populated and fast-paced the twin towns become, nothing changes on the magnificent slopes, and people return to them generation after generation.

Among the town's few architectural highlights, the late-Gothic **Kirche St. Johann** (Church of St. John the Baptist; ⊠ Rathausstutz 2, Davos-Platz) stands out by virtue of its windows by Augusto Giacometti. Nearby is the 17th-century **Rathaus** (Town Hall).

The **Kirchner Museum** houses the world's largest collection of works and documents by and about Ernst Ludwig Kirchner, the German Expressionist artist who came to Davos in 1917 to cure his failing health and stayed to paint. ⊠ *Promenade 82, Davos-Platz,* ☎ *081/4132202,* ▣ *7 SF.* ☼ *Tues.–Sun. 2–6.*

Skiing
More urbane than its connecting cousin resort Klosters, Davos (1,560 m/5,116 ft) extends more than 35 km (22 mi) along a relatively sheltered valley floor, the Prättigau, which opens onto a fantastic panorama at higher elevations. Spanning from Laret (1507 m/4,942 ft) to Monstein (1,626 m/5,333 ft), the commune of Davos is Switzerland's second largest and can accommodate some 24,000 visitors on more than 320 km (196 mi) of runs.

At the southeast end of Davos, the easy west-facing pistes bask in afternoon sun. On the other side of the valley, the steep slopes of the **Parsenn** challenge hordes of experts. Locals and others in the know often prefer to ski on the other side of the valley at **Rinerhorn,** where the slopes, less crowded but nearly as interesting, lead to the hamlet of **Glaris,** 7 km (4½ mi) from the center of Davos. A must for the skilled skier: the **descent** from **Weissfluhgipfel** (2,844 m/9,330 ft) to **Küblis** (814 m/2,670 ft)—a magnificent 15-km-long (9-mi-long) piste with a vertical drop of 2,000 m (6,560 ft). **Lift tickets** to the combined Davos/Klosters areas cost up to 52 SF for one day (depending on which areas you choose to ski in), 259 SF for six days.

Dining and Lodging

$$$$ ✕🏠 **Davoserhof.** With lovely Jakobshorn views from its south side;
★ fresh, pretty rooms in taupe, paisley, and pine; and all-white tile baths, this is one of the most welcoming hotels in town—without taking into account its restaurants, which are two of the region's finest. During the World Economic Forum conference that takes place here every February, you'll be hard-pressed to find a table either in the intimate old Davosstübli, with its burnished Arvenholz and ceramic stove, or in the elegant, piney Jenatschstübe. In spring and summer, everyone eats on the broad terrace overlooking the green hills and mountains. Chef Kurt Jaussi, something of a wunderkind, creates such innovative dishes as salt-encrusted turbot (for two). ⊠ *Berglistutz 2, CH-7270,* ☎ *081/ 4156666,* 𝔽𝔸𝕏 *081/4156667. 22 rooms. 2 restaurants, bar, dance club. AE, DC, MC, V.*

$-$$$$ ✕🏠 **Hubli's Landhaus.** Though on the busy mountain highway between
★ Davos and Klosters, this country inn is quiet as well as comfortable and attractive with its somewhat modernized rustic decor (scarlet, stucco, dark pine, and wrought iron). Its setting in gardens and valley greenery is idyllic. But the strong point by far is the food: Chef Felix Hubli prepares sophisticated international fare (turbot with wild mushrooms and ginger, squab with leeks and truffles) and serves it in two lovely dining rooms: one for visitors, one for demipension guests, who—considering the à la carte prices—are getting a terrific deal. ⊠ *Kantonstr., CH-7265 Davos-Laret,* ☎ *081/4162121,* 𝔽𝔸𝕏 *081/4163342. 20 rooms, 19 with bath. Restaurant. AE, V.*

$$$$ 🏠 **Golfhotel Waldhuus.** Right at the edge of the Davos golf course, with the leisurely *pock-pock* of a tennis game echoing next door, this Relais du Silence property re-creates a suburban country club on the outskirts of an Alpine city. Solid, sunny, and serene, with plenty of pine and stucco to soften its prefab feel, it offers late sun on the terrace, a fireplace in the lobby, and the soothing tunes of a pianist in its bar. The rooms are decorated in country-casual miniature prints and pink linens; public spaces are in pink, lace, and dried flowers. The restaurant serves standards with nouvelle twists (pike quenelles with squid-ink pasta, quail salad with balsamic vinegar). ⊠ *Mattastr. 58, CH-7270,* ☎ *081/ 4168131,* 𝔽𝔸𝕏 *081/4163939. 47 rooms. Restaurant, bar, indoor pool, sauna, driving range, 2 tennis courts, exercise room. AE, DC, MC, V.*

$$$$ 🏠 **Steigenberger Belvedere.** With its neoclassic stone fireplace and wedding-cake white plaster details, this is a grand hotel in the full sense of the word: It sweeps the length of a hillside with south-facing balconies, and its interiors are lavished with period detail. Rooms range from Arvenholz-rustic to period greens and pastels; many have been newly outfitted with hardwood floors: It's worth it to pay for superior class rooms, as rooms with north and end views (and decors) are distinctly inferior. ⊠ *Promenade 89, CH-7270,* ☎ *081/4156000,* 𝔽𝔸𝕏 *081/4156001. 141 rooms. 2 restaurants, bar, café, indoor pool, sauna. AE, DC, MC, V.*

$$$ 🏠 **Ochsen.** Central and urban, with a few upper rooms rising above the street to take in Jakobshorn views, this modest hotel is run by an ambitious young team, which has spent the last few years redoing the rooms in pastels and pine and perfecting Graubündner specialties in the restaurant. The welcoming dining-breakfast room is wall-to-wall Arvenholz, and the *Stübe* (tavern) is down-to-earth enough to draw locals. ⊠ *Talstr. 10, CH-7270,* ☎ *081/4135222,* 𝔽𝔸𝕏 *081/4137671. 47 rooms. Restaurant, bar, stübli. AE, DC, MC, V.*

Nightlife and the Arts

BARS, LOUNGES, AND CASINOS

After 3 AM, hipsters gather for live music and snacks at **EX Bar** (☎ 081/4135645), hopping until 6 AM. **Hotel Europe** (⊠ Promenade 63, ☎ 081/4135921) has two popular bars, the chic **Tonic Piano Bar**, serving until 3 AM, and the homey **Cabanna Bar**. In addition, a **casino** has opened in the hotel, with more than 100 slot machines.

DANCING

At 10:30 PM the Cabanna Bar becomes the **Cabanna Club** (☎ 081/4135921), whose techno decor and loud music lure a rowdy crowd. For dancing, **Pöstli** (☎ 081/4137676) is a winter-only institution with live bands. The **Rotliechtli** (⊠ Davoserhof Hotel; ☞ *above*) has a bar and a dance floor.

Outdoor Activities and Sports

GOLF

Golf Club Arosa (☎ 081/3774242) has a nine-hole course. **Golf Club Vulpera** (☎ 081/8649688) also has nine holes. There's an 18-hole golf course at **Golfplatz Davos** (☎ 081/4165634).

HIKING

Threaded with more than 450 km (280 mi) of marked walks and mountain trails, Davos offers an unusual hiking package. The seven-day itinerary includes walking from Davos to Arosa one day and from Arosa to Lenzerheide the next, with lodging included; contact the tourist office in **Davos** (☎ 081/4152121; ☞ Visitor Information *in* Graubünden A to Z, *below*).

HORSEBACK RIDING

Try **Riding School Flüela** (☎ 081/4131955).

PARAGLIDING

Gleitschirmschule Davos (☎ 081/4136043). **Flugschulcenter Grischa** (☎ 081/4132567).

SAILING AND WINDSURFING

Sailing and windsurfing are done on the Davos lake. To rent boats or take a lesson with a sailing school, call **Segelschule Davosersee** (☎ 081/4161577) or **Hans Heierling** (☎ 081/4165918).

SKATING

Davos has long been reputed as an important ice-sports center, with its enormous **Eisstadion Davos** (☎ 081/4153600) speed-skating rink. The Eisstadion maintains one indoor and two outdoor rinks; you might also look into the skating tournament schedule if you'd like to watch a competition.

SPORTS CENTERS

The **Sports & High Altitude Center Davos** (☎ 081/4153600) offers field and ice-sports facilities for amateurs and Olympians alike.

SWIMMING

Davos has an indoor-outdoor swimming **pool** complex (☎ 081/4136463). You can also swim from the **Strandbad** (open beach; ☎ 081/4161505) in the 65°F waters of the Davosersee.

RACQUET SPORTS

Tennis and Squash Center Davos (☎ 081/4133131) has four indoor and five outdoor tennis courts, plus two squash and four badminton courts.

En Route The main road from Davos leads into the Engadine by way of the spectacular **Flüelapass** (Flüela Pass). For 16 km (13 mi) you climb southeast over mild grades and modest switchbacks. Dense larch forests give way to pine, then to fir, and finally, above the timberline, to a rocky, desolate waste of boulders and jutting cliffs, much of it snow covered except in summer. Ahead, on the left, are the rocky slopes of the **Weisshorn** (3,086 m/10,119 ft), with the **Schwarzhorn** (3,147 m/10,319 ft) to the right. Toward the summit, even in August, you may drive through snow. You'll pass between two small lakes: the Schottensee and the Schwarzsee. At the summit (2,383 m/7,816 ft), 14 km (9 mi) from Davos, is the **Flüela Hospiz** (☎ 081/4161747), a picturesque wooden chalet with a windmill, where you can get refreshments and a night's lodging at reasonable rates. The pass is kept open as much as possible during winter, but you should check its status before setting off; ask a local tourist office or your concierge.

The descent from the Flüela Pass into the Romansh region of the Lower Engadine takes you through a narrow valley and across the River Susasca, in sight of the 3,229-m (10,600-ft) Piz Vadret, to the base of the great **Grialetsch**—a spectacular mass of jagged ice and snow. The road winds, following the increasingly torrential river and its deep, rocky gash, down to Susch, where it flows into the River Inn, or in Romansh, En.

LOWER ENGADINE

Like Dorothy landing in Oz, you may find your sudden arrival in this, the most picturesque and novel of Graubünden's many valleys, something of a shock. You'll hear of people talk of *Schellenursli* (a legendary munchkin of a little boy with a bell), and there's even a sort of Scarecrow—for *Hom Strom* in February the children of Scuol make a figure out of hay to burn the winter away. Festivals and folklore abound, as do dense, fairy-tale forests and quaint village settings. "Allegra!" is the proper greeting on the street, reflecting the Romansh language and Latinate culture that have developed without obstruction here. The Roman roots of the region are also demonstrated in the houses—typically squat cream-color stucco bungalows with deep Etruscan-arch doors, thick Mediterranean walls, and sunken windows. Watch for such functional features as built-in wooden benches at front entrances and for the ever-present expressional sgraffiti—the signature of the Engadine. An underlayer of dark gray stucco is whitewashed; then designs, images, and sometimes sayings are scraped into the paint to reveal the undercolor. The Lower Engadine—more enclosed than its upper counterpart—shares the region's dry, crisp "champagne" climate.

Susch

❼ *27 km (17 mi) east of Davos, 64 km (40 mi) southeast of Landquart.*

Susch guards the entrance to the Lower Engadine, guarded itself by the magnificent Piz d'Arpiglias (3,289 m/9,930 ft). Here the River Susasca tumbles into the Inn, and the small town seems to cling to the banks of the roaring, white-water torrent as it heads on its way to the Danube. Though Susch was partially burned in 1925, its houses remain stubbornly traditional in style, and the streets are lined with sgraffitied structures, their windows spilling geraniums, their heavy wooden doors often half ajar to display interiors quirkily furnished with crockery, copper, antiques, and stuffed game.

The two towers of **Kirche St. Jon** (Church of St. John) stand high over the river, one Romanesque, the other—and the body of the church—dating from 1515. During a restoration in 1742, the late-Gothic style of the windows was changed, but in 1933, on the evidence of recently discovered fragments, they were restored to their original form.

Guarda

★ **⑧** *7 km (4 mi) east of Susch, 71 km (44 mi) southeast of Landquart.*

Between Susch and the resort towns of Scuol, Vulpera, and Tarasp, a scenic valley passes through several gorges and then emerges into flowered plains and a pleasant chain of hamlets: Lavin, Guarda, Ardez, and Ftan. Each offers a new show of fine sgraffitied homes, but Guarda deserves a leisurely exploration among its steep, patterned-cobble streets. The federal government protects the architecture, and row upon row of the vivid dark-on-white etchings, contrasting sharply with the bright red geraniums lined up on the windowsills, draws pedestrians from one photogenic stop to another. As its name implies, Guarda sits high on a hillside looking out over the valley and the 3,001-m (9,840-ft) peaks to the south.

Lodging

$$$$ 🏨 **Meisser.** This brightly colored lodge lives up to its picturesque setting, with sgraffiti and flower boxes outside, antiques and Arvenholz inside. There are a grand Victorian dining hall with pine wainscoting and parquet and a more casual porch restaurant with spectacular valley views. Some rooms are simple and modern, though you can have a splendid carved-pine room if you pay a little bit more. A recently renovated 17th-century farmhouse has six new suites. ⊠ *CH-7545,* ☎ *081/8622132,* 🖷 *081/8622480. 21 rooms, 6 suites. Restaurant, playground. AE, DC, MC, V.*

En Route Between Guarda and Scuol, a small back road leads through Boscha to **Ardez,** with an elaborate botanic Adam-and-Eve fresco on one of the buildings of the main street. The back road continues through Ftan, with its fine view of Schloss Tarasp (☞ *below*).

Scuol, Vulpera, and Tarasp

13 km (8 mi) east of Guarda, 84 km (52 mi) southeast of Landquart.

Sometimes grouped under the name Bad Scuol-Tarasp-Vulpera, these three towns effectively form a vacation and health resort complex whose waters from some 20 mineral springs have historically been used for liver cures. Beautifully located in the open valley of the Inn, with wooded hillsides backed by mountains—the Silvretta on one side and the Engadiner Dolomites on the other—all three towns have been popular summer resorts, frequented most often by Swiss and Germans. Today they fill up in winter as well, thanks to the network of gondolas and ski lifts on the unobstructed south-facing slopes of Motta Naluns—and the reputation of its snowboard school, the oldest in Europe. Scuol, the most urban of the three, has a busy downtown and a small but exemplary *Altstadt* (Old Town) with five functional fountains from which you can make a taste-test comparison of normal tap water with that from a local spring source. If you make a reservation, you can spend a few hours being pampered at **Bogn Engiadina Scuol,** an extensive spa facility—the traditional treatments use moist and dry heat, massage, and mineral baths. The other two towns lie on the other side of the river. Vulpera is draped along the valley floor, with large hotels and the old cure house, the Trinkhalle, with its mineral spring. Tarasp stands apart, little more than a cluster of hotels scattered over green hillsides. ⊠ *Town center,* ☎ *081/8612000.* 🖾 *23 SF.* ☉ *Daily 10–10.*

From Scuol and Vulpera, a bus goes up to the historic **Schloss Tarasp** (Tarasp Castle) in 15 minutes; it's a scenic drive, and you can walk it in 1½ hours. Up close, as well as from across the valley, it's an impressive structure, a rambling fantasy perched 153 m (500 ft) above the valley floor. The main tower and chapel date from the 11th century, when the castle was the stronghold of the knights of Tarasp. Long a source of discord between the powerful bishop of Chur and the count of Tyrol, it was the seat of the Austrian governors until the early 19th century, when Graubünden joined the Swiss Confederation. Some years ago, it was sold to a toothpaste manufacturer that spent 3 million SF restoring it—and then gave it to the prince of Hesse.

Dining and Lodging

$$$ ✕⌗ **Chastè.** Many Swiss hoteliers are proud to claim even a second ★ generation of family ownership; this hidden treasure has spent 500 years under the Pazeller family's care. It started as a farm, then supplied provisions to builders for the Castle Tarasp, which hovers on the hill above; it eventually drew overnight guests—and today it's an impeccable, welcoming inn with every comfort. The Pazellers have preserved the bulging, sgraffitied stucco exterior, and behind the magnificently carved wood door, extraordinary effort has been made to match and modernize. Rudolf Pazeller himself is the chef and offers a small but sophisticated menu; his fish dishes are outstanding. ⌗ *CH-7553 Tarasp,* ☎ *081/8641775,* ℻ *081/8649970. 20 rooms. Restaurant, bar, stübli, sauna, steam room. No credit cards.*

$$$ ⌗ **Guardaval.** This member of the Romantik chain, built in 1693, preserves its original wing, with its stucco vaulting and heavy beams, but has altered the rest to keep rooms up-to-date. The dining/breakfast room shows off mountain views through two stories of windows, and the public areas are dripping with atmosphere (carved and painted antique furniture, ibex antlers). Rooms have spare decor in white and pine. Because the building is protected by historic preservation laws, a few rooms in the older portion still don't have showers—but their arched ceilings and ancient wood compensate. ⌗ *Doess, CH-7550 Scuol,* ☎ *081/ 8641321,* ℻ *081/8649767. 45 rooms. Restaurant, bar, café, sauna, steam room. AE, DC, MC, V.*

$$–$$$ ⌗ **Villa Maria.** This simple hillside retreat above the Trinkhalle has an elite, genteel air, with flowers on the antique furniture and Oriental rugs on the quarry tile. The rooms are homey but fresh, and some have balconies overlooking the forested valley. A little restaurant downstairs has a fireplace and other rustic touches and serves good *cuisine du marché* (menus based on fresh market produce); the chef grows his vegetables out back. ⌗ *CH-7552 Vulpera,* ☎ *081/8641138,* ℻ *081/8649161. 15 rooms. Restaurant, bar, café. No credit cards.*

$$ ⌗ **Engiadina.** This typical Engadiner house, with sgraffiti, oriels, vault- ★ ing, and beams, was built during the 16th century in the lower, older section of Scuol. Newer guest rooms are done in beige tones touched with bright reds or blues, while four older units surround you with Arvenholz. Loftlike apartments can be rented in a second house. The immaculately redone *ustaria* (simple restaurant) and *Arvenstube* (separate dining room) have a welcoming, country feel, with light wood, blue linens, and cushions in every corner. ⌗ *Old Town, near Plaz Fountain, CH-7550 Scuol,* ☎ *081/8641421,* ℻ *081/8641245. 11 rooms, 4 apartments. Restaurant, breakfast room. No credit cards.*

$ ⌗ **Traube.** This fresh, friendly inn reflects the personal touch: The rooms are all wood, the baths are all tile, and the public areas—in parquet and pine, with antiques and a ceramic stove—are pristine. Locals are drawn to the warmth of the pub and the candlelighted restaurant, which serves hearty risottos, gratins, and homemade Nusstorte. Although it's in town, there are a garden and a sun terrace with mountain views. ⌗ *Stradun, CH-7550 Scuol,* ☎ *081/8641207,* ℻ *081/8648408. 19 rooms. Restaurant, stübli, sauna. AE, DC, MC, V.*

Outdoor Activities and Sports

PARAGLIDING

For paragliding and flyovers, call **Hang Loose** (☎ 075/2300705).

RAFTING

Swissraft (☎ 081/9115250) organizes rafting expeditions.

Zernez

★ ❾ *6 km (4 mi) south of Süsch.*

This friendly little crossroads is the last town before the higher valley of the Inn. Here, hordes of serious hikers sporting loden hats, knickers, warm kneesocks, and sturdy boots come to stock up on picnic goods, day packs, and topographical maps before setting off for the Swiss National Park (☞ *below*). A number of moderate hotels make Zernez a great overnight base for park visits.

Dining and Lodging

$$ ✕▣ **Il Fuorn.** This mountain inn was built in 1894 in the middle of
★ what is now the Swiss National Park, and it is the only commercial property that remains there. It makes an ideal base for hikers tackling more than one route, and it's easily accessible from the park's only highway. There are big pine beams inside, a pretty wooden stübli, and a choice of either old-style rooms without bath (though there are sinks in the rooms) or pine-and-stucco rooms with bath in the new wing, added in 1980. The plain, meaty Swiss cooking is augmented by a generous salad bar. ⊠ CH-7530, ☎ 081/8561226, ☏ 081/8561801. 32 rooms, 12 with bath. Restaurant, café, stübli. AE, DC, MC, V.

$ ▣ **Bettini.** This solid old roadhouse is one of the town's best hotels:
★ It's clean, bright, and thoroughly local. Game trophies hang on the knotty pine walls, rustic antiques stand in the hallways, and lovely valley views open from the dining hall, which serves dependable (if predictable) meals. A few back rooms have balconies with the same valley views; two rooms without bathrooms are a real bargain. ⊠ CH-7530, ☎ 081/8561135, ☏ 081/8561510. 25 rooms. Restaurant, café. AE, DC, MC, V.

$ ▣ **Crusch Alba.** Next door to the Bettini, with the same advantageous views, this offers a pleasant alternative—and the policemen relax in its stübli, which speaks well for the local ambience. There's plenty of wood and stucco, and knickknacks in guest rooms add to the already homey atmosphere. The restaurant serves game year-round. ⊠ CH-7530, ☎ 081/8561330, ☏ 081/8561778. 22 rooms. Restaurant, café. AE, DC, MC, V.

$ ▣ **Piz Terza.** This *garni* hotel (one without a restaurant) is completely
★ modern behind its traditional facade; its rooms have slick, plain built-in cabinetry and a spare, utilitarian look. Yet the back rooms have balconies that survey the valley, and each has its own blooming geranium—an indication of the management's friendly approach to bargain hotel service. The public pool is across the street; the Swiss National Park house, just a block beyond. ⊠ CH-7530, ☎ 081/8561414, ☏ 081/8561415. 20 rooms. No credit cards.

Parc Naziunal Svizzer

❿ *Entrance 12 km (7 mi) east of Zernez, 18 km (11 mi) southeast of Susch.*

The Swiss National Park is a magnificent federal preserve of virtually virgin wilderness. Although its 168 square km (64 square mi) cover only 1% or 2% of the territory of a U.S. or Canadian national park, it has none of their developments: no campgrounds, no picnic sites, no residents. It also has few employees: Six administrators and four desk clerks staff the visitor center, and the 10 rangers live outside the park. This is genuine wilderness, every leaf protected from all but nature itself. Dead wood is left to rot, insects to multiply, and only carefully screened scholars are allowed to perform preapproved experiments. As a result, the park contains large herds of ibex with long, curving horns; delicate, short-horned chamois; huge red deer and tiny roe deer; and vast colonies of marmots. They are wild animals, however, and are not likely to line up for Twinkies by the road: Without binoculars (for rent at the visitor center), you're unlikely to get a good look.

The average person's natural urge to see wilderness tends to render the wilderness less wild. Thus the zealous park staff and the tourists are often at odds, and in high seasons, when the hiking hordes descend, rangers watch grimly for visitors who miss the point. The intensity of their philosophy of restriction is everywhere in evidence, as signs, flyers, and brochures adopt a scolding tone in five languages: "Wastepaper and other residues disfigure natural beauty. Take them with you! Don't pick a single flower! Leave your dog at home!" The list of prohibitions includes hunting, fishing, camping, picking berries, collecting roots, grazing cattle, carrying guns, skiing, making commercial movies, even making loud noises. Nonetheless, the wildlife gives a wide berth to paths where, on fine summer days, foot traffic becomes so thick that hikers have to walk in single file and ask permission to pass.

This is no African big-game preserve. You may feel more privileged at the sight of a group of ibex on a distant hill or great herds of male red deer, their antlers silhouetted above a snowy ridge, than when snapping close-up pictures of a dozen Yellowstone bison. If the big game makes no appearance, search your greedy soul and try to follow the park's advice: "Appreciate a butterfly or an ant as much as a herd of chamois."

The trails and settings themselves are magnificent. From small parking lots off the park's only highway (visitors are encouraged to take postbuses into their starting point), a series of wild, rough, and often steep trails takes off into the coniferous forests. From Parking 7, the Il Fuorn–Stabelchod–Val dal Botsch trail marks botanical and natural phenomena with multilingual signs (some in English) and leads to a spectacular barren ridge at 2,340 m (7,672 ft); the round-trip takes about three hours.

Another three-hour route, from picturesque S-chanf (pronounced sss-chonpf) to Trupchun, takes the Höheweg, or high road, into a deep glacial valley where ibex and chamois often gather; the return, by a riverside trail, passes a handy log snack bar—just across the park border and thus permitted. Visitors are restricted to the trails except at designated resting places, where broad circles are marked for hikers to collapse and have lunch. The visitor center provides detailed maps and suggested routes, including time estimates; it also has an introductory film, displays on wildlife and geology, and a new edition of the scientific hiking guide. ⊠ *Nationalpark–Haus, CH-7530, Zernez, leaving the village toward Ofenpass,* ☎ *081/8561378.* ⊡ *4 SF.* ☉ *June–Oct., Mon. and Wed.–Sun. 8:30–6, Tues. 8:30–10* PM.

Outdoor Activities and Sports

HIKING

The **Swiss National Park** (☎ 081/8561378) charts out a series of spectacular all-day or half-day ventures, for large groups only, into the wilderness preserves, some of them covering steep and rough trails.

En Route Drive south along the River Inn from the Swiss National Park toward its source, past S-chanf and Zuoz, the first towns of the Upper Engadine and both full of Engadine-style houses. The drive is lovely, a mild but steady climb past snowcapped peaks and the roaring river. You may notice an increase in Jaguars and Mercedes and the occasional Rolls as you approach Saint-Moritz.

UPPER ENGADINE

Stretching from Saint-Moritz to Zernez and with a gate to the vast Parc Naziunal Svizzer (Swiss National Park) at S-chanf, this is one of the country's highest regions—1,800 m (5,904 ft)—and one of its most dazzling. From mountains peaks, such as Piz Bernina and Piz Corvatsch, you can swoosh down world-class slopes or simply take in the dizzying view from this top-of-the-world plateau. **Engadine Concert Weeks** (✉ Verkehrsverein Oberengadin, CH-7504 Pontresina, ☎ 081/8388300), Switzerland's international chamber music festival, involves some 20 world-class concerts between mid-July and late August held in Sils, Silvaplana, Saint-Moritz, Pontresina, Celerina, Samedan, La Punt, Zuoz, and S-chanf.

Samedan

⓫ *27 km (17 mi) south of Zernez, 33 km (20 mi) southeast of Susch.*

This small, cozy (if less prestigious) resort near Saint-Moritz has an impressive 18-hole golf course (the highest in Europe), is nearest to the Upper Engadine's airport, and gives magnificent views of the awe-inspiring Bernina chain to the south: **Piz Bernina** (4,057 m/13,300 ft), **Piz Palü** and **Piz Roseg** (3,932 m/12,900 ft), **Piz Morteratsch** (3,752 m/12,300 ft), **Piz Tschierva** (3,569 m/11,700 ft), **Piz Corvatsch** (3,447 m/11,300 ft), **Piz Rosatsch** (3,111 m/10,200 ft), and many others. An intricate network of funiculars, cableways, and lifts carries the surrounding resorts' visitors up to overlooks, cafés, hiking trails, and ski pistes that offer an infinite combination of views of these peaks.

Celerina

⓬ *2 km (1 mi) south of Samedan, 3 km (1¼ mi) northeast of Saint-Moritz.*

Though in the shadow of Saint-Moritz, Celerina (Schlarigna in Romansh) still sits in the sunny spotlight as a first-rate ski resort in its own right, with easy access to the facilities of its glamorous neighbor. An attractive cluster of Engadine houses characterizes its oldest neighborhood. Its most striking landmark is the 15th-century church of **San Gian** (St. John), which has a richly painted wooden ceiling.

En Route   Between Celerina and Pontresina, in the direction of the Bernina Pass, you'll find **Punt Muragl,** the base of the funicular up to the summit of **Muottas Muragl.** A 15-minute ride takes you to an altitude of 2,455 m (8,050 ft), 702 m (2,300 ft) above the valley floor. From the top you get an eagle's-eye view of Saint-Moritz, the nearby watershed of **Piz Lunghin,** and the chain of lakes that stretches almost 16 km (10 mi) toward Maloja. In winter you can panorama-sled back down on a rather adventuresome, curvy new 4.2-km (2.6-mi) course through open fields and forests; it's BYO sled, or you can rent one at the top.

Pontresina

⓭ *4 km (2 mi) south of Celerina, 6 km (4 mi) east of Saint-Moritz.*

Lying on a south-facing elevated shelf along the Bernina Valley, Pontresina is an exceptionally picturesque resort. From here you can see clear across to the Roseg Valley, once filled with the Roseg Glacier. The glacier has retreated now to the base of Piz Roseg itself. To the left and southeast, the Flaz River winds down the mountain-framed valley from its source, the Morteratsch Glacier, which oozes down from Piz Bernina. The altitude of Pontresina (1,830 m/6,000 ft) ensures wintry weather, and its access to skiing and snowboarding on the slopes of Diavolezza (2,974 m/9,751 ft) is convenient (☞ Skiing *in* Saint-Moritz, *below*). It is also a superb base for hiking and biking, either to the glaciers or into the heights around them, for fine overviews—and for mountaineering as well. There are concerts presented here summer mornings in the shaggy-pine Tais Woods, and you can take a horse-drawn carriage up the Val Roseg anytime. Though the main streets are built up with restaurants, shops, and services, the dazzling resort still has the feel of a balanced vacation retreat.

Dining and Lodging

$$$$ ✕🏨 **Kronenhof.** Started on this scenic site as a coach stop for post horses
★ running Veltliner wine over the Bernina Pass and developed in three graceful wings, this grandest of luxury structures was completed in 1898, and very little has been changed. If the views from the lobby bay don't dazzle you, the Baroque splendor of the decor will, as the ceilings—already thick with elaborate moldings—are gilded and frescoed to the maximum with pink cherubs and blushing nymphs. Everywhere you'll find original parquet, darkened pine, and restored murals. The rooms are tastefully done, with unassuming pastels and Biedermeier furniture. The lawn that sprawls out toward the Roseg Valley views is a social center in summer and winter, with tennis courts doubling as an ice rink and a pavilion taking in winter sun. The Kronenstübli, all barrel-vaulted Arvenholz, serves international cuisine du marché—such as lobster with ginger butter, and smoked foie gras—and the wine may be drawn from the still-functioning *Veltlinerkeller* (wine cellar) below. ✉ *CH-7504,* ☎ *081/8420111,* 𝔽𝔸𝕏 *081/8426066. 93 rooms. 2 restaurants, bar, café, indoor pool, outdoor pool, beauty salon, massage, 2 tennis courts, boccie, bowling, ice-skating. AE, DC, MC, V.*

$ ✕🏨 **Rosegeletscher.** Hike up the ruggedly beautiful Roseg Valley or take
★ a horse-drawn carriage to this isolated modern hotel in traditional style. The restaurant, where you can either be served or visit the cafeteria line, offers simple regional favorites except in fall, when the owner brings in game from the surrounding countryside; his trophies adorn the walls. This is a very popular lunch spot for hikers, bikers, and cross-country skiers, who reward themselves with a selection from the massive dessert buffet. The rooms are spartan but fresh; besides the usual doubles and singles, there are some larger rooms that can accommodate half a dozen people or more, making it a good spot for hiking parties. ✉ *Via Maistra, CH-7504,* ☎ *081/8426445,* 𝔽𝔸𝕏 *081/8426886. 13 rooms, 3 dorm rooms. 2 restaurants, cafeteria. No credit cards.*

$$$$ 🏨 **Walther.** If the elaborate Kronenhof is Dionysus, the Walther is
★ Apollo, strictly classical with its discreet pastels and sleek, unfussy wood. Though built in 1907, the look is contemporary, save a few ornate moldings. The rooms have built-in pine cabinetry; those with south-facing balconies are most in demand. The state-of-the-art pool is in a glass-and-pine pavilion that opens onto a wooded garden. The clientele is younger than at the Kronenhof. ✉ *Via Maistra, CH-7504,* ☎ *081/8426471,* 𝔽𝔸𝕏 *081/ 8427922. 62 rooms, 9 suites. Restaurant, bar, indoor pool, hot tub, massage, sauna, steam room, health club. AE, DC, MC, V.*

$$$ 🏨 **Saratz.** At a time when grand hotels have been going downhill, if
★ not out of business, this 19th-century hotel has reopened its doors. It's a success story involving four brothers and a family legacy: Now a modern lobby and a 60-room wing, done in porous, toast-color *Tuffstein* in the spirit of the hotel's original stone portals, extend the property lengthwise. The interiors, with their warm schemes of yellow-green and

orange-red, make for an effective bridge between new and old; guests can choose a room with gilt-mirror grandeur or one with stricter '90s lines. The views on the Roseg Valley from the lobby terrace, or anywhere within the hotel's park, are inspiring. Rates are aggressively low for the category, but you're charged an extra fee for rooms on the east and south sides. ⊠ *Via Maistra, CH-7504,* ☎ *081/8426471,* FAX *081/ 8427922. 92 rooms. Restaurant, bar, indoor pool, outdoor pool, hot tub, massage, sauna, steam room. AE, DC, MC, V.*

$$$ 🏨 **Schweizerhof.** This 1904 landmark freshened up its lobbies and common rooms with modern lines and yellow and gray leather. Corner bay rooms have panoramic southwestern views. The public pool is across the street. ⊠ *CH-7504,* ☎ *081/8420131,* FAX *081/8427988. 70 rooms. Restaurant, bar, café, hot tub, sauna. AE, DC, MC, V.*

$$–$$$ 🏨 **Bernina.** This comfortable sports hotel displays modern spring-tone prints, pine furniture, and tile baths. Splendid views can be taken in from balconies and luxury corner doubles or from the restaurant and the stübli's big sun terrace overlooking the mountains. The restaurant serves regional specialties. ⊠ *CH-7504,* ☎ *081/8426221,* FAX *081/8427032. 47 rooms. Restaurant, café, stübli, sauna, steam room. AE, DC, MC, V.*

Nightlife and the Arts

BARS AND LOUNGES

Most bars have piano music until 2 AM. **Sport-Piano-Bar** (⊠ Sporthotel, ☎ 081/8426331). **Pöstli-Keller** (⊠ Hotel Post, ☎ 081/8426318). **Cento Bar** (⊠ Hotel Müller, ☎ 081/8426341). **Bar "Pitschna Szena"** (⊠ Hotel Saratz, ☎ 081/8394000).

DANCING

Dance club **Sarazena** (☎ 081/8426353), in a charming old Engadine house, is open to 3 AM.

MUSIC

Kurorchester Pontresina plays chamber concerts daily during summer at 11 AM in the Taiswald (Tais Forest) free of charge.

Outdoor Activities and Sports

BICYCLING

Conventional and mountain bikes can be rented at **Fähndrich-Sport** (☎ 081/8427155), **Flück Sport** (☎ 081/8426262), and **Michel Massé** (☎ 081/8426824).

FISHING

Trout fishing in the Lej Nair and Lej Pitschen Mountain lakes is free for Pontresina guests. For license information, contact the tourist office (☞ Visitor Information *in* Graubünden A to Z, *below*).

HIKING

Pontresina provides a network of paths of varying difficulty and guided excursions to the Swiss National Park, including sunrise walks, mushroom hunting in season (usually August–September), and glacier hiking. Call the tourist office (☞ Visitor Information *in* Graubünden A to Z, *below*) for info. If you are staying in Pontresina overnight, the tours are free of charge; day visitors pay a small fee.

MOUNTAINEERING AND CLIMBING

Bergsteigerschule Pontresina (Pontresina Mountain Climbing School; ⊠ Via Maistra, CH-7504, ☎ 081/8388333) is the biggest school in Switzerland and offers rock and ice instruction for beginners and advanced climbers, plus private guided tours. Along with the tourist office and the ski school, it's in the new Rondo Congress, Cultural and Information Center.

For excursions on the Flaz river call **Michel Massé** (☎ 081/8426824).

There's a large natural ice-skating rink during winter by the public indoor swimming pool, **Pontresina Hallenbad** (✉ Gemeindeverwaltung, ☎ 081/8427341 or 081/8428257 for both). Ten curling rinks with instructors and ice hockey are available at **Sportpavilion Roseg** (✉ Via Maistra, ☎ 081/8426346 or 081/8426349) from December through March.

In addition to an indoor pool, **Pontresina Hallenbad** (☞ *above*) offers a sauna, a solarium, and a sunbathing terrace.

Thirteen public tennis courts are available in Pontresina at different hotels; inquire at the hotels or at the tourist office. There are two public artificial grass/artificial sand tennis courts and two sand courts at the **Sportpavilion Roseg** (☞ *above*).

Saint-Moritz

★ ⑭ *5 km (3 mi) west of Pontresina, 85 km (53 mi) southeast of Chur.*

Who put the *ritz* in Saint-Moritz? The approach to this celebrated city may surprise newcomers who, having heard the glittering, musical name dropped in the same breath as Paris and Rome, expect either a supremely cosmopolitan old-world capital or a resort whose spectacular natural setting puts other resorts to shame. It is neither. What makes Saint-Moritz's reputation is the people who go there and who have been going there, generation by generation, since 1864, when hotelier Johannes Badrutt dared a group of English resorters—already summer regulars—to brave the Alpine winter as his guests. They loved it, delighted in the novelty of snowy mountain beauty—until then considered something to be avoided—and told their friends. By the turn of the century, Saint-Moritz, Switzerland, and snow were all the rage.

Not that Saint-Moritz had been a stranger to tourism before that. Since 1500 BC, when Druidic Celts first passed through, people have made the pilgrimage here to take healing waters from its mineral springs. The Romans had a settlement here, and later a church was founded on the site, dedicated to Mauritius, an early Christian martyr. The first historical reference to the town dates from 1139, and in 1537 Paracelsus, the great Renaissance physician and alchemist, described the health-giving properties of the Saint-Moritz springs. It is said that during the late 17th century the duke of Parma led a retinue of 25 followers over the mountain passes to taste the waters.

In fact, 70% of the latter-day pilgrims who visit Saint-Moritz come from abroad, still the cosmopolitan mix of socialites, blue bloods, and celebs that made the resort's name. But despite the reputation, not all are glamorous. Saint-Moritz catches social fire around the winter holidays—some New Year's Eve events have guest lists closed a year in advance—but the glitter fades by spring. Very ordinary people fill the streets come summer—the same hikers you might meet in any resort—and hotel prices plummet.

Then visitors see Saint-Moritz for what it really is: a busy, built-up old resort city sprawled across a hillside above an aquamarine lake, the Saint-Moritz See, surrounded by forested hills and by graceful, though not the region's most dramatic, peaks. Piz Rosatsch, with its glacier, dominates the view, with Piz Languard (3,263 m/10,699 ft) on the east and Piz Güglia (2,285 m/7,492 ft) on the west. Saint-Moritz-Dorf is the most like a downtown, with busy traffic and competitive parking in the shopping district. Saint-Moritz-Bad, the original spa-resort at the base of the lake, now bristles with brutish modern housing more worthy of a Costa Moritza than a pedigreed watering place. The town shows its best face from a distance, especially at dusk: From the *See* promenade—the popular walk around the lake—modern edges soften and the lake reflects the darkening mountains, warm hotel lights, and the grace that first made Saint-Moritz a star.

Even a hundred years of hype have not exaggerated its attractions as a winter sports center. The place that twice hosted the Olympic games (1928 and 1948)—and made the shining sun its logo—is still a sports marketing mecca, with excellent facilities for ice-skating, bobsledding, ski jumping, riding, and even winter golf, polo, and horse racing. But it does not have a corner on fine skiing: It shares a broad complex of trails and facilities with Sils, Silvaplana, Celerina, and Pontresina; only the slopes of Corviglia, Marguns, and Piz Nair are directly accessible from town. More complex connections are required to ski Corvatsch/Furtschellas, above Silvaplana, and Diavolezza, beyond Pontresina.

One of the few reminders that the now-contemporary Saint-Moritz was once an Engadine village is the **Engadine Museum,** a reproduction of the traditional sgraffitied home. Tools, furniture, and pottery, all displayed in rooms restored in different styles, explain the local way of life. ⊠ *Via dal Bagn 39,* ☎ *081/8334333.* ⌹ *5 SF.* ☉ *June–Oct., weekdays 9:30–noon and 2–5, Sun. 10–noon; Dec.–Apr., weekdays 10–noon and 2–5, Sun. 10–noon.*

Skiing

As a resort of superlatives—it's the oldest (its thermal springs were known 3,000 years ago), the most snobbish, and the most chichi—Saint-Moritz obviously could not be content with only one ski area. It has three: one on each side of the valley, **Corviglia** and **Corvatsch,** and another in reserve, 20 minutes away by car—**Diavolezza-Lagalp. Piz Corviglia, Piz Nair,** and **Grisch,** on the northwestern slopes of Saint-Moritz, are ideal terrain for family skiing and snowboarding, with 80 km (50 mi) of generally easy runs, wide and well groomed, restaurants here and there, and lift service more than sufficient except for several days in high season. **Corviglia**—site of the principal ski competitions of the Winter Olympics in 1924 and 1948—offers, in spite of its exceptionally sunny location, ideal conditions for intermediate skiers. The elevation (1,647 m/5,400 ft) and the snowmaking machines here and at **Marguns** defy even calamitous snow seasons. **Diavolezza** and **Lagalp** have added new snowmaking capabilities to give slope coverage a boost, and from February on you can ski the awe-inspiring glacier descent from Diavolezza to **Morteratsch.** The long toboganing **Cresta Run** rips from Saint-Moritz to Celerina. Saint-Moritz also has a branch of the official Swiss Ski School (☎ 081/8338090). Lift tickets cost 54 SF for one day, 258 for six.

Dining and Lodging

$$$$ ✕ **Jöhri's Talvò.** Chef Roland Jöhri has moved his highly respected kitchen from Ftan to Champfèr, just outside Saint-Moritz, and established himself in a charmingly renovated 350-year-old Engadine house, where he and his wife make resort guests as comfortable over afternoon tea as over his stellar meals. Both the cooking and decor reflect their philosophy: to marry the best of Graubünden tradition with classic French elegance, from the delicate linens softening weathered woodwork to the light sauces that curb the heartiness of local capuns, pizzocheri, and maluns. There's also a popular lobster menu, with one

whole lobster transformed into three or four inspired courses. Get a table in the open gallery overlooking the ground floor, reserve the cozy familial living room for an intimate meal, or head for the sheltered terrace. Reservations are absolutely required; you should try to get one well ahead of time. ⊠ *CH-7512,* ☎ *081/8334455. AE, DC, MC, V. Closed Mon.*

$$$ ✕ **Chesa Veglia.** This 17th-century *Bauernhof* (farmhouse) retains its raw beams and native carvings within a theme restaurant so self-consciously restored you may think you're in an American mall—an effect enhanced by the restaurant's fragmentation into three theme rooms (an upscale grill, a "stübli," and a pizzeria). Despite the rustic setting, the main menu aspires to international cuisine; you can order *côte de boeuf à la moelle et aux truffes* (beef with marrow and truffles), carpaccio, and terrine *de lièvre* (hare pâté) at prices that are Saint-Moritz–high. There are good fruit tarts at teatime, when the atmosphere is at its most convincing; later, you'll find dinner and dancing with live entertainment and piano music in the grill. ⊠ *CH-7500,* ☎ *081/8372800. AE, DC, MC, V.*

$$ ✕ **Engiadina.** With its plain linoleum and pine, this could pass for a Saint-Moritz diner, though its raison d'être is fondue—with champagne fondue its house specialty. Other favorites are cheap *steak-frites* (steak with french fries), snails, and side orders of Spätzli. It's a popular oddity in this ritzy resort. ⊠ *CH-7500,* ☎ *081/8333265. AE, DC, MC, V.*

$$ ✕🏠 **Meierei.** On a winding, private forest road partway around the
★ lake, this *Landgasthof* (country inn) is a rural mirage, an incongruity in the city but spiritually allied to the mountains and lake. It started in the 17th century as a farm where the bishop stopped over when traveling; later, it became a dairy restaurant and—about 150 years ago— a hotel. Today it's sought out for its restaurant, which serves light meals and such modern combinations as pumpkin gnocchi with lobster. Its sun terrace is also a popular meeting spot for day hikers and walkers. (If you're not a guest, you'll have to walk in, as only guests may drive in.) The rustic themes of the dining areas are loosely translated into guest room decor, with most rooms combining brown tones and wood with green-tone carpet. Some have newer, all-tile baths. ⊠ *CH-7500,* ☎ *081/8333242,* 𝕱𝕏 *081/8338838. 10 rooms. Restaurant, café. No credit cards.*

$–$$ ✕🏠 **Veltlinerkeller.** This plain, bright, genial restaurant has nothing
★ swanky about it—just lots of wood, ancient moldings in the form of grapes, a few outsize game trophies, and a welcoming wood fire where the meat is roasted while you watch. The owner mans the grill, and his touch with Italian-Romansh cooking is light and straightforward. In addition to grilled meats and whole trout, there are good and varied homemade pastas served family style from crockery bowls. The nine double rooms upstairs are finished in slick quarry tile and stucco, with cotton floral prints and all-tile baths. ⊠ *CH-7500,* ☎ *081/8334009,* 𝕱𝕏 *081/8333741. 9 rooms. Restaurant, bar, stübli. No credit cards.*

$$$$ 🏠 **Badrutt's Palace.** With its pseudo-Gothic stone and mismatched sprawl of architectural excess, the Palace is pure Hollywood, all glitz and conspicuous consumption. Winter is its prime time: Flagrant and showy, with Rolls-Royces and Lear jets discharging guests willing to pay more per night than for a transatlantic flight, it is crammed with beautiful people and wealthy wanna-bes who made token appearances on the slopes before checking in at the hairdresser. This place definitely has its standards—like a jacket and tie for public rooms. Nowhere in Switzerland will you find more facilities—the hotel even has private ski instructors and a private cinema. The Restaurant is as vast as a mess hall, beswagged and chandeliered; the Grill-Room is a celadon jewel box and enjoys a culinary reputation beyond the guest

list. Rooms are surprisingly discreet and rather like a lot of other hotel rooms at a third the price—but it's not the drapes you're paying for. ⊠ *CH-7500,* ☎ *081/8371000,* FAX *081/8372999. 180 rooms, 40 suites. 3 restaurants, bar, indoor pool, outdoor pool, hot tubs, massage, sauna, 4 tennis courts, health club, squash, ice-skating, cinema, dance club, nightclub, nursery. AE, DC, MC, V.*

$$$$ ⊞ **Carlton.** If you want luxury without blatant glitz, consider this un-
★ sung hotel, which stands slightly above the city center in a supersunny location with fine views. Built in 1913 and now completely renovated, it's bright and modern, without a scrap of Arvenholz, its white-marble lobby more like a performing-arts center than a Belle Epoque hotel. Blue runners lead upstairs to the plush bar/sitting room and regal dining rooms. Guest rooms have every modern amenity; some lean toward contemporary lines, others evoke eras gone by with crystal chandeliers and fine carpets. The baths are state-of-the-art Euro style, and the beautiful glassed-in pool has views over the lake and a sun terrace. ⊠ *CH-7500,* ☎ *081/8331141,* FAX *081/8332012. 99 rooms, 6 suites. Restaurant, bar, indoor pool, beauty salon, massage, sauna, health club, nursery. AE, DC, MC, V.*

$$$$ ⊞ **Kulm.** This luxury hotel can claim its share of Saint-Moritz superlatives: it was the first hotel here (1856) *and* the first house to have electricity in all of Switzerland (1878). Modern comfort has come a long way since: for example, in the form of the new Panorama Healthclub, with a saltwater grotto and fitness gym. Elsewhere, the hotel's discreetly done in slightly old-fashioned good taste—cream, gold, scarlet. The facilities are top quality, the breakfast room is pure Wedgwood, and the à la carte restaurant—Rôtisserie de Chevaliers—is a romantic vaulted space, serving (predictably enough) old-style haute cuisine. In winter, the outdoor terrace is usually dominated at lunchtime by hardy men just off the icy Cresta Run, Saint-Moritz's exclusive skeleton run up the road. ⊠ *CH-7500,* ☎ *081/8331151,* FAX *081/8332738. 200 rooms. Restaurant, bar, indoor pool, massage, sauna, 3 tennis courts, health club. AE, DC, MC, V.*

$$$$ ⊞ **Schweizerhof.** This big-city hotel in the center of town was built in 1896 and is still grand. Public areas are heavy with carved wood and moldings, and the Victorian splendor is almost oppressive. A lighter touch is the painted ceiling of the guests' dining room, with its glittering birch forest. Guest rooms leave romantic fantasy behind—they're slick postmodern with burled-wood cabinets and contemporary color schemes. There's a popular piano bar and a lively stübli that draws a young après-ski crowd. The Acla restaurant, at street level, serves casual Italian and Austrian meals. ⊠ *CH-7500,* ☎ *081/8370707,* FAX *081/8370700. 72 rooms, 8 suites. 2 restaurants, 4 bars, sauna, health club, nursery. AE, DC, MC, V.*

$$$$ ⊞ **Steffani.** A standard city business-class hotel, this landmark built in 1869 is owned by Best Western and thus tailored to meet American expectations. Despite its age, it now has a heavy, modern look, with some stylized local details but more stress on function and dependability than history. The facilities are ample, and the staff is welcoming. ⊠ *CH-7500,* ☎ *081/8332101,* FAX *081/8334097. 75 rooms, 5 suites. 3 restaurants, 3 bars, indoor pool, hot tub, massage, sauna, bowling, dance club. AE, DC, MC, V.*

$$$–$$$$ ⊞ **Crystal Hotel.** This city-center hotel was built in 1963 but late in 1997 it emerged from a cocoon of serious renovation. The revamp focused on the interior, and if the spacious lobby has a touch of familiarity, it may be because an American interior decorator lent a hand—there's a long, low-slung feel to it. Rooms are all new, done in wood and patterned red fabrics, with luxurious bath products and Arvenholz in the baths. Though there's little hope for a truly broad

view—it's flanked by buildings and a parking garage—the facilities are ample, the fitness center is equipped to get all of Saint-Moritz in shape, and its location is convenience itself—it's steps from the valley station for connections to Corviglia. If you're sore after a tough day on the slopes, try the sauna's Turkish bath. ⊠ *CH-7500,* ☎ *081/8362626,* ℻ *081/8362627. 80 rooms. Restaurant, bar, massage, sauna, health club. AE, DC, MC, V.*

$$$ ⊞ **Waldhaus am See.** This is another world, a good hotel perched on
★ a peninsula overlooking the lake and mountains with a merely peripheral view of Saint-Moritz's urban turmoil (well filtered through double glass) across the highway. With a big, sunny balcony, dining rooms with views, and a clientele ranging from family clans to seniors, it's a vacation lodge geared to leisurely one- to two-week stays. The reasonably priced restaurant, which serves good lake trout, stocks more than 1,500 wines, and owner-entrepreneur Claudio Bernasconi has introduced Switzerland's most extensive whiskey bar (as well as his handpicked selection of ties for sale). Rooms are plain, with pine trim and some dated plumbing, though many modern baths have been added in recent years. Sunny corner doubles have tiny bays over the lake. ⊠ *CH-7500,* ☎ *081/8337676,* ℻ *081/8338877. 50 rooms. Restaurant, sauna, exercise room. DC, MC, V.*

$$–$$$ ⊞ **Eden.** Just up from the center of town, on a hilltop, this small hotel *garni* has been in the same family since it opened in the 1890s. Such personal touches as the buffed original Arvenholz in some guest rooms and an antique swan sleigh that serves as part of the breakfast buffet reflect a genteel air and the owner's singular style. Most rooms have modern lines with wood accents; be prepared for some bright tiles in the bathrooms. ⊠ *CH-7500,* ☎ *081/8336161,* ℻ *081/8339191. 35 rooms. Breakfast room. No credit cards.*

$$–$$$ ⊞ **Landguard.** This delightful little hotel stands between the Eden and
★ the Kulm (☞ *above*), sharing their lovely mountain views. Such restored regional details as sgraffiti, carved ceilings, and fine darkened pine in some rooms preserve the best from its earlier days. The big corner rooms deserve the top price they command; back rooms look over town. All-tile baths add modern sparkle. ⊠ *CH-7500,* ☎ *081/8333137,* ℻ *081/ 8334546. 22 rooms. Breakfast room. AE, DC, MC, V.*

Nightlife and the Arts

To find out what's happening in the arts world, check *Saint-Moritz Aktuell* or the booklet "Engadin," which offers weekly events information for the Upper Engadine resorts.

BARS AND LOUNGES

Bobby's Pub (⊠ Gallaria Badrutt, at Via dal Bagn 52, ☎ 081/8334767) has an English atmosphere. A casual crowd congregates at the **Cava-Bar** in the Steffani (☞ Dining and Lodging, *above,* ☎ 081/8322101). The **Muli Bar,** in the hotel Schweizerhof's (☞ Dining and Lodging, *above*) former library, offers country music après-ski. The Schweizerhof's **piano bar** has a champion bartender who serves exotic cocktails to upscale crowds in a tiny Jugendstil lounge. The hotel's pine stübli, open all year, draws casual young people après-ski with a live guitarist and snacks, including raclette in winter. The **Renaissance Bar** in Badrutt's Palace (☞ Dining and Lodging, *above*), with American-style bar stools and tables, has an open fireplace; the awe-inspiring lobby lounge, also in the hotel, has a pianist evenings.

CASINOS

The casino in **Saint-Moritz** (☎ 081/8321080) has inaugurated 75 slot machines to supplement its roulette.

CLUBS

The **Grand-Bar Nightclub** in Badrutt's Palace (☞ Dining and Lodging, *above*) has dancing to live music. **La Volière** (✉ Suvretta House, ☎ 081/8321132) is a very formal nightclub, requiring evening dress.

DANCING

Absolut (✉ Via Maistra 10, ☎ 081/8336398) draws movers and shakers. **King's Club** of Badrutt's Palace (☞ Dining and Lodging, *above*), with its urban-decay decor—graffiti, neon, dated Keith Haring look—attracts the jet set at holiday time; prepare for a massive cover charge. **Vivai** is a popular disco club in the Steffani (☞ Dining and Lodging, *above*).

MUSIC

The **Saint-Moritz Kurorchester,** a 13-piece summer chamber group, plays free concerts summer mornings at 10:30 in the Heilbadzentrum concert hall—or outside, if the weather is fine.

Outdoor Activities and Sports

BICYCLING

You can rent both conventional and mountain bikes at the **Corviglia Tennis Center** (☎ 081/8331500). Bicycles can be also rented at the **Rhaetian Railway station,** though use of the vehicles is restricted to bike trails. Mountain bikes also are available, but they are rarely permitted on pedestrian trails.

CLIMBING

The school **Bergführerverein** (☎ 081/8337714) will design special programs for you.

GOLF

Saint-Moritz and Samedan share Switzerland's oldest 18-hole golf course, **Engadine Golf Samedan** (☎ 081/8525226), along the River En.

PARAGLIDING

For **hang gliding** or **paragliding** call ☎ 081/8332416.

RAFTING

For white-water rafting expeditions on the River En, call **Swissraft Engadine** (☎ 081/8426824). Tours are run June–September.

SAILING AND WINDSURFING

Arnoud Missiaen (☎ 081/8289229) heads a windsurfing school. The **Segelschule Saint-Moritz** (☎ 081/8334056) gives sailing lessons.

SKATING

Ludains (☎ 081/8335030), an artificial outdoor skating rink in Saint-Moritz-Bad, is open all year.

SPORTS CENTERS

Saint-Moritz/Celerina has an **International Center for Training and Competition** (☎ 081/8376159) with equipment for all Olympic sports.

SWIMMING

You can swim in **Lake Nair** by Saint-Moritz. For indoor swimming, try the **Hallenschwimmbad** (☎ 081/8336025), a municipal pool and sauna in Saint-Moritz-Bad; it has coed and single-sex hours.

TENNIS

Corviglia Tennis Center (☎ 081/8331500) in Saint-Moritz-Bad has four outdoor and four indoor tennis courts, with staff instructors. The local tourist office (☞ Graubünden A to Z, *below*) can tell you about other available courts.

Sils, Sils-Baselgia, and Sils-Maria

⑮ *13 km (8 mi) southwest of Saint-Moritz.*

The Lower Engadine Valley broadens into green meadows punctuated by a series of crystalline lakes: the little Champferer See, just past Saint-Moritz; the larger Silvaplaner See, headed by the small hillside resort of Silvaplana, and the long sprawl of the Silser See, accessible from the land bar that separates the two bodies of water. On this green lowland 13 km (8 mi) from Saint-Moritz stands the resort complex of Sils (Segl in Romansh), connecting Sils-Baselgia and, farther back against the mountains, Sils-Maria. From Sils the highway heads over the Maloja Pass (1,816 m/5,953 ft) and crosses over into Italy.

Although the flat setting and expanding new housing make Sils-Maria look like an American suburban country club, Sils-Maria is a resort with old-Engadine flavor and inspiring views. Nietzsche called it "the land of silver colors" and wrote *Also Sprach Zarathustra* (*Thus Spake Zarathustra*) in his house here, which is now **Stiftung Nietzsche Haus** museum. ⊠ *Next to Hotel Edelweiss,* ☎ *081/8265369.* 🎟 *6 SF.* ☾ *Mid-Dec.–Apr. and June–Nov., Tues.–Sun. 3–6.*

Dining and Lodging

$ ✕🏠 **Chesa Marchetta/Pensiun Andreola.** You won't find a more pleas-
★ ant and complete regional experience than in this tiny twin pension and restaurant run by two sophisticated sisters; not only do they decorate with taste, but they also serve authentic local dishes. The sgraffitied pension is furnished in pine and chic cotton prints, while the neighboring restaurant is an Arvenholz gem, perfectly preserved since 1671. The menu is limited to one main dish a night—homemade pasta with lamb, perhaps, or polenta with veal—with permanent options of *plain in pigna* (potato gratin with homemade sausage) or fondue chinoise; but there are always cold local meats and Engadiner Nusstorte, the region's signature nut cake. Meals are served evenings only, snacks from 3:30 on. ⊠ *CH-7514,* ☎ *081/8265232,* 𝖥𝖠𝖷 *081/8266260. 10 rooms, some without bath. Restaurant, stübli. No credit cards.*

$$$$ 🏠 **Waldhaus.** Hermann Hesse, Thomas Mann, C. G. Jung, Marc Cha-
★ gall, Albert Einstein, and Richard Strauss all found solace in this hilltop forest retreat, high above the meadow that separates Lake Sils and Lake Silvaplana and offers spectacular views in all directions. You can have tea on the terrace, surrounded by tall evergreen woods, or play tennis on the courts just below; either way, you'll be accompanied by the hotel's resident string trio, which adds to the sense of Wagnerian idyll. Even the indoor pool, built of pine and rock, takes in forest views. The building itself is steeped in tradition and creaky grandeur, with its heavy marble pillars, burnished parquet, and Asian runners. The rooms range from spare (chenille and parquet) to splendid (bay windows with fine panoramas), but the public areas are consistently gracious, especially the formal dining room, where in winter the white-draped tables and iciclelike light fixtures mirror the snow-blanketed landscape outside. ⊠ *CH-7514,* ☎ *081/8266666,* 𝖥𝖠𝖷 *081/8265992. 140 rooms. Restaurant, bar, stübli, indoor pool, beauty salon, massage, steam room, miniature golf, 4 tennis courts. MC, V.*

$$ 🏠 **Chesa Randolina.** This hotel in Sils-Baselgia, adjoining Sils-Maria, laps up sun from its position set back from the water. The architecture is low-slung but pure Engadine, with stucco vaulting, beams, and pine in nearly every room; the best have long balconies facing south. There's a broad, spacious lounge with a stone fireplace and a cozy restaurant (hotel guests only) with a sgraffitied ceiling. ⊠ *CH-7515,* ☎ *081/8265151,* 𝖥𝖠𝖷 *081/8265600. 37 rooms. Restaurant, bar. No credit cards.*

$$ ⚏ **Privata.** Tucked into a green corner at the edge of the village, this
★   tidy, fresh little Engadine-style inn is full of personal touches: antiques,
paintings done by past guests, and trophies from the owner's former
days as a ski champion. The parlors have fireplaces and inlaid stone
floors, and there's a lovely garden in back. Decorated in white and pine,
most rooms have good views, though the hotel behind spoils a few. Some
upper rooms have tiny balconies with chairs. The restaurant is open only
to inn guests and the fresh-baked *Zopf* (braided bread) at Sunday
breakfast is a good reason to get up early. ⊠ *Sils-Maria, CH-7514,* ☎
081/8265247, ⅿⅅ *081/8266183. 25 rooms. Restaurant. No credit cards.*

Nightlife and the Arts

Small **chamber ensembles** perform from late June through September
at 4 or 4:30 on the Konzerztplatz in Sils-Maria; in bad weather, they
move to the schoolhouse.

Outdoor Activities and Sports

DOGSLEDDING

Turn yourself over to **Sämy Stöckli** (☎ 079/4404166) and his mush-
ing crew; 12 snow-hungry huskies will pull you across extraordinary
frozen-lake landscapes near Sils.

CLIMBING

Chesa Sur il Lei (⊠ CH-7513 Silvaplana, ☎ 081/8288815).

PARAGLIDING

In Sils–Baseglia, contact instructor **Andrea Kuhn** (☎ 081/8265400).

SAILING AND WINDSURFING

Surf-Schule Malojawind (☎ 081/8265877) is a windsurfing school in
Sils-Maria. **Segel- und Surf-Center** (⊠ CH-7514, ☎ 081/8265877) gives
lessons. Silvaplana's **Surf- und Segelschule** (⊠ CH-7513, ☎ 081/
82655786) has sailing and windsurfing instruction.

SPORTS CENTERS

Silvaplana has the **Sportcentrum Mulets** (⊠ CH-7513, ☎ 081/8289362),
with two sand tennis courts, a soccer field, an ice rink, a playground,
and a training room. Sils's **Muot Marias** (⊠ CH-7513, ☎ 081/8385050)
is a well-equipped sports center.

TENNIS

Sils has two public courts, booked through the **Hotel Waldhaus** (☎ 081/
8266666) or the tourist office (☞ Visitor Information *in* Graubünden
A to Z, *below*).

JULIER ROUTE TO
SAN BERNARDINO PASS

The Julier Pass is one of the three great Alpine passes that are known
to have been used by the Romans (the Grand St. Bernard and the Splü-
gen are the other two)—though even in those days, the Julier was fa-
vored because of its immunity to avalanches. The present road, built
between 1820 and 1826, is dominated by three mountains, Piz Julier,
Piz Albana, and Piz Polaschin, and near the top it is marked by two
pillars, about 1½ m (5 ft) high, which are said to be the remains of a
Roman temple. The terrain here is barren, windswept, and rocky—the
perfect place to imagine an open stage for marching legions.

En Route   About 16 km (10 mi) beyond the summit of the Julier Pass is the vil-
lage of **Bivio**: A former Roman settlement named Stabulum Bivio, it is
called Bivio in Italian and Swiss German, and Beiva in Romansh—and
residents speak all three.

Tiefencastel

⑯ *44 km (27 mi) northwest of Sils, 29 km (18 mi) south of Chur.*

Where the Julia flows into the Albula, you'll find this valley town, buried deep in the mountain forests and accessible only by steep, winding roads; it was entirely destroyed by fire in 1890. Above the rebuilt town, the tall white church of **St. Ambrosius** still stands out against the background of fir trees that cover the encroaching hills.

En Route From Tiefencastel, the road forks: You can drive north on Route 3 toward Chur (☞ *above*) through Lenzerheide (1,525 m/5,000 ft), a year-round resort known for moderate slopes for beginning skiers and a good 18-hole golf course, or cut west to Thusis. The Thusis route is particularly spectacular via the Rhaetian Railway (☞ By Train *in* Graubünden A to Z, *below*), as it passes through 16 tunnels, one of them more than 5 km (3 mi) long, and across 27 bridges and viaducts. The most celebrated of these is the **Solis Viaduct,** the center arch of which is 42 m (137 ft) across and 89 m (293 ft) high.

Thusis, surrounded by high mountains and thick forest, has a late-Gothic church (1506) and the ruins of the old Schloss Hohenhaetien, perched on rocky heights to guard the entrance to the ancient road Via Mala.

Leading south from Thusis, the **Via Mala** writhes south along the bottom of a deep ravine crisscrossed by bridges. It has been replaced by the new highway, but you can still see the old Via Mala by leaving the highway about 5 km (3 mi) after Thusis and following the traffic signs marked VIA MALA toward the San Bernardino Pass. On foot, you can descend 321 steps into the gorge to see the bridges that, in various epochs, have been strung across the treacherous water.

At Zillis, famous for the painted wooden ceiling in its St. Martinskirche (St. Martin's Church), the Via Mala ends, and A13 leads south and west toward the **Splügenpass** (the southbound entrance into Italy). Just west of the Splügenpass is the **San Bernardino Pass** (Little St. Bernard Pass). There is an easy express tunnel through the pass these days, 8 km (5 mi) long, but the tortuous climb up the old highway rewards drivers (and postbus passengers) with astonishing perspectives: As you begin to ascend, the Rheinwald Valley opens below, and you see the first currents of the Hinter, or Lower, Rhine; beyond looms its source, the glacier of the **Zapporthorn** (3,154 m/10,340 ft). This pass is closed in winter; its availability depends on snowfall.

GRAUBÜNDEN A TO Z

Arriving and Departing

By Bus

You can take the Swiss **postbus** system's *Palm Express* (☎ 081/8376764) from Ascona or Lugano in the Ticino over the Maloja Pass and into Saint-Moritz.

By Car

As Graubünden is dense with mountains and thin on major highways, drivers usually enter either by way of the San Bernardino Pass from Ticino or from the north past Liechtenstein, both on **A13,** the region's only expressway; it traces the Rhine to its main source.

By Train

The only main **Swiss Federal Railway** (SBB) trains to enter Graubünden come into Chur at the Rhätische Bahn (☎ 081/2539121). From there, the fine local **Rhaetian Railway** (RhB) takes over, with its broad network of narrow-gauge track. For general **information** on SBB and RhB, call the Rhätische Bahn.

To make the most of the Rhaetian Railway systems, you can take famous scenic train routes in or out of the region. The *Bernina Express* runs from Chur to Saint-Moritz via the Albula route and on to Italy past the spectacular Bernina peaks. The glamorous *Glacier Express* connects Saint-Moritz with Zermatt via the Oberalp Pass and pulls a burnished-wood period dining car. During the 7½-hour trip, the *Glacier Express* crosses 291 bridges and goes through 91 tunnels, covering spectacular Alpine terrain. To reserve a table, contact **Schweizerische Speisewagen Gesellschaft** (✉ CH-7000 Chur, ☎ 081/2521425). For seat reservations for the train (also compulsory), contact the appropriate tourist offices (☞ Visitor Information, *below*) or the railway itself.

Getting Around

By Bus

Postbuses are a dramatic way to lumber up Alpine switchbacks over the region's great passes—that is if you're not inclined to motion sickness. You also can use them to make circle tours, with some careful studying of the schedule. Information is available at all post offices.

By Car

The A13 expressway cuts a swift north–south route through Graubünden. If you want to get back into the deep farmlands, you'll definitely need a car. Fine valley highways connect the rest of the area, though to move from one resort to another you may have to crawl over a mountain pass. If you're traveling in winter, make sure to check up on the status of these passes; weather is obviously a major player. The San Bernardino, Oberalp, and Albula passes are normally closed, but the Bernina, Julier, and Flüela passes are usually open to car traffic. The good news is the imminent opening of the **Vereina Tunnel,** which will stretch from Klosters to Susch/Lavin. Cars will be loaded and sent off twice an hour from each railway terminal. At press time, the tunnel was scheduled to open in late fall 1999.

By Train

The **Rhaetian Railway** (☞ Arriving and Departing, *above*) consists of 375 km (243 mi) of track and 117 tunnels and offers unusually thorough coverage of the terrain. Without resorting to cogwheel supports, some of the trains climb stiff mountain grades of up to 7%. Holders of the Swiss Pass (☞ Train Travel *in* the Gold Guide) travel free on all RhB lines.

Contacts and Resources

Emergencies

Police: Upper Engadine (☎ 081/8641414); Arosa (☎ 081/3771938); Klosters (☎ 081/4221236); Saint-Moritz (☎ 081/8333017).**Ambulance:** Klosters (☎ 081/4221713); Saint-Moritz (☎ 081/8518888). **Hospital**: Upper Engadine (☎ 081/8518111); Davos (☎ 081/4132222).**Doctors**: Upper Engadine referral (☎ 081/8525657). Available doctors, dentists, and emergency pharmacies are listed in local newspapers under "Notfalldienst" (**emergency service**) and in the city or resort's tourist periodical.

Guided Tours

HIKING

Arosa, Davos, and Lenzerheide-Valbella offer an unusual **hiking package**: They'll book your hotel and deliver your bags ahead. You can walk from Davos to Arosa one day and from Arosa to Lenzerheide the next. A seven-day program lets you spend more time in each resort. Contact local tourist offices.

WALKING

The **Arosa** tourist office (☞ Visitor Information, *below*) offers guided tours and nature walks every morning and afternoon from June through October; you can visit a cheese maker, a regional museum, and a 15th-century chapel. The **Pontresina** tourist office (☞ Visitor Information, *below*) offers guided walking tours of its Old Town, full of typical Engadine houses, from mid-June to mid-October. It also offers guided botanical excursions, sunrise viewings, glacier tours, and hiking trips to the Swiss National Park, plus mushroom-picking outings in season (usually August–September). If you are staying in Pontresina, the tours are free; day visitors pay a small fee.

Visitor Information

Verkehrsverein Graubünden (⊠ Alexanderstr. 24, CH-7001 Chur, ☎ 081/3026100, FAX 081/3021414) is tourist information headquarters for the canton. The local **Chur** city tourist office (⊠ Grabenstr. 5, CH-7002 Chur, ☎ 081/2521818) offers leaflets for self-paced walks around the Old Town, as well as guided tours departing from the Town Hall.

Arosa (⊠ Kurverein, Poststr., CH-7050, ☎ 081/3787020). **Davos** (⊠ Promenade 67, CH-7270, ☎ 081/4152121). **Maienfeld** (⊠ Autobahn Raststätte Heidiland, CH-7304, ☎ 081/3026100). **Klosters** (⊠ Kur & Verkehrsverein, Alte Bahnhofstr. 6, CH-7250, ☎ 081/4102020). **Pontresina** (⊠ Rondo Center, CH-7504, ☎ 081/8388300). **Saint-Moritz** (⊠ Kur & Verkehrsverein, Via Maistra 12, CH-7500, ☎ 081/8373333). **Scuol** (☎ 081/8612222). **Sils** (⊠ CH-7514 Sils-Maria, ☎ 081/8385050). **Zernez** (⊠ Verkehrsverein, CH-7530, ☎ 081/8561300).

5 Ticino

Locarno, Lugano

Italian in language, culture, and spirit, Ticino is an irresistible combination of Mediterranean pleasures and Swiss efficiency. With its yacht-filled waterfront promenades of Locarno and Lugano and its constantly sunny climate, Ticino is a canton set apart, a happy harbor for Switzerland's Italian-speaking minority.

NEWCOMERS TO THE OLD WORLD, a little weak on their geography, might hear the names Lugano, Ascona, Locarno, Bellinzona and assume—quite naturally—they're in Italy. Color photographs of the region might not set them straight: Nearly every publicity shot shows palm trees and mimosas, red roofs and loggias, azure waters and indigo skies. Surely this is the Italian Mediterranean or the coast of the Adriatic. But behind the waving date palms are telltale signs: surgical neatness, fresh paint, geometric gardens, timely trains. There's no mistake about it: It's a little bit of Italy, but the canton of Ticino is pure Swiss.

For the German Swiss, it's a little bit of paradise. They can cross over the Saint Gotthard or the San Bernardino passes and emerge in balmy sunshine, eat gnocchi and polenta in shaded *grotti* (rustic outdoor restaurants), drink merlot from ceramic bowls, taste gelato (ice cream) overlooking the waters of Lago di Maggiore (Lake Maggiore)—and still know their lodging will be strictly controlled by the Swiss Hotel Association. They don't even have to change money. The combination is irresistible, and so in spring, summer, and fall they pour over the Alps to revel in low-risk Latin delights.

And the Ticinese welcome them like rich distant cousins, to be served and coddled and—perhaps just a bit—despised. For the Italian-speaking natives of Ticino—a lonely 8% of the Swiss population—are a minority in their own land, dominated politically by the German-speaking Swiss, set apart by their culture as well as by their language. Their blood and their politics are as Mediterranean as their climate: In a battle over obligatory seat belts, the Ticinese consistently voted to reject the federal intrusion. They were voted down by their Germanic neighbors—a 70% majority—and they protested. It was brought to vote again, and again they were defeated. Nowadays the Ticinese defy the federal law—and their policemen, Ticinese themselves, of course, turn a blind and supportive eye.

Their Italian leanings make perfect sense: An enormous mountain chain cuts them off from the north, pushing them inexorably, glacier-like, toward their lingual roots. Most of the territory of Ticino belonged to the pre-Italian city-states of Milan and Como until 1512, when the Swiss Confederation took it over by force. It remained a Swiss conquest—oppressed under the then-tyrannical rule of Uri, Schwyz, and Underwald, the very cantons now revered for forming the honorable Confederation of Switzerland—until 1798, when from the confusion of Napoléon's campaigns it emerged a free canton, and in 1803 it joined the confederation for good.

It remains a canton apart nonetheless, graceful, open, laissez-faire. Here you'll instantly notice differences in manner and body language among Ticinese engaged in conversation; you'll also notice fewer English-speaking Swiss. The climate, too, is different: There's an extraordinary amount of sunshine here—more than in central Switzerland and even in sunny Italy immediately across the border, where Milan and Turin often are haunted by a grim overcast of gray. Mountain-sports meccas aside, this is the most glamorous of Swiss regions: The waterfront promenades of Lugano and Locarno, lined with pollards, rhododendrons, and bobbing yachts, blend a rich social mix of jet-set resorters. A few miles' drive brings the canton's impoverished past into view—the foothill and mountain villages are still scattered with low-roof stone peasants' cabins, but nowadays those cabins often prove to have been gentrified as chic vacation homes.

Although they're prosperous, with Lugano standing third in banking, after Zürich and Geneva, the Ticinese hold on to their past, a mountain-peasant culture that draws them to hike, hunt, and celebrate with great pots of risotto stirred over open outdoor fires. It's that contrast—contemporary glamour, earthy past—that grants travelers a visit that's as balanced, satisfying, and as unique as a good merlot.

Pleasures and Pastimes

Dining

Of all the Swiss regions this can be the most pleasurable to eat in, as the stylish and simple cuisine of Italy has been adopted virtually intact. Because the Ticinese were once a poor mountain people, their everyday cooking shares the earthy delights of another once-poor mountain people, the Piedmontese, whose steaming polenta and rib-sticking gnocchi break bread with game and meaty porcino mushrooms. *Manzo brasato* (savory braised beef with vegetables) and osso buco are standards, as are polenta *con carne in umido* (with meat stew), *busecca* (vegetable soup with tripe), and any number of variations on risotto. If you look and ask, you might be lucky enough to find *trota in carpione* (trout marinated in red wine and vinegar and served as a cold hors d'oeuvre). Game offerings usually include *coniglio* (rabbit), *lepre* (hare), and *capretto* (roast kid).

As in the rest of Switzerland, local cold meats come in a broad variety, from myriad salamis to prosciutto *crudo,* the pearly pink cured raw ham made famous in Parma. Any food product made locally is called *nostrano,* and the prosciutto crudo nostrano is worth asking for at the butcher, as you won't find a match for its forthright, gamey flavor back home. Eat it with bread and sweet butter to balance the salt.

Most cooks import Italian cheeses—Parmigiano-Reggiano, sharp pecorino—though there are good, hard, white mountain varieties (Piora, Gesero) in most shops. The most local treat: tiny *formaggini,* little molds of ultrafresh goat cheese, still shining with whey.

The best place to sample these down-to-earth delicacies is in a grotto, one of the scores of traditional country restaurants scattered across the region. Some of them are set deep in the mountains and forests, little more than a few rows of picnic tables and a string of festive lights. Some serve only cold meats, but a few offer a daily hot dish or two. Wine is poured into an individual *boccalino,* a traditional ceramic pitcher, or a small ceramic bowl, to be drunk from like a cup. Instead of beer to quench locals' thirsts, a mix *gazosa* (lemon-lime soda) and vino nostrano (the house red wine) is de rigueur. If you want a real Italian-style espresso, one-finger deep and frothing with golden foam, ask for *un liscio.* Otherwise they'll serve it with cream, Swiss style—and might even charge you extra. If you want a shot of grappa (grape brandy) thrown in, ask for it *corretto*—literally, "correct." To experience an authentic grotto, avoid the ones with *ristorante* in their names; the categories of eating establishments are carefully regulated, so these will always be pricier—and not the real thing.

CATEGORY	COST*
$$$$	over 80 SF
$$$	50 SF–80 SF
$$	20 SF–50 SF
$	under 20 SF

*Prices are per person for a three-course meal (two-course in the $ category), including sales tax and 15% service charge

Lodging

The hotel industry of this Mediterranean region of Switzerland capitalizes on its natural assets, with lakeside views of Lago di Lugano and Lake Maggiore, and swimming pools and terraces that pay homage to the omnipresent sun. As Ticino is at its best in spring and fall, and packed with sunseekers in summer, many hotels close down for the winter. Tourist offices often publish lists of those remaining open, so if you're planning to come in low season—and even in January the lake resorts can be steamy—check carefully. Although these are vacation resorts, they do not depend on the *demipension* (half-board) system as much as their mountain counterparts, but arrangements can be made.

CATEGORY	COST*
$$$$	over 300 SF
$$$	180 SF–300 SF
$$	120 SF–180 SF
$	under 120 SF

Prices are for a standard double room, including breakfast, tax, and service charge.

Mountain Valleys

Valle Blenio, Valle Maggia, Valle Verzasca, Valle Leventina, and other mountain valleys just a short distance from the major cities are rugged reminders of the region's modest history. Stone-rendered peasant homes, called *rustici,* permeate the valleys, some cut so deeply into the land that the sun never quite reaches bottom. Driving these valleys is a unique experience where time seems to have stopped; you'll encounter whole villages perched on craggy mountainsides, in apparent defiance of gravity.

Waterfront Promenades

Switzerland's sunniest waterfronts—with boating, swimming, charming cafés, fine dining, and shops of all sorts—are in Ticino. Palm-lined promenades in Lugano, Locarno, and Ascona offer tremendous views overlooking rugged Italian Alps. Evenings, harbor lights twinkle as the Ticinese stroll by, enjoying the balmy climate.

Exploring Ticino

The canton is divided into two geographic regions by the small mountain range (554 m/1,817 ft) called Monte Ceneri, which rises up south of the valley below Bellinzona. Extending northeast and northwest of Monte Ceneri in the windswept Sopraceneri region are several mountainous valleys, including Valle Blenio, Valle Maggia, Valle Verzasca, and Valle Leventina. Also north, or literally "above," Monte Ceneri are Locarno and Ascona, which share a peninsula bulging into Lake Maggiore. The more developed southern region, Sottoceneri ("below Ceneri"), is home to business and resort towns, notably Lugano.

Numbers in the text correspond to numbers in the margin and on the Ticino and Lugano maps.

Great Itineraries

Lugano and Locarno alone provide an overview of the region, but completing the picture requires forays to the less touristic waterfront village Ascona, the mountain stronghold Bellinzona, and the rural, rugged mountain valleys beyond.

IF YOU HAVE 1 OR 2 DAYS

Concentrate on ⊞ **Lugano** ⑦–⑮, exploring the waterfront shops, venturing east to the Villa Favorita, and riding a funicular up Monte Brè. On the second day, take in the sights of the serene hillside city **Locarno** ③

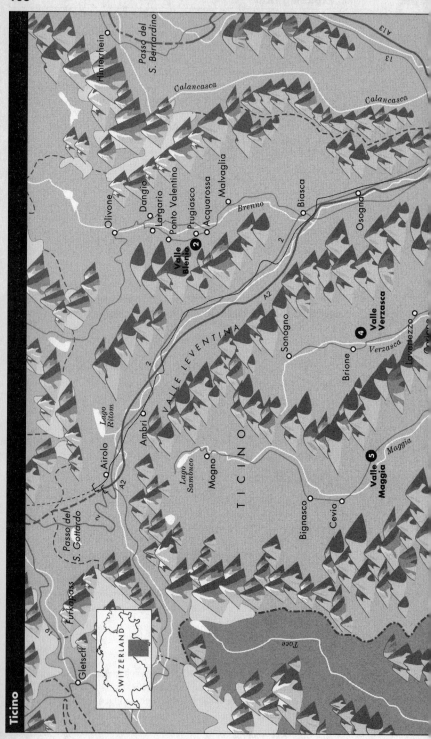

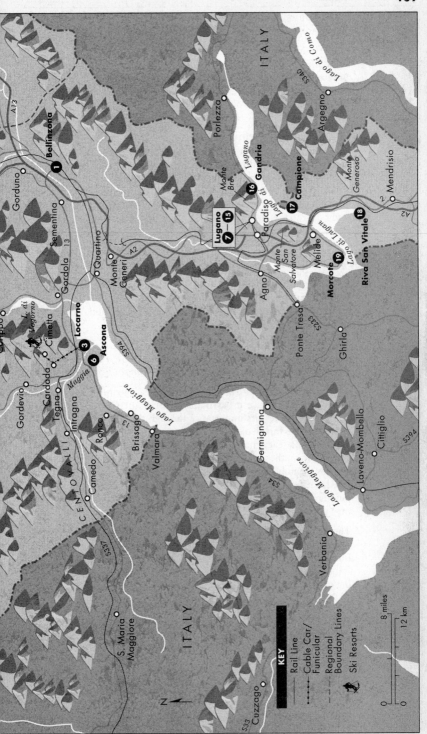

ITALY

Lago di Como

S340

Argegno

Porlezza

Monte
Generoso

Mendrisio

Gandria

Maffe
Brè

Campione

Lago di Lugano

Riva San Vitale

Lugano 7–15

Paradiso

Monte
San
Salvatore

Melide

Morcote

Agno

Ponte Tresa

Ghirla

Citiglio

Laveno-Mombello

Germignana

Lago Maggiore

Verbania

S394

Cuzzago

S33

S. Maria
Maggiore

S337

CENTOVALLI

Camedo

Ronco

Brissago

Valmara

Intragna

Tegna

Gordevio

L. di
Vogorno

Cimetta

Cardada

Maggia

Locarno

Ascona

Monte
Ceneri

Quartino

Gardola

Sementina

Gorduno

Bellinzona

A13

13

S394

S533

S34

Italy

KEY

Rail Line
Cable Car/ Funicular
Regional Boundary Lines
Ski Resorts

0   8 miles

0   12 km

N

and the former fishing village of **Ascona** ⑥, both on the shores of Lake Maggiore.

IF YOU HAVE 3 OR 4 DAYS
In addition to all of the above, explore the medieval fortifications of **Bellinzona** ①, the canton's capital, and tiny **Campione** ⑰, perhaps the most Italian of all Swiss towns. Also take a drive through the wilds of Ticino, into any of the numerous rugged valleys—perhaps **Valle Blenio** ②— where peasant life has carried on virtually unchanged for centuries.

When to Tour Ticino

Lush and Mediterranean, Ticino is gorgeous in springtime; the season starts as early as mid-March here, making the region a popular late-winter escape. In summertime, lakeside activity surges, and the weather can at times be hot. Warm summer nights are incredibly romantic, particularly on the Lago di Lugano. Crowds fill the promenades at Lugano and Locarno throughout summer, but neither waterfront becomes unpleasantly jammed.

SOPRACENERI

Radiating northeast and northwest of Monte Ceneri in Sopraceneri are the mountainous valleys of Valle Blenio, Valle Maggia, Valle Verzasca, Valle Leventina, and the sun-kissed resorts of Locarno and Ascona, both on Italy's famous Lake Maggiore.

Bellinzona

★ ❶ *128 km (79 mi) south of Luzern, 150 km (93 mi) south of Saint-Moritz.*

All roads lead to Bellinzona, the fortified valley city that guards the important European crossroads of the Saint Gotthard and San Bernardino routes. Its importance through the ages makes itself evident: Massive fortified castles—no fewer than three—rise over its ancient center, each named for a strong force: Schwyz, Uri, and Unterwalden, the core cantons of the Swiss Confederation. They were built by the noble Sforza and Visconti families, the dukes of Milan who ruled northern Italy and environs for centuries and held this crucial juncture until 1422, when the Swiss Confederates began a violent century of battling for its control.

The three castles have been exceptionally well restored, and each merits a visit, but the city itself should not be overlooked: It is a classic Lombard town, with graceful architecture and an easy, authentically Italian ambience; it is relatively free of tourists and thus most revealing of the Ticino way of life.

Pick up a map in the tourist office in the **Palazzo Civico** (⊠ Via Camminata, ☎ 091/8252131), a splendid Renaissance structure heavily rebuilt in the 1920s. Its courtyard is framed by two stacked rows of delicate vaulted arcades, with airy loggias at the top. **Old Town,** with its heavy-column arcades, wrought-iron balconies, and shuttered facades, is telling of the direct influence of medieval Lombardy.

The origins of **Castelgrande,** also called the Castle of Uri, date from the 6th century, though the current structure traces to the 1200s. The massive exterior is dominated by two heavy, unmatched towers and the remaining portion of its crenellated wall, which once stretched all the way to the river. Renovations and modern additions have created an elaborate new complex of restaurants (☞ Dining, *below*) and museums, including art and archaeology exhibitions. The newly mounted 14th-century ceiling murals, created to embellish the wooden ceiling of a local villa (now demolished), offer a peek at privately commissioned decorative art. ⊠ *Monte San Michele,* ☎ *091/8258145.* 🎫 *2 SF, 4 SF multiple ticket includes Castello di Montebello and Castello di Sasso Corbaro.* ⊙ *Oct.–Mar., Tues.–Sun. 9–12:30 and 2–4:30; Apr.–Sept., Tues.–Sun. 9–11:30 and 2–5:30.*

The most striking of Bellinzona's three castles is the **Castello di Montebello.** Its oldest, center portion dates from the 13th century; there are a palace and courtyard from the 15th century, with spectacular walkways around the top of the encircling walls. The center structure houses an attractive, modern **Museo Civico** (Civic Museum), with exhibits on local history and architecture, including an impressive collection of Gothic and Renaissance stone capitals. ⊠ *Salita ai Castelli,* ☎ *091/8251342.* 🎫 *2 SF, 4 SF multiple ticket includes Castelgrande and Castello di Sasso Corbaro.* ⊙ *Oct.–May, Tues.–Sun. 10–noon and 2–5; June–Sept., Tues.–Sun. 9–noon and 2–6.*

The lofty **Castello di Sasso Corbaro** (Castle of Sasso Corbaro) is a typical Sforza structure, designed by a Florentine military engineer and built in 1479 for the duke of Milan, who insisted the work be completed in six months. In the dungeon, there's a branch of the **Museo dell'Arte e delle Tradizioni Popolari del Ticino** (Ticino Museum of Popular Arts and Traditions), displaying coins, stamps, historic photographs of Bellinzona, and a fine exhibit of Ticino folk costumes. Ambitious walkers can reach it in about 45 minutes by going uphill from the Castello di Montebello along a switchback road through woods; if you are driving, follow signs. ☎ *091/8255906.* 🎫 *2 SF, 4 SF multiple ticket includes Castello di Montebello and Castelgrande.* ⊙ *Apr.– Oct., Tues.–Sun. 9–noon and 2–5.*

The imposing late-Renaissance facade of the **Chiesa Collegiata di San Pietro e San Stefano** (Church of St. Peter and St. Stephen; ⊠ Piazza Collegiata, ☎ 091/8252605), begun during the 16th century, stands across from the Castelgrande. Its interior is lavishly frescoed in Baroque style by late-18th-century Ticino artists. **Chiesa San Biagio** (Church of St. Biagio), one of Bellinzona's two Italianate churches, is a spare, simple medieval treasure guarded on the exterior by an outsize fresco of a soldierly Christ. The 12th-century late-Romanesque structure suggests a transition into Gothic style. Natural alternating redbrick and gray stone complement fragments of exquisitely colored 14th-century frescoes. ⊠ *Via San Biagio 13, Bellinzona-Ravecchia,* ☎ *091/8252505.*

Built during the end of the 15th century, **Chiesa Santa Maria delle Grazie** (Church of the Holy Virgin Mary) displays a split transept in the Franciscan style, with a dividing wall spectacularly frescoed by an unknown 15th-century Lombard artist. The central image is a crucifixion scene; the surrounding panels depict the life of Christ. ⊠ *Via Convento 5,* ☎ *091/78252663.*

The city's art gallery, **Villa dei Cedri,** sporadically dips into its coffers— made up of a donated private collection—and hangs worthwhile exhibits. Behind the garden and grounds, the city maintains a tiny crop of vines used to produce its very own merlot, available for sale inside. ⊠ *Piazza San Biagio 9,* ☎ *091/8262827.* 🎫 *5 SF.* ⊙ *Mar.–Dec., Tues.–Sun. 10–noon and 2–5.*

Dining

$$–$$$ ✕ **Castelgrande.** Now that the oldest of the city's castles has been ren-
★   ovated, its chic, modern restaurant merits a visit. It's a logical, central place for a serious dining stop. That is, don't expect a quick cafeteria lunch served to shorts-clad tourists: This is a real restaurant, with a daringly cool post-Memphis decor and sophisticated efforts from the

Italian chef: goose liver with blueberries, quail with porcini mushrooms, pigeon and pearl onions in sweet-and-sour sauce. The wine list flaunts more than 70 Ticino merlots. The great terrace has a lighter atmosphere, with views, sunshine, and meals served throughout the day. ⊠ *Monte San Michele,* ☏ *091/8262353. AE, DC, MC, V. Closed Mon.*

$$ ✕ **Osteria Sasso Corbaro.** From the heights of the ancient Castello Sasso Corbaro, this atmospheric restaurant serves meals inside a beautifully restored hall or outside, at stone tables, in the shady, walled-in court-yard. The cooking is simple and regional, with cold and grilled meats, trout, and seasonal vegetables. Good local wines toast a holiday air, as the restaurant opens only in high season. ⊠ *Castello Sasso Corbaro,* ☏ *091/8255532. AE, DC, MC, V. Closed Mon. and Nov.–Apr.*

$–$$ ✕ **Montebello.** At this spot on a hill above the center in the adjoining suburb of Daro, you can relax under a grape arbor at linen-covered tables and enjoy an authentic meal in true Italian style: casual, elegantly simple, and served with easygoing flair. From a standing menu and list of daily specials, sample carpaccio, homemade pasta, and frothy zabaglione (egg whipped with sweet marsala). ⊠ *Via alla Chiesa 3, Bellinzona/Daro,* ☏ *091/8258395. AE, DC, MC, V. Closed Sun.*

En Route　To see the deep countryside of the Ticino—beyond its resorts and cities—follow the A2 expressway north from Bellinzona toward Saint Gotthard; after 17 km (11 mi), exit at **Biasca,** a miniature Bellinzona itself, as it guards two major access roads from the north.

Valle Blenio

❷　*17 km (11 mi) north of Bellinzona, 80 km (49 mi) north of Lugano.*

North of Biasca toward Olivone is the Valle Blenio, a characteristic Ticinese valley cutting deeper and higher into wild, rocky country. Its villages mingle tidy suburban cottages with the architectural signature of Ticino life: ancient stone houses, some little more than huts, with ramshackle roofs of odd-size slab. This is the *rustico* once inhabited by mountain peasants starving under the harsh rule of the Swiss-German confederates. Today the heirs of both those ancient lines happily profit from a new twist: The Ticinese now rent their rustici to wealthy tourists—most of them Swiss-German—who hope to escape the pressures of urban prosperity. In these villages—Largario, Ponto Valentino, Prugiasco—you'll see the real, rural Ticino.

Locarno

❸　*21 km (13 mi) west of Bellinzona, 39 km (24 mi) northwest of Lugano.*

Superbly placed on the sheltered curve of the northernmost tip of Lake Maggiore and surrounded on all sides by mountains, Locarno is Switzerland's sunniest town. Here, subtropical flora flourishes, with date palms and fig trees, bougainvillea, rhododendron, even aloe vera burgeoning on the waterfront. Its fauna is no less colorful: Every spring, summer, and fall the arcaded streets and cafés teem with exotic characters in fur coats and T-shirts, lamé, leather—and sunglasses. You don't show your face in Locarno without a stylish set of shades.

In August, Locarno makes worldwide news with its film festival, showcasing the latest cinema on an outdoor screen in the Piazza Grande; it is also host to international artists in concert. Its facilities haven't just drawn culture hounds: Here, in 1925, Briand, Stresemann, Mussolini, and Chamberlain signed the Locarno Pact, securing the peace—albeit temporarily—in Europe.

Locarno's raison d'être is its waterfront, which has a graceful promenade curving around the east flank of the bay and a beach and public pool complex along the west. Its clear lake is often still as glass, reflecting the Ticinese Alps across to the south. Locarno's Lombard-style shopping arcades and historic landmarks continually draw visitors inland as well.

★ The **Piazza Grande** is the heart of the Old Town and its social center, too: From under the crowded arcades shoppers spill onto open ground to lounge in cafés and watch each other drink, smoke, and pose. **Chiesa Nuova** (New Church; ⊠ Via Cittadella) is an exuberantly decorated Baroque church (1630) with an enormous statue of St. Christopher on the facade. Down the street from Chiesa Nuova, the **Casa dei Canonici** (House of the Canons; ⊠ Via Cittadella) dates from the same period; note the lovely interior courtyard (it's now a private house).

The 17th-century **Chiesa di Sant'Antonio** (Church of St. Anthony) lies at the end of **via Sant'Antonio**, a fine, narrow street lined with splendid old houses in both medieval and flamboyant Baroque styles. Immediately to the right of Chiesa di Sant'Antonio stands the **Casa Rusca,** an 18th-century residence that now serves as the city art gallery. ⊠ *Via Sant'Antonio,* ☎ *091/7563185.* ☜ *5 SF.* ⊙ *Tues.–Sun. 10–noon and 2–5.*

The heavy, frescoed **Chiesa di San Francesco** (Church of St. Francis) and its convent date from the mid-15th century; legend has it that it was founded by St. Anthony of Padua. The emblems on its Renaissance facade show Locarno's social distinctions of the era: The eagle represents the aristocrats; a lamb, the countrymen; and the ox (unkind, surely), the citizens. In its sanctuary, concerts are performed every spring and fall; contact the tourist office (☞ Visitor Information *in* Ticino A to Z, *below*) for more information. ⊠ *Via S. Francesco.*

Built in 1300 as the stronghold of the dukes of Milan, **Castello Visconteo** was soon virtually destroyed by the invading Swiss Confederates. Today it contains a **Museo Municipale e Archeologico** (Municipal and Archaeological Museum), with Roman relics and Romanesque sculpture. ⊠ *Piazza Castello 2,* ☎ *091/7563180.* ☜ *5 SF.* ⊙ *Apr.–Oct., Tues.–Sun. 10–noon and 2–5.*

★ You can get to the **Santuario Madonna del Sasso** (Sanctuary of the Madonna of Sasso) via a five-minute funicular ride to a high plateau (the funicular is close to the train station). The sprawling church complex is where, in 1480, Brother Bartolomeo da Ivrea saw a vision of the Virgin Mary; the sanctuary was begun seven years later and gradually enlarged to include a convent, a museum, and side galleries. Within the sanctuary, you'll find Bramantino's *The Flight to Egypt* (1520) and *Christ Carried to the Sepulcher,* a dramatic, Caravaggiesque procession scene painted in 1870 by Antonio Ciseri, from nearby Ascona. You'll also see naive-art thank-yous to the Madonna from peasants who've survived everything from family tragedies to fender benders. ⊠ *Via Santuario 2, Orselina,* ☎ *091/7436265.* ⊙ *Sanctuary: daily 6:30* AM–8 PM; *church: daily 6:30* AM–7 PM; *museum: weekdays 2–4:30, Sun. 10–noon and 2–5.*

Dining and Lodging

$$$$ ✕ **Centenario.** Set back from the waterfront east of the urban tangle,
★ this gracious ristorante serves innovative Franco-Italian cuisine that is unashamedly nouvelle and absolutely top quality, from its moderately priced business lunch to the all-out *menu de dégustation* (sampling menu). Specialties include risotto in merlot with crayfish tails, rack of roe deer, and tangy lemon soufflé. You can have an aperitif on the lakefront ter-

race before sitting down to a meal amid quarry tile, Persian rugs, and gleaming silver. ⊠ *Lungolago 13, Locarno-Muralto,* ☎ *091/7438222. AE, DC, MC, V. Closed Sun. and Mon.*

$$$$ ✕🏠 **Reber au Lac.** This richly landscaped oasis at the end of the waterfront row holds a roomy, comfortable holiday hotel dating from 1886, with enough amenities—spacious garden, big pool, bathing beach, sheltered terrace dining—to make up for some bold decor. Awning-shaded balconies overlook the lake or pool, and interiors are done in tasteful pastels. Although taking demipension is stressed here, the Grill Room has a reputation with locals for the Franco-Italian cuisine it serves in a Spanish setting. ⊠ *Viale Verbano 55, CH-6600 Locarno-Muralto,* ☎ *091/7358700,* 𝖥𝖠𝖷 *091/7358701. 60 rooms, 8 suites. 2 restaurants, 2 bars, no-smoking rooms, pool, sauna, tennis court, beach, business services. AE, DC, MC, V.*

$$–$$$ ✕🏠 **Belvedere.** Well above the city and somewhat blocked from the
★ best lake views by other developments, this Belle Epoque hotel has gone all out, with interiors in postmodern beech, lacquer, and marble. All rooms face south. There's extra architectural interest in the building's historic core: It started as a private home in 1680, and its florid dining hall remains, with frescoes, elaborately trimmed vaults, and a massive stone fireplace. The combination of gracefully old and smartly new works well, and miles of glass bathe the public areas in sunlight. L'Affresco, the formal restaurant, serves upscale Italian specialties; the Palme has less expensive Italian fare; and the Wintergarden Restaurant basks in the sun with views of the lake, city, and mountains. You can reach the Belvedere by funicular from the train station or on foot in a five-minute uphill walk. ⊠ *Via ai Monti della Trinità 44, CH-6601,* ☎ *091/7510363,* 𝖥𝖠𝖷 *091/7515239. 80 rooms, 12 suites. 3 restaurants, bar, no-smoking rooms, pool, hot tub, sauna, health club, bicycles, playground, business services. AE, DC, MC, V.*

$$–$$$ ✕🏠 **Cittadella.** This popular dining spot in the Old Town along a narrow, historic street offers inexpensive regional food—pizzas, pastas, simple fish—in its casual downstairs trattoria and fine fish dishes in the more formal restaurant upstairs. The preparation is light, the flavors subtle with oils and herbs. Since the restaurant opened hotel rooms upstairs, it has become more commercial and a mite self-promoting. ⊠ *Via Cittadella 18, CH-6600,* ☎ *091/7515885,* 𝖥𝖠𝖷 *091/7517759. 10 rooms. Restaurant. AE, DC, MC, V. Restaurant closed Mon.*

$$ ✕🏠 **Dell'Angelo.** At the end of the Piazza Grande and the long row
★ of Lombardy arcades, this friendly downtown hotel fits right in: It was based on a 1674 structure, with ground-floor arches and iron-trim balconies. Walnut-grain Formica and beige stucco fill the hospital-spare rooms. A lively pizzeria at street level serves pizzas cooked in a wood-burning oven and grilled meats, and you can choose from the same menu in the restaurant upstairs, where you'll eat amid chintz and damask under the faded remains of frescoed vaulting. ⊠ *Piazza Grande, CH-6601,* ☎ *091/7518175,* 𝖥𝖠𝖷 *091/7518256. 49 rooms. Restaurant, pizzeria. AE, DC, MC, V.*

$$ ✕🏠 **Hotel Navegna.** It may not look like much from outside, but this
★ is a true diamond in the rough, right on the lake farther up shore from the promenade. The rooms and decor have recently been entirely refurbished. The inventive Ticinese cooking and desserts earn raves for gregarious owner Enrico Ravelli, a former chef in London, Paris, and Florida. Navegna is close to rail tracks (luckily there are no night trains) so you may wish to request a lake view. ⊠ *Via alla Riva 2, CH-6648 Locarno-Munusio,* ☎ *091/7432222,* 𝖥𝖠𝖷 *091/7433150. 22 rooms. 2 restaurants, bicycles. MC, V. Closed Nov.–mid-Mar.*

$$$ 🏠 **Beau-Rivage.** Small and genteel in a row of ostentatious competi-
★ tors, this lodging built in 1900 (renovated in 1994) retains its gracious

sitting rooms, low vaulting, and terrazzo floors. Although lakeside rooms can be spare and boxy, the views are picture-perfect; back rooms overlook a lush subtropical garden. More trees surround the dining room, which has picture windows that open toward the lake. Demipension is standard. ⊠ *Viale Verbano 31, CH-6600,* ☎ *091/7431355,* FAX *091/7439409. 50 rooms. Restaurant, no-smoking rooms. AE, DC, MC, V. Closed Dec.–Feb.*

Nightlife and the Arts

BARS

Amalur Music Bar (⊠ Via Torretta 7, ☎ 091/7516414) is open year-round; it keeps going until 3 AM or 4 AM. **La Bussola** (⊠ Lungolago, Locarno-Muralto, ☎ 091/7436095) is a favorite among locals; it's closed on Tuesday. **Palm'Arte** (⊠ Hotel La Palma au Lac, viale Verbano 29, Locarno-Muralto, ☎ 091/7353636) is a good piano bar; it's closed Tuesday during the high season and from December to February.

CASINO

The **Kursaal** (Casino; ⊠ Via Largo Zorzi 1, Piazza Grande, ☎ 091/7511535) has 195 slot machines and *boule* (a casino game popular in Switzerland, with a federally imposed 5 SF limit).

FILM

The **Locarno International Film Festival,** gaining ground from Cannes on the prestige front because of the caliber of the films it premieres, takes place every August in the Piazza Grande. In 1999, it runs August 4–14; for information, call ☎ 091/7510232.

MUSIC

From March through July, Locarno hosts **Concerti di Locarno,** offering a series of classical concerts in the Chiesa San Francesco, the Sala Sopracenerina (a conference hall with good acoustics), and the courtyard of the Castello Visconteo. Contact the tourist office for information. (☞ Visitor Information *in* Ticino A to Z, *below*)

OFF THE BEATEN PATH | **CIMETTA** – A winter sports center with views of Monte Rosa, the Swiss Alps, and the Italian Apennines, Cimetta (1,672 m/5,482 ft) can be reached only by chairlift; first you must catch a cable car (near the train station) to Cardada, then a chairlift to the resort. But don't be put off; the ride is part of the fun: As the lake falls away beneath, you sail over flowery meadows and wooded hills. Cimetta is also a hiker's paradise. Renovations are currently being made on both the cable car and chairlift, with reopening planned for spring 1999.

Valle Verzasca

❹ *12 km (7 mi) north of Locarno, 25 km (15½ mi) north of Lugano.*

A short drive along the A13 highway through the wild and rugged mountain gorge of the Valle Verzasca leads to **Corippo,** where a painterly composition of stone houses and a 17th-century church are all protected as architectural landmarks.

About 12 km (7 mi) north of Corippo, in the town of **Lavertezzo,** you'll find a graceful double-arch stone bridge, **Ponte dei Salti,** dating from 1700. The mountain village of Sonogno lies at the end of the 26-km (16-mi) valley.

Valle Maggia

❺ *4 km (2 mi) northwest of Locarno, 30 km (19 mi) northwest of Lugano.*

A drive through this rugged agricultural valley that stretches northwest from Locarno will give you a sense of the tough living conditions endured for centuries by Ticinese peasants, who today mine granite. The valley is cut so far into the earth that sunlight in winter never seems to reaches bottom—a stark contrast to sunny Locarno only a short distance south. Until the 1920s many Valle Maggia natives immigrated to the United States; some returned, bringing with them several English phrases that still pepper the local Ticinese dialect. As you pass through Gordevio, Maggia, Someo, and Cevio—the valley's main village—you'll feel as if you're in a time capsule: There's little commercialization, and the mostly 17th-century houses call to mind a movie set. Bignasco, just beyond Cevio, is the last village before the valley splits in two continuing north.

OFF THE BEATEN PATH **MOGNO** – Beyond Bignasco to the east lies the Valle Lavizzara. There, in tiny Mogno, stands a beautiful, modernist chapel built in 1994 by world-renowned Ticinese architect Mario Botta, who designed the San Francisco Museum of Modern Art. Every Tuesday from April to October, the Locarno tourist office (☞ Visitor Information *in* Ticino A to Z, *below*) leads an excursion and guided tour from Locarno.

Ascona

❻ *3 km (1¼ mi) west of Locarno.*

Though it's only a few minutes from Locarno, tiny Ascona has a life of its own. Little more than a fishing village until the turn of the century, the town was discovered and adopted by a high-minded group of northerners who arrived to develop a utopian, vegetarian artists' colony on **Monte Verità** (☎ 091/7910181), the hillside park behind the waterfront center. Influenced by Eastern and Western religions as well as the new realms of psychology, its ideals attracted thousands of sojourners, including dancer Isadora Duncan and psychologist C. G. Jung. You can visit the group of Monte Verità buildings, including the unusual flat-roof wooden **Casa Anatta,** and view papers and relics of the group's works. ⊠ *Monte Verità, between waterfront and town center,* ☎ *091/7910327.* 🎟 *6 SF.* ☉ *Apr.–June, Sept., and Oct., Tues.–Sun. 2:30–6; July and Aug., Tues.–Sun. 3–7.*

Monte Verità's influence spread through Ascona, its reputation grew throughout the world, and today the still-small village of 5,000 attracts artists, art restorers, and traditional bookbinders to its ancient, narrow streets. On the waterfront, however, it's a sun-and-fun scene, with ★ the **Piazza Motta** (isolated from traffic as a pedestrian zone) crowded with sidewalk cafés and the promenade on the water's edge swarming with boats. Behind Piazza Motta, a charming labyrinth of lanes leads uphill past artisan galleries (not all showing gallery-quality work) to **via Borgo,** lined with contemporary shops and galleries.

OFF THE BEATEN PATH **BRISSAGO ISLANDS** – From Ascona, an easy excursion by car or bus leads to Brissago, a flowery lakefront resort at the lowest elevation in Switzerland. The main attraction, however, lies offshore: The Brissago Islands, two floral gems floating in Lake Maggiore, have been federally preserved as botanical gardens, with more than 1,000 species of subtropical plants. Plaques identify the flora in Italian, German, and French; an English guide to the plants is for sale at the gate (3 SF). You may have lunch or drinks at the island's restaurant, in a beautifully restored 1929 villa that now doubles as a seminar center and offers lodging to groups. Individuals must leave with the last boat back to the mainland—

usually around 6—so check schedules carefully when you plan your excursion. ✉ *Boats depart regularly from Brissago, Porto Ronco, Ascona, and Locarno,* ☎ *091/7914361.* ⛴ *Boat: 19 SF round-trip; island: 6 SF. Buy ticket at entrance or with boat ticket; group and Swiss Boat Pass (☞ Boat Travel in the Gold Guide) discounts apply.*

Dining and Lodging

$$–$$$ ✕ **Da Ivo.** Run by the same family for nearly 30 years, with son Ivo replacing his father in the kitchen, this Ascona institution has something for everyone: fresh, straightforward regional standards as well as refined, contemporary dishes. In the cozy interior, you can dine near a huge fireplace, its flickering glow reflected in the copper pots hanging nearby; in the idyllic arbored garden, ladder-back chairs, and fresh flowers set the informal, summery tone. Specials may include delicate leek tart, *linguetti neri* (pasta flavored with squid ink) with seafood, or Ticino-style lamb with rosemary. ✉ *Via Collegio 11,* ☎ *091/ 7911031. No credit cards. Closed Mon. and late Dec.–mid-Mar.*

$$ ✕ **Ristorante Stazione.** West of Locarno in the picturesque Centovalli is Intragna. Near this tiny burg's train station, you will find this little gem. Agnese Broggini has spent almost 30 years offering a bright, cheerful place to stop and have a special meal of risotto, chicken, or other Ticino specialties. Sixty varieties of merlot are offered. ✉ *Intragna,* ☎ *091/7911212. AE, DC, MC, V.*

$$$$ ✕🏨 **Giardino.** This Relais & Châteaux property would make the Great
★ Gatsby feel in his element; it's as glamorous and atmospheric as a Mediterranean villa. Portuguese ceramics, Florentine floor tiles, Veronese marble, ceramic room-number plaques in della Robbia style, and even a Swiss-Baroque carved-wood conference chamber from Zürich's Bierhalle Kropf have been imported. The luxury borders on decadence: The sheets are pure linen, every room has the latest toilet-bidet combination, and there's a landscaped pool, not to mention a chauffeured Bentley, an antique-bus shuttle service, and pink bicycles for guest use. The restaurants are excellent: Giardino rates among the best in Switzerland for international cuisine; Aphrodite falls not far behind with its vegetarian and Italian specialties. Varied weekly programs include a sunrise mountaintop breakfast, dinner on the hotel's boat, literary/culinary evenings, Sunday classical music performances, and simple hikes and bike tours. Children's activities are organized from mid-July to mid-August. Prepare to be spoiled. ✉ *Via Segnale 10, CH-6612,* ☎ *091/ 7910101,* FAX *091/7921094. 54 rooms, 18 suites, 5 apartments. 3 restaurants, bar, pool, beauty salon, hot tub, steam room, bicycles, cabaret, baby-sitting. AE, DC, MC, V. Closed mid-Nov.–mid-Mar.*

$$$–$$$$ 🏨 **Casa Berno.** This Relais du Silence hotel on a forest road far above the town and lake is tucked into a hillside near the top, so the anonymous rows of concrete balconies offend no one but offer everyone panoramic views—from the Islands of Brissago to Bellinzona. Its absolute isolation and self-containment (there's even a magazine-and-tobacco shop in the lobby) and the aura of dated gentility, projected by the avocado brocade and Picasso prints in cream frames, appeal to relaxed vacationers who want to laze by the big pool overlooking the lake, have drinks and lunch on the broad roof terrace, and get away from it all—completely. Demipension is standard, but menus can be modified. ✉ *CH-6612,* ☎ *091/7913232,* FAX *091/7911114. 65 rooms. 2 restaurants, bar, café, pool, massage, sauna, health club. AE, DC, MC, V. Closed Nov.–Mar.*

$$$–$$$$ 🏨 **Castello Seeschloss.** Dating from 1250 and now completely rebuilt
★ within, this is a romantic enough hotel as is—not even taking into account its garden setting and position across from the waterfront. Its interior is rich with frescoes, beams, vaults, and heavy masonry; other-

wise the decor is light and contemporary—in some cases even industrial-modern. There are a private courtyard for summer-night dining and an isolated pool. Honeymooners, take note: Deluxe rooms in the towers start at prices not much higher than standard doubles and offer lavish appointments. Some rooms even have original 16th- to 18th-century frescoes. ⊠ *Piazza Motta, CH-6612,* ☎ *091/7910161,* 𝖥𝖠𝖷 *091/7911804. 45 rooms. Restaurant, bar, no-smoking rooms, pool, meeting room. AE, DC, MC, V. Closed mid-Nov.–mid-Mar.*

$$$ ⊞ **Tamaro.** Occupying a vaulted and shuttered 17th-century patrician
★ house on the waterfront, this Romantik property really earns the parent company's name: The sitting rooms are richly furnished with antiques, books, and even a grand piano, and the restaurants have a sunny, Mediterranean air that isn't at all contrived. The rooms range from lavish corner doubles with lake views and reproductions of antiques to tiny, bathless quarters overlooking the courtyard that are an excellent value. It's right on the waterfront, and its restaurant and café fill quickly on sunny days. There's a private sun terrace high over the street with fine lake views; you may feel you're on the beach. ⊠ *Piazza G. Motta 35, CH-6612,* ☎ *091/7910282,* 𝖥𝖠𝖷 *091/7912928. 51 rooms. Restaurant, café, pool, bicycles. AE, DC, MC, V. Closed Dec.–Feb.*

$$ ⊞ **Piazza.** This tidy, modest member of the familial Minotel chain, in the middle of the Piazza Motta, looks first and foremost like a coffee shop or café, and you have to wend your way through crowded tables to get to the reception area. The throngs are enjoying at ground level what you'll see better from your room: the pollards, park benches, and blue expanse of the waterfront. The rooms can be tiny, but they're remarkably well planned, with carefully built-in amenities and all-tile baths. (Cheaper rooms are available in the *dépendence,* or neighboring annex, just uphill, but they lack furniture and have a scarlet-and-gold decor dating from the '70s.) ⊠ *Lungolago G. Motta 29, CH-6612,* ☎ *091/7911181,* 𝖥𝖠𝖷 *091/7912757. 24 rooms. Restaurant, café, business services. AE, DC, MC, V. Closed Nov.–Feb.*

Nightlife and the Arts

The ideals that brought Isadora Duncan here still bring culture to Ascona: Every year it hosts the **Ascona New Orleans Jazz** (late June–July), a series of world-class classical music concerts (August–October), and a festival of marionettes (September). The lakefront piazza serves as an open-air stage for almost daily summer entertainment, with mime, theater, and live pop bands. Locarno's August film festival is only a cab ride away across the peninsula.

BARS AND DANCING

Al Lago (⊠ Via Moscia 2, ☎ 091/7910603) is a discotheque for young people, with a piano bar upstairs. Younger disco enthusiasts flock to **Happyville** (⊠ Fontanelle 3, ☎ 091/7914922). More sedate dancers go to **Lello Bar** (⊠ Via Aerodromo 3, ☎ 091/7911374) for live music. **La Tana** (⊠ Via Locarno 110, ☎ 091/7911381) has an orchestra and striptease acts. Note that most bars and clubs are only open during the tourist season (Easter–late October), but La Tana is open year-round.

MUSIC

Ascona New Orleans Jazz (☎ 091/7910090) seeks out performers a cut above standard Dixieland and swing groups and brings them to its open-air bandstands; in 1999 the festival will run from late June to early July. The **Settimane Musicali** (Musical Weeks; ☎ 091/7910093) bring in full orchestras, chamber groups, and top-ranking soloists to Ascona and Locarno; in 1999 they will run from late August to late October.

THEATER

Ascona hosts an **International Festival of Marionettes** with a full schedule of plays—most of them for adults rather than children—from around the world. Most performances take place in the **Teatro San Materno** (⌧ Via San Materno 3, ☎ 091/7918566); in 1999 the performances will run from early to mid-September. The **Teatro di Locarno** (⌧ Kursaal Casino, via Largo Zorzi 1, ☎ 091/7510333) hosts international theatrical companies year-round.

SOTTOCENERI

The Sottoceneri includes the more developed business and resort towns of the south, the foremost being Lugano.

Lugano

❼–**⓯** *45 km (28 mi) southeast of Ascona, 39 km (24 mi) southeast of Locarno.*

Strung around a sparkling bay like Venetian glass beads, with dark, conical mountains rising primordially out of its waters and icy peaks framing the scene, Lugano earns its nickname as the Rio of the Old World. Of the three world-class lake resorts that dominate the waterfront, Lugano tops Ascona and Locarno for architectural style, sophistication, and natural beauty. This is not to say that it has avoided the pitfalls of a successful, modern resort: There's thick traffic right up to the waterfront, much of it manic Italian style, and it has more than its share of concrete waterfront high-rise hotels with balconies skewed to produce "a room with a view" regardless of aesthetic cost. Yet the sacred *passeggiata*—the afternoon stroll to see and be seen that winds down every Italian day—asserts the city's true personality as a graceful, sophisticated old-world resort—not Swiss, not Italian . . . just Lugano.

Much of Lugano—and indeed much of the landscape beyond—can be seen in an afternoon's walk. The **waterfront promenade,** lined with pollarded lime trees, funereal cypresses, and palm trees, affords stunning mountain views: straight ahead, the rocky top of **Monte Generoso** (1,702 m/5,579 ft); flanking the bay at right and left, respectively, the dark wooded masses of **Monte San Salvatore** and **Monte Brè.** The waterfront is also home to another, less natural attraction: the **Casino,** where bets are limited by law to 5 SF.

The serious view hound may want to take at least one **funicular** excursion, up either Monte San Salvatore (☎ 091/9852828) or Monte Brè (☎ 091/9713171). The latter's summit can be reached by car as well. The San Salvatore funicular departs from Paradiso; the Monte Brè funicular, from Cassarate (just east of Lugano). Both afford stunning lake-ward views.

❼ The **Parco Civico** (Town Park) has cacti, exotic shrubs, and more than 1,000 varieties of roses, as well as an aviary, a tiny deer zoo, and another fine view of the bay from its peninsula. ⌧ *Area south of viale Carlo Cattaneo, east of Piazza Castello.* ⌚ *Free.*

❽ In the Parco Civico, the canton's **Museo Cantonale di Storia Naturale** (Museum of Natural History) contains exhibits on animals, plants, and mushrooms, mostly those typical of the region. ⌧ *Viale Cattaneo 4,* ☎ *091/9237827.* ⌚ *Free.* ☉ *Tues.–Sat. 9–noon and 2–5.*

OFF THE BEATEN PATH **VILLA FAVORITA** – This splendid 16th-century mansion in Castagnola houses a portion of the extraordinary private art collection of the Baron von Thyssen-Bornemisza. The villa gardens also have native and exotic

Lugano

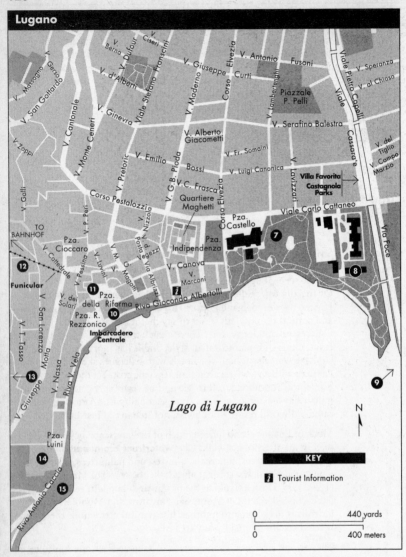

Cattedrale di
San Lorenzo, **12**
Chiesa di Santa Maria
degli Angioli, **14**
Giardino
Belvedere, **15**
Lido, **9**
Museo Cantonale di
Storia Naturale, **8**

Palazzo Civico, **10**
Parco Civico, **7**
Parco del Tassino, **13**
Piazza della
Riforma, **11**

flora. Although, after a scandalous international divorce battle, portions of the collection were temporarily transferred to Spain, a significant display of 19th- and 20th-century paintings and watercolors from Europe and America remains, shown to better advantage than ever in the totally renovated space. Artists represented include Thomas Hart Benton, Giorgio de Chirico, Frederick Church, Lucien Freud, Edward Hopper, Franz Marc, Jackson Pollock, and Andrew Wyeth. Take Bus 1 in the direction of Castagnola or take the 40-minute walk from town. You may want to call ahead, as opening hours and entrance fees can change during special exhibitions. ⊠ *Strada Castagnola, via Rivera 14,* ☎ *091/9721741.* 🖾 *10 SF.* ⊘ *Apr.–Oct., Fri.–Sun. 10–5.*

CASTAGNOLA PARKS – For an idyllic daytime excursion, combine a trip to the Villa Favorita (☞ *above*) with one or both of the parks that neighbor it. The **Parco degli Ulivi** (Olive Park) spreads over the lower slopes of Monte Brè and offers a romantic landscape of silvery olive trees mixed with cypress, laurel, and wild rosemary; you enter it from the Gandria Footpath (Sentiero di Gandria). **Parco San Michele** (St. Michael Park), also on Monte Brè, has a public chapel and a broad terrace that overlooks the city, the lake, and, beyond, the Alps. From Cassarate, walk up the steps by the lower terminus of the Monte Brè funicular.

⑨ The city's **lido** is a stretch of sandy beach with two swimming pools and a restaurant; to reach it, you'll have to cross the Cassarate River, follow the riverbank left to the main street, viale Castagnola, and then turn right; the main lido entrance is just ahead on your right. ☎ *091/ 9714041,* 🖾 *6 SF, changing cabins 3 SF.* ⊘ *May and Sept., daily 9– 6; June and mid–late Aug., daily 9–7; July–mid-Aug., daily 9–7:30.*

⑩ Toward Lugano's center, the pompous **Palazzo Civico** (Town Hall) is a neoclassical structure dating from 1844. Across the street, steamers depart for Lake Lugano from the **Imbarcadero Centrale.** ⊠ *Piazza Civico.*

★ ⑪ The Luganese and their visitors spend endless hours in the lively piazzas that dominate the center of town. **Piazza della Riforma** is so nearly filled with tables it's as if the cafés owned it. Closer to the shore is **Piazza Rezzonico.** Via Luvini is the entrance to the **Old Town,** where narrow streets are lined with chic Italian clothing shops and small markets offering pungent local cheeses and porcini mushrooms. German-Swiss culture subtly asserts itself at lunch stands, where *panini* (small sandwiches) are made not only of prosciutto, tuna, or mozzarella but of sauerkraut and sausage as well.

⑫ The **Cattedrale di San Lorenzo** (Cathedral of St. Lawrence) has a Renaissance exterior and richly frescoed Baroque interior. At the bottom of the staircase leading down and west from the cathedral, a **funicular** mounts from Piazza Cioccaro to the train station. ⊠ *Via Cattedrale.* 🖾 *Free.*

⑬ The luxuriously manicured **Parco del Tassino** lies on a plateau behind the train station and offers lovely bay views from among its rose gardens. Its small deer park and playground make it very child-friendly. ⊠ *Take Bus 2 east to San Domenico stop in Castagnola, or use the funicular from Old Town to the train station.* 🖾 *Free.*

★ ⑭ Via Nassa, Lugano's main shopping street, opens onto the **Piazza Luini,** where the **Chiesa di Santa Maria degli Angioli** (Church of St. Mary of the Angels; ⊠ Piazza Luini), begun in 1455, merits a visit. It contains a magnificent fresco of the *Passion and Crucifixion,* by Bernardino Luini (1475–1532); admission is free. An incongruous **statue of George Washington** stands across the Piazza Luini from Chiesa di Santa Maria degli Angioli. In fact, Washington never visited

Lugano, though this image was erected in 1859 by a grateful Swiss engineer who had made his fortune in America.

⓯ The waterfront **Giardino Belvedere** (Belvedere Gardens) frames a dozen modern sculptures with palms, camellias, oleanders, and magnolias. At the far end there's public swimming. ⊠ *Quai Riva Caccia,* ☎ *091/ 9942035.* ⊑ *4 SF.* ☉ *Mid-May–mid-Sept., daily 9:30–7:30.*

OFF THE
BEATEN PATH
SWISSMINIATUR – Of infinite novelty and surprisingly high quality, this child's paradise is a detailed model of the architectural highlights of Switzerland, built in stone on a scale of 1:25. There's a tiny Chillon, the Cathedral of Lausanne, the Parliament buildings of Bern, a recent reproduction of the Lausanne Olympic Museum, and exquisitely detailed reproductions of Swiss trains, boats, and cable-car systems—all fully functional. Carefully landscaped on the waterfront, the park has a playground for kids who lose interest while Dad is still watching the trains. If you're driving, take the highway going south (direction Mendrisio–Chiasso) and exit at Melide; the train from Lugano to Melide stops right in front of the park. ⊠ *Melide, below Lugano,* ☎ *091/6497951.* ⊑ *10.50 SF.* ☉ *Mid-Mar.–Oct., daily 9–6.*

Dining and Lodging

$$$$ ✕ **Al Portone.** Silver and lace dress up the stucco and stone here, but
★ the ambience is strictly easy, never formal. Chef Roberto Galizzi pursues *nuova cucina* (contemporary cuisine, Italian style) with ambition and flair, and he rarely resorts to gimmickry while putting local spins on Italian classics. You might choose roast veal kidneys with balsamic vinegar, lobster salad, seafood carpaccio, or simple creamed potatoes with priceless white truffle. Or you could *lascia fare a Roberto* (leave it to Robert)—as he calls his menu *de dégustation.* ⊠ *Viale Cassarate 3, Lugano/Cassarate,* ☎ *091/9235511 or 091/9235988. AE, DC, MC, V. Closed Sun. and Mon.*

$$$ ✕ **Galleria.** Though the decor aspires to formal hauteur, with its contemporary appointments and very modern art, family warmth permeates the restaurant, making it a comfortable source of good traditional Italian cooking: pasta, veal favorites, and good, plain grilled fish, as well as a fine little list of local and Italian wines. ⊠ *Via Cantonale 4, Lugano/Manno,* ☎ *091/6108761. AE, DC, MC, V. Closed Sun., 2nd and 3rd wks of Aug.*

$$$ ✕ **Locanda del Boschetto.** The grill is the first thing you see in this no-
★ nonsense, low-key ristorante, a specialist in pure and simple seafood *alla griglia* (grilled). The decor is a study in linen and rustic wood, and the service is helpful and down to earth. ⊠ *Via Boschetto 8,* ☎ *091/ 9942493. AE, DC, MC, V. Closed Mon., 1st and 2nd wks of Nov.*

$$$ ✕ **Santabbondio.** Ancient stone and terra-cotta blend with pristine pas-
★ tels in this upgraded grotto, where subtle, imaginative new Franco-Italian cuisine *du marché* (menus based on fresh market produce)—delicately sauced seafood, painterly desserts—is served in intimate, formal little dining rooms and on a shady terrace. Watch for lobster risotto, scallops in orange-basil sauce, or eggplant ravioli to confirm what locals assert: Chef Martin Dalsass is the canton's best. There's a good selection of open wines. You'll need a cab to get here, but it's worth the trip. ⊠ *Via Fomelino 10, Lugano/Sorengo,* ☎ *091/9932388. AE, DC, MC, V. Closed Mon., 1st wk of Jan., last wk of Feb. No lunch Sat., no dinner Sun.*

$$ ✕ **Al Barilotto.** Despite its generic pizzeria decor and American-style salad bar, this restaurant draws local crowds for grilled meats, homemade pastas, and wood-oven pizza. Take Bus 10 from the city center; the restaurant, inside Hotel de la Paix, is uphill from the main lakefront road. ⊠ *Hotel de la Paix, via Calloni 18, Lugano/Paradiso,* ☎ *091/9949695. AE, DC, MC, V.*

$ ✕ **La Tinera.** Tucked down an alley off via Pessina in the Old Town,
★ this cozy basement taverna squeezes loyal locals and tourists onto
wooden benches for authentic regional specialties, hearty meats, and
pastas. Regional wine is served in traditional ceramic bowls. ⊠ *Via
dei Gorini 2,* ☎ *091/9235219. AE, DC, MC, V. Closed Sun., Aug.*

$ ✕ **Sayonara.** There's nothing Japanese about this place: It's a modern
urban pizzeria, with several rooms that fill at lunch with a mix of tourists
and shoppers. The old copper polenta pot stirs automatically year-round,
and polenta is offered in several combinations, sometimes with mountain hare. ⊠ *Via F. Soave 10,* ☎ *091/9220170. AE, DC, MC, V.*

$$$$ ▢ **Splendide Royale.** This landmark was first converted from a villa to
★ a hotel in 1887, and much of the Victorian luster of its public spaces—
with their marble, pillars, terrazzo, and antiques—has been respectfully
preserved. Since a new wing was added in the '80s, you can choose between solid, well-constructed lodgings decorated in sleek beech, beige,
and gold or more florid period rooms in the original wing. All rooms
are air-conditioned, and there's an attractive S-shape indoor pool.
Rooms offer lake or garden views from their balconies or terraces. The
restaurant La Veranda serves classic French standards to live piano music.
⊠ *Riva A. Caccia 7, CH-6900,* ☎ *091/9857711,* 𝔽𝔸𝕏 *091/9948931 or
091/9857722. 97 rooms, 4 suites. Restaurant, bar, indoor pool, massage, sauna, business services, 3 meeting rooms. AE, DC, MC, V.*

$$$$ ▢ **Ticino.** In this warmly appointed 16th-century row house (protected
★ as a historical monument) in the heart of the Old Town, shuttered windows look out from every room onto a glassed-in garden and courtyard, and there are vaulted halls lined with art and antiques. The
formal restaurant, full of dark-wood wainscoting and leather banquettes,
serves Ticinese specialties. It's a Romantik property, only steps away
from the funicular to the station. ⊠ *Piazza Cioccaro 1, CH-6901,* ☎
091/9227772, 𝔽𝔸𝕏 *091/9236278. 20 rooms. Restaurant, no-smoking
rooms, business services. AE, DC, MC, V. Closed Jan.*

$$$$ ▢ **Villa Principe Leopoldo/Hotel Montalbano.** This extravagantly fur-
★ nished garden mansion, on a hillside high over the lake (Collina d'Oro,
or Golden Hill), offers old-world service and splendor to match. It was
built in 1868 on behalf of Prince Leopold of Hohenzollen. There's a
stunningly arranged pool-and-terrace complex encircled by a double staircase—a slightly Baroque touch of Bel Air. Free transportation to the airport and town is provided. ⊠ *Via Montalbano 5, CH-6900,* ☎ *091/
9858855,* 𝔽𝔸𝕏 *091/9858825. 74 rooms, 4 suites. 2 restaurants, bar, no-
smoking rooms, pool, hot tub, massage, sauna, indoor golf, tennis
court, health club, playground, business services. AE, DC, MC, V.*

$$$–$$$$ ▢ **Du Lac.** This discreet and simple hotel offers more lakefront luxury
than do some glossier hotels down the same beach. Owned by one fam-
ily since it was founded in 1920, Du Lac was rebuilt in 1962 and ren-
ovated over the past few years. Its walls are decked with needlework
art reproductions handmade by its owner. All rooms face the lake; those
on the sixth floor are the quietest and have warm, sleek decor. The hotel
has a private swimming area on the lake. ⊠ *Riva Paradiso 3, CH-6902
Lugano/Paradiso,* ☎ *091/9941921,* 𝔽𝔸𝕏 *091/9941122. 52 rooms, 1 suite.
Restaurant, bar, no-smoking rooms, pool, whirlpool bath, massage,
sauna, exercise room, beach, meeting room. AE, DC, MC, V. Closed
Dec.–Feb.*

$$$ ▢ **Alba.** This solid little hotel, isolated on its own landscaped grounds
★ and lavish inside to the extreme, is ideal for lovers with a sense of camp
or honeymooners looking for romantic privacy. Mirrors, gilt, plush,
and crystal adorn the public areas, and the beds are all ruffles and swags.
The garden is studded with palms—a lovely place for a drink. ⊠ *Via*

delle Scuole 11, CH-6902 Lugano-Paradiso, ☏ *091/9943731,* ℻ *091/9944523. 20 rooms, 1 suite. Restaurant, bar, pool. AE, DC, MC, V.*

$$$ 🏨 **Belmonte.** Five minutes from Villa Favorita, this tall, sun-bleached hotel has a Mediterranean facade of white stucco with tall, powder-blue shutters framing some 40-odd individual balconies. Every room offers a superb view over Lake Lugano, which seems miles below. The terrace in front of the hotel is shaded by a large yellow awning and makes a good spot for lunch or afternoon drinks. ⊠ *Via Serenella 29, CH-6976 Lugano-Castagnola,* ☏ *091/9714033,* ℻ *091/9726139. 45 rooms. Pool. Closed Dec.–Mar.*

$$$ 🏨 **International au Lac.** Just a stone's throw from the lake, this big, old-fashioned, friendly hotel offers many lake-view rooms. The interiors are floridly decorated with Baroque reproductions, heavy plush furniture, and a Victorian dining hall in a tower bay. It's next to the Church of St. Mary of the Angels, on the edge of the shopping district and the Old Town. ⊠ *Via Nassa 68, CH-6901,* ☏ *091/9227541,* ℻ *091/9227544. 80 rooms. Restaurant, pool, free parking. AE, DC, MC, V. Closed Nov.–Mar.*

$$–$$$ 🏨 **Park-Hotel Nizza.** On the lower slopes of Monte San Salvatore and
★ well above the lake, this former villa is an attractive mix of luxurious parlors and modern comforts. Most rooms are small, either with mixed antique reproductions or modern decor; lake panoramic views don't cost extra. An ultramodern bar—of silver vinyl and glass—overlooks the lake, as does a good restaurant that serves vegetable dishes (and even wine) from the hotel's own garden. Summer meals are served in the garden, and there's a weekly special farmer's breakfast and evening cocktail party. It's a hike into town, but there's a shuttle service to Paradiso. ⊠ *Via Guidino 14, CH-6902 Lugano-Paradiso,* ☏ *091/9941771,* ℻ *091/9941773. 29 rooms. 2 restaurants, bar, no-smoking rooms, pool, whirlpool bath, children's playground, business services, free parking. AE, DC, MC, V. Closed mid-Dec.–mid.-Mar.*

$$ 🏨 **San Carlo.** Ideally located on the main shopping street, a block from the waterfront, and only 150 yards from the funicular, this friendly but no-frills hotel is clean, small, quiet, and freshly furnished (it was renovated in 1997); it's one of the better deals in town. ⊠ *Via Nassa 28, CH-6900,* ☏ *091/9227107,* ℻ *091/9228022. 22 rooms. Breakfast room. AE, DC, MC, V.*

$ 🏨 **Flora.** Though it's one of the cheapest hotels in town, this 100-year-
★ old family-run lodging has been well maintained, with tile baths and double-glazed windows. The rooms are minimal, the taste decidedly '60s (red-and-orange prints, wood-grain Formica), and the once-elegant dining hall has seen better days. But some rooms have balconies, and there's a sheltered garden terrace for balmy nights. ⊠ *Via Geretta 16, CH-6902,* ☏ *091/9941671,* ℻ *091/9942738. 50 rooms. Restaurant, bar, outdoor pool, TV room. AE, DC, MC, V. Closed Nov.–Mar.*

$ 🏨 **Zurigo.** Ideally central and handy to parks, shopping, and waterfront promenades, this spartan hotel near the Palais Congrès offers quiet comfort; its rates are affordable even in high season. ⊠ *Corso Pestalozzi 13, CH-6900,* ☏ *091/9234343,* ℻ *091/9234343. 28 rooms. Breakfast room. No credit cards. Closed Nov.–Feb.*

Nightlife and the Arts

BARS AND LOUNGES

There's a piano bar in the **Hotel Eden** (⊠ Via Paradiso 1, ☏ 091/9230121) in Paradiso. The piano player strikes up a tune nightly at **Principe Leopoldo** (⊠ Via Montalbano 5, ☏ 091/9858855). There's also nightly piano music at the **Splendide Royale** (⊠ Riva Caccia 7, ☏ 091/9857711).

CASINO

The **Kursaal** (✉ Via Stauffacher 1, ☎ 091/9235501) has a restaurant, dance club, bar, slot machines, movie theater, and gaming room. There also are Sunday tea dances.

DANCING

La Canva (✉ Riva Paradiso 17, ☎ 091/9941218) is popular among locals. **Capo San Martino** (✉ Via Cantonale, Pazzallo, ☎ 091/9945570) is in nearby Paradiso. **Titanic** (✉ Via Cantonale, Pambio-Noranco, off A2 exit for Lugano-Sud, ☎ 091/9856010) is Ticino's biggest disco, with three dance floors.

MUSIC

There is a free **Blues to Bop Festival** in the Piazza della Riforma during September. The **Estival Jazz** in July offers free outdoor concerts in the Piazza della Riforma. From April to June, the city hosts its **Primavera Concertistica di Lugano** (☎ 091/8007204), with top-level orchestras and conductors.

Gandria

🔟 *7 km (4 mi) east of Lugano.*

Although today its narrow waterfront streets are crowded with tourists, the tiny historic village of Gandria merits a visit, either by boat from Lugano (☞ Getting Around by Boat *in* Ticino A to Z, *below*) or by car, as parking is available just above the town. It clings vertiginously to the steep hillside, and its flower-filled balconies hang directly over open water. Souvenir and crafts shops now fill its backstreet nooks, but the ambience of an ancient fishing village remains.

OFF THE BEATEN PATH

CANTINE DI GANDRIA – Across Lake Lugano from Gandria—almost in Italy—this tiny village has a small **Museo Doganale** (Customs Museum; ☎ 091/9239843), casually known as the "Smugglers' Museum." Here you'll learn the romantic history of clandestine trade through displays of ingenious containers, weapons, and contraband. You can catch a boat from the jetty. ☎ *091/9715223 or 091/9234610 for boat schedule information.* 🎟 *Free.* ⊙ *Apr.–Oct., daily 1:30–5:30.*

Campione

🔢 *18 km (11 mi) south of Gandria, 12 km (7 mi) south of Lugano (take the Paradiso highway across the Melide causeway, then cut north via Bissone).*

In the heart of Swiss Italy lies Campione. Here, in this southernmost of regions, the police cars have Swiss license plates but the policemen inside are Italian; the inhabitants pay their taxes to Italy but do it in Swiss francs.

In the 8th century, the lord of Campione gave the tiny scrap of land to St. Ambrosius of Milan. Despite all the wars that passed it by, Campione remained Italian until the end of the 18th century, when it was incorporated into the Cisalpine Republic. When Italy unified in 1861, Campione became part of the new Kingdom of Italy—and remained so. There are no frontiers between Campione and Switzerland, and it benefits from the comforts of Swiss currency, customs laws, and postal and telephone services. Despite its miniature scale, it has exercised disproportionate influence on the art world: From Campione and the surrounding region, a school of stonemasons, sculptors, and architects emigrated during the Middle Ages to Milan and began working on the cathedrals of Milan, Verona, Cremona, Trento, Modena—and Hagia Sophia in Constantinople.

Nightlife and the Arts

Today, Campione is a magnet for gamblers, as its large, glittering **Casino** (⊠ Piazza Milano 1, ☎ 091/6401111/1184) offers visitors to conservative Switzerland a chance to play for higher stakes than the usual 5 SF: Following Italian law, the sky's the limit here. The casino has a restaurant, dancing, and a show; this is jacket-and-tie territory.

Riva San Vitale

⑱ *9 km (5½ mi) south of Campione, 13 km (8 mi) south of Lugano.*

At the south end of Lake Lugano sits Riva San Vitale, where a 5th-century **Battistero** (Baptistery) remains, still containing its original stone immersion font. Riva San Vitale rivals Campione for its odd history: In 1798 its people objected to new boundaries and declared themselves an independent republic. Their glory lasted 14 days before a small cantonal army marched in and convinced them to rejoin Switzerland. Four kilometers (2 miles) south of Riva San Vitale is little **Mendrisio,** cradle of the Ticinese wine industry. It's known for its medieval processions, which take place on the Thursday and Friday before Easter.

Morcote

★ ⑲ *6 km (4 mi) northwest of Riva San Vitale, 10 km (6 mi) south of Lugano.*

At the southernmost tip of the glorious Ceresio Peninsula waterfront is the atmospheric old resort-village of Morcote, its clay-color Lombard-style houses and arcades looking directly over the waterfront. A steep and picturesque climb leads up to the **Chiesa di Madonna del Sasso** (Church of the Madonna of Sasso), with its well-preserved 16th-century frescoes; its elevated setting affords wonderful views.

TICINO A TO Z

Arriving and Departing

By Bus

The **Palm Express** scenic postbus and train route carries visitors from Saint-Moritz to Lugano or Ascona via the Maloja Pass and Italy. It takes about four hours and is arranged through the appropriate tourist offices (☞ Visitor Information, *below*); you can also contact **Railtour Suisse** (⊠ Piazzale Stazione, 6500 Bellinzona, ☎ 091/8217242).

By Car

There are two major gateways into Ticino: the **Saint Gotthard Pass** (Passo del S. Gottardo) in the northwest and the **San Bernardino Pass** (Passo del S. Bernardino) to the northeast. From the Saint Gotthard Pass, the swift **A2** expressway leads down the Valle Leventina to Bellinzona, where it joins with **A13**, which cuts south from the San Bernardino. A2 directs the mingled traffic flow southward past Lugano to Chiasso and the Italian border, where the expressway heads directly to Como and Milan.

By Plane

The nearest international airport is in Italy. **Malpensa** (⊠ About 50 km/31 mi northwest of Milan), which was enlarged and reopened in fall 1998, is now one of the biggest hubs in southern Europe. Some flights from the international **Linate** (⊠ Less than 10 km/6 mi east of Milan) will be transferred to Malpensa. For air-traffic **information** for

both airports and information on connections with Milan, call 39/
2/74852200. You can continue into Ticino via rail, car, or taxi. **Crossair** (☎ 084/8852000 for central reservations), Switzerland's domestic airline, connects directly into the domestic **Aeroporto Lugano-Agno**
(✉ 7 km/4½ mi west of Lugano, CH-6982 Agno, ☎ 091/6101212)
from **Zurich**'s Kloten Airport (☎ 1571060) and from **Geneva**'s Cointrin (☎ 022/7177111), as well as from other European destinations.

By Train

The Saint Gotthard route connects south from Zürich, cuts through
the pass tunnel, and heads into Bellinzona and Lugano. Side connections lead into Locarno from Brig, crossing the Simplon Pass and cutting through Italy. Swiss Pass (☞ Train Travel *in* the Gold Guide) travelers
do not have to pay Italian rail fares to cross from Brig to Locarno via
Domodossola. Trains connect out of Zürich's airport and take about
three hours; from Geneva, catch the Milan express, changing at Domodossola, Locarno, and Bellinzona. Trains do not go directly into Ascona but stop at Locarno: You must connect by taxi or local bus. For
train information from Lugano, call 1572222 (1.18 SF/min).

Getting Around

By Boat

Like Switzerland's inland lakes, Lake Lugano and northern Lake Maggiore are plied by graceful steamers that carry passengers from one waterfront resort to another, offering excellent perspectives on the
mountains. Steamer travel on Lake Lugano is included in the Lugano
Regional Passes (☞ By Train, *below*) and the Swiss Pass (☞ Train Travel
in the Gold Guide); tickets can be purchased near the docks before departure. On Lake Lugano, the **Navigation Company of Lake Lugano**
(✉ Casella Postale 56, CH-6900 Lugano, ☎ 091/9715223) offers
cruise-boat excursions around the bay to Gandria and toward the
Villa Favorita.

Boats owned by **Navigazione Lago Maggiore-Bacino Svizzero** (✉ Lungolago Motta, CH-6600 Locarno, ☎ 091/7511865) cruise Lake Maggiore. Discounts for Swiss and Swiss Boat passes (☞ Train Travel *and*
Boat Travel *in* the Gold Guide) and the Locarno Regional Pass (☞ By
Train, *below*).

By Bus

There is a convenient postbus sightseeing system here that tourists can
use—easily—to get around the region, even into the backcountry. La Posta
(post and telegraph office) publishes illustrated booklets with suggested
itineraries and prices; you can get them through the **Autopostale Ticino-Moesano** (✉ Via S. Balestra, CH-6905 Lugano, ☎ 091/8078520/28) or
through local tourist and post offices. Postbus excursion prices are reduced with the Locarno or Lugano Regional Pass (☞ By Train, *below*)
and are free with the Swiss Pass (☞ Train Travel *in* the Gold Guide).

By Car

A car is a real asset here if you intend to see the mountain valleys—
and a hindrance in the congested, urban lakeside resorts. Traffic between Bellinzona and Locarno can move at a crawl during high season.

By Train

Secondary rail connections here are minimal and can make all but the
most mainstream rail sightseeing a complicated venture; most excursions will require some postbus connections. Nevertheless there are **Regional Passes**: Lugano's offers seven days' unlimited travel on most
rail and steamer lines, with 50% reductions on various other excursions and modes of transit (92 SF); or three days' travel within seven

consecutive days (70 SF). In Locarno/Ascona, the seven-day Regional Pass offers unlimited travel on local rail and steamer trips and 50% reductions on chairlift and funicular rides (76 SF, available through tourist offices). Compare the Locarno and Lugano passes carefully before choosing; many of their discounted facilities overlap. As the Swiss Pass doesn't cover all the transport facilities of the Lake Lugano region, Regional Passes are offered to its holders at a discount.

Contacts and Resources

Emergencies

Police: 117. **Medical assistance**: 144. Lugano civic **hospital** (☎ 091/8056111). Lugano **dental clinic** (☎ 091/9350180).

Guided Tours

ORIENTATION

The *Wilhelm Tell Express* carries you by paddle steamer and rail from Luzern over the Saint Gotthard Pass and into Locarno and Lugano with a guide and running commentary. Contact **Railtour Suisse** (⊠ Piazzale Stazione, CH-6500 Bellinzona, ☎ 091/8217242) or inquire at rail stations.

Guided walks are available in all regions covering cultural, historical, architectural, and natural interests. Wonderfully detailed brochures with maps are available from local tourist offices for both guided and self-guided tours.

Visitor Information

The principal tourist authority for Ticino is the **Ticino Turismo** (⊠ Villa Turrita, Via Lugano 12, Box 1441, CH-6501 Bellinzona, ☎ 091/8257056, FAX 091/8253614).

Local offices: Ascona (⊠ Casa Serodine, Box 449, CH-6612, ☎ 091/7910090). **Bellinzona** (⊠ Palazzo Civico, CP1419, CH-6500, ☎ 091/8252131). **Biasca** (⊠ CH-6710, ☎ 091/8623327). **Blenio** (⊠ CH-6716 Acquarossa, ☎ 091/8711765). **Brissago Islands** (⊠ CH-6614 Brissago, ☎ 091/7914361). **Locarno** (⊠ Teatro di Locarno, Casino-Kursaal, via Largo Zorzi, CH-6600, ☎ 091/7510333). **Lugano** (⊠ Palazzo Civico, CH-6901, ☎ 091/9214664). **Lugano** (⊠ Palazzo Civico, CH-6901, ☎ 091/9214664). **Mendrisiotto e Basso Ceresio** (⊠ Via Angelo Naspoli 15, CH-6850 Mendrisio, ☎ 091/6465761).

6 Luzern and Central Switzerland

Luzern, Engelberg, Weggis, Schwyz, Zug

Endowed with a sophisticated transportation system that makes it one of the easiest regions to visit, central Switzerland is full of neat little towns, accessible mountains, and modest resorts. Centered around the Vierwaldstättersee, the Lake of the Four Forest Cantons, the region is steeped in history: It is where the Oath of Eternal Alliance is said to have been renewed, and it's also the birthplace of the legend of William Tell.

Updated by
Debbie Ebanks

AS YOU CRUISE DOWN THE LEISURELY sprawl of the Vierwaldstättersee (Lake Luzern), mist rising off the gray waves, mountains—great loaflike masses of forest and stone—looming above the clouds, it's easy to understand how Wagner could have composed his *Siegfried Idyll* in his mansion beside this lake. This is inspiring terrain, romantic and evocative. When the waters roil up, you can hear the whistling chromatics and cymbal clashes of Gioacchino Rossini's thunderstorm from his 1829 opera, *Guillaume Tell*. It was on this lake, after all, that William Tell—the beloved, if legendary, Swiss national hero—supposedly leapt from the tyrant Gessler's boat to freedom. And it was in a meadow nearby that three furtive rebels and their cohorts swore an oath by firelight and planted the seed of the Swiss Confederation.

The Rütli Meadow, a national landmark on the western shores of Lake Luzern, is the very spot where the Confederates of Schwyz, Unterwald, and Uri are said to have met on the night of November 7, 1307, to renew the 1291 Oath of Eternal Alliance—Switzerland's equivalent of the U.S. Declaration of Independence. Through this oath, the world's oldest still-extant democracy was formed, as the proud charter territories swore their commitment to self-rule in the face of the oppressive Hapsburgs and the Holy Roman Empire. Every August 1, the Swiss national holiday, citizens gather in the meadow in remembrance of the Oath of Eternal Alliance, and the sky glows with the light of hundreds of mountaintop bonfires.

William Tell played an important role in that early rebellion, and his story, especially as told by German poet and playwright Friedrich von Schiller in his play *Wilhelm Tell* (1805), continues to stir those with a weakness for civil resistance. Though there are no valid records to prove his existence, and versions of the legend conflict with historical fact, no one denies the reality of his times, when central Switzerland—then a feudal dependent of Austria but, by its own independent will, not yet absorbed into the Holy Roman Empire—suffered brutal pressures and indignities under the rulers in residence. The mythical Gessler was one of those rulers, and his legendary edict—that the proud, resistant Swiss should bow before his hat, suspended on a pole in the village square at Altdorf—symbolizes much crueler oppressions of the time. Schiller's Tell was a hero through and through: brisk, decisive, a highly skilled helmsman as well as marksman, and not one for diplomatic negotiations—he refused to kneel. Tell's famous punishment: to shoot an apple off his young son's head before a crowd of fellow townsmen; if he refused, both would be killed. Tell quietly tucked an arrow in his shirt bosom, loaded another into his crossbow, and shot the apple clean through. When Gessler asked what the second arrow was for, Tell replied that if the first arrow had struck his child, the second arrow would have been for Gessler and would not have missed.

For this impolitic remark, Tell was sentenced to prison. While deporting him across Lake Luzern, the Austrians (including the ruthless Gessler) were caught in a violent storm (remember your Rossini) and turned to Tell, the only man on board who knew the waters, to take the helm. Unmanacled, he steered the boat to a rocky ridge, leapt free, and pushed the boat back into the storm. Later he lay in wait in the woods near Küssnacht and, as Gessler threatened to ride down a woman begging mercy for her imprisoned husband, shot him in the heart. This act of justified violence inspired the people to overthrow their oppressors, swear the Oath of Eternal Alliance around a roaring bonfire, and laid the groundwork for the Swiss Confederation.

Pretty romantic stuff. Yet for all its potential for drama, central Switzerland and the area surrounding Lake Luzern are tame enough turf: neat little towns, accessible mountains, resorts virtually glamour-free—and modest, graceful Luzern (Lucerne) holding forth along the River Reuss much as it has since the Middle Ages.

An eminently civilized region, Zentralschweiz (Central Switzerland) lacks the rustic unruliness of the Valais, the spectacular extremes of the Berner Oberland, the eccentricity of Graubünden. But it's not too sophisticated either and lacks both the snob appeal of jet-set resorts and the cosmopolitan mix of Geneva, Basel, and Zürich. The houses are tidy, pastel, picture-book cottages, deep-roofed and symmetrical, each rank of windows underscored with flowers. The villages, ranged neatly around their medieval centers, radiate tradition; and the wilderness is served by good roads. Luzern, the capital, hosts arts festivals and great shopping but little native industry. Serene and steady as the Reuss that laps at the piers of its ancient wooden bridges, it's an approachable city in an accessible region.

Central Switzerland's popularity with tourists has spawned an infrastructure of hotels, restaurants, museums, excursions, and transportation that makes it one of the easiest places in Switzerland to visit, either by car or by rail—and one of the most rewarding. As Wagner exclaimed, perhaps carried away a bit by his own waterfront idyll: "I do not know of a more beautiful spot in this world!"

Pleasures and Pastimes

Dining

Rooted in the German territory of Switzerland and the surrounding farmlands, central Switzerland's native cuisine is down-home and hearty, though its specialties offer some variety from the veal-and-*Rösti* (hash brown potatoes) found everywhere else. In the heights, there are Alpine cheese specialties (*Aelpler Magrone*—pasta, butter, cheese, and fried onions); in the orchard country around Zug, there are such cherry specialties as *Zuger Kirschtorte,* a rich yellow cake liberally soaked with cherry schnapps. Pears from the local orchards are dried, then spiced and poached in sweetened red *Dole* (wine). Luzern takes pride in its *Kügelipaschtetli,* puff-pastry nests filled with tiny veal meatballs, chicken, or sweetbreads; mushrooms; cream sauce; and occasionally raisins.

But here the real *cuisine du marché,* based on the freshest ingredients available in local markets, focuses on lake fish. Lake Luzern and its neighboring Zugersee (Lake Zug) produce an abundance of *Egli* (perch), *Hecht* (pike), *Forellen* (trout), and *Felchen* (whitefish), and Zug produces its own exclusive *Röteln,* a red-bellied relation to the trout and Geneva's *omble chevalier* (a type of salmon trout found in Lac Léman). Restaurants—especially along waterfronts—trade heavily in these freshwater products, whether they come from the region or not. Ask, and you may get an honest answer: The sources vary, but the tradition and style of preparation remain local. In Zug, whole fish may be baked with sage, bay leaves, shallots, cloves, and plenty of white wine and butter; a Luzern tradition has them sautéed and sauced with tomatoes, mushrooms, and capers.

CATEGORY	COST*
$$$$	over 70 SF
$$$	40 SF–70 SF
$$	20 SF–40 SF
$	under 20 SF

Prices are per person for a three-course meal (two-course meal in $ category), including sales tax and 15% service charge

Hiking

Since Switzerland's 1991 septicentennial, celebrating the 700-year anniversary of its confederation, central Switzerland has marked and developed a historic foot trail, the Swiss Path, which covers 35 km (21½ mi) of lakefront lore along the southernmost branch of Lake Luzern. You'll trace the mythical steps of William Tell and the genuine steps of medieval forefathers and foremothers, climb through steep forests and isolated villages, and visit the holiday resort of Brunnen. Complete information and maps can be requested through Central Switzerland Tourism (☞ Visitor Information *in* Luzern and Central Switzerland A to Z, *below*). The videocassette "Hiking the Swiss Path" is available through branches of Switzerland Tourism.

Lodging

Luzern provides a convenient home base for excursions all over the region, though villages are peppered with small shuttered guest houses, and you may easily find an overnight spot as you drive through the countryside. As the terrain and climate vary radically between balmy lakefronts and icy heights, check carefully for high and low seasons before booking ahead. Such water-sport resorts as Weggis and Vitznau cut back service considerably in winter, just when Engelberg comes alive. Luzern, unlike most Swiss urban areas, has high and low seasons, and prices drop by as much as 25% in the winter, approximately November through March. Rates are usually calculated on a per-person basis, so it is wise to confirm the rates, particularly if you're traveling as anything other than a pair.

CATEGORY	COST*
$$$$	over 350 SF
$$$	250 SF–350 SF
$$	120 SF–250 SF
$	under 120 SF

Prices are for a standard double room, including breakfast, tax, and service charge.

Shopping

Although Luzern no longer produces embroidery or lace, you can find a wide variety of Swiss handiwork of the highest quality, crafts, and watches in all price categories. High-end watch dealers Gübelin and Bucherer offer inexpensive souvenirs to lure shoppers into their luxurious showrooms; smaller shops carry Tissot, Rado, Corum, and others—but prices are controlled by the manufacturers. Watch for closeouts on out-of-date models.

Exploring Luzern and Central Switzerland

Though called the Lake of the Four Forest Cantons, Lake Luzern and its environs take in not only the four cantons that abut the lake—Luzern, Uri, Schwyz, and Unterwalden—but the canton of Zug as well. Unterwalden itself is divided politically into two half-cantons: Obwalden (upper) and Nidwalden (lower). It was the canton of Schwyz that gave Switzerland its name.

The narrow, twisting lake flows from Flüelen, where the Reuss opens into the Urnersee, its southernmost leg. This is the wildest end of the lake, where much of the Tell story was set. The north end of the lake is flanked by the region's highest points, Mt. Pilatus (2,121 m/6,953 ft) and Mt. Rigi (1,798 m/5,894 ft). Luzern lies in a deep bay at the lake's northwest extreme and at the point where the rivers Reuss and

Emme part ways. Zug stands apart, on the northern shore of its own Lake Zug, which is divided from Lake Luzern by the mass of Mt. Rigi.

Numbers in the text correspond to numbers in the margin and on the Central Switzerland and Luzern (Lucerne) maps.

Great Itineraries

When visiting this multiterrain area, you must change modes of transit frequently to see it in all its variety; part of the region's interest is the variety of boat trips, train rides, and drives you'll take to reach the sights. On any given day, you may walk through the lovely Old Town of Luzern, ascend Mt. Pilatus by cable car and descend by cogwheel train, take a lake steamer on the Vierwaldstättersee, or drive through the Rütli Meadow.

IF YOU HAVE 1 OR 2 DAYS

Take in the Old Town sights of ⛰ **Luzern** ①–⑭ and head off the beaten path to the Verkehrshaus, reached easily by car or boat. A boat trip on the **Vierwaldstättersee** gives you the opportunity to see the sights of the region from the lake itself; there are half-day excursions as well as longer ones. **Mt. Pilatus** ⑮ offers central Switzerland's best mountaintop panoramas. Allow yourself a half day to ascend the mountain.

IF YOU HAVE 3 OR MORE DAYS

In addition to all of the above, take a trip to **Einsiedeln** ㉖, with its 9th-century Benedictine monastery. A combined train and cable-car trip from ⛰ **Weggis** ⑲ will take you to the summit of **Mt. Rigi,** where you can see as far as the Black Forest and Mt. Säntis and even spend the night in the hotel at the top. If you're traveling by car, you can follow the course of a lake steamer from Luzern, driving to the Saint Gotthard Pass along the lakefront highway (A2).

When to Tour Luzern and Central Switzerland

If you don't mind negotiating heavy traffic, particularly in Luzern, summer is the ideal season for boat excursions on the lake and great views from the tops of Mt. Pilatus and Mt. Rigi. In fall, when the crowds thin, you'll find crisp, beautiful weather around the mountains and the lake. This isn't a big ski area, so wintertime tends to be quiet, even in Luzern.

LUZERN

Luzern city is a convenient home base for excursions all over central Switzerland, the region indelibly marked by William Tell's legend and Swiss national history. The countryside here is tame, and the vast Vierwaldstättersee (Lake Luzern) offers a prime opportunity for a lake steamer cruise.

Fifty-seven kilometers (36 miles) southwest of Zürich, where the River Reuss flows out of Lake Luzern, Luzern city's Old Town straddles the narrowed waters. The greater concentration of life bustles along the river's right bank. The city's signature sights include Kapellbrücke, a covered wooden bridge, and the moving Löwendenkmal (☞ *below*). There are a couple of passes available for discounts for museums and sights in the city. One is a museum pass that costs 25 SF and grants free entry to all museums for one month. If you are staying in a hotel, you may also want to pick up a special visitor's card; once stamped by the hotel, it entitles you to discounts at most museums and other tourist-oriented businesses as well. Both are available at the tourist office (☞ Visitor Information *in* Luzern and Central Switzerland A to Z, *below*).

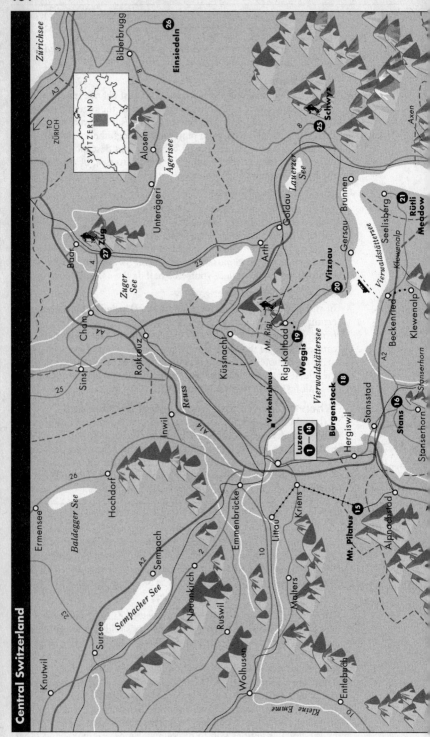

Central Switzerland

Zürichsee

Biberbrugg

Einsiedeln 26

A3

3

8

TO ZÜRICH

SWITZERLAND

Alosen

Ägerisee

Schwyz 25

Axen

Unterägeri

Goldau

Lauerzer See

Gersau

Brunnen

Seelisberg

Rütli Meadow 21

Klewenalp

Zug 27

Arth

Vitznau 20

Vierwaldstättersee

Klewenalp

Beckenried

Baar

Zuger See

25

Mt. Rigi

Rigi-Kaltbad 19

Weggis

A2

Stanserhorn

Cham

Rotkreuz

Küssnacht

Verkehrshaus

Bürgenstock 18

Stansstad

Stans 16

A4

Reuss

Luzern 1 14

Hergiswil

Sins

Inwil

A14

25

26

Hochdorf

Emmenbrücke

Kriens

15 **Mt. Pilatus**

Alpnachstad

Stanserhorn

Ermensee

Baldegger See

Littau

Sempach

A2

2

Neuenkirch

Ruswil

Malters

10

Sursee

Sempacher See

23

Knutwil

Wolhusen

Kleine Emme

Entlebuch

10

KEY

Rail Lines

Cable Car/
Funicular

Tunnels

Regional
Boundary Lines

Ferry

Ski Resorts

4 miles

6 km

Old Town and Beyond

A Good Walk

The main avenue of Luzern, **Rathausquai**, is lined with hotels and cafés. Start at the modern bridge, **Rathaus-Steg**, and head north to **Altes Rathaus** ①, opposite the bridge. Just to the right of the Rathaus is the **Am Rhyn-Haus** ②, now a Picasso museum. Turn right and climb the stairs past the ornately frescoed **Zunfthaus zur Pfistern** (☞ Pfistern *in* Dining and Lodging, *below*), a guildhall dating from the late 15th and early 16th centuries, to the **Kornmarkt**, where the grinding din of the grain market was once heard. Cut left to the **Weinmarkt** ③. Leave the square from its west end, turn right on Kramgasse, and head west across the Mühlenplatz to the **Spreuerbrücke** ④, an unlikely exhibition space for dark paintings of the medieval plague epidemic. On the left bank is the **Natur-Museum** ⑤, a boon for modernist children; next to the museum is the **Historisches Museum** ⑥. From the end of the Spreuerbrücke, cut back upriver along Pfistergasse, veer left on Bahnhofstrasse, and turn right into Münzgasse to the **Franziskanerkirche** ⑦. Return to Bahnhofstrasse and head to the **Jesuitenkirche** ⑧. Going east past the Rathaus-Steg Bridge, you'll see the **Kapellbrücke** ⑨, the oldest of its kind in Europe.

After crossing the Kapellbrücke, break away from Old Town through thick pedestrian and bus traffic at Schwanenplatz to Schweizerhofquai. Double back and take the first right, St. Leodegarstrasse, to the **Hofkirche** ⑩; go back down the church steps, turn right, and continue on to Löwenstrasse. Turn right and continue to Löwenplatz and behold the **Bourbaki-Panorama** ⑪ (at press time—summer 1998—it was closed for renovations until mid-1999), dominating the square like a remnant from a Victorian world's fair. Beyond the plaza, up Denkmalstrasse, is the **Löwendenkmal** ⑫, called by Mark Twain "the most mournful and moving piece of stone in the world." Immediately adjoining the small park that shades the lion lies the **Gletschergarten** ⑬. Return down Denkmalstrasse and, at Löwenplatz, turn right on Museggstrasse, which cuts through an original city gate and runs parallel to the watchtowers and crenellated walls of Luzern, constructed around 1400. The fifth tower is **Zytturm** ⑭.

TIMING

The Old Town is easy to navigate and ideal for walking. You can take in the sights on this route in about three hours; to this add another hour each to see the Natur-Museum and Historisches Museum, and you will want to linger awhile at the Kapellbrücke, Löwendenkmal, and Bourbaki-Panorama (when open). Note that both the Natur-Museum and Historisches Museum are closed Monday; the Gletschergarten is closed Monday from mid-November through February.

Sights to See

❶ **Altes Rathaus** (Old Town Hall). In 1606, the Luzern town council held its first meeting in this late-Renaissance style building, built from 1599 to 1606. It still meets here today. ⊠ *Rathausquai, facing the end of Rathaus-Steg.*

❷ **Am Rhyn-Haus** (Am Rhyn House). Known simply as the Picasso Museum, this spot contrasts a beautiful, 17th-century building with its modern holdings. The collection consists mainly of works from the last 20 years of Picasso's life, along with more than 100 photos of the artist. ⊠ *Furreng. 21,* ☎ *041/4101773.* ⊡ *6 SF.* ◷ *Apr.–Oct., daily 10–6; Nov.–Mar., daily 11–1 and 2–4.*

⓫ **Bourbaki-Panorama.** This enormous conical wooden structure was created between 1876 and 1878 as a genuine, step-right-up tourist attraction and is, in its undiluted period form, as interesting for its novel nature as for its content. At the top of wide entry stairs, the conical roof covers a sweeping, wraparound epic painting of the French Army of the East retreating into Switzerland at Verrières—a famous episode in the Franco-Prussian War. It was painted by Édouard Castres of Geneva, who was aided by many uncredited artists, including Hodler. As you walk around the circle, the imagery seems to pop into three dimensions; in fact, with the help of a few strategically placed models, it does. There's a recorded commentary in English. The Bourbaki-Panorama is closed for renovations until mid-1999. ⊠ *Löwenpl.*, ☎ *041/4109942.* ☜ *3 SF.* ⊙ *Call for hours after reopening.*

❼ Franziskanerkirche (Franciscan Church). After more than 700 years, this church, despite persistent modernization, retains its 17th-century choir stalls and carved wooden pulpit. The barefoot Franciscans once held a prominent social and cultural position in Luzern, which took a firm Counter-Reformation stance and remains more than 70% Roman Catholic today. ⊠ *Franziskanerpl., just off Münzg.*

⓭ Gletschergarten (Glacier Garden). The bedrock of this 19th-century tourist attraction was excavated between 1872 and 1875 and has been dramatically pocked and polished by Ice Age glaciers. A private museum on the site displays impressive relief maps of Switzerland. ⊠ *Denkmalstr. 4*, ☎ *041/4104340.* ☜ *7 SF.* ⊙ *May–mid-Oct., daily 8–6; Mar., Apr., and mid-Oct.–mid-Nov., daily 9–5; mid-Nov.–Feb., Tues.–Sat. 10:30–4:30, Sun. 10–5.*

❻ Historisches Museum (Historical Museum). Housed in the late-Gothic armory dating from 1567, this stylish institution exhibits city sculptures, Swiss arms, and flags. Reconstructed rooms depict rural and urban life; it's also got the original Gothic fountain from the Weinmarkt (☞ *below*). ⊠ *Pfisterg. 24*, ☎ *041/2285424.* ☜ *4 SF.* ⊙ *Tues.–Fri. 10–noon and 2–5, weekends 10–5.*

❿ Hofkirche (Collegiate Church). This sanctuary of St. Leodegar was first founded in 750 as a monastery. Its Gothic structure was mostly destroyed by fire in 1633 and rebuilt in late-Renaissance style, so only the towers of its predecessor were preserved. The carved pulpit and choir stalls date from the 17th century, and the 80-rank organ (1650) is one of Switzerland's finest. It's still used for the church's concerts, which are held several times each month. Outside, Italianate loggias shelter a cemetery for patrician families of old Luzern. ⊠ *St. Leodegarstr. 6*, ☎ *041/4105241. Closed Fri. 10–noon, 2:30–5.*

OFF THE
BEATEN PATH

VERKEHRSHAUS – Easily reached by steamer, car, or Bus 2, the Swiss Transport Museum is almost a world's fair in itself, with a complex of buildings and exhibitions both indoors and out, including dioramas, live demonstrations, and a "Swissorama" (360-degree screen) film about Switzerland. Every mode of transit is discussed, from stagecoaches and bicycles to jumbo jets and space capsules. The museum also has Switzerland's first IMAX theater. If you're driving, head east on Haldenstrasse at the waterfront and make a right on Lidostrasse (it's also signposted). ⊠ *Lidostr. 5*, ☎ *041/3704444.* ☜ *16 SF.* ⊙ *Mar.–Oct., daily 9–6; Nov.–Feb., daily 10–5.*

★ ❽ Jesuitenkirche (Jesuit Church). Constructed from 1667–78, this Baroque church with a symmetrical entrance is flanked by two onion-dome towers, added in 1893. Go inside: Its vast interior, restored to mint condition, is a Rococo explosion of gilt, marble, and epic frescoes. Nearby is the Renaissance **Regierungsgebäude** (Government Building), seat of

Luzern (Lucerne)

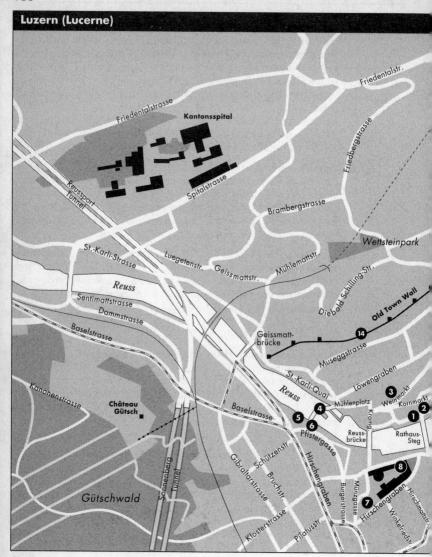

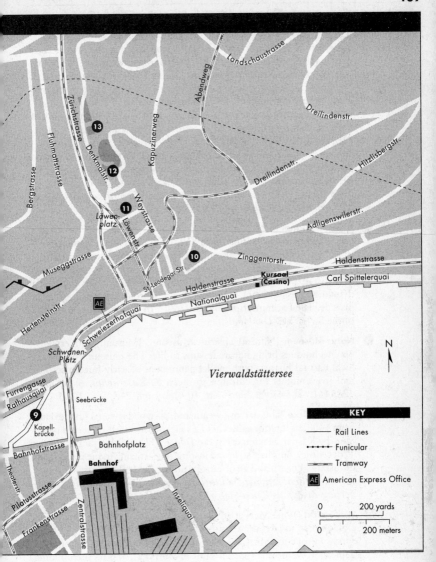

Landschaustrasse

Abendweg

Dreilindenstr.

Zürichstrasse

Denkmalstr.

Fluhmattstrasse

Bergstrasse

Kapuzinerweg

13

12

Weystrasse

Löwen-
platz

Löwenstr.

11

Museggstrasse

Dreilindenstr.

Hitzlisbergstr.

Adligenswilerstr.

10

Zinggentorstr.

Haldenstrasse

St-Leodegar-Str.

Haldenstrasse

**Kursaal
(Casino)**

Carl Spittelerquai

Hertensteinstr.

AE

Schweizerhofquai

Nationalquai

Schwanen-
Platz

Vierwaldstättersee

N

Furrengasse

Rathausquai

Seebrücke

9

Kapell-
brücke

Bahnhofstrasse

Bahnhofplatz

Bahnhof

Theaterstr.

Pilatusstrasse

Frankenstrasse

Zentralstrasse

Inseliquai

KEY	
——	Rail Lines
••••	Funicular
⧓⧓	Tramway
AE	American Express Office

0   200 yards

0   200 meters

the cantonal government. ⊠ *Bahnhofstr., just west of Rathaus-Steg,* ☎ *041/2100756.* ⊙ *Daily 6 AM–6:15 PM.*

★ ⑨ **Kapellbrücke** (Chapel Bridge). The oldest wooden bridge in Europe snakes diagonally across the Reuss. When built during the early 14th century, it served as the division between the lake and the river. Its shingle roof and grand stone water tower are to Luzern what the Matterhorn is to Zermatt, but considerably more vulnerable, as a 1993 fire proved. Almost 80% of this fragile monument was destroyed, including many of the 17th-century paintings inside; restorations are still underway. However, a walk through this dark, creaky landmark will take you past polychrome copies of the 112 gable panels, painted by Heinrich Wägmann during the 17th century and depicting Luzern and Swiss history, stories of St. Leodegar and St. Mauritius, Luzern's patron saints, and coats of arms from local patrician families. ⊠ *Between Seebrücke and Rathaus-Steg, connecting Rathausquai and Bahnhofstr.*

★ ⑫ **Löwendenkmal** (Lion Monument). The Swiss officers and 760 guards officers who died defending Louis XVI of France at the Tuileries in Paris in 1792 are commemorated here. Designed by Danish sculptor Berthel Thorwaldsen and carved out of a sheer sandstone face by Lucas Ahorn of Konstanz, this 19th-century wonder is a simple, stirring image of a dying lion, his chin sagging on his shield, a broken stump of spear in his side. The Latin inscription translates: "To the bravery and fidelity of the Swiss." ⊠ *Denkmalstr.*

⑤ **Natur-Museum** (Natural History Museum). Unusually modern display techniques bring nature lessons to life: The museum focuses on local natural history, with model panoramas of early Luzern settlers and live animals for children to meet. ⊠ *Kasernenpl. 6,* ☎ *041/ 2285411.* ⊡ *5 SF.* ⊙ *Tues.–Sat. 10–noon and 2–5, Sun. 10–5.*

④ **Spreuerbrücke.** This narrow, weathered, all-wood covered bridge dates from 1408. Its interior gables hold a series of eerie, well-preserved paintings (by Kaspar Meglinger) of the *Dance of Death* that date from the 17th century, but their style and inspiration—tracing to the plague that devastated Luzern and all of Europe during the 14th century—are medieval. ⊠ *Between Geissmattbrücke and Reussbrücke bridges, connecting Zeughaus Reuss-Steg and Mühlenpl.*

③ **Weinmarkt** (Wine Market). What is now the loveliest of Luzern's several fountain squares drew visitors from the 15th to 17th centuries from across Europe to witness its passion plays. Its Gothic central fountain depicts St. Mauritius (patron saint of warriors), and its surrounding buildings are flamboyantly frescoed in 16th-century style. ⊠ *Square just west of Kornmarkt, north of Metzgerainli.*

⑭ **Zytturm.** The clock in this fifth watchtower, constructed around 1400, was made in Basel in 1385 and still keeps time. ⊠ *North of and parallel to Museggstr.*

Dining and Lodging

$$$ ✕ **Old Swiss House.** Conceived as self-consciously as its name implies—no doubt to satisfy the romantic expectations of the flood of English tourists heading for the Lion Monument—this popular establishment pleases crowds (and groups) with its beautifully contrived collection of 17th-century antiques, lead glass, and an old-world artifice now pleasantly burnished by more than 130 years of service. The standing menu includes specialties from around the country: cheese croquettes, veal and Rösti, lake fish, and Swiss chocolate mousse. ⊠ *Löwenpl. 4,* ☎ *041/4106171. AE, DC, MC, V. Closed Mon. and Feb.*

$$$ ✕ **Rotes Gatter.** This chic restaurant in the Des Balances hotel (☞ *below*)
★ has a combination as desirable as it is rare: soigné decor, shimmering
river views, and a sophisticated menu with such fish dishes as grilled
omble chevalier in vegetable vinaigrette, steamed perch in chive but-
ter, crayfish soup, or the house specialty, fish fondue. There's a more
casual, less expensive bistro area as well. ⊠ *Weinmarkt,* ☎ *041/
4103010. AE, DC, MC, V.*

$$ ✕ **Galliker.** Step past the ancient facade into a room roaring with local
★ action, where Luzerners drink, smoke, and wish each other *Guten Ap-
petit.* Brisk, motherly waitresses serve up the dishes *Mutti* used to
make: fresh *Kutteln* (tripe) in rich white wine sauce with cumin seeds;
real *Kalbskopf* (chopped fresh veal head) served with heaps of green
onions and warm vinaigrette; and authentic Luzerner Kügelipaschtetli.
Desserts may include dried pears steeped in pinot noir. Occasional experiments in a more modern mode—such as ginger ice cream—prove
that Peter Galliker's kitchen is no museum. ⊠ *Schützenstr. 1,* ☎ *041/
2401002. AE, DC, MC, V. Closed Sun., Mon., and 3 wks in Aug.*

$$ ✕ **Rebstock/Hofstube.** At the opposite end of the culinary spectrum
from Galliker (☞ *above*), this up-to-date kitchen offers modern, in-
ternational fare, including rabbit and lamb, as well as East Asian and
vegetarian specialties. But you're still in Switzerland: The chewy breads,
baked up the street, are so beautiful that they're displayed as objets
d'art. The lively bentwood brasserie hums with locals lunching by the
bar, while the more formal old-style restaurant glows with wood and
brass under a low beam-and-herringbone parquet ceiling. ⊠ *St. Leode-
garpl. 3,* ☎ *041/4103581. AE, DC, MC, V.*

$ ✕ **Pfistern.** One of the architectural focal points of the Old Town wa-
terfront, this floridly decorated old guild house—the guild's origins can
be traced back to 1341—offers a good selection of moderate meals in
addition to higher-price standards. Lake fish and *pastetli* (meat pies
with puff pastry) are worthy local options. Inside, it's woody and pub-
like, if slightly down-at-the-heels, but in summer the small first-floor
balcony may provide the best seat in town. There are also chestnut-
shaded tables directly along the waterfront in the thick of the strolling
crowds. ⊠ *Kornmarkt 4,* ☎ *041/4103650. AE, DC, MC, V.*

$$$$ ✕🏨 **Palace Hotel.** This waterfront hotel drinks in the broadest possi-
★ ble lake views. Built in 1906, it's been brilliantly refurbished so that
its classical look has a touch of postmodernism; it's light, airy, and al-
together sleek. Rooms are large enough for a game of badminton, and
picture windows afford sweeping views of Lake Luzern and Mt. Pila-
tus. The hotel's elegance seeps into its restaurant, Mignon, as well. The
contemporary cuisine—veal tenderloin in tarragon with beet noodles,
for example—is faultlessly prepared and formally presented. Reservations
are essential. ⊠ *Haldenstr. 10, CH-6002,* ☎ *041/4100404,* 🖷 *041/
4101504. 178 rooms, 45 suites. Restaurant, bar, 2 saunas, steam
room, health club, parking (fee). AE, DC, MC, V.*

$$$ ✕🏨 **Wilden Mann.** The city's best-known hotel offers its guests a gra-
★ cious and authentic experience of Old Luzern, with stone, beams,
brass, hand-painted tiles, and burnished wood everywhere. Standard
rooms have a prim 19th-century look. The hotel's reputation extends
to its restaurants; the Burgerstube, which began in 1517 as a rest stop
for Saint Gotthard travelers, is cozy with its dark beams and family
crests, while vaulting and candlelight give the Liedertafel restaurant a
more formal atmosphere. On either side, young chef Andreas Stübi strikes
a fine balance between old-style local cooking and savvy French cuisine: smoked salmon tartare wrapped in Rösti with dill sauce; duck
breast with dandelion honey and balsamic vinegar. ⊠ *Bahnhofstr. 30,
CH-6003,* ☎ *041/2101666,* 🖷 *041/2101629. 35 rooms, 8 suites. 2
restaurants. AE, DC, MC, V.*

$$$$ **Château Gütsch.** This "castle," built in 1888, is not exactly authentic, but honeymooners, gullible romantics, and other neophytes seeking out storybook Europe enjoy the Disneyland-like experience of this hotel: the turrets and towers worthy of a mad Ludwig of Bavaria; the cellars, crypts, and corridors lined with a hodgepodge of relics; not to mention the magnificent hilltop site above Luzern. Fantasy-style rooms are decked out for romance, some with four-poster canopy beds, all with grand baths. The restaurant is known for its dramatic views of Luzern, and there are wine tastings in the atmospheric cellar. You can get a funicular up to the hotel (2 SF); catch it where Pfistergasse meets Baselstrasse. ⊠ *Kanonenstr., CH-6002,* ☎ *041/2494100,* ℻ *041/2494191. 28 rooms, 3 suites. 2 restaurants, pool, free parking. AE, DC, MC, V.*

$$$$ **National Hotel.** In this monumental landmark, founded in 1870 and once home base to Cesar Ritz, the inner sanctums have been restored to florid splendor, down to the last cupola, crown molding, and Corinthian column. The hotel's mansarded facade stretches the length of two city blocks, dominating the lakeside promenade. Rooms are French provincial with brass beds, the domed bar is decked with mahogany and aglitter with crystal, and the marble-column breakfast hall may be the most splendid in Switzerland—even without the lake view. ⊠ *Haldenstr. 4, CH-6003,* ☎ *41/4190909,* ℻ *041/4190910. 78 rooms, 10 suites. 4 restaurants, breakfast room, café, piano bar, indoor pool, sauna, health club, parking (fee). AE, DC, MC, V.*

$$$$ **Schweizerhof.** Built in 1844 and expanded during the 1860s, this imposing structure has hosted Napoléon III, Leo Tolstoy, and Mark Twain—and Richard Wagner lived here while his lakefront home at Tribschen was being completed. Rooms have a sweeping view of the lake and mountains. At press time, the hotel planned to be closed through 1999 for renovation. ⊠ *Schweizerhofquai 3, CH-6002,* ☎ *041/ 4100410,* ℻ *041/4102971. 116 rooms. Restaurant, café, bar, free parking. AE, DC, MC, V.*

$$$ **Des Balances.** This riverfront property, built during the 19th cen-
★   tury on the site of an ancient guildhall, gleams with style. State-of-the-art tile baths, up-to-date pastel decor, and one of the best sites in Luzern (in the heart of the Old Town) make this the slickest in its price class. Rear rooms look toward the Weinmarkt. The restaurant Rotes Gatter (☞ *above*) is so good that you may want to eat every meal in the hotel. ⊠ *Weinmarkt, CH-6000,* ☎ *041/4103010,* ℻ *041/4106451. 50 rooms, 7 suites. Restaurant. AE, DC, MC, V.*

$$$ **Hofgarten.** This gracious and affordable 12th-century house off the end of the Schweizerhofquai reflects the creative mind of owner Claudia Moser. The rooms are an eclectic mix of colors and themes, and all are equipped for people with disabilities. One contains a 5-ft-tall antique oven (still operable) while another is called the Ship Room and resembles the interior of a clipper ship. Hofgarten also offers Luzern's only all-vegetarian restaurant, whose dishes could satisfy even a meat lover. ⊠ *Stadthofdstr. 14, CH-6006,* ☎ *041/4108888,* ℻ *041/4108333. 18 rooms. Restaurant, parking (fee). AE, DC, MC, V.*

$$$ **Montana.** This neoclassic 1910 palace glows with beeswaxed beauty, its luxurious original woodwork, parquet, and terrazzo in superb condition. The public rooms are parlor-fussy, but guest rooms are fresh and new. Those in back overlook a hillside, while the front doubles (slightly costlier) have balconies with views of the city and lake. The building is perched on a slope above town, accessible by funicular from the waterfront or by car. TV is available by request only. ⊠ *Adligenswilerstr. 22, CH-6003,* ☎ *041/4106565,* ℻ *041/4106676. 55 rooms, 10 suites. Restaurant, bar, free parking. AE, DC, MC, V.*

$$ **Des Alpes.** This historic hotel, with a terrific riverfront location in the bustling heart of the Old Town, has an interior resembling a laminate-and-vinyl chain motel. The rooms, however, are generously proportioned, tidy, and even sleek; front doubles, several with balconies, overlook the water and promenade. Cheaper back rooms face the Old Town; those on higher floors have rooftop views and plenty of light. The restaurant has balcony seating, a terrace, and a waterfront café. ⊠ *Rathausquai 5, CH-6003,* ☎ *041/4105825,* 𝖥𝖠𝖷 *041/4107451. 45 rooms. Restaurant, café. AE, DC, MC, V.*

$$ 🏨 **Diana.** This is a city hotel, on the south bank and off the main shopping street, but it's reached through a quiet park. Newly decorated rooms may have built-in fixtures in sleek beech or warm knotty pine; some have French windows that open onto balconies. In the oldest rooms, a bleak Formica look, a holdover from the '60s, prevails. Jugendstil touches remain in the corridors, and the public areas are modern but worn. ⊠ *Sempacherstr. 16, CH-6003,* ☎ *041/2102623,* 𝖥𝖠𝖷 *041/ 2100205. 38 rooms. Breakfast room. AE, DC, MC, V.*

$$ 🏨 **Drei Könige.** This urban inn, far from the Bahnhof (train station) but very handy to bridges to the Old Town, is in a noisy district and has little to offer of Old Luzern, though its restaurant claims roots in the 17th century. Renovated rooms are Scandi-bland and show their age. The higher floors are quieter; ask for a room in back. Bus 2 takes you from the train station to the nearby Hirzenhof stop. Eat at the neighboring Galliker (☞ *above*) and waddle the short stretch home. ⊠ *Bruchstr. 35, CH-6003,* ☎ *041/2408833,* 𝖥𝖠𝖷 *041/2408852. 60 rooms. Restaurant. AE, DC, MC, V.*

$$ 🏨 **Krone.** Spotless and modern, this hotel softens its edges with pastel linens and walls; along the interior walls you may find a stone prayer shrine retained from the original structure. The rooms facing the Weinmarkt have high ceilings and tall windows that let in floods of sunshine. Rooms to the back have no direct sunlight but are still bright and a little larger. Two rooms are completely wheelchair accessible. The restaurant downstairs has a sinful dessert menu (try the crepes!) and sprawls out on to the Weinmarkt in the summer; it has a no-alcohol policy. ⊠ *Weinmarkt 12, CH-6004,* ☎ *041/4194400,* 𝖥𝖠𝖷 *041/4194490. 25 rooms. Restaurant, deli, outdoor café. AE, DC, MC, V.*

$–$$ 🏨 **Goldener Stern.** This plain and pleasant former wine cellar has restored its fine 17th-century exterior to present a scrubbed face to the world. Pristine linens soften the modern rooms; windows, some looking over the Franciscan church, are double-glazed. The stübli is popular with locals. A friendly family business, Goldener Stern is now managed by the second generation. ⊠ *Burgerstr. 35, CH-6003,* ☎ *041/ 2275060,* 𝖥𝖠𝖷 *041/2275061. 18 rooms. Restaurant. AE, MC, V.*

$ 🏨 **Schlüssel.** This spare, no-nonsense lodging on the Franziskanerplatz attracts young bargain hunters; several of its rooms overlook the Franciscan church and fountain. It's a pleasant combination of tidy new touches (quarry tile, white paint) and antiquity: You can have breakfast or a simple hot meal in a low, cross-vaulted "crypt" and admire the fine old beams in the lobby. ⊠ *Franziskanerpl. 12, CH-6003,* ☎ *041/2101061,* 𝖥𝖠𝖷 *041/2101021. 11 rooms. Breakfast room. AE, MC, V.*

$ 🏨 **Tourist.** Despite its friendly, collegiate atmosphere, this cheery dorm-
★ like spot is anything but a backpackers' flophouse. It has a terrific setting on the Reuss around the corner from the Old Town. Its spare modern architecture is brightened with fresh, trendy colors and framed prints, and rooms that don't have the river view face Mt. Pilatus instead. The staff is young and helpful, and the coed four-bed dorms (sex-segregated in high season) draw sociable travelers with their rock-bottom prices. There are also seven private-bath doubles. Shared baths are well maintained. ⊠ *St. Karli Quai 12, CH-6003,* ☎ *041/4102474,* 𝖥𝖠𝖷 *041/ 4108414. 35 dormitory rooms. Coin laundry. AE, DC, MC, V.*

Nightlife and the Arts

For information on goings-on around town, get a copy of the *Luzern City Guide,* published by the city seasonally; it's available at the tourist office (☞ Visitor Information *in* Luzern and Central Switzerland A to Z, *below*). It's bilingual (German/English).

Nightlife

BARS AND LOUNGES

Château Gütsch (⊠ Kanonenstr., ☎ 041/2494141) draws a sedate dinner-and-dancing crowd. **Mr. Pickwick** (⊠ Rathausquai 6, ☎ 041/4105927) serves up pints English style. The **National Hotel** (☞ Dining and Lodging, *above*) mixes drinks in both its glossy American-style bar and its imposing lobby lounge. The **Palace Hotel** (☞ Dining and Lodging, *above*), like the National, has two American-style bars.

CASINOS

The most sophisticated nightlife in Luzern is found in the **Casino** (⊠ Haldenstr. 6, ☎ 041/4185656), a turn-of-the-century building on the northern shore by the grand hotels. You can play *boule* (a type of roulette) in the Gambling Room (5 SF limit, federally imposed), dance in its club **Vegas,** watch the cabaret in the **Red Rose,** or have a Swiss meal in **Le Chalet** while watching a folklore display.

MUSIC

Luzern, the cultural hub of central Switzerland, hosts the **International Music Festival** for three weeks in August every year. The 1998 festival inaugurated the festival's new lakeside home, the Kultur- und Kongresszentrum (⊠ Europapl.). Outstanding performers come from all over the world; 1998 guests included soloist Bryn Terfel, conductor James Levine, and the Berlin Philharmonic. For further information on the festival, contact **International Musikfestwochen** (⊠ Hirschmanttstr. 13, CH-6002, ☎ 041/2103562, FAX 041/2109464). The **Allgemeine Musikgesellschaft Luzern** (AML), the local orchestra in residence, offers a season of concerts from October through June at the Kunsthaus (☎ 041/2105050). For information on its concerts and other performances throughout the year, consult the *Luzern City Guide* (☞ *above*).

THEATER

The **Luzerner Theater** (⊠ Theaterstr. 2, ☎ 041/2106618), directly on the waterfront on the Bahnhof side of town, is home to Luzern's principal theater group, which stages plays in German and operas, usually in the original language. Current productions are detailed in the German/English *Luzern City Guide* published seasonally by the city; it's available at the tourist office (☞ Visitor Information *in* Luzern and Central Switzerland A to Z, *below*).

The Arts

FILM

Movie theaters, concentrated on the south bank of town along Pilatusstrasse and Bahnhofstrasse, usually present films in their original language.

FOLKLORE

The **Night Boat** (☎ 041/3194978), which sails from Landungsbrücke every evening from May through September, offers meals, drinks, and a folklore show during a pleasant lake cruise. Performances at the **Stadtkeller** (⊠ Sternenpl. 3, ☎ 041/4104733) come with Valais-cheese specialties, yodelers, dirndled dancers, and more.

Outdoor Activities and Sports

Bicycling

The standard Swiss practice of renting bicycles from the **train station** (☎ 051/2273261) comes in handy here, as the lake-level terrain offers smooth riding.

Boating

Pedal-, motor-, and sailboats are available in Luzern through **Bucher & Co.** (☎ 041/4102055). **SNG Luzern** (✉ Alpenquai 11, ☎ 041/3680808), open daily 11–6, offers 60-minute boat tours for 13 SF. **Werft Herzog AG** (☎ 041/4104333) specializes in exclusive yacht excursions for as many as 12 passengers.

Golf

Golfplatz Dietschiberg (✉ Just above Luzern, near the city center, ☎ 041/4209787) has an 18-hole course open to visitors.

Swimming

At the **lido** (✉ Lidostr., ☎ 041/3703806), past the casino and near the Verkehrshaus, you can swim in Lake Luzern.

Tennis

Tennisclub Carlton Tivoli (✉ Haldenstr., ☎ 041/3703137) has four outdoor courts available.

Windsurfing

Contact **Kempf Sport AG** (✉ Bahnhofstr. 24, ☎ 041/2101057).

Shopping

The best shopping in the region is concentrated in Luzern, which, although it no longer produces embroidery or lace, still offers a wide variety of Swiss handiwork as well as the high-fashion and luxury goods appropriate to its high profile. During the summer, most shops remain open in the evening until 9 and open on Sunday morning after 11. On Thursday night year-round, shops stay open until 9.

Department Stores

The main department store in town is **Globus** (✉ Pilatusstr. 4, ☎ 041/2270707); it's a good place to hunt for souvenirs. **Migros** (✉ Hertensteinstr. 44 and Letzihof; Hirschengraben 41, ☎ 041/4106363) specializes in groceries and also has inexpensive stationery and office supplies.

Embroidery

For fine handcrafted lace and embroidery, visit **Neff** (✉ Löwenstr. 10, ☎ 041/4101965), if not to buy, just to browse. The main producer of Swiss embroidery is **Sturzenegger** (✉ Schwanenpl. 7, ☎ 041/4101958) of Saint Gallen, which sells its own machine-made lace and embroidered goods as well as Hanro and Calida underwear. The store also stocks a conservative line of women's dresses and blouses.

Handicrafts and Gifts

Aux Arts du Feu (✉ Schweizerhofquai 2, ☎ 041/4101401) offers high-end china and crystal. **Ordning & Reda** (✉ Hertensteinstr. 3, ☎ 041/4109506) is an upscale Swedish stationer featuring precision writing instruments and handmade recycled-paper products. **Schmid-Linder** (✉ Denkmalstr. 9, ☎ 041/4104346) carries an extensive line of Swiss embroidery and linen as well as cuckoo clocks, cowbells, and a large stock of wood carvings from Brienz, in the Berner Oberland.

Markets

A **flea market** takes place every Saturday from 8 to 4 at Untere Burgerstrasse. For locally made crafts, there's a **Handwerksmarkt** on the Weinmarkt on the first Saturday of every month.

Watches

Competition is fierce, and the two enormous patriarchs of the watch business advertise heavily and offer inexpensive souvenirs to lure shoppers into their luxurious showrooms. **Bucherer** (⊠ Schwanenpl., ☎ 041/3697700) represents Piaget and Rolex. **Gübelin** (⊠ Schweizerhofquai, ☎ 041/4105142) is the exclusive source for Audemars Piguet, Patek Philippe, and its own house brand.

Women's Clothing

The czarina of women's fashion in Luzern is **Christina De Boer**, who runs a group of designer boutiques: **De Boer** (⊠ Weggisg. 29, ☎ 041/4102022), **De Boer Rive Gauche** (⊠ Pilatusstr. 14, ☎ 041/2108916), **De Boer's Esprit** (⊠ Kornmarkt, ☎ 041/4102776), and **Christina De Boer** (⊠ Weggisg. 29, Werchlaube, ☎ 041/4106239). **McStore/Maglia Poletti** (⊠ Furreng. 7, ☎ 041/4102115) stocks such hip, upscale Euro designers as Apropos, Annex, Pink Flamingo (all Swiss designers), and Paul Smith, as well as Poletti's own line of knits in wool, silk, and cotton.

LUZERN ENVIRONS

Mt. Pilatus

⑮ *10 km (6 mi) southwest of Luzern.*

This 2,121-m (6,953-ft) mountain was named either from the Latin *pileatus* (wearing a cap), to refer to its frequent cloud covering, or, more colorfully, for the ghost of Pontius Pilate, who supposedly haunts the summit: His body, it was said, was brought here by the devil. For centuries it was forbidden to climb the mountain and enrage the ghost, who was said to unleash deadly storms. Unlike Queen Victoria, who rode to the summit by mule in 1868, you can now reach it by cable car for a hefty 76.20 SF in summer, 42 SF in winter.

Take a trolley from the train station in Luzern to the suburb of Kriens, where you catch a tiny, four-seat cable car that flies silently up to Fräkmüntegg (1,403 m/4,600 ft); then change to the 40-seat cable car that sails through open air up the rock cliff to the summit station (1,696 m/5,560 ft). From here a 10-minute walk takes you to the **Esel** (2,123 m/6,962 ft), at the center of Pilatus's multiple peaks, where views unfold over the Alps and the sprawling, crooked Lake Luzern.

A pleasant variation for the return trip to Luzern from Mt. Pilatus involves riding a steep cogwheel train, often down gradients inclined nearly 48%, through four tunnels that pierce sheer rock face, to Alpnachstad. From there, take a train back to Hergiswil, where you can cross the track and climb aboard the small, private Stans-Engelberg train that heads up the Engelbergertal (Engelberg Valley). By car, simply head from Alpnachstad toward Stans and Engelberg. At lake level, you'll cross a brief neck of land that separates the Alpnachersee and Lake Luzern. If you are coming straight from Luzern, trains run every hour to Engelberg.

Stans

16 *10 km (6 mi) east of Mt. Pilatus, 10 km (6 mi) south of Luzern.*

In the heart of lush valley terrain and mossy meadows, Stans is an old village whose appealing Old Town center is dotted with the deep-roof houses typical of central Switzerland. This was the home of the beloved Heinrich Pestalozzi, the father of modern education. When the French army invaded the village in 1798, slaughtering nearly 2,000 citizens, it was Pestalozzi who gathered the orphaned children in a school, where he applied his progressive theories in the budding science of psychology to the practice of education. Instead of rote memorization and harsh discipline, Pestalozzi's teaching methods emphasized concrete examples (using plant specimens to teach botany, for example) and moral as well as intellectual development—quite a liberal education. He also championed the idea of children's individuality.

The bell tower of Stans's early Baroque **Church of Saints Peter and Paul** is in Italian Romanesque style (with increasing numbers of arched windows as the tower rises), though the incongruous steeple was added during the 16th century; the church as it stands dates from the Renaissance period. ⊠ *Knirig. 1,* ☎ *041/6109261.*

On the town square stands a 19th-century **monument to Arnold von Winkelried,** a native of Stans who martyred himself to lead the Swiss Confederates to victory over the Austrians at the battle of Sempach in 1386. The Austrians, armed with long spears, formed a Roman square so that the Swiss, wielding axes and halberds, couldn't get in close enough to do any damage. Shouting, "Forward, confederates, I will open a path!" von Winkelried threw himself on the spears, clasping as many of them as he could to his breast—creating an opening for his comrades. ⊠ *Knirig., in front of Church of Saints Peter and Paul.*

Another native son, from the neighboring village of Flüeli, is Niklaus von Flüe, who saved the Confederation again, nearly 100 years after von Winkelried, through wise council at the Diet of Stans in 1481. He was canonized in 1947.

En Route A two-part journey on a nostalgic 1893 funicular and an ultramodern cable car takes you to the **Stanserhorn** (1,891 m/6,200 ft), from whose peak you can see the lakes; the Titlis, at 3,050 m (10,000 ft) the highest point in central Switzerland; and even the Jungfrau.

Engelberg

17 *12 km (8 mi) south of Stans, 27 km (17 mi) south of Luzern.*

At the top of the village of Obermatt, Engelberg (1,000 m/3,280 ft) is a popular resort for skiers from nearby Zürich, but its slopes are limited in comparison to Saint-Moritz, Wengen, and Zermatt. Engelberg clusters at the foot of its Benedictine **Kloster** (monastery) founded in 1120; inside there's one of the largest organs in the country. Until the French invaded in 1798, massacring thousands, this monastery ruled the valley. Now, numerous hotels cater to winter skiers and summer hikers. ⊠ *Signposted,* ☎ *041/6371143.* ☉ *Mon.–Sat. 10–4.*

OFF THE
BEATEN PATH

TITLIS – This is perhaps the most impressive of the many rocky peaks that surround the Obermatt's long, wide bowl. Thanks to a sophisticated transportation system that benefits skiers, hikers, climbers, and tourists alike, it's possible to ride a small cable car up to the tiny mountain lake (and famous ski area) called **Trübsee** (1,801 m/5,904 ft). From there change to a larger cable car, which rotates to give 360-degree panoramas, and ascend to Stand and ultimately to the summit station on the Titlis. There's an ice grotto (serving drinks from a solid-ice bar) and a panorama restaurant: Views take in the Jura Mountains, the Graubünden and Bernese Alps, and what, from this perspective, seems like the puny Pilatus. ☜ *73 SF round-trip.*

Skiing

At the base of the 3,021-m-high (9,906-ft-high) **Titlis,** Engelberg has two funicular railways, seven cable cars, 13 lifts, 45 km (28 mi) of downhill runs, 34 km (21 mi) of cross-country trails, 3½ km (2 mi) of toboggan runs, and ice-skating. About half the runs are intermediate level, and there are plenty of easy slopes as well; advanced skiers will have relatively slim pickings. A ski school (☎ 041/6373030) and snowboard school (☎ 041/6374040) are in the **Tourist Center** (☞ Visitor Information *in* Luzern and Central Switzerland A to Z, *below*).

Dining and Lodging

$$–$$$ ✕ **Bierlialp.** The pizzas at this trattoria are incredible: delicious 1½-ft,
★ stone-oven-baked extravaganzas—and that's a single serving! The modern Italian decor is softened by warm candlelight and an even warmer welcome. For a more elaborate entree, try *Tagiatella Nero* (black noodles, fish, and shrimp with a pepper-cream sauce) or the truffle ravioli. ✉ *Dorfstr. 21,* ☎ *041/6371717. AE, DC, MC, V.*

$$ ✕🏨 **Hess.** Though it was gutted and rebuilt inside back in 1984, this old mountain lodge retains the character you expect from a hotel run by the family that founded it in 1884. The pine-and-chintz rooms are fresher than those decorated in dark wood, and corner doubles are bright, with fine views. Southern mountain views look over the road. The public areas are rustic but grand, with parquet floors, a scattering of game trophies, and a huge fireplace in the main lounge. The restaurant, Tudor-Stübli, is known for satisfying such dishes as veal with porcini risotto; Mr. Hess does some of the cooking himself. ✉ *Dorfstr. 50, CH-6390,* ☎ *041/6371366,* ℻ *041/6373538. 40 rooms, 4 suites. Restaurant, piano bar, sauna, exercise room, dance club. AE, DC, MC, V. Closed May and Nov.*

$ ✕🏨 **Alpenclub.** This is a very Swiss find: a cozy, old-fashioned chalet,
★ every square inch pine-paneled and dark-timbered, with down-quilted beds, a glowing fondue stübli, and a quiet sun terrace looking out on snowy peaks. It's lively, casual, and, above all, cheap. It draws mobs of young skiers to its disco-bar and pizzeria, and families to its firelighted restaurant (all serve à la carte only). Though it stands slightly beyond the urbanized center, it's not for quiet retreats, at least at ski time. ✉ *Dorfstr. 5, CH-6390,* ☎ *041/6371243,* ℻ *041/6370337. 8 rooms. Restaurant, bar, pizzeria, stübli. AE, DC, MC, V. Closed May–June.*

$$$ 🏨 **Regina Titlis.** In a resort haunted by fading grand hotels from a bygone Victorian boom, this centrally located high-rise, a little Dallas in the Alps, strikes a jarring note. Built in 1983 on the ashes of its predecessor, it has fresh, solid rooms with warm wood accents, balconies with views, and generous facilities. If you're looking for quiet, reserve a room at the back of the hotel, away from the street. ✉ *Dorfstr. 33, CH-6390,* ☎ *041/6372828,* ℻ *041/6372392. 96 rooms, 28 suites. 2 restaurants, bar, café, indoor pool, sauna, exercise room, free parking. AE, DC, MC, V.*

$$ 🏨 **Schweizerhof.** Though the exterior suggests a once-grande dame,
★ this lovely old fin de siècle structure has been attentively remodeled inside to combine fresh, light, new knotty-pine looks with plush Edwardian comforts. The south-side views are fine, especially from rooms with balconies. Bay corner doubles are worth asking for. Four family

suites with separate bed- and living rooms make this a perfect option for families and small groups. ⊠ *Dorfstr. 42, CH-6390,* ☎ *041/ 6371105,* FAX *041/6374147. 30 rooms, 10 suites. Restaurant, sauna, steam room, exercise room. AE, DC, MC, V.*

$$ 🏨 **Europe.** Built in 1902, this Jugendstil beauty offers modern amenities in a bright, elegant setting. Some of the rooms are simple to the point of being bland, but others have small chandeliers and beautifully detailed, mirrored wardrobes. Step onto the wrought-iron balconies and gaze up at the Titlis or down at the neighboring park; if you score one of the rooms over the front entrance, you'll have especially incredible views. The restaurant, for hotel guests only, serves contemporary cuisine and traditional Swiss favorites. ⊠ *Dorfstr., CH-6390,* ☎ *041/ 6370094,* FAX *041/6372255. 59 rooms, 7 suites. Restaurant, bar. AE, DC, MC, V.*

Outdoor Activities and Sports

MOUNTAIN BIKING

Mountain biking is very popular here; there's a well-traveled path from the Jochpass to the Trübsee. Free biking maps are available at the tourist office. You can rent bikes from **Amstutz** (⊠ Dorfstr. 39, ☎ 041/6371268). Also try **Bike 'n' Roll Rock'n Ice** (⊠ Titlizentru, Dorfstr. 31, ☎ 041/6374691). Another source is **Gisin Sport** (⊠ Klosterg. 8, ☎ 041/6374939).

TENNIS

There are five outdoor tennis courts at the **Hotel Bellevue** (⊠ Bahnhofpl., ☎ 041/6371213). Two indoor courts are maintained at the **Sportcenter Erlen** (⊠ Engelbergstr. 11, ☎ 041/6373494).

VIERWALDSTÄTTERSEE TO SAINT GOTTHARD AND EINSIEDELN

From Luzern, you can take a lake steamer all the way down to the Urnersee (the southern leg of Lake Luzern); or you can drive the same route along the lakefront highway, continuing on to the historic pilgrimage town of Einsiedeln. Either trip will involve switching to train or cable car if you want to climb to Rigi Kulm, the summit of Mt. Rigi.

If you choose to go by boat, depart at any convenient time (schedules are available at the ticket and tourist offices; *see* Visitor Information *in* Luzern and Central Switzerland A to Z, *below*) from the main docks by the train station (or, by car, past the casino along the waterfront drive); the boat will be marked for Flüelen. First-class seats are on top; each level has a restaurant-café. The exterior seats are only slightly sheltered; if you want to sit inside, you may feel obligated to order a drink. Take advantage of the boat's many stops—you can get on and off at will.

Bürgenstock

⓲ *20 km (13 mi) southeast of Luzern.*

Most Flüelen-bound boats go to the base of Bürgenstock, where visitors can take a funicular to the isolated resort at the top of a ridge. Though the plateau isn't terribly high—only 458 m/1,500 ft—it rises dramatically above the water and offers striking views over the lake region; that's why a small colony of luxury hotels has mushroomed, most of them owned by the Frey family. Bürgenstock also can be approached by car, up a narrow, steep road, from Stansstad, on the road between Luzern and Stans.

Weggis

★ *25 km (15 mi) northeast of Bürgenstock, 20 km (12 mi) northeast of Luzern.*

Weggis is a summer resort town known for its mild, almost subtropical climate. There's a pretty waterfront park and promenade; and as it's far from the auto route and accessible only by the secondary road, you get a pleasant sense of isolation. The famed **Mt. Rigi** (1,800 m/5,900 ft) is just a cable-car ride away from Weggis: Follow signs for the Rigibahn, a station high above the resort (a 15-minute walk). From here you can ride a large cable car to **Rigi-Kaltbad,** a small resort on a spectacular plateau; walk across to the electric rack-and-pinion railway station and ride the steep tracks of the Vitznau–Rigi line to the summit of the mountain. Take an elevator to the Hotel **Rigi-Kulm** (☞ *below*) to enjoy the views indoors or walk to the crest (45 minutes) to see as far as the Black Forest in one direction and Mt. Säntis in the other. Or consider climbing to the top, staying in the hotel, and getting up early to see the sun rise over the Alps—a view that has astounded writers from Victor Hugo to Mark Twain. With Lake Luzern on one side and Lake Zug on the other, Mt. Rigi can seem like an island.

You have the option of returning to Luzern from Weggis by taking a different railway down, from Rigi to Arth-Goldau; the two lines were built by competing companies in the 1870s in a race to reach the top and capture the lion's share of the tourist business. The line rising out of the lakefront resort of Vitznau won, but the Arth-Goldau line gets plenty of business, as its base terminal lies on the mainstream Saint Gotthard route. The round-trip fare from Vitznau or Arth-Goldau to Rigi-Kulm is 54 SF.

Skiing

Mt. Rigi, at 1,798 m (5,900 ft), has two funicular railways, three cable cars, seven lifts, 30 km (19 mi) of downhill runs, 14 km (9 mi) of cross-country trails, 14 km (9 mi) of ski-hiking trails, and curling.

Dining and Lodging

$$$ ✕ **Renggli's.** This restaurant is ideally located on the waterfront, with its own private dock and a terrace overlooking the lake. The eclectic cuisine ranges from refined vegetarian dishes to more exotic fare, such as poached guinea fowl with a mango-curry sauce. Standards are jazzed up, too: steamed white fish with apple cider–herb sauce, for instance. ⊠ *Seestr. 21,* ☏ *041/3900370. AE, DC, MC, V.*

$$–$$$ 🏨 **Beau-Rivage.** Built in 1908 but much modernized, this attractive
★ business-class resort concentrates its comforts on a small but luxurious waterfront site, with a restaurant above the manicured lakeside lawn, a swimming pool with mountain views, and lounge chairs at the lake's edge. Its rooms glow with rosy wood, brass, and pastel fabrics. It's at the center of town, near the boat landing. ⊠ *Gotthardstr. 6, CH-6353,* ☏ *041/3901422,* 🖷 *041/3901981. 40 rooms. Restaurant, bar, outdoor pool. AE, DC, MC, V. Closed Nov.–Mar.*

$$$ 🏨 **Posthotel.** This modern establishment caters to business travelers, both for relaxation and for an unavoidable stint of work. All guest rooms face the street, which leads to the lakefront, and a wide range of fitness facilities is available. The old wooden stübli is still here—preserved intact from the original stagecoach café. The restaurant has an interesting departure from a grill; you can have meat or vegetables cooked on a heated, flat stone. The hotel sits directly over the boat landing. ⊠ *Seestr. 8, CH-6353,* ☏ *041/3927200,* 🖷 *041/3927272. 45 rooms. Restaurant, 2 bars, café, stübli, indoor pool, sauna, exercise room, beach, dock, casino, meeting rooms. AE, DC, MC, V. Closed late Dec.–Jan.*

$$ ⊞ **Du Lac Seehof.** Behind its magnificent classic waterfront facade you'll be welcomed on a humbler, homier scale: This is a family-owned-and-run resort hotel, with an arbored terrace café-restaurant. The rooms are bright and spare, with tile baths. Lake-view rooms with balconies cost more but are worth it. The hotel is near the boat landing. ✉ *Gotthardstr. 4, CH-6353,* ☎ *041/3901151,* ☏ *041/3901119. 25 rooms. Restaurant. AE, DC, MC, V.*

$$ ⊞ **Rigi-Kulm.** If you find the novelty of mountaintop stopovers appealing, this high-altitude hotel is for you; built in 1950 and rather generic, it still has the air of a rugged but genteel lodge. Southern rooms have rustic decor and great views. (Be warned, however: Mountainside transportation makes this an awkward home base for excursions, and if it's raining during your stay, the views disappear.) A short walk from the summit, at 1,800 m (5,900 ft), it is accessible by cable car from Weggis to Rigi-Kaltbad, then cogwheel rail; or by cogwheel from Vitznau or Arth-Goldau. Or you can climb up from Weggis, allowing either three hours or, as Mark Twain required, three days, depending on your penchant for resting. If you'd like to follow an old romantic tradition, get up at the crack of dawn to see the sun rise over the Alps. ✉ *CH-6410,* ☎ *041/8550303,* ☏ *041/8550041. 40 rooms. Restaurant, café. AE, DC, MC, V.*

Outdoor Activities and Sports

The tourist office at Weggis (☞ Visitor Information *in* Luzern and Central Switzerland A to Z, *below*) rents **bicycles.** Weggis maintains several public **tennis** courts; call the tourist office for information. Windsurfing lessons and rentals in Weggis are available through the **Hotel Hertenstein** (☎ 041/3901444).

Vitznau

⑳ *4 km (2½ mi) southeast of Weggis, 26 km (16 mi) east of Luzern.*

For a quintessentially scenic, quiet spot, stop over in Vitznau, a tiny waterfront resort that competes with Weggis in balmy weather, although its main claim to fame is the palatial Park Hotel, built in 1902.

En Route From Vitznau, a boat tour will take you across Lake Luzern to **Beck-**
★ **enried,** from which a cable car leads up to **Klewenalp** (1,601 m/5,250 ft), a small winter-sports and summer resort overlooking the lake. The area is excellent for hiking, offering breathtaking panoramic views of the lake and mountains on clear days. (You can get a hiking trail map from newsstands or local tourist offices (☞ Visitor Information *in* Luzern and Central Switzerland A to Z, *below*). If you're driving, follow the north shore until the boat rejoins it at **Gersau,** a tiny lake resort that from 1332 to 1798 was an independent republic—the world's smallest. From Gersau the boat snakes around the sharp peninsula of the Seelisberg; the 1980 completion of a 9¼-km (6-mi) tunnel across the peninsula, south of the lake, opened the way for even swifter north–south travel between Luzern and points north and the Saint Gotthard route and points south.

Lodging

$$$$ ⊞ **Park.** This isolated but lavish retreat dominates the tiny lakefront
★ village of Vitznau like the castle of a feudal lord. Constructed in 1902 and enlarged in 1985, it's a vaulted and beamed Edwardian dream in impeccable modern form. Even the corridors are grand, with massive oak triple doors and Persian runners stretching over quarry tile. Rooms have timeless pastels, and lakefront rooms command dreamy Alpine views. The back rooms overlook the slopes of the Rigi, dotted with grazing cows. With the hotel's restaurants and all the activities available, you

could easily find yourself not wanting to budge. ⊠ *Kantonstr., CH-6354,* ☎ *041/3970101,* ℻ *041/3970110. 74 rooms, 30 suites. 2 restaurants, café, indoor pool, outdoor pool, miniature golf, 2 tennis courts, beach, dock, waterskiing, playground. AE, DC, MC, V. Closed Nov.–Mar.*

$$ ⊠ **Rigi.** Less than half the price of the grandiose Park (☞ *above*), this solid lodging has modernized interiors and a welcoming stübli atmosphere in its public areas. The corner rooms have balconies with a lake view; four rooms have small kitchenettes. The hotel is just one block from the boat landing and close to the Rigibahn (which means there's some traffic noise during the day). Both the restaurant and the less formal stübli serve good, simple fish dishes, and there's a pleasant garden terrace. ⊠ *Hauptstr., CH-6354,* ☎ *041/3972121,* ℻ *041/3971825. 36 rooms. Restaurant, stübli. AE, DC, MC, V.*

$ ⊠ **Schiff.** Commanding much the same view as the Park (though the
★ Park itself clouds some of its lakefront beauty), this plain old roadhouse perches on the hill across the street and offers cheap, no-bath rooms in '50s summer-cottage styles. The vine-trellised terrace restaurant, wide open to the water and mountain skyline, serves inexpensive lake-fish dishes. The hotel says private bathrooms will be added someday, although not too soon, we hope; it's cozy as is. ⊠ *Kantonstr., CH-6354,* ☎ *041/3971357,* ℻ *041/3972498. 6 rooms. Restaurant. AE, DC, MC, V. Closed Oct. and Nov.*

Outdoor Activities and Sports

BIKING
Rent bikes through the **Hotel Vierwaldstättersee** (⊠ Hauptstr., ☎ 041/3972222).

TENNIS
The **Park hotel** (⊠ Hertensteinstr. 34, ☎ 041/3901313) rents court time to nonguests for 35 SF an hour. The **Seehotel Vitznauerhof** (⊠ Seestr., ☎ 041/3997777) has a court and equipment to rent.

WATER SPORTS
Motorboats and paddleboats are for rent through **Anker Travel** (⊠ Zihlstr. ☎ 041/3971707). You can swim in the bay, which is naturally warmer than Luzern's lido.

En Route   At the south end of Lake Luzern, the narrow, majestic **Urnersee** is the wildest and most beautiful leg of the lake. Along its shores lie some of the most historic—or, at least, romantic—landmarks in the region. The **Schillerstein,** on the right as you cruise past the peninsula, is a natural rock obelisk extending nearly 26 m (85 ft) up out of the lake; it bears the simple dedication: TO THE AUTHOR OF WILHELM TELL, FRIEDRICH VON SCHILLER. 1859.

Rütli Meadow

★ ㉑   *15 km (10 mi) northwest of Altdorf on Urnersee, 35 km (22 mi) southeast of Luzern.*

Perhaps the most historically significant site in central Switzerland, the Rütli Meadow, just above the Rütli dock, is where the Confederates of Schwyz, Unterwald, and Uri are said to have met in 1307 to renew the 1291 Oath of Eternal Alliance. **Tellsplatte,** on the east side of the lake, at the foot of the Axen Mountain, is the rocky ledge onto which Tell, the legendary rebellious archer, leapt to escape from Gessler's boat, pushing the boat back into the stormy waves as he jumped. There is a small chapel here, built around 1500 and restored in 1881; it contains four frescoes of the Tell legend, painted at the time of restoration.

Another monumental event took place here centuries later: Amid threats of a 1940 German invasion, General Guisan, Swiss army commander-in-chief, summoned hundreds of officers to the meadow to reaffirm their commitment to the Swiss Confederation in a secret, stirring ceremony.

Altdorf

㉒ *20 km (12 mi) south of Rütli Meadow, 35 km (22 mi) southeast of Luzern.*

Schiller's play *Wilhelm Tell* combines and dramatizes chronicles of the period and sums up the tale for the Swiss, who perform his play religiously in venues all over the country—including the town of Altdorf, just up the road from the Rütli Meadow. Leave the steamer at Flüelen, the farthest point of the boat ride around the lake, and connect by postbus to Altdorf, the capital of the canton Uri and, by popular if not scholarly consensus, the setting for Tell's famous apple-shooting scene. There is a much-reproduced **Tell monument** in the village center, showing a proud father with crossbow on one shoulder, the other hand grasping his son's hand; it was sculpted by Richard Kissling in 1895.

Outdoor Activities and Sports
BIKING

Rent bikes at the train station (☎ 041/8701008) in **Altdorf.** Mountain bikes and motorbikes can be rented and serviced in Altdorf through **Mototreff** (⊠ Flüelerstr. 20, ☎ 041/8709737).

WATER SPORTS

You can rent pedal boats and motorboats in Flüelen at **Herr F. Kaufmann** (⊠ Seestr. 1, Flüelen, ☎ 041/8701575).

Bürglen

㉓ *3 km (1¾ mi) southeast of Altdorf, 40 km (25 mi) southeast of Luzern.*

Tell was supposedly from the tiny town of Bürglen, just up the road from Altdorf. The **Tell Museum** devoted to him displays documents and art on the legend. ⊠ Postpl., ☎ 041/8704155. ☉ *June–Oct., daily 10–11:30 and 2–5; July and Aug., daily 10–5.*

Andermatt

㉔ *25 km (15 mi) south of Bürglen (exit the A2 expressway at Göschenen), 67 km (41 mi) southeast of Luzern.*

Andermatt serves as a crossroads for traffic arriving from the Furka Pass, the Oberalp Pass, and the Saint Gotthard Pass. It's a relaxing little backwater (no tracts of condos here), with lovely valley hiking and, thanks to its level terrain, fine cross-country skiing. It's much more of a local spot than a sunglasses-and-celebrities resort. From the top of **Gemsstock,** approached by cable car from the town, it is said you can see 600 Alpine peaks.

Skiing
A high, sheltered plateau at the crossroads of three passes—the Gotthard, the Furka, and the Oberalp—**Andermatt** (1,449 m/4,750 ft) is easily accessible from all directions. It has five cable cars, 10 lifts, 55 km (34 mi) of downhill runs, and 20 km (12 mi) of cross-country trails and a snowboard fun park. The ski runs are especially suited for intermediate to advanced skiers. The German-only **snow hot line** (☎ 041/8870181) reports on the latest conditions.

Outdoor Activities and Sports

MOUNTAIN BIKING

Mountain biking is popular here; to rent bikes, call **Christen Sport** (⊠ Gotthardstr. 55, CH-6490, ☎ 041/8871251), the leading retailer for summer-sports and snow equipment.

OFF THE
BEATEN PATH

SAINT GOTTHARD PASS – This ancient passage started as a narrow path during the 13th century; a railway was not completed until 1882, and the new tunnel was finished in 1980. In these bleak and icy heights, the watershed source of the Rhine and the Rhône, you may spot eerie, partially concealed military facilities dug deep into the rock and see soldiers drilling in the snow: It's the Swiss army, refining its Alpine defense skills. The pass closes in winter.

Schwyz

㉕ *30 km (20 mi) north of Andermatt (via Hwy. 8 or the A2 expressway—exit just past Altdorf), 44 km (27 mi) east of Luzern.*

This historic town is the capital of the Schwyz canton, root of the name Switzerland, and source of the nation's flag. Switzerland's most precious archives are stored here as well. Traces of an independent settlement at Schwyz have been found from as far back as the Bronze Age (2500 BC–800 BC), but it was its inhabitants' aid in the 1291 Oath of Allegiance that put Schwyz on the map. You can see the beautifully scripted and sealed original document as well as battle flags and paintings of the period in Schwyz's **Bundesbriefmuseum** (Federal Charters Museum), an impressively simple concrete building completed in 1936. ⊠ *Bahnhofstr. 20,* ☎ *041/8192064.* ⊡ *Free.* ☉ *Daily 9:30–11:30 and 2–5.*

Schwyz has several notable Baroque churches and a large number of fine old patrician homes dating from the 17th and 18th centuries, not least being the **Ital-Redinghaus,** with its magnificent interior, antique stoves, and fine stained glass. A visit to this grand house includes a peek inside the neighboring **Bethlehemhaus,** the oldest wooden house in Switzerland, dating from 1287. ⊠ *Rickenbachstr. 24,* ☎ *041/8114505.* ⊡ *2 SF.* ☉ *May–Oct., Tues.–Fri. 2–5, weekends 10–noon and 2–5.*

Curiously, many of Schwyz's splendid houses owe their origin to the battlefield. The men of Schwyz had a reputation as fine soldiers and were in demand in other countries as mercenaries during the 16th and 17th centuries. They built many of the houses you can see today with their military pay.

Einsiedeln

㉖ *27 km (18 mi) northeast of Schwyz, 69 km (43 mi) northeast of Luzern.*

A minor summer and winter resort, Einsiedeln has been a center for pilgrimage since AD 946 and is also the home of the **Black Madonna,** still on display after more than a thousand years. The **Benedictine monastery** was founded during Charlemagne's time—the 9th century—when Meinrad, a Hohenzollern count and monk, chose the remote site to pursue his devotions in solitude. The abbess of Zürich gave him an image of the Virgin Mary, for which he built a little chapel, and Meinrad lived in peace, fed—the story goes—by two ravens who brought him supplies. When he was murdered by brigands seeking treasure, the ravens followed the thieves to Zürich and shrieked over their heads until they were arrested. A monastery was built over Meinrad's grave. When it was completed, the Bishop of Konstanz was invited to

Personal
training for
Europe

Takes the
work out
of your travel

1-800-4-EURAIL
www.raileurope.com

RAIL EUROPE
GROUP

WHEN WAS THE LAST TIME YOU
FELT THIS GOOD **IN THE AIR?**

swissair ✚
1-800-221-4750

Partner in the Delta Air Lines, Midwest Express Airlines
and US Airways frequent flyer programs.

consecrate it, but as he began the ceremony, a voice was heard crying out in the chapel three times, "Brother, desist: God himself has consecrated this building." A papal bull acknowledged the miracle and promised a special indulgence to pilgrims.

Through the ages the monastery of Einsiedeln has been destroyed many times by fire, but the Black Madonna has always been saved. When Napoléon's armies plundered the church, hoping to carry off the sacred image, it had already been taken to the Tirol in Austria for safekeeping. Today the Black Madonna is housed in a black-marble chapel just inside the west entrance to the church. When seen from a distance, its color appears to be a rich bronze, not black, and there is something quaint and gentle about the figure despite its jeweled splendor. The present structure of the abbey was built by Caspar Moosbrugger in 1735 and decorated by the famous brothers Egid Quirid and Cosmos Damian Asam; it is one of the finest late-Baroque churches of its kind, the impressive simplicity and grace of the exterior contrasting vividly with the exuberance of its ornate interior. In front of the church, a grand square surrounds a golden statue of the Virgin Mary with a large gilded crown. Around the base, water trickles from 14 spouts, and pilgrims, to be sure of good luck, traditionally drink from each one in turn.

Einsiedeln is just off the A3 autobahn that connects Zürich with eastern Switzerland. You can take this autobahn to return to Luzern, but a more interesting route is via Alosen and Unterägeri by the Ägerisee, to Zug (☞ *below*), famous for its Old Town.

The Arts
Einsiedeln remains a center for religious pomp and ceremony and celebrates a **Festival of the Miraculous Dedication** every September 14. Every five years some 700 citizens, coached by the monks, perform *Das Grosse Welttheater* (*the Great World Theater*) before the abbey church. A religious drama on life and the problems of humankind, it was first performed before the Court of Spain in 1685. The next performance of this historic pageant takes place in summer 2003.

Outdoor Activities and Sports
For **bicycle** rentals, call the train station (☎ 055/4122158). There are four outdoor **tennis courts** at Grotzenmühle (☎ 055/4124009).

Zug

㉗ *27 km (17 mi) north of Einsiedeln, 28 km (18 mi) northeast of Luzern (via A14 and A4).*

On arriving at the train station in Zug, you may be surprised to find that it is bustling, modern, and full of multinational corporations. Its contemporary life unfurls around the remnants of ancient ramparts, and its lakefront neighborhood seems frozen in another century. From the train station area on Alpenstrasse you can head straight for the waterfront of the **Zugersee** (Lake Zug). This landscaped promenade and park has fine views of Pilatus, Rigi, and the Bernese Alps—including the Eiger, the Mönch, and the Jungfrau.

Zug's Old Town is dominated by the **Rathaus,** which was completed during the early 16th century. Inside, there are exhibits of gold and silver work as well as embroideries, wood carvings, stained glass, and the flag Wolfgang Kolin held until he perished in the battle of Arbedo (1422), when 3,000 Swiss tried valiantly to hold off 24,000 Milanese soldiers. Unfortunately, you'll see these fine furnishings only if you dine in the **Rathauskeller** (☞ Dining and Lodging, *below*), one of the best—

but most expensive—restaurants in central Switzerland. ⊠ *Oberalstadt 1. Closed to the public.*

By passing through a gate under the Zytturm (Clock Tower), you'll come upon the waterfront **Kolinplatz,** dedicated to Wolfgang Kolin and dominated by a fountain in his image. South of the Kolinplatz, up a small hill, is the **Kirche St. Oswald** (Church of St. Oswald), built during the 15th and 16th centuries; it's delicate spires rise high above the town. The Burg, a former Hapsburg residence, has a half-timber exterior so heavily restored it looks like a Disney set for *Snow White.* It now houses the **Burg-Museum,** focusing on archaeology, art, and history from Zug. ⊠ *Kirchenstr. 11,* ☎ *041/7283297.* ⌖ *5 SF, free Sun.* ☉ *Tues.–Fri. 2–5, weekends 10–noon and 2–5.*

NEED A BREAK?	While waiting for your return train, stop at the patisserie-café **Meier** (⊠ Alpenstr. 14, ☎ 041/7111049) for coffee and a slice of the famous Zug Kirschtorte—though the only cherry you'll find is a heavily alcoholic essence that soaks the delicate yellow cake and butter cream.

The most atmospheric streets of Zug are the **Ober-Altstadt** and the **Unter-Altstadt,** tight lanes closed in on each side by narrow, shuttered 16th-century town houses now in the throes of early gentrification: The storefronts are full of arts and crafts, ceramics, jewelry, with a few having trendy baby clothes and toys.

Dining and Lodging

$$$$ ✕ **Rathauskeller.** Upstairs in this historical landmark you are surrounded by a museumlike collection of medieval regional treasures but are served nothing but cutting-edge cuisine. The emphasis is on good fish (scallops marinated in olive oil and lemon juice), meats (tender rabbit fillet with wild mushroom risotto), and a minimum of visual fuss. Downstairs, in the traditional, dark little stübli—and even at a handful of tables on the cobblestones outside—you can order simpler, cheaper dishes from the same kitchen. ⊠ *Oberaltstadt 1,* ☎ *041/ 7110058. AE, V. Closed Sun. and Mon.*

$–$$ ✕ **Aklin.** This 500-year-old Altstadt landmark offers *Grossmutters Küche* (Grandmother's cooking)—*Kalbskopf* (chopped veal head), *Siedfleisch* (boiled beef), and lake fish—on candlelighted wooden tables by a ceramic-tile stove in the upstairs restaurant or in the atmospheric, casual bistro downstairs. ⊠ *Kolinpl. 10,* ☎ *041/7111866. AE, DC, MC, V. Closed Sun.*

$$–$$$ ▥ **Ochsen.** Although the notch-gable facade has been preserved at this 16th-century landmark on the imposing Kolinplatz of Zug's Old Town, the interior is strictly upscale-chain. Hints of architectural detail have been sanded away, and the buffed wood of the restaurant looks more Scandi-sleek teak now than Swiss; it's hard to believe that Goethe was once a guest here. The rooms are high-tech chic; the best are at the far back (above a tiny courtyard) and—of course—looking over the Kolinplatz Fountain, toward the lake. The restaurant deserves its good reputation for fine local dishes: meats, Rösti, and its specialty, lake fish. ⊠ *Kolinpl. 11, CH-6301,* ☎ *041/7293232,* ▧ *041/7293222. 46 rooms. Restaurant. AE, DC, MC, V.*

Outdoor Activities and Sports

At 436 m (1,430 ft), **Zug** has 9 km (6 mi) of **cross-country ski** trails, 17 km (11 mi) of **ski-hiking** trails, and **curling.** You can rent bicycles from the train station (☎ 041/7113988).

LUZERN AND CENTRAL SWITZERLAND A TO Z

Arriving and Departing

By Car

It's easy to reach Luzern from Zürich by road, approaching from national expressway **A3** south, connecting to **A4** via the secondary **E41** in the direction of Zug, and continuing on **A4**, which turns into the **A14**, to the city. A convenient all-expressway connection between the two cities won't be open before the end of the decade. Approaching from the southern, Saint Gotthard Pass route (**A2**) or after cutting through the Furka Pass by rail ferry, you descend below Andermatt to Altdorf, where a tunnel with stifling views sweeps you through to the shores of the lake. If you're heading for resorts on the north shore, leave the expressway at Flüelen and follow the scenic secondary route. From Basel in the northwest, it's a clean sweep by **A2** to Luzern.

By Plane

The nearest international airport is **Zürich-Kloten** (✉ Approximately 54 km/33 mi northeast of Luzern, ☎ 1571060). **Swissair** (☎ 800/221–4750 in the U.S.; 0171/434–7300 in the U.K.) flies in most often from the United States and the United Kingdom.

By Train

Luzern functions as a rail crossroads, with express trains connecting hourly from Zürich, a 49-minute trip, and every two hours from Geneva, a 3½- to 4-hour trip changing at Bern. Trains enter from the south via the Saint Gotthard Pass from the Ticino and via the Furka Pass from the Valais. For rail information, call the **Bahnhof** (train station; ✉ Bahnhofpl., ☎ 1572222).

Getting Around

By Boat

It would be a shame to see this historic region only from the shore; some of its most impressive landscapes are framed along the waterfront, as seen from the decks of one of the cruise ships that ply the lake. Rides on these are included in a **Swiss Pass** (☞ Train Travel *in* the Gold Guide) or a **Swiss Boat Pass** (☞ Boat Travel *in* the Gold Guide). Individual tickets can be purchased at Luzern's departure **docks** (✉ Near the train station, ☎ 041/3676767); the fee is based on the length of your ride. Any combination of transportation can be arranged, such as a leisurely cruise from Luzern to Flüelen at the lake's southernmost point, lasting about 3½ hours and costing 62 SF; the return train trip, via the Arth–Goldau line, takes little more than an hour. If you're staying in a Luzern hotel, you will be eligible for the special **Guest-Ticket**, offering unlimited rides for two days for a minimal fee of 5 SF. The **Tell Pass** (☞ By Train, *below*) gives you free boat rides.

By Bus

The postbus network carries travelers faithfully, if slowly, to the farthest corners of the region. It also climbs the Saint Gotthard and the Furka passes (remember, these are closed in winter). For schedules and prices, check at the post office nearest your home base or pick up a copy of the *Vierwaldstättersee Fahrplan,* a booklet (50 rappen) that covers cruise ships and private railways, available as well at the local tourist office (☞ Visitor Information, *below*). The Tell Pass (☞ By Train, *below*) includes postbus discounts.

By Car

Although Mt. Rigi and Mt. Pilatus are not accessible by car, nearly everything else in this region is. The descent from Andermatt past the Devil's Bridge, which once carried medieval pilgrims from the Saint Gotthard and drew thrill seekers during the 19th century, now exemplifies awe-inspiring Swiss mountain engineering: From Göschenen, at 1,106 m (3,627 ft), to the waterfront, it's a four-lane expressway.

By Train

Swiss National Railways is enhanced here by a few private lines (to Engelberg, Pilatus, the Rigi Kulm) that make it possible to get to most sights. If you don't have a Swiss Pass, there's a central Switzerland regional pass, called the **Tell Pass.** The 15-day pass grants you five days of unlimited free travel on main routes, 10 days at half fare. The seven-day pass gives you two days free, five at half fare. The ticket can be bought at rail or boat ticket offices, on a cruise boat, from travel agencies, or from the tourist office (☞ Visitor Information, *below*). The 15-day pass costs 175 SF second class, 196 SF first class; the seven-day pass costs 128 SF second class, 139 SF first class. Plan your itinerary carefully to take full advantage of all discount rates, and before you buy a regional pass, add up your excursions à la carte. Remember that many routes always charge half price. All boat trips and the private excursions to Rigi and Pilatus are free to holders of regional passes—but getting to the starting point may cost you half price. If you plan to cover a lot of ground, however, you may save considerably. Choose your free days in advance: You must confirm them *all* with the first inspector who checks your pass.

Contacts and Resources

Emergencies

Police (☎ 117). **Medical, dental, and pharmacy referral** (☎ 111). **Auto breakdown**: Touring Club of Switzerland (☎ 140); Swiss Automobile Club (☎ 041/2100155).

Guided Tours

The **Luzern tourist office** (☞ Visitor Information, *below*) offers a guided walking tour of Luzern with English commentary. They last about two hours and cost 15 SF, including a drink. **Schiffahrtsgesellschaft des Vierwaldstättersees** (⊠ Werftestr. 5, CH-6002 Luzern, ☎ 041/3676767) offers historic and Alpine theme cruises with English commentary.

The *Wilhelm Tell Express,* a cooperative effort of Swiss Federal Railways and lake steamers, operates daily from May through October, carrying passengers by steamship and rail to Lugano. The journey, without stopovers, takes six hours. For information, contact the Luzern tourist office (☞ *below*).

Visitor Information

The principal tourist office for the whole of central Switzerland, including the lake region, is the **Zentralschweiz Tourismus** (Central Switzerland Tourism; ⊠ Alpenstr. 1, CH-6002 Luzern, ☎ 041/4184080, FAX 041/4107260). The main tourist office for the city of **Luzern** (⊠ Frankenstr. 1, ☎ 041/4107171) is near the Bahnhof. There's also an accommodations service.

Local offices: **Altdorf** (⊠ Rathauspl., CH-6460, ☎ 041/8720450). **Andermatt** (⊠ Offizielese Verkehrsbüro, Gotthardstr. 2, CH-6490, ☎

041/8871454). **Einsiedeln** (✉ Hauptstr. 85, ☎ 055/4184488). **Engelberg** (✉ Klosterstr., CH-6390, ☎ 041/6373737). **Schwyz** (✉ Bahnhofstr. 32, CH-6440, ☎ 041/8101991). **Stans** (✉ Engelbergstr. 34, CH-6370, ☎ 041/6108833), **Vitznau** (✉ Seestr., CH-6354, ☎ 041/3980035), and **Weggis** (✉ Seestr. 5, CH-6353, ☎ 041/3901155). **Zug** (✉ Alpenstr. 16, CH-6300, ☎ 041/7110078).

7 Basel

At the juncture of France and Germany, German-speaking Basel is a cultural capital with a sense of fun. Cultivated and yet down-home, it has more than 30 museums, Switzerland's oldest university, and some of the most diverse shopping in the country. All the same, beer and sausages are the snack of choice, and the annual Carnival is observed with a boisterousness that's unparalleled in other Swiss towns.

THOUGH IT LACKS THE GILT AND GLITTER of Zürich and the Latin grace of Geneva, in many ways quiet, genteel Basel (Bâle in French) is the most sophisticated of Swiss cities. At the frontier between Europe's two most assertive personalities, France and Germany, and tapped directly into the artery of the Rhein (Rhine), it has flourished on the lifeblood of two cultures and grown surprisingly urbane, cosmopolitan, worldly wise. It is also delightfully eccentric, its imagination as well as its culture fed by centuries of intellectual input: Basel has been host to Switzerland's oldest university (1460) and patron to some of the country's—and the world's—finest minds. A northern center of humanist thought and art, it nurtured the painters Konrad Witz and Hans Holbein the Younger as well as the great Dutch scholar Erasmus. And it was Basel's visionary Lord Mayor Johann Rudolf Wettstein who, at the end of the Thirty Years' War, negotiated Switzerland's groundbreaking—and lasting—neutrality.

Updated by
Kara
Misenheimer

Every day 27,500 French and German commuters cross into Basel, and 10 million tonnes (11 million tons) of cargo pass through its ports. Banking activity here is surpassed only by that in Zürich and Geneva, and every month representatives of the world's leading central banks meet behind closed doors in the city center at the Bank for International Settlements, the world's central bank clearinghouse. Enormous international pharmaceutical firms—such as Novartis and Roche—crowd the riverbanks. Yet Basel's population hovers around a modest 200,000; its urban center lies gracefully along the Rhine, no building so tall as to block another's view of the cathedral's twin spires. Two blocks from the heart of the thriving shopping district you can walk 17th-century residential streets cloaked in perfect, otherworldly silence.

The disproportionate number of museums per capita reflects much about Basel's priorities: The city has more than 30, including the world-class Kunstmuseum (Museum of Fine Arts), the Jean Tinguely Museum, and the Riehen-by-Basel-based Beyeler Foundation. As high culture breeds good taste, Basel has some of the most varied, even quirky, shopping in Switzerland; antique-book stores, calligraphers, and artisans do business next to sophisticated designer shops and famous jewelers. But you can still get a beer and a sausage here: Baslers almost exclusively speak German or their own local version of *Schwyzerdütsch,* called *Baseldütsch.* On Freie Strasse, the main shopping street, dense crowds of shoppers stand outside a local butcher's, holding bare *Wienerli* (hot dogs) and dipping the pink tips into thick golden mustard. They also indulge in *Kaffe und Kuchen*—the late-afternoon coffee break Germans live for—but Baslers do it differently. Instead of the large slices of creamy cake, they select tiny sweet gems—two or three to a saucer, but petite nonetheless—and may opt for a delicate Chinese tea.

The Celts were the first to settle here, some 2,000 years ago, on the site of the Münster (cathedral). During the 1st century BC the Romans established a town at Augst, then called Colonia Augusta Raurica; the ruins and the theater can be visited today, 10 minutes by car outside town. By the 3rd century, the Romans had taken the present cathedral site in Basel proper, naming the town Basilia (royal stronghold). Germanic invaders banished them in 401, and it was not until Henry II, the Holy Roman emperor, took Basel under his wing during the 11th century that stability returned. His image and that of his wife, Kunegunde, adorn the cathedral and the Rathaus (Town Hall). Henry built the original cathedral—on the site of a church destroyed by a raiding band of Hungarian horsemen in 916—and established Basel as one of the centers of his court. In 1006 the bishop of Basel was made ruler of the town, and throughout the Middle Ages these prince-bishops gained and exerted enormous temporal, as well as spiritual, power. Though the bishop-lords are no more, Basel still uses one of their symbols in its coat of arms—a striking black staff.

Yet Basel is first and foremost a Renaissance city in the literal sense of the word: a city of intellectual and artistic rebirth, its flourishing river commerce bringing with it the flow of ideas. In 1431 the Council of Basel, an ecumenical conference on church reform, was convened here, bringing in—over a period of 17 years—the great sacred and secular princes of the age. One of them, who later became Pope Pius II, granted permission for the founding of the university and established Basel as the cultural capital it remains today.

Art and academia over the ages haven't made Basel stuffy, however. The Baslers' Lenten celebration of Fasnacht (related to Mardi Gras, or Carnival) turns the city on its ear. The streets are filled with grotesquely costumed revelers bearing huge homemade lanterns that lampoon local politicians. Although the festivities last only three days, you'll see masks, drums, and fifes displayed and sold everywhere all year and hear strains of fife-and-drum marches wafting from the guild houses' upper windows; they're rehearsing for Fasnacht. Like confetti lodged between the cobblestones, there always seems to be a hint of Fasnacht, age-old and unpredictable, even in Basel's most sedate and cultivated corners.

Pleasures and Pastimes

Dining

When the Alemanni hordes sent the Romans packing, they brought their Germanic cuisine as well; despite persistent bombardment from international cultures, for the most part the German style stuck. When Baslers eat home style, it's inevitably sausage, schnitzel, *Spätzli* (tiny flour dumplings), and beer. The city is full of comfortable haunts lined with carved wood and thick with the mingled odors of cooking meat and cigar smoke.

Yet the proximity of the Rhine has left its *riverains* (riverside dwellers) with a taste for river fish, too, and if Basel could claim a regional specialty, it would be salmon. Salmon made its way from the ocean to the Rhine during the Ice Age and became so commonplace in Basel's golden age that some cooks refused to prepare it more than twice a week. Basel's better restaurants often feature the meaty pink fish (though it's likely imported, as the Rhine has suffered from pollution), served in a white-wine marinade with fried onions on top—*nach Basler-Art* (Basel style). Try it with a bottle of the fruity local Riesling-Sylvaner.

Fasnacht

Originating in the Middle Ages, Fasnacht, Switzerland's best-known Carnival, is a must-see if Basel is on your springtime travel itinerary. Beginning at 4 AM the morning after Ash Wednesday, the Morgenstraich opens the event with a blast of fifes and drums forceful enough to wake the living, the dead, and the hard-of-hearing, too. As it happens, no one's sleeping at all, with most of the population waiting in the freezing darkness for the start of colorful masked processions that traverse the Old Town until dawn and continue for several days more. Nearby Liestal stages its own spectacular and more primitive ceremony the night before, when burning stacks of wood are paraded through the town and heaped together. Early in the procession, the burning wood is carried on participants' backs; as the piles grow, they're put on wagons. The flames flare splendidly against the town's medieval *Tor* (gate) with the rush of each passing group.

Museums

Home to the world's oldest public art collection, the Kunstmuseum (Museum of Fine Arts) is as impressive on the inside as its grand exterior heralds; alone it would qualify Basel as a city with great collections. But that's only the beginning: The city's other museums cover such topics as design, caricature, ethnography, folklife, paper and printing, and pharmaceutical history. The larger museums, such as the Historisches Museum, publish guides in English. Also, the tourist office has a museum guidebook (in English) that describes the highlights of Basel's collections.

EXPLORING BASEL

The Rhine divides the city of Basel into two distinct sections: The whole of the Old Town lies in Grossbasel (Greater Basel), the commercial, cultural, and intellectual center. The opposite, east, bank is Kleinbasel (Little Basel), a tiny Swiss enclave on the "German" side of the Rhine that is the industrial quarter of the city. Unless you are visiting on business and meeting at the convention center east of the river, your time on the right bank will probably be limited to a waterfront stroll and a good night's sleep, as some hotels are here.

Numbers in the text correspond to numbers in the margin and on the Basel map.

Great Itineraries

IF YOU HAVE 1 OR 2 DAYS

Begin with a stroll through Basel's Old Town, seeing its world-class Kunstmuseum and the medieval city gates Spalentor and St. Alban-Tor. Don't miss the Münster and the sweeping views from the church's Rhine terrace, the Pfalz. Beneath the Münster, take one of the little ferries across to the Kleinbasel side for a Rhine-side afternoon stroll along the Oberer Rheinweg.

On the following day, take in some of the city's smaller museums, perhaps in the picturesque St. Alban quarter, where there's a cross-river connection to the Tinguely Museum. Farther afield in Riehen-by-Basel visit the Beyeler Foundation's stunningly well-rounded (and beautifully presented) collection of 20th century art.

IF YOU HAVE 3 TO 5 DAYS

Given the luxury of several days, you can explore even more of Basel's museums. Make sure to take a boat trip to the Roman ruins of Augusta Raurica, east of Basel. You could also take a driving tour of the small villages scattered south of Basel: Balsthal, Holderbank, Oberer Hauenstein, Langenbruck, and Liestal.

Old Town

Standing in the middle of the Marktplatz or even watching river traffic from the Mittlere Rheinbrücke, it's easy to envision the Basel of centuries ago. On a bend of the Rhine, Basel's Old Town is full of majestic Gothic spires and side streets that have remained largely unchanged since the 1600s. Still, much of the delicately preserved architecture of the Old Town incorporates impressive, state-of-the-art museums and miles of pedestrian shopping.

A Good Walk

Six bridges link the two halves of the city; the most historic and picturesque is the **Mittlere Rheinbrücke** ①. Start at its Grossbasel end, near the tourist office. On the corner of what is now a chain restaurant (Churrasco) at Schifflände, you can see a facsimile of the infamous **Lällekönig** ②, a 15th-century gargoyle once mechanized to stick out his tongue and roll his eyes at his rivals across the river.

Walking across the bridge, you'll see Basel's peculiar little gondolalike ferry boats, attached to a high wire and angling silently from shore to shore, powered only by the swift current of the river (you can ride one for 1.20 SF). Across the Rhine, pause to ponder the thoughts of the seated **statue of Helvetia,** one of Basel's many tongue-in-cheek sculptures.

Back across the Mittlere Rheinbrücke in Grossbasel, turn left up a steep little alley called the **Rheinsprung,** banked with 15th- and 16th-century houses and curio shops. Turn right at Archivgässlein, and you'll come to **Martinskirche** ③, the oldest parish church in town, dating from 1288.

Continue along Martinsgasse, on your left, to the elegant neighboring courtyards of the **Blaues und Weisses Haus** ④, meeting place of kings. Just beyond, turn left and head toward the fountain adorned by a mythical green basilisk into the Augustinergasse. At No. 2 is the entrance to the **Naturhistorisches Museum** ⑤, and the **Schweizerisches Museum der Kulturen** ⑥. Under one roof, you will find one of the world's foremost natural history and prehistory collections, as well as European artifacts.

Augustinergasse leads onto the Münsterplatz, dominated by the striking red-sandstone 12th-century **Münster** ⑦, burial place of Erasmus and Queen Anna of Hapsburg. Walk around to the church's river side to a terrace called the **Pfalz,** which offers wide views of the river, the Old Town, and, on a clear day, the Black Forest.

From the Münsterplatz, head down Rittergasse, past its elegant villas and courtyards, to the first busy cross street. Ahead of you is St. Alban-Vorstadt, which leads to the **St. Alban-Tor** ⑧, one of the original 13th-century medieval city gates. St. Alban-Tal runs off St. Alban-Vorstadt and leads down to St. Alban-Rheinweg on the Rhine to the **Basler Papiermühle/Schweizer Papiermuseum und Museum für Schrift und Druck** ⑨ and **Museum für Gegenwartskunst** ⑩.

Leaving the museums by way of the St. Alban-Rheinweg along the riverside, ascend the Wettstein Bridge stairs and head left onto St. Alban-Graben. Here is the imposing **Kunstmuseum** ⑪, home of one of Europe's oldest public collections. Continue down St. Alban-Graben to the next cross street and veer right on Steinenberg, which leads to the **Kunsthalle** ⑫.

Just beyond the gallery, the whimsical Tinguely-Brunnen or **Fasnacht-Brunnen** puts on a show of its own on the Theaterplatz. Rather than head down Steinenberg, you can turn left on Elisabethenstrasse and see the **Haus zum Kirschgarten** ⑬, which houses the collections of the Basel Historical Museum. Or opt to go along Steinentorstrasse to the **Zoologischer Garten** ⑭ directly west of the SBB train station.

At the end of Steinenberg lies the bustling Barfüsserplatz. Here the **Puppenhaus Museum** ⑮ displays toys from the 18th and 19th centuries while the **Historisches Museum** ⑯ exhibits annals and objects out of Basel's proud past, in the mid-14th century Francescan **Barfüsserkirche,** or Church of the Bare Feet.

Behind the tram concourse on Barfüsserplatz, follow the pedestrian zone to Leonardsberg, which leads left up the stairs to the late-Gothic **Leon-**

hardskirche ⑰. Continue along the church walk into the street named Heuberg, the spine of one of the loveliest sections of old Basel. A network of small roads and alleys threads through the quarter, lined with graceful old houses from many periods: Gothic, Renaissance, Baroque, Biedermeier. Heuberg feeds into Spalenvorstadt, which leads ahead two blocks to the **Holbeinbrunnen,** styled from a drawing by Hans Holbein.

The Spalenvorstadt leads farther on to the impressive 14th-century **Spalentor** ⑱, another of Basel's medieval city gates. Spalengraben curves north from here past the buildings of the **Universität,** one of the six oldest universities in German-speaking Europe. Nearby Petersplatz is the site of the 13th-century **Peterskirche** ⑲ and the lively Saturday *Flohmarkt* (flea market).

Petersgasse behind the Peterskirche presents an exemplary row of houses, some only a window's worth wide. Several small streets scale downhill from here, one of which being the Totengässlein, which leads past the **Pharmazie-Historisches Museum** ⑳. The steep stairs wind on in the direction of the **Marktplatz** ㉑, to the historic and modern heart of Basel—with its towering **Rathaus** ㉒.

Leading off the south end of the Marktplatz, main shopping streets Freie Strasse and Gerbergasse are lined with international shops and department stores. The north end leads into **Fischmarkt** ㉓. Marktgasse leads past the historic **Drei Könige Hotel** ㉔ (Three Kings Hotel). If you're feeling energetic, walk to the **Tinguely Museum** ㉕ by crossing over the Mittlere Rheinbrücke or taking the ferry from St. Alban Tal, then heading east toward Solitude Park on Kleinbasel's sunny waterfront promenade Oberer Rheinweg. Or take a tram (No. 6 from Barfüsserplatz, Marktplatz, or Schifflaende; No. 2 from Bankverein or Munstermesse in the direction of Riehen-Grenze) to the **Fondation Beyeler** ㉖, with its modern art collection and green park bordering Germany.

TIMING

Moving at a rather rapid clip you can see the major sights, as well as a cross-section of the cultural and artistic collections, in three to four hours. A more leisurely itinerary, including strolling, Old Town shopping along the Spalenburg, and museums on the Kleinbasel side, will while away the better part of at least one day.

Sights to See

☞ ⑨ **Basler Papiermühle/Schweizer Papiermuseum und Museum für Schrift und Druck** (Basel Paper Mill/Swiss Museum of Paper, Writing, and Printing). Though its name sounds esoteric, this museum is surprisingly accessible, with a functioning waterwheel and live demonstrations of papermaking, typesetting, and bookbinding. It's in a beautifully restored medieval mill house on the waterfront. ✉ *St. Alban-Tal 35/37,* ☎ *061/2729652.* 🎟 *9 SF.* ☉ *Tues.–Sun. 2–5.*

④ **Blaues und Weisses Haus** (Blue House and White House). Built between 1762 and 1768 for two of the city's most successful silk merchants, these were the residences of the brothers Lukas and Jakob Sarasin. In 1777 the emperor Joseph II of Austria was a guest in the Blue House and subsequent visitors, including Czar Alexander of Russia, Emperor Franz of Austria, and King Friedrich Wilhelm III of Prussia, who met for dinner here in 1814, take this historical site's registry list over the top. Restorations through 1999 should restore grandeur and grace to the fading facades behind the respective immense iron and stately wooden gates. ✉ *Martinsg.*

㉔ **Drei Könige Hotel** (Three Kings Hotel). The statues on the facade depict three wise men who visited here nearly a millennium ago, in 1032 to be precise. Rodolphe II, king of Burgundy; Holy Roman emperor Konrad II; and the latter's son, the future Heinrich III, held a meeting here that joined Burgundy to the Holy Roman Empire. The young general Napoléon Bonaparte stayed here in 1797 (the suite has been named for him and redecorated in opulent Empire style), followed by other stellar guests: the kings of Italy, Princess Victoria, Charles Dickens, and Picasso (who once spent the night on the balcony admiring the view). In 1887 the great Hungarian-born Jewish writer Theodor Herzl stayed here during the first Zionist Congress, which laid the groundwork for the founding of the state of Israel. ⊠ *Blumenrain 8.*

Fasnacht-Brunnen (Carnival Fountain). Created by the internationally famous Swiss artist Jean Tinguely, known for his work in mechanized media, this witty, animated construction was commissioned by the city in 1977 to carry on Basel's tradition of fountain sculpture. Its nine busy metal figures, in Tinguely's trademark whimsical style, churn, lash, and spray with unending energy. ⊠ *Theaterpl.*

㉓ Fischmarkt (Fish Market). Fishmongers once kept the catch fresh for the market on this square, whose fountain basin served as a sort of communal cooler. The fountain itself dates from 1390 and features the Virgin Mary, St. Peter, and John the Baptist. ⊠ *Marktg., northwest of Marktpl.*

★ ㉖ Fondation Beyeler (Beyeler Foundation). In the Basel suburb of Riehen, art dealers Ernst and Hedy Beyeler have established a permanent public home for their astonishingly well-rounded collection of 20th-century art. Architect Renzo Piano's building shows few similarities to his bold inside-on-the-outside design for Paris's Pompidou Center; simple, introverted lines direct attention to the 150 paintings and objects. Rightly so, as the collection's catalog reads like a who's-who of modern artists—Cézanne, Matisse, Lichtenstein, Rauschenberg.

In this limpid setting of natural light and openness, Giacometti's wiry sculptures stretch with their shadows toward the ceiling while Monet's water lilies seem to spill from the canvas into an outdoor reflecting pool. Indigenous carved figures from New Guinea and Nigeria stare into faces on canvases by Klee and Dubuffet. And a stellar selection of Picassos is juxtaposed with views on blue skies and neighboring fields.

The harmony of the collection notwithstanding, personal preference is a perceivable theme, and there is a strong sensation of being invited into an intimate space. With local enthusiasm generating capacity crowds on weekends, however, you may feel as though you've brought half of Basel with you. The tram trip from Schifflände takes about 20 minutes. ⊠ *Baselstr. 77, CH-4125 Riehen,* ☎ *061/645–9700.* ☞ *8 SF.* ⊘ *Nov.–mid-Mar., Thurs.–Tues. 11–5, Wed. 11–8; late Mar.–Oct., Thurs.–Tues. 11–7, Wed. 11–8.*

⑬ Haus zum Kirschgarten (Kirschgarten House). This 18th-century home was built as a palace for a young silk-ribbon manufacturer. Nowadays it contains the 18th- and 19th-century collections of the city's Historical Museum, displayed as furnishings in its period rooms. ⊠ *Elisabethenstr. 27,* ☎ *061/2711333.* ☞ *5 SF, 1st Sun. of month free.* ⊘ *Tues.–Sun. 10–5.*

★ ⑯ Historisches Museum (Historical Museum). Housed within the **Barfüsserkirche** (Church of the Bare Feet), which was founded by the barefoot Franciscans in 1250 and built during the mid-14th century, the museum has an extensive collection of tapestries, wooden sculptures, coins, armor, and other vestiges of Basel's past. An underground gallery displays fully reconstructed **medieval and Renaissance guild rooms,** complete with stained glass, ceramic stoves, and richly carved wood. Downstairs, in the back of the church, the **Münster Treasury** contains priceless reliquaries in gold. Despite its status as one of the finest examples of Franciscan architecture north of the Alps, the Church of the Bare Feet was deconsecrated in the 19th century and turned into a warehouse until it was rescued in 1894 and converted to the present-day museum. ⊠ *Barfüsserpl., Steinenberg 4,* ☎ *061/2710505.* 🎟 *5 SF, 1st Sun. of month free.* ☉ *Wed.–Mon. 10–5.*

Holbeinbrunnen (Holbein Fountain). Created by an unknown 16th-century stonemason, this whimsical fountain is a bundle of copies. It depicts a group of dancing farmers, copied from a drawing by Hans Holbein; above stands a bagpiper, copied from a Dürer engraving. The fountain itself is a copy, the original having been moved to the Historical Museum. ⊠ *Spalenvorstadt, 2 blocks up the tram tracks toward Spalentor.*

★ ⑫ **Kunsthalle** (Basel Art Gallery). The first European gallery to show American abstract expressionists mounts changing exhibitions of contemporary art. ⊠ *Steinenberg 7,* ☎ *061/2724833.* 🎟 *9 SF.* ☉ *Tues.–Sun. 11–5, Wed. 11–8:30.*

★ ⑪ **Kunstmuseum** (Museum of Fine Arts). In a city known for its museums, the Kunstmuseum (Museum of Fine Arts) is Basel's heirloom jewel. It was built in 1932–36 to house one of the oldest public collections of art in Europe, owned by the city since 1661; the facade's imposing stonework gives way to an inner courtyard studded with statues. Inside is the world's largest assemblage of paintings by Hans Holbein the Younger, an exceptional group of works by Konrad Witz, and, in fact, such a thorough gathering of the works of their contemporaries that the development of painting in the Upper Rhine is strikingly illuminated. Other Swiss artists are well represented: from the 18th-century Alpine landscapes of Caspar Wolf through Klimt-like Hodler. The museum's other forte is its substantial international 20th-century collection, from George Braque to Jasper Johns. ⊠ *St. Alban-Graben 16,* ☎ *061/2710828.* 🎟 *7 SF includes admission to Museum für Gegenwartskunst; 1st Sun. of month free.* ☉ *Tues.–Sun. 10–5.*

★ ❷ **Lällekönig.** When a famous gate tower on the Grossbasel side was destroyed, with it went the notorious Lällekönig, a 15th-century gargoyle of a king once mechanized by clockworks to stick out his tongue and roll his eyes at the "lesser" citizens across the river. Kleinbasel residents take symbolic revenge even today, though. Every year during the Vogelgryff festival, a birdlike figure dances to the midpoint of the bridge, gives the Lällekönig a flash of his backside, and takes the party back to Kleinbasel. You can see a facsimile of the Lällekönig on the corner of what is now a chain restaurant (Churrasco) at Schifflände 1. The mechanized original still ticks away and sticks out his tongue in the nether regions of the Historical Museum. ⊠ *Schifflände.*

⑰ **Leonhardskirche** (St. Leonard's Church). Like virtually all of Basel's churches, this one was destroyed during the 1356 quake and rebuilt in the Gothic style, although its Romanesque crypt remains. Its High Gothic wooden pulpit is distinctive (the one in the cathedral is stone). Free organ concerts are held on Friday evening. ⊠ *Heuberg.* ☉ *Daily 10–5.*

㉑ **Marktplatz.** Fruits, flowers, and vegetables are sold every morning from open stands in this central square, Basel's historic and modern heart. In fall and winter passersby purchase bags of hot roasted chestnuts, the savory smoke of which fills the square. ⊠ *Tram crossroads at the foot of Rathaus, south of Marktg.* ☉ *Market: Tues., Thurs., and weekends 6–1:30; Mon., Wed., and Fri. 6 AM–6:30 PM.*

168

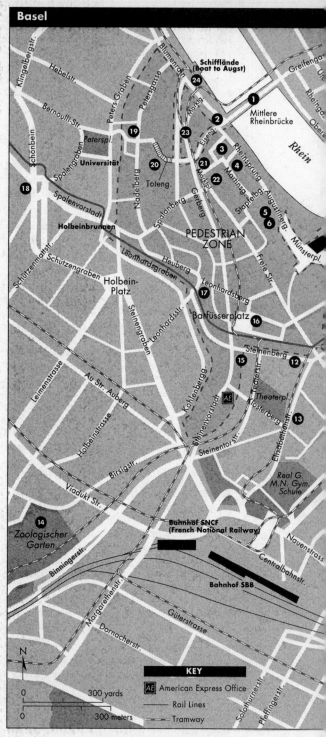

Basel

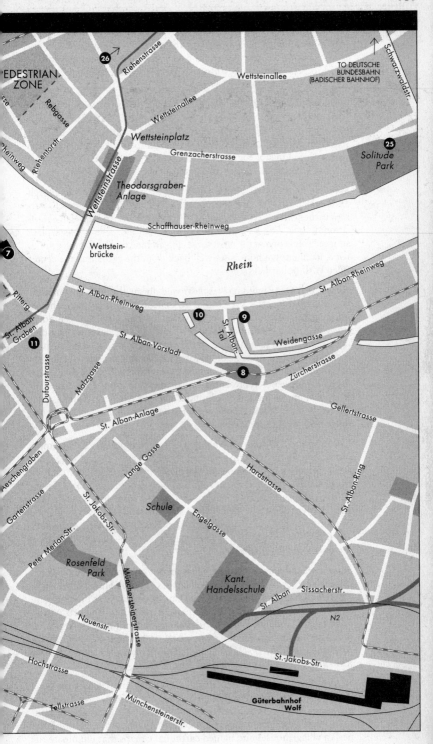

EDESTRIAN
ZONE

Rebgasse

Riehenstrasse

26

Wettsteinallee

Wettsteinallee

Wettsteinplatz

Grenzacherstrasse

Theodorsgraben-
Anlage

Schaffhauser-Rheinweg

Weststeinstrasse

Riehentorstr.

Rheinweg

TO DEUTSCHE
BUNDESBAHN
(BADISCHER BAHNHOF)

Schwarzwaldstr.

25

Solitude
Park

Wettstein-
brücke

Rhein

7

Ritterg.

St. Alban-Graben

St. Alban-Rheinweg

St. Alban-Rheinweg

10

9

St. Alban-Tal

Weidengasse

11

Dufourstrasse

St. Alban-Vorstadt

8

Zürcherstrasse

Malzgasse

St. Alban-Anlage

Gellertstrasse

Aeschengraben

Lange Gasse

Hardstrasse

St. Alban-Ring

Gartenstrasse

St. Jakobs-Str.

Schule

Engelgasse

Peter Merian-Str.

Rosenfeld
Park

Münchensteinerstrasse

Kant.
Handelsschule

St. Alban

Sissacherstr.

N2

Nauenstr.

Hochstrasse

St.-Jakobs-Str.

Tellstrasse

Münchensteinerstr.

**Güterbahnhof
Wolf**

3 **Martinskirche** (St. Martin's Church). The acoustics inside make this church popular for concerts, although it's rarely used for services. The lower portions of the tower date from 1288, making it the oldest parish church in town; the greater part was rebuilt after the earthquake of 1356. The fountain outside, of a warrior dressed for battle, dates from the 16th century. ⊠ *Martinsg.*

★ **1** **Mittlere Rheinbrücke** (Middle Rhine Bridge). This is Basel's most historic and well-known bridge. First built around 1225, the bridge made possible the development of an autonomous Kleinbasel and the consequent rivalry that grew between the two half-towns. The wooden bridge was replaced in stone at the turn of the 20th century, its 1478 chapel reconstructed at the center of the new bridge. ⊠ *Schifflände.*

★ **7** **Münster** (Cathedral). On the site of a 9th-century Carolingian church and replacing a cathedral consecrated by Henry II in 1019, Basel's current cathedral was built during the 12th century in an impressive transitional style, late-Romanesque and pre-Gothic. The Münsterplatz square itself is one of the most satisfying architectural ensembles in Europe, its fine town houses set well back from the cathedral, the center filled with pollarded trees.

Since much of the building was destroyed during the 1356 earthquake, the Romanesque and pre-Gothic influences diminished with the rebuilding of the church in Gothic style. But the facade of the north transept, called the **Galluspforte** (St. Gall's Door), dates to the original structure and stands as one of the oldest carved portals in German-speaking Europe—and one of the loveliest. Slender, fine-tooled columns and rich, high-relief, and freestanding sculptures frame the door. Each of the Evangelists is represented by his animated symbol: the angel for Matthew, an ox for Luke, a bulbous-chested eagle for John, a slim-limbed lion for Mark. Above, around the window, a wheel of fortune flings little men to their destiny.

Inside on the left, following a series of tombs of medieval noblemen, whose effigies recline with their feet resting on their loyal dogs, stands the strikingly simple **tomb of Erasmus.** Below the choir, you can see the delicately rendered death portraits on the double **tomb of Queen Anna of Hapsburg** and her young son Charles, from around 1285. The vaulted **crypt** dates from the original structure and still bears fragments of murals from 1202. ⊠ *Münsterpl.* ☉ *Easter–mid-Oct., weekdays 10–6, Sat. 10–noon and 2–5, Sun. 1–5; mid-Oct.–Easter, Mon.–Sat. 10–noon and 2–4, Sun. 2–4.*

10 **Museum für Gegenwartskunst** (Museum of Contemporary Art). Works from the 1970s to the 1990s of such artists as Frank Stella, Bruce Naumann, and photographer Cindy Sherman are displayed in this museum, a gift of Hoffman–La Roche pharmaceutical heiress and arts patron Maja Sacher. The fittingly modern building looks as though it has shouldered its way in between the street's half-timber houses. ⊠ *St. Alban-Rheinweg 60,* ☎ *061/2728183.* 🎟 *7 SF includes admission to Kunstmuseum; 1st Sun. of month free.* ☉ *Tues.–Sun. 11–5.*

5 **Naturhistorisches Museum** (Natural History Museum). Under the same monumental roof as the Schweizerisches Museum der Kulturen (☞ *below*), this museum outlines the history of the earth, indigenous minerals, mammals, mammoths, and insects. There are even actual-size Polynesian village houses and lighted earthquake maps that illuminate rift zones. ⊠ *Augustinerg. 2,* ☎ *061/2665500.* 🎟 *6 SF for both museums; free Sun.* ☉ *Tues.–Sun. 10–5.*

⑲ Peterskirche (St. Peter's Church). Living evidence of the late-Gothic heyday of Basel, the 13th-century St. Peter's Church sits across from **Petersplatz**, a lovely park next to the **Universität** (University). In the rose-lighted chapel are some interesting 15th-century frescoes. ⊠ *Just across Peters-Graben from Peterspl.*

⑳ Pharmazie-Historisches Museum (Museum of Pharmaceutical History). Although pharmaceuticals as the topic of an entire museum may seem like too much of a necessary thing, this unusual collection showcases Basel's roots in the industry that dominates the banks of the Rhine today. There are recreated old-fashioned pharmacy counters, all kinds of beakers and flacons, plus a bizarre array of old remedies that now seem like candidates for a witches' brew. The museum is housed in Zum Vorderen Sessel, a home once frequented by Erasmus. ⊠ *Totengässlein 3,* ☎ *061/2617940.* ☒ *Free.* ☉ *Weekdays 9–noon and 2–5.*

☞ ⑮ Puppenhaus Museum (Doll House Museum). Bordering on the Barfüsserplatz, this museum, which opened in spring 1998, has several floors stuffed with 18th- and 19th-century toys and classic miniature toy furnishings. The main stars here themselves are stuffed; more than 2,000 teddy bears are exhibited in perhaps the world's most complete collection representing major manufacturers. ⊠ *Steinenvorstadt 1 (at Barfüsserpl.),* ☎ *061/2259595.* ☒ *7 SF.* ☉ *Daily 11–5.*

★ ㉒ Rathaus (Town Hall). This late-Gothic edifice, built to honor the city's entry into the Swiss Confederation in 1501, towers over the Marktplatz. Only the middle portion actually dates from the 16th century; pseudo-Gothic work was added in 1900. A massive clock with figures of the Madonna, the emperor Henry II, and his wife, Kunegunde, adorns the center of the facade, and all around is a series of colorful frescoes, painted in 1608. Step into the courtyard, where the frescoes continue. ⊠ *Marktpl.*

NEED A BREAK?　Choose a few jewel-like pastries and order loose-leaf-brewed tea in the carved-wood, clubby upstairs tearoom of the **Café Schiesser** (⊠ Marktpl. 19, ☎ 061/2616077), steeping since 1870.

Rheinsprung. Fifteenth- and 16th-century houses and a handful of ink makers' shops that reek of alchemy lines this steep little alley in Grossbasel. Number 11 housed Basel's university when it was first founded, in 1460. ⊠ *Grossbasel, parallel to and south of Rhine, between Eiseng. and Stapfelbg.*

---

❻ Schweizerisches Museum der Kulturen (Swiss Museum of World Cultures). Home of one of the world's foremost ethnographic collections, including 32,000 non-European pieces collected from all over the world, the museum can display only a fraction of its holdings at any one time. Of particular interest are its Melanesian and Oceanian pieces, Indonesian artifacts, and items from India and pre-Columbian America. This museum also explores ethnology and Swiss folklife; it shares its space with the Natural History Museum (☞ *above*). ⊠ *Augustinerg. 2,* ☎ *061/2665500.* ☒ *6 SF for both museums; free Sun.* ☉ *Tues.–Sun. 10–5.*

⑱ Spalentor. Like St. Alban-Tor (☞ *below*), Spalentor served as one of Basel's medieval city gates, beginning in the 14th century. More imposing than graceful, it has a toothy wooden portcullis; also note Basel's coat of arms atop the gate. ⊠ *Spalenvorstadt.*

❽ St. Alban-Tor. This original medieval city gate, one of two (☞ *above*), is set amid a lovely garden. Parts of the gate date from the 13th century. ⊠ *St. Alban-Berg.*

Statue of Helvetia. What would the woman pictured on most Swiss coins do if freed from the confines of currency? With spear and shield set aside (and suitcase already packed!) this humanistic interpretation shows her seemingly contemplating the possibilities from a perch not far from the border of her homeland and the wide world beyond. ⊠ *Kleinbasel, right bank of Rhine, near Mittlere Rheinbrücke.*

★ ㉕ **Tinguely Museum.** Ticinese architect Mario Botta, creator of the San Francisco Museum of Modern Art, designed this museum dedicated to the life and work of Switzerland's well-known 20th-century master of mechanized art, Jean Tinguely. Much of the collection is the gift of his widow, artist Niki de Saint Phalle. Born in Fribourg, Tinguely is best known for his whimsical *métamécaniques* (mechanical sculptures), which transform normally inhuman machinery into ironic and often macabre statements: *Le Ballet des Pauvres*, from 1961, suspends a hinged leg with a moth-eaten sock, a horse tail and fox pelt, a cafeteria tray, and a blood-soaked nightgown, all of which dangle and dance on command. The Barca, a wing projecting over the Rhine, offers a splendid river view of Basel; you are obliged to walk through its silent, isolated beauty before entering controlled cacophony. ⊠ *Grenzacherstr. 210,* ☎ *061/6819320.* ⊡ *5 SF.* ☉ *Wed.–Sun. 11–7.*

🦢 ⑭ **Zoologischer Garten** (Zoological Garden). Famed for its armored rhinoceroses (it has had great luck breeding them) as well as its pygmy hippopotamuses, gorillas, and Javanese monkeys, this is no ordinary zoo. It's very child-friendly; there's an arena for elephant riding, and the enormous restaurant-pavilion in the center of the zoo serves kid-size meals. Buy a booklet with a map to find your way, or you may end up wandering in circles. ⊠ *Binningerstr. 40,* ☎ *061/2953535.* ⊡ *10 SF.* ☉ *May–Aug., daily 8–6:30; Mar.–Apr. and Sept.–Oct., daily 8–6; Nov.–Feb., daily 8–5:30.*

OFF THE
BEATEN PATH

LANGENBRUCK AND ENVIRONS – In the German-speaking countryside south of Basel, known as the Baselbiet, a handful of stately little villages offer sturdy old guest houses and a range—from medieval to Roman—of historic sites to explore. Take the winding forest road (A12) west of the freeway between Liestal and Oensingen, watching for Balsthal, Holderbank, Oberer Hauenstein, and Langenbruck; the industrial stretch just south of Liestal is less attractive. Landgasthof Bären (☎ 062/3901414) in Langenbruck offers superb regional cooking, inexpensive prix-fixe menus, and locally brewed beer, as well as attractive, moderately priced rooms.

VITRA DESIGN MUSEUM – Just 10 km (6 mi) across the border in the German town of Weil am Rhein, this museum is a startling white geometric jumble designed by American architect Frank Gehry as part of an avant-garde building complex associated with the Vitra furniture manufacturer. Witty and unexpectedly placed wall openings, asymmetrical skylights, and walkways compete for attention with the collection, some 1,200 items tracing the evolution of furniture design from 1850 to the present. Chair lovers will appreciate the soaring Wall of Chairs and that visitors are encouraged to plop down on many of the pieces. If you like, you can arrange for a guided tour in English. To get here by car, take A5/E35 north from Basel toward Karlsruhe; turn right just after German customs into Route 532, parallel to the parking lot, and turn left after exiting at Weil am Rhein. The museum is 1½ km (about 1 mi) ahead on the right. Or from Deutsche Bahnhof in Basel, take Bus 5 (toward Kandern) to the Vitra stop. Take your passport. ⊠ *Charles-Eames-Str. 1, Weil am Rhein, Germany,* ☎ *49/7621/7023200.* ⊡ *DM 10.* ☉ *Tues.–Fri. 2–6, weekends 11–5. Guided tours Wed.–Fri. at 2.*

Colonia Augusta Raurica (Augst)

Founded in 44–43 BC, Augst is the oldest Roman establishment on the Rhein. Although you can reach it from Basel in 10 minutes by car, Augst is most memorable when visited by boat. To view the restoration sites scattered around the almost suburban neighborhood, be prepared to do some walking.

A Good Tour

A scenic 1½-hour boat ride will take you to the **Old Town** of Augst. From there, walk uphill to the ruins of **Augusta Raurica,** a 2,000-year-old Roman settlement that's been almost entirely rebuilt. Then on to the **Römermuseum,** housed in a vividly reconstructed Roman House containing countless ancient treasures. Boats (Basler Personenschiffahrts-Gesellschaft, ⊠ Depart from the dock at Schifflände, behind the Drei Könige Hotel, ☎ 061/6399500) to Augst leave up to three times a day in high season. The 32 SF round-trip fare takes you slowly up the Rhine, passing the Old Town and the cathedral.

TIMING

Augst merits at least a half day, slightly more if you go by boat. Drinks and cold snacks are available on all cruises, hot meals on some. The last boat returning to Basel each day leaves Augst around 5 PM.

Sights to See

★ **Augusta Raurica.** The remains of this 2,000-year-old Roman settlement have been almost entirely rebuilt (one suspects the Swiss might have done the same had they gotten their hands on that run-down Colosseum in Rome), with substantial portions of the ancient town walls and gates, streets, water pipes, and heating systems all in evidence. The 2nd-century theater has been restored for modern use, and open-air plays and concerts are staged in summer; contact the Roman Museum for details. ⊠ *Above Old Town, Augst.*

Römermuseum (Roman Museum). Housed in a vividly reconstructed Roman house, the Roman Museum contains a substantial treasure trove unearthed in 1962: The objects, dating mostly from the 4th century, are believed to have been buried by the Romans in 350 to protect them from the ravages of the Alemanni, the German tribes who drove the Romans out of Switzerland. Displays include coins thought to depict the emperor Constantine or one of his sons. ⊠ *Giebenacherstr. 17, Augst,* ☎ *061/8162222.* ⌨ *5 SF.* ☉ *Mar.–Oct., Mon. 1–5, Tues.–Sat. 10–5, Sun. 10–6; Nov.–Feb., Tues.–Sat. 10–noon and 1:30–4, Sun. 10–noon and 1:30–5, Mon. 1–4.*

DINING

Of course, Basel can't help but show the sophistication of generations of cosmopolitan influence, and it has a surprising number of innovative French and international restaurants—some of them world class (and priced accordingly). In fact, dining in Basel is a pricey venture, whether your sausage is stuffed with lobster and truffles or merely pork scraps. To keep expenses down, stick to beer-hall fare or watch posted menus for lunch specials.

CATEGORY	COST*
$$$$	over 70 SF
$$$	40 SF–70 SF
$$	20 SF–40 SF
$	under 20 SF

*Prices are per person for a three-course meal (two-course meal in $ category), excluding drinks, tax, and 15% service charge.

$$$$ ✕ **Stucki.** Hans Stucki was one of the finest chefs in the world; ambi-
★   tious young chefs dropped his name the way actors once mentioned
      Stanislavsky. Upon his death in 1998, Jean-Claude Wicky, who worked
      with him for nearly a decade, took his place in the kitchen. Much of
      Stucki's classic menu has been retained, such as pigeon in truffle coulis
      (liquid puree of cooked vegetables), or grilled lobster in tarragon
      sabayon. The service at this restaurant, in the leafy residential neigh-
      borhood of the Bruderholz, is formal and the seating competitive: re-
      serve as far ahead as possible. ⊠ *Bruderholzallee 42,* ☎ *061/3618222.
      Reservations essential. AE, DC, MC, V. Closed Sun.–Mon.*

$$$ ✕ **Chez Donati.** This is where well-heeled Baslers gather, as if at a pri-
★   vate club, to feast on classic old-school Italian cuisine, such as sole and
      rack of veal tantalizingly perfumed with black and white truffles.
      Though the decor borders on kitsch, with its corny murals and abun-
      dance of gilt, the crowds pack in nightly, and Warhol and Tinguely were
      once frequent guests. ⊠ *St. Johanns-Vorstadt 48,* ☎ *061/3220919. AE,
      DC, MC, V. Closed Mon.–Tues. and mid-July to mid-Aug.*

$$$ ✕ **St. Alban-Eck.** This café, a five-minute walk behind the Museum of
      Fine Arts, shows a glimpse of Basel's French blood. In a half-timber
      historic home, it's a real *petit coin sympa* (friendly little corner), with
      plank wainscoting in natural wood, framed historic prints, and net cur-
      tains. The cuisine gracefully mixes German and French favorites: grilled
      entrecôte, sole, salmon, and *foie de veau à la Riehen* (liver with onions,
      apple, and smoked bacon). ⊠ *St. Alban-Vorstadt 60,* ☎ *061/2710320.
      AE, DC, MC, V. Closed Sun. No lunch Sat.*

$$$ ✕ **Schlüsselzunft.** This historic guildhall houses an elegant little restau-
      rant with a ceramic stove and rustic appointments, as well as an in-
      expensive open-atrium courtyard café, called the Schlüsselhöfli. The
      restaurant, which draws business-lunch crowds, serves upscale French
      food and cuisine *Bâloise,* meaning liver with onions and the local
      salmon dish; the café serves shoppers cheap international plates. ⊠ *Freie
      Str. 25,* ☎ *061/2612046. Reservations essential in restaurant. AE,
      DC, MC. Closed Sun.*

$$–$$$$ ✕ **Teufelhof.** Owners Monica and Dominique Thommy have trans-
★   formed a grand old Heuberg mansion into a top gastronomic restau-
      rant, a chic weinstübe, a trendy bar, two theaters, and guest rooms (☞
      Lodging, *below*) decorated by artists; there are even medieval ruins in
      the basement. The formal restaurant Bel Étage's decor is almost min-
      imalist, showcasing a few artworks and a star-pattern parquet floor.
      Michael Baader's masterly guidance might offer such inventions as
      grouper in oyster sauce with *spaghettini* and glazed celery; beef in Stil-
      ton and balsamic vinegar with polenta soufflé; a gratin of raspberries
      and mascarpone with champagne sorbet. Wines by the glass come in
      astonishing variety, and you can buy by the bottle in the new atmo-
      spheric wine shop. The casual, high-tech, and warm-wood weinstübe
      serves a crowd of low-key, upscale bohemians. The café-bar is tiny and
      usually crowded with new-wave artists. ⊠ *Leonhardsgraben 47/
      Heuberg 30,* ☎ *061/2611010. AE, MC, V. Restaurant closed Sun.–
      Mon. No lunch Sat.*

$$ ✕ **Safran-Zunft.** This clublike spot in a grand neo-Gothic hall built in
      1900 has an old-downtown feel and draws retirees and businesspeo-
      ple lunching with their spouses. The food is basic and solid: grilled meats,
      lamb, and trout. The daily three-course menus are a good deal. ⊠ *Ger-
      berg. 11,* ☎ *061/2699494. AE, DC, MC, V. Closed Sun.*

$$ ✕ **Zum Goldenen Sternen.** Dating from 1506, this *Gasthof* claims to
      be the oldest restaurant in Switzerland, though the building has been
      moved from town center to its current Rhine-side site. The impeccable
      restoration retains the antique beams, stenciled ceilings, and unvarnished
      planks, yet without seeming contrived. Though it could easily play a

secondary role, the food almost lives up to the setting: It's classic French, only slightly updated. Game and seafood are specialties. ⊠ *St. Alban-Rheinweg 70,* ☎ *061/2721666. AE, DC, MC, V.*

$ ✕ **Brauerei Fischerstube.** If you're serious about local color, venture a
★ few steps beyond the tourist pale and try a home brew here. Established by a pub keeper who refused the franchise of local brewers, the Fischerstube brews its own lagers and ales in the deep, frothing copper tanks behind the bar. The house label is Ueli Bier, named for a jester-like Fasnacht clown; the timid can taste it at upscale Teufelhof (☞ Lodging, *below*). Pretzels hang on wooden racks on the sanded wooden tables, and the menu includes such local dishes as *Fleischkäse* (sausage loaf) with eggs and *frites* (french fries), rump steak, and just plain *Würstli* (sausage) from the grill. There's a beer garden in back. ⊠ *Rheing. 45,* ☎ *061/6926635. Reservations not accepted. AE, DC, MC, V.*

$ ✕ **Café Pfalz.** This bookish little self-service café, down a narrow street below the cathedral, dishes out veggie plates, muesli, sausage, and quiche in a trim beech-wood-and-black contemporary setting. A salad bar, juicer, and one hot daily special add to the options. ⊠ *Münsterberg 11,* ☎ *061/2726511. No credit cards.*

$ ✕ **Löwenzorn.** This is a classic, comfortable gathering place for plain Germanic food, and though it offers a hodgepodge of fondues, fish, and Italian dishes as well as standard local fare, its regulars come here for beer, a full plate, and some laughs with the friendly staff. With high ceilings, woodwork, ceramic stoves, and a roof garden, it's a nice mix of bistro and beer hall. ⊠ *Gemsberg 2,* ☎ *061/2614213. AE, DC, MC, V. Closed Sun.*

$ ✕ **Zum Schnabel.** This dark-green and aged-wood *Wirtshaus* (inn) has a clubby, unpretentious feel, with multiple variations on Basel-brewed beer. Sausage, pork, and *Rösti* (hash brown potatoes) reign. If you're in the mood for linens, candles, and a more serious meal of fish or veal, climb up to the lovely little wood-lined dining area. ⊠ *Trillengässlein 2,* ☎ *061/2614909. MC, V. Closed Sun.*

LODGING

With its industry, its banking, and its conference center, this is a business city first. As a result, hotel prices tend to be steep, bargains in short supply, and comforts—TV, minibar, phone—more important than atmosphere in the all-out competition for expense-account travelers. There are no guest houses here such as those in the country. When there's a conference in town, every bed for miles can be filled; book well ahead. Hotel reservations can be made through the **Basel Hotel Reservation Service** at the City Information office and at the tourist office, both at the SBB train station (☞ Visitor Information *in* Basel A to Z, *below*).

CATEGORY	COST*
$$$$	over 300 SF
$$$	200 SF–300 SF
$$	140 SF–200 SF
$	under 140 SF

Prices are for a standard double room, including breakfast, tax, and service charge.

$$$$ ▣ **Drei Könige.** An integral part of Basel history even before the first
★ bridges drew the distant banks of the Rhine together, this riverside hotel began in the 11th century as a small inn; it later became a coach stop, and today it's a landmark of the modern city. Expanded to its present form in 1835, it was bought by the family du Boisrouvray in 1976; corridors are lined with a fascinating variety of their portraits, and opulent woodwork, paintings, and furnishings have regained all their 19th-

Dining ●
Brauerei Fischerstube, **13**
Café Pfalz, **14**
Chez Donati, **1**
Löwenzorn, **5**
Safran-Zunft, **9**
St. Alban-Eck, **19**
Schlüsselzunft, **10**
Stucki, **18**
Teufelhof, **8**
Zum Goldenen
Sternen, **20**
Zum Schnabel, **7**

Lodging ○
Bad Schauenburg, **21**
Basel, **6**
Drei Könige, **2**
Euler, **16**
Krafft am Rhein, **12**
Merian am Rhein, **11**
Rochat, **3**
Schweizerhof, **17**
Spalenbrunnen, **4**
Steinenschanze, **15**
Teufelhof, **8**

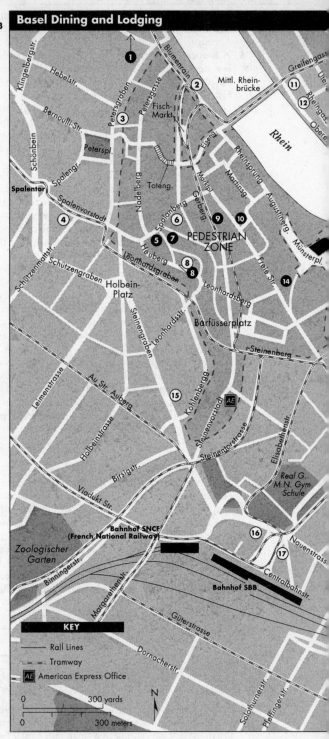
Basel Dining and Lodging

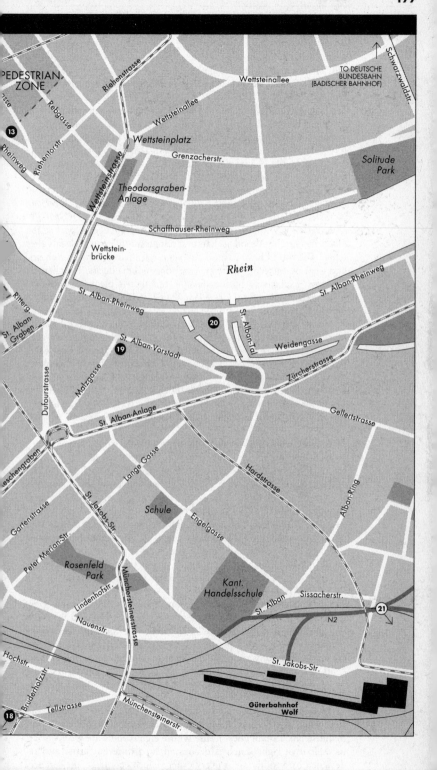

PEDESTRIAN ZONE

Rebgasse

Rheinweg

Riehenstrasse

Riehenstr.

Wettsteinstrasse

Wettsteinallee

Wettsteinallee

Wettsteinplatz

Grenzacherstr.

TO DEUTSCHE BUNDESBAHN (BADISCHER BAHNHOF)

Schwarzwaldstr.

Solitude Park

Theodorsgraben-Anlage

Schaffhauser-Rheinweg

Wettstein-brücke

Rhein

St. Alban-Rheinweg

St. Alban-Rheinweg

St. Alban-Graben

Ritterg.

St. Alban-Vorstadt

Malzgasse

Dufourstrasse

St. Alban-Tal

Weidengasse

Zürcherstrasse

Gellertstrasse

St. Alban-Anlage

Eschengraben

Lange Gasse

St. Jakobs-Str.

Schule

Hardstrasse

Alban-Ring

Gartenstrasse

Peter Merian-Str.

Rosenfeld Park

Lindenhofstr.

Nauenstr.

Münchensteinerstrasse

Engelgasse

Kant. Handelsschule

St. Alban

Sissacherstr.

N2

Hochstr.

Bruderholzstr.

Tellstrasse

Münchensteinerstr.

St. Jakobs-Str.

Güterbahnhof Wolf

13

19

20

21

18

century grandeur, in ravishing colors of cream, gilt, and powder blue. All rooms have big, tile baths; balconied rooms and rooms with serene Rhine views cost more. The formal French restaurant can serve meals on the broad, awning-shaded Rhine terrace, which is heated well into fall. There's also a more casual brasserie. ⊠ *Blumenrain 8, CH-4001,* ☎ *061/2615252,* FAX *061/2612153. 80 rooms, 8 suites. 3 restaurants, bar. AE, DC, MC, V.*

$$$$ ▦ **Euler.** An archetypal little old-world luxury hotel, this landmark on
★ the Centralbahnplatz draws a loyal business clientele, which mingles with local and international bankers over a *Cüpli* (glass of champagne) in the famous leather-and-red-velvet bar. Duvets billow like baking bread out of the bed frames in some of the cushier rooms and suites; standard rooms are furnished in a classic but spare style, with repro-duction antique furnishings. All have triple-glazed windows to cut out tram-traffic noise. ⊠ *Centralbahnpl. 14, CH-4051,* ☎ *061/2724500,* FAX *061/2715000. 55 rooms, 9 suites. Restaurant, bar. AE, DC, MC, V.*

$$$ ▦ **Basel.** This all-modern hotel built in 1975 has become part of the Old Town neighborhood, its bars and restaurants filling with locals after work. The rooms have natural oak veneer, leather-and-chrome chairs, and some pine accents; there are two non-smoking floors. The clientele is almost exclusively businesspeople, but there's plenty of room on weekends. ⊠ *Münzg. 12, CH-4051,* ☎ *061/2646800,* FAX *061/2646811. 68 rooms, 4 suites. 2 restaurants, café, free parking. AE, DC, MC, V.*

$$$ ▦ **Merian am Rhein.** Built in 1972 to blend with the neighboring land-
★ mark Café Spitz, this has a modern, airy look, with touches of gray wood, russet leather, le Corbusier chairs, and live plants. Café Spitz has been a meeting place since the early 13th century, but you wouldn't guess it to look at it; now it's done in light wood, linens, and halo-gen, with fish dominating the wall decor and the menu. There's a lovely, sheltered terrace by the Mittlere Brücke. ⊠ *Rheing. 2, CH-4005,* ☎ *061/6810000,* FAX *061/6811101. 65 rooms. Restaurant, café, in-room VCRs. AE, DC, MC, V.*

$$$ ▦ **Schweizerhof.** This bastion of the station area, once a luxury hotel,
★ now bestows on business travelers the proud personal service once lav-ished on such stars as Toscanini, Menuhin, and Casals. Built in 1864 and in the same family since 1896, it is filled with antiques and faience, though its marble floors and wing chairs mingle with faded updates from the '50s and '60s. The most recently modernized rooms mix Bie-dermeier with beech and pine, though the big front bays feature rose plush and rosewood. The recently refinished restaurant features fish specialties and summer-terrace dining. Staff cuts have cost this land-mark its official fifth star, if not its five-star style. ⊠ *Centralbahnpl. 1, CH-4002,* ☎ *061/2712833,* FAX *061/2712919. 75 rooms. Restau-rant, bar. AE, DC, MC, V.*

$$$ ▦ **Spalenbrunnen.** This unpretentious hotel still has the same great location in a sturdy historic building between the Holbein Fountain and the Spalentor, though now it's under new ownership. The young management has high aspirations for systematically updating the gen-erously sized rooms to include a decor of soft pastels with wood ac-cents, but there's still a transitional feel about it. ⊠ *Schützenmattstr. 2, CH-4051,* ☎ *061/2618233,* FAX *061/2610037. 26 rooms. Restau-rant. AE, DC, MC, V.*

$$$ ▦ **Teufelhof.** In addition to its bars, theaters, medieval ruins, and
★ restaurants (☞ Dining, *above*), this Basel bastion of style and gour-mandise has a small guest house whose eight rooms are works of art in their own right: Each is decorated by a different artist and re-designed by another artist every other year. By contrast, the serenely simple 25 rooms of the adjoining Galerie Hotel function collectively as a canvas for one particular artist; these are also redecorated by an-

other artist annually. There's a food and wine shop in the archaeological cellar. Note that if you'd like a TV in your room, you should request it specifically; one will be hooked up for your stay. ✉ *Leonhardsgraben 47/Heuberg 30, CH-4051,* ☎ *061/2611010,* FAX *061/2611004. 33 rooms. 2 restaurants, bar, café, theaters. AE, MC, V.*

$$ ⊞ **Bad Schauenburg.** Ten kilometers (6 miles) southeast of Basel, this charming country inn has suites done in Biedermeier period antiques and a gourmet restaurant. There's also an informal bistro serving up hearty fare. Take the main road to Liestal, then follow the signs after the turnoff in Frenkendorf. ✉ *Schauenburgerstr., Liestal, CH-4410,* ☎ *061/9011202,* FAX *061/9011055. 34 rooms. Restaurant. AE, DC, MC, V.*

$$ ⊞ **Rochat.** Built in 1898 across from the university, this modest but big and solid brownstone offers plain, if mildly institutional, comforts. Most rooms have a shower; the three without cost less. The restaurant is alcohol free. ✉ *Petersgraben 23, CH-4051,* ☎ *061/2618140,* FAX *061/2616492. 50 rooms. Restaurant, café. AE, DC, MC, V.*

$–$$ ⊞ **Krafft am Rhein.** A rare find in Swiss cities, this is an elegant little
★   mansion of an inn directly on the right-bank waterfront, with mosaic floors, elaborate moldings, chandeliers, and a sinuous atrium stairwell. The proud, accommodating management more than makes up for any wear and tear on the museum-quality architectural details. Some higher-price Rhine-side rooms have polished wood floors, Biedermeier beds, and Oriental runners; others still have '50s mix-and-match. Those without bath fall into the $ category. There's a traditional dining room with peaceful Rhine views for breakfast and dinner, but the downstairs Zem Schnooggeloch (Mosquito's Den) is where everyone gathers for German-style food. The waterfront terrace café is justifiably popular. ✉ *Rheing. 12, CH-4058,* ☎ *061/6909130,* FAX *061/ 6909131. 52 rooms, 45 with bath. Restaurant. AE, DC, MC, V.*

$ ⊞ **Steinenschanze.** Despite its awkward, isolated position above the
★   busy highway and behind the nightlife district, this bargain hotel is clean, welcoming, and bright, with good-size rooms, blue-and-white-tile baths, and tasteful Scandinavian furniture. The harsh parking garage lines have been softened by recessed lighting and a scattering of plants, posters, and knickknacks. Back rooms are quiet; there's a garden behind. ✉ *Steinengraben 69, CH-4051,* ☎ *061/2725353,* FAX *061/ 2724573. 55 rooms. Breakfast room. AE, DC, MC, V.*

NIGHTLIFE AND THE ARTS

For a complete listing of events in Basel, pick up a copy of *Basel Live*, a booklet published every two weeks; it's partially in English. *Basel*, another listings publication, comes out every three months; it's fully bilingual. Both are available at the tourist office and usually at hotel desks. If you'd like to play it by ear, the Steinenvorstadt is crowded with cinemas, bars, and young people, while on the Kleinbasel side, there are more late-night bars along the Oberer Rheinweg.

Nightlife

Bars and Lounges

Brauner Mutz (✉ Barfüsserpl., ☎ 061/2613369) is a big, landmark beer hall with long wooden tables and a beer in every hand. **Campari Bar** (✉ Steinenberg 7, ☎ 061/2728383), behind the Basel Art Gallery and the Tinguely-Brunnen, draws a young, artsy crowd with pop-art paraphernalia, loud pop music, and a thank-God-it's-Friday mood all week. The **Euler Bar** (✉ Centralbahnpl. 14, ☎ 061/2724500), inside the Hotel Euler, draws a conservative business crowd after work. **Zum Sperber** (✉ Münzg. 12, ☎ 061/2612433), behind the Hotel Basel, fills tables and bar stools with well-heeled workers at happy hour; there's live music some evenings.

Dancing and Nightclubs

Atlantis (✉ Klosterberg 13, ☎ 061/2721780) hosts a regular roster of live blues, rock, and alternative bands in a loftlike setting. **Casper's** (✉ Blumenrain 10, ☎ 061/2613050) is an upscale discotheque with a cover charge. **Hazy-Club** (✉ Heuwaage, ☎ 061/2619982) has a top orchestra and show. At **Le Plaza Club** (✉ Am Messepl., ☎ 061/6923206) the DJ spins pop hits. **Singerhaus** (✉ Marktpl., ☎ 061/2616466) is a traditional nightclub with a good show; the bar opens at 7, and dancing starts at 9.

The Arts

Film

Movies in Basel are usually shown in the original language with subtitles. Newspaper listings can be deciphered, but most houses are along Steinenvorstadt in the Old Town, and times are prominently posted. Prices vary depending on how close to the screen you choose to sit.

Music

Stadtcasino (✉ Steinenberg 14, ☎ 061/2726657, FAX 061/2725822), along with its restaurants and piano bar, hosts the Basel Symphony Orchestra, the Basel Chamber Orchestra, and visiting performers. Tickets are sold at the theater box office one hour before performance. Advance bookings can be made at **Musikhaus au Concert** (✉ Aeschenvorstadt 24, ☎ 061/2721176). The **Musik-Akademie der Stadt Basel** (✉ Leonhardsgraben 4–6) is an important European academy with top-quality international performers. Book as for the Stadtcasino (☞ *above*).

Theater

Basel Stadttheater (✉ Theaterstr. 7, ☎ 061/2951133), hosts opera, operetta, dance, and drama in German. Book in advance weekdays 10–1 and 3:30–6:45, Saturday 10–6:45. The box office opens one hour before the performance. The **Komödie** (✉ Steinenvorstadt 63) offers light German-language theater in an intimate atmosphere. Book through the Stadttheater (☞ *above*) or at the box office one hour before the curtain.

OUTDOOR ACTIVITIES AND SPORTS

Golf

Golf and Country Club Basel (✉ Hagenthal-le-Bas in France, ☎ 33/03/89685091) is one of the most beautiful golf courses in Europe, with attractive views of the Jura, Black Forest, and Vosges mountains. It is open to visitors; bring your passport.

Squash

Eglisee (✉ Riehenstr. 315, ☎ 061/6812210) provides squash courts by reservation only. **Sportcenter Paradies** (✉ Bettenstr. 73, ☎ 061/4859580), like Eglisee, has good squash facilities (try to make a reservation if you're going during the week); there are eight courts, and you can rent equipment there.

Tennis

Sporthalle St. Jakob (✉ Schänzli, ☎ 061/3117209) has courts to reserve.

SHOPPING

Though first impressions here may suggest yet another modern pedestrian shopping district, it's worth a closer look. There are still a lot of lone-wolf, private, quirky shops that contain extraordinary treasures.

Department Stores

Whether you're in need of socks, toothpaste, or chocolate-on-the-cheap, department store chains **Manor** (⊠ Greifeng. 22, ☎ 061/6959511) and **EPA** (⊠ Gerberg. 4, ☎ 061/2699250) have items to get by on, plus groceries in the basement. **Globus** (⊠ Marktpl. 2, ☎ 061/2615500) is a nicer version, with gourmet edibles and sleeker clothes. In what can often be a somewhat barren area, **Migros** (⊠ Centralbahnhofpl., ☎ 061/2799745), open at its SBB train station location until 10 PM, is a good place to buy provisions including sandwiches, baked goods, and bottled water.

Flea Markets

There's a large flea market at **Petersplatz** (⊠ Square bordered by Spalengraben on the west and Nadelberg on the east) every Saturday from 9 to 4 that draws serious watch sellers and watch repairmen, despite its garage-sale quality. A small flea market sets up shop on **Barfüsserplatz** (⊠ Just south of Toteng.) every second and fourth Wednesday from 7 to 6:30. This square is also the site of a clothing market every Thursday from 1:30 to 6:30; it offers mostly bohemian batik and tie-dye styles, though you may find cheap China silks.

Shopping Streets

The major, central shopping district stretches along **Freie Strasse** and **Gerbergasse**, though lower-price shops along **Steinenvorstadt** cater to a younger crowd. Streets radiating left, uphill from the Gerbergasse area, feature more one-of-a-kind boutiques. Most antiquarian bookshops concentrate their business on **Klosterberg** through Elisabethenstrasse to Aeschengraben.

Specialty Stores

Antiques
René Simmermacher (⊠ Augustinerg. 7, ☎ 061/2611848) hides away his exquisite, if tiny, collection of European faience from the 17th and 18th centuries in a miniature shop across from the Swiss Museum of World Cultures.

Antique Books
Among many fine competitors, **Erasmushaus/Haus der Bücher** (⊠ Bäumleing. 18, ☎ 061/2723088) carries one of the largest collections of fine old and used books, mostly in German but including some multilingual art publications.

Calligraphic Paraphernalia
Abraxas (⊠ Rheinsprung 6, ☎ 061/2616070) offers not only its own fine writing work but the paraphernalia to go with it; luxurious sealing waxes and reproductions of antique silver seals are available, too. **Scriptorium am Rhysprung** (⊠ Rheinsprung 2, ☎ 061/2613900) mixes its own ink and carries calligraphic pens.

Coins
Münzen und Medaillen AG (⊠ Malzg. 25, ☎ 061/2727544) carries coins and medals dating from antiquity to the mid-19th century.

Crafts and Gifts

Heimatwerk (✉ Schneiderg. 2, ☎ 061/2619178) carries carefully selected and quality-controlled crafts from across Switzerland, from traditional ceramics to linen dish towels and children's wooden toys. Basel-made specialties include embroidered silk ribbons. Highly specialized handiwork comes from **Johann Wanner** (✉ Spalenberg 14, ☎ 061/2614826), who commissions hand-blown, hand-painted, hand-embroidered, and hand-molded ornaments; tin Victorian miniatures; Advent cards; tartan ribbons; cards; and candles—all solely for Christmas. Though primarily specializing in home furnishings, **Atelier Baumgartner** (✉ Spalenberg 8, ☎ 061/2610843) also stocks Swiss and European handicrafts, including much-loved figurines, music boxes, Nutcrackers, and pyramids from the Erzgebirge region of Germany.

Food Specialties

The famous **Läckerli-Huus** (✉ Gerberg. 57, ☎ 061/2612322) sells a variety of sweets but features the local specialty—*Leckerli,* a chewy spiced cookie of almond, honey, dried fruit, and kirsch. It also carries a large line of gift canisters and makes a business of shipping souvenir gifts. **Bachmann** (✉ Gerberg. 51, ☎ 061/2613583; ✉ Blumenrain 1, ☎ 061/2614152; and ✉ Centralbahnpl. 7, ☎ 061/2712627) also carries the lovely little sweets that set Basel apart. **Schiesser** (✉ Marktpl., ☎ 061/2616077), a convivial tearoom, opened in 1870. **Glausi's** (✉ Spalenberg 12, ☎ 061/2618008) ages its own cheeses and offers myriad fresh Swiss specialties.

Linens

Caraco (✉ Gerberg. 77, Falknerstr. entrance, ☎ 061/2613577) sells handmade Swiss lace and embroidered goods as well as imports. **Langenthal** (✉ Gerberg. 26, ☎ 061/2610900) offers mostly Swiss products: tea towels, tablecloths, and folk-style aprons. **Sturzenegger** (✉ Freie Str. 62, ☎ 061/2616867) carries household linens made in Saint Gallen, the Swiss textile capital.

Lingerie

Sturzenegger (☞ Linens, *above*) also carries an extensive line of Hanro and Calida underwear in fine Swiss cottons. **Beldona** (✉ Freie Str. 103, ☎ 061/2731170) stocks Swiss cotton lingerie. **Fogal** sells its famous Swiss hosiery at two locations (✉ Freie Str. 44, ☎ 061/2617461; ✉ Freie Str. 4, ☎ 061/2611220); both branches set out trays of clearance goods.

Men's Clothes

For the smoking-jacket crowd, **Renz** (✉ Freie Str. 2a, ☎ 061/2612991) has a small but impeccable selection of fine Swiss-cotton pajamas, Hanro underwear, and classic Scottish cashmeres. **K. Aeschbacher** (✉ Schnabelg. 4, ☎ 061/2615058) carries unique Swiss silk ties, scarves, robes, and pajamas.

Shoes

Bally Capitol (✉ Freie Str. 38, ☎ 061/2611897) has a wide selection of these conservative Swiss-made shoes. **Rive Gauche** (✉ Schneiderg. 1, ☎ 061/2611080) carries top-quality shoes only. **Kropart** (✉ Schneiderg. 16, ☎ 061/2615133) specializes in trendy, high-end styles. **Müki** (✉ Münsterberg 14, ☎ 061/2712436) sells functional yet stylish European-made kids' shoes—from patent leather loafers to fun-colored fleece house slippers.

Toys

Slightly less folksy than Heimatwerk (☞ Crafts and Gifts, *above*), **Spielhuus** (✉ Eiseng. 8, ☎ 061/2649898) is a good source for board games and reasonably priced children's toys, as well as Fasnacht costumes.

The large, mainstream **Dreamland** (⊠ Freie Str. 17, ☎ 061/2611990) is Switzerland's answer to Toys 'R' Us. **Bercher & Sternlicht** (⊠ Spalenberg 45, ☎ 061/2612550) has miniature trains and accessories.

Women's Clothes

Trois Pommes (⊠ Freie Str. 74, ☎ 061/2729255) dominates the high end, with Jil Sander, Versace, Armani, and Valentino. If you're not too proud to be seen in last year's Valentino, try **Check-out** (⊠ Schnabelg. 4, ☎ 061/2616292), a bargain-bin outlet for Trois Pommes goods.

BASEL A TO Z

Arriving and Departing

By Car

The German autobahn A5 enters Basel from the north and leads directly to the Rhine and the center. From France, the auto route **A35** (E9) peters out at the frontier, and secondary urban roads lead to the center. The A2 autobahn leads off to the rest of Switzerland. As the most interesting and scenic portions of Basel are riddled with pedestrians-only streets, it is advisable to park your car for the duration of your visit.

By Plane

EuroAirport (⊠ Just across the border in France, ☎ 061/3253111) is shared by Basel, Mulhouse, and Freiburg in Germany. Direct flights link Basel to most major European cities. The nearest intercontinental airport is **Kloten** outside **Zürich** (⊠ Approximately 80 km/50 mi southeast of Basel, ☎ 1571060). There are connecting flights from Zürich into Basel's airport on **Crossair** (☎ 061/3253636 for central reservations or 084/8852000 within Switzerland), Switzerland's domestic airline.

BETWEEN THE AIRPORT AND THE CITY CENTER

By Bus. Regular bus service runs between the airport and the train station in the city center. The trip takes about 15 minutes and costs 2.60 SF per person; call 061/3252511 for schedules and information.

By Taxi. One-way fare from the airport to the Basel center costs approximately 35 SF; it takes about 15 minutes in light traffic and up to 30 minutes at rush hours (around noon, 2 PM, and between 5 PM and 7 PM). There are normally cabs at the taxi stand, but if you do need to call one from the airport (in France), you must dial two prefixes: 19 to get out of the country, then 4161, then the number; the cost is negligible. Taxi companies: **Mini Cab** (☎ 061/2711111), **33er Taxi** (☎ 061/6333333), **Taxi-Zentrale** (☎ 061/2712222).

By Train

There are two main rail stations in Basel. The **SBB** (Schweizerische Bundesbahnen; ⊠ Centralbahnstr., ☎ 061/1572222) connects to Swiss destinations as well as to France and its trains. The **DB** (Deutsche Bundesbahn; ⊠ North of the Rhine in Kleinbasel, ☎ 061/6901111) connects to Germany and to the SBB. Arriving in Basel from France, you get off on the French side of the border; carry your bags through a small customs station, where your passport will be checked; then either continue into the open track area to find your connection or exit left into the city center. Arriving from Germany at the DB station, you walk through a customs and passport check as well.

Getting Around

By far the best way to see Basel is on foot or by tram, as the landmarks, museums, and even the zoo radiate from the Old Town center on the

Rhine, and the network of rails covers the territory thoroughly. Taxis are costly, less efficient, and less available than the ubiquitous tram.

By Tram and Bus

Most trams run every six minutes all day, every 12 minutes in the evening. Tickets must be bought at the automatic machines at every stop (most give change). Stops are marked with green-and-white signs; generally the trams run from 5:30 or 6 in the morning until midnight or shortly thereafter. As long as you travel within the central Zone 10, which includes even the airport, you pay 2.80 SF per ticket. If you are making a short trip—four stops or fewer—you pay 1.80 SF. *Mehrfahrtenkarten* (multijourney cards) allow you 12 trips for the price of 10 and can be purchased from the ticket office at Barfüsserplatz and from many of the tram-stop vending machines. *Tageskarten* (day cards) allow unlimited travel all day within the central zone and cost 7.20 SF. You can buy day cards at most hotels as well as through the above sources. Holders of the Swiss Pass (☞ Train Travel *in* the Gold Guide) travel free on all Basel public transport systems.

Contacts and Resources

Emergencies

Police (☎ 117). **Hospital** (✉ Kantonsspital, Petersgraben 2, ☎ 061/2652525). **Medical emergencies and late-night pharmacy** referral (☎ 061/2611515).

English-Language Bookstores

Tanner Books (✉ Streitg. 5, ☎ 061/2724547). **Jäggi** (✉ Freie Str. 32, ☎ 061/2615200).

Guided Tours

Basel Tourismus (☞ Visitor Information, *below*) organizes daily tours of the city by bus, departing at 10 AM from the Hotel Euler by the SBB. The tours last about 1¾ hours and cost 20 SF. They also offer two-hour walking tours Sunday and Monday in summer for 10 SF. Commentary is in English. **Basler Personenschiffahrt** (✉ Departing from Schifflände by Mittlere Brücke, ☎ 061/6399500) offers boat trips on the Rhine to Augst for 32 SF round-trip.

Travel Agencies

American Express (✉ Steinenvorstadt 33, ☎ 061/2813380).

Visitor Information

Basel Tourismus (Basel Tourism; ✉ Schifflände 5, ☎ 061/2686868) is on the Rhine just left of the Mittlere Brücke, at the Schifflände tram stop. The Basel Tourism branch at the **SBB center** (✉ Bahnhof, ☎ 061/1572222) will help you with hotel reservations. **City Information** (✉ Bahnhof, SBB, ☎ 061/2713684) also provides hotel and museum information.

8 Fribourg, Neuchâtel, and the Jura

Un-self-conscious and largely undiscovered, the cantons of Fribourg, Neuchâtel, and the Jura represent three very different worlds. Fribourg, part German and part French, is full of medieval villages; Neuchâtel, French in language and culture, is beginning to shift its focus from watchmaking to tourism; and the isolated Jura Mountains, part German and part French, exist in a realm of their own.

SANDWICHED BETWEEN THE TWO MORE PROMINENT cantons of Bern and Vaud, the three cantons of Fribourg, Neuchâtel, and Jura are often overlooked. The hurried visitor checking off Swiss highlights may sojourn in Lausanne or Bern and make forays into their hinterlands, taking in Gruyères, Fribourg, and little more. That leaves the rest of this ancient green region to the Swiss, who enjoy undisturbed the area's peace, prosperity, and relative lack of touristic development.

Updated by
Beverly
Stearns-
Peterson

The three cantons are almost as diverse, culturally and geographically, as three continents: Fribourg, part German, part French, with its neat emerald hills, tidy farmlands, medieval villages, and magnificent university town; Neuchâtel, low lake lands and forested highlands, as French as a Swiss region can be and the heart of watchmaking country; and the smoky forest heights of the Jura Mountains, cut off from the mainstream, nursing French and German dialects.

Each is a bit of uncut gem, with a minimum of tourist-thronged must-sees and a maximum of untouched beauty, meant to be explored at leisure or sought out as a retreat from the larger-than-life spectacles elsewhere in Switzerland.

Pleasures and Pastimes

Cheese

The name *Fribourg* immediately brings to mind *fondue fribourgeoise*, as the canton combines its two greatest cheese products—Gruyère and Vacherin—for a creamy *moitié-moitié* (half-and-half) blend. Or it may leave out the nutty Gruyère altogether and melt Vacherin alone, adding only water instead of wine or kirsch. Some dip potatoes instead of bread.

As this is cow country, you'll find many places to view cheese being made; but those familiar black-and-white cows that relieve the saturation of green in the Fribourg countryside yield more than cheese: We owe them an additional debt of gratitude for producing *crème-double,* a Gruyères specialty that rivals Devonshire cream. It is a rich, extrathick, high-fat cream that—without whipping—supports a standing spoon. Served in tiny carved-wood *baquets* (vats), it can be poured slowly, in a satiny-thick ribbon, over a bowl of berries, or into a frothy espresso. When it's not pasteurized, you'll get a whiff of green meadows and new-mown hay.

Dining

These three regions enjoy the fruits of rural isolation: sweet fish from Lakes Neuchâtel, Biel, and Murten; trout from the streams of the Jura; game from the forested highlands; and—of course—the dairy products of Fribourg and Gruyères.

Nowhere in Switzerland will you find a greater sense of bounty, and the traditional autumn Fribourg feast, called Bénichon, embodies the region's love of robust, fundamental food. Like the American Thanksgiving, it has come to be a harvest feast, and it fetes not only the return of the cattle from the high pastures to the plains, but the season's final yield: chimney-smoked ham, served hot with green beans; mutton stew with plump raisins and potato puree; and tart *poires-à-Botzi* (pears poached and lightly caramelized). The main feast takes place during the second week of September, but restaurants across the region serve versions of Bénichon all fall.

BONUS MILES MAKE GREAT SOUVENIRS.

Earn Miles With Your MCI Card.

Take the MCI Card along on this trip and start earning miles for the next one. You'll earn frequent flyer miles on all your calls and save with the low rates you've come to expect from MCI. Before you know it, you'll be on your way to some other international destination.

Sign up for MCI by calling 1-800-FLY-FREE

Earn Frequent Flyer Miles.

Is this a great time, or what? :-)

Easy To Call Home.

1. To use your MCI Card, just dial the WorldPhone access number of the country you're calling from.
2. Dial or give the operator your MCI Card number.
3. Dial or give the number you're calling.

# Austria (CC) ♦	022-903-012
# Belarus (CC)	
From Brest, Vitebsk, Grodno, Minsk	8-800-103
From Gomel and Mogilev regions	8-10-800-103
# Belgium (CC) ♦	0800-10012
# Bulgaria	00800-0001
# Croatia (CC) ★	0800-22-0112
# Czech Republic (CC) ♦	00-42-000112
# Denmark (CC) ♦	8001-0022
# Finland (CC) ♦	08001-102-80
# France (CC) ♦	0-800-99-0019
# Germany (CC)	0800-888-8000
# Greece (CC) ♦	00-800-1211
# Hungary (CC) ♦	00▼800-01411
# Iceland (CC) ♦	800-9002
# Ireland (CC)	1-800-55-1001
# Italy (CC) ♦	172-1022
# Kazakhstan (CC)	8-800-131-4321
# Liechtenstein (CC) ♦	0800-89-0222
# Luxembourg	0800-0112
# Monaco (CC) ♦	800-90-019
# Netherlands (CC) ♦	0800-022-9122
# Norway (CC) ♦	800-19912
# Poland (CC) ÷	00-800-111-21-22
# Portugal (CC) ÷	05-017-1234
Romania (CC) ÷	01-800-1800
# Russia (CC) ÷ ♦	
To call using ROSTELCOM ■	747-3322
For a Russian-speaking operator	747-3320
To call using SOVINTEL ■	960-2222
# San Marino (CC) ♦	172-1022
# Slovak Republic (CC)	00-421-00112
# Slovenia	080-8808
# Spain (CC)	900-99-0014
# Sweden (CC) ♦	020-795-922
# Switzerland (CC) ♦	0800-89-0222
# Turkey (CC) ♦	00-8001-1177
# Ukraine (CC) ÷	8▼10-013
# United Kingdom (CC)	
To call using BT ■	0800-89-0222
To call using C&W ■	0500-89-0222
# Vatican City (CC)	172-1022

Flying to France on Friday? Get Francs from Chase on Thursday. Call Currency To Go at 935-9935 for overnight delivery.

Or pounds for London. Or Deutschmarks for Düsseldorf. Or any of 75 foreign currencies. Call **Chase Currency To Go**[SM] **at 935-9935** in area codes 212, 718, 914, 516 and Rochester, N.Y.; all other area codes call 1-800-935-9935. We'll deliver directly to your door.* Overnight. And there are no exchange fees. Let Chase make your trip an easier one.

CHASE. The right relationship is everything.[SM]

In Neuchâtel, Biel and Murten, menus are thick with lake fish: *perche* (perch), *sandre* (a large cousin of the perch), *bondelle* (a pearly fleshed trout found exclusively in Lake Neuchâtel), or *silure* (catfish).

The mountain forests of Jura are known for a woodsy delicacy: *bolets*—fat, fleshy mushrooms with a meaty texture and taste. Served with local rabbit or venison, plus a glass of red Neuchâtel pinot noir, they embody the earthy cuisine of the region.

CATEGORY	COST*
$$$$	over 70 SF
$$$	40 SF–70 SF
$$	20 SF–40 SF
$	under 20 SF

Prices are per person for a three-course meal (two-course meal in $ category), including tax and 15% service charge.

Epicurean Souvenirs

You can buy light, bubbly wines in Neuchâtel; authentic Tête de Moine cheese in Moutier; creamy Vacherin cheese in Fribourg; or crème-double in Gruyères. Gruyères has the most concentrated selection of local crafts, with shops up and down its single street hawking lovely hand-carved wooden kitchen tools, including a traditional shallow double-cream ladle, often with a pretty (if inappropriate) blossom of edelweiss carved through its handle.

Hiking and Walking

Uncluttered, solitary, only moderately strenuous—and greener than any other canton—Fribourg is ideal hiking country. The wildest country is concentrated along the French border west of Lac Neuchâtel (Lake Neuchâtel), in the low Jura Mountains. If city wandering is more your style, the city of Neuchâtel has one of the country's largest pedestrian zones, the first Swiss city to designate such a zone. The town center is built on a hill; from there, paths lead directly down to the picturesque Lake Neuchâtel shoreline, ideal for a stroll.

Lodging

As relatively untouristed cantons, Fribourg, Neuchâtel, and Jura have a less developed hotel infrastructure, which means fewer lodging choices but also more authentic hotels—almost all are unpretentious, old, and homey. Fribourg is by far the best equipped, with guest houses in every village, though there's only a handful of choices in the city itself. In Neuchâtel, most lodgings are along the lake, but as you venture inland into the hills, there are fewer and fewer available. In Jura, hotels are downright rare—one or two per town, holiday retreats scattered sparsely across the countryside; lacking a central inn as home base, you may prefer to make excursions from Neuchâtel. If you plan to take refuge in the Jura for a week of exploring, consider renting a holiday flat or house; ask tourist offices for listings.

CATEGORY	COST*
$$$$	over 250 SF
$$$	180 SF–250 SF
$$	120 SF–180 SF
$	under 120 SF

Prices are for a standard double room, including breakfast, tax, and service charge.

Snowshoeing

This newly updated winter sport, involving lightweight plastic *raquettes de neige* that allow snow hikers to leave the trail, was revived in the Jura resort of St-Cergue a few years ago. You'll find hook-sole snowshoes in many Swiss sports shops and plenty of company on the relatively gentle Jura Mountain slopes.

Exploring Fribourg, Neuchâtel, and the Jura

The long ellipse of Lake Neuchâtel divides these regions in two, with its northern tip dipping into canton Bern and its southern into Vaud. Both of these cantons have fingers of territory that reach deep into their neighbor's turf, with bits of Vaud alternating with Fribourg along the southern shore, and one tiny claw of Bern actually reaching the French border. Below the lake, Fribourg spreads southeast to the Simmental; above it, the Neuchâtel region runs along the French border and rises into the modest but rugged heights of the Jura Mountains.

Numbers in the text correspond to numbers in the margin and on the Fribourg, Neuchâtel, and the Jura map.

Great Itineraries

Though the major sights themselves require only a little time, they are grouped together in distant regions. You can explore much of this area by train with great ease, but renting a car will save you some time and allow you to go at your own pace.

IF YOU HAVE 1 OR 2 DAYS

Plan your itinerary according to your starting point. If you're coming from the east (Bern, Basel, or Zürich), start with the Old Town and lakefront promenade of ⛳ **Neuchâtel** ⑩, with a brief detour to medieval **Murten** ⑨ just down the road; then spend the second day in medieval ⛳ **Fribourg** ① to the south, with a quick side trip to **Gruyères** ③. If you're coming from the south (Geneva or Lausanne), start with Gruyères and Fribourg, then move north to Neuchâtel and Murten.

IF YOU HAVE 3 OR MORE DAYS

More time allows you to whistle-stop in lakefront villages, seeing Roman ruins and châteaus. Visit ⛳ **Fribourg** ①, then cut south to the castle at **Gruyères** ③ and circle northwest through Neuchâtel's ancient towns of **Bulle** ④, **Romont** ⑤, **Payerne** ⑥, **Avenches** ⑧, and **Murten** ⑨. From ⛳ **Neuchâtel** ⑩, head south along the lakeshore to the château town of **Grandson** ⑪ and the spa town of **Yverdon-les-Bains** ⑫. Travel northwest from Neuchâtel into watch country, stopping at the peculiarly fascinating watchmaking city of **La Chaux-de-Fonds** ⑬, and take in the natural beauty of canton Jura, perhaps stopping at **Saignelégier** ⑭ to go horseback riding or cross-country skiing.

When to Tour Fribourg, Neuchâtel, and the Jura

Throughout the year you'll encounter lighter tourist traffic here than in any other region. Summer is a particularly lovely time in the Jura, when forest glades become ripe with the smells of the woods. Fribourg is also pleasant in summer, but crowds tend to pick up, especially in Gruyères. Spring and fall are beautiful times to visit anywhere in this region.

FRIBOURG

With its landscape of green, rolling hills punctuated by craggy peaks, Fribourg is Switzerland's most rural canton; its famous Fribourgeois cows—almost all Holstein (black and white)—provide the canton with its main industry. Fondue was invented in these green hills; Gruyère cheese and Switzerland's famous double cream both originated here.

Fribourg

★ ❶ *34 km (21 mi) southwest of Bern.*

Between the rich pasturelands of the Swiss plateau and the Alpine foothills, the Sarine River twists in an S-curve, its banks joined by webs of arching bridges. From the heights in the upper half of the curve, the narrow medieval town houses—well maintained, comfortably lived in, utterly ungentrified—of the city Fribourg seem to tumble down into the river, shored up by foundations at least as tall as their livable space. It's an astonishing city on first sight from the highway, as if a 16th-century engraving had popped into three dimensions and bloomed into tones of terra-cotta and ocher. It's just as impressive from its Old Town center; though scarcely developed to accommodate visitors, it's worth a day's leisurely reconnaissance.

Fribourg was a stronghold of the Counter-Reformation and championed Catholicism while a large part of Europe experienced a religious transformation. There is evidence everywhere of that faith, and walking through the Old Town's streets today, with spires and steeples and pealing bells everywhere, even a pagan might be impressed. Fribourg University was founded in 1889 and today remains the only Catholic university in Switzerland. It is also the only bilingual institution of its kind and reflects the region's peculiar linguistic agility. Two-thirds of the people of canton Fribourg are native French speakers, one-third are native German speakers, and most switch easily between the two. The city of Fribourg is totally bilingual, down to its street signs and the confessionals in the Cathedral.

The **Hôtel de Ville** (Town Hall), in Fribourg's Haute-Ville (Upper City), is the seat of the cantonal parliament and a 16th-century clock tower gem; it was built on the foundations of the château of Berthold of Zähringen, who founded the village in 1157. The symmetrical stairways were added during the 17th century, as was the clock. On the square of the Town Hall a market takes place every Saturday morning. ⊠ *Upper City.*

Across the river along the Pont de St-Jean (St. John Bridge) is the **Planche-Supérieure,** a sloping, open triangular *place* (square) now lined with cafés. This **Basse-Ville** (Lower City) was once the sole approach to the main upper quarters, and it thrived as such; when sophisticated bridges were built joining the upper peninsula to the land mass, the lower quarter was literally passed over and it faded.

Next to the **Pont du Milieu** (Middle Bridge) and back across the river is the **Pont de Berne** (Bridge of Bern), the oldest bridge in a city of bridges, built entirely of wood and roofed with wooden shingles. All Fribourg's bridges were once like this but were modernized; during the 19th century, engineers even built a series of spectacular suspension bridges, strung high across the valley. Those bridges have been replaced by the solid, concrete arches you see today.

The **Pont de Zähringen** (Bridge of Zähringen) spans the river in the Upper City, with views over the Pont de Berne and the Pont de Gotteron as well as down to the remaining towers, which once guarded the entrance to the city. You are now standing on the narrow peninsula on which Berthold first founded Fribourg; the Hotel Duc Berthold (☞ Dining and Lodging *below*) claims that he lived on their site.

The **Cathédrale St-Nicolas** (St. Nicholas Cathedral) rears up above the Upper City in striking Gothic unity, its massive tower built during the 15th century, though the body of the cathedral was begun in 1283. It draws the Catholic powers of not only Fribourg but also Geneva and Lausanne, whose cathedrals now serve the Protestant faith. Above the

Fribourg, Neuchâtel, and the Jura

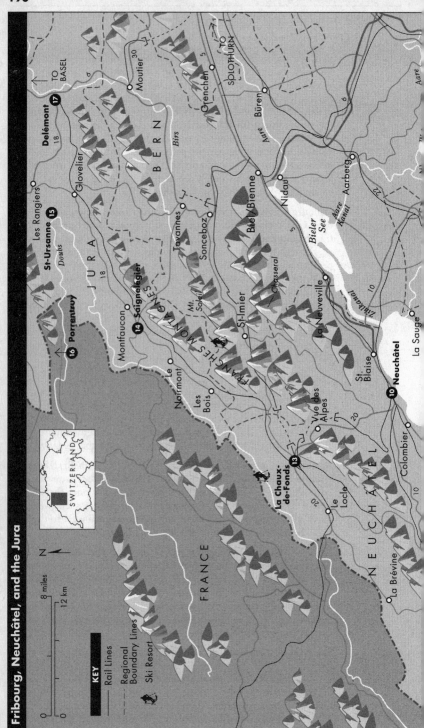

KEY

— Rail Lines

--- Regional Boundary Lines

🎿 Ski Resort

0 ____ 8 miles

0 ____ 12 km

N

SWITZERLAND

TO BASEL

Moutier 30

Delémont 18 **17**

Grenchen 5

TO SOLOTHURN

Glovelier

Büren

Aare

BERN

Birs

Les Rangiers

St-Ursanne **15**

Doubs

Tavannes

Sonceboz 5

Biel/Bienne

Nidau

Aare Kanal

Aarberg

22

JURA

18

Porrentruy **16**

Saignelégier **14**

Montfaucon

Mt. Soleil

St-Imier

Chasseral

La Neuveville

Bieler See

Zihlkanal 10

FRANCHES MONTAGNES

Le Noirmont

Les Bois

St Blaise

Neuchâtel **10**

La Sauge

FRANCE

Vue des Alpes

20

La Chaux-de-Fonds **13**

Le Locle

20

La Brévine

NEUCHÂTEL

10

Colombier

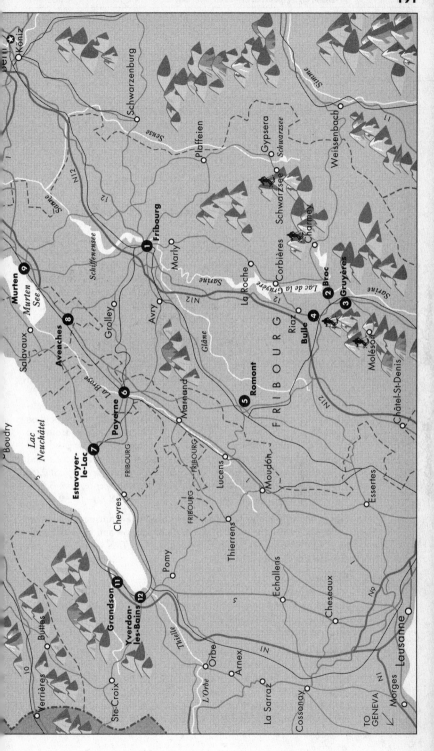

main portal, a beautifully restored tympanum of the Last Judgment shows the blessed being gently herded left toward Peter, who holds the key to the heavenly gates; those not so fortunate head right, led by pig-face demons, into the cauldrons and jaws of hell. Inside the enormous structure you'll see its famous 18th-century organ, built by Fribourger Aloys Mooser, and exceptional stained-glass windows dating from 1895 through 1936. Though perhaps incongruous in the Gothic setting, they are beautifully executed in a pre-Raphaelite and Art Nouveau style, suggestive of America's Tiffany; the Polish artist Joseph Mehoffer won a competition for the commission. In the **Chapelle du St-Sépulcre** (Chapel of the Holy Sepulcher) a moving group of 13 figures portrays the entombment of Christ. It dates from 1433 and, despite its prosaic composition, suggests intense emotion. ✉ *3 rue des Chanoines,* ☎ *026/ 3223945.* ✉ *Free.* ⊘ *Mon.–Sat. 7:30–7, Sun. 9–7.*

The 13th-century **Église des Cordeliers** (Church of the Franciscan Friars), up the hill from the Cathédrale St-Nicolas, is nearly as impressive as the latter. Attached to the Franciscan friary, it has a 16th-century polytych on the high altar by the anonymous Nelkenmeisters, or Maîtres à l'Oeillet (two artists who signed their works only with red and white carnations), a carved-wood triptych believed to be Alsatian, and a 15th-century retable depicting St. Anthony in temptation by the Fribourg artist Hans Fries. ✉ *6 rue de Morat,* ☎ *026/3471160.* ✉ *Free.* ⊘ *Mon.–Sat. 9–6, Sun. noon–6.*

The **Musée d'Art et d'Histoire de Fribourg** (Fribourg Museum of Art and History) occupies a Renaissance mansion and, incongruously, an old slaughterhouse. The graceful gray-stone Ratzé mansion, built in 1581–84, displays a concentration of local art from the 11th to 18th centuries as well as a strong collection on Fribourg archaeology. The museum's most striking aspect, however, is the 19th-century slaughterhouse, a stark stone structure modernized with steel and block glass to display a provocative mix of sacred sculptures (many from the cathedral) and the black whimsy of Jean Tinguely. The sun-washed attic gallery displays 19th- and 20th-century paintings from Delacroix and Courbet to Ferdinand Hodler. ✉ *12 rue de Morat, Upper City,* ☎ *026/ 3228571.* ✉ *Permanent collection free; temporary expositions 5 SF– 10 SF.* ⊘ *Tues.–Sun. 10–5, additional hrs Thurs. 8 PM–10 PM.*

Espace Jean Tinguely–Niki de Saint Phalle, a new museum opened in 1998, showcases the work of the city's native son and his artist wife. ✉ *2 rue de Morat,* ☎ *026/3055140.* ✉ *5 SF.* ⊘ *Tues.–Sun. 10–5, additional hrs Thurs. 8 PM–10 PM.*

Skiing

Winter sports in the *Alpes fribourgeoises* are popular; there are a variety of areas and possibilities for alpine skiing, cross-country, snowboarding, and luge (sledding). A bilingual (French/German) report on ski conditions for this entire area is available by calling ☎ 1573821.

Schwarzsee, a tiny family resort village in canton Fribourg, lies at the very end of a valley road 26 km (16 mi) southeast of Fribourg, nestled below several 2,000-m (6,560-ft) peaks; its lifts can carry you up to 1,750 m (5,740 ft) for medium runs with spectacular views. At 1,050 m (3,449 ft), the mountain has three ski areas with 10 lifts, 25 km (15 mi) of downhill runs, and 10 km (6 mi) of cross-country trails. For the ski report in German, call ☎ 026/4121660.

Dining and Lodging

$$–$$$ ✕ **L'Aigle Noir.** This slick, contemporary restaurant, on a narrow, cob-
★ bled backstreet in the Old Town, comes as something of a surprise,
with a casual dinette decor—new beech chairs, ceramic floors—on the
café side, and sleek paneling and Biedermeier chairs in the restaurant.
The food is a step above *cuisine bourgeoise*—beef with béarnaise sauce
comes with delicate waffle chips instead of *frites* (french fries), and there
are touches of ginger and fashionable fruit. ✉ *10 rue des Alpes,* ☎
026/3224977. AE, DC, MC, V. Closed Sun.–Mon.

$$–$$$ ✕🏨 **Auberge de Zaehringen.** The oldest private house in Fribourg has
★ become a lovely auberge, after having had only members of three families as owners during its 700 years. This marvelous Old Town inn offers two of the best restaurants in the area and a spectacular view over
the Sarine. The warmly lighted brasserie, with its great 17th-century
wooden beams overhead, serves bistrolike specialties: wild mushrooms
cooked on a bed of crisp cabbage and served on puff pastry with a delicate thyme and rosemary sauce, or a saffron fish soup. In the more
formal dining room, you can sample juniper-perfumed rack of lamb
with sweetbreads and admire a view little changed for nearly eight centuries. The two guest rooms are vast and luxurious, furnished with antiques, lush fabrics, and marble baths. Free cab service to the hotel is
offered from the train station if you telephone in advance. Reservations are essential at the restaurant on weekends. ✉ *13 rue de Za-
ehringen, CH-1700,* ☎ *026/3224236,* 🄵🄰🄷 *026/3226908. 2 rooms. 2
restaurants, bar. DC, MC, V. Closed Mon. No dinner Sun.*

$$$ 🏨 **De la Rose.** Though managed in a laissez-faire style that's dis-
tinctly un-Swiss, this convenient, historic property has a spartan, ser-
viceable style (built-in wood cabinetry, shades of beige), while its
public spaces still retain details of its 17th-century origins. There's a
vaulted cellar bar, and a front terrace with views toward the cathe-
dral. An emphasis on quiet comforts—trouser press, electric kettle—
softens the rock and roll blaring at the reception. ✉ *1 rue de Morat,
CH-1700,* ☎ *026/3510101,* 🄵🄰🄷 *026/3510100. 40 rooms. Restaurant,
bar, café. AE, DC, MC, V.*

$$$ 🏨 **Golden Tulip.** This modern, 1970s glass-and-concrete box is near
the Bahnhof at the head of Grand Places, a city park studded with a
Tinguely fountain. Though its aesthetic clashes with the medieval grace
that characterizes Fribourg, it is the only business hotel in the area,
with comfortable if small rooms, simple decor, and a spare but functional work space (you can get a hold of projection screens and other
business necessities). The restaurant and bar are popular with the
suits. ✉ *14 Grand Places, CH-1700,* ☎ *026/3519191,* 🄵🄰🄷 *026/3519192.
130 rooms. 2 restaurants, bar, free parking. AE, DC, MC, V.*

$$–$$$ 🏨 **Hotel Duc Berthold.** Berchtold V himself is said to have lived in this
ancient building during the 12th century. There's nothing medieval about
it now, although the smallish rooms have a comfortable, old-fashioned
air with their delicate florals, creamy linens, and reproduction antique
furniture. Triple-glazed windows keep out the din from the heavily traf-
ficked Zähringen Bridge. ✉ *5 rue des Bouchers, CH-1700,* ☎ *026/
3508100,* 🄵🄰🄷 *026/3508181. 37 rooms. 2 restaurants, bar, coffee shop.
AE, DC, MC, V.*

$$ 🏨 **Elite.** This modest lodging is convenient to the Old Town, with
spare but functional furnishings (circa 1970). Rooms on the univer-
sity side have views over the campus lawns. ✉ *7 rue du Criblet, CH-
1700,* ☎ *026/3223836,* 🄵🄰🄷 *026/3224036. 36 rooms. Restaurant, 2 bars,
café. AE, V.*

Broc

❷ *33 km (20 mi) south of Fribourg.*

Here there's a **Nestlé *chocolaterie*** (chocolate factory) that, in the right
weather conditions, floods the air with the scent of warm, rich milk
chocolate. You can watch a 30-minute film demonstrating the process
of converting harmless little brown beans into vast, unctuous tar pits
of creamy brown paste; a tasting follows. ✉ *CH-1636,* ☎ *026/
9215151.* ✍ *Free.* ☉ *May–Oct., weekdays 9–11 and 1:30–4. Reservations essential.*

Gruyères

★ ❸ *5 km (3 mi) south of Broc, 35 km (21 mi) south of Fribourg.*

The castle village of Gruyères rises above the plain on a rocky crag,
its single main street lined with Renaissance houses in perfect condition. With its traditional crest bearing a crane (*grue* in French), Gruyères
is a perfect specimen of a medieval stronghold: It was once the capital of the idyllic Alpine estates of the Burgundian counts of Gruyères.
The town is entirely car-free, so if you're driving, you'll need to park
in the lot outside town and walk in (a short distance).

There were 19 counts, from 1080 to 1554; the last was Michael of
Gruyères, a lover of luxury and a big spender, who expanded the estates and then fled his creditors, leaving vast holdings to Fribourg and
Bern. In 1848 a wealthy Geneva family bought the old **château.** As patrons of the arts, they hosted the artist Corot; panels by him grace the
castle's drawing room. In a tour of the castle, you can also see the 13th-
century dungeon and the living quarters, decorated in 16th- and 17th-
century styles with tapestries, frescoes, and grand fireplaces. In high
season the parking lots below the castle swell with tour buses, and the
street fills quickly with crowds. Arrive early to beat the onslaught. ✉
CH-1663, ☎ *026/9212102.* ✍ *5 SF.* ☉ *June–Sept., daily 9–6; Mar.–
May and Oct., daily 9–noon and 1–5; Nov.–Feb., daily 9–noon and
1–4:30.*

Wooden spoons make a good souvenir, as Gruyères is known not only
for its mild, nutty cheese (always spelled without the *s*) but also for its
48% butterfat crème-double, which pours slowly over a bowl of
berries; it is sold at creameries up and down the street and in restaurants as well. In the village below the castle, you can visit the **fromagerie**
(cheese dairy), where the famous Gruyère is produced with fully modernized equipment. ✉ *Village below castle,* ☎ *026/9211410.* ✍ *Free.*
☉ *Daily 8–7; demonstrations 10 and 2.*

OFF THE
BEATEN PATH

CHARMEY, CRÉSUZ, LA VALSAINTE – If you're traveling by car, head
north from Gruyères on the road to the small family ski resort of
Charmey. Once you've passed Crésuz but before reaching Charmey,
cut left and take the attractive drive into the narrow, hill-framed La Valsainte. It's barely populated, except for a few villages and some fine examples of the low-roof, silvery-shingle Fribourg barns rising out of the
pastures. There are two charming places to eat along the way (☞ Dining and Lodging, *below*).

Skiing

Gruyères/Moléson, at 1,100 m (3,609 ft), offers skiing up to 2,002 m
(6,568 ft), with wraparound views of the pre-Alps and on to Lake
Geneva. It has three cable cars, four lifts, 20 km (12 mi) of downhill
ski runs, and 8 km (5 mi) of cross-country trails. **Charmey,** at 900 m
(2,953 ft), lies in a bowl surrounded by forested peaks; its one ski area

stretches between Vounetz, at 1,627 m (5,337 ft), and the village it-self. Slopes are of medium difficulty at best. The resort's charms lie more in its bucolic isolation and familial ways. Charmey has eight lifts, in-cluding a gondola; 20 km (12 mi) of downhill runs; and 25 km (16 mi) of cross-country trails.

Dining and Lodging

$$ ✕ **Pinte des Mossettes.** For a local treat, head up the tiny road from
★ Gruyères into picturesque La Valsainte. Near the road's end, just past the Chartreux convent, a tiny restaurant perches on a hilltop overlooking the green valley, with tables set up on the terrace in summer creating an atmosphere of a Ticinese grotto. Inside is casual and rustic, too. Owner-chef Judith Baumann, who won acclaim in 1998 as Switzer-land's female chef of the year, prepares a simple daily menu based on local and often homegrown ingredients—mushrooms, cheeses—that are worth your trip. Dishes plunge deep into the season; a spring menu could include milk-fed veal or elder-flower ice cream. ⊠ *Road between Gruyères and La Valsainte, Cerniat,* ☎ FAX *026/9272097. AE, DC, MC, V. Closed Dec.–Jan.*

$ ✕ **Le Chalet.** This local institution nestled into the foot of the castle at the end of the only thoroughfare is frankly touristic, but it's not with-out regional charm. Carved pine and gingham create a faux-authen-tic atmosphere that's pleasant if contrived. Upstairs, a vast loft shelters a collection of farm implements, and on both floors, waitresses wear traditional costumes. You can sample fondue Fribourg style (with potatoes), raclette, and berries with crème-double. ⊠ *CH-1663,* ☎ *026/ 9212154,* FAX *026/9213313. AE, DC, MC, V.*

$ ✕⊡ **Le Vieux Chalet.** This plain, old-fashioned country inn is off the beaten path, on the road between Gruyères and Charmey; though it was built in 1960, every effort was made to reproduce authentic wood-work and architectural detail. There are only six bedrooms, all done in knotty pine. But, the downstairs is roomy and welcoming: The rus-tic wood-lined café is filled with stools and rough-hewn tables, the restau-rant warmed by a stone fireplace. Inexpensive daily plates, cheese specialties, local ham, and berries with Gruyère crème-double are some of the treats. The restaurant is closed Tuesday. ⊠ *Road from Gruyères to Charmey, in direction of Jaun Pass, CH-1653 Crésuz,* ☎ *026/ 9271286. 6 rooms. Restaurant, 2 cafés. AE, MC, V.*

$$–$$$ ⊡ **Hostellerie des Chevaliers.** You need never mingle with the busloads
★ except in passing the parking lots, as this idyllic, atmospheric hotel stands aloof, well off the main tourist drag. It even has the same views as the castle, and back rooms overlook the broad valley. The decor is a warm regional mix of antiques, handsome woodwork, and ceramic stoves—sometimes a little eccentric, as in the baths, which have been outfitted with teal or pumpkin tiles, and rooms, festooned with rich jewel tones and lavish prints. It's near the town's parking lot. ⊠ *CH-1663,* ☎ *026/ 9211933,* FAX *026/9212552. 32 rooms. Restaurant. AE, DC, MC, V.*

$$ ⊡ **Fleur de Lys.** From its vaulted, stenciled reception area to its pine-
★ and-beam restaurant, this is a welcoming little hotel, with pretty wood-paneled rooms and a wonderful rear terrace looking over the mountains. ⊠ *CH-1663,* ☎ *026/9212108,* FAX *026/9213605. 10 rooms. Restau-rant, 2 cafés. AE, DC, MC, V.*

$–$$ ⊡ **De Ville.** Directly on the picturesque main street, with back rooms overlooking the valley, this small family inn has been modernized with quarry tile, stucco, and pine. Five rooms are doubles with a shower instead of a full bath; there are also a triple and a pair of quads, all with full bath. ⊠ *CH-1663,* ☎ *026/9212424,* FAX *026/9213628. 8 rooms. Restaurant, café. AE, DC, MC, V. Closed Jan.*

Bulle

❹ *5 km (3 mi) northwest of Gruyères (toward the A12 expressway), 31 km (19 mi) southwest of Fribourg.*

You can learn about Gruyères farming traditions at the **Musée Gruérien,** where a display of folk costumes, art, and farm tools is enhanced by a reproduction of a flagstone farmhouse kitchen and dining room. ⊠ *pl. du Cabalet,* ☎ *026/9127260.* 🎟 *4 SF.* ☉ *Tues.–Sat. 10–noon and 2–5, Sun. 2–5.*

Romont

❺ *15 km (9 mi) northwest of Bulle, 49 km (30 mi) southwest of Fribourg.*

The best way to approach this 13th-century town of two broad streets is to leave the highway and drive up to its castle terrace. The fortress's 13th-century ramparts surround the town, forming a belvedere from which you can see the Alps—from Mont Blanc to the Berner Oberland—as well as other notable buildings: the 12th-century **Cistercian convent,** the 17th-century **Capuchin monastery,** and the lovely 13th-century *collégiale,* one of the purest examples of a Gothic church in Switzerland, with period windows, sculptures, choir stalls, a screen, and an altarpiece. Inside the castle is the **Musée du Vitrail,** a museum of contemporary (and some older) stained glass. A slide presentation traces the development of the craft. ⊠ *Château,* ☎ *026/6521095.* 🎟 *6 SF.* ☉ *Apr.–Oct., Tues.–Sun. 10–noon and 2–6; Nov.–Mar., weekends 10–noon and 2–6.*

Payerne

❻ *15 km (9 mi) north of Romont, 18 km (11 mi) southwest of Fribourg.*

The market town of Payerne has a magnificent 11th-century **église abbatiale** (abbey church), one of the finest examples of Romanesque art in Switzerland. Recent efforts have restored it to its functioning austere abbey, with a grand barrel-vaulted sanctuary and original, primitive capital carvings on the pillars. ☎ *026/6626704.* 🎟 *3 SF.* ☉ *Weekdays 10:30–noon and 2–5, weekends 10:30–noon.*

Estavayer-le-Lac

❼ *7 km (4 mi) northwest of Payerne, 51 km (32 mi) southwest of Neuchâtel.*

On the shores of Lake Neuchâtel, this modest but charming lake resort has retained much of its medieval architecture, from arcades to the enormous, multitower medieval **Château de Chenaux.** Much less traditional is the quirky **Musée de Grenouilles** (Frog Museum), which displays 108 embalmed frogs posed like people in scenes of daily life from the 19th century up through today. Other exhibits include an authentic 17th-century kitchen, various military and household artifacts dredged from Lake Neuchâtel, and more than 200 Swiss railroad lanterns, some up to 100 years old. ⊠ *rue des Musées, CH-1470,* ☎ *026/6632448.* 🎟 *3 SF.* ☉ *Mar.–June and Sept.–Oct., Tues.–Sun. 9–11 and 2–5; July–Aug., daily 9–11 and 2–5; Nov.–Feb., weekends 2–5.*

Avenches

★ **❽** *5 km (3 mi) northeast of Estavayer-le-Lac, 13 km (8 mi) northeast of Fribourg.*

Avenches is the old capital of the Helvetians, which, as Aventicum, grew into an important city that reached its halcyon in the 2nd century AD.

In its prime, the Roman stronghold was surrounded by some 6 km (4 mi) of 2-m-high (6-ft-high) stone walls. The Alemanni destroyed it in the 3rd century. You can still see the remains of a Roman forum, a bath-house, and an amphitheater—today the **Musée et Théâtre Romains** (Roman Museum and Theater)—where bloodthirsty spectators once watched the games. The collection of Roman antiquities at the museum is noteworthy, including an excellent copy of a gold bust of Marcus Aurelius, unearthed at Avenches in the 1920s, the original of which is in Lausanne. ☎ *026/6751730.* ▦ *2 SF.* ☉ *Apr.–Sept., Tues.–Sun. 10–noon and 1–5; Oct.–Mar., Tues.–Sun. 2–5.*

Murten

★ ❾ *6 km (4 mi) northeast of Avenches, 17 km (11 mi) north of Fribourg.*

The ancient town of Murten, known in French as Morat, is a popular resort on Lac de Murten (Murten Lake), with a boat-lined waterfront. It was here, on June 22, 1476, that the Swiss Confederates—already a fearsomely efficient military machine—attacked with surprising ferocity and won a significant victory over the Burgundians, who were threatening Fribourg under the leadership of Duke Charles the Bold. Begun as a siege 12 days earlier, the battle cost the Swiss 410 men; the Burgundians 12,000. The Burgundian defeat at Murten prevented the establishment of a large Lothringian kingdom and left Switzerland's autonomy unchallenged for decades. Legend has it that a Swiss runner, carrying a linden branch, ran from Murten to Fribourg to carry the news of victory. He expired by the town hall, and a linden tree grew from the branch he carried. Today, to commemorate his dramatic sacrifice, some 15,000 runners participate annually on the first Sunday in October in a 17-km (11-mi) race from Murten to Fribourg. As for the linden tree, it flourished in Fribourg for some 500 years, until 1983, when it was ingloriously felled by a car—one driven, no doubt, by a Burgundian.

Bilingual Murten/Morat has a superbly preserved medieval center. The modern highway enters and leaves the old part of town through 13th-century gates; the houses and shops that line the broad main street, the Hauptgasse, look out from under vaulted arcades. Its **Musée Historique** (Historical Museum) is in a renovated mill, complete with two water-powered mill wheels; on view are prehistoric finds, ancient military items, and trophies from the Burgundian Wars. ✉ *Historic center,* ☎ *026/6703100.* ▦ *4 SF.* ☉ *Oct.–Dec. and Mar.–Apr., Tues.–Sun. 2–5; May–Sept., Tues.–Sun. 10–noon and 2–5; Jan.–Feb., weekends 2–5.*

Dining and Lodging

$$$$ ✕▦ **Le Vieux Manoir au Lac.** One kilometer (½ mile) south of Murten
★ on Lake Murten, this stately mansion is a graceful mix of half-timbers and turrets, with a deep Fribourg roofline. Sprawling comfortably across a manicured park near the lakefront, it exudes a manorial grace you won't find elsewhere in Switzerland, even in other Relais & Châteaux properties. The decor is an eclectic mix of parquet and Persian rugs, wing chairs, Biedermeier, and country prints; rooms are a rich blend of chintz, gingham, and toile de Jouy. The restaurant offers a choice of seasonal sampling menus, each with a French/Continental bent; options might include roast lamb with mustard sauce or a lasagna of asparagus with truffle butter. A winter garden allows you to dine in a room bathed with light, just yards from the shore of the lake. ✉ *rue de Lausanne, CH-3280 Meyriez,* ☎ *026/6786161,* ℻ *026/6786162. 30 rooms. Restaurant, café. AE, DC, MC, V.*

$$$ ✕⊞ **Schiff.** Over an all-modern structure directly on the waterfront, below the Old Town, homey touches have been determinedly super-imposed: Persian rugs, antiques, and gilt. The setting is ideal, with a sheltered terrace and access to the lakeside promenade. The restaurant, Lord Nelson, wraps around the garden and serves ambitious French cuisine on the terrace or in a room with a nautical theme, both with lake views. Specialties may include risotto with porcini mushrooms and pigeon breast or classic local trout, perch, or pike, sold by weight. ⊠ *Ryf 53, CH-3280,* ☎ *026/6702701,* 𝖥𝖠𝖷 *026/6703531. 15 rooms. Restaurant, bar, café. AE, DC, MC, V.*

$$–$$$ ✕⊞ **Weisses Kreuz.** Though it shares great lake views with other ho-
★   tels in town, this lodging has more to offer: the devotion—even ob-session—of its owners (it has been in one family since 1921). There are two buildings, and though you might be tempted by lakeside panoramas, consider the wing with Old Town views across the street; it's furnished in extraordinary style with complete antique bedroom sets—Biedermeier, Art Nouveau, Louis XVI, Empire. Simpler rooms, in Scandinavian pine or high-tech style, cost less. The lovely formal din-ing room is known for its broad array of fish specialties: whitefish with chanterelle mushrooms and cucumbers, timbale of three lake fish, pike braised in dill. ⊠ *Rathausg. 31, CH-3280,* ☎ *026/6702641,* 𝖥𝖠𝖷 *026/ 6702866. 27 rooms. Restaurant, café. AE, DC, MC, V.*

$$ ⊞ **Krone.** Its best features are its shuttered facade on the Old Town side and the spectacular terrace in back, looking over the lake and wa-terfront. In between, you'll find a mix of splashy '60s prints and as-sertive chintz, with massive carved antiques in the halls. The rooms are solid if occasionally small, but the lake views in the back are great. ⊠ *5 Rathausg., CH-3280,* ☎ *026/6705252,* 𝖥𝖠𝖷 *026/6703610. 33 rooms. Restaurant, bar, 2 cafés. AE, DC, MC, V.*

LAC NEUCHÂTEL

The region of Neuchâtel belonged to Prussia from 1707 to 1857, with a brief interruption caused by Napoléon and a period of double loy-alty to Prussia and the Swiss Confederation between 1815 and 1857. Yet its French culture remains untouched by Germanic language, diet, or culture. Some boast that the inhabitants speak "the best French in Switzerland," which is partly why so many summer language courses are taught here.

Neuchâtel

★ ⑩ *28 km (17 mi) north of Murten, 48 km (30 mi) northwest of Fribourg.*

The city of Neuchâtel, at the foot of the Jura, flanked by vineyards and facing southeast, enjoys remarkable views across Lac Neuchâtel and the whole crowded range of the middle Alps, from the majestic mass of Mont Blanc to the Bernese Oberland. (Lac Neuchâtel, at 38 km/24 mi long and 8 km/5 mi wide, is the largest in the country.) A prosper-ous city, Neuchâtel was known for its watchmaking from the early 18th century on. It possesses an air of almost tangible dignity; in the lower part of town, bordering the placid lake, broad avenues are lined with imposing yellow-sandstone buildings that inspired author Alexandre Dumas to call it a city carved in butter. The overall effect is of unruf-fled but compact grandeur—yet the city's cafés and marketplace throng with lively, urban street life and the Gallic, bony-chic Neuchâtelois.

The extent of French influence in Neuchâtel is revealed in its monu-ments and architecture, most notably at the **Église Collégiale** (Colle-giate Church), a handsome Romanesque and Burgundian Gothic structure dating from the 12th century, with a colorful tile roof. (For anyone not wanting to climb steep streets, the church and prison tower may be reached from the Promenade Noire off the place des Halles by an inconspicuous elevator—*Ascenseur publique.*) The church contains a strikingly realistic and well-preserved grouping of life-size painted figures called *le cénotaphe,* or monument to the counts of Neuchâtel; dating from the 14th and 15th centuries, this is considered one of Europe's finest examples of medieval art. Under restoration since 1997, it is scheduled to be on display again in 1999. Grouped around the church are the ramparts and cloisters of the 12th-century **château,** which today houses the cantonal government. ⊠ *12 rue de la Collegiale,* ☏ *032/8896000.* ⬛ *Free.* ☉ *Daily 8–6.*

The **Tour des Prisons** (Prison Tower), which adjoins the Église Collégiale, affords panoramic views from its turret. On your way up, you'll see a series of models of Neuchâtel as it evolved from the 15th through the 18th centuries. ⊠ *rue Jeanne de Hochberg, adjoining Église Collégiale,* ☏ *032/8896000.* ⬛ *50 centimes.* ☉ *Daily 8–6.*

The **architecture of the Old Town** demonstrates a full range of French styles, far beyond the Gothic. Along rue des Moulins are two perfect specimens of the Louis XIII period, and—at its opposite end—a fine Louis XIV house anchors the place des Halles (market square), also notable for its turreted 16th-century **Maison des Halles.** The **Hôtel de Ville** (⊠ Rue de l'Hôtel de Ville), opened in 1790 east of the Old Town, is by Pierre-Adrien Paris, the architect of Louis XVI. There are several fine patrician houses, such as the magnificent **Hôtel DuPeyrou,** the mansion of Pierre-Alexandre DuPeyrou (⊠ 1 av. DuPeyrou, east of Old Town), the friend, protector, and publisher of Jean-Jacques Rousseau, who studied botany in the nearby Val-de-Travers. Most of the Old Town is a pedestrian zone, though public buses do run through it.

★ For connoisseurs not only of art but of art museums, the **Musée d'Art et d'Histoire** (Museum of Art and History) merits a pilgrimage. Thanks to a remarkably unprovincial curator, it displays a deep collection of paintings gathered under broad themes—nature, civilization—and mounted in a radical, evocative way. Fifteenth-century allegories, early Impressionism, and contemporary abstractions pack the walls from floor to ceiling: interacting, conflicting, demanding comparison. You may climb a platform (itself plastered with paintings) to view the higher works. This aggressive series of displays is framed by the architectural decorations of Neuchâtel resident Clement Heaton, whose murals and stained glass make the building itself a work of art.

This novel museum also has the honor of hosting three of this watchmaking capital's most exceptional guests: the **automates Jaquet-Droz,** three astounding little androids, created between 1768 and 1774, that once toured the courts of Europe like young mechanical Mozarts. Pierre Jaquet-Droz and his son Henri-Louis created them, and they are moving manifestations of the stellar degree to which watchmaking had evolved by the 18th century. One automaton is called **Le Dessinateur** (the Draughtsman). A dandy in satin knee pants, he draws graphite images of a dog, the god Eros in a chariot pulled by a butterfly, and a profile of Louis XV. **La Musicienne** (the Musician) is a soulful young woman who plays the organ, moving and breathing subtly with the music, and actually striking the keys that produce the organ notes, also authentic. **L'Écrivain** (the Writer) dips a real feather in real ink and writes 40 different letters, capital and lowercase; like a primitive computer, he can be programmed to write any message simply by changing a steel disk. The automates are viewable only on the first Sunday of the month, at 2, 3, or 4, or by appointment, but an audio-visual show and a close-up view of them is enough to re-create the thrill. ✉ *quai Léopold-Robert,* ☎ *032/7177925.* 🎫 *7 SF; free Thurs.* ⊙ *Tues.– Sun. 10–5, Thurs. 10–9.*

☞ The **Papiliorama** and **Nocturama** literally crawl with life. Under a vast glass dome, a complete tropical garden biosphere, the **Papiliorama** in-cludes tropical plants, lily ponds, more than a thousand living butter-flies, dwarf caimans (*crocodilians*), tortoises, birds, fish, and gigantic tropical insects—the latter, fortunately, in cages. A second dome, **Noc-turama,** is filled with tropical nocturnal mammals, bats, and owls. They're just 5 km (3 mi) from Neuchâtel; you can get there by car or train. ✉ *Marin,* ☎ *032/7534344.* 🎫 *Both domes: 11 SF.* ⊙ *Apr.–Sept., daily 9–6; Oct.–Mar., daily 10–5.*

Dining and Lodging

$–$$ ✕ **Du Banneret.** This restaurant, next to the hotel of the same name and similarly built of yellow Neuchâtel sandstone in late Renaissance style, is across from a colorful fountain. Lying at the foot of the rue du Château, the brasserie is a cozy gathering place, where the chef often emerges to greet his guests. The brasserie has a low beamed ceiling with huge stones framing the windows toward the fountain; the dishes are mostly regional fare, such as homemade pasta with fresh wild mush-rooms or lake trout. In summer tables are set up on the small terrace facing the fountain. In the upstairs dining room, the food takes a strong Italian twist. ✉ *1 rue Fleury,* ☎ *032/7252861,* 🖷 *032/7254630. AE, DC, MC, V. Closed Sun.*

$$ ✕🏨 **Auberge de l'Aubier.** Just a 10-minute drive west from Neuchâ-tel but already in the countryside, this small auberge is akin to an eco-retreat. There are solar panels on the barn, rainwater is used in the washing machines, and you can be sure the kitchen's ingredients are fresh—the auberge runs its own organic farm. Each guest room has an individual theme, and on a clear day you can make out Mont Blanc. ✉ *CH-2205 Montézillon,* ☎ *032/7303010,* 🖷 *032/7303016. 15 rooms. Restaurant, shop, meeting rooms. AE, MC, V.*

$ ✕🏨 **Du Marché.** Opening directly onto the place du Marché, this is a delightful place for a hearty plat du jour or a carafe of local wine. In-side, pass through the lively bar-café to the steamy, old-wood brasserie for a bowl of tripe in Neuchâtel wine or salt pork with lentils. Upstairs, a pretty little dining room serves more sophisticated fare. Plain, func-tional rooms with tidy tile bathrooms down the hall are an excellent value. ✉ *4 pl. des Halles, CH-2000,* ☎ *032/7245800,* 🖷 *032/7214742. 10 rooms. Restaurant, café. AE, DC, MC, V.*

$$$$ 🏨 **Beau-Rivage.** This restored 19th-century building occupies a prime spot in the city, giving a splendid view of the Alps on a clear day. Its warmly lighted, high-ceiling, polished-oak interior exudes a feeling of stately calm. There are fax machines in every room. ✉ *1 esplanade du Mont Blanc, CH-2001,* ☎ *032/7231515,* 🖷 *032/7231616. 65 rooms. Restaurant, bar. AE, DC, MC, V.*

$$$ 🏨 **Beaulac.** In a city with few lodging options, this one, across from the Musée d'Art et d'Histoire and directly on the waterfront, has one of the most attractive locations. Despite its foursquare modern exte-rior—avant-garde in 1957—its decor and facilities are state-of-the-art, with burled wood and jewel tones, an English-style piano bar, confer-ence rooms with panoramic views, and even a Web site corner. Views from most of the rooms extend toward the Alps, and a broad terrace café juts directly over the lake. ✉ *2 esplanade Léopold-Robert, CH-2000,* ☎ *032/7231111,* 🖷 *032/7256035. 80 rooms. 2 restaurants, bar, sauna, exercise room, meeting rooms. AE, DC, MC, V.*

$$–$$$ 🏨 **La Maison du Prussien.** This 16th-century mill, restored and brought into the Romantik hotel chain, sits alongside a roaring woodland stream above Neuchâtel and packages itself for honeymooners and business groups on retreat—but individuals are also welcome. There are polished beams, terra-cotta floors, and verdant views on all sides; three of the suites have fireplaces. Take the tunnels under Neuchâtel toward La Chaux-de-Fonds, exit toward Pontarlier-Vauseyon, and then watch for the hotel's signs. ⊠ *Au Gor du Vauseyon, CH-2006,* ☎ *032/7305454,* FAX *032/7302143. 6 rooms, 4 suites. Restaurant, brasserie, café. AE, DC, MC, V.*

Nightlife and the Arts

A new breed of nightlife, *restaurants de nuit* and *bars musicaux,* has swept through the city; these places stay open all night, plying customers with food and entertainment. The **Garbo Café** (⊠ *5–7 rue des Chavannes,* ☎ *032/7243181)* and the **Dakota** (⊠ *3 av. de la Gare,* ☎ *032/7100705)* draw dinner crowds from 9 PM to 6 AM, and such discos as **La Rotonde** (⊠ *14 Faubourg du Lac,* ☎ *032/7244848)* and **Le Shakespeare** (⊠ *7 rue des Terreaux,* ☎ *032/7258588)* are very popular with the younger set. The year's biggest celebration, however, remains the annual grape harvest of nearby vineyards (☞ En Route, *below),* celebrated the last weekend of September with parades and fanfares in the city center.

Outdoor Activities and Sports

BIKING

Neuchâtel has about 400 km (248 mi) of marked mountain-bike trails. You can rent mountain bikes at **Alizé** (⊠ pl. du 12-Septembre, ☎ 032/7244090). Free trail maps are available at the tourist office (☞ Visitor Information *in* Fribourg, Neuchâtel, and the Jura A to Z, *below).*

GOLF

There's an 18-hole golf course at **Voëns sur St-Blaise** (☎ 032/7535550).

SWIMMING

There are **public beaches** at nearly every village and resort around Lake Neuchâtel and Lake Murten, plus a **municipal complex** (⊠ Nid du Crô Rte des Falaises 30, ☎ 032/7214848) with outdoor and indoor pools, open daily, in Neuchâtel.

En Route   Just a few miles west of Neuchâtel lie some of Switzerland's best **vineyards,** their grapes producing chiefly white wine that is light and somewhat sparkling. The wines are bottled before the second fermentation, so they have a rather high carbonic-acid content. If you'd like to arrange a tasting, your best bet would be to call the vintner and set up an appointment.

Grandson

❶❶ *29 km (18 mi) southwest of Neuchâtel.*

This lakeside village in canton Vaud has a long history. It is said that in 1066 a member of the Grandson family accompanied William of Normandy (better known as the Conqueror) to England, where he founded the English barony of Grandison. Otto I of Grandson took part in the Crusades, and one of his descendants was a troubadour praised by Chaucer. When the Burgundian Wars broke out during the late 15th century, the **Château de Grandson** (Grandson Castle), built during the 11th century and much rebuilt during the 13th and 15th centuries, was in the hands of Charles the Bold of Burgundy. In 1475 the Swiss won it by siege, but early the next year their garrison was surprised by Charles, and 418 of their men were captured and hung from the apple trees in the castle orchard. A few days later the Swiss returned to Grandson and, after crushing the Burgundians, retaliated by stringing their prisoners from the same apple trees. After being used for three centuries as a residence by the Bernese bailiffs, the castle was bought in 1875 by the de Blonay family, which restored it to its current impressive state, with high, massive walls and five cone turrets. Inside, you can see a reproduction of a Burgundian war tent, *oubliettes* (dungeon pits for prisoners held *in perpetua*), torture chambers, and a model of the Battle of Grandson, complete with 20-minute slide show. Cassette-guided tours of the town are available at the castle reception desk. ☎ *024/4452926.* ⌑ *8 SF.* ☉ *Mar.–Oct., daily 9–6; Nov.–Feb., Sat. 1–5 and Sun. 9–5 or by request.*

Yverdon-les-Bains

⑫   *6 km (4 mi) southwest of Grandson, 36 km (22 mi) southwest of Neuchâtel.*

This busy lakefront market town is known for its natural thermal baths, first developed by the Romans, now accessible through a state-of-the-art **thermal center** (✉ ave. des Bains 22; ☎ 024/4230232). Its turreted **château,** built in the mid-13th century, has now been restored and modernized; it was in the castle here that the famous Swiss educator Johann Heinrich Pestalozzi, born in 1746, opened an experimental school that attracted other reformers from both Germany and England. ☎ *024/4259310.* ⌑ *6 SF.* ☉ *Tues.–Sun. 2–5.*

In front of Yverdon's Hôtel de Ville (Town Hall)—notable for its Louis XV facade—stands a bronze monument of Pestalozzi, grouped with two children. The town center has been closed for pedestrians; there are also waterfront promenades, a pretty campground, and 5 km (3 mi) of beaches. From this southernmost tip of Lake Neuchâtel, there's an easy sweep by expressway (A1) to Lausanne or Geneva.

THE JURA

Straddling the French frontier from Geneva almost all the way to Basel are the Jura Mountains, an area that remains remote and something of a secret. (Those mountains falling within the canton of Neuchâtel are known as the Montagnes Neuchâteloises.) By Alpine standards the mountains are relatively low; few peaks exceed 1,500 m (4,920 ft). It is a region of pine forests; lush pastures; and deeply cleft, often craggy valleys where the farmers lived in relative isolation until the invasion of railways and roads. In winter some parts of the Jura can be very cold: La Brévine, a windswept hamlet between Le Locle and Les Verrières on the border, is known as the Swiss Siberia. Horse breeding and watchmaking make odd industrial bedfellows in this region, with most of the watchmaking concentrated around Le Locle and La Chaux-de-Fonds, and the horse business flourishing in Franches-Montagnes, farther north.

En Route   From Neuchâtel into the Jura Mountains, Highway A20 climbs 13 km (8 mi) from Neuchâtel to the **Vue des Alpes,** a parking area on a high ridge that affords, as the name implies, spectacular views of the Alps, including Mont Blanc.

La Chaux-de-Fonds

⑬   *22 km (14 mi) north of Neuchâtel.*

During the early 18th century, watchmaking began as a cottage industry here; over the years, the town became the watchmaking capital of Switzerland. The town was destroyed by fire at the end of the 18th century; it was then rebuilt on a stiff grid plan, its broad avenues lined with mansarded town houses. Beyond this stately center, bald, white, modern housing has sprung up in its bleak industrial zone.

Yet La Chaux-de-Fonds takes pains to document its architectural history and—unfettered by its tradition—makes the most of its modern elements. Perhaps this heightened consciousness of architecture, good and bad, inspired its native son: Charles-Édouard Jeanneret, the famed architect who called himself Le Corbusier, was born here. His birthplace can be seen, although not toured, along with the École d'Art, where he taught, and several villas he worked on between 1906 and 1917. Only one is open to the public: the **Villa turque,** made of reinforced concrete and faced with terra-cotta tiles. The tourist office has a brochure outlining a walk by this and the other buildings.

The **Musée des Beaux-Arts** (Museum of Fine Arts), itself a striking neoclassical structure, was designed by Le Corbusier's teacher L'Éplattenier; it contains a furniture set, an oil painting (*Seated Woman*, 1933), and a tapestry (*Les Musiciens*, 1953–57) by Le Corbusier. There also works by such other Swiss artists as Léopold Robert and Ferdinand Hodler. ⊠ *33 rue des Musées,* ☎ *032/9130444.* ◰ *6 SF, Sun. free 10– noon.* ⊙ *Tues.–Sun. 10–noon and 2–5.*

★ The **Musée International d'Horlogerie** (International Timepiece Museum) displays a spectacular collection of clocks and watches that traces the development of timekeeping and the expansion of watchmaking as an art form. Unfortunately, the objects are mounted with a minimum of commentary, though most labels have English descriptions. There are also audiovisual presentations on the history and science of the craft, an open work area where you can watch current repairs on pieces from the collection, and a frankly commercial section displaying current models by the stellar local watchmaking firms (Corum, Girard-Perregaux, Ebel, and so on). ⊠ *29 rue des Musées,* ☎ *032/ 9676861.* ◰ *8 SF.* ⊙ *Oct.–May, Tues.–Sun. 10–noon and 2–5; June– Sept., Tues.–Sun. 10–5.*

Lodging

$$ ☷ **Moreau.** Chocoholics will especially like this hotel; the ornate corner building includes the Moreau family confectionery on the ground floor, which specializes in hand-dipped chocolates. The atmosphere is subdued, and many of the comfortable rooms are furnished with antiques. The hotel is especially attractive in summer when a sidewalk café is set up outside under the tall trees; it's near the town center, the museums, and the train station. ⊠ *45 av. Léopold-Robert, CH-2300,* ☎ *032/9132222,* ℻ *032/9132245. 45 rooms. 2 restaurants, bar, sauna, solarium, exercise room, meeting rooms. AE, DC, MC, V.*

$–$$ ☷ **De la Fleur-De-Lys.** This popular spot along the main thoroughfare is the hotel equivalent to a pair of khakis—it's plain and serviceable. The atmosphere is relaxed; the rooms upstairs are quiet and modestly furnished. ⊠ *13 av. Léopold-Robert, CH-2300,* ☎ *032/9133731,* ℻ *032/ 9135851. 28 rooms. Restaurant, bar, meeting rooms. AE, DC, MC, V.*

Skiing

A fair-size city in the Montagnes Neuchâteloises, La Chaux-de-Fonds is known as a fine cross-country ski area, although there are some modest downhill runs nearby as well. The **Tête de Ran,** beyond Vue des Alpes, tops 1,400 m (4,592 ft) and allows skiers to take in panoramic views toward the Bernese Alps. At 1,120 m (3,675 ft), the resort has facilities at **La Vue des Alpes, Tête-de-Ran, La Corbatière,** and **Le Locle,** with 18 lifts, 27 km (16 mi) of downhill runs, and 56 km (35 mi) of cross-country trails. Call ☎ 157/160130 for a bilingual (French/German) bulletin on ski conditions.

En Route   Between La Chaux-de-Fonds and Delémont (just 11 km/6½ mi south of Delémont), the medieval town of **Moutier** produces the firm, piquant Tête de Moine cheese, the only reminder of the once-renowned monastery of Bellelay.

Saignelégier

⑭ *26 km (16 mi) northwest of La Chaux-de-Fonds, 36 km (22 mi) southwest of Delémont.*

A small, fairly modern town set in rolling pastures, Saignelégier is known mostly for its lush surroundings, horseback riding, and cross-country skiing. The *Marché-Concors National de Chevaux* (National Horse Fair) on the second Sunday in August draws crowds from throughout Switzerland and France, as does the *fête des Montgolfières* (Hot-Air Balloon Festival) the second weekend of October.

OFF THE   ★ **LE NOIRMONT** – Just five minutes by car or train from Saignelégier,
BEATEN PATH   nearly on the French border, is one of Switzerland's top gourmet restaurants, Hôtel-Restaurant de la Gare. Chef Georges Wenger extracts culinary inspiration from his rural location, and he has made himself an expert on updating the Jura's regional specialties. The seasonal menu might include sautéed porcini mushrooms or sausage in Jura wine. There's a trio of rooms upstairs if you plan to stay put after the meal. ✉ *2 rue de la Gare, CH-2340,* ☎ *032/9531110,* Ⅺ *032/951059. 3 rooms. Restaurant. AE, MC, V. Closed Mon. and Tues.*

Lodging

$$–$$$ 🏠 **De la Gare et du Parc.** On the main road through town, this carefully renovated hotel with the charm of a stately home offers a peaceful atmosphere, complete with a large garden for its guests. Rooms are modern and conservative. Cheerful bright awnings, shutters, and flags greet you outside; inside the scene is more muted and elegant. ✉ *CH-2350,* ☎ *032/9511121,* Ⅺ *032/9511232. 17 rooms. Restaurant, café, terrace. AE, DC, MC, V.*

Outdoor Activities and Sports

HORSEBACK RIDING

At the **Manège de Saignelégier** (☎ 032/951755) you can rent horses; the town's setting makes it perfect for a ride.

SPORTS CENTER

The modern **Centre de Loisirs** (☎ 032/9512474) has an impressive array of facilities: a covered 25-m swimming pool, indoor ice rink, gymnasium, weight room, even conference rooms and restaurant. There are cross-country ski tracks nearby. A map in front of the sports center displays a network of nearby trails for biking or hiking.

St-Ursanne

⑮ *22 km(14 mi) west of Delémont, 27 km (17 mi) from Saignelégier.*

This lovely, quiet medieval town in a valley carved by the River Doubs is best known to outdoors enthusiasts—fishermen, bicyclists, canoeists, and kayakers. The 12th-century church, **la Collégiale,** is a mixture of Romanesque and early Gothic architecture; the large cloisters are Gothic. The old stone bridge over the River Doubs, with its statue of St. John Nepomucene, the patron saint of bridges, best catches the romantic spirit of St-Ursanne. Local restaurants often serve perch and trout from the Doubs, as well as the region's smoked meats and mushrooms.

Porrentruy

16   *13.5 km (8 mi) northwest of St-Ursanne, 28 km (mi) from Delémont.*

A small detour toward the French border brings you to the center of the Ajoie region and to this city that has an excellently preserved medieval town center. It is worth the journey just to view the impressive **Château de Porrentruy** towering over the Old Town, now used by cantonal offices. This was once the seat of the prince bishops of Basel; the 13th-century Tour Réfouse (refuge tower) next to the castle provides a beautiful view and is always open to the public. The Porte de France, a remnant of the walls of the city, and the old stone houses alongside dramatically reflect a medieval character.

Delémont

17   *81 km (50 mi) northeast of Neuchâtel.*

Nestled in a wide, picturesque valley, this is the chief town of canton Jura; though it's on the edge of the French-German language divide, the official language is French. From the 11th century until the 18th century, Delémont was annexed by the bishop-princes of Basel, who often used it as a summer residence; portions of its center retain their 18th-century air. You'll see 500-year-old fountains and classical houses and, a mile northeast of town, the pilgrimage church **Chapelle du Vorbourg,** perched on a wooded outcropping. The door is usually open; masses are held Sunday and holidays at 9:30 AM.

FRIBOURG, NEUCHÂTEL, AND THE JURA A TO Z

Arriving and Departing

By Car

An important and scenic trans-Swiss artery, the **A12** expressway, cuts from Bern to Lausanne, passing directly through Fribourg; a parallel northwestern route approaches from Basel by expressway (**A1**) to Solothurn, then changes to a secondary highway and follows the northwestern shore of Lake Neuchâtel, with brief sections of expressway at Neuchâtel itself and from Yverdon on down to Lac Léman. A slow but scenic route along A18 cuts from Basel through the Jura by way of Delémont.

By Plane

Geneva's **Cointrin** Airport (✉ 138 km/86 mi southwest of Fribourg, ☎ 022/7993111) is the second-busiest international airport in Switzerland. Frequent flights from the United States and the United Kingdom arrive on **Swissair** and other international carriers via Cointrin. Bern's small airport, **Belp** (✉ 34 km/21 mi northeast of Fribourg, ☎ 031/9613411), services **Crossair** (☎ 061/3253636 for central reservations or ☎ 1553636 toll-free within Switzerland) to major European cities.

By Train

The main train route between Basel, Zürich, and Geneva passes through the Fribourg station (☎ 157/2222) between Bern and Lausanne. Trains generally arrive twice an hour.

Getting Around

By Boat

There are boat trips on the lakes of Neuchâtel, Murten (Morat), and Biel (Bienne), as well as on the Aare River and the Broye Canal, a natural wildlife sanctuary. Schedules vary seasonally, but in summer are frequent and include evening trips. Contact **Compagnie de la Navigation** (☎ 032/7534012) for more information.

By Bus

Postbus connections, except in the principal urban areas, can be few and far between; plan excursions carefully using the bus schedules available at the train station.

By Car

The charms of this varied region can be seen best by car, and there are scenic secondary highways throughout. Keep in mind that some towns, like Gruyères, are car-free or have pedestrians-only centers; in these cases, parking lots are easy to find.

By Train

Secondary connections are thin, but they allow visits to most towns. To visit Gruyères, you must take a bus out of Broc.

Contacts and Resources

Emergencies

Police: (☎ 117). **Fribourg** (☎ 117 or 026/3051818). **Neuchâtel** (☎ 117 or 032/7222222). **Ambulance or medical emergency:** (☎ 026/4225500). **Fribourg and Neuchâtel** (☎ 117). **Medical and dental referrals:** Fribourg (☎ 026/3223343). **Neuchâtel** (☎ 032/7222222).

Guided Tours

Guided walks of Neuchâtel depart from the front of the Tour de Diesse (⌂ rue du Châteaux) in July and August for 8 SF. The tour lasts about two hours.

Visitor Information

The regional office for canton Fribourg is based in **Fribourg** (⌂ 1107 rte. de la Glâne, CH-1700, ☎ 026/4025644). The regional office for canton Neuchâtel (as well as its city tourist office) is based in **Neuchâtel** (⌂ Hôtel des Postes, CH-2000, ☎ 032/8896890). The Jura's regional office holds forth in **Saignelégier** (⌂ 1 rue de la Gruyère, CH-2350, ☎ 032/9521952).

Local tourist offices: **Estavayer-le-Lac** (⌂ Pl. du Midi, CH-1470, ☎ 026/6631237). **Fribourg** (⌂ 1 av. de la Gare, CH-1700, ☎ 026/3213175, FAX 026/3223527). **Gruyères** (⌂ CH-1663, ☎ 026/9211030). **La Chaux-de-Fonds** (⌂ 1 Espacité, CH-2302, ☎ 032/9196895). **Murten** (⌂ 6 Franz-Kirchg., CH-3280, ☎ 026/6705112). **Porrentruy** (⌂ 5 Grand Rue, CH-2900, ☎ 032/4665959). **St-Ursanne** (⌂ CH-2882, ☎ 032/4613716). **Yverdon-les-Bains** (⌂ 1 pl. Pestalozzi, CH-1400, ☎ 024/4236290).

9 Bern

With an Excursion to the Emmental

Humble and down-to-earth, Bern is a city of broad medieval streets, farmers' markets, and friendly, slow-spoken people. It is also the federal capital of Switzerland and, more remarkably, a World Cultural Heritage city known for its sandstone arcades, fountains, and thick, sturdy towers. A short drive outside the city will take you to the farm-sprinkled lowlands of the Emmental region.

Updated by
Susan Tuttle-
Laube

THOUGH BERN IS THE SWISS CAPITAL, you won't find much cosmopolitan nonsense here: The *cuisine du marché,* based on the freshest ingredients available in the local market, features fatback and sauerkraut; the annual fair fetes the humble onion; and the president of the Swiss Confederation often takes the tram to work. It's fitting, too, that a former Swiss patent office clerk, Albert Einstein, began developing his theory of relativity in Bern. Warm, friendly, down-to-earth, the Bernese are notoriously slow-spoken; ask a question and then pull up a chair while they formulate a judicious response. Their mascot is a common bear; they keep some as pets in the center of town. Walking down broad medieval streets past squares crowded with farmers' markets, past cafés full of shirt-sleeve politicos, you might forget that Bern is the geographic and political hub of a sophisticated, modern, and prosperous nation.

Although Bern is full of patrician houses and palatial hotels, there is no official presidential residence: The seven members of the coalition government, each of whom serves a year as president, have to find their own places to live when in Bern.

Bern wasn't always so self-effacing. It earned its pivotal position through a history of power and influence that dates from the 12th century, when Berchtold V, duke of Zähringen and one of the countless rulers within the Holy Roman Empire, established a fortress on this gooseneck in the River Aare. An heir to the German Alemanni tribes, whose penetration into Switzerland can roughly be measured by the areas where Swiss German is spoken today, he chose Bern not only for its impregnable location—it's a steep promontory of rock girded on three sides by the river—but also for its proximity to the great kingdom of Burgundy, which spread across France and much of present-day French-speaking Switzerland.

By the 14th century Bern had grown into a strong urban republic. When the last Zähringens died, the people of Bern defeated their would-be replacements and, shedding the Holy Roman Empire, became the eighth canton to join the rapidly growing Swiss Confederation. It was an unlikely union: aristocratic, urban Bern allied with the strongly democratic farming communities of central Switzerland. But it provided the Bernese with enough security against the Hapsburg Holy Roman Empire to continue westward expansion.

Despite a devastating fire that laid waste to the city in 1405, by the late 15th century the Bernese had become a power of European stature—a stature enhanced exponentially by three decisive victories over the duke of Burgundy, in 1476 and 1477. Aided by the other cantons and prompted by Louis XI, king of France and bitter enemy of the Burgundians, the Bernese crushed Charles the Bold and drove him out of his Swiss lands. Not only did the Bernese expand their territories all the way west to Geneva, but they also acquired immense wealth—great treasures of gold, silver, and precious textiles—and assumed the leading role in Switzerland and Swiss affairs.

Bern stayed on top. Through the 17th and 18th centuries, the city's considerable prosperity was built not so much on commerce as on the export of troops and military know-how. The city and her territories functioned essentially as a patrician state, ruled by a nobility that saw its raison d'être in politics, foreign policy, the acquisition of new lands, and the forging of alliances. At the same time, her landed gentry continued to grow fat on the fruits of the city's rich agricultural lands.

Napoléon seized the lands briefly from 1798 until his defeat in 1815, but by the 1830s the Bernese were back in charge, and when the Swiss Confederation took its contemporary, democratic form in 1848, Bern was a natural choice for its capital.

Yet today it's not the massive Bundeshaus (Houses of Parliament) that dominates the city but instead its perfectly preserved arcades, fountains, and thick, stalwart towers—all remnants of its heyday as a medieval power. They're the reason UNESCO granted Bern World Cultural Heritage status, along with the Egyptian pyramids, Rome, Florence, and the Taj Mahal.

Pleasures and Pastimes

Arcades

Like a giant cloister, Bern is crisscrossed by *Lauben* (arcades) that shelter stores of every kind and quality. Stout 15th-century pillars support the low vaulted roofs, which extend to the edge of the pavement below. At the base of many arcades, nearly horizontal cellar doors lead down into interesting underground eateries and businesses. Combined with Bern's sturdy towers and narrow cobbled streets, the arcades distinguish the city as one of the country's best-preserved medieval towns.

Flowers

Geranium-filled window boxes are as common a sight in Bern as ruins are in Rome. In 1897 Bern formed a preservation society to encourage the population to decorate their houses with flowers. In 1902 this society began to decorate the public fountains and then a few years later, the windows of buildings in the Old Town. In 1984 Bern won the title of Europe's most floral city, and the geranium is the city's official flower. The hillside Rosengarten (Rose Garden), flourishing with some 160 varieties, and the city's flower market have added to Bern's renown as a blossoming city.

Fountains

Throughout Bern, scores of brilliantly colored and skillfully carved fountains—their bases surrounded by flowers—provide relief from the structural severity of the medieval houses that form their background. Like the stelae of Athens, these fountains remind the Bernese of their moral forbears: Witness the Anna Seilerbrunnen, an ode to temperance and moderation, and the Gerechtigkeitsbrunnen (Justice Fountain) whose statue depicts the goddess Justice standing over several severed heads. Most of the fountains are the work of Hans Gieng, who created them between 1539 and 1546.

Markets, Old and New

In the Middle Ages, Bern was a great marketing center, and markets today—with stands hawking everything from geraniums to meats—are still an integral part of daily life. The lone surviving market from medieval Bern is the Zibelemärit (Onion Market), which takes place on the fourth Monday in November. Draped from scores of stalls are long strips of onions woven into the shapes of dolls, animals, and even alarm clocks. The Onion Market dates from the 1405 fire: In gratitude for assistance given by Fribourg, Bern granted farmers the right to sell their onions in the city's market square.

Museums

Being the nation's capital, Bern offers a satisfying concentration of museums, including the stellar Kunstmuseum, full of fine art, and its massive Historisches Museum, displaying war trophies and church treasures. All uniquely Swiss are the original Museum für Kommunikation (formerly the PTT Museum); the Schweizerisches Alpines Museum, exploring the Alps and their conquest; and the Schützenmuseum (Swiss Rifle Museum), about the innately Swiss love of sharpshooting.

EXPLORING BERN

Because Bern stands on a high, narrow peninsula formed by a gooseneck in the Aare, its streets seem to follow the river's flow, running in long parallels to its oldest, easternmost point; from afar, its uniform red-tile roofs seem to ooze like glowing lava down the length of the promontory. The Old Town was founded on the farthest tip and grew westward; its towers mark those stages of growth like rings on a tree.

Numbers in the text correspond to numbers in the margin and on the Bern map.

Great Itineraries

IF YOU HAVE 1 OR 2 DAYS

You can visit Bern's Old Town in a single day; but two days will allow you a more leisurely pace, with plenty of time for museums and shopping. Starting at the main train station, the Hauptbahnhof, you can move eastward through the towers, fountains, and arcades of the Old Town to the founding site of Bern at Nydeggkirche. Across the Aare are more museums, the Rosengarten, and the embassy row of Thunstrasse. Back on the north side of the river to the west and south, the Münster and the Bundeshaus are not to be missed.

IF YOU HAVE 3 TO 5 DAYS

If you're making an extended stay in Bern, spend the first few days as above, exploring the town. To help round out the city's history, visit the Historisches Museum, or try the Naturhistorisches Museum, which is considered one Europe's best natural history museums. Then escape for a half or full day drive through the Emmental to experience a landscape that has been left virtually untouched since the 19th century (☞ Excursion to the Emmental, *below*). If you're anxious to get an even closer look at the mountains, head into the Berner Oberland, one hour away. You can visit the Jungfrau region by train, taking the Interlaken–Grindelwald–Klein Scheidegg–Jungfraujoch route (and, weather permitting, Wengen) in a single long day (☞ Chapter 10).

Old Town

Now a pedestrian zone, the old city center west of the river retains a distinctly medieval appeal—thanks to the 1405 fire that destroyed its predominantly wooden structures. The city was rebuilt in sandstone, with arcades stretching on for some 6 km (4 mi).

As medieval as it may look, the Old Town is decidedly modern, with countless shops concentrated between the Hauptbahnhof (main train station) and the Zytgloggeturm (Clock Tower)—especially on Spitalgasse and Marktgasse. Beyond, along Kramgasse and Gerechtigkeitsgasse and, parallel to them on the north, Postgasse, there are quirkier, bohemian spots and excellent antiques stores. You may hear the Bernese calling this area the *Altstadt* (Old Town), as its 800 years of commerce give it seniority over the mere 15th-century upstarts to the west.

A Good Walk

Start on the busy Bahnhofplatz in front of the grand old Schweizerhof Hotel, facing the Hauptbahnhof. To your left is the **Heiliggeistkirche** ①. If you turn right down the Bollwerkstrasse, away from the church, and veer right down Genfergasse, ahead you'll see the **Kunstmuseum** ② on the right at Hodlerstrasse. Retrace your steps back to Spitalgasse and walk *outside* the arcades (keeping an eye out for trams) to see some of the city's stunning architecture; if you walk inside the sheltered walkways, you'll be seduced by modern shops and cafés.

Head for the **Pfeiferbrunnen,** or Bagpiper Fountain. At the edge of the Bärenplatz stands the **Käfigturm** ③, once a medieval city entrance and now a small library. Continue down Marktgasse past the **Anna Seilerbrunnen,** an allegory on moderation, and the **Schützenbrunnen,** or Marksman Fountain, a tribute to a troop commander from 1543.

Just beyond and spreading to your left lie the Kornhausplatz and the imposing 18th-century **Kornhaus** ④, now a popular restaurant (☞ Dining, *below*). In the Kornhausplatz, the ogre depicted in the **Kindlifresserbrunnen** is worth a second look: He's munching on a meal of small children.

Dominating town center, the mighty **Zytgloggeturm** ⑤ entertains with its hourly mechanical puppet performance. Continue down Kramgasse, a lovely old street with many guild houses, some fine 18th-century residences, more arcades, and, of course, more fountains: first the **Zähringerbrunnen,** or Zähringen Fountain, a monument to Bern founder Berchtold V; then the powerful depiction of Samson, **Simsonbrunnen.** Between the fountains on your right at No. 49 is the **Einsteinhaus** ⑥, once Albert Einstein's apartment and workplace.

Turn left at the next opening (Kreuzgasse) and make a brief diversion to the Rathausplatz and, at its north end, the **Rathaus** ⑦ itself. Across from it stands the **Vennerbrunnen,** or Ensign Fountain, of a Bernese standard-bearer.

Return as you came and turn left on the main thoroughfare, now called Gerechtigkeitsgasse. You'll pass the **Gerechtigkeitsbrunnen,** the Justice Fountain. Beyond are some lovely 18th-century houses. Hospiz zur Heimat, at No. 50, was constructed between 1760 and 1762 and has a lovely Louis XV facade. At No. 7 is the Gasthaus zum Goldenen Adler (☞ Lodging, *below*). Built between 1764 and 1766, it has a particularly captivating coat of arms by locksmith Samuel Rüetschi.

A left turn at the bottom of Gerechtigkeitsgasse will take you steeply down Nydegg Stalden through one of the oldest parts of the city; **Nydeggkirche** ⑧ is on your right. Down the hill stands the **Läuferbrunnen,** the image of a city herald. Take the Untertorbrücke, or Lower Gate Bridge, across the Aare.

From here, it's a short, steep climb to the east end of the high Nydeggbrücke. If you're feeling energetic, it's well worth crossing the road and either climbing a small path to the left, turning right at the top; or turning right and then left to walk up the broader Alter Aargauerstalden, where you'll turn left. Either will bring you to the **Rosengarten** ⑨, its roses in spectacular bloom from June to October.

Head back down to the Nydegg Bridge but don't cross it yet: On your left, facing the Old Town, you'll find the famous **Bärengraben** ⑩, home to the city's mascots.

Cross the bridge and turn left up Junkerngasse, notable for its fine old houses. Number 59 is the elegant 15th-century **Béatrice von Wattenwyl House,** where the Swiss government gives receptions. At the top of Junkerngasse, you come to the pride of the city: the magnificent Gothic **Münster** ⑪. On leaving the cathedral, head left to the terrace on its south side. Look east, in the direction from which you've come, for a view of the impressive south-side facades of the patrician houses and their gardens leading down to the **Matte** neighborhood.

Cross the Münsterplatz, passing by the **Mosesbrunnen.** Follow Münstergasse and at its end turn left into Casinoplatz, where you'll find the so-called **Casino** (actually a restaurant and concert locale). At this point, by crossing the river on the panoramic Kirchenfeldbrücke to Helvetiaplatz, you can visit six major museums that are conveniently grouped together. Just across the bridge, immediately on your left, you'll see the contemporary **Kunsthalle** ⑫. On your right is the **Schweizerisches Alpines Museum** ⑬, for armchair climbers and real ones, too. Across the square behind the massive fountain of Mother Helvetica is the **Historisches Museum** ⑭, where armor and arms, tapestries, and church treasures illustrate Bern's 15th-century victory over Burgundy.

Leaving the history museum, turn left and follow Bernastrasse a half block down. Adjoining the museum at the back is the **Schweizerisches Schützenmuseum** ⑮. Continue down Bernastrasse to the **Naturhistorisches Museum** ⑯. On leaving the museum, head left and then turn left onto Hallylerstrasse, then left again onto Helvetiastrasse, where you'll find the **Museum für Kommunikation** ⑰, tracing the evolution of the Swiss mail system. When you are done with the museums, you can nip down the Thunstrasse for a look at the impressive buildings in this quiet neighborhood that make up Embassy Row.

Head back over the Kirchenfeldbrücke, toward Casinoplatz, but turn left into the little alley just after crossing the bridge and stroll along the terrace behind the **Bundeshaus** ⑱. This spot affords another fine view across the river and, in good weather, to the distant Alps; at the bridge end of the parapet is a diagram to help you pick out the principal peaks. You can walk around the Bundeshaus into the Bundesplatz and then into the traffic-free Bärenplatz. On Tuesday and Saturday mornings, a lively market spills into surrounding streets.

TIMING

You can tour the Old Town in a single day, leaving extra time for the Bärengraben, Münster, and Rosengarten (in clear weather). If you'll be in Bern longer, leave an afternoon for at least one of the many museums, or indulge your whims in the arcade shops. Crowds can be considerable on weekends, so plan accordingly. Arrive at the Zytgloggeturm five minutes before the hour at the very latest: The mechanical figures spring into action at precisely four minutes before, and it's best to leave time to claim a spot on the street.

Sights to See

★ ☙ ⑩ **Bärengraben** (Bear Pits). Since the late 1400s, the Bear Pits have been digs for the city's mascots: fat brown bears that clown and beg for carrots, which vendors provide for tourists and loyal townsfolk. According to legend, Berchtold V announced that he would name the new city for the first animal he killed. It was a bear, of course; in those days the woods were full of them. The German plural for bears is *Bären,* and you'll see their images everywhere in Bern: on flags, the city coat of arms, buildings, statues, chocolates, and umbrellas, and—of course—as stuffed toys. Note that, in spite of its name, you won't find the real critters at Bärenplatz, but rather at the east end of the peninsula just across the river. ⊠ *South side of Nydeggbrücke.*

★ ⑱ **Bundeshaus** (Houses of Parliament). This hulking, domed building is the beating heart of the Swiss Confederation and meeting place of the Swiss National Council. Free guided tours (in English) include entry to the parliamentary chambers. ⊠ *Bundespl.,* ☎ *031/3228522.* ☉ *Free tours on Mon.–Sun. at 9, 10, 11, 2, 3, and 4 (Sun. until 3.) Can vary according to Parliament sessions.*

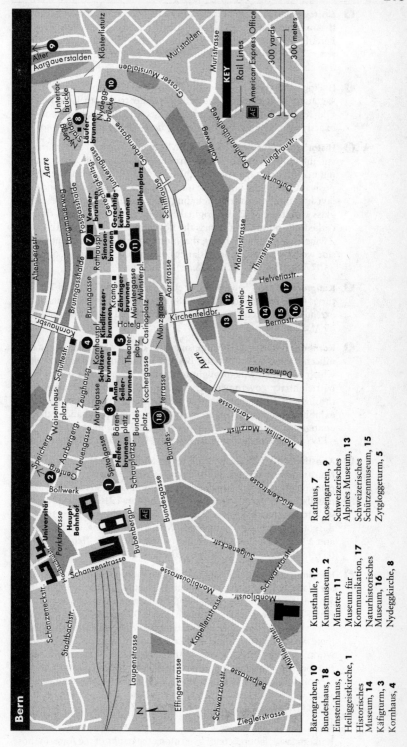

Bern

KEY

Rail Lines

AE American Express Office

0 / 300 yards
0 / 300 meters

Bärengraben, 10
Bundeshaus, 18
Einsteinhaus, 6
Heiliggeistkirche, 1
Historisches Museum, 14
Käfigturm, 3
Kornhaus, 4

Kunsthalle, 12
Kunstmuseum, 2
Münster, 11
Museum für Kommunikation, 17
Naturhistorisches Museum, 16
Nydeggkirche, 8

Rathaus, 7
Rosengarten, 9
Schweizerisches Alpines Museum, 13
Schweizerisches Schützenmuseum, 15
Zytgloggeturm, 5

⑥ Einsteinhaus (Einstein's House). For a bit of recent history, you can visit the apartment and workplace of Albert Einstein. It was during his stay here that, at the age of 26, he published his "Special Theory of Relativity." ⊠ *Kramg. 49,* ☎ *031/3120091.* 🎫 *2 SF.* ⊙ *Tues.–Fri. 10–5 and Sat. 10–4. Closed Dec.–Jan.*

❶ Heiliggeistkirche (Church of the Holy Ghost). Completed in 1729, the sanctuary adds a bit of Baroque flamboyance to the otherwise medieval Old Town. The ornateness also contrasts with the neighborhood—not exactly Bern's nicest. ⊠ *Spitalg. 44, across from Hauptbahnhof.*

★ **⑭ Historisches Museum** (Historical Museum). Much of this enormous, enlightening collection is booty from victories over Burgundy, including magnificent tapestries "acquired" in 1476–77, when the Bernese pushed Charles the Bold back into France. There are armor and arms, lavish church treasures (including 15th- and 16th-century stained-glass windows), and the original Last Judgment sculptures from the cathedral's portal. Don't miss the novel three-way portrait of Calvin, Zwingli, and Luther. Among the important exhibitions about the outside world is an exceptional Islamic collection. ⊠ *Helvetiapl. 5,* ☎ *031/3507711.* 🎫 *5 SF.* ⊙ *Tues.–Sun. 10–5.*

❸ Käfigturm (Prison Tower). A city entrance from the 13th and 14th centuries (later restored during the 18th century), when the limits of Bern extended only this far west, the Käfigturm served as a prison until 1897. ⊠ *Marktg. 67.*

❹ Kornhaus (Granary). The imposing 18th-century Kornhaus has a magnificent cellar, now a popular Bernese restaurant (☞ Dining, *below*), which once held wine brought to town by farmers as a tribute to the patrician city government. Extensive renovations have taken place throughout 1998, including the addition of a museum that will host exhibitions and events on architecture, photography, handicrafts, and contemporary culture. ⊠ *Zeughausg. 2/Kornhauspl. 18.* ☎ *031/3129110.* 🎫 *Not available at press time.* ⊙ *Not available at press time.*

⑫ Kunsthalle (Art Gallery). Not to be confused with the traditional Kunstmuseum, this ground-breaking contemporary art venue has no permanent collection, but displays temporary exhibits of living artists, usually before you've heard of them. Built in 1918 in heroic classical style to boost local artists—Kirchner, Klee, Hodler—it grew to attract the young Kandinsky, Miró, Sol LeWitt, Richard Long, Cy Twombly—and a parade of newcomers of strong potential. ⊠ *Helvetiapl. 1,* ☎ *031/3510031.* 🎫 *6 SF.* ⊙ *Tues. 10–9, Wed.–Sun. 10–5.*

❷ Kunstmuseum (Art Museum). Just down the hill and three blocks from the Hauptbahnhof, this important museum displays the third-largest art collection in Switzerland—and the largest gathering of works by Paul Klee in the world, with more than 2,000 examples of this native son's skills. From another Bern native, the symbolist Ferdinand Hodler, there are striking allegories (some enormous), landscapes, and portraits; works by Swiss artists Stauffer, Anker, and Böcklin are also featured. But the Kunstmuseum's concentration is not entirely Swiss, with masterworks ranging from Fra Angelico to Cézanne, Rouault, and Picasso. There are a cafeteria and cinema, too. ⊠ *Hodlerstr. 8–12,* ☎ *031/3110944.* 🎫 *6 SF.* ⊙ *Tues. 10–9, Wed.–Sun. 10–5.*

Matte. In the narrow row houses below the patrician residences of Junkerngasse, laborers once lived along the banks of the Aare. In those days, as today, the neighborhood was called *Matte* and was the most sociable, raucous part of town. There developed a bizarre dialect—*Mattenenglisch*—that can still be heard today, though it has grown so rare that its proponents have formed a club to keep it alive. Spotted with Yiddish and Gypsy terms, the dialect derives its name from *Matten* (lowland or meadow) and *Englisch* (unintelligible). Even if you don't hear the local tongue, Matte is a lovely old neighborhood to wander. From the cathedral terrace, take the 183 steps or ride the funky little outdoor elevator (1 SF) down to the river. There's a flea market here on Mühleplatz, every third Saturday from May through October. ⊠ *Off Gerberg. and below Junkerng.*

★ ⑪ **Münster** (Cathedral). Started in 1421 by master mason Matthäus Ensinger, Bern's famous cathedral was planned on lines so spacious that half the population could worship in it at one time. Its construction went on for centuries. Even the Reformation, the impact of which converted it from a Catholic to a Protestant church, did not halt the work. Daniel Heinz directed construction for 25 years (from 1573 to 1598), completing the nave and the tower. The finishing touch, the tip of the 100-m (328-ft) steeple (the highest in Switzerland), was not added until 1893. Today you can ascend it by a dizzying 254-step spiral staircase to enjoy a panorama of red roofs, the Aare, and if the weather is clear, the Bernese Alps off in the distance.

The cathedral has two outstanding features, one outside and one in. Outside is the **main portal,** with a magnificent sculpture representation of the Last Judgment (1490) composed of 234 carved figures—on the left is heaven and on the right, hell. This work was completed immediately before the Reformation, but it escaped destruction by the iconoclasts who emptied the niches of the side portals. The main portal was recently restored and painted in vivid—some may say jarring—colors. Green demons with gaping red maws and ivory-skin angels with gilt hair appear with Technicolor intensity.

Inside the church, while the elaborately carved pews and choir stalls are worth attention, note the **stained glass,** especially the detailed 15th-century windows of the choir, dealing as much with local heraldry as with Christian iconography. ⊠ *Münsterpl. 1,* ☎ *031/3110572.* ☉ *Easter Sun.–Oct. 31, Tues.–Sat. 10–5 and Sun. 11–5; Nov.–Easter Sun. Tues.–Sat. 11–noon and 2–4, (Sat. until 5), Sun. 11–2.*

⑰ **Museum für Kommunikation** (Museum of Communication). Housed in a modern building behind the Historical Museum, this high-concept, interactive museum (formerly known as the Schweizerisches PTT Museum) has detailed documents, art, and artifacts of early technology relating to the history of the mails in Switzerland. There's a magnificent stamp and postmark collection, one of the largest and most valuable in the world, exhibited in sleek sliding-glass trays. ⊠ *Helvetiastr. 16,* ☎ *031/3575555.* ▨ *5 SF.* ☉ *Tues.–Sun. 10–5.*

★ ☾ ⑯ **Naturhistorisches Museum** (Museum of Natural History). Considered one of Europe's finest museums of natural history, this beloved institution has a huge display area with a slick, skylighted four-story wing. It has enormous, evocative wildlife dioramas, as well as row upon row of Victorian oak-and-beveled-glass cases mounting varied species of mammals like so many butterflies. Its quirkiest trophy: the stuffed body of Barry, a St. Bernard that saved more than 40 people in the Alps during the last century. There's also a splendid collection of Alpine minerals. ⊠ *Bernastr. 15,* ☎ *031/3507111.* ▨ *3 SF, free Sun.* ☉ *Mon. 2–5, Tues.–Sat. 9–5, Sun. 10–5.*

OFF THE BEATEN PATH
TIERPARK DÄHLHÖLZLI – Here is a zoo with a difference: Parts of it are in a natural woodlands park along the Aare river and can be visited anytime day or night. The habitats back onto public walkways; come by

at the right moment, and you'll get a peek at the animals behind the trees. The proper zoo part has some exotic species and a vivarium full of reptiles and fish. The majority of the zoo's creatures are European: wolves, chamois, lynx, seals, and—of course—bears. The zoo is an easy trip south on Bus 18. ✉ *Tierparkstr. 1,* ☎ *031/3571515. Zoopark:* ✇ *Free.* ☉ *Daily 24 hrs. Zoo, Vivarium, Petting Zoo:* ✇ *6 SF.* ☉ *Apr.–Sept., daily 8–6:30; Oct.–Mar., daily 9–5.*

❽ Nydeggkirche (Nydegg Church). Built in 1341–46, the Nydegg Church stands on the ruins of Berchtold V's first fortress (destroyed about 1260– 1270), the founding place of Bern. You can see parts of the original foundation below the chancel; there's also a wooden pulpit from 1566. ✉ *Nydeggasse,* ☎ *031/3116102.* ☉ *Daily 10–noon and 2–5:30; closed Sun. afternoon.*

★ ❼ Rathaus (Town Hall). Bern's stately Town Hall is the seat of the cantonal government. Along with the city's arcades, it was built after the great fire of 1405 and still retains its simple Gothic lines. It's not open to the public. ✉ *Rathauspl. 2.*

❾ Rosengarten (Rose Garden). At the splendidly arranged and kept Rose Garden, some 160 varieties of roses bloom from June to October. One of Bern's most popular gathering places, this is a great vantage point for the Jungfrau, Eiger, and Mönch—on clear days only. ✉ *Alter Aargauerstalden.* ✇ *Free.* ☉ *Daily sunrise–sunset.*

⓭ Schweizerisches Alpines Museum (Swiss Alpine Museum). This arcane but eye-opening museum of the Alps has topographical maps and reliefs—their own evolution fascinating—and displays illustrating the history of mountain climbing, alongside epic art and fine old photos. There's an enormous model of the Berner Oberland (indispensable for getting your bearings if you're headed for that region) under a magnificent Hodler mural of the tragic conquest of the Matterhorn. ✉ *Helvetiapl. 4,* ☎ *031/3510434.* ✇ *5 SF.* ☉ *Mid-May–mid-Oct., Mon. 2–5, Tues.–Sun. 10–5; mid-Oct.–mid-May, Mon. 2–5, Tues.–Sun. 10–noon and 2–5.*

⓯ Schweizerisches Schützenmuseum (Swiss Rifle Museum). Run by the Swiss Marksmen's Association, this institution pays homage to this very Swiss art. Through a large collection of guns in every imaginable form, the museum traces the evolution of firearms from 1817; with trophies, it celebrates centuries of straight shooting, as Swiss markspeople have always measured themselves against the apple-splitting accuracy of archer William Tell. ✉ *Bernastr. 5,* ☎ *031/3510127.* ✇ *Free.* ☉ *Tues.–Sat. 2–4, Sun. 10–noon and 2–4.*

★ ❺ Zytgloggeturm (Clock Tower). Bern's oldest building, the mighty Clock Tower, was built in 1191 as the west gate to the then-smaller city. Today it dominates the town center with its high copper spire and a massive astronomical clock and calendar, built on its east side in 1530. As an added attraction, a delightful group of mechanical figures performs every hour. To see the puppet show, it's best to take up position at the corner of Kramgasse and Hotelgasse at least five minutes before the hour: You won't be the only one there.

At four minutes to the hour, heralded by a jester nodding his head and ringing two small bells, the puppet show begins. From a small arch on the left appear a couple of musically inclined bears—a drummer and a piper—leading a procession of a horseman with a sword, a proud bear wearing a crown, and lesser bears, each carrying a gun, a sword, or a spear. When the procession comes to an end, a cockerel on the left crows and flaps his wings, a knight in golden armor above hammers out the hour, and Father Time, on a throne in the middle, beats time with a scepter in one hand and an hourglass in the other. ⊠ *Kramg.*

DINING

Although Bern strikes a diplomatic balance in heading French-Swiss and German-Swiss politics, its Teutonic nature conquers Gaul when it comes to cuisine. Dining in Bern is usually a down-to-earth affair, with Italian home cooking running a close popular second to the local standard fare: German-style meat and potatoes. The most widespread specialty is the famous *Bernerplatte,* a meaty version of Alsatian *choucroûte*—great slabs of salt pork, beef tongue, smoky bacon, pork ribs, and mild pink pork sausages cooked down in broth and heaped on a broad platter over juniper-scented sauerkraut, green beans, and boiled potatoes. When a waitress eases this wide load onto the table before you, you may glance around to see who's sharing: One serving can seem enough for four. Another meaty classic is the Berner version of *Ratsherrtopf,* traditionally enjoyed by the town councillors: veal shank cooked in white wine, butter, and sage. The busy market provides plenty of local produce, so hearty soups are abundant, and everyone looks forward to a fat pastry and coffee in the late afternoon.

CATEGORY	COST*
$$$$	over 80 SF
$$$	50 SF–80 SF
$$	20 SF–50 SF
$	under 20 SF

Prices are per person for a three-course meal (two-course meal in $ category), including sales tax and 15% service charge.

$$$$ ★ ✕ **Bellevue-Grill.** When Parliament is in session, this haute-cuisine landmark in the Bellevue Palace (☞ Lodging, *below*) is transformed from a local gourmet mecca to a political clubhouse where the movers and shakers put their heads together over such unusual dishes as roast breast of duck in sauce with a hint of coffee, or poached lamb with capers. ⊠ *Kocherg. 3–5,* ☎ *031/3204545. Reservations essential. Jacket and tie. AE, DC, MC, V.*

$$$$ ★ ✕ **Schultheissenstube.** The intimate, rustic dining room, with a clublike bar and an adjoining, even more rustic, all-wood *stübli* (taverncafé), looks less like a gastronomic haven than a country pub; folksy piped-in music furthers the illusion. Yet the cooking is sophisticated, international, and imaginative—consider pigeon mousse with black truffles, quail breast and duck liver on choucroûte, oyster and champagne risotto—and the wine list, encyclopedic. ⊠ *Hotel Schweizerhof (☞ Lodging, below), Bahnhofpl. 11,* ☎ *031/3114501. Jacket and tie in dining room. AE, DC, MC, V. Closed Sun.*

$$$ ✕ **Jack's Brasserie.** Sometimes referred to by locals as Stadt Restaurant (City Restaurant), this dining room at street level, with high ceilings, wainscoting, and roomy banquettes is airy, bustling, urbane, and cosmopolitan. Enjoy a drink here by day at bare-top tables or settle in at mealtime for smartly served Swiss standards, French bistro classics, or a hefty Wiener schnitzel. ⊠ *Hotel Schweizerhof (☞ Lodging, below), Bahnhofpl. 11,* ☎ *031/3114501. AE, DC, MC, V.*

$$$ ✕ **Verdi.** Named for the Italian opera composer, this restaurant is nothing if not theatrical. There are framed pieces of opera memorabilia, carved wood ceilings, chandeliers, velvet drapes, and occasionally even opera singers to entertain guests between courses. Amazingly, it isn't the least bit kitschy. Chef Giovanni D'Ambrogio even cooks specialties from Verdi's hometown region of Emilia-Romagna. Try his spaghetti Scarpara, with an excellent, garlicky tomato sauce, or the sliced

steak on a bed of arugula with Parmesan. Reservations are essential if you want to even get near this popular spot on weekends. ⊠ *Gerechtigkeitsg. 5,* ☎ *031/3126368. AE, DC, MC, V.*

$$$ ✕ **Zimmermania.** This deceptively simple bistro has been in business
★ for more than 150 years and is a local favorite for authentic French bourgeois cooking. The owner visits Paris regularly to update his exceptional seasonal menu. Try their cheese soufflé or veal kidneys in mustard sauce or any of their ocean fish specialties. For a special vintage, ask for the separate French wine list. ⊠ *Brunng. 19,* ☎ *031/3111542. AE, MC, V. Closed Sun.–Mon.*

$$ ✕ **Brasserie zum Bärengraben.** Directly across from the Bear Pits, this
★ popular, easygoing little local institution is a place to settle in with a newspaper and a *Dezi* (deciliter) of wine. You'll find old-style basics— *Kalbskopf an vinaigrette* (chopped veal head in vinaigrette), pigs' feet, stuffed cabbage—as well as French-accented brasserie fare (lamb with rosemary, for instance) and wonderful pastries. Stick to daily specials and one-plate meals; dining à la carte can be expensive. ⊠ *Muristalden 1,* ☎ *031/3314218. AE, MC, V.*

$$ ✕ **Della Casa.** You can stay downstairs in the steamy, rowdy stübli,
★ where the necktied businessmen roll up their sleeves and play cards, or head up to the lovely wood-lined linen-and-silver restaurant, where they leave their jackets on. The independent waitresses are "wonderfully prickly dragons," according to one Swiss food magazine, but no one seems to mind. An unofficial Parliament headquarters, the restaurant has a solid Italian menu and generous platters of local specialties; it's a good place to try the Bernerplatte. The fragrant Czech-brewed Pilsner Urquell drawn from the tap is a treat. ⊠ *Schauplatzg. 16,* ☎ *031/3112142. DC, MC, V. Closed Sun. No lunch Sat.*

$$ ✕ **Harmonie.** Run by the same family since 1900, this lively lead-glass and old-wood café-restaurant is pleasantly dingy, very friendly, and welcoming to foreigners. Expect the basics: sausage and *Rösti* (hash brown potatoes), *Käseschnitte* (cheese toast), *Bauern* omelets (farm style, with bacon, potatoes, onions, and herbs), and fondue. ⊠ *Hotelg. 3,* ☎ *031/3113840. MC, V. No dinner Sat., no lunch Sun. and Mon.*

$$ ✕ **Il Grissino.** In a busy Bernese square, this very popular haunt specializes in pizzas cooked in a wood-fired oven—26 colorful varieties— and such traditional pastas as *fettuccine nere Stefano* (black noodles with salmon and broccoli). Run by a Swiss-Italian family, it has a bright, contemporary interior with curious ceiling lamps dressed up with glass beads and metallic leaves. The wine list is all Italian. ⊠ *Waisenhauspl. 28,* ☎ *031/3110059. AE, DC, MC, V.*

$$ ✕ **Lorenzini.** After a few days of Bern's rib-sticking cooking, plain and
★ simple Italian food may sound more appealing than ever: This hip, bright spot is a breath of fresh Tuscan air. Delicious homemade pastas and specialties of various Italian regions—say, Alba truffles—are served with authentic, contemporary flair. ⊠ *Theaterpl. 5,* ☎ *031/ 3117850. DC, MC, V.*

$$ ✕ **Menuetto.** A reaction against meaty Bern cuisine, this refreshing veg-
★ etarian oasis represents the city's Green (also very Germanic) side, creating sophisticated, imaginative cooking—*rouladen* (roulades) of spinach and feta with tamari beer sauce, raspberry sorbet with thick almond milk and chunks of fresh fruit. The sleek, chic, white-on-white decor is warmed with parquet floors and hanging greens. ⊠ *Münsterg. 47 and Herreng. 22 (2 entrances),* ☎ *031/3111448. AE, DC, MC, V. Closed Sun.*

$$ ✕ **Zunft zu Webern.** Part of a weavers' guildhall built in 1704, the ground floor of this classic building has been redesigned to marry clean, modern, and traditional styling, with gleaming fresh wood and bright lighting. The upgraded standards on the menu—lamb stew with saffron,

In case you want to see the world.

In case you want to be welcomed there.

We're here to see that you're always welcomed at establishments everywhere. That's why millions of people carry the American Express® Card – for peace of mind, confidence, and security, around the world or just around the corner.

do more®

Cards

In case you're running low.

We're here to help with more than 118,000 Express Cash locations around the world. In order to enroll, just call American Express before you start your vacation.

do more

Express Cash

And just in case.

We're here with American Express® Travelers Cheques
and Cheques *for Two*.® They're the safest way to carry
money on your vacation and the surest way to get a
refund, practically anywhere, anytime.
Another way we help you…

do more ®

**Travelers
Cheques**

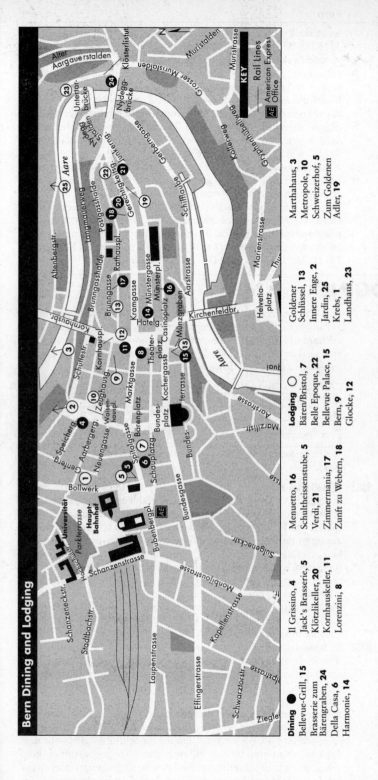

Bern Dining and Lodging

Dining ●
Bellevue-Grill, **15**
Brasserie zum
Bärengraben, **24**
Della Casa, **6**
Harmonie, **14**

Il Grissino, **4**
Jack's Brasserie, **5**
Klötzlikeller, **20**
Kornhauskeller, **11**
Lorenzini, **8**

Menuetto, **16**
Schultheissenstube, **5**
Verdi, **21**
Zimmermania, **17**
Zunft zu Webern, **18**

Lodging ○
Bären/Bristol, **7**
Belle Epoque, **22**
Bellevue Palace, **15**
Bern, **9**
Glocke, **12**

Goldener
Schlüssel, **13**
Innere Enge, **2**
Jardin, **25**
Krebs, **1**
Landhaus, **23**

Marthahaus, **3**
Metropole, **10**
Schweizerhof, **5**
Zum Goldenen
Adler, **19**

KEY
— Rail Lines
AE American Express
Office

for example—are generously portioned. ✉ *Gerechtigkeitsg. 68,* ☎ *031/ 3114258. MC, V. Closed Sun.–Mon.*

$–$$ ✕ **Klötzlikeller.** This cozy wine cellar dates from 1635 and is the old-
★ est in Bern. Since 1885 only unmarried women have been permitted to own and run the place—a tradition begun by the daughters of Mr. Klötzli himself. Monthly musical theater dinner programs and a chang-ing menu featuring foods and wine from selected regions make this place unique. Or try their satisfying traditional Bernese dishes on the stan-dard menu, like tripe and Rösti. ✉ *Gerechtigkeitsg. 62,* ☎ *031/ 3117456. AE, MC, V. Closed Sun.–Mon.*

$ ✕ **Kornhauskeller.** This spectacular vaulted old wine cellar under the
★ Granary is a must for its magnificent old-world architecture, frescoes, and bustling atmosphere—but not necessarily for the food and service. Harried waiters can be impatient with tourists—the restaurant's lifeblood—but people continue to pour in. The food is stick-to-your-ribs standards, like Rösti and veal, but at press time a change in own-ership (and an upswing in food quality) was forecast. ✉ *Kornhauspl. 18,* ☎ *031/3111133. AE, DC, MC, V. No dinner Sun.*

LODGING

As a frequent host to conventioneers, tourists, and visiting members of Parliament, Bern is well equipped with hotels in all price ranges. Rooms are hard to find when Parliament is in session; this is one town where you need to book well ahead. All but the bargain hotels are concen-trated around the Old Town.

CATEGORY	COST*
$$$$	over 300 SF
$$$	180 SF–300 SF
$$	140 SF–180 SF
$	under 140 SF

Prices are for a standard double room, including breakfast, tax, and service charge.

$$$$ ▦ **Bellevue Palace.** As the name implies, this 1865 landmark, set on the high bank above the river, is considerably more palatial than the Schweizerhof, its friendly rival. There are a sweeping staircase and a spectacular Belle Epoque stained-glass ceiling in the lobby; the rooms are up to the same standard, discreetly colored in shades of powder blue, cream, and orchid. The chief advantage over the Schweizerhof is the view, which is best from the back rooms; these face the river and the snowcapped Alps, including the Eiger and the Jungfrau. The Belle-vue-Grill (☞ Dining, *above*) draws crowds of nonguests, many of them politicos from the Parliament building next door. ✉ *Kocherg. 3– 5, CH-3001,* ☎ *031/3204545,* 🖷 *031/3114743. 131 rooms, 14 suites. 3 restaurants, bar. AE, DC, MC, V.*

$$$$ ▦ **Schweizerhof.** This landmark just across from the Hauptbahnhof is decidedly nonpalatial: The lobby is on a human scale, though deluxe, and the broad corridors are lined with the antiques and objets d'art of the Gauers, the hotel's founding family. Each room's decor is differ-ent—you might be assigned to one of four rooms designed by young Bernese artists representing the ultramodern streak in Swiss design, or you might find a room drenched in sea-blue toile de Jouy. They're well equipped for business meetings, but the thoughtful touches—the next day's weather report on your pillow beside the requisite truffle—keep it welcoming, not just efficient. And you won't go hungry; there's the Schultheissenstube (they say the peephole in the door was installed for a local politician), Jack's Brasserie (☞ Dining, *above*), and Yamato, the first Japanese restaurant in Bern, offering sushi and tempura. ✉

Bahnhofpl. 11, CH-3001, ☎ 031/3114501, FAX 031/3122179. 70 rooms, 15 suites. 3 restaurants, bar, nightclub. AE, DC, MC, V.

$$$ 🏨 **Bären/Bristol.** These adjoining, connected Best Western properties are the hotel equivalent of Siamese twins; both are dependable business-class hotels, with all-modern interiors and first-class comforts. The Bärenbar (technically in the Bären) serves drinks and snacks, and bears figure heavily in the decor. ⊠ *Bären: Schauplatzg. 4–10, CH-3011, ☎ 031/3113367 or 800/5281234, FAX 031/3116983, 57 rooms; Bristol: ☎ 031/3110101, FAX 031/3119479, 92 rooms. Both hotels: Snack bar, sauna, solarium, bicycles. AE, MC, V.*

$$$ 🏨 **Belle Epoque.** Its historic theme has nothing to do with Bern's me-
★ dieval background, but this relatively new hotel (1989) has made itself into a period museum nonetheless, more suggestive of Gay Paris than Berchtold's lair. Every inch of the arcaded row house has been filled with authentic Art Nouveau or Jugendstil antiques, from the stylized wooden vines on the reception desk to the vintage posters and stunning light fixtures. Despite the aged opulence of the furnishings, the amenities are state-of-the-art, with electric blinds and a no-smoking floor. The glowing, snug hotel bar is one of the most beautiful in the city; look for the photos of Henri de Toulouse-Lautrec over the door. ⊠ *Gerechtigkeitsg. 18, CH-3011, ☎ 031/3114336, FAX 031/3113936. 14 rooms, 2 suites. Breakfast room, bar. AE, DC, MC, V.*

$$$ 🏨 **Bern.** Behind a severe and imposing neoclassic facade, this former theater and once-modest hotel has been transformed into a slick, business-class lodging, with air-shaft gardens supplying light to the inner rooms. All the rooms are a bit heavy on the wine-red color scheme, so for the most light, ask for one on the top floors, either facing the back or the traffic-free street. The restaurant, Seven Stuben, consists of seven rooms—each with its own motif—within one restaurant. There is also a separate, chic French restaurant. The bar is cozy and well stocked. ⊠ *Zeughausg. 9, CH-3011, ☎ 031/3121021, FAX 031/3121147. 98 rooms, 1 suite. 2 restaurants, bar. AE, DC, MC, V.*

$$$ 🏨 **Innere Enge.** In 1992 this early 18th-century inn was transformed into a deluxe business hotel. Spacious, light, and airy—thanks to generous windows that take in views toward the Bernese Alps—it's outside the city center, with trees and lawns to compensate for the bus or cab ride into town. Top-story rooms have sloped ceilings as they're under the eaves. Marian's Jazzroom, in the Louis Armstrong Bar, features top jazz acts Tues.–Sat. (☞ Nightlife, *below*). Take Bus 21 (marked BREM-GARTEN) from the train station. ⊠ *Engestr. 54, CH-3012, ☎ 031/3096111, FAX 031/3096112. 13 rooms, 15 suites. Restaurant, bar, café. AE, DC, MC, V.*

$$ 🏨 **Krebs.** A small, scrupulously maintained hotel, the Krebs is solid
★ and impeccable, thanks to the ownership's eye for detail. The self-service laundry facilities (rare in Switzerland) and on-line access in the rooms prove they've got your interest at heart. Rooms are spare but pristine, and there's a pleasant ground-floor café-bar. The five rooms without bath offer excellent value. ⊠ *Genferg. 8, CH-3001, ☎ 031/3114942, FAX 031/3111035. 46 rooms, 41 with bath. Breakfast room, café, coin laundry. AE, DC, MC, V.*

$$ 🏨 **Metropole.** Centrally located between the Old Town and the train station, Metropole buzzes with activity in its tiny lobby. Interiors and rooms are clean but plain. The Brasserie, on street level, serves moderately priced Swiss fare and is always crowded. ⊠ *Zeughausg. 28, CH-3011, ☎ 031/3115021, FAX 031/3121153. 58 rooms. 3 restaurants, piano bar. AE, DC, MC, V.*

$$ 🏨 **Zum Goldenen Adler.** Built in a magnificent patrician town house
★ in the Old Town, this guest house has been lodging travelers since 1489, though the current structure dates from 1764. One family has run it

for 100-odd years. Despite the striking exterior with its coat of arms, the interiors are modest and modern, with linoleum baths and severe Formica furniture, but the ambience is comfortable and welcoming nonetheless. ⊠ *Gerechtigkeitsg. 7, CH-3001,* ☎ *031/3111725,* FAX *031/3113761. 16 rooms. Restaurant. AE, DC, MC, V.*

$ ☎ **Glocke.** Although it's very plain, there's a young, friendly management here and two lively restaurants—one a Swiss chalet, with dancing and folklore shows, and the other a haunt for an arty crowd (the starting-out kind, not the divas). The 19 rooms without bath are an especially good deal. ⊠ *Rathausg. 75, CH-3011,* ☎ *031/3113771,* FAX *031/3111008. 26 rooms, 7 with bath. 2 restaurants. AE, DC, MC, V.*

$ ☎ **Goldener Schlüssel.** This bright, tidy little hotel in the heart of the Old Town has standard-issue rooms with fresh linens and tile baths. As the building looks over the Rathausgasse, you'll find the back rooms quieter. The good, inexpensive restaurant on the ground floor serves home-cooked meat-and-Rösti favorites in a dinette-with-paper-place-mat ambience. The seven rooms without bath are a bargain. ⊠ *Rathausg. 72, CH-3011,* ☎ *031/3110216,* FAX *031/3115688. 29 rooms, 22 with bath. Restaurant, stübli. AE, MC, V.*

$ ☎ **Jardin.** In a commercial neighborhood far above the Old Town, this
★ is a solid, roomy, middle-class hotel, with friendly management and fresh decor. It's easily reached by Tram 9 to Breitenrainplatz. ⊠ *Militärstr. 38, CH-3014,* ☎ *031/3330117,* FAX *031/3330943. 20 rooms. Restaurant, bowling, free parking. AE, DC, MC, V.*

$ ☎ **Landhaus.** In the old town just across the river from the Altstadt,
★ this 90-year old apartment building has been freshly renovated into a simple, clean, and bright hotel/hostel, with old natural-wood floors, soothing pastel walls, and modern, metal-frame beds. Pick anything from a dorm-style cubicle to a double room with shower; value-for-money-wise, it's a great bargain. Cook for yourself in the community kitchen or dine at the hotel's trendy restaurant. You can get a modem connection at the front desk; there's live jazz at the bar on Thursday. ⊠ *Altenbergst. 46, CH-3013,* ☎ *031/3314166,* FAX *031/3326904. 4 rooms, plus 3 4- or 6-bed dormitories. Restaurant, 2 bars, food shop, bicycles, coin laundry. AE, DC, MC, V.*

$ ☎ **Marthahaus.** This cheap, cheery pension stands at the end of a
★ quiet cul-de-sac in a residential neighborhood north of the Old Town. All the rooms have been freshly decorated in white, and the squeaky-clean look is reinforced with hospital-style metal beds. It's an easy ride over the Kornhaus Bridge on Bus 15 or via Lorrainebrücke on Bus 20. ⊠ *Wyttenbachstr. 22a, CH-3013,* ☎ *031/3324135,* FAX *031/3333386. 38 rooms. Breakfast room. MC, V.*

NIGHTLIFE AND THE ARTS

This Week in Bern, edited every week by the tourist office, carries listings on concerts, museums, and nightlife; it's available at the tourist office (☞ Visitor Information *in* Bern A to Z, *below*) and hotels. *Bern Aktuell,* published every two weeks and also distributed by the tourist office, has listings in English.

Nightlife

Bars and Lounges

On the ground floor of the little hotel **Belle Epoque** (☞ Lodging, *above*) there's a lovely small bar where you can drink surrounded by Art Nouveau treasures. For a nightcap in a formal hotel venue, go to the **Bellevue Palace** (☞ Lodging, *above*). The **Schweizerhof** (☞ Lodging, *above*) is a hotel with a small American-style bar. **Arlequin** (⊠

Gerechtigkeitsg. 51, ☎ 031/3113946) is a cozy wine bar where small meals are served. For history, head for **Klötzlikeller,** said to be the oldest wine bar in Bern (☞ Dining, *above*). The chic bar **CoCo** (✉ Genferg. 10, ☎ 031/3111551), has Gauguin-esque murals on the walls.

Casino

Bern's **Kursaal** (✉ Schänzlistr. 71–77, ☎ 031/3331010) has a disco with live music as well as gambling in the **Jackpot Casino,** which stays within the federally mandated 5 SF bet limit.

Dancing

The popular **Mocambo** (✉ Aarbergerg. 61, ☎ 031/3115041) is under new management and has been slickly redone with lots of mirrors to reflect the Beautiful People. Along with dancing to live and DJ music until 3 AM on weeknights, 3:30 AM on Saturday, it also has a revolving stage and three bars. **Babalu** (✉ Gurteng. 3, ☎ 031/3110808) draws crowds for dancing with live music. Do note that places for dancing often also have a separate "cabaret" that is actually a strip club.

Jazz Club

Marian's Jazzroom (✉ Engestr. 54, ☎ 031/3096111), in the Innere Enge(☞ Lodging, *above*), a hotel, offers top live acts nightly and has become one of Bern's best-known jazz clubs. There are shows from Tuesday to Saturday at 7:30 PM and 10:30 PM; Sunday there's a jazz brunch at 10:30, 11:45, and 12:45.

The Arts

Film

Bern's 23 movie theaters show films in their original language. Current listings can be found in hotels, the daily newspapers *Der Bund* (weekly events supplement "Die Berner Woche") and *Die Berner Zeitung* (weekly events supplement "Die Berner Agende"), and the tourist office (☞ Visitor Information *in* Bern A to Z, *below*).

Music

The **Bern Symphony Orchestra** (☎ 031/3114242 for tickets) is the city's most notable musical institution. Concerts take place at the **Casino** (✉ Casinopl.) and the **Stadttheater** (✉ Kornhauspl. 20). There also is a five-day **International Jazz Festival** every April or May, with tickets available at Ticket Corner, at the Schweizerischer Bankverein (Swiss Bank Corporation; ✉ Bärenpl., ☎ 031/3362539).

Opera

Bern's resident company is famous for its adventurous production standards. Performances are at the **Stadttheater** (✉ Kornhauspl. 20, ☎ 031/3110777); tickets are sold next door (✉ Kornhauspl. 18) Monday–Saturday 10–6:30 and Sunday 10–12:30.

Theater

Although you can see traditional and modern plays at the **Stadttheater** (✉ Kornhauspl. 20, ☎ 031/3110777), a characteristic of Bern is its range of little theaters, mostly found in the cellars in the Old Town.

Avant-garde plays, satires, and burlesques (in Swiss-German), plus pantomime and modern dance, are performed at **Theater am Käfigturm** (✉ Marktg. 67, ☎ 031/3116100). **Kleintheater** (✉ Kramg. 6, ☎ 031/3113080) has a modern repertoire; buy tickets at the **Müller & Schade** store (✉ Kramg. 52, ☎ 031/3202626). **Berner Puppentheater** (✉ Gerechtigkeitsg. 31, ☎ 031/3119585) produces funny, action-packed puppet shows—enjoyable even if you don't speak the language.

OUTDOOR ACTIVITIES AND SPORTS

Bicycling

There are about 300 km (185 mi) of marked trails around Bern; ask for routes at the tourist office. Bikes can be rented at the Hauptbahnhof, the main train station. You can also get them at **Ski- und Velocenter** (⊠ Hirschengraben 7, ☎ 061/321–0031).

Golf

The **Golf and Country Club Blumisberg** (⊠ 18 km/11 mi west of town, ☎ 026/4963438) has 18 holes and a clubhouse with a restaurant, bar, showers, and swimming pool. The club admits visitors weekdays, provided they are members of any golf club with handicaps. Only local members and their guests are admitted on weekends.

Riding

The riding school **Reitsportanlage Eldorado** (⊠ Könizstr. 21–23, CH-3098 Köniz, ☎ 031/9714840) is easily reached by bus 17.

Swimming

Hallenbad Hirschengraben (⊠ Maulbeerstr. 14, ☎ 031/3813656) is an indoor swimming pool. Below the Parliament building you can swim in the river at the **Aarebad Marzili** waterfront (⊠ Marzilistr. 29, ☎ 031/3110046). **Aarebad Eichholz** (☎ 031/9612602), in the town of Wabern, is a bathing facility. The beach at **Aarebad Lorraine** (⊠ Uferweg, ☎ 031/3322950) is on the right bank northwest of the Kursaal.

SHOPPING

Shop hours are generally weekdays 8:15–6:30, Thursday to 9 PM, and Saturday 8:15–4; Sunday most stores are closed, and many remain closed Monday morning.

Department Stores

Globus (⊠ Spitalg. 17–21, ☎ 031/3118811), one of the city's largest department stores, has a wide variety of designer labels. **Loeb** (⊠ Spitalg. 47–57, ☎ 031/3207111) is known for its high-quality clothes.

Markets

Every Tuesday and Saturday mornings, colorful farmers' markets (fruits, vegetables, and flowers) take place on the **Bärenplatz,** where buskers perform pantomime and music. There's a meat-and-dairy market on **Münstergasse.** A general market holds forth on **Waisenhausplatz.** From May through October, a flea market sets up shop every third Saturday on **Mühleplatz,** behind the cathedral. On the first Saturday of the month, **Münsterplatz** is the site of an arts-and-crafts fair. Mid-May brings a one-day geranium market to the **Münsterplatz.**

Shopping Streets

The **Old Town** is one big shopping center, and its 6 km (4 mi) of arcades shelter stores of every kind and quality. Many of the modern, mainstream shops are concentrated between the Bahnhof and the Clock Tower, especially on **Spitalgasse** and **Marktgasse.** Beyond, along **Kramgasse** and **Gerechtigkeitsgasse** and, parallel to them on the north, **Postgasse,** are quirkier, artsy spots and excellent antiques stores. Good shopping can be had at **Junkerngasse** and **Münstergasse,** especially in art galleries and avant-garde fashion.

Specialty Stores

Antiques
The best antiques shops line Gerechtigkeitsgasse and Postgasse; their wares range from cluttery *brocante* (collectibles) to good antiques from all over Europe. The **Puppenklinik** (⊠ Gerechtigkeitsg. 36, ☎ 031/3120771) is just this side of a museum, with its shelves and window densely packed with lovely—if slightly eerie—old dolls and toys.

Chocolate
Tschirren (⊠ Kramg. 73, ☎ 031/3111717) has been making chocolates and sweets for more than 40 years. **Abegglen** (⊠ Spitalg. 36, ☎ 031/3112111) is a local favorite. **Eichenberger** (⊠ Bahnhofpl. 5, ☎ 031/3113325) has a fine selection of chocolates and candies. **Beeler** (⊠ Spitalg. 29, ☎ 031/3112808) is another top chocolatier.

Souvenirs/Gifts
Heimatwerk Bern (⊠ Kramg. 61, ☎ 031/3113000), a branch of this excellent Swiss chain of handicraft stores, offers a broad and high-quality line of ceramics, wood carvings, and linens—all Swiss-made. There are also souvenirs with the now-ubiquitous cowhide pattern.

EXCURSION TO THE EMMENTAL

The great city of Bern stands alone in a large and lovely region tourists usually overlook: the Berner Mittelland, the rural lowlands of the enormous canton Bern, which comprises not only the city of Bern but the Alps of the Berner Oberland as well. The Mittelland stretches from the Bielersee (Lac de Bienne) and its officially bilingual city of Biel (Bienne) all the way south to Thun, and its green farmlands border Solothurn to the north; central Switzerland to the east; and Fribourg, Neuchâtel, and the Jura to the west. Heading south toward Thun, you climb mist-wrapped green-velvet foothills and approach wraparound views of the Bernese Alps. Driving on back roads, you will see neat, prosperous old towns and farms, a handful of castles, and—most of all—verdant, undulating patchwork countryside.

Its most famous—though as yet unspoiled—region is the **Emmental,** the valley of the River Emme, where Switzerland's trademark cheese is made: Emmentaler cheese, the one with the holes. Here you can visit a cheese factory and admire some of Switzerland's most beautiful farmhouses—plump, broad boxes topped with deep-curving roofs that slope nearly to the ground. In the 19th century Swiss clergyman Jeremias Gotthelf found the virtues of family life and Christian beliefs in this breathtaking valley to be so inspiring that he turned to writing novels and short stories about the Emmentalers. His efforts revealed a prodigious literary talent, making him one of Switzerland's most famous writers.

Not much has changed in the Emmental since Gotthelf's time, and within a half hour of leaving the city of Bern on Highway 10 going toward Worb/Langnau, bedroom communities dissolve into small farm villages with picturesque curved-roof country inns, their emblems suspended from wrought-iron brackets. After about 10 km (6 mi) you'll be in **Zäziwil.** Follow the signs heading to Langnau, then turn left at Bowil for the small road up the hill to the summit point of **Chuderhüsi** (6 km/4 mi). At the top (1103 m/3650 ft) the road opens to a panorama of the Bernese Alps in all their glory. There is a restaurant, whose only claim to fame is the view; save your appetite for another local spot.

Heading down on the other side of Chuderhüsi, you'll come to the **Würzbrunnen Church**, featured in the films made about Jeremias Gotthelf. Take the road down into the valley at Rothenbach and then follow the signs for Eggiwil, where the road meets up with and then follows the Emme, the river from which the valley got its name. You'll cross or pass seven covered bridges by the time you reach the village of Schüpbach (about 11 km/6½ mi), where you can turn left for a stop in the pretty little village of **Signau** (2 km/1 mi), a good place to see examples of the local architecture, or head right for a side trip to **Langnau** (about 10 km/6 mi) and on to **Trubschachen** (7 km/4½ mi), where you can visit some small, local museums and a demonstration pottery studio. From Langnau and Trubensachen, double back to Emmenmat and continue north, following the signs to **Sumiswald**. Take your time— the scenery is nothing short of spectacular.

Here the gentle hills begin to roll out village after beautiful village. The scenery is dotted with many impressive examples of the classic Emmental farmstead. The enormous *Bauernhaus* (main building) shelters the living quarters of the farmer and his family; at the back of the house, built into the central plan, is the cowshed; and grains and feed are stored upstairs, under the deep roof. Next door, in a separate house, lives the older generation: When a farmer retires, he passes the entire farm on to his youngest son and moves into the *Stöckli,* a kind of guest house, conceding the home to the new family. The third building, standing apart, is the *Spycher,* for storing the harvest of food, grains, and in olden days, the family's savings. If the farm caught fire, this building would be saved over the main house.

Continue north in the direction of Huttwil, turning left at Weier (7 km/4½ mi) to visit the cheese museum in **Affoltern**. Follow signs to **Burgdorf** to complete the circuit, where you can pick up the highway back to Bern (about 20 km/13 mi).

TIMING

If you are based in Bern and have a car, a 90-km (56-mi) round-trip begun late morning with lots of stops for photos, lunch, shopping, and coffee can get you back in time for dinner in the city. If you plan to spend some time visiting the cheese factory and museums, get an earlier start.

Numbers in the margin correspond to points of interest on the Emmental map.

Signau

❶ *24 km (15 mi) east of Bern*

Signau is a pretty little village, typical for the region. There are some rather impressive examples of the classic Emmental farmstead to be seen here.

Dining and Lodging

$ ✕ **Zum Wysse Rössli.** In Zäziwil (9 km/6 mi southwest of Signau), this grand old Emmental inn, its roof spreading out like the wings of a mother hen, shelters innumerable halls for local sports clubs and family events, but its main pub and restaurant serve the natives daily. Read a newspaper, meet your card-playing neighbors, and tackle a little local dialect—the menu is in Swiss-German. Rösti, mixed salads, and smoked farm ham are outstanding; heavier meat dishes and meringue with ice cream may do you in (pleasantly). ✉ *Thunstr. 10, Zäziwil,* ☎ *031/ 7111532. AE, DC, MC, V. Closed Tues.*

$ ✕🏨 **Bären.** Look for the enormous bear jutting out above the entrance of this inn, on Signau's main street. The restaurant keeps the locals happy

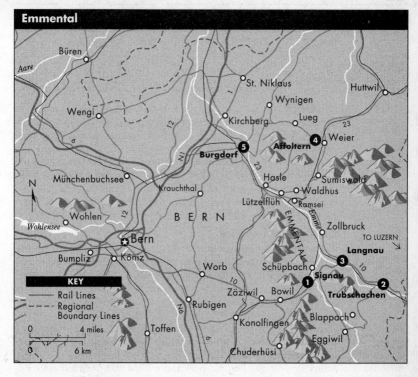

Emmental

with uncompromising Emmental cooking: fluffy cheese tarts, golden Rösti, enormous mixed salads, local game, and silky wild mushrooms in season. The rooms upstairs offer impeccable modern comfort. ✉ *Dorfstr. 48, CH-3534 Signau, ☎ 034/4971364. 4 rooms. V, MC. Closed Mon.*

Trubschachen

② *13 km (8 mi) east of Schüpbach, 37 km (23 mi) east of Bern.*

Trubschachen, a center for the region's folk-style ceramics, sits in the shadow of the 1,195-m (3,920-ft) ridge Blappach. (If you brave the narrow farm road up the ridge, you'll find more good views toward the Bernese Alps.) There's a **Heimatmuseum** (Hometown Museum) arranged in the three traditional buildings of a farm, with crafts and household antiques displayed in the *Spycher* and *Stöckli*. If you plan to visit by appointment, call a few days in advance. ✉ ☎ *034/4956038. 🎫 4 SF. ☉ Apr.–Nov., Sun. only 2–4, or by request.*

For a chance to watch local craftspeople at work, visit the *Schautöpferei* (demonstration pottery studio), in the Bauernhaus building of the Heimatmuseum. There you'll also find a shop full of the local ceramics and a cozy café upstairs open for coffee and snacks. ✉ ☎ *034/4956029. 🎫 Free. ☉ Weekdays 8–noon and 1:30–5:30, Sat. 9–noon and 1:30–5:30.*

Langnau

③ *7 km (4 mi) west of Trubschachen, 30 km (19 mi) east of Bern.*

This graceful old market town serves as capital of the region and clearinghouse for its cheese. There you will find the **Heimatmuseum Lang-**

nau, a museum of traditional crafts, tools, and furniture as well as military paraphernalia, all in an enormous chalet. ⊠ *Bärenpl. 2a, Langnau,* ☎ *034/4021819.* ☜ *3 SF.* ☉ *Tues.–Sun. 1:30–6. Closed Dec.–Mar.*

Affoltern

❹ *30 km (19 mi) northwest of Langnau, 35 km (22 mi) northeast of Bern.*

In Affoltern, the *Schaukäserei* (demonstration dairy) allows you to see Swiss cheese in the making. From a glassed-in balcony, you can watch gallons of milk being stirred in copper cauldrons, its curd being separated from its whey in great sieves, with the heavy solids eased into molds to be brine-soaked and then stored. Try to be here between 9 AM–11 AM or 2 PM–4 PM, when the most active stages of cheese making take place. In a restored *Stöckli* from 1741 old-fashioned ways of cheese making over a wood fire are sometimes demonstrated. ⊠ *Affoltern,* ☎ *034/4351611.* ☜ *Free.* ☉ *Daily 8:30–6:30.*

Dining and Lodging

$ ✕ **Emmentaler Schaukäserei.** After you've toured the factory and exhibits on cheese making, you can sate your appetite at the factory's simple restaurant, where the menu features a wide variety of cheese dishes—fondue, *Käseschnitte*—as well as local cold meats. Special cheese breakfasts are served daily until 11:30. In fine weather, picnic on the self-service terrace. ⊠ *Affoltern,* ☎ *034/4351611. AE, DC, MC, V.*

$$ ✕▥ **Sonne.** This is an archetypal Emmental guest house: weathered but pristine, steeped in tradition but airy and bright, and serving rich, hearty cooking based on ingredients straight off the farm. There are satiny soups, flaky *Pastetli* (puff pastry filled with creamed veal), unusually well-executed veal dishes, and freshwater fish. Make a heroic effort to leave room for the meringue, fluffed to enormous proportions with farm-fresh Emmental egg whites. It's set on a sunny hill with valley views, not far from the demonstration cheese dairy. There are a few simple bedrooms upstairs. The restaurant is closed to nonguests on Thursday and for lunch on Friday. ⊠ *CH-3416 Affoltern,* ☎ *034/4358000,* FAX *034/4358019 12 rooms. AE, DC, MC, V. Closed Jan.*

OFF THE BEATEN PATH | **Lueg.** From Affoltern, make a side trip northwest to Lueg (887 m/2,909 ft) for views toward the Alps: It's a brief walk uphill to the crest to take in the great panorama and to catch the Alps in a different light as seen earlier in the day from Chuderhüsi.

Burgdorf

❺ *12km (7 mi) west of Affoltern and 25 km (15 mi) north of Bern.*

In Burgdorf there's a sizable Gothic castle built by the Zähringens during the 12th century, the family responsible for the founding of the cities of Bern, Fribourg, Murten, and Burgdorf. The castle was turned into a museum more than 100 years ago: The **Schlossmuseum Burgdorf** (Castle Museum of Burgdorf). A walk through the Knights' Hall and the various rooms, towers, and battlements of the original castle reveals the history and culture of Burgdorf and the Emmental. Regional costumes, ceramics, and period furniture are displayed along with alternating exhibitions. ⊠ *Burgdorf,* ☎ *034/4230214.* ☜ *5 SF.* ☉ *Apr. 1–Nov. 1, Mon.–Sat. 2–5, Sun. 11–5.*

The **Kornhaus,** a former granary, now houses the Swiss Center for Folk Culture, a collection of Swiss costumes, historic phonographs, musical instruments, and a yodeling hall. ⊠ *Kornhausg. 16, Burgdorf,* ☎

034/4231010. ✉ 10 SF. ☉ *Tues.–Fri. 10–12:30 and 1:30–5; weekends 10–5.*

Emmental A to Z

Getting Around

BY CAR

Driving is by far the best way to experience this rural region because
good, small highways carry you from town to town through countryside often untouched by modern architecture.

BY TRAIN AND BUS

If you plan your itinerary carefully, you can arrange a comfortable though
limited tour of the region combining trains from Bern into Burgdorf,
connecting to Hasle; from there you can take a postbus to Affoltern,
for instance, to visit the cheese factory. Or stay on the train all the way
to Langnau and enjoy the countryside as you travel.

Guided Tours

Badertscher (✉ Freiburgstr. 430, CH-3018 Bern, ☎ 031/9919100) offers coach excursions through the region. **Emmental Tours** (✉ CH-3454
Sumiswald, ☎ 034/4312161) is another resource.

One of the most novel and effective ways to experience the region is
by plodding down its back roads in a Gypsy wagon, complete with
two horses and lodging in typical Emmentaler inns. You can pack a
picnic or stop for lunch at a guest house along the way. Contact **Eu-
rotrek/Unitours** (✉ Malzstr. 17–21, CH-8036 Zürich, ☎ 01/4620203).

Visitor Information

Pro Emmental (✉ Schlossstr. 3, CH-3550 Langnau, ☎ 034/4024252),
FAX 034/4025667.

BERN A TO Z

Arriving and Departing

By Car

Bern is connected conveniently by expressway to Basel via **A1,** to the
Berner Oberland via **A6,** and to Lac Léman and thus Lausanne, Geneva,
and the Valais via **A12.**

By Plane

The small airport **Belp** (✉ Belpmoos, 9 km/6 mi south of Bern, ☎ 031/
9613411) has flights to Amsterdam, Brussels, Frankfurt, and most other
major European airports connecting through **Crossair** (☎ 031/9602121
for reservations), Switzerland's domestic airline. **Air Engiadina** (☎
0848848328 toll-free for reservations), a regional airline, offers direct
flight connections with Munich and Vienna.

BETWEEN THE AIRPORT AND THE CENTER

A city **bus** runs regularly between Belp and the city's Hauptbahnhof (main
train station). The fare each way is 14 SF. A **taxi** from the airport to
the Hauptbahnhof costs about 35 SF and takes about 15 minutes.

By Train

Bern is a major link between Geneva, Zürich, and Basel, and **fast
trains** run almost every hour from the enormous central station, the
Hauptbahnhof (☎ 157/2222). Bern is the only European capital to have
three **high-speed trains**: the ICE, the TGV, and the Pendolino. The ICE
from Berlin takes nine hours; the TGV from Paris takes 4½ hours; the
Pendolino from Milan takes 3–4 hours.

Getting Around

The best of Bern is concentrated in a relatively small area, and it's easy to get around on foot.

By Bus and Tram

Bus and tram services are excellent, with fares ranging from 1.50 SF to 2.40 SF. Buy individual tickets from the dispenser at the tram or bus stop: Find the name of the stop closest to your destination on the map, then check to see the fare on the list of stops. There is an unlimited Visitors Card available—6 SF for 24 hours, 9 SF for 48 hours, and 12 SF for 72 hours—at the tourist office in the Hauptbahnhof (☞ Visitor Information, *below*) or at the public-transportation ticket office in the passageway leading down to the Hauptbahnhof (take the escalator in front of Loeb's department store and turn right through the Christoffel Tower). A Swiss Pass (☞ Train Travel *in* the Gold Guide) includes free travel in Bern.

By Taxi

Taxis are actually a cumbersome alternative to walking, especially when streets are dominated by trams. It costs between 12 SF and 15 SF to cross town.

Contacts and Resources

Embassies

United States (✉ Jubiläumstr. 93, ☎ 031/3577011). **Canada** (✉ Kirchenfeldstr. 88, ☎ 031/3526381). **United Kingdom** (✉ Thunstr. 50, ☎ 031/3525021).

Emergencies

Police (☎ 117). **Ambulance** (☎ 144). **Hospital** (✉ Insel Spital, Freiburgstr., ☎ 031/6322111). **Medical and dental referrals** (☎ 031/3112211). **All-night pharmacy referrals** (☎ 031/3112211).

English-Language Bookstore

Stauffacher (✉ Neueng. 25, ☎ 031/3112411) has the broadest selection of books in English.

Guided Tours

ORIENTATION TOURS

A two-hour English-commentary bus tour around the Old Town, covering all the principal sights, is offered for 22 SF by the tourist office, where you meet.

PERSONAL GUIDES

To arrange for a private guide, contact the tourist office (☞ *below*).

Travel Agency

American Express Travel Agency (✉ Bubenbergpl. 9, ☎ FAX 061/3122116). **Carlson Wagonlit Travel** (✉ Von Werdt-Passage 5, ☎ 031/3282828).

Visitor Information

Berne Tourismus (✉ Bahnhofpl., at the main train station, CH-3001, ☎ 031/3116611) has several special services, including Clock Tower visits, walking tours, and even a city tour by raft along the Aare.

10 Berner Oberland

Gstaad, Interlaken, Wengen

The Bernese Alps concentrate the very best of rural Switzerland: panoramas of the treble peaks of the Eiger, Mönch, and Jungfrau mountains; crystalline lakes, gorges, and waterfalls; and emerald slopes dotted with gingerbread chalets and cows with bells—not to mention world-class skiing. It's no secret, though: Berner Oberland is the most touristic canton in Switzerland.

Updated by
Susan Tuttle-
Laube

THERE ARE TIMES WHEN THE REALITY OF Switzerland puts postcard idealization to shame, surpassing tinted-indigo skies and advertising-image peaks with its own astonishing vividness. Those times happen often in Berner Oberland. Though the Valais and Graubünden areas offer stiff competition, this rugged region concentrates the very best of rural Switzerland: mountain panoramas that can't be overrated, massive glaciers, crystalline lakes, gorges and waterfalls, chic ski resorts, and emerald slopes scattered with gingerbread chalets.

It was the Romantics who first beat a path to this awe-inspiring region. After contemplating the Staubbach Falls in 1779, the great German writer Johann Wolfgang von Goethe was moved to write one of his most celebrated poems, *Gesang der Geister über den Wassern* (*Song of the Spirits over the Waters*). Rousseau spread word of its astounding natural phenomena to Paris society. Then Lord Byron came to investigate; it's said he conceived *Manfred* in barren, windswept Wengernalp. Shelley followed, then William Thackeray, John Ruskin, and Mark Twain; the landscape master painter J. M. W. Turner and the composer Johannes Brahms took in the views; finally, Queen Victoria herself came, beginning a flood of tourism that changed Berner Oberland's—and Switzerland's—profile forever.

Before the onslaught of visitors inspired the locals to switch from farming to innkeeping, agriculture was the prime industry—and is still much in evidence today. As if hired as props to style a photo opportunity, Swiss-brown cows pepper the hillsides wherever rock gives way to grass, and the mountains echo with their bells. The houses of Berner Oberland are classics, the definitive Swiss chalets: The broad, low, deep-eaved roofs cover gables that are scalloped, carved, and painted with the family dedication; the wood weathers to dark sienna after generations of harsh cold and clear sun. From early spring through autumn, every window box spills torrents of well-tended scarlet geraniums, and adjacent woodpiles are stacked with mosaiclike precision.

The region is arranged tidily enough for even a brief visit. Its main resort city, Interlaken, lies in green lowlands between the gleaming twin pools of the Brienzersee and the Thunersee, linked by the River Aare. Behind them to the south loom craggy, forested foothills with excellent views, and behind those foothills stand some of Europe's noblest peaks, most notably the snowy crowns of the Eiger (3,970 m/13,022 ft), the Mönch (4,099 m/13,445 ft), and the fiercely beautiful Jungfrau (4,158 m/13,638 ft). Because nature laid it out so conveniently, the region has become far and away the most popular for tourism, with its excursion and transportation systems carrying enormous numbers of visitors to its myriad viewpoints, overlooks, and wonders of the world. The railroad to the Jungfraujoch transports masses of tour groups to its high-altitude attractions, and on a peak-season day its station can resemble the Sistine Chapel in August or the Chicago Board of Trade. But the tourist industry can handle the onslaught, offering such an efficient network of boats, trains, and funiculars; such a variety of activities and attractions; and such a wide range of accommodations, from posh city hotels to rustic mountain lodges, that every visitor can find the most suitable way to take in the marvels of the Bernese Alps.

Pleasures and Pastimes

Dining

Meals in Berner Oberland tend to be down-to-earth, starting with hearty soup or a mixed slawlike salad, followed by lake fish or meat and potatoes, and then a sizable dessert. Fried or broiled *Egli* (perch) and *Felchen* (whitefish) are frequently local and lake-fresh; such waterfront resorts as Spiez, Brienz, and Iseltwald specialize in fish. Meat dishes represent Bernese and Zürich cuisines: *Ratsherrentopf* is a mixed grill, *geschnetzeltes Kalbsfleisch* is veal or calves' liver in cream sauce. Colorful mixed salads include crisp shredded celery root, beet, carrot, and cabbage. Because the Alpine experience demands it, the Oberland has adopted the French territories' cheese fondue and raclette (a dish of melted cheese served with potatoes and pickles) as winter-night staples.

The valley town of Meiringen claims to have invented meringue; whether or not this is true, its region consumes enough to corner the culinary market. Enormous, crisp, ivory meringue puffs may be served with or without vanilla ice cream; regardless, they are buried under mounds of heavy piped whipped cream. You may find a half portion more than adequate.

CATEGORY	COST*
$$$$	over 70 SF
$$$	40 SF–70 SF
$$	20 SF–40 SF
$	under 20 SF

Prices are per person for a three-course meal (two-course meal in $ category), including sales tax and 15% service charge

Hiking

Partly because of its spectacular ski transport network woven throughout the region, Berner Oberland offers a wealth of highly developed walking and hiking options. The scenery is magnificent—what can surpass the views from the Mürren plateau toward the Jungfrau, Eiger, and Mönch?—and the options varied, from rough trails toward glaciers to smooth postbus roads. From May through October you'll be unlikely to find yourself alone for long on any given trail; now resorts are clearing more and more winter hiking trails as well. A wide variety of topographical maps and suggested itineraries is available at local tourist offices, especially the Jungfrau region central office on the Höheweg in Interlaken.

Lake Cruises

Steamers crisscross the lakes of Brienz and Thun, trailing leisurely across crystal waters past rolling panoramas of forested hills and craggy, snowcapped peaks. They provide an alternative to high-speed car cruises and limited train runs and, with their buslike schedule, allow passengers to step off at any port for a visit; they need only choose the best boat to catch next. Drinks and meals in the glassed-in cafés (both first and second class) offer respite on windy days.

Lodging

Berner Oberland tradition mandates charming chalet-style exteriors replete with scalloped-wood balconies, steeply sloped roofs, and cascades of scarlet geraniums, no matter what architectural era a hotel dates from. But many hotels in the region have interiors that reflect their roots in the '60s ski boom, with their no-nonsense, Scandinavian-spare, avocado-beige and walnut-grain Formica furnishings. Some of the most recently renovated have softened the '60s edge with such folksy touches as carved knotty pine. A few landmarks have preserved quaint interiors that reflect their lovely facades. Although a vast majority of the hotels are still family owned and run, big businesses are creeping in, scooping up properties that private families can no longer carry and creating competition that forces even more family-run places to go under, a sad scenario that is actively being fought in some communities. Small towns may not have street addresses; in those cases, hotels large and small are clearly signposted. Prices below are average for Berner Oberland; note that such car-free resorts as Wengen and Mürren run well above this curve, especially during ski season. Half-board, or *demipension* (breakfast and one hot meal), and full-board (three meals) plans are often the thrust of regional hotels. Remember that many properties post rates on a per-person basis.

CATEGORY	COST*
$$$$	over 250 SF
$$$	200 SF–250 SF
$$	120 SF–200 SF
$	under 120 SF

Prices are for a standard double room, including breakfast, tax, and service charge.

Shopping

Berner Oberland is known for its spindle-made *torchon* lace from Lauterbrunnen and the wood carvings of Brienz, especially fine nativity scenes. Traditional hand-painted pottery from around Steffisburg is gaining popularity. Such winter resorts as Grindelwald, Mürren, and Wengen have their share of state-of-the-art ski boutiques, with Gstaad adding international designer shops.

Skiing

As one of Switzerland's capitals of winter sports, Berner Oberland provides a dazzling variety of choices to skiers. Each resort offers its own style of transit and its own peculiar terrain, from the nursery slopes to the deadly narrow pistes of the Schilthorn. The lift lines are a fair bit more tolerable here, although the region as a whole is not as snow-sure as is, for example, the Engadine.

Exploring Berner Oberland

The central, urban-Victorian resort of Interlaken makes a good base for excursions for visitors who want to experience the entire Jungfrau region, which includes the craggy bluff-lined Lauterbrunnen Valley and the opposing resorts that perch high above it: Mürren and Wengen. Both busy, sporty Grindelwald, famous for scenic rides and sports, and isolated Kandersteg, ideal for hiking and cross-country skiing, can be visited out of Interlaken, but they make good home bases themselves; they both lie at the dead end of gorge roads that climb into the heights. Spreading east and west of Interlaken are Brienzersee and Thunersee lakes, both broad, crystalline, and surrounded by forests, castles, and picturesque waterfront resorts, including Brienz and Thun. From Spiez on the Thunersee, you can head west through the forest gorge of the Simmental to the Saanenland and glamorous Gstaad. Connections by rail or car keep most highlights within easy reach.

Numbers in the text correspond to numbers in the margin and on the Berner Oberland map.

Great Itineraries

Ten days in Berner Oberland gives you the luxury of exploring each of the valleys and lakes of this varied region, but you can experience it *en passage* as well, depending on your travel pace and your ability to take excursions.

IF YOU HAVE 3 DAYS
Base yourself in ⊞ **Interlaken** ① or **Bönigen** ②, one day taking a boat
trip across the Thunersee to **Thun** ⑫, the next day a driving tour around
the Brienzersee to **Brienz** ⑨ and the Freilichtmuseum Ballenberg. The
third day (or best-weather day) head up the Lauterbrunnen Valley and
take the famous rail trip from **Wengen** ⑥ to the **Jungfraujoch** ⑤, returning via **Grindelwald** ⑦.

IF YOU HAVE 5 DAYS
Follow the tours above, and while in the Lauterbrunnen Valley, take
the cable cars or cogwheel rail up to **Mürren** ④ and the Schilthorn. On
day five, drive up to **Kandersteg** ⑮ to hike to the Oeschinensee, or wind
through the forest to visit famous ⊞ **Gstaad** ⑯.

IF YOU HAVE 10 DAYS
Rent an apartment or settle in on a half-board (breakfast and one hot
meal) or full-board (three meals) plan in one of the cozier hotels of Interlaken or any crossroads resort (Grindelwald and Lauterbrunnen also
offer easy access to sights), taking in the lesser sights as you cruise around
the varied region. Visit the Trümmelbach Falls in the Lauterbrunnen
Valley, see the castles at **Hilterfingen** ⑬ and **Oberhofen** ⑭ on the
Thunersee and take another high-altitude excursion out of Interlaken
to Harder Kulm, Heimwehfluh, or Schynige Platte. You might even hop
on a train and make a day trip into the capital city of Bern, only an
hour away (☞ Chapter 9).

When to Tour Berner Oberland

In high summer, Berner Oberland is the most popular tourist area in
Switzerland and can feel overrun, so aim for the cusp—mid-June, late
September—when the weather still holds but the crowds thin. Ski season begins in mid-December and runs through Easter vacation. May
and November are low season, and prices drop—but some hotels and
cable cars shut down for maintenance; depending on snow conditions,
some excursions may be closed into June or shut down mid-October.
But fear not: The Jungfraujoch rail trip (☞ *below*) runs 365 days a
year, even in pea-soup fog.

JUNGFRAU REGION

The thriving resort town of Interlaken holds forth between two spectacularly sited lakes, the Brienzersee (Lake Brienz) and the Thunersee
(Lake Thun) and is the gateway to two magnificent mountain valleys,
one leading up to the popular sports resort of Grindelwald, the other
into Lauterbrunnen and the famous car-free resorts of Wengen and Mürren. Rearing over both valleys, the Jungfrau and its partner peaks, the
Eiger and Mönch, can be viewed to advantage from various high-altitude overviews.

Interlaken

❶ *58 km (36 mi) southeast of Bern.*

The name *Interlaken* has a Latin source: *interlacus* (between lakes); as
a gateway to Berner Oberland, this bustling Victorian resort town is
the obvious home base for travelers planning to visit the region's two
lakes and the mountains towering behind them. At 570 m (1,870 ft),
Interlaken dominates the Bödeli, the branch of lowland between the
lakes that Interlaken shares with the adjoining towns of Unterseen,
Wilderswil, Bönigen, and Matten. The town's two train stations, Interlaken East and Interlaken West, are good orientation points; most
sights are just a few minutes' walk from one of the stations. There are

SWITZERLAND

TO BERN

TO LUZERN

Wiggen

Flühli

Marbach

Kleinteil

TO LUZERN

Oberei

Glaubenbüelenpass

Lungernsee

chwarzenegg

Brienzer-
Rothorn

Lungern

4

Niederhorn

6–11

Brienz

9

Freilichtmuseum
Ballenberg

eatenberg

Harder
Kulm

Brienzersee

Giessbach

10

Meiringen

St. Beatus-
höhlen

8

Iseltwald

cht

Unterseen

Bönigen

First

unersee

Heimwehfluh

1

2

Interlaken
Matten

Schynige Platte

Wilderswil

Gundlischwand

7

Grindelwald

OBERER GRINDELWALD GLETSCHER

Zweilütschinen

6

Wengen

Lauberhorn

Lauterbrunnen

3

Staubbachfälle

Kleine Scheidegg

Eiger

Trümmelbachfälle

Mönch

Schilthorn

Mürren

4

5

Mürrenbachfälle

Jungfraujoch

Jungfrau

ALETSCH
GLACIER

see

BLÜMLISALP

Breithorn

KEY

Rail Lines

Funicular/
Cable Car

Regional
Boundary Line

Ski Resort

N

0   6 miles

0   9 km

unlimited excursion options, and it's a pleasant, if urban, place to stay put as well, as its setting is spectacular and its ambience genteel.

The **Höheweg** (⊠ East of Hotel Metropole, town center, ☞ *below*) is the city's main promenade, its tree- and flower-lined walkways cutting through the edge of the broad green parklands of the **Höhematte**. This 35-acre park once pastured the herds of the Augustinian monastery, which dominated medieval Interlaken. Cows are still pastured there in fenced-off areas that are moved to different spots on the field daily.

Mark Twain once sojourned at the **Grand Hotel Victoria-Jungfrau** (☞ Dining and Lodging, *below*), on the Höheweg, conceived to take in the view of the snowy Jungfrau that towers above town. The hotel originated as two humbler inns, the Jungfrau (1864) and the Chalet Victoria (1865); these were merged and expanded in 1895, and the facade redesigned and landmark tower added in 1899.

Between the Höheweg and the River Aare, you'll find the landscaped **Kursaal** (Casino) grounds, complete with a floral clock. Built in 1859 in a dramatic combination of Oberland chalet and Victorian styles, the Kursaal was renovated in 1968 and has become once again a social focal point for the city. Plays and concerts are presented here, mostly during the high season, and there are folklore evenings in the adjoining *Spycher* (the Swiss name for a farm storage barn). The **casino** here has gambling nightly, including 120 slot machines, but bets are limited by federal law to 5 SF (☞ Nightlife and the Arts, *below*). ⊠ *Off Höheweg,* ☎ *033/8276100.*

The **Schlosskirche** (Reformed Church) was once the chapel for the Augustinian monastery. Though founded in 1133, the monastery and the convent that shared its grounds during the 13th century have left only a 14th-century chancel and a branch of the cloister. The rest of the convent was built into a private castle in 1745, which, attached behind the church, now provides office space to the community. ⊠ *At the end of the Höhematte south of the Hotel du Nord.*

On the north side of the River Aare is the tiny town of **Unterseen,** with its picturesque Old Town and Marktplatz (Marketplace). Founded in 1279 on lands rented from the Augustinians, Unterseen retains some of the region's oldest buildings, including the 17th-century **Stadthaus** (city hall) and the 14th-century **church,** its steeple dating from 1471. The **Schloss Unterseen** (Unterseen Castle), built in 1656 for the reigning Bernese nobleman, stands at the opposite end of the square, near a medieval arched gateway. You can get here via a short (10-minute) bus ride from Interlaken's center, or even by walking; it's near the Interlaken West train station.

Fronting on the Unterseen Marktplatz is the **Touristik-Museum der Jungfrau Region** (Museum of Tourism of the Jungfrau Region), which traces the history of tourism and excursions in the Jungfrau region over the last 200 years. Exhibits include models of early transportation and examples of primitive mountain-climbing and skiing equipment. ⊠ *Obereg. 26,* ☎ *033/8229839.* ☞ *3 SF.* ⊙ *May–mid-Oct., Tues.–Sun. 2–5.*

OFF THE
BEATEN PATH

HEIMWEHFLUH – An old-fashioned red funicular railway leads to the top of this 669-m (2,194-ft) mountain, where you will get views over both lakes and an elevated peek at the Jungfrau, the Eiger, and the Mönch. A restaurant and playground have been built at the top, complete with a 300-m bob-run, and there's a show of model trains every 30 minutes. The funicular station is a five-minute walk from the Interlaken West station down the

Rugenparkstrasse. ⊠ *Funicular station: south of Interlaken West,* ☎ *033/ 8223453.* 🎫 *16 SF (includes the model train show).* ⊙ *Apr.–Oct.*

HARDER KULM – Take the 12-minute funicular ride up Harder Kulm (1,310 m/4,297 ft); from there, hike uphill to views south over the city, the lakes, and the whole panorama of snowy peaks. A turreted Gothic chalet-style restaurant offers Friday-evening visitors more than food: From mid-June through September, there are folk music and dancing, too, and you're free to join in. ⊠ *Funicular station north of the River Aare near Interlaken East, across the Beaurivagebrücke,* ☎ *033/8287339.* 🎫 *Funicular round-trip: 20 SF; music: 4 SF.* ⊙ *Funicular: June–Oct., daily; music: Fri. only.*

SCHYNIGE PLATTE – For the most splendid overview in the region, make the ambitious trip to this 1,965-m (6,445-ft) peak for a picnic, a wander down any of numerous footpaths, or a visit to the Alpine Botanical Garden, where more than 500 varieties of mountain flowers grow. You may opt to walk either up or (more comfortably) down: Specify when you buy your ticket. Train service runs from approximately 7:40 AM to 6 PM. ⊠ *Take 6-min ride on Bernese Oberland Railway from Interlaken East to Wilderswil; take 50-min cogwheel train ride to peak,* ☎ *033/ 8387111.* 🎫 *Round-trip 54 SF; one-way 31.80 SF.* ⊙ *Late May or early June–late Oct., daily, depending on snow conditions.*

Dining and Lodging

$$$–$$$$ ✕ **Alpenblick.** Just 2 km (1 mi) south of Interlaken in Wilderswil, this
★ hotel restaurant is one of the best in Berner Oberland (competing with Grindelwald's Fiescherblick). It is a carved-wood-and-shingle 17th-century landmark in the quiet old Oberdorf (Upper Village) and serves a varied clientele, including loyal gastronomes who make a pilgrimage to try chef Richard Stöckli's international cuisine. Locals dine here regularly, too, seeking out old-style classics (Rösti with wild mushrooms) and upscale bistro fare (marinated lake fish tartare, duck liver pâté with onion confit). ⊠ *CH-3812 Wilderswil,* ☎ *033/8220707. AE, DC, MC, V.*

$$–$$$ ✕ **Schuh.** With a luxurious shady terrace spilling into the Höhematte in summer and cocktail piano enhancing the dated elegance inside, this sweet shop and café-restaurant serves everything from tea to rich, hot meals. Leave room for the pastries, like the glossy strawberry tarts, which you'll find in the adjoining shop. ⊠ *Höheweg 56, across from the Metropole,* ☎ *033/8229441. AE, DC, MC, V.*

$$–$$$ ✕ **Stellambiente.** For something nicely out of the ordinary, try this restau-
★ rant in the Stella (☞ Lodging *below*) hotel. The modern, highly flavored cuisine includes several vegetarian options, with locally grown ingredients and an extraordinary variety of salads—from 40 to 50 kinds in the Thursday salad buffet. Order the "surprise" menu in advance, and you'll be served five courses of unexpected delights on beautiful, individually selected pieces of china. There's an exceptional attention to detail. An attractive terrace, complete with fountain, turns summer dining into a garden idyll. Though it's not absolutely required, try to make reservations in advance. ⊠ *Waldeggstr. 10,* ☎ *033/8228871. AE, DC, MC, V.*

$$ ✕ **Im Gade.** This welcoming hybrid of carved-wood coziness and sleek
★ formality fills up night after night with appreciative locals who recognize fresh, fine cooking and alert service. Details count here: Even that dab of smoky sauerkraut in your crisp mixed salad is homemade. Seasonal specialties (game, mushrooms) stand out. Fondues are available but are not the restaurant's forte: Stick to the hearty veal dishes, the lovely lake fish, or the generous daily specials. ⊠ *Höheweg 70, Hotel du Nord,* ☎ *033/8222631. AE, DC, MC, V. Closed mid-Nov.–mid-Dec.*

$$ ✕ **Krebs.** The sunny front-porch serving area looks over the street, but head for the more formal dining room, glassed-in yet still opening onto the main promenade. You may feel you've forgotten your parasol: This is a classic old-world resort spot and serves its upscale Swiss classics and homey daily plates with starched-collar style. It has been in Interlaken—and the Krebs family—since 1875. ⊠ *Bahnhofstr. 4,* ☎ *033/8227161. AE, DC, MC, V. Closed Nov.–Apr.*

$–$$ ✕ **Laterne.** You'll find this unpretentious local favorite a bit off the tourist
★   track, east of the center near the A8 ring road (a 10-minute walk from Interlaken West). There's a sports-bar ambience, complete with piles of photo albums chronicling what seems to be every party ever held there, and a rustic, woody setting. Besides the big meat dinners there are good Swiss specialties: seven kinds of *Rösti* (hash brown potatoes) served in iron skillets, vegetarian meals, and eight kinds of cheese fondue at reasonable prices. There's also live Swiss folk music every second Friday. ⊠ *Obere Bönigstr. 18,* ☎ *033/8221141. AE, DC, MC, V.*

$$$$ ⌂ **Beau Rivage.** Its Belle Epoque grandeur glossily revisited, this In-
★   terlaken old-timer offers more intimate luxury than the Grand Hotel Victoria-Jungfrau (☞ *below*). From the tastefully decorated rooms there are views of either the mountains or the quiet Aare, and the hotel is just a stone's throw from the Interlaken East train station. As it's set well back from the road and surrounded by gardens, though, it maintains an unruffled calm. Delicate *cuisine du marché* (based on the freshest ingredients available) is served in the highly rated hearth-warmed restaurant La Bonne Fourchette. ⊠ *Höheweg 211, CH-3800,* ☎ *033/8216272,* ℻ *033/8232847. 99 rooms. 2 restaurants, 2 bars, indoor pool, sauna, health club, bicycles. AE, DC, MC, V.*

$$$$ ⌂ **Grand Hotel Victoria-Jungfrau.** Follow in Mark Twain's footsteps
★   to this 1865 landmark, a splendid, block-long, wedding-cake sprawl that dominates the Höheweg. A bit different today than in Twain's time, its restoration has taken it firmly into the 20th-century, with a glitzy postmodern black-and-burled-wood entry and plenty of facilities, including indoor master golf. The flashy formal restaurant, La Terrasse, is a vision of marble and glass overlooking the promenade and the Höhematte. A jacket and tie are required at the restaurant. ⊠ *Höheweg 41, CH-3800,* ☎ *033/8282828 or 800/223–6800,* ℻ *033/8282880. 215 rooms. 2 restaurants, 2 bars, indoor pool, outdoor pool, beauty salon, spa, 7 tennis courts, billiards. AE, DC, MC, V.*

$$$$ ⌂ **Hotel Metropole.** As Berner Oberland's only skyscraper, this 18-story concrete high-rise gobbles up the scenery and ruins everyone's view but its own—which is spectacular. If you turn your back on the picture windows framing the lake-and-mountain scenery, you'll think you're in the United States: It's slick, airtight, dependable, and banal; there's even an atrium lobby-lounge. The rooftop restaurant serves Italian food along with staggering views. ⊠ *Höheweg 37, CH-3800,* ☎ *033/8286666,* ℻ *033/8286633. 97 rooms. Restaurant, snack bar, indoor pool, massage, sauna. AE, DC, MC, V.*

$$$ ⌂ **Du Lac.** Don't be put off by the views over the tracks of Interlaken East: The trains run only in the day. Moreover, the waterfront restaurant and pricier back rooms have one of the most peaceful situations in town—a wide, woodsy bank of the Aare. The hotel's musty grandeur has been maintained by a single family for more than 100 years. Most of the rooms were refurbished in 1997; they're straightforward and comfortable. The stübli is a casual restaurant for Swiss snacks from the region. ⊠ *Höheweg 225, CH-3800,* ☎ *033/8222922,* ℻ *033/ 8222915. 40 rooms. Restaurant, stübli. AE, DC, MC, V.*

$$$ ⌂ **Royal–St. Georges.** If you are a fan of Victoriana, this impeccably restored gem is a dream come true, with original moldings, built-in furnishings, and fantastical bath fixtures reproduced in gleaming Jugendstil–Art Nouveau. A few rooms were done in ho-hum modern, as some guests object to bathtubs with feet, but you can ask for a period version. The street-side rooms—the ones with Jungfrau views—are noisier. ⊠ *Höheweg 139, CH-3800,* ☎ *033/8227575,* 𝔽𝔸𝕏 *033/8233075. 89 rooms, 6 suites. Restaurant, bar, hot tub, sauna. AE, DC, MC, V.*

$$$ ⌂ **Stella.** This small, family-run gem defies its outdated '60s exterior
★ and residential neighborhood setting—inside you'll find marvelous, friendly service; innovative, cozy rooms; and special, personal touches, such as rose petals strewn across your duvet in welcome. This is a small hotel that truly does try harder—and does so successfully. The personal touch carries over to their restaurant, the Stellambiente (☞ Dining *above*). ⊠ *Waldeggstr. 10 CH-3800,* ☎ *033/8228871,* 𝔽𝔸𝕏 *033/8226671. 29 rooms. Restaurant, indoor pool. AE, DC, MC, V.*

$$ ⌂ **Chalet Oberland.** A vacation-intensive combination of rustic decor and city-crossroads position, this downtown lodge attracts the young with its popular pizzeria and Tuesday-night Swiss folklore show. The all-wood stübli offers traditional Swiss food and fondue. The rooms are sleek but minimal; the Art Deco–style 1988 wing is slicker. ⊠ *Postg. 1, CH-3800,* ☎ *033/8278787,* 𝔽𝔸𝕏 *033/8278770. 148 rooms. Bar, coffee shop, pizzeria, stübli. AE, DC, MC, V.*

$$ ⌂ **Hirschen.** This dark-beam 17th-century guest house, in one family
★ since 1666, has old, deep-shingle eaves and rooms with private baths, fresh knotty-pine walls, and built-in furniture. The stübli, paneled in aged pine, and the highly acclaimed restaurant, scattered with antiques, serve local specialties; veal, beef, cheese, vegetables, and even honey come from the owner's farm. There are a sheltered terrace and balcony overlooking a lovely garden. The hotel's location on an outskirts crossroad makes it convenient for drivers who are covering the region rather than staying in town. ⊠ *Hauptstr. 11, CH-3800,* ☎ *033/ 8221545,* 𝔽𝔸𝕏 *033/8233745. 20 rooms, 1 suite. Restaurant, stübli. AE, DC, MC, V.*

$$ ⌂ **Splendid.** Location is key here: You can't get more central to shopping and nightlife. Renovations have ironed out the wrinkles in this modest little family-run Victorian palace, and you'll find new baths, sleek beige decor, and cozy spindle beds. The back rooms overlook a quiet backstreet; the corner bays are prettiest. The proprietor is a hunter, so game in season is fresh and local. ⊠ *Höheweg 33, CH-3800,* ☎ *033/ 8227612,* 𝔽𝔸𝕏 *033/8227679. 35 rooms. Restaurant, pub. AE, MC, V.*

$$ ⌂ **Toscana.** This former downtown pizzeria has evolved into a sleek, sizable hotel. The stress on technical perfection (intercom, elevators, cable TVs, indoor parking, angled mountain views) doesn't preclude the personal touch of good Tuscan cooking, prepared by the Italian owners. ⊠ *Jungfraustr. 19, CH-3800,* ☎ *033/8233033,* 𝔽𝔸𝕏 *033/ 8233551. 20 rooms. Restaurant, café, free parking. V.*

$ ⌂ **Alp Lodge.** This is possibly the best bargain in town. The tiny,
★ cheery rooms have bunk beds, doubles, or twins, and murals painted by local art students. You won't find a better deal. ⊠ *Marktg. 59, CH-3800,* ☎ *033/8224748,* 𝔽𝔸𝕏 *033/8229250. 20 rooms. No credit cards.*

$ ⌂ **Balmer's.** This popular private youth hostel offers families and
★ young travelers bare-bones bedrooms at rock-bottom prices. Kitchen access, washers and dryers, videos, two fireplaces, convenience store, and self-service suppers make you feel at home in this lively, collegiate, international atmosphere. The English-speaking staff is especially helpful in finding you the cheapest deals in skiing and other outdoor activities. Rooms are available with one to five beds, all with sinks. There's even a massive group tent pitched at the edge of town roughly from June through September. Check-in is required by 5 PM, checkout by 10 AM; there are no lockers or day storage. It's a quick bus ride from either rail station—they even offer a free shuttle bus May–September.

⊠ *Hauptstr. 23–25, CH-3800,* ☎ *033/8221961,* F̄Ā̄X̄ *033/8233261. 50 rooms. Bar, library, coin laundry. AE, MC, V.*

$ 🖬 **Alphorn Garni.** Formerly called Pilgerruhe, this lovely Victorian bed and breakfast, on a quiet side street between Interlaken West and the Heimwehfluh, offers quintessential middle European pristine stuffiness—waxed parquet, brocade, and heavy florals—and an equally typical, impeccable garden. ⊠ *Rugenaustr. 8, CH-3800,* ☎ *033/8223051,* F̄Ā̄X̄ *033/8233069. 20 rooms. Breakfast room, bar. AE, DC, MC, V.*

Nightlife and the Arts

BARS

Buddy's Pub (⊠ Hotel Splendid, ☎ 033/8227612) is a popular conversation spot where locals and visitors actually mingle. Riverside in the **Hotel Bellevue** (☎ 033/8224431) is a well-frequented hotel bar. **Sternen** (☎ 033/8223425), on the pedestrian stretch of the Jungfraustrasse, offers a good selection of wines by the glass and summer seating on the sidewalk.

CASINOS

The **Kursaal** (☎ 033/8276100) has *boule* (a type of roulette) and 120 slot machines; it's open from 8 PM till 2:30 AM daily. It's not exactly Vegas, but there's a friendly atmosphere. Remember there's a 5 SF gambling limit.

DANCING

The disco **Black and White,** in the Hotel Metropole (☎ 033/8236633), attracts an upscale crowd. **High-life** (⊠ Rugenparkstr. 2, ☎ 033/8221550), near Interlaken West, brings back easygoing oldies. **Hollywood** (⊠ Hotel Central, ☎ 033/8231033) pumps in beats with up-to-date sound equipment. **Johnny's Club** (⊠ Hotel Carlton, ☎ 033/8223821) draws a rougher crowd.

FOLKLORE

Folklore shows—yodeling and all—are presented at Interlaken's **Folklore-Spycher** in the Kursaal (⊠ Off Höheweg, ☎ 033/8276100), with admission including meals (44 SF to 54 SF) or not (16 SF), as space allows. Priority is given to diners. Meals are at 7:30, shows at 9. At the restaurant at **Harder Kulm** (☎ 033/8223444), reached by funicular, on Friday only from June through September you can hear typical *ländler* (traditional dance) music and try a little regional dancing.

THEATER

For a real introduction to the local experience, don't miss the **Tellfreilichtspiele,** an outdoor pageant play presented in Interlaken every summer by a cast of Swiss amateurs. Wrapped in a rented blanket—which you'll need, since evenings can be chilly and the show goes on regardless of weather June through September—and seated in a 2,200-seat sheltered amphitheater that opens onto illuminated woods and a permanent village-set, you'll see 250 players in splendid costume acting out the epic tale of Swiss hero William Tell. The text is Schiller's famous play, performed in German with the guttural singsong of a Schwyzerdütsch accent—but don't worry; with galloping horses, flower-decked cows, bonfires, parades, and, of course, the famous apple-shooting climax, the operatic story tells itself. Tickets are available through the **Tellbüro** (⊠ Bahnhofstr. 5A, ☎ 033/8223722), travel agents, and some hotel concierges; prices range from 12 SF to 32 SF.

Outdoor Activities and Sports

HORSEBACK RIDING

The area between Lake Thun and Lake Brienz offers a number of scenic marked bridle paths through woods, over fields, and by streams.

Guided rides and classes are available from **E. Voegeli** (⊠ Scheidg. 66, Unterseen, ☎ 033/8227416 and 079/3545289).

MOUNTAIN CLIMBING

Contact **Alpinzentrum Jungfrau** (⊠ CH-3812 Wilderswil, ☎ 033/8235523) for placement with accredited mountain guides. **Adventure World** (⊠ CH-3800 Interlaken, ☎ 033/8267711) can also assist you with guides.

SAILING

Lake Thun provides the area's most beautiful sailing. From April through mid-October, Interlaken's **Swiss Sailing School** (☎ 033/8228330) offers courses and boat rental.

TENNIS

In Interlaken, there are four outdoor courts on the **Höhematte** (☎ 033/8221472). Three outdoor and four indoor courts are maintained at **Tennis- und Sportcenter Interlaken** (⊠ Behind the Grand Hotel Victoria-Jungfrau, ☎ 033/8260000).

Shopping

An excellent central source for handicrafts and goods typical of the region as well as throughout Switzerland is **Heimatwerk** (☎ 033/8221653), on Interlaken's Höheweg, past the Casino.

Bönigen

❷ *2 km (1 mi) east of Interlaken.*

With Interlaken so close, Bönigen never got a fair chance to develop into a resort town in its own right. All the better for the tourist who wants to be near the action but not exactly in it, as well as for those who like a base for excursions a bit out of the tourist crowds. This quiet lakeside village is a leisurely half-hour stroll or five-minute car or bus ride from Interlaken and offers its own quaint charm. Somehow Bönigen escaped major fires in its 750-year history so there remains a nice collection of *beschnitzten Häuser,* original wooden houses dating from the 16th to the 18th centuries. The homes are covered with elaborate carvings—curling along posts and window frames, dripping off balconies and underscoring the eaves. Arrowed signs lead you past 18 of the nicest. Many of the sightseeing boats on **Brienzersee** or Lake Brienz start or stop here, and the open expanse of lake is a welcome sight after all the narrow valleys.

Dining and Lodging

$$$$ ✕⛏ **Seiler au Lac.** Give this hotel a point for trying harder. With some
★ heavy competition down the road in Interlaken, this cheerful, personal lakefront hotel makes up for its less prestigious address with wonderful views of the lake and mountains, a genuinely friendly ambience, rigorous attention to detail, and individually designed rooms reflecting the rather novel tastes of the owners. A bathroom could have decorative tiles or perhaps a triangular mirror, or draperies could swag the head of your bed. In the same family for more than 100 years, it has kept up with the times, at the same time retaining a conservative decency. The rustic pizzeria is very popular and reasonably priced. The classier restaurant specializes in lake fish dishes. ⊠ *Am Quai 3, CH-3806,* ☎ *033/8223021,* ⅎ𝕏 *033/8223001. 45 rooms. Restaurant, bar, grill, pizzeria, lake access. AE, DC, MC, V.*

$ ⛏ **Hotel Oberländerhof.** Comfortably worn at the edges, this century-old family-run hotel next door to the Seiler au Lac (☞ *above*) is worth a second look. Ignore the need for fresh paint and the worn red linoleum. Instead, notice the carved gargoyles making faces from the woodwork, the angels looking down from the plaster ceilings, the dusty red-velvet curtains, and the central atrium, all recalling a glamorous past. The rooms are clean and up to par, some with lake views; although they don't have bathtubs, they all have showers and toilets. The service is friendly, and the café is filled with locals. ⊠ *Am Quai 1, CH-3806,* ☎ *033/8221725.* 𝔽𝔸𝕏 *033/8232866. 18 rooms. Breakfast room, café. MC, V.*

Lauterbrunnen

★ ❸ *10 km (6 mi) south of Interlaken.*

Below Interlaken the mountains seem to part like the Red Sea into the awesome, bluff-lined Lauterbrunnen Valley. Around the village of Lauterbrunnen, grassy meadows often lie in shadow, as 460-m (1,508-ft) rocky shoulders rise on either side. This tidy town of weathered chalets serves as a starting point for the region's two most spectacular excursions: to the Schilthorn and to the Jungfraujoch. Lauterbrunnen's airportlike, superefficient parking and rail terminal allows long- and short-term parking for visitors heading for Wengen, Mürren, the Jungfraujoch, or the Schilthorn. Consider choosing this valley as a home base for day trips by train, funicular, or cable, thereby saving considerably on hotel rates.

Magnificent **waterfalls** adorn the length of the Lauterbrunnen Valley, the most famous being the 300-m (984-ft) **Staubbachfälle** (Staubbach Falls) and, just beyond, the spectacular **Trümmelbachfälle** (Trümmelbach Falls), a series of seven cascades hidden deep inside rock walls at the base of the Jungfrau, which you can access by underground funicular. Approach the departure point via a pretty, creek-side walkway and brace yourself for some steep stair climbing. Be sure to bring along a light jacket—the spray can be more than refreshing in the cool Alpine air. ⊠ *Follow signs and walkway,* ☎ *033/8553232.* 🖭 *10 SF.* ☉ *Apr.– June, daily 9–6; July–Aug., daily 8–6; Sept.–Nov., daily 9–5.*

Dining and Lodging

$ ✕🏠 **Stechelberg.** At the very end of the Lauterbrunnen Valley, where the road peters out into a beautiful foot trail, this isolated old lodging offers unspoiled comforts with a hard-core local touch: heavy smoke, muddy boots, and yodeling on Saturday night. Rooms upstairs are creaky, cozy, and all wood, with balconies that open to the sound of the roaring river. In the restaurant, stick to simple sausage-and-Rösti specials; more ambitious attempts fall short. ⊠ *CH-3824,* ☎ *033/8552921,* 𝔽𝔸𝕏 *033/8554438. 16 rooms. Restaurant, café. AE, DC, MC, V.*

$ ✕🏠 **Waldrand.** If you really want to get away from it all but still take in Jungfrau/Eiger/Mönch views, drive or take the postbus up a narrow, winding mountain road from Lauterbrunnen to Isenfluh, the poor man's Mürren. Its sole, tiny pension provides contemporary knotty-pine rooms and flower-lined balcony views as well as plain, hot café food downstairs. The hiking possibilities are endless. On request, the owners will pick you up at the rail station in Lauterbrunnen. ⊠ *CH-3822,* ☎ *033/8551227,* 𝔽𝔸𝕏 *033/8551392. 4 rooms. Restaurant. AE, V.*

$–$$ 🏠 **Sternen.** In Lauterbrunnen center, near the parking and rail complex, this century-old, weathered-wood hotel has rooms that show some wear, but clean, sociable public spaces, dramatic views, and low prices should make up for frayed edges. Daily rates go down the longer you stay. ⊠ *CH-3822,* ☎ *033/8551231,* 𝔽𝔸𝕏 *033/8554431. 12 rooms, 4 with bath. Restaurant, café. MC, V.*

Shopping

A good source of Lauterbrunnen lace is **Handwärch Lädeli** (⊠ Near the old schoolhouse, ☎ 033/8553551).

Mürren

★ ④ *7 km (4 mi) southwest of Lauterbrunnen, 16 km (10 mi) south of Interlaken, plus a 5-min cable-car ride from Stechelberg.*

This lofty sports mecca (elevation 1,000 m/3,280 ft) offers panoramic hiking trails in summer and unrivaled views toward the Jungfrau, the Mönch, and the Eiger. Skiers may want to settle here for daredevil year-round skiing at the top; hikers may combine staggering views and bluff-top trails with extraordinarily peaceful mountain nights. Remember that this is a car-free resort.

Mürren is one of the stops along the popular cable-car ride up the south side of the **Schilthorn** (2,970 m/9,742 ft), famed for its role in the James Bond thriller, *On Her Majesty's Secret Service*. The peak of this icy Goliath is accessed by a four-stage cable-lift ride past bare rock cliffs and stunning slopes. At each level, you step off the cable car, walk across the station, and wait briefly for the next cable car up. At the top is a revolving restaurant, Piz Gloria. The cable-car station that accesses the Schilthorn actually has its base in nearby Stechelberg, near the site of the **Mürrenbachfälle** (Mürrenbach Falls), which at 250 m (820 ft) are among the tallest in Europe. ☎ 033/8562141. ⌨ *Round-trip cable car Stechelberg–Schilthorn 83 SF (64 SF between 7:25 AM and 8:55 AM); for funicular/cogwheel alternative.* ☉ *Departures daily year-round, twice hourly 6:25 AM–11:25 PM; last departure from the top 6:03 PM in summer, 5:03 PM in winter.*

If you can't stomach (or afford) the route via cable car, you may approach Mürren by funicular out of Lauterbrunnen's train station, then connect by cogwheel rail from Grütschalp, following the track along the run of the cliff and looking toward magnificent views of the Big Three. The whole trip takes about 30 minutes and drops you at the Mürren rail station, at the opposite end of town from the cable-car stop. The trains run every 15–20 minutes, and they're much cheaper than the cable car. If you're not settling in to stay in a Mürren hotel, this is an ideal takeoff point for a day hike along the bluff top. Point your binoculars at the gleaming dome on the Jungfraujoch across the valley: You can almost hear the winds howling off the Aletsch Glacier.

Skiing

Mürren provides access to the **Schilthorn** (2,970 m/9,742 ft)—the start of a 15-km (9-mi) run that drops all the way through Mürren to Lauterbrunnen. At 1,650 m (5,413 ft), the resort has one funicular railway, two cable cars, seven lifts, and 65 km (40 mi) of downhill runs. A one-day pass covering the Schilthorn region costs 50 SF; a seven-day pass costs 216 SF.

Lodging

$$ 🏠 **Alpenblick.** This simple, comfortable, modern pension is in a spectacular setting and has balconies with astonishing views. Friendly owners (and their good home cooking) round out the experience. It's just beyond the center, near the train (not the cable-car) station, so you may choose to take the funicular up if you have loads of luggage. ⊠ CH-3825, ☎ 033/8551327, ⅜ 033/8551391. *14 rooms. Restaurant, café. AE, MC, V.*

$$ 🏠 **Bellevue-Crystal.** Distinguished from surrounding chalets by its sturdy brick-and-shutter construction, this older landmark presents itself as a traditional ski lodge with full modern comforts. Each room has a tiny balcony with fine views, and the decor is fresh pine and ging-ham. ⊠ *CH-3825,* ☎ *033/8551401,* ℻ *033/8551490. 15 rooms. Restaurant, café, sauna. MC, V.*

Jungfraujoch

★ **⑤** *½-day cog-railway excursion out of Interlaken, Lauterbrunnen, or Grindelwald.*

The granddaddy of all high-altitude excursions, the famous journey to the Jungfraujoch, site of the highest railroad station in the world, is one of the most popular tourist goals in Switzerland. From the station at Lauterbrunnen you take the green cogwheel Wengernalp Railway nearly straight up the wooded mountainside as the valley and the village shrink below. From the hilltop resort of **Wengen** (☞ *below*) the train climbs up steep grassy slopes past the timberline to **Kleine Scheidegg,** a tiny, isolated resort settlement surrounded by vertiginous scenery. Here you change to the **Jungfraubahn,** which tunnels straight into the rock of the Eiger, stopping briefly for views out enormous picture windows blasted through its stony face.

The **Jungfraujoch terminus** stands at an elevation of 3,475 m (11,400 ft); you may feel a bit light-headed from the altitude. Follow signs to the **Top of Europe** restaurant, a gleaming white glass-and-steel pavilion. The expanse of rock and ice you see from here is simply blinding.

If you're not sated with the staggering views from the Jungfraujoch terminus, you can reach yet another height by riding a high-tech 90-second elevator up 111 m (364 ft) to the **Sphinx Terrace:** To the south crawls the vast Aletsch Glacier, to the northeast stand the Mönch and the Eiger, and to the southwest—almost close enough to touch—towers the tip of the Jungfrau herself. Note: Even in low season, you may have to wait in long lines for the elevator up.

More than views are offered to the hordes that mount the Jungfraujoch daily. You can take a beginner's **ski lesson** or a **dogsled ride,** or tour the chill blue depths of the **Ice Palace,** a novelty attraction on the order of a wax museum, full of incongruous and slightly soggy ice sculptures. Admission is included in the price of the excursion (the ski lessons and dogsled rides cost extra).

A few things to keep in mind for the Jungfraujoch trip: Take sunglasses, warm clothes, and sturdy shoes; even the interior halls can be cold and slippery at the top. Return trains, especially toward the end of the day, can be standing-room only. To save money, take the 6:30 AM train. Guided tours with escort and English commentary (called Jungfrau Tour as opposed to *Jungfrau individuell*) also cost less; these leave once a day from Interlaken East. You can get to Lauterbrunnen or Grindelwald (☞ *below*) on your own steam (or using your Swiss Pass, ☞ Train Travel *in* the Gold Guide) and then buy a ticket to the top; if you've driven, of course, you'll have to return the way you came and miss the full round-trip tour. ☎ *033/8287111, 033/8287233 for Jungfrau Tour, 033/8551022 for Jungfraujoch weather information.* 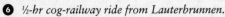 *Round-trip Interlaken East–Lauterbrunnen–Wengen–the Jungfraujoch (back via Grindelwald) 158.20 SF; 6:30 AM 119.20 SF. ☉ Daily June–Sept. 6:30 (first train up)–6:10 (last train down).*

Wengen

⑥ *½-hr cog-railway ride from Lauterbrunnen.*

This south-facing hilltop resort perched on a sunny plateau over the Lauterbrunnen Valley has magnificent panoramas down the valley toward the Breithorn. It rivals Mürren for its quiet, chic, and challenging skiing, which connects with the trail network at Grindelwald; loyalists prefer Wengen for its memorable sunsets. You can aim for central, upscale hotels, near resort shopping and active bars, or head downhill to pleasant, more isolated lodgings, all artfully skewed toward the view. It's a car-free town; most hotels have porters meeting the trains.

Skiing

Just over the ridge from Grindelwald, the sunny resort of **Wengen** (1,300 m–3,450 m/4,265 ft–11,316 ft) nestles on a sheltered plateau high above the Lauterbrunnen Valley; from there, a complex lift system connects to Grindelwald, Kleine Scheidegg, and Männlichen. Wengen has six funicular railways, one cable car, 31 lifts, and 250 km (155 mi) of downhill runs. The Lauberhorn run is tough; it's often used for skiing competitions.

Lodging

$$$ 🏨 **Beausite Park Hotel.** As Wengen's only grand hotel, the Beausite Park
★ has spacious, traditional rooms with windows overlooking the town and the valley below. Service is efficient and geared more toward couples than families: Pampering is encouraged. A 10-minute walk from the village, the hotel is near the cable-car station. ⊠ CH-3823, ☎ 033/8565161, ᐧᐧ 033/8553010. 46 rooms, 7 apartments. Restaurant, piano bar, indoor pool, massage, sauna. AE, DC, MC, V.

$$$ 🏨 **Regina.** Guests can ski to the door of this hotel and then walk five minutes to the village center for a cup of hot chocolate. The Victorian-style decor is cozy, and every room is different. Ask for a corner room; these overlook the valley. ⊠ CH-3823, ☎ 033/8551512, ᐧᐧ 033/8551574. 96 rooms. Restaurant, bar. AE, DC, MC, V.

$$$ 🏨 **Silberhorn.** Its 19th-century origins evident only in the roofline, this all-modern resort lodge has a young, lively staff and ambience. Rooms are full of pine and chintz; the ones in the older wing are a tad bit fancier. ⊠ CH-3823, ☎ 033/8565131, ᐧᐧ 033/8552244. 70 rooms. 2 restaurants, pub, hot tub, sauna, dance club, nursery. AE, DC, MC, V.

$$–$$$ 🏨 **Alpenrose.** Run by one family for more than 100 years, this wel-
★ coming inn has fresh decor that's all knotty pine and painted wood. Rooms with south-facing balconies are only slightly more expensive and worth it. It's downhill and away from the center, with an emphasis on good half-board food. The restaurant is for guests only. ⊠ CH-3823, ☎ 033/8553216, ᐧᐧ 033/8555518. 50 rooms. Restaurant. AE, DC, MC, V.

$$–$$$ 🏨 **Victoria Lauberhorn.** Since 1895, this gabled bastion of mountain
★ tourism has offered knee-buckling views to its guests—especially those paying slightly more for the southern panorama that put Wengen on the map, though north and west village-and-hillside views are nothing to sniff at, either. The public spaces mix rustic with funeral-parlor swank, but the room decor has discreet regional flair with its pretty painted furniture. ⊠ CH-3823, ☎ 033/8565151, ᐧᐧ 033/8553377. 72 rooms. Restaurant, bar. AE, DC, MC, V.

$–$$ 🏨 **Bären.** This lodging just past the center is straightforward and modern, with good views and low rates. Each balcony room has a bath and toilet; others have only running water. There are a pleasant terrace café and a good family restaurant. For cheap sleeps (about 35 SF, including breakfast), you can stay in one of the two dormitory-style rooms, each with 10 beds. ⊠ CH-3823, ☎ 033/8551419, ᐧᐧ 033/8551525. 14 rooms. Restaurant, café. AE, DC, MC, V.

$–$$ 🏨 **Eden/Eddy's Hostel.** A shingled, Victorian jewel box joins forces with an unpretentious crash pad—the Eden Hotel providing marvelous southern views, rooms with or without bathrooms, and pretty gardens and a terrace, and Eddy's Hostel providing a no-frills bed, a shower, and a breakfast buffet across the street at the Eden. There are plenty of occasions to mix at barbecues, over aperitifs on the terrace or stone-grilled meats in the restaurant, or at one of many live music events. ⊠ *CH-3823,* ☎ *033/8551634,* FAX *033/8553950. 18 rooms, 6 dorms. Restaurant, café. AE, DC, MC, V.*

$–$$ 🔲 **Schweizerheim.** It's worth the hike to this old-fashioned family-run
★ pension nestled well below the beaten path: The full-valley views are flawless, the gardens pristine, and the terrace picnic tables balance precariously over the Lauterbrunnen Valley. The good restaurant, once frequented by locals, now serves pension guests only. ⊠ *CH-3823,* ☎ *033/8551112,* FAX *033/8552327. 24 rooms. Restaurant. MC, V.*

Outdoor Activities and Sports

SKATING

Wengen has a natural **rink** (Natureisbahn) and a partially sheltered indoor rink (Kunsteisbahn); for hours, contact the tourist office (☎ 033/8551414).

TENNIS

Five **public courts** are available for rental through the tourist office (☎ 033/8551414).

Nightlife and the Arts

DANCING

You can dance at **Club Anonym** (⊠ Hotel Silberhorn, ☎ 033/8565131); it's closed Sunday. If you'd like to look at something besides pretty people, try **Carousel** at the Regina hotel (☞ *above*), which has a beautiful view.

Grindelwald

➐ *27 km (17 mi) east of Interlaken.*

Strung along a mountain highway with two convenient train stations, Grindelwald (1,050 m/3,445 ft) is the most easily accessible of the region's high resorts. It makes an excellent base for skiing and hiking, shopping and dining—if you don't mind a little traffic.

★ From Grindelwald you can drive, take a postbus, or hike up to the **Obererigletscher,** a craggy, steel-blue glacier. You can admire its icy grandness from a distance while comfortably seated at the Hotel Wetterhorn's outdoor café (☞ Dining and Lodging, *below*), or approach at the base along wooded trails. There's an instrument at the base to measure the glacier's daily movement.

Also out of Grindelwald, you can take the **Firstbahn,** a 30-minute gondola ride to the lovely views and pistes of the **First** ski area (2,163 m/7,095 ft). The **Alpine garden** flourishes within easy walking distance (it's even wheelchair accessible) of the first cable car. Without hiking into the heights, you can see gentians, edelweiss, anemones, and Alpine asters in their natural habitat.

Skiing

An ideal base camp for the Jungfrau ski area, Grindelwald (1,050 m/3,445 ft) provides access to the varied trails of Grindelwald First and Kleine Scheidegg/Männlichen. Grindelwald has eight funicular railways, three cable cars, 22 lifts, and 165 km (103 mi) of downhill runs. Some long runs go right down to the village; there are special areas for snowboarders and beginning skiers.

Dining and Lodging

$ ✕ **Onkel Tom's Hütte.** With all the upscale hotels and restaurants avail-
★ able in this resort town, it's a nice change of pace to eat someplace sim-

ple. This tiny, smoke-free pizza parlor, set in a rustic A-frame cabin on the main drag, is as cozy as they come. Rough wooden floors accommodate ski boots, and eight wooden tables share space with a huge iron cookstove, where the young owner produces fresh pizzas in three sizes (the smallest of which is plenty for a normal appetite!). There are also generous salads, homemade desserts, and a surprisingly large international wine list. Its popularity outstrips its size, so enjoy the good kitchen smells while you wait. ⊠ *Across from the Firstbahn,* ☎ *033/ 8535239. MC, V. Closed Nov.*

$$$$ ✕⊡ **Belvedere.** As you wind your way into Grindelwald, this large, ★ pink structure, precariously perched above the road, comes into view. Rustic styling has given way to tastefully designed interiors; the Salon Louis Phillippe is a particularly pleasant place to relax, with its period furniture and wood-inlay games tables. There are drop-dead views of the Eiger and surrounding peaks from almost every room. The staff and management radiate genuine warmth and absolute professionalism; the owner is an active outdoorsman and takes groups of guests skiing, hiking, and golfing weekly. The restaurant offers fresh, creative menus that change according to the delicious whims of their trusted chef. ⊠ *CH-3818,* ☎ *033/8545454,* ℻ *033/8535323. 51 rooms. Restaurant, stübli, piano bar, indoor pool, hot tub, 2 saunas, exercise room, playroom. AE, DC, MC, V. Closed Nov.*

$$$$ ✕⊡ **Schweizerhof.** Behind a dark-wood Victorian chalet facade dat- ★ ing from 1892, this big, comfortable, homelike hotel has attracted a loyal clientele for more than 30 years. Wingbacks and bookcases in the lobby lounge and dining rooms—of scrubbed pine and hand-painted (and carved) trim—are inviting on rainy days. Rooms are decorated in cozy carved pine and have tile baths, along with luxurious bathrobes. The emphasis here is on demipension (half board), and the generous nightly smorgasbord includes entrée, soup, meat course from an open grill, salad (grown in the hotel's own garden), cheese, and fruit; the breakfasts are big, too. The à la carte Schmitte stübli is lovely for fondue. Reserve well in advance and keep in mind that there's a slight surcharge for stays of less than three nights. ⊠ *CH-3818,* ☎ *033/ 8532202,* ℻ *033/8532004. 53 rooms. Restaurant, stübli, indoor pool, beauty salon, sauna, bowling, health club. AE, MC, V.*

$$–$$$ ✕⊡ **Fiescherblick.** This is the place to eat in Grindelwald, whether as ★ a pension hotel guest or day-tripper: The serious cuisine in the intimate restaurant continues to draw kudos and devoted food lovers, and the low-priced Swiss Bistro in the adjoining bar allows casual lunchers to enjoy the talents of the same chef. Sample *tête de veau bouilli* (a rugged head-scrap stew with vinaigrette), Rösti with farm cheese and chives, wild garlic sausage with onion sauce, or veal *geschnetzeltes* (finely sliced veal in wine-and-mushroom cream sauce). The fresh pine decor carries into the guest rooms, too. ⊠ *CH-3818,* ☎ *033/8534453,* ℻ *033/8534457. 25 rooms. Restaurant, stübli. AE, DC, MC, V.*

$–$$ ✕⊡ **Hotel Wetterhorn.** Overlooking the magnificent ice-blue upper glacier—as well as the sprawling parking lot where hikers leave their cars—this modest inn offers generous lunches outdoors, with full glacier views, and good regional dining inside its comfortable restaurant. Portions of veal favorites are large and delicious, and there is a good selection of Swiss wines. The adjoining Gletscherstübli attracts locals as well as the hordes of tourists and hikers who come to marvel at its namesake. Up the creaky old stairs, there are simple aged-pine rooms—some have glacier views—with sink and shared bath. They have renovated the neighboring farmhouse and chalet into four vacation apartments. ⊠ *CH-3818,* ☎ *033/8531218,* ℻ *033/8535818. 9 rooms. Restaurant, café, stübli. AE, DC, MC, V.*

$$$$ 🏨 **Regina.** Although its turreted exterior dates from the turn of the century, Grindelwald's pricey establishment became a hotel in 1953 and exudes '50s glamour; its spare beige-and-avocado sprawl is packed with a boggling array of wing chairs, Baroque antiques, and Swiss kitsch, all from the founder's collection. The views are flawless, the location central, and the tennis courts may be the most spectacularly sited in the world. ⊠ *CH-3818,* ☎ *033/8545455 or 800/2236800,* 📠 *033/8534717. 100 rooms. Restaurant, indoor pool, pool, beauty salon, massage, sauna, 2 tennis courts, nightclub. AE, DC, MC, V.*

$$$ 🏨 **Gletschergarten.** In the same family for three generations, this atmospheric pension radiates welcome, from the heirloom furniture and paintings (by the grandfather) to the tea roses cut from the owner's garden. There's heraldry in the stained-glass windows, a ceramic stove with built-in seat warmer, and every amenity, including a piano, a solarium, and a ski-drying room. All rooms have balconies, some with glacier views, others overlooking the emerald green hills. Refined home cooking is served to guests only; demipension is de rigueur. ⊠ *CH-3818,* ☎ *033/8531721,* 📠 *033/8532957. 26 rooms. Restaurant, bar, sauna, steam room, Ping-Pong, billiards, coin laundry. MC, V.*

$$–$$$ 🏨 **Alpina.** The cinder-block construction of this vacation lodging, built in 1973, is stone cold to all appearances. But its lofty perch makes for sensational views from its front balconies—and the edges are softened within and without by parlor-plush public areas, geraniums below every window, and warm, personal service. Tile bathrooms, most with showers, accompany no-nonsense rooms. It's a five-minute walk straight uphill from the station. ⊠ *CH-3818,* ☎ *033/8533333,* 📠 *033/8533376. 30 rooms. Restaurant. AE, DC, MC, V.*

$ 🏨 **Säumertaverne.** Outside Gündlischwand, in the forested gorge be-
★   tween Interlaken and Grindelwald, you'll find an impeccable little country inn, with rustic room decor (painted cabinetry, farm implements), modern baths, forest and valley views, and cowbells *thunking* outside the windows. A sunny terrace café and a comfortable family restaurant offer cheese specialties. It's convenient only if you're traveling by car. ⊠ *CH-3815,* ☎ *033/8553276,* 📠 *033/8552351. 9 rooms. Restaurant, café. MC, V.*

Nightlife and the Arts

DANCING

Challi Bar (☎ 033/8545492) in the Hotel Kreuz has a DJ who plays requests. The **Plaza Club** (⊠ Sunstar Hotel, ☎ 033/8534240) is a Swiss self-styled "ethno disco," which plays off the stereotypical Swiss images of cows, cheese, and mountains, although the music is strictly modern (no yodeling here). There's also the **Regina Bar-Dancing** (⊠ Grand Hotel Regina, ☎ 033/8545455).

Outdoor Activities and Sports

MOUNTAIN CLIMBING

The **Bergsteigerzentrum** (⊠ Grindelwald center, ☎ 033/8535200) offers daily and weekly courses to mountain and glacier hikers.

SKATING

The **Sportzentrum Grindelwald** (☎ 033/8541212) has indoor and natural rinks.

TENNIS

Grindelwald has six **public courts;** for permits, call the tourist office (☎ 033/8541212).

BRIENZERSEE

Reputedly the cleanest lake in Switzerland—which surely means one of the cleanest in the world—this magnificent bowl of crystal-clear water mirrors the mountain-scape and forests, cliffs, and waterfalls that surround it. You can cruise alongside Lake Brienz at high speed on the A8 freeway or crawl along its edge on secondary waterfront roads; or you can cut a wake across it on a steamer, gliding quietly from port to port, exploring each stop on foot, then cruising to your next destination.

Iseltwald

❽ *9 km (6 mi) northeast of Interlaken.*

This isolated peninsula juts out into the lake, its small hotels, cafés, and rental chalets clustered at the water's edge. Every restaurant prides itself on its lake fish, of course. From the village edge, you may want to take off on foot; a lovely forest walk of about 1½ hours brings you to the falls of the **Giessbach** (Giess Brook), which tumbles in several stages down through the rocky cliffs to the lake. The most scenic route to Iseltwald from Interlaken is via the south-shore road; follow the black-and-white ISELTWALD signs. You can also take the A8 expressway, following the autoroute signs for Meiringen.

Brienz

★ **❾** *12 km (7 mi) northeast of Iseltwald, 21 km (13 mi) northeast of Interlaken.*

The romantic waterfront village of Brienz, world renowned as a wood-carving center, is a favorite stop for boat tourists as well as drivers. Several artisan shops display the local wares, which range in quality from the ubiquitous, winningly simple figures of spotted cows to finely modeled nativity figures and Hummel-like portraits of William Tell. Brienz is also a showcase of traditional Oberland architecture, with some of its loveliest houses (at the west end of town, near the church) dating from the 17th century. Once an important stage stop, Brienz hosted Goethe and Byron at its landmark Hotel Weisses Kreuz (☞ Dining and Lodging, *below*); their names, along with the 1688 date of construction, are proudly displayed on the gable.

At Brienz you may want to try your own hand at wood carving: In one lesson at the atelier of **Paul Fuchs** you can learn to carve the typical Brienzer cow. Make a reservation through the tourist office in Brienz or directly with Mr. Fuchs. ⊠ *Scheidweg 19D, in Hofstetten, between Brienz and Ballenberg,* ☎ *033/9511418.* ⊡ *18 SF.* ☉ *2-hr workshops Apr.–Oct., Thurs. 6:15 PM.*

Switzerland's last steam-driven cogwheel train runs from the center of Brienz, at the waterfront, up to the summit of **Brienzer-Rothorn,** 2,346 m (7,700 ft) above the town. Trains run at least every hour, but to avoid long waits at peak times, purchase your ticket for a particular train in advance on the day you will make the trip; they do not accept reservations. ☎ *033/9514400.* ⊡ *64 SF round-trip.* ☉ *Daily June–Oct.*

OFF THE
BEATEN PATH
☼ **FREILICHTMUSEUM BALLENBERG –** Just east of Brienz, a small road leads to this child-friendly, outdoor museum-park, where 80 characteristic Swiss houses from 18 cantons have been carefully dismantled and transported to the site. Linen weaving, basket making, and baking are demonstrated. ⊠ *CH-3855,* ☎ *033/9511123.* ⊡ *14 SF.* ☉ *Mid-Apr.–Oct., daily 10–5.*

Dining and Lodging

$–$$ ✗ **Steinbock.** Whether you dine on the broad flower-lined terrace or
★   inside the wonderful old (1787) carved-wood-and-homespun chalet,
you'll feel the atmosphere of this proud local institution. Choose from
no fewer than nine interpretations of Lake Brienz whitefish, regional
pastas, or veal classics. ✉ *Hauptstr. 123, CH-3855,* ☎ *033/9514055.
AE, DC, MC, V. Closed Tues. and Feb.*

$$ ✗🖿 **Hotel Weisses Kreuz.** Generic modern improvements have erased
some of the fine origins of this structure, built in 1688 and host to Goethe
and Byron, but the current version has a tidy, cozy charm of its own.
The location is across the highway from the waterfront, close to
Rothorn Railway excursion crowds. But if you are a history buff, the
idea of its antiquity and the hallowed names on the gable may be al-
lure enough, and the woody stübli draws loyal locals for a chat and a
daily paper. The pine and homespun-linen restaurant offers omelets and
Käseschnitte (cheese and bread baked in its own whey) as well as lake
fish, steaks, and strudel. Some rooms have lake views, and the sunny
lake-view terrace café draws locals as well as tourists fresh off the boat.
✉ *Hauptstr. 143, CH-3855,* ☎ *033/9511781,* FAX *033/9514117. 14
rooms. Restaurant. AE, DC, MC, V. Closed mid-Nov.–mid-Dec.*

$$ ✗🖿 **Lindenhof.** In a 1787 lodge high above the touristy lakefront, dis-
★   cerning German and Austrian families settle in for a week or two of
evenings by the vast stone fireplace, dinners in the panoramic winter
garden (or on the spectacular terrace), and nights in dressed-up theme
rooms with such evocative names as Marmot Cave and Hunter's Hut.
The grounds are vast and beautifully manicured, the atmosphere familial and formal at once. Families with small children dine together
by the fire, apart from other guests. ✉ *Lindenhofweg 15, CH-3855,*
☎ *033/9511072,* FAX *033/9514072. 40 rooms, 4 suites. Restaurant, bar,
café, kitchenettes, indoor pool, sauna. AE, MC, V.*

$$ 🖿 **Schönegg und Spycher.** Clinging to a steep, garden-covered hillside
★   over town, this tidy little pension is run by house-proud Christine Math-
yer, who sees to it that all three small lodgings maintain their old-fash-
ioned charm. There's a 1957 fireplace lounge, with flagstone floors and
wood carvings, and rooms with rustic painted furniture, flower-sprigged
duvets, checked bedspreads, and chocolates on the pillow at night. Guests
can play Ping-Pong and lounge in the sunny garden overlooking the
lake, and it's an easy walk up to the Lindenhof or down to the Stein-
bock (☞ *above*) for dinner. ✉ *Talstr. 8, CH-3855,* ☎ *033/9511113.*
FAX *033/9513813. 16 rooms. Bar, breakfast room, Ping-Pong. MC, V.*

$$ 🖿 **Seehotel Bären.** The modern construction and 1960s room decor
are upstaged by the gracious dining room, flower-framed terrace café,
and private waterfront promenade. Lakeside rooms, which have serene
water views, are considerably pricier in high season; back rooms open
over the main road. A small beach gives access to the crystalline water.
✉ *Hauptstr. 72, CH-3855,* ☎ *033/9512412,* FAX *033/9514022. 32
rooms. Restaurant, café, lake, beach. AE, DC, MC, V.*

Shopping

Brienz is the place for good selections of local wood carvings. **Ed Jobin**
(✉ Hauptstr. 111, ☎ 033/9511414) has traditional carvings from
model cows to wall plaques. **H. Huggler-Wyss** (✉ Fischerbrunnenpl.,
☎ 033/9511679) is another worthwhile source.

Meiringen

⓾   *12 km (7 mi) east of Brienz, 35 km (22 mi) northeast of Interlaken.*

Set apart from the twinned lakes and saddled between the roads to the
Sustenpass and the Brünigpass, Meiringen is a resort town with 300

km (186 mi) of marked hiking trails and 60 km (37 mi) of ski slopes. Its real claim to fame, though, is **Reichenbachfälle** (Reichenbach Falls), where fictional detective Sherlock Holmes and his archenemy Professor Moriarty plunged into the "cauldron of swirling water and seething foam in that bottomless abyss above Meiringen." Visitors can now view the dramatic fall where Conan Doyle intended to end his series of mysteries. A nearby hotel bears the detective's name, and in the center of town, the **Sherlock Holmes Museum** has created an "authentic" replica of Holmes's front room at 221b Baker Street. ⊠ *Bahnhofstr. 26,* ☎ *033/9714221.* ⊡ *3.80 SF.* ☉ *May–Sept., Mon.–Tues. 1:30–6, Wed.– Sun. 3–6; Oct.–Apr., Wed.–Sun. 3–6.*

Dining and Lodging

$$ ✕⊡ **Sporthotel Sherlock Holmes.** This sports-oriented hotel is ideal for hikers and skiers. Though the building is modern and unspectacular, most rooms look out on Reichenbach Falls. Rooms are functional and simple, but wood cabinetry gives them a cozy, Alpine feel. The restaurant serves wholesome Swiss food. ⊠ *Alpbachallee 3, CH-3860,* ☎ *033/9729889,* 𝔽𝔸𝕏 *033/9729888. 60 rooms. Restaurant, indoor pool, sauna, health club, Ping-Pong, billiards. AE, MC, V.*

Outdoor Activities and Sports

HIKING

The private, 20-km (12½-mi) **road to Grindelwald** permits no cars but provides a beautiful, seven-hour Alpine hike. For maps of other local hiking trails, hit the tourist office (☞ Visitor Information *in* Berner Oberland A to Z, *below*).

THUNERSEE

If you like your mountains as a picturesque backdrop and prefer a relaxing waterfront sojourn, take a drive around the Thunersee (Lake Thun)—or crisscross it on a leisurely cruise boat. More populous than Lake Brienz, its allurements include the marina town of Spiez and the large market town of Thun, spread at the feet of the spectacular Schloss Zähringen (Zähringen Castle). There are more castles along the lake, and yet another high-altitude excursion for rising above the waterfront to take in Alpine panoramas—a trip up the Niederhorn.

Spiez

🄫 *19 km (11¾ mi) west of Interlaken.*

The town of Spiez is a summer lake resort with marinas for water-sports enthusiasts. Its enormous waterfront castle, **Schloss Spiez,** was home to the family Strättligen and, in the 13th century, its great troubadour, Heinrich. The structure spans four architectural epochs, starting with the 11th-century tower; its halls contain beautiful period furnishings, some from as long ago as Gothic times. The early Norman church on the grounds dates from the last millennium. ☎ *033/6541506.* ⊡ *4 SF.* ☉ *Apr.–June and Sept.–Oct., Tues.–Sun. 10–5, Mon. 2–5; July–Aug., daily 10–6.*

Dining and Lodging

$$–$$$ ✕⊡ **Seegarten Hotel Marina.** With a pizzeria corner in one wing and two dining rooms that stretch comfortably along the marina front, this is a pleasant, modern family restaurant, and its lake fish specialties are excellent, served in generous portions. The Spiez castle looms directly behind you, unfortunately out of sight. The rooms upstairs are spare and modern. ⊠ *Schachenstr. 3, CH-3700,* ☎ *033/6556767,* 𝔽𝔸𝕏 *033/ 6556765. 42 rooms. Restaurant, bar, café, pizzeria. AE, DC, MC, V.*

$$$$ ⌘ **Strandhotel Belvedere.** A member of the Hotel Suisse Silence chain, this graceful old mansion-hotel has beautiful lawns and gardens, and its manicured waterfront on Lake Thun offers secluded swimming. The decor hearkens back a few decades; rooms are done in blue and old rose, with canopy beds. Corner and lakeside rooms are worth the higher price. Guests have free access to the city's heated outdoor pool, 100 m (328 ft) away. ✉ *Schachenstr. 39, CH-3700,* ☎ *033/6543333,* FAX *033/6546633. 30 rooms. Restaurant, beach. AE, DC, MC, V. Closed Oct.–Mar.*

Outdoor Activities and Sports
TENNIS AND SWIMMING

Spiez has municipal tennis courts at the bay, by the municipal pool (☎ 033/6544917).

Thun

⑫ *10 km (6 mi) north of Spiez, 29 km (18 mi) northwest of Interlaken.*

Built along an island on the River Aare as it leaves Lake Thun, the picturesque market town of Thun is laced with rushing streams crossed by wooden bridges, and its streets are lined with arcades. The main shopping thoroughfare of the Old Town may be unique in the world: Pedestrians stroll along flowered terrace sidewalks built on the roofs of the stores' first floors and climb down stone stairs to visit the "sunken" street-level shops.

From the charming medieval Rathausplatz (Rathaus Square), a cov-
★ ered stair leads up to the great **Schloss Zähringen** (Zähringen Castle), its broad donjon cornered by four stout turrets. Built in 1191 by Berchtold V, duke of Zähringen, it houses a fine **historical museum** and provides magnificent views from its towers. In the **knights' hall** are a grand fireplace, an intimidating assortment of medieval weapons, and tapestries, one from the tent of Charles the Bold. Other floors display local Steffisburg and Heimberg ceramics, 19th-century uniforms and arms, and Swiss household objects, including charming Victorian toys. ✉ *Rathauspl.,* ☎ *033/2232001.* ⊞ *5 SF.* ☽ *Apr.–May and Oct., daily 10–5; June–Sept., daily 9–6; Feb., daily 1–4.*

Dining and Lodging
$$ ✕⌘ **Krone.** Positioned directly on the lovely Rathausplatz in the Old Town, this landmark has some fine bay-window tower rooms and river views. Despite its historic setting and classic exterior, the slick new interior is tile-and-wood modern. The Chinese restaurant, Wong-Kun, has a cross-cultural menu, and an upscale bistro whips up chic versions of regional dishes. ✉ *Ob. Hauptg. 2, CH-3600,* ☎ *033/2228888,* FAX *033/2278890. 27 rooms. 2 restaurants. AE, MC, V.*

$ ✕⌘ **Zu Metzgern.** This grand old shuttered and arcaded *Zunfthaus* (guild house), at the base of the castle hill, provides fresh pastel rooms (bathrooms down the hall) with Rathausplatz views. There's atmospheric dining, too, whether in the wood-and-linen restaurant or on the intimate little terrace, tucked behind an ivy-covered trellis. It's ideally placed for a castle climb and Old Town shopping and touring. ✉ *Untere Hauptg. 2, CH-3600,* ☎ *033/2222141,* FAX *033/2222182. 8 rooms. Restaurant, café. MC, V.*

Shopping
A Thun branch of **Heimatwerk** (✉ Ob. Hauptg. 66, ☎ 033/2223441) offers a wide variety of Swiss handicrafts—good pottery, fine embroidery, music boxes, pressed flowers. Swiss Army knives, linens, and general gifts are also widely available. A good spot for traditional and artisan pottery in Thun is **Töpferhaus** (✉ Ob. Hauptg. 3, ☎ 033/2227065).

Just outside Thun in Heimberg, the **Museum Hänn** (✉ Bahnhofstr. 4, ☎ 033/4381242) demonstrates and displays its traditional ceramic work, as it has since 1731.

Hilterfingen

⑬ *4 km (2½ mi) southeast of Thun, 18 km (11 mi) northwest of Interlaken.*

Hilterfingen's castle, **Schloss Hünegg** (Hünegg Castle), was built in 1861 and furnished over the years with a bent toward Jugendstil and Art Nouveau. The stunning interiors have remained unchanged since 1900 and give a good look at how opulent 19th-century castle life was. ✉ *Staatsstr.*, ☎ *033/2431982.* 🎫 *4 SF.* ☉ *Mid-May–mid-Oct., Mon.– Sat. 2–5, Sun. 10–noon and 2–5.*

Oberhofen

⑭ *2 km (1 mi) southeast of Hilterfingen, 16 km (10 mi) northwest of Interlaken.*

Oberhofen is topped with its own **Schloss Oberhofen** (Oberhofen Castle), this one a hodgepodge of towers and spires on the waterfront. Begun during the 12th century, it was repeatedly altered over a span of 700 years. Inside, a historical museum has a display on the lifestyle of Bernese nobility. ☎ *033/2431235.* 🎫 *4 SF.* ☉ *Mid-May–mid-Oct., Tues.–Sun. 10–noon and 2–5, Mon. 2–5.*

OFF THE BEATEN PATH

NIEDERHORN – Thirteen km (8 mi) east of Oberhofen, the town of Beatenbucht has a shore terminal that sends funiculars to Beatenberg daily in high season. From there you can either walk up a trail or catch a chairlift to the Niederhorn (1,919 m/6,294 ft), from which an astonishing panorama unfolds: Lake Thun and Lake Brienz, the Jungfrau, and even, on a fine day, Mont Blanc.

ST-BEATUSHÖHLEN – Just west of Beatenberg, the illuminated St-Beatushöhlen caves have been heavily developed, complete with a wax figure of Irish missionary St. Beatus himself, isolated in his cell as he was during the 6th century. This is less a center for pilgrimage than a simple cave tour with stalactites and stalagmites in dripping grottoes. 🎫 *12 SF.* ☉ *Apr.–Oct., daily 9:30–5:30. Guided tours every 30 mins.*

KANDER VALLEY

Easily reached by car or the Lötschberg rail line from Interlaken via Spiez, the spectacular, high-altitude Kander Valley leads up from Lake Thun toward Kandersteg, an isolated resort strewn across a level plateau. From Kandersteg, you can make a hiker's pilgrimage to the silty blue Oeschinensee. And en route to the lakes below, you may want to visit the touristy but pleasant Blausee.

Kandersteg

⑮ *45 km (28 mi) southwest of Interlaken.*

At 1,176 m (3,858 ft), Kandersteg stands alone, a quiet resort spread across a surprisingly broad, level—and thus walkable—plateau. Lofty bluffs, waterfalls, and peaks—including the **Blümlisalp**, at 3,664 m (12,018 ft), and the **Doldenhorn**, at 3,643 m (11,949 ft)—surround the plateau, and at the end of its 4-km (2½-mi) stretch, the valley road ends abruptly.

Exploration above Kandersteg must be accomplished by cable or on foot, unless (depending on Swiss army training schedules and weather) you find the tiny paved road into the magnificent **Gastern Valley** open: Carved into raw rock, portions of the road are so narrow that cars must take turns coming and going. You can usually call the local tourist office (☞ Visitor Information *in* Berner Oberland A to Z, *below*) to see if the road is passable.

Don't miss the **Oeschinensee,** an isolated, austere bowl of glacial silt at 1,578 m (5,176 ft); from Kandersteg you can walk there in about 1½ hours, and it's also accessible by chairlift to the Oeschinen station, with a downhill walk of approximately 30 minutes through peak-ringed meadowlands. You also may choose to hike back down to Kandersteg from the Oeschinensee, but be prepared for the severe downhill grade. Less ambitious hikers can circle back to the chairlift at the end of a relatively level walk.

Although it's a dead-end valley for cars confining themselves to Berner Oberland, Kandersteg is the source of one of Switzerland's more novel modes of transit: the rail-ferry tunnel through the **Lötschenberg.** After driving your car onto a low-slung railcar, you will be swept along piggyback through a dark and airless tunnel to Goppenstein, at the east end of the Valais region (☞ Chapter 11). Travel time is 15 minutes; the cost is 25 SF.

Dining and Lodging

$$ ✕🏨 **Ruedihus.** This beautifully, painstakingly restored all-wood chalet,
★ set in a meadow beyond the village center, is one of the best hotels to open in Switzerland in years. With bulging lead-glass windows, authentically low ceilings and doors (watch your head), and raw, aged woodwork throughout, it re-creates the atmosphere of the 1753 original. Antique beds with bleached homespun linens are counterbalanced by modern baths, and every corner has its waxed cradle, pewter pitcher, or crockery bowl. Upstairs, the Biedermeier restaurant offers excellent meat specialties, but eat downstairs at least once: The Käse-und Wystuben serves nothing but Swiss products—Vaud and Valais wines, greens and sausages, and a variety of fondues. (No credit cards are accepted in the restaurants.) It's a proud, tasteful, informed effort to serve travelers in search of a true regional experience; the Maeder family, owners of the Waldhotel Doldenhorn (across the road; ☞ *below*) and this one, are the ones to thank for this. As the hotel has only nine rooms, reservations are key. ⊠ CH-3718, ☎ 033/6758182, FAX *033/6758185. 9 rooms. 2 restaurants, café. AE, DC, MC, V.*

$$–$$$ 🏨 **Waldhotel Doldenhorn.** Nestled into a forest hillside far from the
★ road through the center, this retreat—a member of the Relais du Silence group, inns specializing in peace and quiet—offers several options: large rooms with balconies and mountain views, smaller rooms opening onto the woods, or modest lodging in a separate budget chalet. The rooms gracefully combine modern and rustic styles. A cross-country ski trail starts at the hotel's door. There's a formal Swiss-French restaurant and a casual stübli, too. For those with a do-it-yourself approach, one apartment has a kitchenette. ⊠ CH-3718, ☎ 033/6758181, FAX *033/6758185. 33 rooms. Restaurant, stübli. AE, DC, MC, V.*

$ 🏨 **Edelweiss.** Built in 1903 by the current owner's grandfather, this cozy old inn has sleek, impeccable rooms and an old-fashioned atmosphere, complete with low ceilings and burnished wood. There's a comfortable checkered-cloth stübli for drinks only. The pretty garden makes you forget you're on the main road, five minutes from the train station. ⊠ *CH-3718,* ☎ *033/6751194. 8 rooms. Breakfast room, stübli. No credit cards.*

OFF THE
BEATEN PATH

BLAUSEE (Blue Lake) – If you're traveling with a family, you may want to visit the much-vaunted Blausee, a naturally blue pool above Frutigen. Be warned: It's privately owned and so developed, with a restaurant, boat rides, and a shop, that you may think the lake itself is artificial. Admission includes a boat ride, a visit to the trout nursery, and use of the picnic grounds. ⊠ *4 km (2½ mi) north of Kandersteg, above Frutigen,* ☏ *033/6711641.* ◪ *4.50 SF.* ☉ *Late Apr.–mid-Oct., daily 8–5.*

SIMMENTAL AND GSTAAD

Separate in spirit and terrain from the rest of Berner Oberland, this craggy forest gorge follows the Lower Simme into a region as closely allied with French-speaking Vaud as it is with its Germanic brothers. Here the world-famous winter resort of Gstaad has flexed the muscle of its famous name to link up with a handful of neighboring ski resorts, creating the almost limitless sports opportunities of the Gstaad "Super-Ski" region. From Gstaad, it's an easy day trip into the contrasting culture of Lac Léman (Lake Geneva) and the waterfront towns of Montreux and Lausanne.

En Route From Interlaken, take A8 toward Spiez, then cut west on A11 toward Gstaad. The wild forest gorges of the Simmental Valley lead you through **Zweisimmen,** the principal sporting center of the surrounding area, to the Saanenland. The total distance from Spiez is about 40 km (25 mi).

Gstaad

16 *49 km (30 mi) southwest of Spiez, 67 km (42 mi) southwest of Interlaken.*

The peak-ringed valley called the Saanenland is anchored by this, the Oberland's most glamorous resort. Linking Berner Oberland with the French-accented territory of the Pays-d'Enhaut (Highlands) of canton Vaud, Gstaad blends the two regions' natural beauty and their cultures as well, upholding such Pays-d'Enhaut folk art traditions as *papier découpé* (paper cutouts) as well as decidedly Germanic ones (cowbells, wood carvings). Even Rösti and fondue cohabit comfortably on heavy tooled-pine tables—which here are decked in delicate French-style linens.

But in Gstaad, neither local culture wins the upper hand: The folksy *gemütlichkeit* (homeyness) of the region gives way to jet-set international style, and although the architecture still tends toward weathered-wood chalets, the main street is lined with designer boutiques, which seem oddly out of context. Prince Rainier of Monaco, Julie Andrews, Roger Moore, and Elizabeth Taylor have all owned chalets in Gstaad, rubbing elbows at local watering holes, and Yehudi Menuhin founded his annual summer music festival here as well. (The Menuhin festival takes place every August, and hotels fill quickly then—as they do for the Swiss Open Tennis tournament, held here every July.)

This is a see-and-be-seen spot, with less emphasis on its plentiful but moderate skiing than on the scene—après-ski, *après*-concert, or *après*-match. The Christmas–New Year's season brings a stampede of glittering socialites to rounds of international dinner parties, balls, and elite soirees. Occasionally, the jet-setters even hit the slopes. Despite a few family-style hotels, the number of deluxe lodgings is disproportionate, and prices tend to be high, on the scale of those at Saint-Moritz. Yet Gstaad's setting defies its socialite pretensions: Richly forested slopes, scenic year-round trails, and, for the most part, stubbornly authentic chalet architecture keep it firmly anchored in tradition. The village has been car-free since fall 1997.

Skiing

Gstaad does not hesitate to call itself a "Super-Ski" region, and the claim is not far from the truth. It has become increasingly popular since the beginning of the century, both for its ideal situation at the confluence of several valleys and for the warmth of its slopes, which—at 1,100 m (3,608 ft), stay relatively toasty compared to other resorts.

Skiing in Gstaad is, in terms of numbers, the equivalent of Zermatt: 69 lifts can transport more than 50,000 skiers per hour to its network of 250 km (155 mi) of marked runs. In fact, these lifts are spread across an immense territory, 20 km (12 mi) as the crow flies, from Zweisimmen and Saint-Stefan in the east (where German is spoken, as in Gstaad) to Château-d'Oex, a Vaud town where French is spoken; to understand one another, people sometimes use English.

Gstaad's expansive area means that most of its lifts are not reachable by foot: Since parking is in short supply, public transport is the best option. The flip side is that except in very high seasons (Christmas, February, Easter) and in certain places, such as the lift for the Diablerets Glacier, or the Pillon, the crowds are not heavy, and lift-line waits are tolerable. A one-day ticket costs 50 SF; a six-day pass costs 233 SF.

Dining and Lodging

$$$$ ✕ **Chesery.** This lively late-night dining scene, complete with piano bar, manages to combine the height of upscale chic with summits of culinary excellence—all at 1,100 m (3,608 ft). Chef Robert Speth marries exotic flavors, such as ginger or mango, with market-fresh ingredients: Watch for veal and salmon in pastry with spinach, or duck in kumquat sauce. Crowds pack in, ordering dinner until 11:30 PM, so book well ahead in high season. ⊠ *Lauenenstr.,* ☎ *033/7442451. AE, DC, MC, V. Closed Mon.*

$$–$$$ ✕🏠 **Posthotel Rössli.** This comfy, modest pension-style inn, the oldest
★ inn in town, combines down-home knotty-pine decor with soigné style: Despite the mountain-cabin look, its staff and clientele are young and chic, and the café, a local-landmark watering hole, draws crowds. The restaurant, full of linens and candlelight, serves simple daily menus at reasonable prices. ⊠ *CH-3780,* ☎ *033/7484242,* FAX *033/7484243. 18 rooms. Restaurant, café. AE, DC, MC, V.*

$–$$ ✕🏠 **Gasthof Alte Post/Weissenburg.** This graceful, isolated old coach
★ stop is on the magnificent forested Simmen Valley road, about halfway between Spiez and Gstaad. Dating from 1808, it has been lovingly restored; you'll find much carved and painted wood, many antiques, and good home cooking. The back rooms look over the Simmen River. ⊠ *CH-3764 Weissenburg,* ☎ *033/7831515,* FAX *033/7831578. 10 rooms. Restaurant. AE, MC, V.*

$$$$ 🏠 **Grand Hotel Park.** A little bit of Vail comes to the Alps in this enormous modern hotel, opened in 1990 to cater to health-conscious socialites unwilling to pay Palace (☞ *below*) prices. The facilities are state of the art, right down to the antistress program and indoor saltwater pool, and treatment weeks offer an irresistible mix of glamour and virtue. The rooms, though, are far from the ultramodern crowd; flowered wallpaper, wooden furniture, and wardrobes painted with folk-arty Swiss scenes keep things down to earth. ⊠ *CH-3780,* ☎ *033/7489800,* FAX *033/7489008. 82 rooms, 11 suites. 5 restaurants, 2 bars, indoor pool, outdoor pool, beauty salon, tennis court, squash. AE, DC, MC, V. Closed late Sept.–mid-Dec. and Apr.–early June.*

$$$$
★

Palace. Towering over tiny Gstaad like Mad Ludwig's castle, this fantasyland burlesque packs a wallet-wallop. Although it cozily refers to itself as a "family pension" (albeit the largest in Switzerland), it has an indoor swimming pool with underwater music and water-jet massage, chauffeured Rolls-Royces, and oxygen cures, among other amenities. The rooms have rustic touches but are undeniably lavish; you could play hockey in the sprawling tile baths. Be prepared for the steep 15-minute walk uphill. ⊠ CH-3780, ☎ 033/7485000 or 800/2236800, FAX 033/7485001. 111 rooms. 4 restaurants, piano bar, indoor pool, outdoor pool, 2 saunas, steam room, 4 tennis courts, health club, squash, ice-skating. AE, DC, MC, V.

$$$–$$$$

Bernerhof. This modern chalet-style inn, in the center of town a half block from the station, was built on the site of an older hotel dating from 1904. The crowds of young couples, families, and singles who came during its opening season, in 1974, are still returning and stay in touch by means of the hotel's newsletter. It's simple, solid, and surprisingly cozy, with tile baths, lots of natural pine, and a balcony for every room. There are good play facilities for children. Though considerably lower than those at the Grand Hotel Park (☞ above), prices remain very expensive by Berner Oberland standards. Homemade pasta is the highlight of the restaurant, and local and Asian dishes are served in the café. ⊠ CH-3780, ☎ 033/7488844, FAX 033/7488840. 42 rooms. 3 restaurants, café, indoor pool, sauna, health club. AE, DC, MC, V.

$$$–$$$$
★

Olden. In the middle of downtown, this charming Victorian inn has artisan woodwork in every niche and an air of cozy-chic. The rooms are fresh, folksy, and atmospheric but have slick, modern baths. The adjoining chalet wing, slightly pricier, is lovely; the views from the pretty dormer window in Room 39 are worth a special request. See and be seen at the sidewalk café. ⊠ CH-3780, ☎ 033/7443444, FAX 033/7446164. 15 rooms. 3 restaurants, café. AE, DC, MC, V.

Outdoor Activities and Sports

GOLF

Gstaad-Saanenland (☎ 030/7442636) in Saanenmöser, a little past Schönried on Route 11, has 18 holes in an idyllic setting.

HORSEBACK RIDING

In Gstaad, the **M. J. Lieber Reitzentrum** (☎ 030/7442460) offers guided outings for experienced riders only.

MOUNTAIN CLIMBING

Great day climbs can be had from Gstaad. **Alpinzentrum Gstaad** (☎ 033/7274006) can supply you with mountain guides and snow-sports teachers. **Experience Gstaad** (☎ 033/7448800) is the place to go for guides for off-trail skiing, ice climbing, and snowshoe trekking. **Beats Adventure** (☎ 033/7441521) aims its tough sport excursions at very fit people.

TENNIS

Gstaad Tennishalle (☎ 033/7441090) has three indoor and two outdoor courts.

Nightlife and the Arts

CONCERTS

The **Gstaad Musiksommer** brings violinist and conductor Yehudi Menuhin to the Alps to head a summer music school and lead a few world-class concerts. After his departure, the concerts continue as part of the **Alpengala.** To reserve seats in advance, write to the **Festivalbüroxx** (⊠ Verkehrsverein, CH-3780 Gstaad, ☎ 033/7488338). Information on the next summer's programs is generally available in December.

The **"Club 95"** disco (☎ 033/7441431) is in the Sporthotel Victoria.

BERNER OBERLAND A TO Z

Arriving and Departing

By Car

There are swift and scenic roads from both Bern and Zürich to Interlaken. From **Bern,** the autoroute A6 leads to Spiez, then A8 continues as the highway to Interlaken. From **Zürich,** the planned autoroute link with Luzern (Lucerne) is incomplete; travel by Highway E41 south, then pick up the autoroutes A4 and A14 in the direction of Luzern. From **Geneva,** the autoroute leads through Lausanne and Fribourg to Bern, where you catch A6 south, toward Thun. A long, leisurely, scenic alternative: Leave the autoroute after Montreux, and head northeast on A11 from Aigle through Château-d'Oex to Gstaad and the Simmental.

By Plane

Belp (⊠ Belpmoos, ☎ 031/9613411) Airport in Bern brings you within an hour via train to Interlaken, the hub of Berner Oberland. **EuroAirport** (⊠ Just across the border in France, ☎ 061/3253111), near Basel, is within 2¼ hours by train. The **Zürich-Kloten** (☎ 1571060) Airport is within 2½ hours. Geneva's **Cointrin** (☎ 022/7177111) is an almost 2¾-hour trip.

By Train

Trains from **Bern** to Interlaken run once an hour between 6 AM and 11 PM, some requiring a change at Spiez. From **Zürich,** a direct line leads through Bern to Interlaken and takes about 2½ hours, departing hourly; a more scenic trip over the Golden Pass route via Luzern takes about two hours. From **Basel** trains run twice an hour via Olten (approximately a 2½-hour trip). Trains run hourly from **Geneva** (a 2¾-hour ride). Trains stop at the **Interlaken West** (☎ 033/8264750) station first. Next stop is **Interlaken East** (☎ 033/8222792). West is the more central, but check with your hotel if you've booked in advance: Some fine hotels are clustered nearer the East station, and all Brienzersee boat excursions leave from the docks nearby. For **train information** in Interlaken, ask at Interlaken West.

Getting Around

By Boat

Frequent round-trip boat cruises around Lake Thun and Lake Brienz provide an ever-changing view of the craggy foothills and peaks. The round-trip from Interlaken to **Thun** takes about four hours; the trip to Spiez takes about two hours and includes stopovers for visits to the castles of Oberhofen, Spiez, and Thun. A round-trip from Interlaken to **Brienz** takes around 2½ hours, to Iseltwald about 1¼ hours. These boats are public transportation as well as pleasure cruisers; just disembark whenever you feel like it and check timetables when you want to catch another. Tickets are flexible and coordinate neatly with surface transit: You can cruise across to Thun and then take a train home for variety. Buy tickets and catch boats for Lake Thun at **Interlaken West** station. For Lake Brienz, go to **Interlaken East.**

By Bus

Postbuses travel into much of the area not served by trains, including many smaller mountain towns. In addition, a number of private motorcoach tours cover points of interest. Schedules are available from tourist offices or Die Post (the mail, telephone, and telegraph office).

By Cable Car

More than 30 major cableway and lift systems climb Bernese Oberland peaks, including one of the largest cableways in the world, which stretches up to the Schilthorn above Mürren.

By Car

Driving in Berner Oberland allows you the freedom to find your own views and to park at the very edges of civilization before taking off on foot or by train. If you are confining yourself to the lakefronts, valleys, and lower resorts, a car is an asset. But several lovely resorts are beyond the reach of traffic, and train, funicular, and cable-car excursions take you to places ordinary tires can't tread; sooner or later, you'll leave the car behind and resort to public transportation. For maximum flexibility, rent a car in Bern if you fly into Belp.

By Train

Berner Oberland is riddled with federal and private railways, funiculars, cogwheel trains, and cable lifts designed with the sole purpose of getting you closer to its spectacular views. A **Swiss Pass** lets you travel free on federal trains and lake steamers, and it gives reductions on many private excursions (☞ Train Travel *in* the Gold Guide). If you're concentrating only on Berner Oberland, consider a 15-day **Regional Pass,** which offers 450 km (279 mi) of free rail, bus, and boat travel for any five days of your visit, with half fare for the remaining 10 days, as well as discounts on some of the most spectacular (and pricey) private excursions into the heights. For adults, the price is 235 SF (first class) and 190 SF (second class); children pay half those amounts. A seven-day pass allows you three free travel days for 185 SF (first class) and 150 SF (second class) for adults, half-price for children. These regional passes also grant a 50% discount for travel to Luzern, Zermatt, and Brig. With a **Family Card** (20 SF; ☞ Children & Travel *in* the Gold Guide), children up to 16 accompanied by at least one parent travel free. Discount passes pay for themselves only if you're a high-energy traveler; before you buy, compare the price à la carte for the itinerary you have in mind.

On Foot

You can cover a lot of ground without wheels, as this region (like most others in Switzerland) has highly developed, well-groomed walking trails leading away from nearly every intersection. Most are comfortably surfaced and are marked with distances and estimated walking times. Several itineraries are available from the Berner Oberland tourist office; these combine hikes with lodging along the way. The less ambitious walker may take advantage of postbus rides uphill and a leisurely stroll back down—though descents prove more taxing for calf muscles and knees than novice hikers imagine.

Contacts and Resources

Car Rental

Interlaken: Avis (✉ Waldeggstr. 34a, ☎ 033/8221214). **Hertz** (✉ Harderstr. 44, ☎ 033/8226172).

Emergencies

Police (☎ 117). **Hospital** (☎ 033/8262626). **Doctor referral** (☎ 033/8232323). **Dentist and pharmacist referral** (☎ 111).

Guided Tours

Auto AG Interlaken offers guided coach tours and escorted excursions within Berner Oberland. There are **bus** tours to Mürren and the Schilthorn (including **cable car**), to Grindelwald and Trümmelbach Falls, to Kandersteg and the Blausee, and to Ballenberg. Guests are picked up at either Interlaken West or East station or at the Metropole or Interlaken hotel (☎ 033/8221512 for reservations). The tourist office (☞ Visitor Information, *below*) is the best source for tour information.

If you're traveling without either a Swiss Pass or a Regional Pass (☞ By Train, *above*), note that guided tours to the Jungfraujoch or to the Schilthorn, arranged through the railway and cable companies themselves, cost less than independent round-trip tickets.

For a nostalgic tour of the streets of greater Interlaken by **horse-drawn carriage,** line up by the Interlaken West station (✉ Ernst Voegeli Kutschenbetrieb, ☎ 033/8227416).

Travel Agencies

Interlaken: Kuoni (✉ Höheweg 3, ☎ 033/8283636). **Jungfrau Tours** (✉ Strandbadstr. 3, ☎ 033/8283232). **Vaglio** (✉ Höheweg 72, ☎ 033/8270722).

Visitor Information

Berner Oberland Tourismus dispenses tourist information for the entire region, though it's not oriented toward walk-ins, so write or call (✉ Jungfraustr. 38, CH-3800 Interlaken, ☎ 033/8230303, FAX 033/8230330). The **Interlaken Tourist Office,** at the foot of the Hotel Metropole Höheweg (☎ 033/8222121, FAX 033/8225221) provides information on Interlaken and the Jungfrau region. Arrange your excursions here.

Other tourist offices: **Brienz** (✉ CH-3855, ☎ 033/9528080). **Grindelwald** (✉ CH-3818, ☎ 033/8541212). **Gstaad** (✉ CH-3780, ☎ 033/7488181). **Kandersteg** (✉ CH-3718, ☎ 033/6758080). **Lauterbrunnen** (✉ CH-3822, ☎ 033/8551955). **Meiringen** (✉ CH-3860, ☎ 033/9725050). **Mürren** (✉ CH-3825, ☎ 033/8568686). **Spiez** (✉ CH-3700, ☎ 033/6542138). **Thun** (✉ CH-3600, ☎ 033/2222340). **Wengen** (✉ CH-3823, ☎ 033/8551414).

11 Valais

Crans, Verbier, Zermatt

Alpine villages, verdant vineyards, world-class resorts, and that rocky celebrity the Matterhorn—all are good reasons to visit the valley (valais) of the Rhône. This is wilderness country, where tumbledown huts and state-of-the-art sports facilities share steep green hillsides and forests. Long isolated from the world by mountains, it remains a land apart.

THIS IS THE VALLEY OF THE MIGHTY Rhône, a river born in the heights above Gletsch (Glacier), channeled into a broad westward stream between the Bernese and the Valais Alps, lost in the depths of Lac Léman (Lake Geneva), and then diverted into France, where it ultimately dissolves in the marshes of the Camargue. Its broad upper valley forms a region of Switzerland that is still wild, remote, beautiful, and slightly unruly, its *mazots* (barns balanced on stone columns to keep mice out of winter food stores) romantically tumbledown, its highest slopes peopled by nimble farmers who live at vertiginous angles.

Updated by
Ian Plenderleith

The birthplace of Christianity in Switzerland, Valais was never reformed by Calvin or Zwingli, nor conquered by the ubiquitous Bernois—one reason, perhaps, that the west end of Valais seems the most intensely French of the regions of the Suisse Romande.

Its romance appeals to its fellow Swiss, who, longing for its rustic atmosphere, build nostalgic Valais theme huts in their modern city centers to eat raclette under mounted pitchforks, old pewter pitchers, and grape pickers' baskets. For vacations, the Swiss come here to play: to escape, to hike, and, above all, to ski. Zermatt, Saas-Fee, Crans-Montana, and Verbier—renowned resorts for serious sports lovers—are all in Valais, some within yodeling distance of villages barely touched by modern technology.

Pleasures and Pastimes

Dining
Though the French influence in the western portion of this region means a steady diet of cuisine *bourgeoise,* leading newcomers to think entrecôte with peppercorn sauce is a native dish, the elemental cuisine of Valais is much simpler. In a word: cheese.

Fondue, of course, is omnipresent. Often it is made with the local Bagnes or Orsières, mild cheeses from near Martigny. But the noblest application for these regional products is raclette (melted cheese with potatoes and pickles), an exclusive invention of this mountain canton (though the French of Haute-Savoie embrace it as their own). Ideally, the fresh-cut face of a half wheel of Orsières is melted before an open wood fire, the softened cheese scraped onto a plate and eaten with potatoes (always in their skins), pickled onions, and tiny gherkins. Nowadays, even mountain *carnotzets* (cellar pubs) with roaring fires depend on electric raclette-heaters that grip the cheese in a vise before toasterlike elements. The beverage: a crisp, bubbly, fruity Fendant.

Valais rivals the Graubünden in its production of *viande séchée* (air-dried beef), a block of meat marinated in herbs, pressed between planks until it takes on its signature bricklike form, and then dried in the open air. Shaved into thin, translucent slices, it can be as tender as a good *prosciutto crudo*—or as tough as leather. The flavor is concentrated, the flesh virtually fat-free.

CATEGORY	COST*
$$$$	over 70 SF
$$$	40 SF–70 SF
$$	20 SF–40 SF
$	under 20 SF

*Prices are per person for a three-course meal (two-course in $ category), including sales tax and 15% service charge

Hiking

As skiing is to winter, hiking is to summer in Valais, and the network of valleys that radiate north and south of the Rhône provides almost infinite possibilities. Sociable hikers can follow trails out of the big resorts—especially outside Saas-Fee and Zermatt, where the mountains' peaks and glaciers are within tackling distance—but don't overlook wilder, more isolated alternatives in the less developed Val d'Hérens and Val d'Anniviers. Good maps and suggested itineraries are available through the Valais regional tourist office in Sion (☞ Visitor Information *in* Valais A to Z, *below*).

Lodging

The most appealing hotels in Valais seem to be old. That is, historic sites have maintained their fine Victorian ambience; postwar inns, their lodgelike feel. Most of those built after about 1960 popped up in generic, concrete-slab, balconied rows to accommodate the masses that arrived with the 1960s ski boom. They are solid enough but, for the most part, anonymous, depending on the personality and dedication of their owners.

Valais is home to some of Switzerland's most famous resorts, and prices vary widely between top-level Zermatt lodgings and those in humbler towns. To indicate the relationship between resort prices and simple, wayside auberges (inns), the price categories below have been equally applied, so remember: The standards in a $$$-rated hotel in expensive Zermatt may be moderate compared to nonresort towns. When you write for information, check prices carefully. *Demipension*, or half board (includes breakfast and a hot meal, either lunch or dinner), is often included in the price, and rates may be listed per person. And when planning a vacation in fall or spring, research your itinerary carefully: Many of the resorts shut down altogether during the November and May lulls and schedule their renovations and construction projects for these periods. That means that while some places offer low-season savings, others simply close their doors. The broad price category spectrum indicated—sometimes from $ to $$$—shows the sometimes enormous differences between high- and low-season prices.

CATEGORY	COST*
$$$$	over 250 SF
$$$	180 SF–250 SF
$$	120 SF–180 SF
$	under 120 SF

Prices are for a standard double room, including breakfast, tax, and service charge.

Skiing

With plateaus and cavernous gorges radiating out from the valley, Valais has nurtured ski resorts for centuries. Zermatt, with its rustic, historic atmosphere, contrasts sharply with its high-tech peers to the west: Verbier, Crans-Montana, and Anzères are virtually purpose-built, with every amenity and connection—and considerably less focus on charm. You can find all ranges of difficulty and all kinds of snow—even, above Crans, in July.

Exploring Valais

Valais is an L-shape valley with Martigny at its angle; the eastern, or long, leg of the L is the most characteristic and imposing. This wide, fertile riverbed is flanked by bluffs and fed from the north and south by remote, narrow valleys that snake into the mountains. Some of these valleys peter out in desolate Alpine wilderness; some lead to its most famous landmarks—including that Swiss superstar, the Matterhorn. Not all of Valais covers Alpine terrain, however: The western stretch—between Martigny and Sierre—comprises one of the two chief sources of wine in Switzerland (the other is in Vaud, along Lake Geneva; *see* Chapter 12). Valais wines, dominated by round, fruity Fendant and light, ruby Dôle, come from verdant vineyards that stripe the hillsides flanking the Rhône.

The Val d'Entremont leads southward down an ancient route from Lake Geneva to the Col du Grand St-Bernard (Great St. Bernard Pass), traversing the key Roman crossroads at Martigny. Up the valley, past the isolated eagle's-nest village of Isérables, two magnificent castle-churches loom above the historic Old Town at Sion. From Sion, the Val d'Hérens winds up into the isolated wilderness past the stone Pyramides d'Euseigne and the Brigadoon-like resorts of Évolène and, even more obscure, Les Haudères. The Val d'Anniviers, the valley winding south from Sierre, leads to tiny, isolated skiing and hiking resorts, such as Vissoie and Grimentz. The most famous southbound rib of Valais valleys leads from Visp to the stellar resort of Zermatt and its mascot mountain, the Matterhorn. The fork in that same valley leads to spectacular Saas-Fee, another car-free resort in a magnificent glacier bowl. Back at the Rhône, the valley mounts southward from Brig to the Simplon Pass and Italy or northeastward to the glacier-source Gletsch and the Furka Pass out of the region.

Numbers in the text correspond to numbers in the margin and on the Valais map.

Great Itineraries

It's not necessary to explore every wild valley that ribs out from the Rhône in order to experience Valais; better to choose one region and spend a few days hiking, driving, or skiing. However, you will want to see the sights of the main river valley: Martigny, Sion, and at least one of the great Alpine passes, depending on your next travel goal.

IF YOU HAVE 2 DAYS

If you're using the Rhône Valley Highway as a means to cover ground scenically, enter from Lac Léman and cruise directly to **Sion** ⑦, where you'll walk through the Old Town and climb up to the church fortress of Valére. Although you won't have time to cut north or south into a radiating valley, any pass you use to exit the region will cover magnificent terrain: either the climb from **Martigny** ② to the **Col du Grand St-Bernard** ⑤ into Piedmont in Italy, the dramatic ascent from Brig over the **Simplon Pass** ⑰, or the slow, isolated approach to **Gletsch** ⑲ and the **Furka Pass** ⑳. Whenever time and road conditions permit, opt for the slow switchback crawl over the mountain passes rather than more efficient tunnels.

IF YOU HAVE 5 DAYS

Enter from Lac Léman and visit the museums of **Martigny** ②. Spend the night and next day exploring **Sion** ⑦, then make your selection: If you have never seen the Matterhorn, head directly for **Zermatt** ⑬ and spend three nights shutter-snapping, riding cable cars for better views, and shopping for state-of-the-art sports equipment. Other Alpine resort options are magnificently sited: **Saas-Fee** ⑯, glamorous **Verbier** ③, and trendy **Crans-Montana** ⑩. If you prefer wilderness and old-fashioned retreat, shun the famous spots and head up the Val d'Hérens to pretty little **Évolène** ⑧, up the Val d'Anniviers to **Grimentz** ⑪, or up the Mattertal to charming **Grächen** ⑭, teetering on a high plateau.

IF YOU HAVE 10 DAYS

En route to the mountains, take time to visit **St-Maurice** ① and **Martigny** ②, then head directly into the mountains and spend four quiet days wandering up the Val Hérens to **Évolène** ⑧, with side trips to see the Grande Dixence Dam and the Pyramides d'Euseigne and time for wilderness walks or cross-country skiing. Set aside a full day for the monuments and museums of 🖼 **Sion** ⑦ before heading back into the heights. You'll feel the contrast when you reach highly developed, Germanic 🖼 **Zermatt** ⑬, where another four nights will give you time to exploit its facilities. From Zermatt, you can exit Valais via the **Simplon Pass** ⑰ or the **Furka Pass** ⑳.

When to Tour Valais

Valais is at its sunny best in high summer and mid-winter, with foggy dampness overwhelming the region in late autumn (its low season). Mid-December to Easter is peak ski season in the resorts. As Europeans vacation here for weeks at a time, book well ahead if you want to compete for lodging in August, at Easter time, and at Christmas and New Year's. And remember: May and November are renovation and repair time, with many facilities closed.

VAL D'ENTREMONT TO THE COL DU GRAND ST-BERNARD

The Rhône River at Villeneuve broadens deltalike into a flat valley that pours into Lake Geneva. But heading south, up the valley, the mountains already begin to crowd in on either side. Once you cross the Rhône and officially enter the canton of Valais, leaving Vaud behind, the valley and the river begin to change character. The mountains—the Dents du Midi in the west and the Dents de Morcles to the east—come closer; the Rhône no longer flows placidly but gives a foretaste of the mountain torrent it will become as you approach its source. This most ancient of Alpine routes leaves the Rhône at the Martigny elbow and ascends due south to 2,469 m (8,098 ft) at the pass before descending into Italy's Valle d'Aosta.

St-Maurice

❶ *46 km (28 mi) west of Sion, 56 km (35 mi) southeast of Lausanne.*

The **St-Maurice Abbey** is an important stop on this ancient route to the Great St. Bernard Pass. Here, at the end of the 3rd century, a Theban leader named Maurice was massacred, along with most of his men, for refusing to worship the pagan gods of Rome. Christianity was first established in Switzerland here in Valais, and its fierce Catholicism—at both the French and the German ends—reflects this early zeal. The abbey was built in AD 515 to commemorate the martyrdom, and excavations near the Baroque *église abbatiale* (abbey church) have revealed the foundations of this original building. The abbey treasury contains an exceptionally precious collection of Romanesque and Gothic objects. ☎ *024/4851181.* 🎟 *Free.* ☉ *Guided tours July–Aug., Tues.–Sat. 10:30, 2, 3:15, 4:30, and Sun. 2, 3:15, 4:30; May–June and Sept.–Oct., Tues.–Sat. 10:30, 3, 4:30, and Sun. 3, 4:30; Nov.–Apr., Tues.–Sun. 3.*

Martigny

❷ *17 km (11 mi) south of St-Maurice, 23 km (14 mi) southwest of Sion.*

This valley crossroads, once used as a Roman camp, is still on the map today thanks to the Foundation Pierre Gianadda, which sponsors a clus-

SWITZERLAND

Gruyères
Im Fang
Zweisimmen
Frutigen
Montbovon
Château-
d'Oex
Gstaad
Kandersteg
BERN
OBERL
l'Etivaz
Lauenen
Lenk
Abelboden
Gsteig
Glacier de la
Plaine-Morte
Gletscherhorn
Wildstrubel
Leysin
Les Diablerets
Leukerbad
Gopper
Villars-sur-Ollon
Crans-
Montana
VALAIS
Vermala
Gan
TO MONTREUX
Anzère
10
Bex
Sierre
Niouc
St-Léonard
Chandolin
TO
CHAMPÉRY
Sion
7
Vex
VAL D'ANNIVIERS
St-Maurice
Rhône
Ardon
Veysonnaz
Thyon
Saillon
Nendaz
Grimentz
11
Dorénaz
Riddes
Pyramides
d'Euseigne
Ayer
Isérables
6
La Tsoumaz
(Mayens-de-Riddes)
12
Zinal
Mt. Gelé
VAL D'HÉRENS
Martigny
2
Verbier
3
Mt. Fort
Évolène
8
Sembrancher
Le Châble
Les Ruinettes
Les Haudères
9
Weisshorn
TO
CHAMONIX
Orsières
Lac des
Dix
Dent
Blanche
Champex
4
VAL D'ENTREMONT
Liddes
Arolla
Zerm
Mt. Collon
Tête
Blanche
Zmutt
Matterhorn
Col du Grand
St-Bernard
5
Klein
Matterhorn
ITALY

Grindelwald
Lauterbrunnen
Mönch
Handegg
Grimsel Pass
Gletsch **19** **20** Furka Pass
Schilthorn
Jungfrau
Oberwald
ER AND
Münster
Breithorn
Aletschhorn
Val de Conches
Grosser Aletschgletscher
Rhône
19
18 Riederalp
Mörel
stein
Lonza
Brig **16**
pel
Rhône
Turtmann
9
Visp
Simplon Tunnel
Stalden
17 Simplon Pass
St.-Niklaus **14** Grächen
Gondo
Gstein-Gabi
Saas-Grund
Domodossola
15 Saas-Fee
Längfluh
Mittelallalin
Alphübel
Feegletscher
Täsch
Allalinhorn
att
Unterrothorn
13
Gornergrat
Trockener Steg
MONTE
Dufourspitze
Breithorn
ROSA
I T A L Y

KEY

——— Rail Lines

········ Cable Car/
Funicular

– – – Regional
Boundary Lines

Ski Resort

N

| 0 | | 6 miles |
| 0 | | 9 km |

ter of world-class museums. Leonard Gianadda created the foundation in 1976 after the death of his brother, Pierre, in an airplane accident. Its first application: To develop Gallo-Roman ruins discovered during a building project. This became the **Musée Gallo-Romain** (Gallo-Roman Museum), which displays relics excavated from a 1st-century temple: striking bronzes, statuary, pottery, and coins. A marked promenade leads visitors through the antique village, baths, drainage systems, and foundations to the fully restored 5,000-seat amphitheater, which dates from the 2nd century.

Exhibitions—say, a recent Manet retrospective—are often installed in the museum. Hours vary with each temporary show; you'll see posters throughout major Swiss cities. And don't be surprised if you see posters for a concert by an international classical star—the Roman museum not only doubles as an art gallery but as a concert hall as well. ⊠ *Rue de Forum, 59,* ☎ *027/7223978.* ⊡ *12 SF.* ⊙ *Mid-June–Oct., daily 9–7; Feb.–June, daily 10–6; Nov.–Jan., daily 10–noon and 1:30–6.*

The Foundation Pierre Gianadda also sponsors a sizable **Musée de l'Automobile** (Automobile Museum), which contains some 50 antique cars, including an 1897 Benz, the Delauneay-Belleville of Czar Nicholas II of Russia, and a handful of Swiss-made models—all in working order. ⊠ *Rue de Forum 59,* ☎ *027/7223978.* ⊙ *Mid-June–Oct., daily 9–7; Feb.–June, daily 10–6; Nov.–Jan., daily 10–noon and 1:30–6.*

In the gracefully landscaped garden surrounding the Foundation Pierre Gianadda's museums, a wonderful **Parc de Sculptures** (Sculpture Park) displays works of Rodin, Brancusi, Miró, Calder, Moore, Dubuffet, and Segal.

Verbier

❸ *29 km (18 mi) east of Martigny (exit at Sembrancher), 58 km (36 mi) southwest of Sion.*

It's the skiing, not the social life, that draws Diana Ross; Björn Borg; Sarah Ferguson, the Duchess of York; and thousands of other committed sports lovers to Verbier, a high-tech, state-of-the-art sports complex that connects to several nearby resorts (including Thyon and Nendaz). Verbier has the biggest aerial cableway in Europe, with two cabins accommodating 150, and some 86 smaller transportation installations. Summer sports are equally serious: Hang gliding and its variations compete with golf as the principal sports. Though it's perched on a sunny shelf high above the Val de Bagnes, with the 3,023-m (9,915-ft) Mont Gelé towering behind and wraparound views, Verbier itself is too modern to be picturesque, but thanks to its compact layout and easygoing locals, the town has a friendlier feel to it than the traffic-ridden sprawl of Crans-Montana or hotel-packed Zermatt. You won't have any trouble finding your way around; all hotels are clearly signposted.

Skiing

At 1,500 m (4,921 ft), Verbier is the center of Switzerland's most famous transit network, **Televerbier**—which consists of 12 gondolas, 7 cable cars, 34 chairlifts, and 47 ski lifts giving access to 400 km (247 mi) of marked pistes. From this resort an immense complex of resorts has developed—some more modest, others more exclusive—covering four valleys in an extended ski area whose extremities are 15 km (9 mi) or so apart as the crow flies and several dozen kilometers apart by way of winding mountain roads.

Les Ruinettes gives access to Verbier's entire upper ski area, which culminates at **Mont-Fort,** at 3,300 m (10,825 ft). This is reached by an aerial tram, *Le Jumbo,* equipped with a cab that accommodates 150, the largest in Switzerland. This entire sector is crisscrossed by a dense network of astonishingly varied pistes. There are several strategic passes, including **Les Attelas, Mont-Gelé, Col des Gentianes, Lac des Vaux,** and **Tortin.** One-day lift tickets cost 56 SF; six-day passes cost 282 SF.

Dining and Lodging

$$–$$$ ✗ **Le Bouchon Gourmet.** Away from the main drag of generic fondue cabins and no-surprise pizza houses, this warmly decorated spot serves an excellent range of French-influenced poultry dishes (including gizzard pâté) and tongue-melting desserts. Especially worth sampling are the succulent duck in red wine sauce and for dessert the brandy-inflamed apple tart. ⊠ *Rue de la Poste,* ☎ 027/7717296. AE, DC, MC, V.

$$$$ ✗⊞ **Rosalp.** The honey-gold pine rustic-chic decor makes a surprisingly
★ warm and comfortable setting for one of Switzerland's great meals. Chef Roland Pierroz continues to earn the highest gastronomic kudos and an international following for his prawn bisque, squab with truffles, and apple tarts, as well as for the variety of fine local cheeses he presents. A glorious finish to a day on the slopes: Dine here, then roll upstairs to the fine little hotel, a member of the Relais & Châteaux chain. Built in 1946, it has been renovated several times since then; ask for the newer rooms, which have marble baths. The upper rooms are smaller but quieter, with better views. Reservations are essential at the restaurant. ⊠ *CH-1936,* ☎ 027/7716323, ℻ 027/7711059. *19 rooms, 3 apartments. Restaurant, café, hot tub, sauna. AE, DC, MC, V.*

$$$$ ⊞ **Hotel Vanessa.** This comfortable, quiet, centrally located hotel offers mainly southern views and spacious, pine-decorated rooms complete with balcony, kitchenette (even including a dishwasher), as well as a large number of two- and three-room suites. The questionably decorated but convivial bar plays host to a regular in-house pianist. ⊠ *CH-1936,* ☎ 027/7752800, ℻ 027/7752828. *35 rooms, 21 suites. Restaurant, bar, sauna. AE, DC, MC, V.*

$$$–$$$$ ⊞ **Grand Combin et Golf.** As modern and central as most of its Verbier rivals, this chalet hotel is a bit softer around the edges, thanks to some knotty pine, overstuffed chairs, a fireplace, and a cocktail club ambience in Jacky's Piano Bar, a plush late-night venue for an established clientele. In summertime, barbecues and raclette dinners promote mingling. The 18-hole golf course offers magnificent views, although even guests will have to pay for the privilege of a round. The hotel runs private buses to the cable cars. ⊠ *CH-1936,* ☎ 027/7716515, ℻ 027/ 7711488. *30 rooms. Restaurant, bar, sauna, steam room, 18-hole golf course, exercise room. AE, DC, MC, V.*

$$$–$$$$ ⊞ **Rhodania.** Built, like its peers, in the mid-1960s, this generic, centrally located property is coolly chic with its carved wood fixtures and the occasional cozy accent. South balconies have the famous view. There's a spot for spaghetti and the humming Farm Club (☞ *Nightlife and the Arts, below*) for dancing and darting glances. ⊠ *CH-1936,* ☎ 027/ 7716121, ℻ 027/7715254. *44 rooms. 2 restaurants, bar, dance club. AE, DC, MC, V.*

$ ⊞ **Les Touristes.** If you're here for the world-class skiing and want to pass on the anonymous comforts of chic but pricey Verbier, head for this old-style pension. Built in the 1940s in a dark-wood roadhouse style, it's in the village below the main resort, where a few traditional chalets are still evident. The rooms are spare, and the bare-bones shower and toilet are down the hall, but the stübli-restaurant attracts locals disenchanted with the uptown scene. Staying here means one more connection to get you to the slopes—a brief bus ride—but you save a

bundle. ⊠ CH-1936, ☎ 027/7712147, ₣ 027/7712147. *14 rooms.
Restaurant, stübli. AE, MC, V.*

Nightlife and the Arts

DANCING

The **Farm Club** (⊠ Rhodania Hotel, ☎ 027/7716121; closed Sun.) is
the place to be seen in Verbier, with lines often forming in the street
for the privilege of jiving to pop's back catalog while quaffing a bottle of vodka costing well into three figures in both franc and dollar terms.
Apparently it is not the done thing to turn up before 1 AM. In the meantime you could head to the less pretentious **Scotch** (⊠ Rue de la Poste,
☎ 027/7711656), whose slogan reads: "We may be small but we're
cheap." **Marshal's** (⊠ Hotel Farinet, ☎ 027/7713572) caters to the
techno generation; the popular **Crock** bar (⊠ Route des Creux, ☎ 027/
7716934) has live music on weekends.

MUSIC

For more than two weeks overlapping July and August the **Verbier Festival and Academy** hosts an impressive classical music festival, which
in recent years has attracted such names as conductor Sir Neville Mar-
riner, violinist Nigel Kennedy, and soprano singer Barbara Hendricks.
To order tickets, call ☎ 027/7718282 or fax ₣ 027/7717057.

Outdoor Activities and Sports

BICYCLING

Jet Sports (☎ 027/7712067) rents mountain bikes.

GOLF

The **Golf Club** (☎ 027/7715314) has two 18-hole courses.

MOUNTAIN CLIMBING

Les Combins (☎ 027/7716825) provides guides and training. **École
d'Alpinisme de Verbier** (☎ 027/7712212) offers guides and training too.

PARAGLIDING

The **Centre Parapente** (☎ 027/7716818) gives paragliding lessons and
sells equipment. **L'Envol** (☎ 027/7715131) paragliding school offers
training and rentals.

SPORTS CENTERS

Verbier's **Centre Polysportif** (☎ 027/7716601) has indoor skating as
well as a swimming pool, saunas, whirlpools, a solarium, curling, tennis courts, and squash.

TENNIS

The **Centre Polysportif** (☎ 027/7716601) has nine courts. There are
three private courts available for rental through **Gérard Besson** (☎ 027/
7712333).

Champex

❹ *31 km (19 mi) south of Martigny, 51 km (32 mi) southwest of Sion.*

Clinging high above the Orsières Valley (famous for its raclette cheese),
this delightful little family resort lies wrapped around a tiny mirror of
a lake and surrounded by forested peaks, concentrating some of the
prettiest scenery in the region—including views dominated by the massive Combin (4,314 m/14,150 ft).

Dining and Lodging

$$ ✕▥ **Belvédère.** This is the prototypical *relais de campagne* (country inn):
★   full of warm wood, cozy old-style rooms with balconies, creaky pine-
    panel halls hung with historic photos, and doilies everywhere, cro-
    cheted by the owner herself. Set on a wooded hill above the lake and

town, it offers breathtaking views all the way down to the Val d'Entremont. The café attracts local workers, and the restaurant serves the owners' fresh, straightforward *cuisine bourgeoise* as well as a variety of fondues. Watch for garlic-sautéed porcini mushrooms on toast, lamb fillet in sage with *Rösti* (hash brown potatoes), and muscat mousse with grape compote. Vegetables are local and organically grown. The list of local wines includes some rare bargains. ⊠ *CH-1938,* ☎ *027/7831114,* FAX *027/7832576. 9 rooms. Restaurant, café. MC, V.*

$ ✕⊞ **Auberge de la Forêt.** On a quiet street facing the lake, this place has a few lake-view rooms with a comfortable, modern look. The fireplace and grill turn out authentic raclette. ⊠ *CH-1938,* ☎ *027/ 7831278,* FAX *027/7832101. 15 rooms. Restaurant, café. MC, V.*

Col du Grand St-Bernard

★ ❺ *40 km (25 mi) south of Martigny, 69 km (43 mi) southwest of Sion.*

The Great St. Bernard Pass, breasting the formidable barrier of the Alps at 2,069 m (6,786 ft), is the oldest and most famous of the great Alpine crossings, and the first to join Rome and Byzantium to the wilds of the north. Known and used for centuries before the birth of Christ, it has witnessed an endless stream of emperors, knights, and simple travelers—think of Umberto Eco's *The Name of the Rose,* with two friars crossing on donkey back in howling winter winds. Napoléon took an army of 40,000 across it en route to Marengo, where he defeated the Austrians in 1800.

You'll have an easier time crossing today than Napoléon did: If you simply want to get to Italy quickly, you can take the swift tunnel that opens out on the other side, above the Valle d'Aosta. But by skipping the tiny winding road over the top, you'll miss the awe-inspiring, windswept moonscape at the summit and the hospice that honors its namesake. In 1038, the story goes, Bernard of Menthon, bishop of Aosta, came to clear the pass of brigands. When he reached the top, he found a pagan temple, which he covered with his chasuble. The shrine immediately crumbled to dust and, by the same power, the brigands were defeated. There Bernard established his hospice.

The **hospice of St. Bernard** served international travelers throughout the Middle Ages. Kings and princes rewarded the hospice by showering estates upon the order. By the 12th century, it owned 79 estates in England, including the site of the present-day Savoy Hotel in London. Nowadays its residents—Augustinian canons—train as mountain guides and ski instructors and accommodate young groups. Behind the hospice, there's a kennel full of the landmark's enormous, furry namesakes: the famous St. Bernard dogs, who for centuries have helped the monks find travelers lost in the snow. They supposedly came to Switzerland with silk caravans from central Asia and were used by Romans as war dogs; nowadays they're kept more for sentimental than functional reasons. The most famous was Barry, who saved more than 40 people during the 19th century and today stands stuffed in the Bern Naturhistorisches Museum (Museum of Natural History; ☞ Chapter 9). Souvenir stands sell plush versions of St. Bernards on either side of the pass. ☎ *027/7871236.* ⌨ *Kennel: 6 SF.* ☉ *July–Aug. 8 AM–10 PM.*

ISÉRABLES, SION, AND THE VAL D'HÉRENS

The Rhône Valley just east of Martigny is at its most fertile, its flatlands thick with fruit orchards and vegetable gardens, its south-facing slopes striped with vineyards. The region nurtures a virtual market basket of apples, pears, carrots, and delicate white asparagus, a specialty of early spring. The blue-blood crop of the region is grapes: This is one of the primary wine-producing regions in the country, and the fruity Fendant and hearty red Dôle (a blend of pinot noir and gamay grapes) appear on every region's lists, as well as the Dôle Blanche, actually a rosé, often taken as an aperitif. Once Valais wines were poured from hinged-lid tin or pewter pitchers called *channes*; reproductions are displayed and sold throughout the region. Also from the orchards come potent but intensely perfumed eaux-de-vie (or schnapps), especially *abricotine* (from apricots) and *williamine* (from pears).

This patch of Valais demonstrates the contrasts of this dramatic region: Over the fertile farmlands looms the great medieval stronghold of Sion, its fortress towers protecting the gateway to the Alps. Yet jutting sharply up into the bluffs to the south are the once-primitive, isolated mountain villages of Isérables and Évolène.

Isérables

★ ❻ *24 km (15 mi) southwest of Sion.*

This is a rare opportunity to visit one of the scores of eagle's-nest towns you'll glimpse as you pass through the region's valleys. Set on a precarious slope that drops 1,000 m (3,280 ft) into the lowlands, it has narrow streets that weave between crooked old stone-shingle mazots, the typical little Valais barns balanced on stone disks and columns to keep mice out of winter food stores.

Since the arrival of the cable car in recent times, Isérables has prospered and modernized itself considerably. Yet the inhabitants of this village still carry the curious nickname Bedjuis. Some say it is derived from "Bedouins" and that the people are descended from the Saracen hordes who, after the battle of Poitiers in 732, overran some of the high Alpine valleys. Certainly some of the people here—stocky, swarthy, and dark-eyed—seem different from most in the canton.

Sion

★ ❼ *158 km (98 mi) south of Bern.*

Rearing up spookily in the otherwise deltalike flatlands of the western Valais, two otherworldly twin hills flank the ancient city of Sion. Crowning the first, **Tourbillon,** is a ruined **château** built as a bishop's residence at the end of the 13th century and destroyed by fire in 1788. On the other, **Valère,** is an 11th-century **church.** The two together are a powerful emblem of the city's 1,500-year history as a bishopric and a Christian stronghold. From the top of either hill, you'll have a dramatic view of the surrounding flatlands and the mountains flanking the valley. Tourbillon is the higher of the two hills, so its view is a touch more spectacular; it's also possible to visit the château. 🎫 *Free.* 🕐 *Mid-Mar.–mid-Nov., Tues.–Sun. 10–6.*

Sion folk are seen as a little "different" not just by the Swiss at large but even by their fellow inhabitants of the Valais. The town is not as hospitable as the tourist-oriented ski resorts around it, and there is a dearth of quality hotels. The people of Sion are fiercely proud and independent, as reflected in the fanatical support for their soccer team (very rare in a country much keener on winter sports) and their dogged attempts to stage the Winter Olympics. They failed in 2002 but are trying again for 2006 (a decision will be made in fall 1999).

The town can be comfortably explored on foot in an afternoon, unless you lose yourself in one of its museums or labyrinthine antiques shops. The **Old Town,** down rue de Lausanne (take a left when leaving the tourist office, map in hand), is a comfortable blend of shuttered 16th-century houses and modern shops. The grand old **Maison Supersaxo** (House of Supersaxo) was built in 1505 by Georges Supersaxo, the local governor, to put his rivals to shame. This extravagantly decorated building features a Gothic staircase and a grand hall whose painted wood ceiling is a dazzling work of decorative art. ⊠ *Tucked into a passageway off rue Supersaxo.* ☜ *Free.* ☉ *Weekdays 8–noon and 2–6.*

The imposing **Hôtel de Ville** (Town Hall) has extraordinary historic roots: Though it was built during the 1650s, there are transplanted stones in the entrance bearing Roman inscriptions, including a Christian symbol from the year 377. The 17th-century doors are richly carved wood, and the tower displays an astronomical clock. Upstairs the **Salle du Conseil** (Council Hall) is also adorned with ornate woodwork. ⊠ *At the intersection of rue de Conthey and rue du Grand-Pont.* ☜ *Free interior visits only with guided walking tour of the town (8 SF) from the Sion tourist office.* ☉ *Tues. and Thurs. only; mid-July through Aug., 4–6.*

The **Musée Cantonal d'Archéologie** (Museum of Archaeology) displays a cantonal collection of excavated pieces, including fine Roman works found in Valais. The narrow old cobbled rue des Châteaux leading up toward the twin fortifications passes graceful old patrician houses, among them the museum. ⊠ *12 rue des Châteaux,* ☎ *027/ 6064700.* ☜ *4 SF.* ☉ *Tues.–Sun. 10–noon and 2–6.*

★ In the **Église-Forteresse de Valère** (Church-Fortress of Valère), high above the town and valley, you'll observe a striking example of sacred and secular power combined—as in the church's heyday it often subjugated rather than served its parishioners. Built on Roman foundations, massive stone walls enclose both the **château** and the 12th-century **Église Notre Dame de Valère** (Church of Our Lady of Valère).

This structure stands in a relatively raw form, rare in Switzerland, where monuments are often restored to Disneyland perfection: Over the engaging Romanesque carvings, 16th-century fresco fragments, and 17th-century stalls, painted with scenes of the Passion, there hangs a rare jewel of an **organ** in "swallow's-nest" form, its cabinet painted with two fine medieval Christian scenes. Dating from the 14th century, it is the oldest playable organ in the world, and an organ festival celebrates its musical virtues annually (☞ Nightlife and the Arts, *below*). The church also houses the **Musée d'Histoire et Ethnologie** (Museum of History and Ethnology), which displays a wide array of medieval chests and sculptures. There are periodic guided tours of the Église-Forteresse, but they're not given in English. ☎ *027/6064710.* ☜ *5 SF.* ☉ *Tues.–Sun. 10–noon and 2–6. Guided tours 1st Sat. of the month, 2:30.*

The Cathedral **Notre-Dame du Glarier** (Our Lady of Glarier) is dominated by its Romanesque tower, built in the Lombard, or Italian, style and dating from the 12th century; the rest of the church is late-Gothic style. ⊠ *rue de la Cathédral.*

Just up from the cathedral grounds, the **Tour des Sorciers** (Sorcerers' Tower) is the last remnant of the walls that once ringed the town. ☜ *2 SF.* ☉ *Tues.–Sun. 2–6.*

Dining and Lodging

$$$$ ✕ **Supersaxo.** One of the few restaurants in Sion enjoying a reputation beyond the city walls, Supersaxo serves quality nouvelle cuisine in modern, sleek surroundings. If the elaborate evening menus are beyond your price range then you can always pop in at lunchtime and treat yourself to a *plat du jour* (daily special) for a little over 20 SF, and if you're wearing jeans and scuffed shoes, you can amuse yourself at the sight of other diners looking down their noses at you. ⊠ *Passage Supersaxo*, ☎ 027/3238550. AE, DC, MC, V.

$$ ⌂ **Du Rhône.** This spare, cinder-block urban property could be an American motel if it weren't for the illuminated antiquities visible from the north windows. At the edge of the Old Town and handy to the castle walks, it makes a comfortable, no-frills base for your explorations. ⊠ *CH-1950*, ☎ *027/3228291*, ⑆ *027/3231188. 45 rooms. Restaurant. AE, DC, MC, V.*

$ ⌂ **Du Midi.** On the edge of the Old Town, and now absorbed into the upper floors of a downtown shopping block, this was once a freestanding roadhouse, a loner in the shadow of the city's twin citadels. Its small rooms are sparkling and attractive despite their vibrant color scheme. ⊠ *CH-1950*, ☎ *027/3231331*, ⑆ *027/3236173. 12 rooms. Restaurant, brasserie. AE, DC, MC, V.*

Nightlife and the Arts

Sion attracts world-class musicians and scholars to its festivals celebrating the medieval organ in its church-fortress Valère (☞ Exploring, *above*). The **Festival International de l'Orgue Ancien Valère** (International Festival of the Ancient Valère Organ; ⊠ CH-1950 Sion, ☎ 027/3235767) takes place from July through the beginning of September.

Nightlife in Sion is sparse, but if you're hoping to offload some cash in the presence of minimally clad females then you might wish to seek out **La Matze** (⊠ rue de Lausanne 51, ☎ 027/3224042). **Le Galion** (⊠ Rue de Lausanne 130, ☎ 027/3220950) bills itself as a cabaret.

OFF THE BEATEN PATH	**GRANDE DIXENCE DAM –** Veer right past Vex up the narrow mountain road that leads about 16 km (10 mi) up the Val d'Hérémence to the Grande Dixence Dam, a gargantuan monolith of concrete built during the mid-1960s at the improbable altitude of 2,364 m (7,754 ft). Only the Swiss could have accomplished such a feat of Alpine engineering—an achievement that brings them millions on millions of kilowatt hours every year. The potential energy is impressively apparent because the now-vast Lac des Dix backs up some 4 km (2½ mi) into the barren, abandoned valley.

En Route South of Sion, the Val d'Hérens is a valley lined with improbably high mountain farms and pastures. Here you will find the **Pyramides d'Euseigne** (Pyramids of Euseigne), a group of bizarre geological formations: stone pillars formed by the debris of glacial moraines and protected by peculiar hard-rock caps from the erosion that carved away the material around them. The effect is that of enormous, freestanding stalagmites wearing hats. A car tunnel has been carved through the base of three of them.

Évolène

➑ *23 km (14 mi) southeast of Sion, cross the main highway and head south toward Vex.*

In a broad, fertile valley, Évolène is a town of ramshackle mazots and wooden houses edged with flower-filled window boxes that provide a picturesque setting for vacationers—mostly French—and mountaineers, who tackle nearby Mont-Collon and the Dent-Blanche. If you're lucky, you'll see some of the older women villagers in the traditional dress of kerchiefs and flowered cottons that they still favor. Évolène is known for its rough homespun wool.

Les Haudères

❾ *5 km (3 mi) south of Évolène, 28 km (17 mi) southeast of Sion.*

This tiny but popular vacation retreat south of Les Haudères is little more than a scattering of chalets in a spectacular, isolated mountain valley. Farther on, the little skiing and mountaineering resort of **Arolla** (2,010 m/6,593 ft) is custom-made for those seeking a total retreat in Alpine isolation.

CRANS-MONTANA AND THE VAL D'ANNIVIERS

Spiking north and south of the crossroads of Sierre, you'll find polar extremes: the sunny, open plateau, home to the glamorous resorts of Crans and Montana, and the wild, craggy Val d'Anniviers that leads to the isolated forest retreat of Grimentz.

Crans-Montana

❿ *12 km (7 mi) north of Sierre, 19 km (11¾ mi) northwest of Sion.*

This well-known twin sports center rises above the valley on a steep, sheltered shelf at 1,495 m (4,904 ft) and commands a broad view across the Rhône Valley to the peaks of Valais Alps; its grassy and wooded plateau shares the benefits of Sierre's sunshine. Behind it, the **Rohrbach-stein** (2,953 m/9,686 ft), the **Gletscherhorn** (2,943 m/9,653 ft), and the **Wildstrubel** (3,243 m/10,637 ft) combine to create a complex of challenging ski slopes. Every September, the 18-hole golf course is the site of the annual Swiss Open, a period the locals describe as "party week." The most direct route to Crans-Montana is from Sierre, just southeast, either by car or funicular.

The resort towns themselves are highly developed and charmless, lacking the regional color and grace of Zermatt. The streets are lined with modern shops and hotels, and car traffic is almost always heavy. As in Verbier, all hotels are signposted. The crowds are young, wealthy, and international, although only a cynic would go so far as to describe the ambience as overbearingly vacuous.

Skiing

The pearl of the region is the **Plaine Morte,** a flat glacier 5 km–6 km (3 mi–3½ mi) long, perched like a pancake at an elevation of 3,000 m (9,840 ft), which has snow year-round. A cross-country ski trail (watch out for your lungs at this altitude) of 10 km–12 km (6 mi–7½ mi) is open and maintained here seven months of the year. You can also downhill-ski on the gentle slopes in summer; in winter, the descent from the Plaine Morte follows wide and relatively easy pistes as far as one or two chutes. The ascent on the gondola from **Violettes Plaines-Morte,** virtually under assault during the high season and in good weather, will in itself justify your stay in Crans-Montana. Expert skiers may prefer the **Nationale Piste,** site of the 1987 world championships. The incredibly steep-pitched **La Toula** is also a challenge for pros. A one-day lift ticket costs 54 SF; a six-day pass costs 255 SF.

Dining and Lodging

$$$–$$$$ ✕🏠 **Aïda-Castel.** In a resort that mushroomed during the 1960s and
★ seems to be frozen in time, this warm and welcoming complex is refreshingly au courant. The public areas have carved or aged wood, terra-

cotta, and stucco; the rooms have hand-painted furniture and some stenciled ceilings. The amenities are all top quality. The very popular public restaurant, La Hotte, serves Italian fare, some prepared on the open grill, as well as real raclette made at fireside—so good that reservations are essential. The hillside location is moderately isolated, with great southern views from nearly every balcony. ⊠ *CH-3962 Montana,* ☎ *027/4817060,* FAX *027/4817062. 61 rooms. 3 restaurants, pool, hot tub, sauna, exercise room, meeting room. AE, DC, MC, V.*

$$$$ ⊞ **Grand Hôtel du Golf.** This is the blue blood of the lot, a grand, gen-
★ teel old resort oasis with urbane good taste and every amenity. Built by English golfers in 1907 and owned by the same family since 1914, it's been postmodernized outside and carefully tended within. In addition to a formal restaurant and a homey café, there's a fine bar completely paneled in oak. Manicured grounds adjoin the 9- and an 18-hole golf courses. An annex to the hotel with around 20 additional suites is due for completion by the end of 1998. ⊠ *CH-3963 Crans,* ☎ *027/ 4814242,* FAX *027/4819758. 72 rooms, 8 suites. Restaurant, bar, café, in-room VCRs, indoor pool, beauty salon, sauna. AE, DC, MC, V.*

$$$–$$$$ ⊞ **Crans-Ambassador.** A stylized château with a three-peak roofline and direct access to the slopes, this dramatic modern structure stands apart from the twin towns and offers some of the resorts' finest views south. Each room has a balcony or terrace, and the back rooms look onto shaggy pine forests. The interiors are anonymously sleek, warmed up by occasional touches of wood; all the baths sparkle. The classic French restaurant also has a terrace. ⊠ *CH-3962 Montana,* ☎ *027/ 4814811,* FAX *027/4819155. 70 rooms. Restaurant, indoor pool, sauna, exercise room. AE, DC, MC, V.*

$$–$$$$ ⊞ **Le Green.** What was once a rustic, welcome alternative to Crans glitz has succumbed: Completely renovated and redecorated in jazzy, bright *style golf,* and with a floor constructed on top, this has become another pricey four-star option. Facilities include a brasserie, a pine-deck bar, and a sauna-solarium. ⊠ *CH-3963 Crans,* ☎ *027/4813256,* FAX *027/4811781. 32 rooms, 2 suites. Restaurant, bar, brasserie, sauna, exercise room. AE, DC, MC, V.*

$$–$$$$ ⊞ **Mirabeau.** Completely redone in pastels straight out of suburbia, this attractive midtown property has views of the street—or of other hotels. It's at the hub, however, of the downtown restaurant and shopping scene. ⊠ *CH-3962 Montana,* ☎ *027/4802151,* FAX *027/4813912. 45 rooms. Restaurant, bar, sauna, exercise room. AE, DC, MC, V.*

$–$$$ ⊞ **La Prairie.** Wally Cleaver might have stayed here on a school ski trip: There are rough-hewn fireplaces everywhere, and the young, rec-room atmosphere is downright wholesome. Built in the 1930s, the updated rooms glow with pine, and the baths are very modern. The hotel is away from the noisy center but conveniently placed. ⊠ *CH-3962 Montana,* ☎ *027/4814421,* FAX *027/4818586. 32 rooms. Restaurant, bar, pool. AE, DC, MC, V.*

$–$$ ⊞ **Regina.** On the main shopping street in Montana, this is a spare, tidy city inn with the rare option of inexpensive rooms (bathrooms are down the hall). Although their decor is dated (wood paneling, all-weather carpet), some rooms have balconies that overlook the valley. There's a cozy lounge downstairs as well as a wonderful bakery—so breakfasts are homemade and fresh. ⊠ *CH-3962. Montana,* ☎ *027/4813522,* FAX *027/4801868. 24 rooms. Breakfast room. AE, DC, MC, V.*

Nightlife

DANCING

If you've ever wondered what Salvador Dali would have produced if he'd illustrated a vodka ad, then head for the **Absolut** (☎ 027/4816596), a nightclub in Crans. At 15 SF for a beer you might find the prices pretty surreal, too. The American-theme club **Go Crazy** (☎ 027/4819200) nearby is around half the price; **The Pub** (☎ 027/4815496) is a lively international meeting place with a DJ every night of the season. Up in Montana the small but convivial **Amadeus** (☎ 027/4812495), beneath the Olympic Hotel, is a popular après-ski venue with the young crowd; the disco **Number One** (☎ 027/4813615) is comparatively cheap, popular with locals, and described by some as a bit wild.

Outdoor Activities and Sports

BICYCLING

Alex Sports (☎ 027/4814061) rents mountain bikes by the day and week.

GOLF

Crans and Montana have one 18-hole **golf course** and two nine-hole courses (☎ 027/4812168).

TENNIS

The **Centre de Tennis Au Lac Moubra** (☎ 027/4815014) has seven indoor courts.

En Route   East of the city limits of Sierre and south of the Rhône, follow signs southward for Vissoie. Here you will enter the **Val d'Anniviers,** a wild and craggy valley said to derive its name from its curious and famous (among anthropologists, at least) nomads, known in Latin as *anni viatores* (year-round travelers). Some claim they are descended from the Huns who straggled into the area during the 5th century. Since the development of modern roads, the Anniviards no longer follow their ancient pattern: to migrate down into the valley around Niouc in spring, move to Sierre in summer to cultivate collectively owned vineyards, and return to their isolated villages to hole up for the winter. The ancient practice disappeared in the 1950s, but many residents are the nomads' descendants.

Grimentz

⑪ *20 km (12½ mi) south of Sierre.*

With a population of 370, this ancient little 13th-century village has preserved its weathered-wood houses and mazots in its tiny center, although anonymous new hotels have sprung up near the ski facilities above.

Skiing

Grimentz shares transit facilities with **Zinal** (☞ *below*) and **Chandolin** in the Val d'Anniviers. Though they're separated by wilderness, each can provide a day's skiing, with easy access for variety the next day. Grimentz's trails, while limited, should meet everyone's needs. There's a hair-raising expert run from **Pointe de Lona** (at 2,900 m/9,512 ft) all the way back down to the parking lot (at 1,570 m/5,150 ft). Beginners can enjoy equally spectacular sweeps from **Orvizal,** starting at 2,780 m (9,118 ft), back to town. The upper runs are reached by ski tows only; a cable car has been added to the first level. **Grimentz,** at 1,570 m (5,150 ft), has eight tows, one chairlift, one cable car, 50 km (31 mi) of downhill runs, and 22 km (14 mi) of cross-country trails. A ski pass, which costs 36 SF for one day, 172 SF for six days, offers access to all Val d'Anniviers facilities, including 46 lifts and 250 km (155 mi) of downhill runs.

Dining

$ ✕ **Le Mélèze.** Warm your feet by the central fireplace, open on all sides, in the old, all-wood café and restaurant on the edge of Grimentz that serves raclette, crepes, and generous hot meals. ☎ *027/4751287. AE, DC, MC, V. Closed June and Nov.*

Zinal

⑫ *25 km (16 mi) south of Sierre.*

Summer travelers can veer down a tiny forest road from Grimentz toward Zinal, with the Weisshorn dominating the views. Zinal (1,675 m/5,494 ft) is another isolated mountaineering center with well-preserved wood houses and mazots. It is worth building enough time into your itinerary to stop over in one of these windswept mountain aeries and walk, climb, ski, or relax by the fire.

ZERMATT AND SAAS-FEE

Immediately east of Sierre, you'll notice a sharp change: *vals* become *-tals,* and the sounds you overhear at your next pit stop are no longer the throaty, mellifluous tones of Suisse Romande but the lilting, guttural Swiss-German dialect called Wallisertiitsch, a local form of Schwyzerdütsch. Welcome to Wallis (*vahl*-is), the Germanic end of Valais.

This sharp demographic frontier can be traced back to the 6th century, when Alemannic tribes poured over the Grimsel Pass and penetrated as far as Sierre. Here the middle-class cuisine changes from *steak-frites* (steak with french fries) to veal and Rösti, though the mountain peasants' basics—cheese, bread, and wine—are found throughout.

Zermatt

★ **⑬** *29 km (18 mi) south of Visp, plus a 10-km (6-mi) train ride from Täsch.*

Despite its fame—which stems from that mythic mountain, the Matterhorn, and from its excellent ski facilities—Zermatt is a resort with its feet on the ground, protecting its regional quirks along with its wildlife and its tumbledown mazots, which crowd between glass-and-concrete chalets like old tenements between skyscrapers. Streets twist past weathered-wood walls, flower boxes, and haphazard stone roofs until they break into open country that slope, inevitably, uphill. Despite the crowds, you are never far from the wild roar of the silty river and the peace of a mountain path.

★ Hordes of package-tour sightseers push shoulder to shoulder to get yet another shot of the **Matterhorn** (4,477 m/14,685 ft). Called one of the wonders of the Western world, the mountain deserves the title: Though it has become an almost self-parodying icon, like the Eiffel Tower or the Empire State Building, its peculiar snaggle-tooth form, free on all sides of competition from other peaks, rears up over the village, larger than life and genuinely awe-inspiring. Leaving the train station and weaving through the pedestrian crowds, aggressive electric taxi carts, and aromatic horse-drawn carriages along the main street, Bahnhofstrasse, you are assaulted on all sides by Matterhorn images: On postcards, on sweatshirts, on calendars, on beer steins, on candy wrappers, it looms in multiples of a thousand, the original obscured by resort buildings (except from the windows of pricier hotel rooms). But breaking past the shops and hotels onto the main road into the hills, visitors seem to reach the same slightly elevated spot and stop dead in their tracks: There it is at last, up and to the right, its twist of snowy rock blinding in the sun, mink-brown weathered mazots scattered romantically at its base. Surely more pictures are taken from this spot than from anywhere else in Switzerland.

It was Edward Whymper's spectacular—and catastrophic—conquering of the Matterhorn, on July 14, 1865, that made Zermatt a household word. Whymper stayed at the Hotel Monte Rosa (☞ Dining and Lodging, *below*) the nights before his departure and there revealed the names of his party of seven for the historic climb: Michel Croz, a French guide; old Peter Taugwalder and his son, young Peter, local guides; Lord Francis Douglas, a 19-year-old Englishman; Douglas Hadow; the Reverend Charles Hudson; and Whymper himself. They climbed together, pairing "tourists," as Whymper called the Englishmen, with experienced locals. They camped at 11,000 ft and by 10 AM had reached the base of the mountain's famous hook. Wrote Whymper of the final moments:

The higher we rose the more intense became the excitement. The slope eased off, at length we could be detached, and Croz and I, dashing away, ran a neck-and-neck race, which ended in a dead heat. At 1:40 PM, the world was at our feet, and the Matterhorn was conquered!

Croz pulled off his shirt and tied it to a stick as a flag, one that was seen in Zermatt below. They stayed at the summit one hour, then prepared for the descent, tying themselves together in an order agreed on by all. Croz led, then Hadow, Hudson, Lord Douglas, the elder Taugwalder, then the younger, and Whymper, who lingered to sketch the summit and leave their names in a bottle.

I suggested to Hudson that we should attach a rope to the rocks on our arrival at the difficult bit, and hold it as we descended, as an additional protection. He approved the idea, but it was not definitely decided that it should be done.

They headed off, "one man moving at a time; when he was firmly planted the next advanced," Whymper recalled.

Croz . . . was in the act of turning around to go down a step or two himself; at this moment Mr. Hadow slipped, fell against him, and knocked him over. I heard one startled exclamation from Croz, then saw him and Mr. Hadow flying downward; in another moment Hudson was dragged from his steps, and Lord Douglas immediately after him. All this was the work of a moment. Immediately we heard Croz's exclamation, old Peter and I planted ourselves as firmly as the rocks would permit; the rope was taut between us, and the jerk came on us both as on one man. We held; but the rope broke midway between Taugwalder and Lord Francis Douglas. For a few seconds we saw our unfortunate companions sliding downward on their backs, and spreading out their hands, endeavoring to save themselves. They passed from our sight uninjured, disappeared one by one, and fell from precipice to precipice on to the Matterhorn glacier below, a distance of nearly 4,000 feet in height. From the moment the rope broke it was impossible to help them. So perished our comrades!

A "sharp-eyed lad" ran into the Hotel Monte Rosa to report an avalanche fallen from the Matterhorn summit; he had witnessed the deaths of the four mountaineers. The body of young Lord Douglas was never recovered, but the others lie in the grim little cemetery behind the Zermatt church, surrounded by scores of other failed mountaineers, including a recent American whose tomb bears the simple epitaph: I CHOSE TO CLIMB.

In summer, the streets of Zermatt fill with sturdy, weathered climbers, state-of-the-art ropes and picks hanging at their hips. They continue to tackle the peaks, and climbers have mastered the Matterhorn literally thousands of times since Whymper's disastrous victory.

In Zermatt it's quite simple to gain the broader perspective of high altitudes without risking life or limb; the train trip up the **Gornergrat** on the *Gornergratbahn* functions as an excursion as well as ski transport. Part of its rail system was completed in 1898, and it's the highest open-air rail system in Europe (the tracks to the Jungfraujoch, though higher, bore through the face of the Eiger). It connects out of the main Zermatt train station and heads sharply left, at right angles with the track that brings you into town. Its first stop is the **Riffelberg,** which, at 2,582 m (8,469 ft), offers wide-open views of the Matterhorn. Farther on, from **Rotenboden,** at 2,819 m (9,246 ft), a short downhill walk leads to the **Riffelsee,** which obligingly provides photographers with a postcard-perfect reflection of the famous peak. At the end of the 9-km (5½-mi) line, the train stops at the summit station of **Gornergrat** (3,130 m/10,266 ft), and passengers pour onto the observation terraces to take in the majestic views of the Matterhorn, Monte Rosa, Gorner Glacier, and an expanse of scores of peaks and 24 other glaciers. If you ski or hike down, the cost of the trip is just 37 SF. ⊠ *Leaves from Zermatt station.* 🚠 *63 SF round-trip.* ☽ *Departures every 24 mins 7–7. Bring warm clothes, sunglasses, and sturdy shoes.*

Zermatt lies in a hollow of meadows and trees ringed by mountains— among them the broad **Monte Rosa** (4,554 m/14,937 ft) and its tallest peak, the **Dufourspitze** (at 4,634 m/15,200 ft, the highest point in Switzerland)—of which visitors hear relatively little, so all-consuming is the cult of the Matterhorn. In the mid-19th century, Zermatt was virtually unheard-of; the few visitors who came to town stayed at the vicarage. It happened, however, that the vicar had a nose for business and a chaplain named Seiler. Joseph Seiler convinced his little brother, Alexander, to come to this spectacular mountain valley and start an inn. Opened in 1854 and named the Hotel Monte Rosa, it remains as one of five Seiler hotels in Zermatt. In 1891, the cog railway between Visp and Zermatt took its first summer run and began disgorging tourists with profitable regularity—though it didn't plow through in wintertime until 1927.

Skiing

Zermatt's skiable terrain lives up to its reputation: The 73 lift installations are capable of moving well above 50,000 skiers per hour to reach its approximately 245 km (152 mi) of marked pistes—if you count those of Breuil in Italy. Among the lifts are the cable car that carries skiers in several minutes up to an elevation of 3,820 m (12,532 ft) on the Klein Matterhorn, the small *Gornergratbahn* that creeps up to the Gornergrat (3,100 m/10,170 ft), and a subway through an underground tunnel that gives more pleasure to ecologists than it does to sun-loving skiers.

This royal plateau has several less-than-perfect features, however, not least of which is the separation of the skiable territory into three sectors. **Sunegga-Blauherd-Rothorn** culminates at an elevation of 3,100 m (10,170 ft). **Gornergrat-Stockhorn** (3,400 m/11,155 ft) is the second. The third is the region dominated by the **Klein Matterhorn;** to go from this sector to the others, you must return to the bottom of the valley and lose considerable time crossing town to reach the lifts to the other elevations. The solution is to ski for a whole day in the same area, especially during high season (mid-December to the end of February, or even until Easter if the snow cover is good). On the other hand, thanks to snowmaking machines and the eternal snows of the Klein Matterhorn, Zermatt is said to guarantee skiers 2,200 m (7,216 ft) of vertical drop no matter what the snowfall—an impressive claim. A one-day lift ticket costs 60 SF; a six-day pass costs 296 SF. A ski school (Skischulbüro; ⊠ Banhofstr., ☎ 027/9662466) operates during the high season, from mid-December until April.

Dining and Lodging

$$ ✕ **Findlerhof.** Whether for long lunches between sessions on the slopes,
★ for the traditional wind-down après-ski, or for a panoramic meal
break on an all-day hike, this mountain restaurant in tiny Findeln,
perched high between the Sunnegga and Blauherd ski areas, is de
rigueur with hip young Brits and Americans. The Matterhorn views
from the wraparound dining porch are astonishing, the winter dining
room cozy with pine and stone, and the food surprisingly fresh and
creative. Franz and Heidi Schwery tend their own Alpine garden to pro-
vide spinach for the bacon-crisped salad and rhubarb and berries for
their hot desserts. It's about a 30-minute walk down from the Sunnegga
Express stop and another 30 minutes back down to Zermatt. ✉ *Find-
eln,* ☎ *027/9672588. No credit cards. Closed May–mid-June and
mid-Oct.–Nov.*

$$ ✕ **Zum See.** This alternative to Findlerhof, beyond Findeln in a tiny
★ village (little more than a cluster of mazots) of the same name, serves
up light meals of a quality and inventiveness that would merit acclaim
even if it weren't in the middle of nowhere at 1,766 m (5,792 ft). In
summer, its shaded picnic tables draw hikers rewarding themselves at
the finish of a day's climb; in winter, its cozy, low-ceiling log dining
room sets skiers aglow with an impressive assortment of brandies. Regional specialties are prepared with masterly care, from wild mushrooms
in pastry shells to rabbit, Rösti, and *foie de veau* (calves' liver). ✉ *Zum
See,* ☎ *027/9672045. Reservations essential après-ski. AE, MC, V.
Closed May–June and Oct.–mid-Dec.*

$ ✕ **Elsie's Bar.** This tiny log cabin of a ski haunt, directly across from
the Zermatt church, draws an international crowd for cocktails American style. Light meals include cheese dishes and snails. ✉ *Kirchepl.,*
☎ *027/9672431. AE, DC, MC, V.*

$$$$ ✕🏨 **Hotel Monte Rosa.** Alexander Seiler founded his first hotel in the
★ core of this historic building, expanding it over the years to its current
scale. Behind the Monte Rosa's graceful shuttered facade you find an
ideal balance between modern convenience and history in the abundance of brass, stained and beveled glass, burnished pine, the fine old
flagstone floors, the original ceiling moldings, the fireplaces, and the
candlelighted Victorian dining hall. The room decor, while impeccably up to date, favors prim Victorian prints and gleaming cabinetry.
Southern views go quickly and cost more. The bar is an après-ski
must. ✉ *CH-3920,* ☎ *027/9673333,* FAX *027/9671160. 44 rooms, 5
suites. Restaurant, bar, sauna (at Mont Cervin). AE, DC, MC, V.*

$$$$ ✕🏨 **Mont Cervin.** One of the flagships of the Seiler dynasty, which
★ founded and still dominates the hotel business in Zermatt, this sleek,
luxurious, and urbane mountain hotel is never grandiose, in either scale
or attitude. First built in 1852, it's unusually low-slung for a grand hotel,
with dark beams and a color scheme of burnished jewel tones that en-
hances the womblike impression. Jacket and tie are required in the guests'
dining hall, and for the Friday gala buffet it's black tie only. There's
an attractive stübli-style *dancing* (dance bar) with live music and a grill
and a sparkling sports center. ✉ *CH-3920,* ☎ *027/9668888,* FAX *027/
9672878. 101 rooms, 43 suites. Restaurant, 2 bars, grill, indoor pool,
sauna, health club, dance club. AE, DC, MC, V.*

$$$$ ✕🏨 **Pollux.** This modern hotel is simple and chic, with its straightforward rooms trimmed in pine and leatherette. It's small-scale, and
none of its windows looks onto the Matterhorn, but its position directly on the main pedestrian shopping street puts guests in the heart
of resort activities. There are a French restaurant and an appealing old-
fashioned stübli that draws locals for its low-price lunches, snacks, and
Valais cheese dishes, enjoyed street-side. Children in adjoining rooms,
complete with toilet and shower, get a 60% reduction. ✉ *CH-3920,*

☎ 027/9664000, ℻ 027/9664001. 33 rooms. Restaurant, stübli, sauna, dance club. AE, DC, MC, V.

$$$–$$$$ ✕⌘ **Julen.** The 1937 chalet architecture, the local *Arvenholz* (Alpen
★ pine) within, and the impeccable 1981 renovation qualify this second-generation lodge for membership in the Romantik chain, which assures guests of authentic regional comforts. The rooms are simple, with carved pine beds, beige carpet, and warm brown ceramic-tile baths; those on the south have balconies with Matterhorn views. The cozy but elegant main restaurant offers French cooking—the daily menu is an excellent value—but downstairs the welcoming stübli, all pine, beams, and cowbells, serves unusual dishes prepared with lamb (such as lamb's tongue in capers) from local family-owned flocks. ⌂ *CH-3920*, ☎ 027/9667600, ℻ 027/9667676. 37 rooms. Restaurant, café, sauna. AE, DC, MC, V.

$$–$$$$ ✕⌘ **Riffelalp.** If you want to experience all the beauty of Zermatt's
★ spectacular setting and none of the bustle of a popular, urbanized resort, consider staying partway up the Gornergrat cogwheel run on a sunny, isolated plateau. This Victorian inn was burned and rebuilt from the ground up in 1988, and now it's a trim, solid, airy structure with pretty rooms and stunning views. The restaurant has a terrace that's popular with day-trippers and offers such unusual local specialties as *Walliser noodle gratin* (noodle and cheese casserole) and ravioli with morel cream sauce. It's a 400-m (1,312-ft) walk through the woods from the cog-rail stop; if you have luggage and equipment, the owners will meet you. ⌂ *CH-3920*, ☎ 027/9664646, ℻ 027/9675109. 20 rooms. Restaurant, sauna, tennis court. AE, DC, MC, V.

$$$$ ⌘ **Schweizerhof.** Despite its location on Zermatt's main pedestrian street and the ranks of storefronts on its ground floor, this member of the Seiler group is surprisingly tranquil, and some of its angled windows have Matterhorn views. A solid building, it has been warmed with tooled pine and cozy fabrics, and its facilities are top quality, including a terrace garden in the back. As a Seiler hotel, it participates in the Dine-Around plan, which allows pension guests to eat in any of the Seiler restaurants, including Mont Cervin, Monte Rosa, and others. ⌂ *CH-3920*, ☎ 027/9676767, ℻ 027/9676769. 103 rooms. Restaurant, indoor pool, sauna. AE, DC, MC, V.

$$$$ ⌘ **Zermatterhof.** If you can afford no-limits luxury, then you might as
★ well go for the best and indulge in all that this faultless amenity has to offer. Built in 1879 and totally renovated during the 1980s and '90s, they have had more than a century to get things exactly right. Rooms in multifarious shades and styles of wood have either granite or marble bathrooms, where you can lie back and enjoy the ultimate in alpine decadence—nibbling a chocolate Matterhorn while your back is massaged by Jacuzzi bubbles. The formal restaurant, where you feel like a grand orchestra would be a suitable accompaniment to dinner, is for guests only, but the quality of its French-Italian-influenced cuisine meets the hotel's overall five-star standard. The glass-dome Rôtisserie La Broche is open to nonguests. ⌂ *CH-3920*, ☎ 027/9666600, ℻ 027/9666699. 60 rooms, 26 suites. 2 restaurants, bar, indoor pool, hot tub, sauna, tennis court, health club. AE, DC, MC, V.

$$–$$$ ⌘ **Alphubel.** Although it's surrounded by other hotels and is close to the main street, this modest, comfortable pension built in 1954 feels off the beaten track—and it offers large, sunny balconies to lodgers on the south side. The interiors are a little institutional, but there's a sauna in the basement, available to guests for a small charge. ⌂ *CH-3920*, ☎ 027/9673003, ℻ 027/9676684. 31 rooms. Restaurant, sauna. AE, MC, V.

$$–$$$ ⌘ **Parnass.** Across the street from the roaring river, with views east and south to the Matterhorn, this simple '60s construction offers a cozy, clublike lounge, knotty-pine rooms, and private pension dining with unusually adventurous and successful cooking. In winter, annual regulars rub shoulders by the fireplace in this exceptionally welcoming hotel. ⊠ *CH-3920,* ☎ *027/9671179,* FAX *027/9674557. 31 rooms. Restaurant. MC, V.*

$–$$$ 🏨 **Romantica.** Among the scores of anonymously modern hotels cloned all over the Zermatt plain, this modest structure—unremarkable at first glance—offers an exceptional location directly above the town center, no more than a block up a narrow mazot-lined lane. Its tidy, bright gardens and flower boxes, its game trophies, and its old-style granite stove give it personality, and the plain rooms—in beige, white, and pine— benefit from big windows and balconies. Views take in the mountains, though not the Matterhorn, over a graceful clutter of stone roofs. ⊠ *CH-3920,* ☎ *027/9662650,* FAX *027/9662655. 13 rooms. AE, MC, V.*

$–$$$ 🏨 **Touring.** Its reassuringly traditional architecture and snug, sunny rooms full of pine, combined with an elevated position apart from town and excellent Matterhorn views, make this an appealing choice for travelers avoiding the chic downtown scene. Hearty daily menus are served to pension-guests in the cozy dining room, and a sunny enclosed playground has lounge chairs for parents. ⊠ *CH-3920,* ☎ *027/9671177,* FAX *027/9674601. 21 rooms, 10 with bath. Restaurant, stübli, exercise room. MC, V.*

$ 🏨 **Mischabel.** One of the least, if not *the* least, expensive hotels in this pricey resort town, the Mischabel provides comfort, atmosphere, and a central situation few places can match at twice the price: Southern balconies frame a perfect Matterhorn view—the higher the better. Creaky, homey, and covered with Arvenholz aged to the color of toffee, its rooms have sinks only and share the linoleum-lined showers on every floor. A generous daily menu, for guests only, caters to families and young skiers on the cheap. ⊠ *CH-3920,* ☎ *027/9671131,* FAX *027/9676507. 28 rooms. Restaurant. MC, V.*

Nightlife

Grampi's Bar (☎ 027/9677788), on the main drag, is a lively young people's bar, where you can get into the mood for dancing downstairs with a Lady Matterhorn cocktail. The newly renovated **T-Bar** (☎ 027/ 9674000), below the Hotel Pollux, plays more varied music then the generic disco-pap of the ski resorts, and its walls and ceilings are interestingly adorned with ancient skiing equipment, which somehow looks more comfortable than the garish space-age wear of today.

Outdoor Activities and Sports

MOUNTAIN BIKING AND CLIMBING

Mountain biking is severely limited by Zermatt authorities to prevent interference with hiking on trails. About 25 km (15 mi) have been set aside, however. A new map is available at the tourist office (☞ Visitor Information *in* Valais A to Z, *below*). Bikes can be rented at **Slalomsport** (☎ 027/9671116). For mountain-climbing guides and instruction, contact the **Alpin Center Zermatt** (☎ 027/9662460).

TENNIS

The **Tennisstar/Club** (☎ 027/9663000) has three courts. The **Gemeinde** (☎ 027/9673673) maintains nine courts.

Shopping

Zermatt may be Switzerland's souvenir capital, offering a broad variety of watches, knives, and logo clothing. Folk crafts and traditional products you'll find include large, grotesque masks of carved wood and lidded channes in pewter or tin, molded in graduated sizes; they are sold everywhere, even in the grocery stores of tourist-conscious resorts.

SPORTS EQUIPMENT AND APPAREL

Zermatt's streets are lined with stores offering state-of-the-art sports equipment and apparel, from collapsible grappling hooks for climbers to lightweight hiking boots in psychedelic colors. You'll see plenty of the new must-have walking sticks—pairs of lightweight, spiked ski poles for hikers to add a bit of upper-body workout to their climb and a touch of neon flash as well. Although prices are consistently high, the array of choices is dazzling.

Bayard (⊠ Bahnhofpl., ☎ 027/9664950; ⊠ Bahnhofstr., ☎ 027/9664960) heads the long list of sporting-goods stores. **Glacier Sport** (☎ 027/9672719) specializes in ski equipment and accessories. **La Cabane** (☎ 027/9672249) is the best source for trendy sports clothing.

Grächen

⑭ *28 km (17 mi) south of Visp.*

From the valley resort village of St. Niklaus, a narrow, winding road crawls up to this small, tame family resort nestled comfortably on a sunny shelf at 1,617 m (5,304 ft). Little more than a picturesque scattering of small hotels, chalets, and mazots, it concentrates its business near a central parking lot and closes the rest of its streets to car traffic. Small and isolated as it is, there are butchers, grocers, and enough shops and cafés to keep visitors occupied on a foggy day. This is a place to escape tourist crowds, hike high trails undisturbed by the traffic you find near the larger resorts, or ski a variety of fine trails on the Hannigalp. Grächen makes a heroic effort to keep families happy, offering a staffed and supervised winter-sports area, with ski and toboggan lifts, playgrounds, and even igloos, for children under six years old, free of charge.

Dining and Lodging

$$ ✕☐ Désirée. Though the rooms are institution-modern, the balconies take in valley views and the restaurant-stübli downstairs is rich in smoky, meaty, local atmosphere. It's in the center but above traffic; access is by electric cart. ⊠ CH-3925, ☎ 027/9562255, FAX 027/9562070. 22 rooms. Restaurant, stübli, exercise room. AE, DC, MC, V.

$$ ✕☐ Walliserhof. Directly in the center of town, this eye-catching dark-wood Valais-style chalet is ringed with balconies; in summer geraniums spill from every window. The interior is bright and elegant, and rooms glow with warm knotty pine. The south-side suites hog the magnificent views. The restaurant, serving basic French fare, has a formal air, with candles and linens. ⊠ CH-3925, ☎ 027/9561122, FAX 027/9562922. 25 rooms. Restaurant, café, dance club. AE, MC, V.

$–$$ ✕☐ Hannigalp. The oldest hotel in town, this welcoming landmark built
★ in 1909 and run by the same family for 80 years has been completely modernized without losing its regional character. The rooms have been updated to spare, blond-wood simplicity; most have balconies. The amenities are remarkable for the price. Headed by the owner himself, the kitchen creates straightforward French cuisine for the restaurant and regional specialties to serve in the cozier bar. It is in a quiet, car-free zone. ⊠ CH-3925, ☎ 027/9562555, FAX 027/9562855. 22 rooms. Restaurant, bar, indoor pool, hot tub, sauna, tennis court. MC, V.

Saas-Fee

⑮ *36 km (22 mi) south of Visp.*

At the end of the switchback road to Saas-Grund (1,559 m/5,114 ft) lies a parking area where visitors must abandon their cars for the length of their stay in Saas-Fee. It might be enough to simply stay in the parking lot, for the view even on arriving at this lofty (1,790 m/5,871 ft) plateau is humbling. Saas-Fee lies in a deep valley that leaves no doubt about its source: It seems to pour from the vast, intimidating **Fee Glacier,** which oozes like icy lava from the broad spread of peaks above. *Fee* can be translated as "fairy," and Saas-Fee is indeed fairy-like: It's at the heart of a cirque of mountains, 13 of which tower to more than 4,000 m (13,120 ft), among them the **Dom** (4,545 m/14,908 ft), the highest mountain entirely on Swiss soil.

The village itself, draped along the valley floor, combines the modern-resort look with its weathered chalets with some success. The 1963 **church** (✉ Town center) is a stylized and inoffensive homage to the shingle steeples all across the country.

Skiing

The first glacier to be used for skiing here was the **Längfluh** (2,870 m/9,414 ft), accessed by gondola, then cable car. The run is magnificent, sometimes physically demanding, and always varied. From the Längfluh you can take the new ski lift to reach *the* ski area of Saas-Fee, the **Felskinn-Mittelallalin** sector (3,000 m–3,500 m/9,840 ft–11,480 ft). Felskinn harbors its own surprise: In order to preserve the land and landscape, the Valaisans have constructed a subterranean funicular, the Métro Alpin, which climbs through the heart of the mountain to Mittelallalin, that is, halfway up the Allalinhorn (4,027 m/13,210 ft); tourists debark in a rotating restaurant noted more for the austere grandeur of its natural surroundings than for the quality of its food. Felskinn-Mittelallalin's exceptional site, its high elevation, its runs (15 km/9 mi), and its ample facilities (cable car, funicular, and five ski lifts) have made Saas-Fee the number one summer-skiing resort in Switzerland. A one-day lift ticket costs 56 SF; a six-day pass costs 260 SF.

Dining and Lodging

$$$$ ✕🏨 **Waldhotel Fletschhorn.** High on a forested hillside above the re-
★ sort, this quiet *Landgasthof* (country inn) is a sophisticated retreat for gourmets who like to rest undisturbed after an excellent meal. The baths are sizable, and although the rooms have ultramodern fittings, they're mellowed with pine paneling, antiques, and serene views. Half board includes innovative French cuisine cooked by Switzerland's 1994 Chef of the Year, Irma Dütsch, featuring local products and specialties: reindeer with wild mushrooms, stuffed quail with polenta in pinot noir, straw-roasted chicken. Ms. Dütsch published her own cookbook in early 1998 and also runs culinary courses at the hotel. Reservations are essential at the restaurant. Manager Hansjörg Dütsch provides transportation from town. ✉ CH-3906, ☎ 027/9572131, ℻ 027/9572187. *15 rooms. Restaurant, sauna. AE, DC, MC, V.*

$$$$ 🏨 **Ferienart Walliserhof.** The slightly battered woodwork of the rooms suggests it may soon be time for renovation, but it is hard to believe you are in the same hotel when you come downstairs and take advantage of the unrivalled facilities this friendly hotel has to offer. The pool with the mock-glacier roof is an unusual in-water experience, and you can peruse the labyrinth of bars and restaurants offering a choice ranging from Thai to Italian cuisine. The hotel's location in the town's very center doesn't deprive it of great panoramas on all sides. ✉ CH-3906, ☎ 027/9581900, ℻ 027/9581905. *43 rooms, 9 suites. 3 restaurants, café, piano bar, indoor pool, barbershop, beauty salon, massage, sauna, pro shop, nightclub. AE, DC, MC, V.*

$$$–$$$$ 🏨 **Allalin.** Families especially will appreciate the flexibility and up-to-
★ date design of the apartment quarters available here, all with kitchen equipment as well as balconies. In high season, guests must pay half pension and eat one meal per day in the restaurant—no great punishment, as the

kitchen is surprisingly sophisticated. Built in 1928, the hotel feels warm, bright, and natural. It's on the hill just east of the center and a block from the main parking, and all doubles have a spectacular southern or southeastern view. ⊠ *CH-3906*, ☎ *027/9571815*, FAX *027/9573115. 27 rooms. Restaurant, bar, café, kitchenettes, sauna. AE, DC, MC, V.*

$$$–$$$$ 🏨 **Saaserhof.** Renovation in 1994 brought the dated decor of this Saas-Fee institution up to date attractively, and the location near the best lift facilities is excellent. ⊠ *CH-3906*, ☎ *027/9573551*, FAX *027/9572883. 36 rooms, 5 suites. Restaurant, bar, hot tub, sauna. AE, DC, MC, V.*

$–$$$ 🏨 **Britannia.** Compensating for its brand-new architecture with light carved pine in every corner, this tidy, fresh, simple lodging is in the heart of town, near resort shopping on the main pedestrian street. The best balconies face south and east. ⊠ *CH-3906*, ☎ *027/9571616*, FAX *027/ 9571942. 19 rooms. Restaurant, bar. AE, MC, V.*

Outdoor Activities and Sports

MOUNTAIN CLIMBING

The **Swiss Mountaineering School** (☎ 027/9574464) conducts daily guided forays.

SPORTS CENTER

The **Bielen Recreation Center** (☎ 027/9572475) has a four-lane swimming pool, children's pool, whirlpools, steam baths, sauna, solarium, fitness center, and games.

TENNIS

Kalbermatten Sports Ground (☎ 027/9572454) has two tennis courts available. **Bielen Indoor Tennis Courts** (☎ 027/9572475) also has a pair.

BRIG AND THE ALPINE PASSES

This region is the Grand Central Station of the Alpine region; all mountain passes lead to Brig, and traffic pours in (and through) from Italy, the Ticino, central Switzerland, the Berner Oberland—and, via the latter, from Paris, Brussels, and London and Rome.

Brig

16   *209 km (129 mi) southeast of Bern.*

A rail and road junction joining four cantons, this small but vital town has for centuries been a center of trade with Italy. It guards not only the Simplon route but also the high end of the Rhône Valley, which leads past the Aletsch Glacier to Gletsch and the Grimsel Pass (toward Meiringen and the Berner Oberland) or the Furka Pass (toward Andermatt and central Switzerland). The fantastical **Stockalperschloss,** a massive Baroque castle, was built between 1658 and 1678 by Kaspar Jodok von Stockalper, a Swiss tycoon who made his fortune in Italian trade over the Simplon Pass. Topped with three gilt onion domes and containing a courtyard wrapped by elegant Italianate arcades, it was once Switzerland's largest private home and is now completely restored. ⊠ *Alte Simplonstr., from station walk up Bahnhofstr. to Sebastienpl., turn left onto Alte Simplonstr.,* ☎ *027/9231901.* 🎟 *5 SF.* ☉ *May–Oct., Tues.–Sun., guided tours at 10, 11, 2, 3, 4, and 5.*

En Route   Above the eastern outskirts of Brig is the entrance to the **Simplon Tunnel,** which carries trains nearly 20 km (12 mi) before emerging into Italian daylight. The first of the twin tunnels—the world's longest railway tunnels—was started in 1898 and took six years to complete.

Simplon Pass

⑰ *23 km (14 mi) southeast of Brig.*

Beginning just outside Brig, this historic road meanders through deep gorges and wide, barren, rock-strewn pastures to offer increasingly beautiful views back toward Brig. At the summit (2,010 m/6,593 ft), the **Simplon-Kulm Hotel** shares the high meadow with the **Simplon Hospice,** built 150 years ago at Napoléon's request and now owned by the monks of St. Bernard. Just beyond stands the bell-towered **Alt Spital,** a lodging built during the 17th century by Kaspar Jodok von Stockalper.

From the summit you can still see parts of the old road of the tradesmen and Napoléon, and it is easy to imagine the hardships travelers faced at these heights. Look north toward the Bernese Alps and a portion of the massive Aletsch Glacier. Beyond the pass, the road continues through Italy, and it's possible to cut across the Italian upthrust and reenter Switzerland in the Ticino, near Ascona.

Riederalp

⑱ *13 km (8 mi) north of the Brig.*

The bleak and stony ascent of the Val de Conches follows the increasingly wild, silty Rhône to its source, with mountain resorts threading into the flanking heights. Within the Val de Conches, Riederalp is best known as the home of Art Furrer, who became famous in the United States as one of the pioneers of freestyle skiing. On his return to Switzerland, he came to this resort and established a freestyle ski school available to nearly every good skier.

On a rugged, treeless plateau, the resort is accessible only by cable car from **Mörel,** and its views over the Italian Alps are rivaled only by the staggering views over the Aletsch Glacier on secondary ascent by cable car up to **Moosfluh.** A swift new (1995) gondola up to Moosfluh, reputedly the fastest in Europe, holds 12 people. Riederalp borders the preserved pine stands of the **Aletsch Forest,** one of the highest in Europe. From Fiesch, just up the valley from Mörel, you can ascend by cable car all the way to the top of the **Eggishorn** (2,927 m/9,600 ft). This extraordinary vantage point looks over the entire sweep of the Aletsch and its surrounding peaks.

Skiing

At 1,900 m (6,232 ft), with a peak of 2,700 m (8,856 ft), **Riederalp** has seven lifts and 30 km (19 mi) of downhill runs, a third of which are expert. A one-day lift ticket (including access to the whole Aletsch ski area) costs 43 SF; a six-day pass costs 203 SF. Stretching from Münster to Oberwald, the **Val de Conches** offers superior snow conditions and villages straight out of the Middle Ages, as well as the most beautiful cross-country skiing trails in the Alps, with the exception of those in the Upper Engadine (☞ Saint-Moritz *in* Chapter 4) at 1,300 m (4,265 ft), with a peak of 1,450 m (4,757 ft); it has 85 km (53 mi) of trails and an ice-skating rink. Freestyle skier Art Furrer's ski school (Skischule Forum Alpin; ☎ 027/9272121) is still up and running.

Gletsch

⑲ *48 km (30 mi) northeast of Brig.*

Summer travelers may want to travel the distance to the tiny resort of Gletsch, named for its prime attraction: the glacier that gives birth to the Rhône. The views over the Bernese and Valais Alps are magnificent. From Gletsch, you can drive over the Furka Pass directly or over the scenic Grimsel Pass (2,130 m/7,101 ft) to the Bernese Oberland.

Furka Pass

★ ⑳ *11 km (7 mi) east of Gletsch, 59 km (37 mi) northeast of Brig.*

Making the final ascent of Valais, drivers arrive at Oberwald, source of the train tunnel through the Furka Pass, which cuts over the heights and leads down to central Switzerland. Spectacular views and stark moon-scapes are punctuated by the occasional Spielberg-esque military oper-ations—white-clad soldiers melting out of camouflaged hangars carved deep into solid-rock walls. The sleek, broad highway that snakes down toward Andermatt shows Swiss Alpine engineering at its best.

VALAIS A TO Z

Arriving and Departing

By Car
Valais is something of a dead end by nature: A fine expressway (**A9**) carries you in from Lac Léman (Lake Geneva), but to exit—or enter—from the east end, you must park your car on a train and ride through the **Furka Pass** tunnel to go north, or take the train through the tun-nel through the **Simplon Pass** to go southeast. (The serpentine roads over these passes are open in summer; weather permitting, the Sim-plon road stays open all year.) You also may cut through from or to Kandersteg in the Berner Oberland by taking a car train to Goppen-stein or Brig. A summer-only road twists over the **Grimsel Pass** as well, heading toward Meiringen and the Berner Oberland or, over the **Brünig Pass**, to Luzern.

By Plane
Geneva's Cointrin (☎ 022/7993111) serves international flights and is nearest the west (French) end of Valais; it's about two hours away by train or car. **Zürich's Kloten** Airport (☎ 1571060) brings you closer to the east (German) side, but the Alps are in the way; you must con-nect by rail tunnel or drive over one of the passes.

By Train
There are straightforward rail connections to the region by way of Lau-sanne to the west and Brig/Brigue to the east. The two are connected by one clean rail sweep that runs the length of the valley. For infor-mation, call ☎ 040/671040.

Getting Around

By Car
If you want to see the tiny back roads—and there's much to be seen off the beaten path—a car is the only means. The **A9** expressway from Lausanne shrinks, at Sierre, to a well-maintained highway that con-tinues on to Brig. Distances in the north and south valleys can be de-ceptive: Apparently short jogs are full of painfully slow switchbacks and distractingly beautiful views. Both Zermatt and Saas-Fee are car-free resorts, though you can drive all the way to a parking lot at the edge of Saas-Fee's main street. Zermatt must be approached by rail from Täsch, the end of the line for cars. Car ferries over mountain passes, either to Kandersteg or over the Furka Pass, can be claustrophobic and time-consuming: Think of them as the world's longest car wash.

By Train

The main rail service covers the length of the valley from Lausanne to Brig, but routes into the tributary valleys are limited. There is a train station in the main tourist magnet, Zermatt (☎ 027/9664711).

On Foot

This is one of the hiking capitals of Switzerland, and it's impossible to overstate the value of getting away from wheeled transit and setting off on a mountain path through the sweet-scented pine woods and into the wide-open country above timberline. The trails are wild but well maintained here, and the regional tourist office (☞ Visitor Information, *below*) publishes a thorough map with planned and timed walking tours. Ask for *Sentiers valaisans;* it's written in English, French, and German.

Contacts and Resources

Emergencies

Police: Crans-Montana (☎ 027/4812450); **Sion** (☎ 027/6065656); **Verbier** (☎ 027/7713069); **Zermatt** (☎ 027/9666920). **Medical assistance: Crans-Montana** (ambulance, ☎ 027/4551717); **Sion** (ambulance, ☎ 027/3233333); **Verbier** (☎ 027/7220144); **Zermatt** (ambulance, ☎ 027/9672000). **Late-night pharmacies** (☎ 111).

Guided Tours

BUS

Guided coach tours of Valais, including lodging and dining packages, are offered by **Valais Incoming** (✉ 3 av. de Tourbillon, Sion, ☎ 027/3292422), a tour company based in Sion.

HELICOPTER

Sion's **Air-Glaciers** (☎ 027/3226464) proposes several itineraries out of Sion for groups of four or six that want a bird's-eye view of Valais—from a helicopter. Prices range from 341 SF for 10 minutes on up into the thousands for personalized itineraries.

VINEYARDS

Wine lovers can trace the best Valais *vignobles* (vineyards) firsthand by following a list provided by the **OPAV** (Office de Promotion des Produits de l'Agriculture Valaisanne; ✉ 5 av. de la Gare, ☎ 027/3222247), which promotes agriculture in the region; you must arrange the visits yourself.

Visitor Information

The main tourist office for Valais is in **Sion** (✉ 6 rue Pré-Fleuri, CH-1951, ☎ 027/3223161, ℻ 027/3231572).

Local offices: **Brig** (✉ Train station, ☎ 028/222222). **Crans-sur-Sierres** (✉ CH-3963, ☎ 027/4850800). **Montana** (✉ av. de la Gare, CH-3962, ☎ 027/4850404). **Riederalp** (☎ 027/9271365). **Saas-Fee** (✉ CH-3906, ☎ 027/9581858). **Sion** (✉ pl. de la Planta, CH-1950, ☎ 027/3228586). **Verbier** (✉ CH-1936, ☎ 027/7753888). **Zermatt** (✉ CH-3920, ☎ 027/9670181).

12 Vaud

Lausanne, Montreux,
Les Alpes Vaudoises

The verdant vineyards of La Côte and
Lavaux, the rugged Alpes Vaudoises,
and two graceful waterfront cities—
Lausanne and Montreux—comprise
one of Switzerland's most diverse
regions. Centered around Lac Léman,
also known as Lake Geneva, this
French-speaking canton harbors
some of the country's most famous
cathedrals and castles, as well as Alpine
retreats, balmy lake resorts, and
picturesque coastal wine villages.

FORCED TO CONCENTRATE ON JUST ONE region of Switzerland, a visitor could do worse than choose Vaud (pronounced Voh). Its cultural and geographic diversity covers the spectrum: It has a world-class Gothic cathedral (Lausanne) and one of Europe's most evocative châteaux (Chillon), Edwardian mansions and weathered-wood chalets, sophisticated culture and ancient folk traditions, snowy Alpine slopes and balmy lake resorts, simple fondue and the legerdemain of some of the world's great chefs. And everywhere there are the roadside vineyards that strobe black-green, black-green, as the luxurious rows of vines alternate with the rich, black loam.

Updated by
Jennifer Quale

This is the region of Lac Léman, or Lake Geneva, a grand and romantic body of water crowned by Lausanne's cathedral and the castle of Chillon. Its romance—Savoy Alps looming across the horizon, steamers fanning across its surface, palm trees rustling along its shores—made it a focal point of the budding 19th-century tourist industry, an object of literary fancy, an inspiration to the arts. In a Henry James novella, the imprudent Daisy Miller made waves when she crossed its waters unchaperoned to visit Chillon; Byron's Bonivard languished in chains in its dungeons. From their homes outside Montreux, Stravinsky wrote *The Rite of Spring* and Strauss his transcendent *Four Last Songs*. Yet at the lake's east end, romance and culture give way to wilderness and farmlands, to mountains with some peaks so high they grow grazing grass sweet enough to flavor the cheese. There are resorts, of course—Leysin, Villars-Gryon, Château-d'Oex—but none so famous as to upstage the region itself.

Throughout the canton, French is spoken, and the temperament the Vaudoise inherited from the Romans and Burgundians sets them apart from their Swiss-German countrymen. It's evident in their humor, their style, and—above all—their love of their own good wine.

Pleasures and Pastimes

Châteaux
Home to magnificently restored Chillon, the most visited if not the best château in Switzerland, Vaud offers a variety of smaller draws as well, including Coppet, Nyon, Prangins, Rolle, Allaman, Aubonne, and Rougemont, among others. Most house museums and offer baronial views.

Dining
Because of its fortuitous position, draped along a sloping, sunny coast and facing a sparkling lake and the looming peaks of the French Alps, the Lake Geneva coast draws weekenders and car tourists who speed along the waterfront highway, careening through cobbled wine towns, tops down, gastronomy guides on the dashboard, in search of the perfect lunch. As in all great wine regions, *dégustation* and *haute gastronomie* go hand in hand, and in inns and auberges throughout La Côte and Lavaux (the two stretches of vineyard-lined coast) you'll dine beside ascoted oenophiles who lower their half-lenses to study a label and order a multicourse feast to complement their extensive tastings.

The culinary delights of Vaud range from the *cuisine du marché* (cuisine based on fresh market produce) of top-drawer chefs to the simplest fare: *papet Vaudois,* a straightforward stew of leeks, potatoes, and cream served with superb local sausages; delicate *filets de perche* (local perch fillets, sautéed in butter and served by the dozen); and even *malakoffs,* egg-and-Gruyère fritters, which trace back to soldiers of La Côte fighting in the Crimean Wars.

Though nowadays fondue is de rigueur in any Alpine setting, Vaud is the undisputed capital of the Swiss national dish and one of its most loyal custodians. In the Pays-d'Enhaut (Highlands) and on the slopes of the Jura Mountains, the cattle head uphill every summer, and production of the local cheese soars—the nutty hard cheese known as Gruyère, whether or not it comes from that Fribourgeois village. It is sold at various stages of its production: young and mild, ripe and savory, or aged to a heady tang.

The concept of fondue is elementary: Grated cheese is melted in a pot with white wine, garlic, and a dash of kirsch, and diners sit in a circle around the pot, dipping chunks of bread into the bubbling mixture with long, slender forks. Many restaurants prefer to serve it in an adjoining *carnotzet,* or stübli (the French and German version of a cozy drinking parlor)—not only to re-create a rustic Alpine experience but also to spare fellow diners the heavy fumes of Sterno, which is used to keep the cheese warm and liquid.

It is a dish at its best when the windows are thick with frost. To wash it down, you drink fruity white wine or plain black tea—never red wine, beer, or (shudder) cola. And halfway through, you down a stiff shot of kirsch—the reviving blast called the *coup du milieu* (shot in the middle). A mixed salad of winter crudités—grated carrots, celery root, beets, or cabbage—is indispensable to digestion.

Another Alpine cheese specialty of Vaud is *tomme,* mild white pressed patties of fresh, raw cow's-milk cheese, often breaded and fried and served whole, piping hot and oozing through the golden crust.

To experience Vaud's best cuisine, look for *déjeuners d'affaires* (business lunches), plats du jour, and prix-fixe menus, which can offer considerable savings over à la carte dining.

CATEGORY	COST*
$$$$	over 70 SF
$$$	40 SF–70 SF
$$	20 SF–40 SF
$	under 20 SF

Prices are per person for a three-course meal (two-course meal in $ category), including sales tax and 15% service charge.

Lodging

It's a pleasure unique to Vaud to wake up, part floor-length sheers, and look out over Lake Geneva to Mont Blanc; a series of 19th-century grand hotels with banks of balconied lake-view rooms were created to offer this luxury to such grand-tourists as Strauss, Twain, Stravinsky, and Henry James. Yet there's no shortage of charming little inns that offer similar views on an intimate scale. Up another 1,200 m (3,936 ft) you'll find the antithesis to an airy lakefront inn: the cozy, honey-gold Alpine chalet, with down quilts in starched white envelopes, homespun doilies, balustrade balconies with potted geraniums, and panoramic views.

The hotels of Lausanne and Montreux are long on luxury and grace, and low prices are not a strong suit, though they do offer an occasional bargain. Especially at peak periods—Christmas–New Year's and June–August—it's important to book ahead. Plenty of small auberges in the villages along the lake offer traditional dishes and simple comforts. Up in the Pays-d'Enhaut and the Alps southeast of the lake, there are comfortable mountain hotels in all price ranges—though rates are naturally higher in the resorts themselves. Charges are generally not as steep as those in the Alpine resorts of Graubünden or Valais.

CATEGORY	COST*
$$$$	over 300 SF
$$$	200 SF–300 SF
$$	120 SF–200 SF
$	under 120 SF

Prices are for a standard double room, including breakfast, tax, and service charge.

Museums

Lausanne is a city of museums and galleries, not only covering history, science, and the beaux arts, but eclectic subjects as well—the Olympics and *l'art brut* (raw art), for example. And all along the coast you'll find tiny, meticulous museums covering local history, from the strong influence of the Romans to wine making, the military, and, at Nestlé's Alimentarium, the history of food.

Skiing

The Alpes Vaudoises are home to lovely, not-overdeveloped high-altitude resorts—Leysin, Villars-Gryon, Les Diablerets, Château-d'Oex—where you can experience all levels of skiing difficulty and all the Swiss Alps atmosphere you could wish for.

Wine

As one of the main wine production regions in Switzerland, Vaud can't be savored without sampling the local wares. If you're only tangentially interested, check the blackboard listings in any café for local names on *vins ouvert* (open wines), sold by the deciliter: the fruity whites of Épesses and St-Saphorin of Lavaux (between Lausanne and Montreux); the flinty Luins, Vinzel, and La Côte variations between Lausanne and Geneva. If time allows, plan a drive worthy of Albert Finney and Audrey Hepburn in *Two for the Road,* steering that rent-a-car through narrow, fountain-studded stone streets in tiny wine villages, stopping at inns and *vignobles'* (vineyards'), dégustations to compare. (Do designate a driver.) And head for a market Saturday in Vevey, where vendors sell wine wholesale and tasters carry a glass from booth to booth. If you're planning a visit in the summer of 1999, play your cards right and come during the Fête des Vignerons (Winegrowers' Festival), one of Switzerland's greatest folk pageants. Based in Vevey (☞ *below*), the festival takes place roughly every 20 years; parades and celebrations go on for about two weeks.

Exploring Vaud

Lac Léman, or Lake Geneva, is a graceful swelling in the Rhône River, which passes through the northern hook of the Valais, channels between the French and Vaudoise Alps, then breaks into the open at Bouveret, west of Villeneuve. Its northern shore hosts three of Switzerland's great French cities, grandes dames of the Suisse Romande: Lausanne, Montreux, and Geneva (☞ Chapter 13). The southern shore falls in France's Haute-Savoie, providing those famous shore cities with magnificent views of the French Alps. The north portion of the lake with its green hillsides and the cluster of nearby Alps that loom over its east end make up the canton of Vaud.

Numbers in the text correspond to numbers in the margin and on the Vaud and Lausanne maps.

Great Itineraries

You could easily spend a full Swiss vacation in Vaud, flying directly in and out of Geneva Cointrin without setting a toe in Geneva: By rail or car, you could head straight for such coastal towns as Coppet, Nyon, and Morges, dig into Lausanne's urban graces, crawl through delightful wine villages en route to Montreux, then head straight up into those mountains that have been looking over your shoulder. In three days, you could visit the wine villages of Lavaux, also taking in Lausanne and Montreux's Chillon Castle. In five, you could slow your pace to explore La Côte as well. In 10 days, you could expand your castle touring along the lake, see more museums and head into the Pays-d'Enhaut for a few days of mountain walking.

IF YOU HAVE 3 DAYS

Drive the coastal highway through **Coppet** ① to **Nyon** ② to visit the Roman museum and medieval castle that juts over the lake. Spend a day exploring a few select sights in the charming waterfront city of ⊞ **Lausanne** ⑥–⑱, then set out for the winding road, La Corniche de la Vaud, visiting a vignoble or two at Épesses or St-Saphorin. You'll end up at the lakefront town of ⊞ **Montreux** ㉑, with its fabled **Château de Chillon** ㉒.

IF YOU HAVE 5 DAYS

After a drive through **Coppet** ① and a trip to the château and Roman museum at **Nyon** ②, spend a leisurely day cruising the Route du Vignoble to Rolle, Aubonne, **Allaman** ③, **Morges** ④, and **St-Sulpice** ⑤; then spend two days exploring ⊞ **Lausanne** ⑥–⑱. On your last day, explore the Corniche Road en route to ⊞ **Montreux** ㉑ and the **Château de Chillon** ㉒.

IF YOU HAVE 10 DAYS

Spend a night in the **Nyon** ② environs, tour the Route du Vignoble to Rolle, Aubonne, **Allaman** ③, **Morges** ④, and **St-Sulpice** ⑤; then spend three nights in ⊞ **Lausanne** ⑥–⑱. Spend a day winding along the Corniche Road, with stops to wander Épesses and St-Saphorin, tasting the local wines and eating a leisurely lunch. Then drive into ⊞ **Vevey** ⑳, the genteel sister to glittery **Montreux** ㉑; its Old Town, museums, and Saturday wine market merit an overnight stop. A half day allows you to take in the magic of the **Château de Chillon** ㉒ before you leave Lake Geneva to head into the Alpes Vaudoises. Two nights in **Leysin** ㉖ or ⊞ **Villars-Gryon** ㉔ will allow you to hike, ski, or sit on a sunny balcony, enjoying spectacular views. Then cross the Col des Mosses and the Gorges du Pissot into ⊞ **Château-d'Oex** ㉘, where two more nights allow you to breathe the pure air, walk the mellow hills, and study the folkloric chalets that link the region culturally to Gstaad and the Berner Oberland (☞ Chapter 10).

When to Tour Vaud

The lake sparkles and clouds lift from Mont Blanc from spring to fall; November tends to be drizzly gray, then winter brightens things up above the plain (as they call the flatter terrain surrounding the lake). Crowds monopolize Montreux and Chillon year-round but overwhelm it in July (jazz festival time) and August (Europe-wide vacations). It's worth aiming for concert and dance season in Lausanne: from September through May. Prime ski time in the Alpes Vaudoises is from late December through Easter, and prices go up accordingly. Early spring is daffodil season in Les Avants, over Montreux, where the hillsides come alive with the wild yellow flowers.

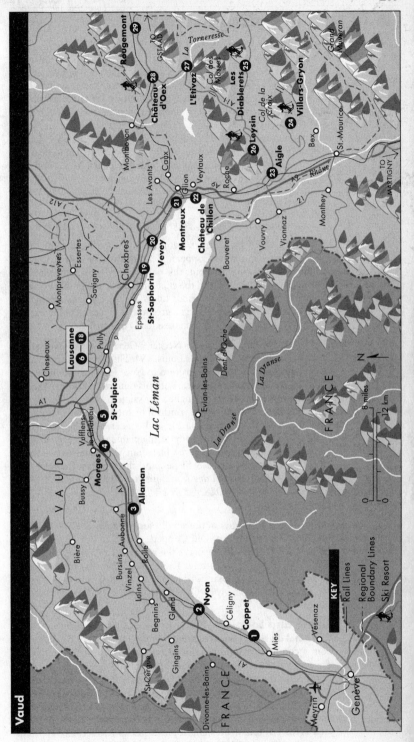

Vaud

Rougemont ❷❾
La Torneresse
TO GSTAAD
Château ❷❽
d'Oex
L'Etivaz ❷❼ Col des
Mosses
Les ❷❺
Diablerets
Villars-Gryon
Grand
Muveran
A11
Col de la
Croix
❷❹
St-Maurice
Montbovon
Leysin ❷❻
Bex
Caux
Les Avants
Gilon Veytaux
❷❸ Aigle
Rhône
TO
Esserles
Savigny
Chexbres
Montpreveyres
Montpreveyres
Epesses
St-Saphorin ❶❾
Vevey
❷❶ Montreux
Château de
Chillon
Roche
Vouvry
Vionnaz
Monthey
Cheseaux
Lausanne
❻ — ❶❽
Pully
A1
Bouveret
St-Sulpice ❺
Vufflens-
le-Château
Epesses
La Dranse
Evian-les-Bains
Dent d'Oche
Lac Léman
N
VAUD
Bussy
Morges ❹
Aubonne
Allaman ❸
8 miles
12 km
Bière
Bursins
Vinzel
Rolle
Luins
FRANCE
La Dranse
La Dranse
Nyon ❷
Céligny
Coppet ❶
Mies
Begnins
Gland
Gingins
St-Cergue
Divonne-les-Bains
FRANCE
Vésenaz
Meyrin
Genève

KEY
Rail Lines
Regional
Boundary Lines
Ski Resort

LA CÔTE AND LAUSANNE

Just northeast of Geneva, La Côte (the Coast) of Lac Léman (Lake Geneva) has been settled since Roman times, with its south-facing slopes cultivated for wine. It is thus peppered with ancient waterfront and hillside towns, castles, and Roman remains. A car is a must if you want to wind through tiny wine villages, but do get out and walk—if only to hear the trickling of any number of Romanesque trough fountains. Be willing to zigzag a few times from the slopes to the waterfront and back if you're determined to cover all the region's charms; sticking exclusively to either the diminutive Route du Vignoble or the coastal road deprives you of some wonderful sights. You'll end your rural tour in the sophisticated city of Lausanne.

Coppet

❶ *10 km (6 mi) south of Nyon, 46 km (28 mi) southwest of Lausanne.*

Its pretty, arcaded main street, with occasional peeks through to the jettied waterfront, makes Coppet a pleasant stop for a stroll, but it is

★ the **Château de Coppet** that puts this natty lake village on the map. Enclosed within vast iron gates, the château has been kept in its original 18th-century form, with luxurious Louis XVI furnishings arranged in a convincingly lived-in manner; its grounds, with grand old trees, hidden courtyards and stone stairs, are equally evocative.

The château was built by Jacques Necker, a Genevan banker who served as financial minister to France's Louis XVI. The turmoil of the French Revolution and Necker's opposition to Napoléon led him into exile in this splendid structure, where, with his remarkable wife, Madame de Staël, he created the most sought-after salon in Europe. Never mind that she had been jilted by the youthful historian Edward Gibbon in 1756; her own intellectual sparkle and concern for the fiery issues of the day attracted the company of the giants of the early Romantic period: Lord Byron, the Swiss historian Jean-Charles Sismondi, the German writer August Schlegel, and the faithless Edward Gibbon himself. ⊠ *3 chemin des Murs, just uphill from the waterfront highway,* ☎ *022/7761028.* ⊡ *7 SF.* ☉ *Guided tours Apr.–Oct., daily 2–6.*

For the house-tour hound, the small **Musée Régional du Vieux-Coppet** (Regional Museum of Old Coppet), a 15th-century residence on the arcaded Grand-rue, displays the restored furnishings of a local 19th-century bourgeois family. There's a noteworthy instrument in the music room: part piano, part violin. ⊠ *30 Grand-rue,* ☎ *022/7763688.* ⊡ *3 SF.* ☉ *Apr.–Oct., Tues.–Sat. 2–5. Guided tours by request.*

Dining and Lodging

$$$$ ✕⊡ **Hôtel du Lac.** First classed a *grand logis* in 1628 to distinguish it from a common roadhouse, this historic inn still feels like an exclusive men's club, catering to power-lunchers and well-heeled travelers. It fronts on the main road but opens directly onto the water, with a sycamore-shaded terrace; a lake-view porch with awning for diners; and rooms with beams, niches, and antiques. Its inventive French restaurant draws a regular clientele for its exquisite fish presentations, such as fillet of tuna with shallots and bordelaise sauce. ⊠ *51 Grand-rue, CH-1296,* ☎ *022/7761521,* ℻ *022/7765346. l2 rooms, 6 suites. Restaurant (reservations essential), bar. AE, DC, MC, V.*

Nyon

❷ *9 km (4 mi) north of Coppet, 27 km (17 mi) southwest of Lausanne.*

Lovely Nyon, with its waterfront drive, shops, museums, and a castle dominating its cliff-top Old Town, was founded by Julius Caesar around 56 BC as a camp for war veterans. The Romans called it Noviodunum and developed the entire region for miles around, charting, building, and developing sophisticated systems. Flanked by a statue of ★ Caesar himself, the **Basilique et Musée Romain** (Basilica and Roman Museum) contains an attractively mounted collection of sumptuously detailed architectural stonework, fresco fragments, statuary, mosaics, and earthenware. A pristine miniature model inside and an excellent trompe-l'oeil artist's impression of the basilica on the outside wall of the museum make clear the remarkable feat of the original structure. ✉ *rue Maupertuis,* ☎ *022/3617591.* ▣ *6 SF; pass for all 3 Nyon museums 12 SF.* ☉ *Apr.–Oct., Tues.–Sat. 10–noon and 2–5, Sun. 10–5; Nov.–Mar., Tues.–Sat. 2–5, Sun. 10–5. Guided tours by request.*

Dominating Nyon's hilltop over the waterfront, the **Château de Nyon** is a magnificent multispire 12th-century fortress with a terrace that takes in sweeping views of the lake and Mont Blanc. Within its massive rooms, you can visit the **Musée Historique et des Porcelaines** (Museum of History and Porcelain), which covers the history of Nyon and focuses on a fascinating part of its heritage: After the French Revolution, Nyon became a great porcelain center, creating flower-sprigged tea sets, vases, and bowls, of which fine examples are on display. ✉ *Place du Château,* ☎ *022/3615888.* ▣ *6 SF; pass for all 3 Nyon museums 12 SF.* ☉ *Apr.–Oct., Tues.–Sat. 10–noon and 2–5, Sun. 10–5. Guided tours by request.*

Along with the views from the château-museum's terrace, don't miss the town's waterfront promenade below, where boats and swans bob in the waves. Nestled in a charming floral park that parallels the water, the **Musée du Léman** exhibits models of Lake Geneva boats through the ages as well as sizable lake-water aquariums, housed in a shuttered 18th-century hospital. ✉ *8 quai Louis Bonnard,* ☎ *022/3610949.* ▣ *6 SF; pass for all 3 Nyon museums 12 SF.* ☉ *Apr.–Oct., Tues.–Sat. 10–noon and 2–5, Sun. 10–5; Nov.–Mar., Tues.–Sat. 2–5, Sun. 10–5.*

The **Château de Prangins**, built in the 18th century by a Parisian banker who thus fulfilled his wish to become a baron, was opened in 1998 as the Swiss Romand branch of the **Musée National Suisse** (Swiss National Museum). Although its doors were still closed at press time, the château's reincarnation was nearly two decades in the making, with its four floors detailing (in four languages including English) Swiss life and history from 1750 to 1920. Surrounded by parks and gardens (the estate once stretched all the way to Rolle), the new museum promises to be a major venue for cultural events as well. If you're traveling with kids, you'll get a price break; there's free admission for children up to age 16. ✉ *3 km (2 mi) northeast of Nyon,* ☎ *022/9948890.* ▣ *5 SF.* ☉ *Tues.–Sun. 10–5.*

OFF THE BEATEN PATH | **ST-CERGUE –** From Nyon you can take a beautiful ride into verdant Jura-range resort country on the little mountain railway Nyon–St-Cergue–Morez up to St-Cergue, 20 km (12 mi) to the north, and beyond. Note the contrast between the old rolling stock, museum pieces in themselves, and the bright red coaches. St-Cergue is a quaint, time-capsule resort that flourishes in both summer and winter—the first hint in Vaud of bigger Alpine sprawls to come—with good ski facilities for children, modest skiing for adults, mushing (dog-sledding races), and fine cross-country trails. It's also the birthplace of snowshoeing, the hot winter sport that involves lightweight, plastic *raquettes de neige,* with which you can leave the trail and move with streamlined efficiency across the surface. If you find yourself here in late September or the first week of October, be sure to take in the annual *Fête Desalpe,* the ritual parade of cows coming down from the mountains. It lasts all of a Saturday morning, allowing hundreds of the noble beasts to file through the streets in amazing floral headgear. ☒ *20 km (12 mi) northwest of Nyon.*

★ **CÉLIGNY –** Six kilometers (4 miles) north of Coppet on the coastal road, bear left inland at the first sign for Céligny, where you'll discover the endearing village that was home to Richard Burton during the last years of his life. With its lakefront, small port, lawns for sunbathing, and a rock-solid pier, it provides the best swimming opportunities for miles around. The enclave is endowed with the prerequisites of charm: rows of vineyards, a historic (but private) château and church, a village square adorned with flowers, a fountain, and its best-kept secret, the wonderfully *sympa* (friendly) Auberge du Soleil. From there you can walk to the village cemetery, the smaller one hugging the edge of the forest, to visit Burton's simple grave. Rumor has it that Elizabeth Taylor has already purchased the adjacent plot.

ROUTE DU VIGNOBLE – Parallel to the waterfront highway, threading through the steep-sloping vineyards between Nyon and Lausanne, the Route du Vignoble unfolds a rolling green landscape high above the lake, punctuated by noble manor-farms and vineyards. Luins, home of the flinty, fruity white wine of the same name, is a typical pretty village. Just up the road, the village of Vinzel develops its own white wines on sunny slopes and sells them from the wine cellars that inspired its name (*vin-cellier*). It is also the best source for a very local specialty, the malakoff. These rich, steamy cheese-and-egg beignets have always been a favorite of the Vaudois, but after the Crimean Wars they were renamed after a beloved officer who led his army of Vaud-born mercenaries to victory in the siege of Sebastopol. For a great spot to sample them, head to Au Coeur de la Côte (☞ Dining and Lodging, *below*). The Route du Vignoble continues through Bursins, home of an 11th-century Romanesque church—and of the venerable actor Peter Ustinov. Drivers can choose to follow it all the way to Morges, or to cross under the autoroute to view lakefront castles and the new Swiss National Museum in Prangins. ☒ *Route between Nyon and Lausanne, parallel to the waterfront highway.*

Dining and Lodging

$$ ✕ **Auberge du Château.** This reliable restaurant, just steps from Nyon's Musée Romain, serves straightforward Swiss fare and reasonable plats du jour, including veal five different ways (such as scalloped veal with lime and fresh ginger) and game in autumn. In summer, a big terrace lets diners study the château; in winter, broad windows take in the view. ☒ *8 pl. du Château,* ☏ *022/3616312. AE, DC, MC, V. Closed Wed. Oct.–Apr.*

$ ✕ **Au Coeur de la Côte.** Following ROUTE DU VINOBLE signs on the Jura side of the A1 autoroute after exiting at Gland, head up the vine-lined slopes to Vinzel (wine cellar), where this modest village inn and its flowered terrace overlook the vineyards and the lake beyond. Here you can taste the commune's Vinzel, or fill up on two or three hot, rich, Gruyère-based malakoffs, served with pickles and mustard, any time of day from 11:30 AM to 9:30 PM. ☒ *Vinzel, along Rte. du Vignoble,* ☏ *021/8241141. No reservations. MC, V. Closed Mon.*

\$–\$\$ ✕🏨 **Auberge du Soleil.** Lured by the charm of Céligny and the chance
★ to own a 300-year-old building, Californian chef John Olcott and his
German wife, Catrin, have established a wonderful auberge. For years
the auberge lay dormant, until the couple took it over in 1996 and renovated every nook and cranny, including the seven sweet guest rooms
up the old winding stone staircase. Whether in the café up front or the
quieter restaurant in back, the decor is a minimalist showcase for the
chef's fetching presentations, such as mâche (lamb's lettuce) salad with
seared fresh scallops in a blood orange vinaigrette. Although the inventive side of the menu changes frequently, the local standards, which
include Rösti, perch, and fondue, never vary. Be sure to save room for
the *tarte crème brûlée.* You'll need a reservation in order to snatch a
table from the locals, essential in summer for a table on the terrace.
✉ *10 Rte. des Coudrées, Céligny,* ☎ *022/9609633. AE, DC, MC, V.
Restaurant closed Tues. No dinner Mon.*

En Route Twelve kilometers (7 miles) northeast of Nyon, the lakefront village
of **Rolle** merits a detour for a look at its dramatic 13th-century **château,**
built at the water's edge by a Savoyard prince. Equally dramatic in its
concept is the early 19th-century **Château de Beaulieu,** 2 km (1 mi)
before entering Rolle on the coastal road. You could call it a decora-
tor's show house on a grand scale—it's the exclusive domain of the
prestigious Moinat Antiques and Decoration enterprise based in Rolle.
Except for a single corner of modern plumbing, not a stone has been
altered; period furnishings and Aubusson carpets fill the labyrinth of
its three creaky floors, making it easy to imagine life as it was for the
rich Geneva family that built this country retreat. But this is no hands-
off museum; the carpets and furniture are for sale.

Allaman

❸ *17 km (10 mi) northeast of Nyon, 20 km (12 mi) west of Lausanne.*

You can wander the interior of the stately 16th-century **Château d'Allaman,** built first during the 12th century by the barons of Vaud, then
rebuilt by the Bernois after a 1530 fire. It has been converted to a stunning antiques mall, its narrow halls and stairwells lined with beeswaxed
armoires and ancestral portraits, all for sale at lofty prices through private entrepreneurs who rent space within. The château's vaulted crypt
offers wine dégustations for potential buyers as well. For antiques, collectibles, and art at more reasonable prices, head to the annex next door,
known as **La Grange,** the château's erstwhile stables and barn. ✉ *Between Aubonne and Allaman, signposted,* ☎ *0218073805.* 🎫 *Free. Shops:
☉ Wed.–Sun. 2–6. Wine crypt:* ☎ *021/8088239. ☉ Wed.–Sun. 11–7.*

Morges

❹ *9 km (5 mi) northeast of Allaman, 8 km (5 mi) west of Lausanne.*

On the waterfront just west of the urban sprawl of Lausanne, Morges
is a pleasant lake town favored by sailors and devotees of its *Fête de
la Tulipe* (Tulip Festival), held annually from mid-April to mid-May.
Its château, built by the duke of Savoy around 1286 as a defense
against the bishop-princes of Lausanne, now houses the **Musée Militaire Vaudois** (Vaud Military Museum), which displays weapons, uniforms, and a collection of 10,000 miniature lead soldiers. In the Général
Henri Guisan Hall, you'll find memorabilia of this World War II general, much honored for keeping both sides happy enough to leave
Switzerland safely alone. ✉ *Le Château,* ☎ *021/8012616.* 🎫 *5 SF. ☉
Feb.–June and Sept.–mid-Dec., weekdays 10–noon and 1:30–5,
weekends 1:30–5; July–Aug., daily 10–5.*

One kilometer (half mile) west of Morges, the tiny village of Tolochenaz honors a beloved long-term resident in the **Pavillon de Audrey Hepburn.** Founded in 1996, the contemporary, white shoebox-y building is a few minutes' walk from the village cemetery where the star is buried, a bit farther from La Paisable, the gracious, shuttered manor house where she lived for 26 years. Exhibits of photographs, posters, and Academy Awards chronicle her artistic and humanitarian achievements, but equally touching is the sentiment with which the villagers volunteer their time to keep her memory alive. ⊠ *Chemin des Plantées, Tolochenaz,* ☎ *021/8036464.* ◻ *10 SF.* ⊙ *Mid-Mar.–mid-Nov., Tues.–Sun. 10–6; mid-Nov.–mid-Mar., Tues.–Sun. 11–3.*

Dining

$$$$ ✕ **L'Ermitage.** Eager to fill the void left by Fredy Girardet's retirement, Bernard Ravet offers visitors to the Lausanne area a once-unthinkable alternative. While branching out with bold visuals and confident combinations—say, rabbit tartare with caviar, *omble chevalier* (salmon trout) in court bouillon with fried frogs' legs in *pistou* (the French version of Italy's pesto) or lightly house-smoked Bavarian salmon—and enriching his sophisticated *cave* (cellar), he and his wife still extend a warm, even casual welcome, with a glass of local St-Saphorin by the huge fire downstairs. These are a French chef and a French restaurant to be reckoned with. It's about a 15-minute drive west of Lausanne, in a former wine maker's 17th-century farmhouse, with beams and fireplaces inside and grand old trees in the garden. ⊠ *Vufflens-le-Château, 2 km (1 mi) west of Morges,* ☎ *021/8022191. Reservations essential. DC, MC, V. Closed Sun.–Mon.*

OFF THE **VUFFLENS-LE-CHÂTEAU –** Two kilometers (1 mile) northwest of Morges,
BEATEN PATH   this village is known for its namesake château, a 15th-century Savoyard palace with a massive donjon and four lesser towers, all trimmed in fine Piedmont-style brickwork.

St-Sulpice

❺ *5 km (3 mi) east of Morges, 3 km (1¼ mi) west of Lausanne.*

Just west of Lausanne, turn right toward the waterfront to visit St-Sulpice, an ancient village and site of one of the best-preserved 12th-century
★ Romanesque churches in Switzerland, **l'Église de St-Sulpice** (Church of St. Sulpice). Severe but lovely, it was built by monks from the Cluny Abbey in Burgundy; its painted decoration softens the spare purity of its lines. Three original apses remain, although the nave has disappeared; the short bell tower is built of small stone blocks likely brought from the ruined Roman township at nearby Vidy. At one time the home of 40 monks, the adjoining priory was converted into a private residence during the 16th century. Today the church earns new renown as a venue for classical music concerts. ⊠ *chemin du Crêt, at the dock.* ◻ *Free.*

Lausanne

❻–⓲ *66 km (41 mi) northeast of Geneva.*

"Lausanne is a block of picturesque houses, spilling over two or three gorges, which spread from the same central knot, and are crowned by a cathedral like a tiara. . . . On the esplanade of the church . . . I saw the lake over the roofs, the mountains over the lake, clouds over the mountains, and stars over the clouds. It was like a staircase where my thoughts climbed step by step and broadened at each new height," wrote Victor Hugo of this grand and graceful tiered city, which reigns like a queen with a tiara over the lake and surrounding mountains. Voltaire, Rousseau, Byron, and Cocteau all waxed equally passionate about Lausanne—and not only for its visual beauty. It has been a cultural center for centuries, the world drawn first to its magnificent Gothic cathedral and the powers it represented, then to its university, and during the 18th and 19th centuries, to its vibrant intellectual and social life. In the 1990s, the Swiss consider Lausanne the most desirable city in which to live.

Lausanne's importance today stems from its several disparate roles in national and world affairs. Politically, it is the site of the Tribunal Fédéral, the highest court of appeals in Switzerland. Commercially, although it is by no means in the same league as Zürich or Bern, it figures as headquarters for many multinational organizations, corporations, and sports federations. On a major international rail route and a vital national junction, Lausanne serves as a trade center for most of the surrounding agricultural regions and the expanding industrial towns of Vaud. This prosperity spills over into the arts; there's a surprising concentration of dance companies—including that of Maurice Béjart—as well as several theaters, jazz cellars, and a pair of excellent orchestras. Lausanne is also the world's Olympic capital; the International Olympic Committee has been based here since 1915 (its founder, Baron Pierre de Coubertin, is buried nearby at Montoie Cemetery). Ironically, the citizens of Lausanne voted against hosting the 1994 Winter Olympics, afraid, in part, of upsetting the delicate balance of old and new they cautiously sustain.

The balance has not always been kept. The first 20 years after World War II saw an immense building boom, with old buildings and whole neighborhoods pulled down to make way for shining new office blocks and apartment buildings—an architectural exuberance that has given Lausanne a rather lopsided air. Rising in tiers from the lakeside at Ouchy (360 m/1,181 ft) to more than 600 m (2,000 ft), the city covers three hills, which are separated by gorges that once channeled rivers; the rivers have been built over, and huge bridges span the gaps across the hilltops. On one hill in particular, modern skyscrapers contrast brutally with the beautiful proportions of the cathedral rising majestically from its crest. For the sake of hygiene, atmospheric alleys and narrow streets have mostly been demolished, yet the Old Town clustered around the cathedral has been painstakingly and attractively restored—perhaps too much so, leaving the area somewhat lifeless, as if it were all an open-air museum. Yet Lausanne continues to develop its assets: Two slick museum complexes have been opened, one devoted to the city's Roman roots, the other to the worldwide glories of the Olympics.

For walking in Lausanne you should bring comfortable shoes, as the city's steep inclines and multiple layers add considerable strain to getting around. There are plenty of buses and a Métro (subway system), but to see the concentrated sights of the Old Town, it's best to tackle the hills on foot.

A Good Walk

Begin in the commercial hub of the city, the **place St-François** ⑥ (nicknamed Sainfe by the Lausannois), where you'll see the former Franciscan **Église St-François**. Behind the Église St-François, take a near hairpin turn right to the east on the fashionable main shopping street, the ancient **rue de Bourg** ⑦. At the top of rue de Bourg, opposite the plush Hermès emporium, rue Caroline leads you left and left again over the **Pont Bessières,** where you can see the city's peculiar design spanning gorges and covered rivers.

Lausanne

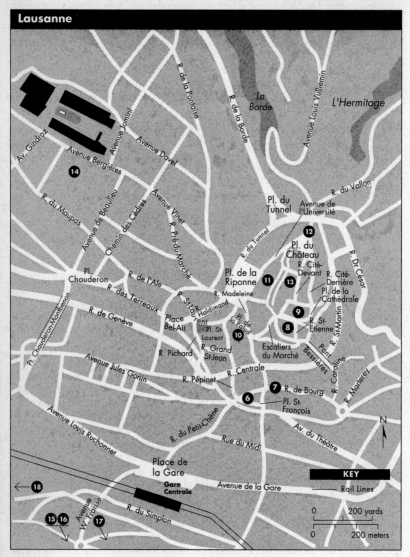

Ancienne-
Académie, **13**

Cathédrale de Notre-
Dame, **9**

Château St-Maire, **12**

Collection de l'Art
Brut, **14**

Débarcadère, **16**

Hôtel de Ville, **10**

Musée Historique de
Lausanne, **8**

Musée
Olympique, **17**

Musée Romain de
Lausanne–Vidy, **18**

Ouchy, **15**

Palais de Rumine, **11**

Place St-François, **6**

Rue de Bourg, **7**

Crossing the bridge and bearing right brings you up into the Old Town. On your left, the imposing palace of the Old Bishopric now houses the **Musée Historique de Lausanne** ⑧. Straight ahead, at the top of rue St-Étienne in the Place de la Cathedral, towers the tremendous **Cathédrale de Notre-Dame** ⑨, which is on par with some of France's and England's best.

With the cathedral on your left, walk up the narrow passage of rue Cité Derrière to the Place du Château and its namesake monument, the **Château St-Maire** ⑫, a stern, castellated structure. As you face the château, turn left and walk down the Rue Cité Devant. On your right you will see the **Ancienne-Académie** ⑬ halfway between the château and the cathedral. As you pass the cathedral, again on your left, veer right toward a flight of wooden steps that leads down to the second, more dramatic **Escaliers du Marché**, a wood-roof medieval staircase. At the bottom of the 150 covered steps, you'll run into the Place de la Palud and the **Hôtel de Ville** ⑩, the seat of the municipal and communal councils. Turning right, just up rue Madeleine from the Place de la Palud, you will come upon the Place de la Riponne and the imposing **Palais de Rumine** ⑪, which houses a pack of museums covering subjects from archaeology to zoology.

Some of Lausanne's other worthwhile museums take a bit of extra effort to reach. A long hike up avenue Vinet, northwest of the Old Town, will take you to the **Collection de l'Art Brut** ⑭, an unusual museum of fringe art. South of the Old Town, the waterfront community of **Ouchy** ⑮ can be easily reached by the steep funicular Métro across from the Gare Centrale (train station) and from the Flon (city center, a bit west of the Old Town). Ouchy's **Débarcadère** ⑯ has all the typical quaiside attractions—vendors, people strolling on a promenade, and a relaxed atmosphere. Just east of Ouchy, on a hillside overlooking the lake, the dramatic **Musée Olympique** ⑰ conveys the history and disciplines of the Olympic Games. It's less than half a mile from the Débarcadère along the quai de Belgique, which turns into the quai d'Ouchy. West of Ouchy at Vidy (just off the Lausanne-Maladière exit from E25/A1) is the **Musée Romain de Lausanne–Vidy** ⑱, where you can see a reconstructed private Roman home. Like the Musée Olympique, this is easy to get to on foot; it's just under a mile from the Débarcadère.

TIMING

You can tour the Old Town, despite the hills, in a couple of hours following the above route (do not reverse the order unless you're keen to walk up instead of down the Escaliers du Marché). But that's without stopping: If you have time, plan a full day to include visits to at least a few of the museums and the cathedral—not to mention some unique shops off the Place du Palud. Count on lunch in one of the minuscule cafés near the cathedral. Or you could spend your afternoon in Ouchy and the nearby museums; getting to Ouchy by car or funicular takes under 10 minutes, while walking down the Avenue d'Ouchy from the Gare Centrale to the Débarcadère takes about 15 minutes. Remember that museums are never open on Monday.

Sights to See

⑬ **Ancienne-Académie** (Old Academy). Originally the first school of Protestant theology in Europe (1536), the edifice later became home of the city's university and is now a secondary school. ⊠ *7 rue Cité-Devant.*

★ ⑨ **Cathédrale de Notre-Dame** (Cathedral of Our Lady). A Burgundian-Gothic architectural treasure, this cathedral is Switzerland's largest church—and probably its finest. Begun during the 12th century by Italian, Flemish, and French architects, it was completed in 1275. Pope Gregory X came expressly to perform the historic consecration ceremony—of double importance, as it also served as a coronation service for Rudolph of Hapsburg as the new emperor of Germany and of the Holy Roman Empire. Emperor Rudolph brought his wife, eight children, seven cardinals, five archbishops, 17 bishops, four dukes, 15 counts, and a multitude of lesser lords, who must have crowded the church's exquisitely proportioned nave.

Viollet-le-Duc, a renowned restorer who worked on the cathedrals of Chartres and Notre-Dame-de-Paris, brought portions of the building to Victorian-Gothic perfection in the 19th century. His repairs are visible as paler stone, in contrast to the weathered local sandstone; his self-portrait appears in the face of King David, harp and scroll in hand, to the right of the main portal. Streamlined to the extreme, without radiating chapels or the excesses of later Gothic trim, the cathedral wasn't always so spare; in fact, there was brilliant paintwork. Zealous Reformers plastered over the florid colors, but in so doing they unwittingly preserved it, and now you can see portions of these splendid shades restored in the right transepts. The dark and delicate choir contains the 14th-century tomb of the crusader Otto I of Grandson and exceptionally fine 13th-century choir stalls, unusual for their age alone, not to mention their beauty. The church's masterpiece, the 13th-century painted portal—considered one of Europe's most beautiful—was reopened in 1997 after more than a decade of restoration.

Protestant services (the cathedral was Reformed in the 15th century) exclude nonworshiping visitors on Sunday from 10 to 11:30. You may want to come instead for the evening concerts given on an almost-weekly basis in spring and autumn; call ahead for a precise schedule. ⊠ *pl. de la Cathédrale,* ☎ *021/3167161.* ☉ *Apr.–Oct., weekdays 7–7, weekends 8–7; Nov.–Mar., weekdays 7–5:30, weekends 8–5:30.*

★ ⑫ **Château St-Maire.** The fortresslike elements of this 15th-century stone cylinder certainly came into play. The castle was built for the bishops of Lausanne; during the 16th century, the citizens wearied of ecclesiastic power and allied themselves with Bern and Fribourg, against the bishops protected within. Before long, however, Bern itself marched on Lausanne, put a bailiff in this bishops' castle, and stripped the city fathers of their power. The Bernese imposed Protestantism on the Lausannois, and their Catholic churches and cathedral were ransacked to fill the coffers of Bern. Today the Château St-Maire is the seat of the cantonal government. ⊠ *pl. du Château.*

★ ⑭ **Collection de l'Art Brut.** This singular museum focuses on the genre of fringe or "psychopathological" art, dubbed *l'art brut* in the 1940s by French artist Jean Dubuffet. His own collection forms the base of this ensemble of raw material from untrained minds—prisoners, schizophrenics, or the merely obsessed. Strangely enough, the collection is housed in the Château de Beaulieu, a former mansion of Madame de Staël, she of the sophisticated salons. You can get here by walking up avenue Vinet or by taking Bus 2 from Place St-Laurent in the direction of Le Désert. ⊠ *11 av. des Bergières,* ☎ *021/6475435.* 🎫 *6 SF.* ☉ *Tues.– Sun. 11–1 and 2–6.*

⑯ **Débarcadère** (Wharf). The main boat traffic comes from the white steamers that land here. In fine weather, the waterfront buzzes with nightlife—strollers, diners, people lingering in outdoor cafés, roller skaters, artisans selling their wares. It's as if sedate Lausanne lifts her skirts a bit at the shoreline. ⊠ *pl. du Port, Ouchy.*

❿ **Hôtel de Ville** (Town Hall). This building on the Place de la Palud, constructed between the 15th and the 17th centuries, is the seat of municipal and communal councils. A painted medieval **Fontaine de la Justice** (Justice Fountain) draws strollers to lounge on its heavy rim. Across from the Town Hall, you can watch the **animated clock,** a modern work with moving figures that was donated to the city by local merchants; the figures appear every hour on the hour. A street market is held here every Wednesday and Saturday mornings. ⊠ *2 Pl. de la Palud.*

❽ **Musée Historique de Lausanne** (Historical Museum of Lausanne). The Ancien-Évêché (Old Bishopric) holds a wealth of both temporary and permanent historical exhibits about the city. Don't miss the 250-square-ft scale model of 17th-century Lausanne, with its commentary illuminating the neighborhoods' histories; also look for the re-created 19th-century shop windows. ⊠ *4 pl. de la Cathédrale,* ☎ *021/3128454.* ☜ *7 SF.* ☉ *Tues., Wed., and Fri.–Sun. 11–6, Thurs. 11–8.*

⑰ **Musée Olympique** (Olympic Museum). With high-tech presentation and touching mementos, this complex pays tribute to the athletic tradition in ancient Greece, to the development of the modern Games, to the evolution of the individual sports, and to the athletes themselves. There are art objects—an Etruscan torch from the 6th century BC, Rodin's *American Athlete*—7,000 hours of archival films and videos, interactive displays, photographs, coins and stamps, and medals from various eras throughout Olympic history. You'll even see the running shoes Carl Lewis wore to win the 200-m gold medal at Los Angeles in 1984. A museum shop, stocked with books, posters, and Olympic-logo clothes, a lovely café overlooking the lake and sculpture park, and occasional Sunday-afternoon classical concerts complete this ambitious, world-class endeavor. Cynics may find the slick displays short on substance (despite the emotional *Chariots of Fire*–style music throbbing in the background) and some of the video archives skimpy, if technologically intriguing. Video viewings are limited to two selections at a time to keep zealots from commandeering a machine for the afternoon. ⊠ *1 quai d'Ouchy,* ☎ *021/6216511.* ☜ *14 SF.* ☉ *May–Sept., Mon.–Wed. and Fri.–Sun. 10–7, Thurs. 10–8; Oct.–Apr., Tues., Wed., and Fri.–Sun. 10–6, Thurs. 10–8.*

⑱ **Musée Romain de Lausanne-Vidy** (Lausanne-Vidy Roman Museum). This is the current incarnation of the restored remains of the late Roman communities Lousonna and Vidy, which both flourished here from 15 BC into the 4th century. A private home, complete with a well and painted murals, has been reconstructed and used as the centerpiece for a permanent exhibition on the ancient settlements; a small treasure trove of coins, votive figures, and objects from daily life—carved combs, toga pins, jewelry—is displayed. You can get guided tours in English of the museum and neighboring archaeological sites on request. The site is west of Ouchy, just off the Lausanne-Maladière exit from E25/A1. ⊠ *24 chemin du Bois-de-Vaux, Vidy,* ☎ *021/6251084.* ☜ *4 SF.* ☉ *Tues., Wed., and Fri.–Sun. 11–6, Thurs. 11–8.*

⑮ **Ouchy.** Officially a separate township, Ouchy can be easily reached by the steep funicular Métro across from the Gare Centrale (train station) and from the Flon (city center). It serves as Lausanne's port, and it's a fashionable place to live. The resort area is dominated by the **Château d'Ouchy** (Ouchy Castle), now a hotel; its tower dates from the Middle Ages.

⑪ **Palais de Rumine.** Built at the turn of the century, this enormous neo-Renaissance structure houses several museums, all with a local spin. The **Musée Cantonal de Géologie** (Cantonal Museum of Geology) has an excellent fossil collection, including a mammoth skeleton. Besides its collection of regional fauna, the **Musée Cantonal de Zoologie** (Cantonal Museum of Zoology) has a rare collection of comparative anatomy. The top exhibit at the **Musée Cantonal d'Archéologie et d'Histoire** (Cantonal Museum of Archaeology and History) is the gold bust of Marcus Aurelius discovered at nearby Avenches in 1939. The **Musée Cantonal des Beaux-Arts** (Cantonal Museum of Fine Arts) is also found in the Palais, with an enlightening collection of Swiss art, not only by the Germanic Hodler and Anker but also by Vaud artists—especially Bocion, whose local landscapes are well worth study during a visit to this region. ⊠ *Palais de Rumine, 6 pl. de la Riponne. Museum of Geology:* ☎ *021/3204192.* 🎟 *Free.* ☉ *Tues.–Thurs. 11–6, Fri.–Sun. 11–5. Museum of Zoology:* ☎ *021/3128336.* 🎟 *Free.* ☉ *Tues.–Thurs. 11–6, Fri.–Sun. 11–5. Museum of Archaeology:* ☎ *021/3128334.* 🎟 *Free.* ☉ *Daily 10–noon and 2–5. Museum of Fine Arts:* ☎ *021/3128332.* 🎟 *6 SF.* ☉ *Tues.–Wed. 11–6, Thurs. 11–8, Fri.–Sun. 11–5.*

❻ Place St-François (St. Francis Square). The brick-paved square is dominated by the massive post office and the former Franciscan **Église St-François** (Church of St. Francis), built during the 13th and 14th centuries. From 1783 to 1793, Edward Gibbon lived in a house on the site of the post office and there finished work on *The Decline and Fall of the Roman Empire.* In those days, the square, now reserved for pedestrians, was a popular riding circuit.

❼ Rue de Bourg. Once a separate village isolated on this natural ridge, this is now the fashionable main shopping street (☞ Shopping, *below*). Narrow and cobblestoned, it's lined with platinum-card stores like Hermès; boutiques have been built into the centuries-old buildings, though some have added fittingly modern facades. Tony stores notwithstanding, the street has its down-to-earth moments; on weekends a fresh-produce market makes things even more crowded.

Dining and Lodging

$$$$ ✕ **La Grappe d'Or.** In this relaxed but classic firelighted French restaurant, imaginative modern cooking of a high standard is prepared by Bavarian chef Peter Baermann and impeccably served under the discreet supervision of his wife, Angelika. Try the fillet of venison with a sauce of figs and red wine, scallops with potato gnocchi, or the hearty *cardons* (cardoons; an artichokelike vegetable cultivated in Geneva and Lyon) in foie gras. Pastries are extraordinary. ⊠ *3 Cheneau de Bourg,* ☎ *021/3230760. Reservations essential. AE, MC, V. Closed Sun. No lunch Sat.*

$$$$ ✕ **Restaurant Rochat.** After 17 years working in the kitchen of the legendary Fredy Girardet, Philippe Rochat stepped in to replace the culinary giant, who finally made good on threats of retirement and turned the restaurant over at the end of 1996. Now secure in his own right, Rochat has changed the name of this gourmet shrine, although he maintains his mentor's tradition with such specialties as artichoke Bavarian with lobster, preserved duckling in lemon and spices, or glazed sweetbreads with wild mushrooms. Consider one of the artfully orchestrated prix-fixe menus: Your choice, fish or fowl, will be carved table-side and consumed in hushed, perhaps reverent appreciation. Leave room for selections from the immense cheese cart and for the celestial desserts. Service and presentation are spectacular, less ceremonious than in Girardet's era. It's a quick drive east of Lausanne in a surprisingly understated former Hôtel de Ville. Make reservations as far ahead as possible. Trivia bit: Rochat's wife (and the restaurant's maître d'hôtel), Franziska, has made her own contribution to his renown; she was the surprise female winner of the 1997 New York City Marathon, the first Swiss ever to win a major marathon. ⊠ *1 rue d'Yverdon, Crissier, 7 km (4 mi) east of Lausanne,* ☎ *021/6340505. Reservations essential. AE, MC, V. Closed Sun.–Mon., end July–mid-Aug.*

$$–$$$ ✕ **Café Beau-Rivage.** As if turning its back on the aristocratic splendor of the Beau-Rivage Palace that shelters it, this young, lively brasserie-café faces the lake and the Ouchy waterfront scene. Its flashy brass-and-Biedermeier dining area and bar fill with smart Lausannois and Grand-Tour internationals enjoying upscale, trendy cuisine du marché, duck with wild mushrooms, and salmon tartare. Despite the brasserie atmosphere, there are no paper place mats: Linen, silver, and monogrammed damask set the BCBG (*bon chic, bon genre*) tone. Summers, the pillared terrazzo terrace is the place to be seen. ⊠ *pl. du Général-Guisan, Ouchy,* ☎ *021/6133330. Reservations essential. AE, DC, MC, V.*

$$ ✕ **À la Pomme de Pin.** In the Old Town behind the cathedral, this winsome *pinte* (wine pub)—one of Lausanne's oldest—produces an eclectic menu ranging from French to Italian to Swiss (rabbit and Rösti, anyone?) along with reasonable plats du jour, served both in the casual café and the adjoining linen-decked restaurant. ⊠ *11–13 rue Cité-Derrière,* ☎ *021/3234656. AE, MC, V. Closed Sun. No lunch Sat.*

$$ ✕ **Café du Grütli.** Tucked in between the place de Palud and the covered stairs to the cathedral, this is a typical old-style Swiss-Romand restaurant, with a bentwood-and-net-curtain café on the ground floor and a simple, more formal dining room upstairs. There are several fondues as well as brasserie classics—boiled beef vinaigrette, rabbit in mustard sauce, profiteroles, and *tart Tatin* (upside-down apple tart). Have one of several open Vaud wines or a *café pomme* (coffee with a side shot of apple eau-de-vie) with the locals, who unwind here with the daily papers. There are a handful of tables outdoors if you want to make the *American in Paris*–style street scene. ⊠ *4 rue de la Mercerie,* ☎ *021/3129493. DC, MC, V. Closed Sun. No dinner Sat.*

$ ✕ **Bleu Lézard.** A complete cross-section of Lausanne urbanites—hip artists, yuppies, shoppers, university students—fight for tables at this laid-back, stylish restaurant, where you can sample aubergine carpaccio, duck breast in violet vinegar sauce, and marrow crisps and grapes, all for remarkably low prices. A tongue-in-cheek decor of found-object art and easygoing waiters dressed in whatever khakis and flannels they found near the bed that morning add to the New Age ambience. Mixed drinks along with live jazz, Latino, and disco music draw a nocturnal clientele downstairs in the cellar. ⊠ *10 rue Enning,* ☎ *021/ 3127190. AE, MC, V.*

$ ✕ **Café Romand.** All the customers seem to know each other at this vast, smoky, parquet dining institution, where shared wooden tables and clattering china create the perfect ambience for fondue feasts, smoked fish platters, mussels, *choucroûte,* or a sausage plate. Prominent members of Lausanne's arts community swarm here after rehearsals and concerts and are known to toast each other loudly across the crowded room. ⊠ *2 pl. St-François,* ☎ *021/3126375. MC, V. Closed Sun.*

$ ✕ **Manora Crocodile.** If you're fed up with heavy Vaud cheese dishes and local sausage, this cheery self-service chain offers startlingly inexpensive options, chopped fresh and cooked before your eyes in huge woks under silent no-smoke hoods. The light, bright, woody decor increases the greening effect of iced pitchers of fresh-squeezed fruit juices, four sizes of salad, a fruit bar, pasta station, and a daily risotto. Hot food is served nonstop from 11 AM to 10 PM, and no one dish costs more than 14 SF. A no-smoking dining room is a lifesaver in this city of chain-smokers. ⊠ *17 pl. St-François,* ☏ *021/3209293. Reservations not accepted. No credit cards.*

$$$$ ⊡ **Beau-Rivage Palace.** Of the scores of deluxe hotels in Switzerland,
★   this gleaming grande dame stands apart, its neoclassic structure seamlessly restored to period opulence, its vast waterfront grounds manicured like a country manor estate. It opened in 1861 as the Beau-Rivage (the Palace wing and Renaissance cupola were added in 1908), but every inch of marble, crystal, and polished mahogany sparkles like new. The Palace was renovated from the roots up in 1994: Rooms now have remote light controls, doorbells, maid lights, towel heaters, piped-in music over the tub and walk-in shower, and phones sprouting from every surface—as well as classic comforts: wing chairs, Asian rugs, and balconies with lake views. Among the facilities are three first-class restaurants including the gourmet La Rotonde, La Résidence with fish and Mediterranean specialties, and the Café Beau Rivage with up-to-the-minute brasserie fare. Jacket and tie are required at La Rotonde. ⊠ *chemin de Beau-Rivage, CH-1000 Ouchy 6,* ☏ *021/6133333,* 𝗙𝗔𝗫 *021/ 6133334. 174 rooms, 6 suites. 3 restaurants, 3 bars, pool, beauty salon, sauna, 2 tennis courts, exercise room, piano, playground. AE, DC, MC, V.*

$$$$ ⊡ **Lausanne Palace.** New management and a complete face-lift confirm there are two luxury Palaces in town. This Edwardian landmark—smaller than the Beau-Rivage and distinctly urban in setting and style—stands on a hill high over the lake, with layers of city scenery draped behind. It faces a city street, so to take advantage of its views, you need a back room—though three-quarters of the rooms have balconies. The room decor varies from Empire reproduction to cool modern, with occasional period details, such as inlaid wood and marble fireplaces. The fitness center, complete with indoor pool, a childcare facility, and its own restaurant, is the largest of its kind in the Lake Geneva region. Although the main restaurant, Le Relais, serves ambitious French cuisine, the Parisian-style Brasserie du Grand-Chêne opening onto the street is decidedly less formal. ⊠ *7–9 rue du Grand Chêne, CH-1002,* ☏ *021/3313131,* 𝗙𝗔𝗫 *021/3232571. 134 rooms, 16 suites. 3 restaurants, bar, beauty salon, pool, sauna, health club. AE, DC, MC, V.*

$$$–$$$$ ⊡ **De la Paix.** This turn-of-the-century business-class hotel in the center of town has all the amenities of a Best Western property and wonderful lakeside views. The rooms facing the lake are done in warm shades of pumpkin and terra-cotta; those on the backstreet side are considerably humbler. Its bar, Jacky's, is a Lausanne institution. ⊠ *5 av. Benjamin-Constant, CH-1002,* ☏ *021/3107171,* 𝗙𝗔𝗫 *021/3107172. 111 rooms, 6 suites. Restaurant, bar, café. AE, DC, MC, V.*

$$$–$$$$ ⊡ **La Résidence.** Within three graceful 18th- and 19th-century villas
★   near the waterfront at Ouchy, this polished small hotel complex has been modernized without ruffling its gentility or disturbing its graceful stone arches, marble floors, or discreet gardens. You may think you're in a country manor—especially in the rooms that overlook the Beau-Rivage's park. Room decor was revamped in 1998, while freshly cut flowers and personal service from the caring staff make this the delightful antithesis of a grand-hotel experience. Guests may use the facilities of the Beau-Rivage Palace next door. ⊠ *15 pl. du Port, CH-1006,* ☏ *021/6133434,* 𝗙𝗔𝗫 *021/6133435. 44 rooms. Restaurant, pool. AE, DC, MC, V.*

$$$–$$$$ ⊡ **Royal Savoy.** Here you can not only stay in an enormous Victorian
★   castle but also enjoy a broad, private landscaped garden and park, with outdoor swimming pool, terrace restaurant, and strolling musicians. The rooms themselves are lovely—something more expensive hotels often seem unable to achieve—with florals and jewel tones, delicate

period reproduction desks and chairs, and French doors that open onto balconies over the lawns and lake. ⊠ *40 av. d'Ouchy, CH-1000,* ☎ *021/6148888,* 𝔽𝔸𝕏 *021/6148878. 99 rooms, 9 suites. 2 restaurants, bar, pool, exercise room, sauna. AE, DC, MC, V.*

$$$ 🏨 **Agora.** Certainly one of the most novel lodgings in Lausanne—and
★ in Switzerland—this hotel seems a vision, almost a hallucination. Built from scratch in 1987, it sits like a landed spaceship on an otherwise ordinary city block. From its sculptural marble facade to its high-tech bathrooms, it is decked in metallic tones and cool blues; even the leather upholstery has a silvery glow. All rooms have air-conditioning, videos in four languages, windows that open, and wet bars—and the light fixtures are Michael Graves–cum–Jetsons. The cool-tone restaurant features contemporary, market-fresh cuisine; it's closed weekends and from mid-July to mid-August. ⊠ *9 av. du Rond-Point, CH-1006,* ☎ *021/6171211,* 𝔽𝔸𝕏 *021/6162605. 83 rooms. Restaurant, bar, minibars, in-room VCRs. AE, DC, MC, V.*

$$$ 🏨 **Château d'Ouchy.** Here, you pay for the privilege of staying in a 12th-century castle that was converted into a pseudo-medieval hotel during the 19th century. The interiors are dated-modern and a little faded, and the glassed-in terrace restaurant is like most others on the waterfront. If you really want medieval atmosphere, spring for the deluxe $$$$ top tower room, which has wraparound views through Romanesque windows. There's a Parisian-style brasserie and a popular waterfront veranda with pasta and pizzas. ⊠ *2 pl. du Port, CH-1006,* ☎ *021/6167451,* 𝔽𝔸𝕏 *021/6175137. 34 rooms. 2 restaurants, bar, dance club. AE, DC, MC, V.*

$$$ 🏨 **Mövenpick Radisson.** This is a business-style chain hotel across the street from a busy marina. One of the nicer of the newest hotels that stretch along the lake in Ouchy, it's a five-minute drive from the city center. Rooms, à la Laura Ashley, are spacious for a European hotel, but those facing the lake can be noisy. A generous buffet breakfast in one of the three restaurants costs extra. ⊠ *4 av. de Rhodanie, CH-1000,* ☎ *021/6172121,* 𝔽𝔸𝕏 *021/6161527. 260 rooms, 5 suites. 3 restaurants, piano bar, no-smoking rooms, sauna, exercise room. AE, MC, V.*

$$-$$$ 🏨 **Des Voyageurs.** In a narrow town house in the city center, this is a comfortable, friendly hotel, with fresh decor and impeccable maintenance. Although it was renovated in 1994 to provide more modern services (copy machines, fax machines, VCRs), Victorian details are still in evidence; the oak stairways, stained glass, and Victorian breakfast room are just enough to keep you interested in what could have been an anonymous urban space. ⊠ *19 rue Grand-St-Jean, CH-1003,* ☎ *021/3199111,* 𝔽𝔸𝕏 *021/3199112. 33 rooms. Breakfast room, no-smoking rooms. AE, DC, MC, V.*

$$-$$$ 🏨 **Elite.** Directly uphill from the train station on a surprisingly quiet street,
★ this hotel is a tranquil little enclave. Most rooms have a view of fruit trees and a garden; ask for a fourth-floor room for a spectacular lake view. The hotel has been in one family for 50 years, and it shows—from the solid renovation and modern touches (electric doors, piped-in music) to the squeaky-clean maintenance. There are kitchenettes available. ⊠ *1 av. Ste-Luce, CH-1003,* ☎ *021/3202361,* 𝔽𝔸𝕏 *021/3203963. 33 rooms. Breakfast room, no-smoking rooms. AE, DC, MC, V.*

$$ 🏨 **L'Angleterre.** A plaque by the door says Lord Byron wrote *The Prisoner of Chillon* here in 1817, and it looks as if it hasn't been kept up since. Behind the classic symmetry of the 18th-century facade, you'll find chipped mix-and-match furniture, rumpled carpet, and postwar bathrooms. Nevertheless, the terrace café is popular, and above it, each shuttered window opens directly onto the lake. The view might inspire you to poetry, too. ⊠ *9 pl. du Port, CH-1006,* ☎ *021/6164145,* 𝔽𝔸𝕏 *021/6168075. 28 rooms. Restaurant, café. AE, DC, MC, V.*

$–$$ **City.** Under the same management as the Agora (☞ *above*), this once-faded urban hotel, at the hub of the downtown crossroads, has undergone a profound and daring renovation, transforming itself from a steam-heated dump into a spectacular architectural showcase with curving chrome planes, a two-way escalator flanked by a sleek waterfall, and breathtaking views of the city, especially from the glassed-in breakfast room. Slick and soundproof, with fresh duvets, pink-tile baths, videos, hair dryers, and room service, the City is a value-priced model for its peers. ⊠ *5 rue Caroline, CH-1007,* ☎ *021/3202141,* FAX *021/3202149. 51 rooms. Breakfast room, in-room VCRs. AE, DC, MC, V.*

$–$$ **Regina.** This tiny old lodging near the Old Town has spruced up its public areas and, in 1997, totally refurbished its guest rooms—they're now squared away with color-coordinated carpets and upholstery. Those in the back are quiet, with roofline views; although the rooms don't have bathtubs, they all have private bathrooms with showers. The best thing about this place, though, is the owners' friendly service; the couple spent over a decade in the United States, so the language barrier is nonexistent. ⊠ *18 rue Grand-St-Jean, CH-1003,* ☎ *021/ 3202441,* FAX *021/3202529. 15 rooms. Breakfast room. MC, V.*

Nightlife and the Arts

Lausanne is one of the arts capitals of Switzerland, sharing with Geneva the **Orchestre de la Suisse Romande.** It also hosts the great ballet company of **Maurice Béjart** since his exodus from Brussels. For ticket outlets contact the Lausanne Convention and Tourist Office (⊠ 2 av. de Rhodanie, ☎ 021/6137321); the tourist office's calendar of monthly events, as well as the publication *Reg'art* (published bimonthly in French), offers information on upcoming activities. Check out the daily newspaper *24 Heures* for listings as well.

BARS AND LOUNGES

One of the most chic and lively gathering spots in Lausanne is the **Café Beau-Rivage** (☎ 021/6133330), in the luxury hotel of the same name (☞ Dining and Lodging, *above*); there's an American-style bar with stools, the wicker-and-marble decor of a Parisian brasserie, and live music nightly. The Lausanne Palace (☞ Dining and Lodging, *above*) serves drinks in its lobby bar **Le Relais** (☎ 021/3313131). The Royal Savoy (☞ Dining and Lodging, *above*) serves drinks at one end of its bowered garden restaurant, **La Terrasse** (☎ 021/6148888), throughout the warm season, with guitarists or small ensembles; its interior bar is an intimate, armchaired lounge.

CLASSICAL MUSIC

Théâtre-Municipal Lausanne (⊠ 12 av. du Théâtre, ☎ 021/3126433), like a tattered bomb shelter deep underground in the heart of Lausanne, is one of the city's central performance venues for concerts, operas, and ballets, including the riveting experiments of Maurice Béjart. The **Théâtre de Beaulieu** (⊠ 10 av. des Bergières, ☎ 021/6432111), right across from the Collection de l'Art Brut (☞ Exploring, *above*), hosts full-scale performances of orchestral music, opera, and dance in its larger hall; this is where the Orchestre de la Suisse Romande performs. The Orchestre de Chambre de Lausanne plays at the **Salle Métropole** (☎ 021/3111122).

DANCING

The hot new discotheque, the **D Club** (⊠ 4 rue de Grand Pont, ☎ 0213124041), is decked out with works of contemporary European sculptors. Within the discotheque **La Griffe** (⊠ 2 pl. de la Gare, ☎ 021/ 3110262) you'll find a disc jockey, video screen, and light show. **Le Gibo** (⊠ Galeries St-François, ☎ 021/3120935) offers tropical atmosphere and dance music.

Le Chorus (✉ 3 av. Mon Repos, ☎ 021/3232233) has a renowned jazz cellar and also serves food and drinks.

The Lausanne Palace's upscale **Brummell** (✉ 7 rue du Grand-Chêne, ☎ 021/3120920) has dancing and a cabaret.

Théâtre Vidy-Lausanne (✉ 5 av. Émile-Jacques-Dalcroze, ☎ 021/61945445), west of Lausanne's center, presents classical and contemporary theater in French. **Théâtre Kléber-Méleau** (✉ 9 chemin de l'Usine-à-Gaz, Renens, ☎ 021/6258400), at Vidy, offers a variety of French-language theater, old and new.

Outdoor Activities and Sports
La Nautique (✉ 1 pl. du Vieux-Port, ☎ 021/6160023) has a clubhouse, changing rooms, and a crane. The **École de Voile de Vidy** (✉ Port de Vidy, ☎ 021/6179000) is a sailing school with rentals.

Five open-air skating rinks in the Lausanne area stay open from October to March. **Patinoire de Montchoisi** (✉ 30 av. du Servan, ☎ 021/6171163) has 35,000 square ft of surface. **Patinoire de la Pontaise** (✉ 11 rte. Plaines-du-Loup, ☎ 021/6468163) attracts urban crowds. Three rinks are operated by **Centre Intercommunal de Glace de Malley** (✉ 14 chemin du Viaduc, in nearby Prilly, ☎ 021/6206500). The new skate park **La Fièvre du Roller** (✉ 36 av. de Sévelin, ☎ 021/6263793), with half pipes for roller bladers, stays open year-round.

In Lausanne, the pool **Piscine de Montchoisi** (✉ 20 av. du Servan, ☎ 021/6161062) makes artificial waves; it's open from May through August. **Bellerive Beach** (✉ 23 av. de Rhodanie, ☎ 021/6178131) has access to the lake and three pools, one Olympic size, plus generous lawns and a self-service restaurant. The covered pool at **Mon-Repos** (✉ 4 av. du Tribunal-Fédéral, ☎ 021/3234566) stays open all winter, closing only July–August.

Shopping
The main shopping circle centers on **place St-François, rue St-François, rue de Bourg,** and **rue du Grand-Pont.** Less expensive shopping is along **rue St-Laurent** and **rue de l'Ale.**

Librairie Payot (✉ 4 pl. Pépinet, ☎ 021/3413331) carries mass-market French books and a good assortment in English.

In Lausanne, **Bon Génie** (✉ 10 pl. St-François, ☎ 021/3204811) carries a broad and varied line of upscale designer goods. The large department store **Globus** (✉ rue Centrale at rue du Pont, ☎ 021/3429090) has splendid new food halls at the basement level and a restaurant.

Langenthal (✉ 8 rue de Bourg, ☎ 021/3234402) is the central source for towels, sheets, and embroidered handkerchiefs, mainly Swiss made. **Drafil** (✉ pl. St-Laurent, ☎ 021/3235044) carries a lovely line of trousseau goods, all made in Suisse Romande. **Coupy** (✉ 4 Madeleine, ☎ 021/3127866) has a large selection of duvets, pillows, and linens.

There are fruit and vegetable markets in Lausanne along **rue de l'Ale, rue de Bourg,** and **place de la Riponne** every Wednesday and Saturday mornings. **Place de la Palud** adds a flea market to its Wednesday and Saturday produce market and is the site of a handicrafts market the first Friday of the month from March through December.

TOYS

Franz Carl Weber is the main Swiss source for international toys (⊠ 23 rue de Bourg, ☎ 021/3201471). **Davidson Formation** (⊠ 20 rue Grand St-Jean, ☎ 021/3232522) has a unique collection of educational toys and English-language books.

WATCHES

The place St-François has most of the watch shops. **Bucherer** (⊠ No. 5, ☎ 021/3206354) sells Rolex and Piaget. **Junod** (⊠ No. 8, ☎ 021/3122745) carries Blancpain. **Grumser** (⊠ No. 11, ☎ 021/3124826) specializes in Baume & Mercier. **Roman Mayer** (⊠ 12 bis pl. St-François, ☎ 021/3122316) carries Audemars Piguet, Ebel, and Omega.

LAVAUX VIGNOBLES AND MONTREUX

To the east of Lausanne stretches the Lavaux, a remarkably beautiful region of vineyards that rise up the hillsides all the way from Pully, on the outskirts of Lausanne, to Montreux—a distance of 24 km (15 mi). Brown-roof stone villages in the Savoy style, old defense towers, and small baronial castles stud the green-and-black landscape. The vineyards, enclosed within low stone walls, slope so steeply that all the work there has to be done by hand. Insecticides, fungicides, and manure are carried in baskets, and containers are strapped to men's backs. Harvest in early October is a time for real rejoicing, with the women picking the heavy, round fruit and the men carrying the loads to the nearest road, emptying them into vats and driving them by tractor to the nearest press. Some Lavaux vintages are excellent and in great demand, but unfortunately, as with so much of Switzerland's wine, the yield is small, and the product is rarely exported. From May to October, especially on weekends, you'll find a winegrower's cellar in every village and some of the private châteaux-vignobles open for tastings (and, of course, sales).

En Route   The scenic **Corniche Road** stretches some 17 km (10 mi) through Lavaux, threading above the waterfront from Lausanne to Vevey, between the autoroute and the lakeside Route 9. This is Switzerland at its most Franco-European, reminiscent in its small-scale, humble way of the Riviera or the hill towns of Alsace. You'll careen around hairpin turns through villages' narrow cobbled streets, with the Savoy Alps glowing across the sparkling lake and the Dents du Midi looming ahead, hand-painted signs beckoning you to stop and taste the wines from the vine rows that stripe the hills above and below the road. Stop to gaze at roadside overlooks or wander down a side lane into the fields of **Riex, Épesses, Rivaz,** or the **Dézaley,** the sources of some of Switzerland's loveliest white wines, and typically magical little Vaudois villages. Toward the end of the road, you can follow new hiking trails (signposted with informative tidbits about the vineyards) from **Chexbres,** a spick-and-span summer lake resort about 600 m (2,000 ft) above sea level.

St-Saphorin

⑲ *15 km (9 mi) southeast of Lausanne.*

At the end of the Corniche Road just east of Vevey, St-Saphorin is perched just above the water. With its impossibly narrow, steep cobbled streets and ancient wine makers' houses crowded around fountains and crooked alleys, this is a village that merits a stop.

Dining

$$ ✕ **Auberge de l'Onde.** Once the main *relais* (stagecoach stop) between ★ the Simplon and Geneva, this is a vineyard inn out of central casting, groaning with history and heady with atmosphere: Igor Stravinsky and Charlie Chaplin were among the artists loyal to its charms. The ambience is equally seductive in its tiny wood-panel café, where locals read the papers over a chipped pitcher of St-Saph, as they call it, and a plate of butter-fried lake perch, or in its dainty beamed dining room lined with ancient crockery and lighted with grape-wood sconces. The latter is worth the splurge, with silver-platter service (two helpings) of very local *omble chevalier* (salmon trout) in sorrel sauce and bubbling hot fruit gratins, served by white-bloused waitresses who hover with a good bottle of the local *récolte* (vintage) while day-tripping connoisseurs sniff and roll the almond-perfume wine over their tongues. ✉ *St-Saphorin,* ☎ *021/9213083. AE, DC, MC, V.*

Vevey

★ ⑳ *2 km (1 mi) east of St-Saphorin, 19 km (12 mi) east of Lausanne.*

This soigné waterfront town was the setting for Anita Brookner's evocative 1985 novel *Hotel du Lac,* about a woman retreating to a lake resort to write; her heroine was attracted to the site, in part, because of its slightly stuffy 19th-century ways. In the 1870s, Henry James captured this mood of prim grace while writing (and setting) *Daisy Miller* in the Hotel des Trois Couronnes. Indeed, despite its virtual twinning with glamorous Montreux, Vevey retains its air of isolation, of old-world gentility. Loyal guests have been returning for generations to gaze at the **Dent d'Oche** (2,222 m/7,288 ft) across the water in France and make sedate steamer excursions into Montreux and Lausanne: today there are some who come just to see the bronze statue of Charlie Chaplin in the waterfront Rose Park and to take the funicular or mountain train up to Mont Pelerin. Yet Vevey is a great walking town, with more character in its shuttered **Old Town,** better museums, landmarks, and shops, and more native activity in its wine market than cosmopolitan Montreux can muster. In 1999, from July 29 to August 15, Vevey celebrates the **Fête des Vignerons** (Winegrowers' Festival), a tremendous, traditional festival held roughly every quarter century since 1783. Pageants, parades, musicians, and allegorical and mythical figures flood the town; there is even a coronation ceremony for prize-winning winegrowers.

Vevey is a marketing center for wines of the region, and the local white is sold in summer at its Saturday market on the waterfront, alongside fruits and vegetables; you buy your own glass and taste *à volonté* (at will). Vevey is also the hometown of Nestlé, which dominates the global food market (including chocolate and milk products); its laboratories and world headquarters are based here.

Among the notables attracted to live or sojourn in Vevey were Graham Greene, Victor Hugo, Jean-Jacques Rousseau (who set much of *La Nouvelle Heloise* here), Dostoyevsky, the French artist Gustave Courbet, Oskar Kokoschka, Charlie and Oona Chaplin (buried in the cemetery at Corsier), and Swiss native Édouard Jeanneret, known as Le Corbusier. By following an excellent brochure/map published by the tourist office, you can travel "On the Trail of Hemingway"—and to the homes and haunts of some 40 other luminaries.

★ Le Corbusier's **Villa le Lac,** a low-slung, one-story white house built directly on the Vevey waterfront, was constructed for his parents in 1923; it remains unaltered, with his original furnishings and details preserved within. Shingled in corrugated sheet metal, with a white-metal railed balcony looking over the water and a "birdhouse" chimney in molded concrete, it is typically sculptural and, in a modest way, visionary. ⊠ *On the western outskirts of Vevey, just west of the marina,* ☎ *021/9235371.* ⚎ *Free.* ☉ *Guided tours Wed. 2–5; closed mid-Nov.–mid-Mar.*

Ⓒ A controlling financial power in the region, Nestlé sponsors an unconventional museum in Vevey, the **Alimentarium.** This well-funded, unusually presented exhibition addresses three aspects of food and food production: science (the food chain), ethnology (food in different world cultures), and history (eating habits through the ages). Displays are in a grand 19th-century mansion; in addition, there are films, computers, and—if the subject matter makes you feel a bit hungry—a snack bar. Though many of the displays are esoteric and even unfocused, the downstairs interactive exhibits on nutrition—based on your personal statistics—are straightforward and informative. A children's section offers kids a chance to cook and to visit a model digestive tract. ⊠ *quai Perdonnet,* ☎ *021/9244111.* ⚎ *5 SF.* ☉ *Tues.–Sun. 10–noon and 2–5.*

The **Musée Jenisch** owes its considerable inventory of the works of the Expressionist Oskar Kokoschka to his retirement on Vevey's shores. Its partner wing, the **Cabinet Cantonal des Estampes** (Cantonal Print Collection) contains a rich assortment of engravings, some by Dürer and Rembrandt. ⊠ *2 av. de la Gare,* ☎ *021/9212950,* ⚎ *8 SF–12 SF.* ☉ *Tues.–Sun 10:30–noon and 2–5:30.*

The **Musée Historique du Vieux Vevey** (Historical Museum of Old Vevey) occupies a grand 16th-century manor house, briefly home to Charlotte de Lengefeld, wife of Friedrich von Schiller. It retains some original furnishings as well as collections of arms, art, keys, and vintner paraphernalia. ⊠ *2 rue du Château,* ☎ *021/9210722.* ⚎ *4 SF.* ☉ *Tues.–Sun. 10:30–noon and 2–5:30.*

Dining and Lodging

$–$$ ✕ **Café de La Clef "chez Manu."** Jean Jacques Rousseau stayed here in 1730, making this café as much a landmark as the pillared marketplace in front of it. No one seems to mind the uninspired decor of tile floors, salmon-pink walls, and the odd potted palm; rather the locals line up for lunchtime tables to savor such well-prepared traditional specialties as fondue and *filets de perches* (perch fillets—for something different try them curried) along with *julienne de légumes au bouillon safrané* (fresh fish and vegetable soup with saffron). The walls are occasionally brightened with exhibitions of regional artists. ⊠ *1 rue du Théâtre,* ☎ *021/9212245. MC, V. Closed Sun.*

$$$$ ☖ **Des Trois Couronnes.** Honeycombed by dramatic atrium stairwells and thick with alabaster and faux *marbre* (marble), this regal landmark was Henry James's home base in writing (and setting) the novella *Daisy Miller.* (The antiheroine, on her grand tour of Europe's finest, strayed unchaperoned to Chillon and, having thus flown in the face of Victorian propriety, met a richly deserved demise.) In filming his version of the story, Peter Bogdanovich cast the hotel as itself: Its halls are indeed evocative of an era of grand tours, and even guest rooms still exhibit period sensibility. A vast lakefront terrace overlooks the pollards, the promenade, and the steamers that still carry their cargo of headstrong women toward Chillon. Reservations are essential at the restaurant, which has tempting French cuisine at unexpectedly reasonable prices. ⊠ *49 rue d'Italie, CH-1800,* ☎ *021/9213005,* ℻ *021/9227280. 55 rooms, 10 suites. Restaurant, bar, café, exercise room. AE, DC, MC, V.*

$$$ 🏨 **Du Lac.** Anita Brookner set her novel *Hotel du Lac* in this lesser sister of the Trois Couronnes (☞ *above*): Its readers may be disappointed to find the hotel lacking the discretion, refinement, and even the stuffiness she so precisely described. Instead there are sandwich boards proclaiming the next theme feast in the restaurant, along with plenty of reminders that this is a link in the Best Western chain. Though some rooms are done up with prim florals or chic burled wood, others retain the kelly-green carpet and mustard chenille of another era in decorating. Its location is the hotel's main attraction, as there are a sheltered terrace restaurant, garden, and pool all just across the street from the waterfront. ⊠ *1 rue d'Italie, CH-1800,* ☎ *021/9211041,* 🖷 *021/9217508. 56 rooms. Restaurant, café, pool. AE, DC, MC, V.*

$–$$ 🏨 **Des Négociants.** Handy to the market, in the Old Town by the lake, this is a comfortable, no-nonsense lodging. Its arcaded, shuttered facade is in sharp contrast to the laminated, foursquare interiors, but the top floor has a dormer room of knotty pine that is suitable for families, and all baths are tiled. The restaurant serves standard brasserie fare, cooked by the owner himself. ⊠ *27 rue du Conseil, CH-1800,* ☎ *021/ 9227011,* 🖷 *021/9213424. 23 rooms. Restaurant. AE, DC, MC, V.*

Outdoor Activities and Sports

Pedal boats for splashing along the sunny waterfront can be rented from **José Justo** (⊠ pl. du Marché, ☎ 021/9213880).

Montreux

㉑ *4 km (2 mi) southeast of Vevey, 21 km (13 mi) southeast of Lausanne.*

Petite Montreux could be called the Cannes of Lake Geneva—though it might raise an eyebrow at the slur. Spilling down steep hillsides into a sunny south-facing bay, its waterfront thick with magnolias, cypress, and palm trees, the historic resort earns its reputation as the capital—if not the pearl—of the Swiss Riviera; unlike the French Riviera, it has managed, despite overwhelming crowds of conventioneers, to keep up appearances. Its Edwardian-French deportment has survived considerable development, and though there are plenty of harsh new high-rises with parking-garage aesthetics, its mansard landmarks still unfurl orange awnings to shield millionaires from subtropical sun.

The site where Stravinsky composed *Petrouchka* and *Le Sacre du Printemps* and where Vladimir Nabokov resided in splendor, Montreux and its suburbs have attracted artists and literati for 200 years: Byron, Shelley, Tolstoy, Hans Christian Andersen, and Flaubert were drawn to its lush shoreline. When its casino opened in 1883, tourism began in earnest. Today, Montreux is best known for its history-making Montreux Jazz Festival, which takes place each July; with Vevey, it also sponsors a Festival International de Musique (International Festival of Music) in September.

★ **㉒** Certainly the greatest attraction at Montreux and one of Switzerland's must-sees is the **Château de Chillon,** the awe-inspiring 12th-century castle that rears out of the water at Veytaux, just down the road from and within sight of Montreux. On Roman foundations, Chillon was built under the direction of Duke Peter of Savoy with the help of military architects from Plantagenet England. For a long period it served as a state prison, and one of its shackled guests was François Bonivard, who supported the Reformation and enraged the Savoys. He spent six years in this prison, chained most of the time to a pillar in the dungeon, before being released by the Bernese in 1536.

While living near Montreux, Lord Byron visited Chillon and was so transported by its atmosphere and by Bonivard's grim sojourn that he was inspired to write his famous poem *The Prisoner of Chillon*. Like a true tourist, he carved his name on a pillar in Bonivard's still-damp and -chilly dungeon; that graffito is protected under a plaque today.

Visitors to Chillon now must file placidly from restored chamber to restored turret, often waiting at doorways for entire busloads of fellow tourists to pass. Yet the restoration is so evocative and so convincing, with its tapestries, carved fireplaces, period ceramics and pewter, and elaborate wooden ceilings, that even the jaded castle hound may become as carried away as Byron was. While you're waiting your turn, you can gaze out the narrow windows over the sparkling, lapping water and remember Mark Twain, who thought Bonivard didn't have it half bad. ⊠ *CH-1820 Veytaux, less than 3 km/2 mi south of Montreux,* ☎ *021/9633912.* ▱ *7 SF.* ☉ *Nov.–Feb., daily 10–noon and 1:30–4; Mar., daily 10–noon and 1:30–4:45; Apr.–June and Sept., daily 9–5:45; July, daily 9–6:15; Aug., Fri.–Wed. 9–6:15, Thurs. 9–8; Oct., daily 10–4:45.*

Dining and Lodging

$$$–$$$$ × **Le Pont de Brent.** Tucked on a hillside next to its namesake bridge
★ in the unassuming Montreux suburb of Brent, this small but elegant restaurant ties with Rochat (formerly Girardet) for the honor of the best table in Switzerland. Who would guess that the green shuttered windows and pale stone exterior of this unassuming building screen showstopping cuisine? Norman chef Gérard Rabaey performs alchemy with local ingredients to turn out dishes almost too pretty to eat: Morels stuffed with truffles, leeks, and green asparagus, red mullet with new cabbage in sweet-peppered sabayon, or fanned rhubarb with hazelnut ice cream and honey. Apart from the slightly stiff decor, all is warm here, from the ocher walls to the welcome and service. ⊠ *Rte. de Brent, 7 km/4½ mi northwest of Montreux, Brent,* ☎ *021/9645230. Reservations essential. MC, V. Closed Sun. and Mon., last 2 wks of July, late Dec.–early Jan.*

$$ × **Du Pont.** In the Old Town high on the hill over Montreux's water-
★ front, this bustling, old restaurant-café takes its food and its customers seriously. You can relax in the smoky café (where jeans aren't out of place) or enjoy full service and pink linens in the lovely dining room upstairs. Suit your whim: The menu and the prices are exactly the same, including a cheap daily special—and whether you order them upstairs or down, the German-born chef (who spent years in Italy) will personally grate your white Alba truffle. There are big portions and definitive versions of veal *piccata*, pastas, steaks, and game, and toothsome risotto. ⊠ *12 rue du Pont,* ☎ *021/9632249. AE, DC, MC, V.*

$$$–$$$$ ×▱ **Hotel Victoria.** Noël Coward stayed in Room 49 some 40 years
★ ago while his chalet was being renovated in nearby Les Avants (the playwright had a penchant for high places). Since 1869, this superb hotel set in its own park in the heights of Glion above Montreux has drawn its share of celebrities and royalty, who come not to be seen but to see the glories of the lake from this unique vantage point—and to be pampered without pomposity. The current owner oversees every detail from the foot-high down seat cushions in the grand salon to the hand-painted stenciling in the corridors and the freshly cut flowers everywhere. The dining room could be a Coward stage set, its opulence tempered by the occasional eccentric guest, a dog or two, and the brief appearance of unbuttoned children. Room decor mixes fine art with soothing pastels, swish amenities, and often a balcony. A lap pool, a lighted tennis court, and a French restaurant serving excellent light cuisine complete this elegant country-house fantasy. ⊠ *CH-1823 Glion,* ☎ *021/9633131,* ℻ *021/9631351. 50 rooms, 9 suites. Restaurant, bar,*

breakfast room, minibars, pool, tennis court, sauna, exercise room, piano, library, meeting room. AE, DC, MC, V.

$$$–$$$$ ✕⌂ **L'Ermitage.** Freestanding on its own waterfront-garden grounds,
★ this genteel, intimate retreat offers top-drawer haute gastronomie and a few luxurious rooms upstairs. The guest rooms are lightened with fresh flowers, lacquered cane furniture, and lake views; many rooms have balconies. Chef Étienne Krebs's exceptional cuisine may include ray wing in saffron-potato emulsion with oil and smoked tomato bouillon, breast of duck in a celery-root casserole, or hot chestnut soufflé with kirsch ice cream. The ultimate splurge: his seven-course laissez-faire menu, a parade of delicately orchestrated surprises. The main restaurant is closed Sunday and Monday; there's a terrace for alfresco dining open daily in summer. ⊠ *75 rue du Lac, CH-1815,* ☎ *022/ 9644411. 7 rooms. AE, DC, MC, V.*

$$$$ ⌂ **Le Montreux Palace.** Dominating the hillside over the Grand-rue and the waterfront, the silver mansards and yellow awnings of this vast institution flag the Palace as a landmark, though its aristocratic origins have been compromised considerably in an era of business-convention crowds. It was first opened in 1906, a colossal Belle Epoque folly of stained glass, frescoes, and flamboyant molded stucco; author Vladimir Nabokov lived among the furbelows for almost 20 years before dying in his suite. Much of that excess has been tempered with age and updated with touches of modern glitz, including a glossy, modern shopping arcade, a pavilion across the street (Le Petit Palais) with two nightclubs, and Switzerland's first Harry's Bar. Lakeside rooms are appropriately posh; mountainside rooms, in the back, miss out on the hotel's raison d'être: a commanding Lake Geneva view. Reservations are essential in all restaurants. ⊠ *10 Grand-rue, CH-1820,* ☎ *021/ 9621212,* ⅢX *021/9621717. 210 rooms, 25 suites. 4 restaurants, 2 bars, no-smoking rooms, pool, beauty salon, tennis court. AE, DC, MC, V.*

$$$ ⌂ **Suisse et Majestic.** Despite its grand Victorian facade, this is a business-class hotel, offering standard services to groups and conferences. Renovation has revived some of its fin de siècle appeal, even imposing period details to enhance the vaguely ice-cream-parlorish theme. The results: a comfortable lodging that might have popped up anywhere—though it's in the heart of old Montreux. ⊠ *43 av. des Alpes, CH-1820,* ☎ *021/9635181,* ⅢX *021/963506. 150 rooms. Restaurant, bar, café, meeting rooms. AE, DC, MC, V.*

$$ ⌂ **Masson.** If you're traveling by car or you enjoy being away from
★ the downtown resort scene, look up this demure little inn on a hillside in Veytaux, between Chillon and Montreux. Since it was built in 1829, it's had only four owners, and the current family takes pride in its genteel period decor and up-to-date technology, including color television with remote headphones so one guest won't disturb another. There are floral prints, brass beds, pristine linens, buffed parquet, and expansive lake views from the numerous balconies. The breakfast buffet is generous, with homemade jams. A simple evening meal is served for half-board guests. The dinner-only restaurant is for guests only; reservations are essential. ⊠ *5 rue Bonivard, CH-1820 Veytaux,* ☎ *021/9638161,* ⅢX *021/9638166. 30 rooms. Restaurant. AE, MC, V.*

$–$$ ⌂ **Hostellerie du Lac.** This rambling, quirky old Swiss-Victorian house
★ stands directly on the waterfront promenade and offers smashing lake views from the front rooms. The decor is eclectic, with fussy, flocked Victoriana jumbled in with mixed '60s styles; some rooms have a fireplace or a balcony. Its popular restaurant and front-porch terrace café serve solid renditions of old favorites and cheap daily plates. ⊠ *12 rue du Quai, CH-1820,* ☎ *021/9633271,* ⅢX *021/9631835. 8 rooms. Restaurant, café. MC, V.*

Nightlife and the Arts

Montreux's famous festivals and arts events are listed in a seasonal booklet published by the tourist office; tickets are sold from its booth at the waterfront. The renowned **Montreux Jazz Festival** takes place every July. Its more sedate, classical **Festival International de Musique** (International Festival of Music) shares venues with Vevey from August through September. For tickets to these popular events, contact their **ticket office** (☎ 021/9622119) as far in advance as possible. In summer, Montreux offers a variety of free outdoor concerts from its bandstand on the waterfront near the landing stage.

BARS

In Montreux, the **Montreux Palace** (☞ Dining and Lodging, *above*; ⊠ 100 Grand-rue, ☎ 021/9621212) now has a **Harry's Bar** with a pianist after 5. The **Royal Plaza** (⊠ 97 Grand-rue, ☎ 021/9635131) has a piano bar with jazz in the summer and an American-style bar in the lobby.

CASINO

The **Casino** (⊠ 9 rue du Théâtre, ☎ 021/9628383) at Montreux, established in 1883, was burned in 1971 and rebuilt in 1975; now you'll find dancing, slot machines, a billiards room, and a Mongolian restaurant. The usual 5 SF gambling limit applies.

DANCING

The **Backstage Club** (⊠ 100 Grand-rue, ☎ 021/9633444) is the newest scene in Montreux for dancing, with disc jockeys and sushi bar. You can glide along the lake as you dance on the **Bateau Dansant,** (☎ 084/8811848), which departs from the landing stage on Wednesday at 7:25 PM and 9 PM throughout July and August. **Caesar's** (⊠ 55 Grand-rue, ☎ 021/9637559) makes room for lakefront dancing and cabaret.

Outdoor Activities and Sports

SAILING AND WATER SPORTS

Pedal boats are popular along Montreux-Vevey's waterfront. Rentals are available at **Albert Morisod** (⊠ By the convention center, ☎ 021/9633936). **Jean Morisod** (⊠ At the quai du Casino, ☎ 021/9633160) also rents them.

Cercle de la Voile de Montreux (⊠ Clarens, ☎ 021/9643898) is the local sailing club. Montreux offers guests of its hotels free and supervised use of its waterfront facilities for windsurfing and waterskiing; afternoons, there's a fee at the **Ski-Nautique Club** (☎ 021/9634456).

La Maladaire (☎ 021/9645703) in adjoining Clarens has an Olympic-size indoor pool. The **Casino** (⊠ 9 rue du Théâtre, ☎ 021/9628383) has a pool on an outdoor terrace with a bar.

OFF THE
BEATEN PATH

BLONAY–CHAMBY RAILROAD – The allure for travelers to Montreux is not limited to the shoreline scene. Out of Montreux, a number of railways climb into the heights, which, in late spring, are carpeted with an extravagance of wild narcissi. If you like model railroads, you will especially enjoy a trip on the Blonay–Chamby Railroad line, whose real steam-driven trains alternate with electric trains on weekends only between Blonay and Chamby above Montreux, with a stop at a small museum of railroad history in between. You can depart from either end; the trip takes about 20 minutes each way, not including a browse in the museum. ⊠ *Case Postale 366, CH-1001 Lausanne,* ☎ *021/9432121.* ☞ *Round-trip ticket 12 SF.* ☺ *Trains run May–Oct., Sun. 9:40–6 and Sat. 2–6.*

LES AVANTS – The Montreux–Oberland–Bernois Railroad (MOB) line leads to the resort village of Les Avants (970 m/3,181 ft)—and then on to Château-d'Oex, Gstaad, and the Simmental. The Simmental isn't mentioned below (but note that the Simmental Valley *is* discussed in Chapter 10), though Chateau-d'Oex has its own section, below, with mentions of Gstaad within it. Noël Coward bought his dream home in Les Avants, at No. 8, Route de Sonloup; Ernest Hemingway wrote to his family and friends of its fields of daffodils—and, more in character, of its bobsled track.

LES ALPES VAUDOISES

At the eastern tip of Lake Geneva, the Alps on the French and Swiss sides close in on the Rhône, and the lakefront highways begin a gradual, ear-popping ascent as the scenery looms larger and the mountains rise around you. The high-altitude Alpine resorts of Villars-Gryon, Leysin, and Les Diablerets each have their charms for winter-sports fans and summer hikers; a visit to any one of the three would suffice for a mountain retreat. On the other hand, the Pays-d'Enhaut, over the Col des Mosses, is a rustic, lower-altitude region surrounded by rocky ridges and velvet hillsides, flecked with snow and sprinkled with ancient carved-wood chalets; either Château-d'Oex or Rougemont would serve well as home base for a sojourn in this gentle resort area. You can make a beeline from one to another, but rail connections are limited and driving often torturous; you'd do well to choose one dreamy spot and stay put—by the fireplace, on the balcony—for as many days as your itinerary allows.

The resorts of the Vaud Alps, although anything but household words to most ski buffs, offer the bonus of a transportation linkup and lift-ticket package with the sprawling Gstaad "Super-Ski" region (☞ Chapter 10). This skiing mecca takes in the entire Saanen Valley from Zweisimmen to Château-d'Oex and even dovetails with the parallel valley resorts of Adelboden and Lenk, justifying a visit for skiers who want to cover a lot of territory during their stay.

En Route At **Roche,** on the highway between Villeneuve and Aigle, there's a massive 15th-century stone barn that was built by the monks of Grand St-Bernard, on a scale as big as an airplane hangar, and divided into three great pillared naves. The building itself would be worth the detour, but today—after extensive restorations—it houses the **Musée Suisse de l'Orgue** (Swiss Organ Museum), a vast collection of instruments that had been without the cathedral-scale space required for display until it arrived in this gargantuan barn. There's an ornate Louis XVI organ case, an 18th-century pedal board, a neo-Gothic harmonium, and even an Emmental home organ. The curator leads three one-hour tours a day (in French) and demonstrates the instruments. ⊠ *Association des Amis du Musée Suisse de l'Orgue, 5 pl. St-François, CH-1003 Lausanne,* ☎ *021/3200277.* ☎ *Free.* ☉ *May–Oct., Tues.–Sun. 10–noon and 2–5.*

Aigle

㉓ *17 km (10 mi) south of Montreux, 38 km (24 mi) southeast of Lausanne.*

On a smooth plain flanked by the sloping vineyards of the region of Le Chablais, Aigle is a scenic wine center. Its spired and turreted **Château de Savoie,** originally built during the 13th century, was almost completely destroyed—and was then rebuilt—by the 15th-century Bernese.

The **Musée de la Vigne et du Vin** (Museum of the Vine and Wine), in the Château d'Aigle, displays casks, bottles, presses, and wine makers' tools within its wood-beam chambers. Some living quarters are reproduced, and there's even a collection of costumes worn over the centuries for the local Fête des Vignerons. ⊠ *Château d'Aigle, CH-1860,* ☎ *024/4662130.* ⊞ *6 SF.* ☉ *Apr.–June and Sept.–Oct., Tues.–Sun. 10–12:30 and 2–6; Jul.–Aug., daily 10–6; Nov.–Mar., tours by appointment.*

OFF THE
BEATEN PATH

SWISS VAPEUR PARC – Where the Rhône empties into Lake Geneva, between Vaud and France, families may want to visit the Swiss Vapeur Parc (Swiss Steam Park), a miniature railway circuit laid out in a green park. There you can straddle the tiny models and cruise around a reduced-scale landscape. ⊠ *CH-1897 Le Bouveret,* ☎ *024/4814410.* ⊞ *8.50 SF (includes ride).* ☉ *Mid-May–late Sept., weekdays 1:30–6, weekends 10–6; late Apr.–mid-May and late Sept.–Oct., Wed. and weekends 1:30–6.*

Villars-Gryon

★ ㉔ *15 km (9 mi) southeast of Aigle, 53 km (33 mi) southeast of Lausanne.*

At 1,300 m (4,264 ft), this welcoming ski center spreads comfortably along a sunny terrace, the craggy peaks of Les Diablerets (3,210 m/10,528 ft) behind it and before it a sweeping view over the Rhône Valley all the way to Mont Blanc. Balanced along its ridge and open to the vast space below, its busy little downtown—sports shops, cafés, resort hotels—tapers off quickly into open country. Though it's thriving with new constructions, Villars retains a sense of coziness and tradition, and some of its family-owned hotels have preserved the feel of mountain lodges that's rare these days in Switzerland. What Villars lacks in the glitz of Gstaad, it amply compensates with unpretentious good cheer. A network of lifts connecting with Les Diablerets make this a good choice for skiers or hikers who want to experience Suisse Romande relatively unspoiled.

Skiing

For serious skiers, Villars itself nicely balances sophistication and Alpine isolation, offering some of the best-developed options and including a new and very accessible link to **Les Diablerets Glacier.** The main ski area over the village can be reached easily either by cable car to **Roc d'Orsay** (2,000 m/6,560 ft) or by cog railway from the center to **Bretaye;** either site allows access to the lifts that fan out over a sunny bowl riddled with intermediate runs and off-trail challenges. From Bretaye, you also can take lifts up to **Grand Chamossaire** (2,120 m/6,954 ft) for gentle, open runs. Ski **Petit Chamossaire** for a more taxing expert descent. Trails from **Chaux Ronde** and **Chaux de Conches** are easy enough for beginners, but the more advanced can find jumps and trees enough to keep them more than alert. Just beyond Villars, the linking resort of **Gryon** presents a few more options and a change of scenery, again with trails for all levels of skill. **Villars,** at 1,300 m (4,264 ft), has 45 lifts, 120 km (75 mi) of downhill runs (including the **Diablerets Glacier**), and 44 km (27 mi) of cross-country trails.

Dining and Lodging

$–$$ ✕ **Le Refuge de Frience.** A few scenic kilometers from Villars en route
★ to Gryon, this 18th-century Heidi-esque chalet combines the grist of Alpine legend with good, honest food. Three cheery rooms glowing with log fires under low, beamed ceilings give way to unfettered views of the mountains and in summer, of cows roaming the slopes. You won't

see tourists here; it's a word-of-mouth place that packs in locals and weekend expats in the know. They go for the fondue and raclette, river trout, and plates of fresh regional mushrooms—and wine spouting from an old *fontaine,* a wrought-iron contraption rarely seen in restaurants. ✕ ⊠ *Alpe des Chaux, 4½ km (3 mi) from Villars,* ☎ *024/4981426. MC, V. Closed Tues. and Apr.–May.*

$$$–$$$$ ⊞ **Le Bristol.** This resort hotel, the poshest in town, rose from the ashes of an older landmark and—despite the Colorado-condo exterior and the jutting balcony for every room—is now furnished with a light, bright, and convincingly regional touch. The interiors are mostly white with mauve touches and carved blond pine, and picture windows are angled to take in the views. There are good health facilities and a choice of attractive restaurants, including a terrace above the valley. Activities and theme events abound. ⊠ *av. Centrale, CH-1884,* ☎ *024/4963636,* FAX *024/4963637. 110 rooms. 2 restaurants, bar, indoor pool, hot tub, sauna, exercise room, squash. AE, DC, MC, V.*

$$ ⊞ **Alpe Fleurie.** From the minute you check in, you'll know this is a
★ family-run, family-oriented hotel: There are snapshots of children and dogs over the reception desk. Launched in 1946 and maintained by the second generation, which lives on the top floor, this chalet-hotel has been updated steadily, and the rooms show a thoughtful mix of modern textures and classic pine. It stands on the main street along the valley side, and south-facing rooms have terrific views. Local residents hit the restaurant for their favorite Vaudoise specialties. ⊠ *av. Centrale, CH-1884,* ☎ *024/4953464,* FAX *024/4963077. 17 rooms. Restaurant, bar, café. AE, DC, MC, V.*

$$ ⊞ **Écureuil.** Although there's a restaurant downstairs and a carnotzet
★ for fondue, nearly every room in this warm, family-run inn has a kitchenette, so you can make yourself at home, mountain cabin–style. Opened in 1947 and run by the son of the founder, the hotel has lots of homey touches: books and magazines, swing sets, and a piano parlor. An older, stone-base chalet on the grounds offers bigger rooms; both buildings stand across the street from the Bristol and therefore don't have direct access to those Villars views. ⊠ *av. Centrale, CH-1884,* ☎ *024/4952795,* FAX *024/4954205. 27 rooms. Restaurant, café, Ping-Pong. MC, V.*

$$ ⊞ **La Renardière.** This group of three classic chalets, set back from the
★ resort center and surrounded by tall firs, was opened as a hotel in 1957 and still looks like a '50s mountain lodge, with its golden pine, plaid curtains, and log bar. The lounges and sitting areas have fireplaces; the rooms are simple, done in pine and chenille, with the customary color scheme of orange and brown. In the traditional restaurant, linens, crystal, and fresh flowers soften the rustic edges, and there's an agreeable terrace café that serves good lunches under the firs. ⊠ *Rte. des Liyeux, CH-1884,* ☎ *024/4952592,* FAX *024/4953915. 21 rooms, 4 suites. Restaurant, bar, café. AE, DC, MC, V.*

Outdoor Activities and Sports

GOLF

The precipitously sited **Golf Alpin** (⊠ Av. Central, ☎ 024/4954214) has 18 holes.

SKATING

Nonskiers can amuse themselves at a centrally located indoor **skating rink** (⊠ Chemin de la Gare, ☎ 024/4951221).

SWIMMING

In the same building as the skating rink in Villars, there's an **indoor pool** (☎ 024/4952128). There's an outdoor pool at **New Sporting** (⊠ Rte. du Col de la Croix, ☎ 024/4951969).

OFF THE   Ⓒ **MINE DU SEL** – Children inured to the thrill of cable cars, narrow-gauge
BEATEN PATH   railroads, and steam trains might brighten at a journey to the center of
the earth in the Mine du Sel (Salt Mine) at Bex, just off the southbound
Route 9. First dug in 1684, this ancient underground complex bores into
the mountain as far as Villars and covers some 50 subterranean km (30
mi). After an introductory audiovisual show, you ride a narrow-gauge
train into the depths and take a guided walk through the works. Wear
sturdy shoes and warm clothing as the temperature stays at 63°F (17°C)
year-round. ⊠ CH-1880 Bex, ☎ 024/4630330. ⊡ 13 SF. Prior booking essential, even for individuals. ⊙ Apr.–mid-Nov., with 2¼-hr-long
tours leaving promptly daily at 10, 2, and 3.

Les Diablerets

⑥ *19 km (12 mi) northeast of Aigle, 59 km (37 mi) southwest of Lausanne.*

In summer, car travelers can cut along spectacular heights on a tiny
13%-grade road over the Col de la Croix (1,778 m/5,832 ft) to get
from Villars to the small neighboring resort of Les Diablerets (1,160
m/3,806 ft). Train travelers will have to descend to Bex and backtrack
to Aigle. Les Diablerets lies at the base of the 3,209-m (10,525-ft) peak
of the same name—which sheds the dramatic namesake 3,000-m
(9,840-ft) glacier.

Skiing

The ski facilities at Les Diablerets have been updated with new lifts,
and the new connection with Villars adds considerably to ski options—including summer skiing on the glacier itself, some dramatic intermediate peak-top runs at **Quille du Diable** and **Scex Rouge.** There's
one gravity-defying expert slope, directly under the gondola, from
Pierre-Pointes back to the valley. From Scex Rouge, a popular run carries you around the top of the **Oldenhorn** and down to **Oldenegg,** a
wide-open intermediate run through a sheltered valley. At 1,250 m (4,100
ft), **Les Diablerets** has six cable cars, 18 lifts, 120 km (75 mi) of downhill runs, 30 km (19 mi) of cross-country trails, and 6 km (4 mi) of
prepared tobogganing trails. A one-day lift ticket, valid at Villars,
Gryon, and Les Diablerets, costs 42 SF; a six-day pass costs 210 SF.

Leysin

⑦ *16 km (10 mi) northeast of Aigle, 54 km (33 mi) southeast of Lausanne.*

From the switchback highway A11, a small mountain road leads up
to this family resort, which has easy skiing and a spectacular sunny
plateau setting and looks directly onto the Dents du Midi.

Skiing

Small-scale and cozy, Leysin offers a widespread network of lifts that
allow you to cover a lot of varied ground on easy-to-medium slopes.
From Berneuse, you can muster up your courage in the revolving
restaurant and head for the **Chaux de Mont** (2,200 m/7,216 ft), where
an expert run winds along a razorback and back through the forests
to town. At 1,250 m (4,100 ft), it has two cable cars, 18 lifts, a shuttle train, and 60 km (37 mi) of ski runs, as well as skating, curling, ski
bob, and 36 km (22 mi) of cross-country trails. A one-day lift ticket
costs 34 SF; a six-day pass costs 170 SF.

PAYS-D'ENHAUT

Separated from the high-altitude Alpine resorts by the modest Col des Mosses (1,445 m/4,740 ft) and isolated, high-altitude family ski centers (Les Mosses, La Lécherette), the Pays-d'Enhaut (Highlands) offers an entirely different culture from its Vaud cousins. Here the architecture begins to resemble that of the Berner Oberland, which it borders: Deep-eave wooden chalets replace the Edwardian structures of the lakelands, and the atmosphere takes on a mountain-farm air. The Pays-d'Enhaut once belonged to Gruyères, then was seized by Bern; when Vaud was declared a canton, the Pays-d'Enhaut went with it. A stone's throw up the valley, you cross the Sarine/Saanen and the so-called Rösti Border, where the culture and language switch to Bernese German. This is still Gruyère cheese country and also the source of one of Switzerland's most familiar decorative arts: *papier découpé,* delicate, symmetrical paper cutouts, an ornate and sophisticated version of America's grade-school snowflakes. They are cut in black, often with simple imagery of cattle and farmers, and fixed on white paper for contrast. The real thing is a refined craft and is priced accordingly, but attractive prints reproducing the look are on sale at reduced prices throughout the region.

L'Etivaz

㉗ *21 km (13 mi) northeast of Aigle, 59 km (37 mi) southeast of Lausanne.*

Visitors to the Pays-d'Enhaut who cross the Col des Mosses first pass through the village of L'Etivaz, where a Gruyère-style cheese is made from milk drawn exclusively from cows grazed on pastures of elevations between 1,000 m and 2,200 m (3,280 ft–7,216 ft) elevation. The sweet, late-blooming flowers they eat impart a flavor that lowland cheeses can't approach. The very best L'Etivaz cheese—*Rebibes*—is aged for three years in the cooperative here until it dries and hardens to a Parmesan-like texture; then it's shaved into curls and eaten by hand. Feel free to stop in at the **cooperative;** one of the workers in cream-color rubber boots will be happy to sell you brick-size chunks of both young and old cheeses at prices well below those at resort groceries.

Dining and Lodging

$ ✕ⓘ **Du Chamois.** For four generations, one family has coddled guests
★ in this weathered-wood chalet. Its bookcases are full of rainy-day reading, and its meals simple, impeccable presentations of trout, cheese, omelets, and steaks marvelously prepared and garnished by the current generation's man of the house. Warm gold pine planking covers nearly every surface, and historic photos, lace curtains, and local paper cutouts add the grace notes. The baths are up to date, while the rooms are simple and genuinely homey. ✉ *CH-1831,* ☎ *026/9246266,* FAX *026/9246016. 18 rooms. Restaurant, café, tennis court, playground. AE, DC, MC, V.*

En Route   Clinging to a precarious cliff-side road between L'Etivaz and Château-d'Oex, drivers penetrate the canyon wilderness of the **Gorges du Pissot,** where sports lovers in wet suits "canyon"—literally, hike the river bottom—under the white waters of the Torneresse River.

Château-d'Oex

㉘ *33 km (20 mi) northeast of Aigle, 64 km (40 mi) east of Lausanne.*

At the crossroads between the Col des Mosses highway to Aigle and the Valais and the route to the Berner Oberland lies Château-d'Oex (pronounced day), a popular sports resort that connects, in these days of sophisticated ski transit, with the greater Gstaad ski region. Its perhaps even greater claim to fame these days is ballooning, with periodic hot-air-balloon competitions that draw mobs of international enthusiasts and fill hotels throughout the region. Mixing Edwardian architecture with weathered-wood chalets, the town spreads over a green, forest-top hillside above the highway and heads the French end of the valley of the Sarine River—also known, in the Berner Oberland, as Saanenland.

★ In Château-d'Oex's small center, the **Musée Artisanal du Vieux Pays-d'Enhaut** (Artisan and Folklore Museum of the Old Highlands) gives you real insight into life in these isolated parts. Complete interiors are evocatively reproduced: two kitchens, a farmer's home, a cheese maker's house, and a carpenter's studio. Marvelous woodwork and ironwork, a variety of ceramics, plus displays of old papier découpé, furniture, and popular art round out the collection. ⊠ *Grand-rue, CH-1837,* ☎ *026/9246520.* ⊠ *3 SF.* ⊙ *Nov.–Sept., Tues., Thurs., and Fri. 10–noon and 2–4:30, weekends 2–4.*

Le Chalet is a rather commercialized reproduction of a mountain cheese maker's place, with afternoon demonstrations over an open fire. Visitors sit at café tables (and are sold drinks or cheese dishes) while they watch the hot labor of stirring milk in a vast copper vat. Regional crafts and dairy products are on sale downstairs. ⊠ *CH-1837,* ☎ *026/9246677.* ⊠ *Free (a purchase or consumption is expected).* ⊙ *Sat.–Thurs. 9–6, Fri. 9 AM–11 PM; demonstrations Tues.–Sun.*

Skiing

Château-d'Oex itself has cable-car links to **La Braye** and the expert and intermediate trails that wind back down. At 1,000 m (3,280 ft), it has one cable car, two chairlifts, 10 lifts, 50 km (31 mi) of downhill runs, and 30 km (19 mi) of cross-country trails. A one-day lift ticket costs 36 SF; a six-day pass costs 171 SF.

Dining and Lodging

$ ✕ **Buffet de la Gare.** Though you'd be better off driving five minutes up to L'Etivaz for equivalent (but better prepared and served) middle-class cuisine, this easygoing and convenient train-station café draws a regular local crowd for light meals and a dependable plat du jour. Stick with *croûtes* (rich toasted-cheese sandwiches) and salads, and opt for the casual—and smoky—café rather than the more formal restaurant, though it's fun to watch the trains roll by the latter. ⊠ *CH-1837,* ☎ *026/9247717. MC, V.*

$$ ✕🏠 **Bon Accueil.** Occupying a beautifully proportioned, weathered-
★ wood chalet that has been sitting on a green hillside looking over the valley since the 18th century, this is the quintessential French-Swiss country inn. The rooms mix aged pine planking, spindle furniture, and antiques, and under the old low-beam ceilings the floors creak agreeably. If you prefer quieter though smaller accommodations, take a room—perhaps with a sun terrace—in the new building (connected by lawn and tunnel to the old). Up-to-date amenities, immaculate appointments, pastel accents, and fresh flowers—inside and out—keep standards at a well-above-rustic level. The restaurant (reservations are essential) is even more civilized, and the menu offers a range of specialties, from simple lake fish to such intricate creations as flash-fried freshwater fish with tarragon-shallot sauce. Meals are served in a warm dining room with a brick fireplace, much waxed wood, and pewter accents. For winter nights, there's a fire-lighted stone cellar bar with low-key jazz. ⊠ *CH-1837,* ☎ *026/*

9246320, FAX *026/9245126. 20 rooms. Restaurant, bar, sauna. AE, DC, MC, V.*

$$ 🏨 **De L'Ours.** Built in 1801 in the heart of Château d'Oex, this old inn now follows the ubiquitous postrenovation format: standard, dependable beige and Formica. The rooms on the top floor have more character, with their attic timbers and touches of fresh pine. There's a shady courtyard and an inexpensive, understated restaurant that serves regional specialties. ✉ *CH-1837,* ☎ *026/9242280,* FAX *026/9242279. 40 rooms. Restaurant, café. AE, DC, MC, V.*

$$ 🏨 **Ermitage.** This 1965 chalet-style hotel on the highway is full of bright colors and splashy prints and aspires to the rustic Victorian look. The restaurant mixes French and Ticinese specialties. ✉ *CH-1837,* ☎ *026/9246003,* FAX *026/9245076. 20 rooms. Restaurant, café. AE, DC, MC, V.*

$$ 🏨 **Richmont.** The exterior is authentic (weather-blackened wood, flower boxes on the balconies), but the interior is a study in florid Victorian excess—the colors intense, the upholstery heavy, and the half-timbering an apparent afterthought. There are a lively pizzeria and a steak house downstairs. ✉ *CH-1837,* ☎ *026/9245252,* FAX *026/9245384. 10 rooms. Restaurant, bar, café, pizzeria. AE, DC, MC, V.*

$ 🏨 **Printannière.** This creaky old cottage offers simple, cheap lodging without bathrooms, just beyond the town center. The linens are fresh, the decor is straightforward, and the windows frame astonishing views. There's a pretty garden terrace behind. The restaurant is for guests only; it's best to make reservations. ✉ *CH-1837,* ☎ *026/9246113. 8 rooms. Restaurant. No credit cards.*

Outdoor Activities and Sports

BALLOONING
The hot-air-ballooning center in Château-d'Oex offers accompanied flights. To arrange one, contact the tourist office (☞ Visitor Information *in* Vaud A to Z, *below*). An annual festival gets off the ground in January.

BICYCLING
In this graceful region of rolling hills and steep, verdant climbs, mountain bikes can be rented at **Roch Sports** (☎ 026/9247251). Also try **Château Sports** (☎ 026/9245858).

RAFTING, HYDROSPEED, AND CANYONING
Several gorges near Château-d'Oex offer excellent rafting, as well as two unusual white-water sports: Hydrospeed involves floating the waters in flippers and wet suit; canyoning has you hiking the river bottom clad in wet suit, life jacket, and helmet. Arrange supervised initiations into these sports through the tourist office (☞ Visitor Information *in* Vaud A to Z, *below*).

SKATING
There's an outdoor rink at the **Parc des Sports** (☎ 026/9246700).

SWIMMING
In summer, **Château-d'Oex** opens a heated, 50-m open-air pool with restaurant (☎ 026/9246234).

Rougemont

29 *40 km (25 mi) northeast of Aigle, 71 km (44 mi) east of Lausanne.*

Though this historic village is now being encroached on by sporty Gstaad—its beautiful wooden barns and ornately decorated chalets crowded out by modern resort lodgings—it retains its ancient monuments. The striking Romanesque **church,** with its deeply raked roof and needle-sharp spire, was built between 1073 and 1085. The exterior wall of the 16th-century **château** behind the church is emblazoned with the *grue* (crane) of Gruyères, harking back to the Pays-d'Enhaut's earliest loyalties. (The château is privately owned and closed to the public.)

Skiing

Rougemont has **La Videmanette,** a cable run that drops you off for leisurely, moderate skiing back to the village, or on up to trails that wind over toward **Gstaad,** the glamour resort across the invisible German-language frontier. From the second stop up the Videmanette, there's also a 4½-km (3-mi) sledding run.

VAUD A TO Z

Arriving and Departing

By Car

There are two major arteries leading to Lac Léman (Lake Geneva), one entering from the north via Bern and Fribourg (**A12**), the other arcing over the north shore of Lake Geneva, from Geneva to Lausanne (**A1**), then to Montreux and on south through the Alpes Vaudoises toward the Grand St. Bernard Pass (**A9**) in canton Valais. They are swift and often scenic expressways, and the north-shore artery (A1 and A9) traces a route that has been followed since before Roman times. Secondary highways parallel the expressways, but this is one case where, as the larger road sits higher on the lakeside slopes, the views from the expressway are often better than those from the highway. Be sure, however, to detour for the Corniche Road views between Lausanne and Montreux.

By Plane

Geneva's **Cointrin** (✉ 55 km/34 mi southwest of Lausanne, ☎ 022/7993111) is the second-busiest international airport in Switzerland, servicing frequent flights from the United States and the United Kingdom on **Swissair** as well as on other international carriers. From Cointrin, **Crossair** (☎ 061/3253636 for central reservations or 1553636 toll free within Switzerland), Switzerland's domestic line, connects to secondary airports throughout the country.

By Train

Lausanne lies on a major train route between Bern and Geneva, with express trains connecting from Basel and Zürich. From Geneva, trains take about 30 minutes and arrive in Lausanne up to four times an hour; from Bern, they take a little more than an hour and arrive twice an hour. TGVs (high-speed trains) run from Paris four times a day and take 3 hours and 40 minutes.

Getting Around

By Boat

Like all fair-size Swiss lakes, Lake Geneva is crisscrossed with comfortable and reasonably swift **steamers.** They carry you scenically from port to port and sometimes run more often than the trains that parallel their routes. With a Swiss Pass (☞ Train Travel *in* the Gold Guide) you travel free.

By Bus

A useful network of **postbus** routes covers the region for the resourceful traveler with plenty of time; some routes are covered only once or twice a day. Schedules are available from tourist offices (☞ Visitor Information, *below*) and rail stations. Lausanne has a good bus network; if you have a Swiss Pass, you can travel free on city buses in Montreux, Vevey, and Lausanne.

By Car

A web of **secondary highways** cuts north into the hills and winds east of the southbound expressway into the Alpine resorts, giving the driver maximum flexibility.

By Train

Trains along the waterfront, connecting major Lake Geneva towns, are swift and frequent. There also are several **private rail systems** leading into small villages and rural regions, including the **Montreux–Oberland–Bernois Railroad Line** (MOB; ☎ 021/9898181), which climbs sharply behind Montreux and cuts straight over the pre-Alps toward Château-d'Oex and the Berner Oberland. There is also the **Blonay–Chamby Railroad Line** (✉ Case Postale 366, CH-1001, Lausanne, ☎ 021/9432121).

Lausanne itself has a tiny but essential **Métro** that every seven minutes connects the waterfront at Ouchy to the train station and the place St-François above. It runs until midnight; tickets are under 3 SF.

Contacts and Resources

Emergencies

Vaud (☎ 117). **Police: Château-d'Oex** (☎ 026/9244421); **Montreux** (☎ 021/9632121); **Villars** (☎ 024/4955321).**Ambulance: Château-d'Oex** (☎ 026/9247593); **Montreux** (☎ 144); **Villars** (☎ 024/4951537). **Hospitals: Aigle** (☎ 024/4688688); **Lausanne Centre Hospitalier Universitaire Vaudois** (emergency services; ☎ 021/3141111); **Montreux** (☎ 021/9666666); **Pays-d'Enhaut** (☎ 026/9247593). **Medical and dental referrals: Lausanne** (☎ 021/6529932). **Late-night pharmacies** (☎ 111). **Auto breakdown: Touring Club of Switzerland** (☎ 140).

Guided Tours

ORIENTATION

The **Lausanne tourist office** sponsors a two-hour coach trip into the Old Town, including a visit to the cathedral and an extended city coach tour that takes in the Lavaux vineyards. There also are three general tours during the summer: one to Gruyères; one to Chamonix and Mont Blanc; and one to the Alps by coach and the Montreux–Oberland–Bernois Railroad Line *Panoramic Train* to Les Diablerets and Château-d'Oex (☞ Getting Around, *above*).

SPECIAL INTEREST

Vignoble Tours. The **Office des Vins Vaudois** (✉ 6 chemin de la Vuachère, CH-1005 Lausanne, ☎ 021/7296161) offers carefully marked walks—not personally guided—through the vineyards, passing production centers, winegrowers' homes, and *pintes* (pubs) for tasting along the way. Write for the *Guide du Vignoble Vaudois* for itineraries, hours, and addresses of suggested stops. For tickets to the **Fête des Vignerons** (Winegrowers' Festival) and information regarding its programs and hotel packages, contact the Vevey Tourist Office (✉ Box 27, CH-l800 Vevey, ☎ 021/9222020, FAX 021/9222025).

Visitor Information

The **Office du Tourisme du Canton de Vaud** (✉ 60 av. d'Ouchy, CH-1006 Lausanne, ☎ 021/6132626) has general information on the region.

Regional offices: **Château-d'Oex** (⊠ CH-1837, ☎ 0264/9242525). **Lausanne** (⊠ 2 av. de Rhodanie, ☎ 021/6137321). **Leysin** (⊠ CH-1854, ☎ 024/4942244). **Nyon** (⊠ Av. Viollier 7, ☎ 022/3616261, FAX 022/3615396). **Montreux** (⊠ pl. du Débarcadère, CH-1820, ☎ 021/9628484). **Vevey** (⊠ Box 27, CH-l800 Vevey, ☎ 021/9222020, FAX 021/9222025). **Villars** (⊠ CH-1884, ☎ 024/4953232).

13 Geneva

As the headquarters of the United Nations, the World Health Organization, and the International Red Cross; an international mecca for writers and thinkers of every stripe; and a stronghold of luxurious stores and extravagant restaurants, Geneva is Switzerland's most cosmopolitan city. This is a city of wealth and influence, where the rustic chalets of hilltop villages seem worlds away.

**Updated by
Nancy Coons**

DRAPED AT THE FOOT OF THE JURA and the Alps on the westernmost tip of Lac Léman (Lake Geneva), Geneva is the most cosmopolitan and graceful of Swiss cities and the soul of the French-speaking territory. Prodding into France as though dipping a delicate toe into Gallic waters—bordered on the north by the Pays de Gex and the south by Haute-Savoie, and lying little more than 160 km (100 mi) from Lyon—the city emits an aura of Gallic hauteur. Grand, mansarded mansions stand guard beside the River Rhône, where yachts bob, gulls dive, and Rolls-Royces purr past manicured promenades. The combination of Swiss efficiency and French savoir faire gives Geneva a chic polish, and the infusion of international blood from the UN adds a heterogeneity rare in a population of only 180,000. The canton has a population of 400,000, many of whom work in Geneva; still others commute by the thousands from the relatively cheap housing in Saint-Julien, to the south, in France.

Geneva has long been a city of enlightened tolerance, offering refuge to the writers Voltaire, Victor Hugo, Alexandre Dumas, Honoré de Balzac, and Stendhal, as well as the religious reformers John Calvin and John Knox. Lord Byron, Percy Bysshe Shelley, Richard Wagner, and Franz Liszt all fled from scandals elsewhere into Geneva's sheltering arms.

Although many left Geneva to escape the narrow austerity and bigotry of 16th-century Calvinism—whose namesake reformed the city that sheltered him, preaching fire and brimstone and stripping the cathedral of its papist icons—masses of Protestants fled *to* it nonetheless. The English fled Bloody Mary, Protestant Italians the wrath of the pope, Spaniards the Inquisition, French Huguenots the oppressive French monarchy—and Geneva flourished.

Yet to this day the conservative Genevois seem to hear Calvin tsk-tsking in their ears as they do a little *lèche-vitrines* (window-shopping, literally window-licking) at some of the world's most expensive stores and most excessive restaurants; it's the cosmopolitan foreign population that seems to indulge itself the most. Some say that during the 1970s, there was more Middle Eastern oil money in Geneva than in the Middle East, and stories abound of sheikhs taking over half a hotel for month-long shopping sprees.

Nowadays, Geneva lets down her discreet chignon only once a year, to celebrate the Escalade. On the night of December 11–12, 1602, the duke of Savoy—coveting Geneva and hoping to restore it to Catholicism—sent his men to scale the city walls with ladders. They were ignominiously defeated when a housewife, seeing the Savoyards clambering up the walls, emptied a *marmite* (pot) of hot soup over their heads and gave the alarm. The event is commemorated every year by the Festival of the Escalade, when uniforms come out of museums to be worn in reenactments of the battle, chocolate versions of the marmite are filled with marzipan vegetables for the children, and throughout the Old Town the usually decorous Genevois take to the streets in costume.

Pleasures and Pastimes

Antiquing
Catering to the public that frequent auctions at Sotheby's and Christie's, Geneva's Old Town and Pâquis neighborhood are chock-full of atmospheric shops bulging with 16th-century books, ancient engravings, carved picture frames, and fine old jewelry and silver.

Churches

The Gothic and neoclassic Cathédrale St-Pierre, with its early Christian excavations, and the Temple de l'Auditoire, where Jean Calvin preached and taught, offer an illuminating overview of Geneva's Catholic and Reformed personae.

Dining

Connoisseurs of *haute gastronomie* will not be disappointed by a city that persuades great French chefs to cross the border. But budget diners can experience earthy Geneva cuisine—sausage, pigs' feet—in unpretentious bistros, too. With only 160 km (100 mi) separating it from one of France's culinary capitals, Geneva is a blood brother to Lyon: Its traditional cuisine emphasizes *abats* (organ meats), *andouillettes* (chitterling sausages), potatoes, and onions. And like that of Lyon, its haute cuisine rivals the best in the world.

There are some dishes to watch for: *Cardon* (cardoon, an artichoke-like vegetable cultivated in Geneva and Lyon) is often baked with cream and Gruyère in rich gratins; *omble chevalier,* a kind of salmon trout, is native to Geneva's Lake Geneva. The city's two most traditional dishes are even more down to earth: *pieds de cochon* (pigs' feet), served in a variety of ways; and fricasée (savory wine-based stew) of chicken or pork. *Longeole*—a novel sausage blending spinach, cabbage, and leeks with pork by-products—is a specialty of Geneva and Haute Savoie. And you may find *petit salé* (salt pork) with lentils, tripe, or *boudin*—rich, rosy-brown blood pudding.

Yet for all its robust, old-fashioned favorites, Geneva cultivates an astonishing number of great restaurants—many of them headed by chefs imported from across the French border. Prices at these gastronomic meccas can be dry-mouth high, but—as in most Swiss cities—you can save considerably by choosing a lunchtime prix-fixe menu. If you want to splurge, starting with tiers of briny oysters and finishing with good *vieille prune* (a plum-base eau-de-vie), and plumbing the depths of great French-Swiss wine lists, there's no limit to what you can spend (and enjoy) here in Switzerland's culinary cosmopolis.

Museums

Not only are there grand, world-class public museums of art and natural history here, but also privately sponsored, eclectic collections—of new sculpture, primitive art, Asian ceramics, musical instruments, and more. The Palais des Nations, although fully functional as home to the UN, serves as a living museum, with its radio-age translation devices and socialist-realist murals; the Musée Internationale de la Croix-Rouge (International Red Cross Museum) puts the horrors of the modern age into uncomfortable perspective.

Neighborhoods

In addition to its beautifully preserved and atmospheric Vieille Ville, Geneva packs in various residential and commercial areas through which to wander, many with strong personalities: the honky-tonk sleaze behind the *gare*/rue des Pâquis, the stately homes above the Parc des Bastions, the Sardinian architecture in Carouge, south of the city center, the glittering shops on the rue du Rhône, the avant-garde galleries west of the Plaine de Plainpalais.

EXPLORING GENEVA

Geneva lies between the southwest corner of Lac Léman and the canton of Geneva, which bulges even farther west into France. The city itself crowds along the tapering shores of Lake Geneva, which, at the

Pont du Mont-Blanc, narrows back into the Rhône. Thus Geneva is as much a river town as a lake town, and its Rive Droite (Right Bank, on the north side) and Rive Gauche (Left Bank, on the south side) have strong identities. Most of the central city's best is concentrated on the Rive Gauche, but the Rive Droite is where the waterfront and many handsome hotels are.

Numbers in the text correspond to numbers in the margin and on the Geneva map.

Great Itineraries

IF YOU HAVE 2 DAYS

Allow yourself an hour to stroll the Right Bank before crossing to the Left Bank and entering the Old Town. Save time for the Gothic-neo-classic hybrid Cathédrale St-Pierre. Then window-shop your way through ancient streets to the Musée d'Art et d'Histoire, where such Swiss masterworks as Ferdinand Hodler's Impressionist landscapes are on view. The next day, head for the International Area and spend the morning at the Palais des Nations, the afternoon at the Musée Inter-nationale de la Croix-Rouge. Nights are for concerts and hearty dinners with a beaker or two of Lake Geneva wines.

IF YOU HAVE 3 DAYS

Museum hounds will want to devote their first day to a brief stroll along the Right Bank, then head for the Musée Rath for a world-class temporary exposition. Visit the Monument de la Réformation, then climb up into the Old Town to visit the cathedral and its excavations, the Temple de l'Auditoire, the 14th-century Maison Tavel, and any number of bookstores and antiques shops. The next day, concentrate on the museums behind the Old Town, such as the Collection Baur or the Musée d'Histoire Naturelle. On your third day, head north to the International Area and spend the morning at the Palais des Nations, the afternoon at the Musée Internationale de la Croix-Rouge. If time remains, there's also the Musée Ariana, devoted to ceramics and glass.

IF YOU HAVE 4 DAYS

With another day, you can absorb even more of the art museums—spend a morning at the Musée Barbier-Mueller, studying primitive and ancient art from Oceania, as well as an afternoon at the cutting-edge Musée d'Art Moderne et Contemporain.

Right Bank, Left Bank, and Old Town

This is the heart of Geneva. On the Right Bank, grand hotels line the banks of the Rhône and monuments, with parks and fountains relieving the big-city modernity. Over the bridges, the Left Bank bristles with dangerously expensive world-class shops. Once you climb into the ancient and peaceful heights of the *Vieille Ville*, or Old Town, cosmopolitan, world-class museums pepper the neighborhoods—though walkers may be so seduced by the stores and sidewalk cafés that they may not have time to explore them all.

A Good Walk

Begin your walk from Cornavin, the long rail station. As it's awkward to cross the **place de Cornavin** ① directly, take the pedestrian underpass from the shopping center below the station. You'll emerge above rue du Mont-Blanc, a partially pedestrian shopping street that slopes down to the lake. If you venture into the neighborhood to the north (Les Pâquis), you may be surprised at the prevalence of daytime red-light life, a source of not-so-Calvinist (and not-so-original) sin. To the south, rue du Mont-Blanc opens onto the Pont du Mont-Blanc, a broad bridge that spans the last gasp of Lake Geneva as it squeezes back into the Rhône. From the middle of the bridge you can see the snowy peak of Mont Blanc itself, and from March to October you'll have a fine view of the **Jet d'Eau** ②.

Heading back north over the bridge, turn right onto quai du Mont-Blanc and walk along the pollard-lined waterfront promenade toward the *débarcadères,* the docks used by Swissboat, Mouettes, and the CGN steamers. Across the quai stands the elaborate neo-Gothic **Monument Brunswick** ③, the tomb of a duke of Brunswick who left his fortune to the city. Across the street at the Hôtel Beau-Rivage, you'll see the discreet sign for Sotheby's auction house (☞ Shopping, *below*). Some of the city's most glamorous hotels stand beyond the Beau-Rivage; just past them you'll reach the **Pâquis-Plage,** a swimming area with changing rooms, restaurants, and plenty of space to swim and sunbathe.

Head back southwest along the Right Bank waterfront on quai des Bergues. Here you'll find a novelty that shows Geneva's Swiss accent: Beneath the water alongside the opposite (left) bank is a four-story, electronically controlled parking lot. In the center of the river, off the Pont des Bergues, is **Ile Rousseau** ④, whose namesake is memorialized with a statue.

The next bridge west along the quai is the Pont de la Machine, where the crystal-clear Rhône—its waters having lost the mud they carried when entering the east end of the lake—tumbles in a tumult of foam over a dam. By crossing the river at yet the next bridge, the Pont de l'Ile, you will pass the **Tour de l'Ile** ⑤, a onetime prison.

On the left bank, cross the place Bel-Air, the center of the business and banking district. Cut west (right) to the rue de la Corraterie, during the 17th century the riding circuit of the best Geneva horsemen; follow it south to the **place Neuve** ⑥. On the north end, opposite the entrance to the park, stands the arts venue, the **Grand Théâtre.** To its right is the Conservatoire de Musique. To the left is the **Musée Rath** ⑦.

Behind imposing gates, the Parc des Bastions is the site of **Geneva University,** founded as an academy in 1599 by Calvin himself. Enter the park and keep to your left. Almost immediately, at the foot of the ramparts, you will come to Geneva's most famous monument, the **Monument de la Réformation** ⑧; sit down on the terrace steps—made of Mont Blanc granite—to take it all in. Afterwards, walk on to the back of the park and exit by a gate on the left; then turn left onto rue St-Léger, passing under an ivy-hung bridge.

As you climb the winding street, the present quickly falls away, and thick-walled houses with weathered shutters take you into the atmospheric *Vieille Ville* (Old Town). You'll soon reach the tiered plateau of the historic **place du Bourg-de-Four** ⑨. From the *place,* angle uphill on rue de l'Hôtel-de-Ville, past the chic shops and *antiquitaires* (antiques shops). Then cut right into place de la Taconnerie, past Christie's auction house (☞ Shopping, *below*). Calvin certainly would not have approved of such a material establishment being so near his turf: Just beyond lies the small Gothic church that served as his **Temple de l'Auditoire** ⑩—the lecture theater where he taught missionaries his doctrines of reform.

Just past the Auditoire rises the magnificent mongrel **Cathédrale St-Pierre** ⑪, where Calvin galvanized the faltering souls of Geneva. After exploring its austere interior, take the stairs on the left side to the *site archéologique*ŇXtags error: No such tagŇđ ⑫, where you can spend an hour or so exploring the restored remains of the churches that once stood on the site of the present-day cathedral. From there, head to the ancient rue du Puits St-Pierre, where the **Maison Tavel** ⑬, now a historical museum, stands as the oldest house in town.

Turn left on rue Jean-Calvin. Number 11, now a stately neoclassic facade, was the address of John Calvin himself. (Just beyond, a plaque commemorates George Sand's sojourn here from 1849 to 1859.) Next door, the **Musée Barbier-Mueller** ⑭ has a private collection of African, Oceanian, and Southeast Asian art in permanent rotation.

Head back up rue du Puits St-Pierre, passing some ancient cannons from the Swiss Republic under vaulted arcades of the old arsenal. Beyond stands the imposing facade of the **Hôtel de Ville** ⑮, where the Geneva Convention was signed in 1864. Just down the Grand-Rue to your right, you'll see the birthplace of Rousseau (No. 40). Ferdinand Hodler, the Swiss Impressionist, lived at No. 33 from 1881–1902; you'll see his works at the Musée d'Art et d'Histoire.

But before you head there, cross the place du Bourg-de-Four and follow rue Etienne-Dumont, curving left onto the pont St-Victor and continuing up rue St-Victor. Framed by two statues, you'll find the Petit Palais, a parqueted mansion housing a private **Musée d'Art Moderne** ⑯, focused entirely on French art from 1870 to 1940.

On leaving the Petit Palais, follow the pedestrian bridge over the Boulevard Helvetique to rue Charles Galland, where the vast **Musée d'Art et d'Histoire** ⑰ spreads before you, its broad corridors packed with international paintings and sculpture. Leaving the museum, turn right and follow rue Charles-Galland to rue Lefort; turn left and look for the spiraling cupolas of the late-19th-century Église Russe, completely decorated within in neo-Byzantine styles. Turn right on rue Lefort, left on rue Munier-Romilly. On the right is the **Collection Baur** ⑱, an elegantly mounted collection of Asian decorative art objects.

Return to rue Charles-Galland and follow it right to boulevard des Tranchées; turn left and head for place Émile Guyénot. Veer right on route de Malagnou and walk to the **Musée d'Histoire Naturelle** ⑲. Just beyond it, on the same side of the street, is the **Musée de l'Horlogerie et de l'Émaillerie** ⑳, a bijou in itself. From here you can retrace your steps to the Old Town or catch Bus 6 back to place Bel-Air.

Sights to See

★ ⑪ **Cathédrale St-Pierre** (St. Peter's Cathedral). Built during the 12th and 13th centuries in Gothic style, the cathedral lost its aesthetic balance and some of its grandeur when a sternly beautiful but incongruous neoclassic portico was added in the 18th century. The church interior remains wholly Romanesque and Gothic, however, and its austerity reflects its change of role—from a Catholic cathedral to a Protestant church, stripped of its ornaments by followers of Calvin. His chair, according to tradition, remains on the left, in front of the last pillar before the transept. You can climb the **north tower** and the **south tower** to take in grand views over Geneva. ⊠ *pl. de la Taconnerie,* ☎ *022/ 3102929.* ⊠ *North and south towers 3 SF.* ☉ *Oct.–May, Mon.–Sat. 9–7, Sun. 11–7; June–Sept., Tues.–Sat. 2–5, Sun. 10–noon and 2– 5 (except during services).*

★ ⑱ **Collection Baur.** A broad and exquisite array of Japanese and Chinese objects collected by businessman Alfred Baur fills this graceful mansion. Over a period of 50 years, Baur acquired rose and celadon porcelains from China, smooth-lined medieval Japanese stoneware, ceramics and jade, Samurai swords, lacquer boxes, and more. ⊠ *8 rue Munier-Romilly,* ☎ *022/3461729.* ⊠ *5 SF.* ☉ *Tues.–Sun. 2–6.*

⑮ **Hôtel de Ville** (Town Hall). This 16th-century building shelters the **Alabama Hall,** where, on August 22, 1864, the Geneva Convention was signed by 16 countries, laying the foundation of the International Red Cross. Eight years later, in 1872, a court of arbitration was convened in this same room to settle the Alabama dispute between Great Britain and the United States, which was unhappy over British support to the Confederacy during the Civil War. The hall is still used for civil functions. ⊠ *rue de l'Hôtel-de-Ville,* ☎ *022/3192209.* ⊙ *Individual visits by request.*

④ **Ile Rousseau.** This small island is known for its statue of the Geneva-born French philosopher Jean-Jacques Rousseau, who did much to popularize both the city and Switzerland during the 18th century. ⊠ *Rhône center, off the Pont des Bergues.*

② **Jet d'Eau.** Europe's tallest fountain, gushing 145 m (475 ft) high, is visible from the Pont du Mont-Blanc from March through October. ⊠ *Lake Geneva.*

★ ⑬ **Maison Tavel.** Dating from the 14th century, the oldest house in Geneva has been studiously restored. Several rooms have period furnishings, while others house collections of architectural details, arms, and arcane souvenirs of Geneva's past—including a guillotine and a garishly painted miter, worn by convicted pimps in Calvin's day. In the large attic, there's a relief map of the city as it was around 1850; a recorded commentary (in English) and timed lights illuminate various landmarks and neighborhoods. Good temporary expositions occasionally focus on details of local lore. ⊠ *6 rue du Puits St-Pierre,* ☎ *022/3102900.* 🎫 *Free.* ⊙ *Tues.–Sun. 10–5.*

③ **Monument Brunswick.** This tomb of a duke of Brunswick who died in Geneva in 1873 and left his fortune to the city is modeled on the Scaglieri monument in Verona. ⊠ *Bounded by rue des Alpes, quai du Mont-Blanc, and rue Adhémar-Fabri.*

★ ⑧ **Monument de la Réformation.** Built between 1909 and 1917, this gigantic wall—more than 90 m (295 ft) long—is as impressive for its simplicity and clean lines as for its sheer size. A central group of sculptures has four statues of the great leaders of the Reformation—Bèze, Calvin, Farel, and Knox—each more than 15 ft high. On either side of these giants are smaller statues (a mere 9 ft tall) of other personalities, such as Oliver Cromwell. Between the smaller figures are bas-reliefs and inscriptions that tell the story of important events connected with the Reformation. Carved in the wall to the right of Cromwell is the presentation by the English Houses of Parliament of the Bill of Rights to King William III, in 1689. Above it, in English, are listed the bill's main features—the guiding principles of democracy. To the left of Cromwell is a bas-relief of the Pilgrim fathers praying on the deck of the *Mayflower;* farther left another relief shows John Knox preaching with obvious passion. Flanking the monument are two memorials, one on the left to Martin Luther, one on the right to Ulrich Zwingli. ⊠ *Just off promenade des Bastions, in Parc des Bastions.*

OFF THE BEATEN PATH
MUSÉE D'ART MODERNE ET CONTEMPORAIN (Museum of Modern and Contemporary Art) – This is the gritty venue for a collection of stark, profound, mind-stretching art works, none dating from before 1965. Opened in September 1994 and funded by a private foundation of seven Genevois, the museum occupies a former factory whose original concrete floors and fluorescent lighting remain. Its spare, bleak lines serve as a foil to the often overscaled artworks it houses: Paintings, sculptures, and structures by Gordon Matta-Clark, Jenny Holzer, Sol Le-

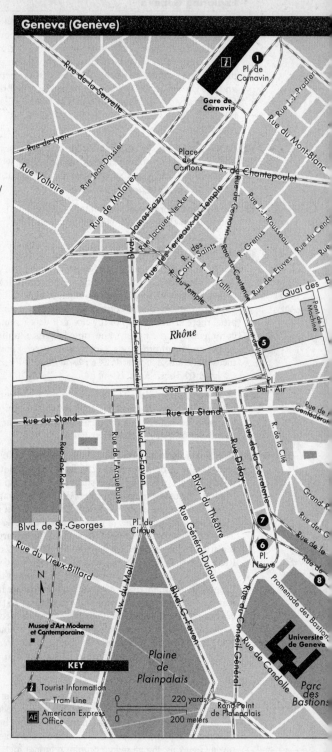

Geneva (Genève)

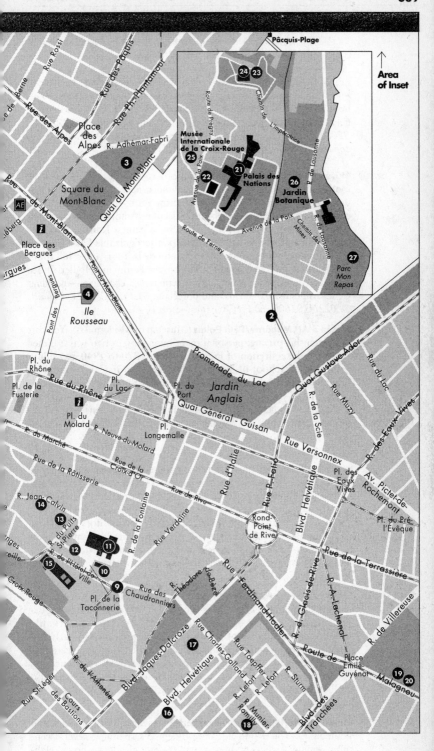

Pâcquis-Plage

↑
Area
of Inset

Rue Rossi

Rue des Pâquis

Rue de Berne

Rue Ph. Plantamour

Rue des Alpes

Place
des
Alpes

R. Adhémar-Fabri

3

Rue du Mont-Blanc

Quai du Mont-Blanc

Square du
Mont-Blanc

AE

i

Place des
Bergues

Pont des Bergues

Pont du Mont-Blanc

4

Ile
Rousseau

Pl. du
Rhône

Pl. de la
Fusterie

Rue du Rhône

Pl.
du Lac

Pl. du
Port

Jardin
Anglais

Promenade du Lac

Quai Gustave-Ador

Quai du Lac

i

Pl. du
Molard

R. Neuve-du-Molard

Quai Général - Guisan

R. du Marché

Pl.
Longemalle

Rue Versonnex

R. de la Scie

Rue Muzy

R. des Eaux-Vives

Rue de la Rôtisserie

Rue de la
Croix-d'Or

Rue d'Italie

Rue de Rive

R. Pictet-de-Rochemont

Av. Pictet-de-Rochemont

Pl. des
Eaux
Vives

R. Jean-Calvin

14

13

R. du Puits-St-Pierre

12

11

R. de la Fontaine

Rue Verdaine

R. P. Fatio

Blvd. Helvétique

Rond-
Point
de Rive

Pl. du Pré-
l'Evêque

15

R. de l'Hôtel-de-
Ville

10

9

Pl. de la
Taconnerie

Rue des
Chaudronniers

R. Théodore-de-Bèze

Rue Ferdinand-Hodler

Clécis-de-Rive

Rue de la Terrassière

R. A.-Lachenal

R. de Villereuse

Croix-Rouge

17

Rue Charles-Galland

Rue Toepffer

R. Lefort

R. Lefort

R. Sturm

Route de

Place
Emile-
Guyénot

19 **20**

Malagnou

Rue St-Léger

Cours
des Bastions

Blvd. Jaques-Dalcroze

Blvd. Helvétique

16

R. Munier-Romilly

18

Blvd. des Tranchées

Inset

Musée
Internationale
de la Croix-Rouge

24 **23**

Route de Pregny

Chemin de l'Impératrice

R. de Lausanne

25

22

21

Palais des
Nations

26

Jardin
Botanique

Avenue de la Paix

Avenue de la Paix

Route de Ferney

Chemin des Mines

R. de Lausanne

27

Parc
Mon
Repos

2

witt, Nam June Paik, Dennis Oppenheim, and Jean Basquiat, among others. Of particular interest is a permanent reconstruction of art collector Ghislain Mollet-Viéville's Paris apartment, where he lived in a state of pure modernism among works of Sol Le Witt and Carl André. To get here from the city center, take Tram 12 toward Plaine de Plainpalais; at its main stop, get off and walk straight across the park. Head up rue des Vieux-Grenadiers and turn right into the entrance. Note: Don't go in the front door, the separate Centre d'Art; enter the "court" and pass through the massive metal doors. ⊠ *10 rue des Vieux-Grenadiers,* ☎ *022/ 3206122.* ☜ *9 SF.* ☉ *Wed.–Sun. noon–6, Tues. noon–9 pm. Walking commentary tour (in French):* ☜ *4 SF.* ☉ *Tues. 6:30* PM.

★ ⑰ **Musée d'Art et d'Histoire** (Museum of Art and History). A massive mother lode of world culture that administrates several other museums, including the Maison Tavel and the Rath, this 1910 landmark contains an enormous beaux-arts collection. Among its holdings are the 15th-century *Fishing Miracle,* by Swiss painter Konrad Witz, depicting Christ walking on the waters of a recognizable Lake Geneva; several masterworks of Maurice-Quentin de la Tour; and a full room of Alpine landscapes by Swiss Impressionist Ferdinand Hodler. Other gems include six period rooms and collections on archaeology—including Genevan prehistory—arms, and porcelain. ⊠ *2 rue Charles-Galland,* ☎ *022/4182600.* ☜ *Free.* ☉ *Tues.–Sun. 10–5.*

⑯ **Musée d'Art Moderne/Petit Palais** (Museum of Modern Art). You can approach this private, personal mansion-gallery in two ways: Either you'll see the collection of French art from 1870 to 1940 as a dilute gathering of school-of-Seurats, also-ran Renoirs, and wanna-be Braques. . . or as a rare illustration of the evolution of French modernism, laced with works of unknown female artists and pillared by a few masters' experiments—some, as in the three-dimensional Gaugins, unexpected joys. ⊠ *Terrasse St-Victor 2,* ☎ *022/3461433.* ☜ *10 SF.* ☉ *Tues.–Fri. 10–6; weekends 10–5.*

★ ⑭ **Musée Barbier-Mueller.** Since Josef Mueller began collecting so-called primitive art in 1907, his family has amassed a staggering quantity of fine pieces from Africa, Oceania, Southeast Asia, and the Americas. Only a small selection is on view at any given time in this private museum—but each is exquisitely lighted, framed, and juxtaposed with similar and contrasting works. Labels in English guide visitors from ivory fly-whisk handles from Zaire to massive carved masks from New Ireland. The museum building, a restored Old Town vault of scrubbed terra-cotta and halogen-lighted stone, is a work of art itself. ⊠ *10 rue Calvin,* ☎ *022/3120270.* ☜ *5 SF.* ☉ *Daily 11–5.*

⑲ **Musée d'Histoire Naturelle** (Museum of Natural History). Among natural history museums, this one is exceptional. Its dense, fascinating exhibit on the history of man includes "Lucy," the remarkably well-preserved remains of a female Australopithecus, an early hominid. Lucy was found in Ethiopia; she's about 3 million years old. Besides the evolutionary displays, there are aquariums, vivariums, and evocative wildlife dioramas, complete with sound effects. There's also an illuminating display on Swiss geology. ⊠ *1 rte. de Malagnou,* ☎ *022/4186300.* ☜ *Free.* ☉ *Daily 9:30–5.*

⑳ **Musée de l'Horlogerie et de l'Émaillerie** (Museum of Watchmaking and Enameling). You'll find not only timepieces spanning several centuries—many of them crafted in Geneva—but also music boxes, elaborately enameled watchcases, and even a collection of Art Nouveau jewelry. They're mounted in a mansion as impressive as its contents.

Try to be there on the hour for the chiming of the clocks. ✉ *15 rte. de Malagnou,* ☎ *022/4186470.* 🎟 *Free.* ⏱ *Wed.–Mon. 10–5.*

❼ Musée Rath. Geneva's first art museum, opened in 1825, hosts eclectic, often international temporary exhibitions. Upcoming shows include a selection of works by Swiss artists on Swiss themes, and an exhibit on pre-Columbian Mexican art. ✉ *pl. Neuve,* ☎ *022/4183340.* 🎟 *Up to 10 SF, depending on the exposition.* ⏱ *Tues. and Thurs.–Sun. 10–5, Wed. noon–9.*

❶ Place de Cornavin. The train station square is the hub of Geneva's Right Bank commerce. From here streets radiate into the key neighborhoods and across the Rhône to the Left Bank and Old Town. You can catch a bus here to the International Area (☞ *below*).

★ ❾ Place du Bourg-de-Four. This atmospheric, sprawling Old Town "square" was once the crossroads of some important routes leading to southern France via Annecy and Lyon, to Italy, to the Chablais, and beyond. Before that, it served as a Roman forum and as a cattle and wheat market. Today it's a crossroads still, where shoppers, workers, and students meet in open cafés and lounge around its fountain, striking a delicate and charming balance among scruffy bohemia, genteel tradition, and slick gentrification. ✉ *At intersection of rue Verdaine and rue des Chaudronniers.*

NEED A BREAK?

Have a coffee or *apero* (aperitif) at the lively **La Clémence** (✉ 20 pl. du Bourg-de-Four, ☎ 022/3122498), a sidewalk café spilling out into the middle of the place du Bourg-de-Four. You can people-watch or read for hours Paris style.

❻ Place Neuve. From this imposing crossroads you'll see a high rock wall, part of the city's ancient ramparts, towering over all surrounding landmarks. The noble old houses at the top of the wall are home to some of Geneva's wealthiest families. ✉ *Intersection of bd. du Théâtre, rue de la Corraterie, and Parc des Bastions.*

⓬ Site archéologique. In the 1980s the floors of the Cathédrale St-Pierre (☞ *above*) were lifted and the foundations of previous churches excavated. Today, walkways allow visitors to examine the different levels of these excavations. Portions remain of a Christian baptistery that dates from the late 300s, when the Roman Empire was still vacillating about its conversion to the new faith. Especially striking is a 5th-century room with an ornate mosaic floor. There also are remains of several early cathedrals as well as the first Romanesque cathedral on this site, dating from 1000; its ruins serve as the foundation for the cathedral today. There are markers and charts to guide you through the different eras and a collection of sculptures from the site. ✉ *pl. de la Taconnerie, under the nave of Cathédrale St-Pierre (entrance outside),* ☎ *022/3102929.* 🎟 *5 SF.* ⏱ *June–Sept., Tues.–Sat. 11–5, Sun. 10–5; Oct.–May, Tues.–Sat. 2–5; Sun. 10–noon and 2–5.*

❿ Temple de l'Auditoire (Protestant Lecture Hall). In this former Catholic chapel built on the foundations of a 5th-century predecessor, Jean Calvin taught missionaries his doctrines of radical, puritanical reform. From 1556 to 1559, the Scots reformer John Knox also preached here. During the heat of the Reformation battles, the temple became a haven of worship for Protestant refugees, encouraged by Calvin to hold services in their native English, Italian, Spanish, and Dutch; today it is a multinational center of worship, with Sunday services in English and Dutch. The austerity is striking, the period furniture still in use. Printed information and historic documents are also on display. Sadly, due to lack of funds the temple is officially closed to the public. Serious aficionados might attend the Scots service Sunday morning at 11; groups may organize (well in advance) a visit for a token fee. ⊠ *pl. de la Taconnerie,* ☎ *022/3118533.*

NEED A BREAK?	Have an exotic, elegantly served tea, an exquisite hot snack, or a hot plat du jour (daily special) in the **Darjeeling Salon de Thé** (⊠ 9 pl. du Bourg-de-Four, at Étienne Dumont, ☎ 022/3112979), an intimate, upscale, postmodern corner tearoom with sculptural, if uncomfortable, leather chairs.

⑤ Tour de l'Ile. Dating from the epoch of the bishops' rule, this one-time prison off the main Pont de l'Ile is today almost swallowed up by modern buildings on either side. ⊠ *Just off the main Pont de l'Ile.*

International Area

Well north of the city center, a modern area of open grassland and hills is scattered with a handful of museums, embassies, and landmarks. Graceful estates surround most, and a serene botanical garden is a good place to digest the heavy historical and political fare you will encounter within.

A Good Walk

To visit the **Palais des Nations** ㉑, an architecturally unusual building created to house the well-intentioned League of Nations, take Bus 8 to the place des Nations. On weekends, get off here and enter directly past the guard gates. On weekdays, when security is in full swing in front, stay on the bus for another stop, getting off at Appia. In addition to the Palais des Nations, the Appia bus stop gives you access to the palatial Italianate **Musée Ariana** ㉒, a subsidiary of the Museum of Art and History housing the **Musée Suisse de la Céramique et du Verre.** Consider a brief stop, but if you're pressed for time, forge ahead to the Musée Internationale de la Croix-Rouge (☞ *below*).

Past the parklands of the Palais des Nations—which do not belong to Geneva but have their own territorial rights—head back uphill on avenue de la Paix, which becomes route de Pregny, and turn right on chemin de l'Impératrice to the Château de Penthes. This 1852 mansion has been converted to house the **Musée des Suisses à l'Étranger** ㉓, a permanent exhibition addressing Switzerland's relations with the outside world—many of them military. It neighbors the **Musée Militaire Genevois** ㉔, which focuses exclusively on local history.

Head back down route de Pregny and right into a cut in the hill. You'll arrive at the **Musée Internationale de la Croix-Rouge** ㉕, a fiercely moving and important permanent exhibition tracing the history of humanitarian assistance. You may want to follow this with a 20-minute contemplative stroll down the length of avenue de la Paix, heading toward the lake and the peaceful **Jardin Botanique** ㉖.

If you are traveling by car or have on your walking shoes, continue toward the lake and cross the Parc Mon Repos to the **Musée d'Histoire des Sciences** ㉗ in the lovely Villa Bartholoni (1826). Bus 4-44 will carry you back to the center.

TIMING

You could easily devote a full day to this area, spending the morning in the Musée Internationale de la Croix-Rouge, the early afternoon in the Musée des Étrangers, and touring the Palais des Nations after. You might even hike home via the Jardin Botanique if your feet hold out, but take note: The International Area's suburban landscape stretches over the equivalent of many city blocks—the grounds of the Palais des Nations cover more surface than the entire Old Town—so prepare for a lot of walking. This neighborhood's museums and the Palais (off-season) are closed on Tuesday.

Sights to See

㉖ Jardin Botanique (Botanic Garden). Fans of living flora and fauna will enjoy this botanical garden, with its deer park, exotic hothouses, rose garden, and collection of Alpine rock plants. There's even a section devoted to scent and touch. ⊠ *North of av. de la Paix, east of International Complex,* ☎ *022/4185100.* ⊡ *Free.* ⊙ *Daily 8–7:30.*

㉒ Musée Ariana. Home to the **Musée Suisse de la Céramique et du Verre** (Swiss Museum of Ceramics and Glass), this grand 1884 edifice displays a massive collection, spanning seven centuries, of pottery, porcelain, and faience from Europe, Asia, and the Near East, as well as from regions of Switzerland. The exchange of style and techniques between East and West is emphasized. Downstairs, a 20th-century hall showcases Art Nouveau and Art Deco ceramics and glass; another area illuminates production and firing techniques. ⊠ *10 av. de la Paix,* ☎ *022/4185450.* ⊡ *Free.* ⊙ *Wed.–Mon. 10–5.*

㉗ Musée d'Histoire des Sciences (Museum of the History of Science). A collection of scientific instruments, with videos demonstrating their use, illustrates the evolution of modern science, giving viewers a glimpse of Geneva's role as intellectual capital of Europe during the 18th century. The Italianate mansion alone is worth visiting. ⊠ *Villa Bartholoni, 128 rue de Lausanne,* ☎ *022/7316985.* ⊡ *Free.* ⊙ *Tues.–Sun. 1–5.*

★ **㉕ Musée Internationale de la Croix-Rouge** (International Red Cross Museum). In a country that, despite its neutrality, seems sometimes to idealize warfare, where military museums are as prevalent as mountains, this painstakingly nonjudgmental museum sends a different message to the world. Housed in a grim glass-and-concrete structure designed to reflect the contents' sobering themes, it uses state-of-the-art technology in several media to illuminate human kindness in the face of disasters both natural and man-made.

Good deeds are dramatized, from the proverbial Samaritan's to Clara Barton's, and through film, you not only learn how Henri Dunant was inspired by the Battle of Solferino to found the Red Cross but also see for yourself the postbattle horrors that moved him to action. Every effort is made to project a telling image, since mere dates and numbers might leave you unmoved. The sometimes bleak displays include endless monolithic aisles of file boxes containing records of World War I prisoners—recorded on 5 million cards—and a reconstruction of a 3 m-by-2 m (10 ft-by-6½ ft) concrete prison cell, reported by a Red Cross observer, that once contained 17 political prisoners—34 footprints make the inhumane conditions instantly, poignantly clear. And then you learn what people did to help: The Red Cross alerted families of the World War I prisoners to their sons' and husbands' moves and lodged formal protests that resulted in improved conditions for this cell's inhabitants.

The masterpiece of the exhibition is the astonishing **Mur du Temps** (Wall of Time), a simple time line that traces, year by year, wars and natural disasters that have killed 100,000 people or more. At first the list starts short, with earthquakes, volcanoes, and plagues dominating; as you enter the modern age, the lists stretch long and heavy with wars—even the natural disasters seem to increase, as if the sophisticated man-made devastation had unleashed evil into the atmosphere.

Though it seems no expense has been spared in creating this exhibition and its building, no funds were drawn from the Red Cross itself; the project relied on corporate donors. Commentaries and captions are in English, French, and German. ⊠ *17 av. de la Paix,* ☎ *022/7345248 or 022/7332660 for recorded information (in French).* ☜ *10 SF.* ☉ *Tues.–Sun. 10–5.*

㉔ Musée Militaire Genevois (Geneva Military Museum). On the same site as the Musée des Suisses à l'Étranger, this museum highlights the city's history, including the Geneva hero Général Henri Guisan, who rallied the Swiss to unity during World War II. ⊠ *8 chemin de l'Impératrice,* ☎ *022/7335381.* ☜ *5 SF.* ☉ *Tues.–Sun. 2–5.*

★ **㉓ Musée des Suisses à l'Étranger** (Museum of Swiss Citizens Abroad). Since Swiss neutrality began during the early 16th century, the Swiss have remained consummate soldiers—for other countries' wars. Sometimes they were even hired to fight on opposing sides in the same war. So impressive was their reputation as mercenary soldiers that the pope himself hired them as bodyguards—and they continue to serve at the Vatican today. This museum, housed inside the circa-1852 **Château de Penthes,** sheds light on Swiss military history with documents, models, prints, and a multitude of flags and uniforms. There are also displays on nonmilitary topics, from the Swiss postal system to Swiss participation in the California gold rush. ⊠ *8 chemin de l'Impératrice,* ☎ *022/7349021.* ☜ *5 SF.* ☉ *Wed.–Mon. 10–noon and 2–6.*

NEED A BREAK? | Have a prix-fixe meal, a plat du jour, or a slice of homemade fruit tart at **Cent Suisses** (⊠ 19 chemin de l'Impératrice, ☎ 022/7344865), a simple, comfortable lunch-only spot adjoining the Musée des Suisses à l'Étranger.

★ **㉑ Palais des Nations** (Palace of Nations). To create a home for the League of Nations, the Palais des Nations was built between 1929 and 1937; it was inaugurated in 1938 but dissolved in 1940, when the former Soviet Union withdrew. In 1945, when the United Nations was formed in the United States, the Palais des Nations took on the European branch of the organization. The original wing was built according to plans selected in an architectural competition: Le Corbusier's modernist designs were rejected in favor of those of a group of international architects who followed a style that has, ironically, come to be known as fascist. Indeed, this is a superb example of the severe blend of Art Deco and stylized classicism that Mussolini and Hitler idealized, and its details, both architectural and decorative, have been preserved practically untouched—the bronze torchères, the gleaming cold marble, and the exaggerated stylistic references that foreshadow the postmodernism of the 1980s.

You can visit the **Assembly Hall,** where the original system for simultaneous translation, including earpieces that must surely qualify as antiques, remains virtually as it was in 1937. Here, in 1988, Yasir Arafat met with the remaining UN delegates when he was denied a U.S. visa. In the **Council Chamber** you'll see splendid allegorical murals in heroic style painted by Catalan artist José Maria Sert in 1934; in shades of gold and sepia, they depict humankind's progress in health, technology, freedom, and peace. In the corridors, you'll see rows of delegates' overcoats, which, while their owners negotiate global disarmament, hang trustingly under signs marked VESTIAIRE NON GARDÉ (coatrack unsupervised). Buy your ticket at the booth outside and wait in the lobby, where you can watch videos on world hunger or browse through the bookstore, full of literature on international issues and demographics.

The tour lasts about an hour, not including the initial wait. ⊠ *Palais des Nations,* ☎ *022/9074560.* 🎫 *8.50 SF.* ☉ *Apr.–June and Sept.–Oct., daily 10–noon and 2–4; July–Aug., daily 9–6; Jan.–Mar. and Nov.–mid-Dec., weekdays 10–noon and 2–4. Last 2 wks in Dec. by appointment only.*

DINING

Many restaurants close on weekends, especially Sunday night. In Geneva, not only is the food French but the style of dining is as well—late, leisurely, with seasonal specialties celebrated like the annual visit of an old friend. Brasseries and bistros are social centers, and open-air cafés spill into every square.

CATEGORY	COST*
$$$$	over 90 SF
$$$	50 SF–90 SF
$$	30 SF–50 SF
$	under 30 SF

*Prices are per person for a three-course meal (two-course meal in $ category), excluding drinks, sales tax, and 15% service charge

$$$$ ✕ **Le Béarn.** Directed by precocious young French chef Jean-Paul Goddard, this elegant, intimate little place produces modern, light, and creative cuisine: duck-breast carpaccio with apricot chutney, rabbit with sage and nettles, subtly sweet tarragon sorbet, and any number of truffle specialties, including a spectacular truffle soufflé. The dining room is done in Empire style; the only somber notes are struck by diplomat and politician guests. Both the dessert cart and the wine list, which has mostly Swiss and French vintages, are remarkable. ⊠ *4 quai de la Poste,* ☎ *022/3210028. Reservations essential. AE, DC, MC, V. Oct.–Apr., closed Sun., no lunch Sat. May–Sept., closed weekends.*

$$$$ ✕ **Le Chat Botté.** Prepared in a kitchen as silent and concentrated as
★ an operating theater, this seafood challenges that of the best coastal establishments without resorting to stylish gimmicks. Savor the likes of pan-crisped cod on a bed of peppers and eggplant or meaty scallops interspersed with medallions of porcini mushrooms. A mine of oeno-knowledge, the sommelier will introduce you to surprising local wine finds and unexpected *mariages* (combinations). The wood-paneled dining room is sedate without being stuffy, and the flower-decked lakefront balcony-terrace offers the ultimate summer dining experience. ⊠ *Hotel Beau Rivage, 13 quai du Mont-Blanc,* ☎ *022/7166920. Reservations required. AE, DC, MC, V. Closed weekends.*

$$$$ ✕ **Les Continents.** Chef Patrick Domon, who apprenticed with Fredy Girardet and earned his wings in London, Hong Kong, and Singapore, flaunts his expertise (and Asian influences) in his prawn salad in curry vinegar; marbled terrine of pigeon and foie gras with lentils; a mushroom-stuffed breast of Bresse hen in crisp potato crust; and pastry-wrapped pear with crème brûlée. Set within the Intercontinental Hotel (☞ *Lodging, below*), it functions as a virtual branch of the UN. ⊠ *7–9 chemin du Petit-Saconnex,* ☎ *022/9193350. Reservations essential. AE, DC, MC, V. Closed weekends.*

$$$$ ✕ **Le Cygne.** This handsome and luxurious restaurant of the Noga-Hilton, all sleek lacquered wood and modern architectural style, offers splendid views over the bay, the Jet d'Eau, and, in the distance, Mont Blanc. It features Parisian chef Philippe Jourdin's soigné, if conservative, creations: seafood reigns, but don't miss the rabbit stuffed with tomato confit, garnished with eggplant tartare. There's a fabulous cellar of French wines (including some little-known ones), as well as Swiss, Italian, and American vintages. The real show: the caravan

of six constantly changing dessert carts. ☒ *19 quai du Mont-Blanc,* ☎ *022/9089085. Reservations essential. AE, DC, MC, V.*

$$$$ ✕ **Le Lion d'Or.** On the lakeside bluff of Cologny—the Beverly Hills
★ of Geneva—the summer terrace of this culinary landmark is a little paradise, with an overwhelming view of the bay and the UN. Though the chic decor is strictly Louis XV–Louis XVI, the cuisine is modern, light, sophisticated, and glories in seafood and seasonal cuisine. The alliance of local celebrity chefs Gilles Dupont and Tommy Birne has brought the cooking back into a competitive gastronomic class, finessing such winners as duck wings with ginger and lime, lobster in herb vinaigrette, and just about any seafood, exquisitely grilled. Take Bus G or A in the direction of Corsier Village, or take a cab—it's not far beyond quai Gustave-Ador. ☒ *5 pl. Gautier, Cologny,* ☎ *022/7364432. Reservations essential. AE, DC, MC, V. Closed weekends.*

$$$$ ✕ **Le Neptune.** As its name suggests, this chic clubhouse of bankers and financiers is the king of the sea, offering a vast variety of fish and shellfish prepared with superb sophistication: a clever mille-feuille of tuna sashimi, grilled sea bass in a coulis of fennel, pan-crisped lobster served warm in a salad. Prices are uncompromising but justified. ☒ *Hotel du Rhône, 1 quai Turrettini,* ☎ *022/7319831. Reservations essential. Jacket required. AE, DC, MC, V. Closed weekends.*

$$$ ✕ **L'Ange du Dix Vins/Le Dix Vins.** The imaginative cuisine of young
★ chef Réné Fracheboud now serves two crowds, one in the main restaurant, the other in the cozier, antiques-cluttered bistro. (If you get mixed up, you can cross from one to the other through the kitchen.) Novel specialties, vividly flavored with dried tomatoes, curry oil, cocoa, and even coffee, are served in a warm Mediterranean decor of gold and ocher. There's a good list of lesser-known wines by the glass; the list of bottled wines is prestigious. Prices are comparable between the two restaurants; the bistro has a looser, livelier ambience. ☒ *31–29 rue Jacques Dalphin, Carouge,* ☎ *022/3420318. AE, MC, V. Closed weekends.*

$$$ ✕ **La Glycine/Chez Jipek'à.** This is a classic *caboulot* (downscale cabaret-bistro) and a picturesque *caf' conc'* (café-concert), complete with a little Italian-style terrace under the *glycine* (hanging wisteria). Jipek'à—a Czech turned Swiss—is the soul of the popular spot, which is always smoky, noisy, and full to bursting. The food is only average, but you come here for the ambience, to sing or laugh with the pianist and *les bohèmes* who frequent the place. People have been known to dance between tables here. ☒ *21 rue de Montbrillant,* ☎ *022/7336285. No credit cards. Closed weekends.*

$$$ ✕ **Roberto.** Roberto Carugati and his daughter, Marietta, have made
★ this spot the meeting point and melting pot of table-hopping Genevans, chic Italians from Milan and Rome, and Parisian artists and political stars. You'll find classic Italian dishes—risotto and gnocchi, *bollito misto* (boiled meat with herb sauce), osso buco, and grilled sole—as well as great Italian wines, a lively atmosphere, and swift service. ☒ *10 rue Pierre-Fatio,* ☎ *022/3118033. AE, MC, V. Closed Sun. No dinner Sat.*

$$–$$$ ✕ **La Perle du Lac.** This grand wooden chalet, set alongside a swan-populated lake in a vast, romantic park-promenade, has a lovely summer terrace where you can order simple grilled meats and salads, and an elegant but intimate panoramic restaurant called L'Orangerie that serves more sophisticated cuisine: *rouget barbet* (red mullet) on zucchini julienne with saffron; *dorade* (dorado, a lean, delicate Mediterranean fish) on rhubarb compote with orange butter; puff pastry with seasonal berries. After your meal, you can take a walk through the flower gardens in one of Geneva's prettiest landscapes. ☒ *128 rue de Lausanne,* ☎ *022/7317935. AE, DC, MC, V. Closed Mon.*

$$ ✕ **Boeuf Rouge.** Despite the contrived decor—a send-up of a Lyonnais
★ bistro, jam-packed with kitschy ceramics and Art Nouveau posters—
this cozy, popular spot delivers the real thing: rich, unadulterated Ly-
onnais cuisine, from the bacon-egg-and-greens *salade Lyonnaise* and
hand-stuffed, pistachio-studded sausage to the *boudin noir* (blood
sausage) with apples and tender quenelles *de brochet* (of pike). The am-
bience is relaxed, and the service is brisk and flamboyant: All dishes
are presented on a flower-crowded tray before they're served at table-
side. Dine late to avoid crowds of foreign business travelers; chic
Genevois slum here for comfort food after 10. ⊠ *17 rue Alfred-Vin-
cent,* ☎ *022/7327537. AE, DC, MC, V. Closed weekends.*

$$ ✕ **Brasserie Lipp.** This white-tile clone of one of Paris's favorite hangouts for politicians and intellectuals is out of place on the third floor
of a slick shopping center, but this is a failing more than compensated
for in summer by a spectacular terrace at the foot of the Old Town.
The menu is mostly basic brasserie fare, with good *choucroûte*
(sauerkraut) and heaping platters of seafood. A choice of small or large
portions on many dishes, as well as a cheap daily lunch plate, helps
keep prices down. ⊠ *In Confédération-Centre mall, 8 rue de la Confédération,* ☎ *022/3111011. AE, DC, MC, V.*

$$ ✕ **Le Carnivore.** This restaurant's name sums up the experience: Great
slabs of sizzling meat and mountains of golden *frites* (fries) are rushed
to the tables by red-swathed waiters. There are good salads, too—with
lentils and smoked duck breast, or walnuts and Roquefort. ⊠ *30 pl.
du Bourg-de-four,* ☎ *022/3118758. AE, DC, MC, V.*

$$ ✕ **Chez Bouby.** At the corner of rue Grenus, this popular, modernized
bistro serves a mixed and arty crowd until 1 AM. The cooking is earthy,
with an emphasis on abats, game, mussels, and good wines by the glass.
⊠ *1 rue Grenus,* ☎ *022/7310927. MC, V. Closed Sun.*

$$ ✕ **Chez Jacky.** Despite the predictable wood-and-copper bistro look,
the cuisine of Jacky Gruber is more than a cut above average, exhibiting
a nouvelle influence in the sauces and combinations but not in the por-
tions, which are sizable. Try the omble chevalier, which comes in a sauce
of Swiss red wine, or the *cuisson de lapin* (rabbit thigh) with cabbage
and mustard sauce. ⊠ *9–11 rue Jacques-Necker,* ☎ *022/7328680. AE,
MC, V. Closed weekends.*

$$ ✕ **L'Entrecôte Couronnée.** Exclusive and clubbish, this little bistro isn't
exactly gentrified—it's at the edge of the Pâquis quarter and the red-
light district, and it's run by a retired chanteuse. The entrecôte is excellent, which is a blessing: The house specialty is the only menu
choice. The restaurant's name means "the Crowned Steak," but it's
not just the steaks that are crowned—the prominent clientele has included the Archduke of Hapsburg and Marie-Astrid de Luxembourg.
⊠ *5 rue des Pâquis,* ☎ *022/7328445. MC, V. Closed weekends.*

$$ ✕ **La Favola.** Run by a young Ticinese couple from Locarno, this
★ quirky little restaurant may be the town's most picturesque. The tiny
dining room, at the top of a vertiginous spiral staircase, strikes a del-
icate balance between rustic and fussy, with its lace window panels,
embroidered tablecloths, polished parquet, and rough-beam ceiling
sponge-painted in shades of ocher and rust. The food echoes this ac-
cent, part country-simple and part city-chic: Try carpaccio with olive
paste or white truffles, bollito of venison in Barolo, ravioli with as-
paragus, or rabbit in Gorgonzola. Lunch menus offer excellent value.
⊠ *15 rue Jean-Calvin,* ☎ *022/3117437. MC, V. Closed weekends.*

$$ ✕ **Hôtel-de-Ville.** Behind its prim lace curtains, this steamy, clattering
brasserie packs in local antique furniture—and art dealers, who settle
onto wooden banquettes for mussels, longeole, beautifully garnished
game platters, and a selection from the varied cheese cart. Don't let

Dining 🔴
Boeuf Rouge, **8**
Brasserie Lipp, **31**
Café du Grütli, **29**
Chez Bouby, **22**
Chez Jacky, **17**
Chez Léo, **44**
Hôtel-de-Ville, **34**
La Favola, **33**
La Glycine/Chez
Jipek'à, **15**
La Perle du Lac, **1**
Le Béarn, **25**
Le Carnivore, **36**
Le Chat Botté, **4**
Le Cygne, **3**
Le Jardin, **5**
Le Lion d'Or, **46**
Le Neptune, **23**
L'Opera Bouffe, **45**
Le Pied-de-Cochon, **37**
Le Saint-Germain, **27**
L'Ange du Dix Vins/
Le Dix Vins, **38**
L'Echalotte, **26**
L'Entrecôte
Couronnée, **7**
Les Armures, **35**
Les Continents, **14**
Les Fous de la
Place, **30**
Roberto, **43**
Taverne de la
Madeleine, **39**

Lodging ⚪
Ambassador, **21**
Beau-Rivage, **4**
Beau-Site, **28**
Bernina, **12**
Central, **32**
D'Allèves, **19**
De Berne, **9**
De la Cigogne, **40**
De la Cloche, **2**
Des Bergues, **20**
Des Tourelles, **24**
Intercontinental, **14**
International et
Terminus, **11**
Le Richemond, **6**
Les Armures, **35**
Lido, **16**
Métropole, **42**
Montana, **10**
St-Gervais, **18**
Strasbourg-
Univers, **13**
Touring-Balance, **41**

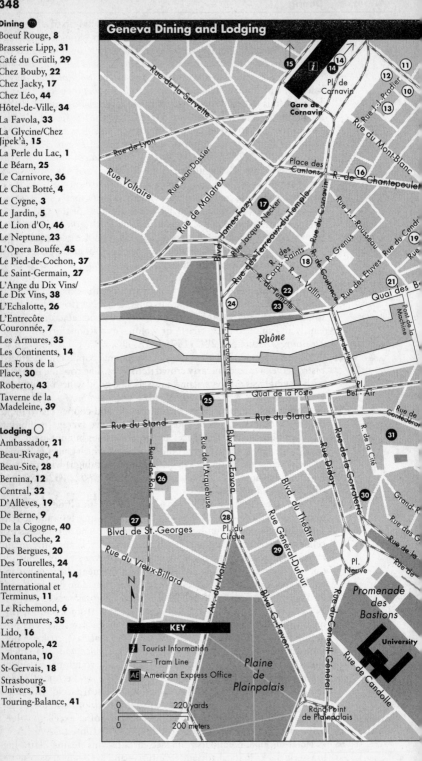

Geneva Dining and Lodging

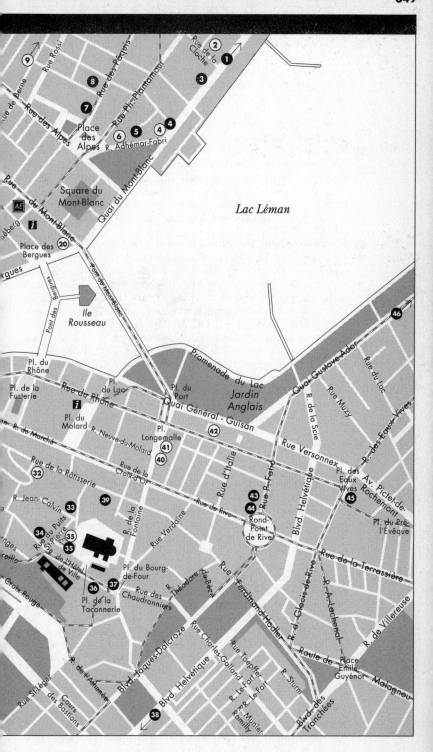

the brusque service deter you; they're like that to everyone. ✉ *39 Grand-rue,* ☎ *022/3111887. AE, DC, MC, V. Closed Sun.*

\$\$ ✕ **Les Fous de la Place.** This chic spot, just off the Place Neuve, pulls ★ in an arty, young-pro crowd for imaginative cuisine at reasonable prices: oyster gratin with fennel, zucchini flan with caramelized grapefruit, spicy pumpkin gnocchi on a bed of spinach, and *tarte Tatin* (apple tart) with Gruyère cream. The setting is spare but warm, with bookcases, slim red settees, saffron tasseled drapes, and scarlet cone lamps. ✉ *21 rue Corraterie,* ☎ *022/3105340. AE, DC, MC, V. Closed Sun., Mon., and Sat. noon.*

\$\$ ✕ **Le Jardin.** Ensconced in the grandiose Hotel Le Richemond, this Mediterranean-accented lunch spot is another local favorite. Businesspeople choose light daily menus here, while elegant bourgeois order salads and salmon carpaccio. The summer terrace is lovely, and the whole place hops when Christie's, also in the hotel, has an auction. ✉ *Hotel Le Richemond, 8 rue Adhémar-Fabri,* ☎ *022/7311400. AE, DC, MC, V.*

\$\$ ✕ **L'Opera Bouffe.** This extremely popular spot offers almost-classic ★ Geneva bistro food, with a small selection of light daily specials, many with a special twist courtesy of the Syrian chef, such as spinach salad topped with Parmesan or monkfish brochette with lime. The setting is chic and postmodern, with thrilling strains of Puccini pouring over the diners—often in competition with conversation. ✉ *5 av. de Frontenex,* ☎ *022/7366300. AE, DC, MC, V. Closed Sun. in July–Aug.*

\$\$ ✕ **Le Pied-de-Cochon.** Crowded, noisy, smoky, and packed shoulder ★ to shoulder with hip young legals spilling over from the Palais de Justice, this is the authentic Genevan ur-bistro, before which all others look like theme restaurants. Under ancient beams, by the worn zinc bar, you'll sample good, simple Lyonnais dishes, including petit salé, ham, grilled andouillettes, tripe, and salads. The namesake pigs' feet are served grilled, with mushrooms or lentils, or *désossés* (boned). ✉ *4 pl. du Bourg-de-Four,* ☎ *022/3104797. AE, DC, MC, V. Closed Sun. May–Sept.*

\$\$ ✕ **Le Saint-Germain.** In this intimate little establishment near the place du Plainpalais the specialty is seafood: delicate raw fish salad, poached St-Pierre (John Dory). The *patronne* presents the fish whole before serving. The prices are reasonable for such high quality. ✉ *61 bd. St-Georges,* ☎ *022/3282624. AE, DC, MC, V. Closed weekends.*

\$ ✕ **Les Armures.** Everyone from workers to politicians comes to this ★ picturesque and historic restaurant at the summit of the Old Town, in the hotel of the same name (☞ Lodging, *below*). There are several dining halls, all decorated with authentic arms from the Middle Ages, but despite the tourist kitsch it's good food, *pas cher.* There's a broad menu of Swiss specialties, from fondue to choucroûte to *Rösti* (hash brown potatoes), but some of the dishes are pure Genevois, including *longeole* (sausage) in cabbage and leeks, and chicken fricasée. ✉ *1 rue du Puits St-Pierre,* ☎ *022/3103442. AE, DC, MC, V.*

\$ ✕ **Café du Grütli.** This is a high-tech, high-style student canteen in the postmodernized Maison Grütli, where Geneva offers creative space to its painters, sculptors, photographers, and filmmakers. The light lunches (Gruyère carpaccio with dried fruit, grilled duck, preserved lamb stew) and late snacks (quiches, melted-cheese salads) are as hip as the regulars, who spill out into the atrium lobby. In summer, check out the broad terrace. ✉ *16 rue Général-Dufour,* ☎ *022/3294495. No credit cards.*

\$ ✕ **Chez Léo.** This tiny, charming bistro, on the corner next door to Roberto (☞ *above*), features the simple Italian cuisine of Roberto's son, Léo. Here you'll find veal piccata in lemon sauce and homemade tortellini in an old-fashioned bentwood-and-posters setting. ✉ *12 rue Pierre-Fatio,* ☎ *022/3115307. MC, V. Closed Sun. No dinner Sat.*

$ ✕ **L'Echalotte.** Big and brightly lighted, with polished wood banquettes and paper place mats, this comfortable spot draws Genevois of all social levels. There's a generous amount of choices on the prix-fixe menu, and the cooking is eclectic and homey—such dishes as scallops wrapped in fresh and smoked salmon, snails in puff pastry, and butter-thick chocolate terrine are all highly flavored and served with casual flair. ⊠ *17 rue des Rois,* ☎ *022/3205999. AE, MC, V. Closed weekends.*

$ ✕ **Taverne de la Madeleine.** Tucked into the commercial maze between
★ rue de la Croix-d'Or and the Old Town, overlooking l'Église de la Madeleine, this casual café claims to be the oldest eatery in Geneva. Run by the city's temperance league, it serves no alcoholic beverages and thus loses the business-lunch crowd, which insists on a pitcher of Fendant with meals. That means that there's all the more room for you to relax over homemade choucroûte, perch, or fresh-baked fruit tarts in the charming Victorian dining room upstairs. The kitchen closes at 6 in summer, at 4 on Saturday. ⊠ *20 rue Toutes-âmes,* ☎ *022/3106070. No credit cards. Closed Sun.*

LODGING

Spending the night in Geneva is as financially taxing as eating a meal: This is a sophisticated European city, and the prices reflect its stature. It is also a popular convention center, and rooms can sell out in blocks, whole groups of hotels snatched up at a time. Book well in advance and brace yourself: You will have to pay more than 400 SF a night for posh lodgings and more than 120 SF simply to have a toilet in your room.

CATEGORY	COST*
$$$$	over 300 SF
$$$	200 SF–300 SF
$$	120 SF–200 SF
$	under 120 SF

Prices are for a standard double room, including breakfast, sales tax, and service charge. Note that luxury hotels start at 500 SF.

$$$$ 🏨 **Les Armures.** This historic treasure in the heart of the Old Town
★ dates from the 17th century, but its original stonework, frescoes, and stenciled beams are now complemented with impeccable modern comforts. Its intimate rooms embellish appropriate old-world furnishings with slick marble baths. Despite the luxury, prices are lower than grand hotels on the Rive Droite. The casual restaurant is an Old Town must (☞ Dining, *above*). Approach by car can be difficult: from the Place Neuve, head into the Old Town via rue de la Tertasse. ⊠ *1 rue du Puits St-Pierre, CH-1204,* ☎ *022/3109172,* FAX *022/3109846. 28 rooms. Restaurant, bar. AE, DC, MC, V.*

$$$$ 🏨 **Beau-Rivage.** Hushed, genteel, and a trifle creaky, this grand old
★ Victorian palace maintains much of its original 1865 splendor. The bar and some suites are particularly florid, and most rooms, updated with dramatic swagged fabrics and rich marble baths, retain fine old architectural details; the front doubles take in Right Bank views. The opposite of Hilton-slick, this discreet landmark banks on the warm hospitality of the Mayer family, which has been watching over individual needs since the hotel's founding. Historic guests include Richard Wagner, Jean Cocteau, and Sissi, the empress Elizabeth of Austria, who died here after being stabbed only 100 m (328 ft) away. The Beau Rivage and its neighbor, Le Richemond (☞ *below*), really create their own price category, with doubles starting at more than 500 SF. ⊠ *13 quai du Mont-Blanc, CH-1201,* ☎ *022/7166666,* FAX *022/7166060. 91 rooms, 6 suites. 2 restaurants, bar, café. AE, DC, MC, V.*

$$$$ ⊡ **Des Bergues.** Having emerged from its chrysalis of renovation in
★ 1997, this 1834 Right Bank landmark pulled off a revival most Swiss
hotel-palaces only dream of—it made the bathrooms state of the art,
installed new cabinetry, and restored the mansarded facade. The lush
room decor—heavy gold medallion prints in doubles, taupe toile de
Jouy in suites—still features the extraordinary collection of heirloom
engravings, now tastefully reframed. The air is thick with discretion;
registering guests are seated in the low-key marble lobby as if they were
shopping for jewels. The choicest rooms have views of the lake, but
the quietest are on the inside court. ✉ *33 rue des Bergues, CH-1201,*
☏ *022/7315050,* ⅏ *022/7321989. 40 rooms, 10 suites. Restaurant,
bar. AE, DC, MC, V.*

$$$$ ⊡ **De la Cigogne.** Every room in this offbeat luxury hotel showcases
a different, sometimes excessive decorative style—always romantic, usually neo-medieval. It's a great place to enjoy antiques, tapestries, some
working fireplaces, and lovely slate-roof-and-chimney views in the
heart of the luxury shopping area, steps from the Old Town. ✉ *17 pl.
Longemalle, CH-1204,* ☏ *022/8184040,* ⅏ *022/8184050. 50 rooms.
Restaurant, bar. AE, DC, MC, V.*

$$$$ ⊡ **Intercontinental.** This modern high-rise is as big as an airport terminal, with every amenity amassed on floor after solidly constructed
floor. Rooms with lake views are magnificent, no more expensive than
rooms without them, and much in demand. Soft beige, flame-stitch fabrics, and brass warm a generic decor. As it's in the international neighborhood, the hotel draws a diplomatic crowd to its restaurant, Les
Continents (☞ Dining, *above*), but caters to large groups as well. ✉
7–9 chemin du Petit-Saconnex, CH-1211, ☏ *022/9193939,* ⅏ *022/
9193838. 278 rooms, 67 suites. 2 restaurants, bar, snack bar, pool, beauty
salon, health club, free parking. AE, DC, MC, V.*

$$$$ ⊡ **Métropole.** Built in 1855, lent to the city of Geneva to house the
★ Red Cross prisoners-of-war archives and now restored by its long-stand-
ing management, the Métropole has as much riverside splendor as its
Right Bank sisters—at a lower price. The ambience is relaxed and un-
fussy despite the grand scale, with leather and hunting prints mixed in
with discreet pastels. The riverside rooms are noisier because of traffic, but the view is superb; request the quieter third or fourth floors.
It's seconds from the best shopping and minutes from the Old Town.
✉ *34 quai Général-Guisan, CH-1204,* ☏ *022/3183200,* ⅏ *022/
3183300. 127 rooms. 2 restaurants, bar, café. AE, DC, MC, V.*

$$$$ ⊡ **Le Richemond.** No longer under the proud management of the Arm-
leder dynasty, this oh-so-gorgeous 1875 luxury landmark seems to com-
pensate by intensifying the already extravagant decor. Fringed braid,
gilt, beveled mirrors, velour, moiré, and dizzying floral-print carpet stretch
on for miles. Opulence takes the place of lake views; of all the Right
Bank palaces, this is the only one set back and turned away from the
water. It is nonetheless a splendid hotel, smothering guests with staff-
intensive attention. ✉ *8–10 rue Adhémar-Fabri, CH-1211,* ☏ *022/
7311400,* ⅏ *022/7312414. 67 rooms, 31 suites. 1 restaurant, bar, beauty
salon, exercise room. AE, DC, MC, V.*

$$$ ⊡ **Ambassador.** Perched directly over the roaring torrents of the Pont
de la Machine, this business-class lodging softens its modernized rooms
(air-conditioning, white-tile baths) with sleek wood and muted colors.
Double-window corner rooms (in the 11 series) are especially desir-
able. ✉ *21 quai des Bergues,* ☏ *022/7317200,* ⅏ *022/7389080. 86
rooms. Restaurant, bar, free parking. AE, DC, MC, V.*

$$$ ⊡ **De Berne.** Despite its unfortunate position on the fringe of the red-
light district, this is a solid, spacious, and well-maintained business-
class hotel. It was built during the mid-'60s, but most of its harshest
edges have been softened with spindled wood, touches of brass, and

a warm cocoa color scheme. Rooms on the rue Sismondi side are quietest. ⊠ *25 rue de Berne, CH-1201,* ☎ *022/7316000,* FAX *022/7311173. 89 rooms. Restaurant, bar. AE, DC, MC, V.*

$$$ 🏨 **Touring-Balance.** Now owned and managed by the neighboring Cigogne (☞ *above*), this no-nonsense lodging will remain midlevel, but watch for an upgrade in style. For the moment it has a sharp laminate lobby and old-style lower floors with French doors; the higher floors are slick and high-tech. There are gallery-quality lithos in every room, and the location, in the midst of Left Bank luxury shopping, is ideal. ⊠ *13 pl. Longemalle, CH-1204,* ☎ *022/3104045,* FAX *022/3104039. 58 rooms. Restaurant, coffee shop, bar. AE, DC, MC, V.*

$$ 🏨 **D'Allèves.** This simple hotel on a quiet square between the station and the Right Bank is crowded with the owner's art and antiques collection and decorated with a kind of dark elegance (velvet, red carpet, chenille) no longer in vogue. There's a modest but good restaurant and a coffee shop. ⊠ *13 rue Kléberg, CH-1211,* ☎ *022/7321530,* FAX *022/ 7383266. 35 rooms. Restaurant, coffee shop. AE, DC, MC, V.*

$$ 🏨 **Montana.** This station-area property offers sharp rooms with a
★ taupe-and-salmon color scheme, double-glazed windows, modular built-in furniture, and all-tile baths. The scale is small, but the warm welcome from the multilingual staff sets this spot heads above its drab neighbors. ⊠ *23 rue des Alpes, CH-1201,* ☎ *022/7320840,* FAX *022/ 7282511. 40 rooms. Breakfast room. AE, DC, MC, V.*

$$ 🏨 **Strasbourg-Univers.** Though this station-area hotel has a slick
★ wood-and-marble look, its prices remain well below those of much shabbier competitors. The new rooms have glossy burled-wood details and chic florals. ⊠ *10 rue Jean-Jacques Pradier, CH-1201,* ☎ *022/9065800,* FAX *022/7384208. 49 rooms. Restaurant, café. AE, DC, MC, V.*

$-$$ 🏨 **Bernina.** Directly across from the train station, this mildly gloomy city hotel offers several combinations to suit your budget, from cheap double beds with sink and bidet to full doubles with the works. Most rooms have neutral colors and tile baths; the oldest rooms are done in florid prints. Breakfasts are served with some of the niceties you find in fancier hostelries. ⊠ *22 pl. de Cornavin, CH-1211,* ☎ *022/7314950,* FAX *022/7327359. 80 rooms. Breakfast room. AE, DC, MC, V.*

$-$$ 🏨 **International et Terminus.** This keep-it-simple spot near the station has made an effort to warm its public areas with antiques and to freshen the rooms with clean, neutral decor (walnut laminate, pastel polyester quilts). The long-standing staff may negotiate prices, depending on demand. ⊠ *20 rue des Alpes, CH-1201,* ☎ *022/7328095,* FAX *022/7321843. 53 rooms. Restaurant. AE, DC, MC, V.*

$-$$ 🏨 **Lido.** This is another no-frills-but-close-to-the-station choice. Despite the black-and-white-tile baths that reveal this hotel's age, rooms have fresh, pale carpet, wood veneer furnishings, and double-glazed windows; those over the square are quietest, and those in the 33–43 series are largest. Three rooms lack showers. ⊠ *9 rue de Chantepoulet, CH-1201,* ☎ *022/7315530,* FAX *022/7316501. 31 rooms. Breakfast room. AE, DC, MC, V.*

$ 🏨 **Beau-Site.** Although the flea-market furniture and creaky parquet, exposed wiring, and thick paint may be grim, there are big windows, high ceilings, and rock-bottom prices. Some rooms have showers, though (with one exception) all toilets are down the hall. A few rooms retain old fireplaces. Rooms on the courtyard side are quietest, as the neighborhood—the lively Place du Cirque—is very downtown. ⊠ *3 pl. du Cirque, CH-1204,* ☎ *022/3281008,* FAX *022/3292364. 25 rooms. Breakfast room. AE, MC, V.*

$ 🏨 **Central.** Despite being at the top of an anonymous urban building
★ on a back shopping street, this bargain hotel merits the elevator ride:

Most rooms are freshly decorated with grass-cloth wallpaper and carpet, and all have tile bathrooms. Prices are the lowest in town for rooms with bath. ⊠ *2 rue de la Rôtisserie, CH-1204,* ☎ *022/8188100,* FAX *022/8188101. 30 rooms. AE, DC, MC, V.*

$ 🏠 **De la Cloche.** Think of yourself as a privileged border in the doily-★ trimmed flat of a sweet *dame d'un certain age.* The once-luxurious apartment has been carved into eight bedrooms, with toilets down the hall and a familial shower (two rooms have their own). The homey decor (flocked wallpaper, bookcase loaded with travel guides) matches the spirit of the place; feel free to make a cup of tea in the kitchen. The courtyard setting is so quiet that you can hear birds chirping in the garden. ⊠ *6 rue de la Cloche, CH-1201,* ☎ *022/7329481,* FAX *022/7381612. 8 rooms, 2 with shower. Breakfast room. AE, DC, MC, V.*

$ 🏠 **St-Gervais.** On a historic block in the Right Bank town center, this low-budget inn offers garretlike rooms that are well maintained, with fresh linens and framed prints. Families should ask for the large, old room with ancient beams. A tiny pub on the ground floor serves snacks. Two rooms have baths. ⊠ *20 rue des Corps-Saints, CH-1201,* ☎ *022/7324572,* FAX *022/7384369. 21 rooms, 2 with bath. Pub. AE, MC, V.*

$ 🏠 **Des Tourelles.** Once worthy of a czar, now host to backpackers, this ★ stripped-down Victorian vision offers enormous bay-window corner rooms, many with marble fireplaces. French doors open over the Rhône. The furnishings are scarce and strictly functional, but the staff is young and friendly. Bring earplugs: Though drapes are thick and the windows insulated, the location is noisy, over roaring bridge traffic. New modular showers mean nearly all rooms now have complete bathrooms. ⊠ *2 bd. James-Fazy, CH-1201,* ☎ *022/7324423,* FAX *022/7327620. 23 rooms, most with bath. Breakfast room. AE, DC, MC, V.*

NIGHTLIFE AND THE ARTS

Geneva Agenda, which has bilingual (English and French) weekly listings of films, concerts, museum exhibitions, and galleries, is available free in most hotels.

Nightlife

Bars and Lounges

If you want a cocktail with piano music in the background, go to one of the luxury hotels and sink into an armchair. The **Métropole** (☞ Dining, *above*; ⊠ 34 quai Général Guisan, ☎ 022/3111344) is particularly comfortable; you can sit in the lobby or in the bar itself. **La Coupole** (⊠ 16 rue Pierre-Fatio, ☎ 022/7356544) has piano music from 7 PM on. **Griffin's Café** (⊠ 36 bd. Helvétique, ☎ 022/7351218) has a singer-pianist. Many Genevois drink in cafés, bistros, and brasseries; you'll see a different local scene by joining them (☞ Dining, *above*).

Casino

Geneva has its own casino in the **Grand Casino** complex (⊠ 19 quai du Mont-Blanc, ☎ 022/7326320), but there's a 5 SF gambling limit. The big money changes hands only 15 minutes away at the **Casino de Divonne** in France (⊠ Divonne, ☎ 0033/450403434). Take the Geneva-Lausanne autoroute and exit at Coppet-Divonne (☞ Getting Around by Car *in* Geneva A to Z, *below*)

Dancing

Arthur's (⊠ 20 Rte. de Pré-Bois, ☎ 022/7881600), in the Mövenpick Hotel, is Switzerland's largest disco, accommodating some 1,500 guests (most of them blond) in several dance areas. **Club 58** (⊠ 15 rue des Glacis-de-Rive, ☎ 022/7351515) draws carefully coiffed thirtysomethings. **Griffin's** (⊠ 36 bd. Helvétique, ☎ 022/7351218) is a chic, exclusive nightclub/restaurant with dancing. Quai du Seujet is an area dense with clubs: Try **L'Interdit** (⊠ 18 quai du Seujet, ☎ 022/7389091) for classic disco dancing; **Le Loft**(⊠ 20 quai du Seujet, ☎ 022/7382828) is as much a gay bar as a disco. Just over the French border in Saint-Julien is **Macumba** (⊠ Rte. Annecy, cross the border at Perly, ☎ 023/0450492350), which claims to be the biggest disco in Europe. **Le Petit Palace** (⊠ 6 rue Tour-de-Boël, ☎ 022/3110033) is popular with young people eager to burn their latest paycheck. **Rêve d'O** (⊠ 4 quai des Forces-Motrices, ☎ 022/3290133) is the place for techno.

Jazz Clubs

Halles de l'Ile (⊠ pl. de l'Ile, ☎ 022/3115221) features jazz and views over the Rhône. **Sud des Alpes** (⊠ 10 rue des Alpes, ☎ 022/7323095) is frequented by true aficionados.

The Arts

Film

Most movies are dubbed in French. To find English-language films in English, watch listings in the local newspapers or *Geneva Agenda* for the initials *v.o.*, meaning *version originale*. They are often shown in the late afternoon and after 10 PM.

Music

Various concerts and an important annual solo competition take place in the **Conservatoire de Musique** (⊠ pl. Neuve, ☎ 022/3117633). The **Grand-Théâtre de Genève** (⊠ pl. Neuve, ☎ 022/3112311) burned down in 1951 when a rehearsal of *Die Walküre*'s fire scene became too realistic. It reopened in 1962 and now features concerts of classical music as well as opera, operetta, and dance; watch for listings of Sunday-morning chamber music recitals in the foyer. Recent productions have been displaced during a new renovation project; it may be reopened by publication time. **Radio-Suisse Romande** (⊠ Passage de la Radio, 66 bd. Carl-Vogt, ☎ 022/7087711) has a concert hall, and audiences are welcome at some of the live broadcasts. The gilt-and-velvet bijou **Victoria Hall** (⊠ 14 rue Général-Dufour, ☎ 022/3288121) is the main venue of **L'Orchestre de la Suisse Romande**, which was conducted for 50 years by Ernest Ansermet and through him had close links with Stravinsky. For information on the orchestra's season, call 022/3170017.

Theater

Performances are mostly in French, but during the summer, amateur companies of a high standard present plays in English as well.

The **Comédie de Genève** (⊠ 6 bd. des Philosophes, ☎ 022/3205001) stages classic drama. For something more experimental, head to the **Théâtre de Grütli** (⊠ 16 rue Général-Dufour, ☎ 022/3289878). **Marionettes de Genève** (⊠ 3 rue Rodo, ☎ 022/3296767) puts on great kids-oriented puppet shows.

OUTDOOR ACTIVITIES AND SPORTS

Golf

The **Golf Club de Genève** (⊠ 70 Rte. de la Capite, Cologny, ☎ 022/7357540) welcomes visitors and rents equipment.

Sailing

The **École Club Migros** (⊠ 3 rue du Prince, ☎ 022/3106555) offers sailing courses. **Bateaux École Léman** (⊠ Across from 44 quai Gustave-Ador, ☎ 022/7352263) provides rentals and classes.

Skating

Patinoire des Vernets (⊠ 4–6 rue Hans-Wilsdorf, Acacias, ☎ 022/4184000) has indoor skating from October to March. For outdoor folly October–March, bring your skates to **Patinoire de Meyrin,** (⊠ chemin Louis Rendu, ☎ 022/7821300).

Skiing

Though Geneva is not a ski destination, those in need of a quick fix should head for the **Gare Routière de Genève** (bus station; ⊠ pl. Dorcière, just off rue du Mont-Blanc, ☎ 022/7320230), which provides daily trips to many local French resorts, including Chamonix. The trip takes 1–1½ hours, and the 50 SF fare includes a ski-lift pass.

Swimming

The skating rink at Meyrin becomes an outdoor pool in summer. As for swimming in Lake Geneva, Geneva residents are divided: Some have been swimming in it for years, while others offer dire predictions that you'll catch cystitis, strep throat, and worse from its polluted waters. There are two access points close to the center: **Pâquis-Plage** (☎ 022/7322974), a sheltered area above quai Mont-Blanc, with a restaurant and changing rooms. The other is **Genève-Plage** (⊠ quai Gustave-Ador, ☎ 022/7362482), beyond the Jet d'Eau.

Tennis

Visitors are welcome at the **New Sporting Club** (⊠ 51 Rte. de Collex, Bellevue, ☎ 022/7741514); the **Tennis du Bois Carré** (⊠ 204 rte. de Veyrier, Carouge, ☎ 022/7843006); and the **Tennis Club des Eaux-Vives** (⊠ Parc des Eaux-Vives, ☎ 022/7355350).

SHOPPING

Auctions

As a jewelry capital rivaled only by New York, Geneva is home to the world's two most famous auction houses. **Christie's** (⊠ 8 pl. de la Taconnerie, ☎ 022/3111766), often consigns wines and ornaments to complement its jewelry sales. It holds its glamorous auctions in the equally glamorous Hotel Le Richemond. **Sotheby's** (⊠ 13 quai du Mont-Blanc, ☎ 022/7328585), at the Hôtel Beau-Rivage, often has previews, the lots soon to be snatched up by erudite collectors.

Department Stores

Grand Passage (⊠ 50 rue du Rhône, ☎ 022/3106611) is the granddaddy of Geneva department stores, with a full line of upscale goods. **Bon Génie** (⊠ 34 rue du Marché, ☎ 022/3108222) has attentive service to match its luxurious goods.

Flea Markets

There is a flea market in the **plaine de Plainpalais** with plenty of *brocante* (one man's junk, another man's antiques) every Wednesday and Saturday year-round. An arts-and-crafts market on the **place de la Fusterie** holds forth every Thursday in summer. A clothing and book market takes place daily year-round on **place de la Madeleine.**

Shopping Streets and Malls

The two principal shopping streets run parallel along the Left Bank. For luxury shopping the first is **rue du Rhône.** The other is the neighboring street that changes names and is known variously as: **rue de la Confédération, rue du Marché, rue de la Croix-d'Or,** and **rue de Rive.**

The **Grande-Rue** in the Old Town is lined with galleries, antiques shops, and bookstores. Streets radiating down from **place du Bourg-de-Four** are boutique havens. **Rue du Mont-Blanc** on the Right Bank has less expensive watch and souvenir shops. The **Centre-Confédération** is a glitzy three-story shopping center that opens at the bottom onto place Bel-Air and from the top leads into the Old Town. **Les Cygnes,** a small, glossy urban mall just north of the train station on rue de Lausanne, has everything from shoes to gourmet food.

Specialty Stores

Antiques

Antiquorum (⊠ 2 rue du Mont-Blanc, ☎ 022/9092850) deals exclusively in the sale of antique watches. **Ars Nova** (⊠ 6 rue Jean-Calvin, ☎ 022/3118660) has a gallery-quality selection of treasures from the early 20th century, including Art Deco jewelry. **Au Vieux Canon** (⊠ 40 Grande-Rue, ☎ 022/3105758) deals in extravagant English silver. **Buchs** (⊠ 34–36 Grande-Rue, ☎ 022/3117485) sells beautifully restored antique frames of old-master vintage and quality. **Jadis** (⊠ 21 Grande-Rue, ☎ 022/7812402) sells an unusual selection of antique watches and jewelry. **Rue des Belles Filles** (⊠ 6 bis rue Étienne-Dumont, ☎ 022/3103131) offers a crowded treasure hunt for vintage clothing, jewelry, and knickknacks.

Books

Librairie Jullien (⊠ 32 pl. du Bourg-de-Four, ☎ 022/3103670) has sold new and antique books since 1839. The commercial chain **Librairie Payot** (⊠ 5 rue Chantepoulet, ☎ 022/7318950; ⊠ 5 rue de la Confédération) carries English as well as French titles. **À Montparnasse** (⊠ 39 Grande-Rue, ☎ 022/3116719) collects lovely old books and prints. **Galerie Bernard Letu** (⊠ 2 rue Calvin, ☎ 022/3104757) carries an inspired collection of art and photography books. **Elm** (⊠ 3 rue Versonnex, ☎ 022/7360945) sells a mix of English and American books. **Oreille Cassé** (⊠ 8 pl. Grenus, ☎ 022/7324080) sells hardcover French comic books (*bandes dessinées*) and children's books.

Chocolate

Arn (⊠ 12 pl. du Bourg-de-Four, ☎ 022/3104094) is an Old Town institution for handmade chocolates, pastries, and sweets. **Du Rhône** (⊠ 3 rue de la Confédération, ☎ 022/3115614) has an excellent, expensive selection of its famous chocolates. **Jenny** (⊠ 8 rue Kléberg, ☎ 022/7314811) has fine sweets and a tearoom to sample them in. **Rohr** (⊠ 3 pl. de Molard, ☎ 022/3116303; ⊠ In the covered passageway at 42 rue du Rhône, ☎ 022/3116876) also has its devotees.

Jewelry

There's no ceiling on the price of world-famous baubles in Geneva. At **Chopard** (⊠ 8 rue de la Confédération, ☎ 022/3113728) you can wrap your wrist with a diamond-studded watch. **Cartier** (⊠ 35 rue du Rhône, ☎ 022/3118066) is a wonderful source for traditional stones (rubies, emeralds, diamonds), sometimes set in a variation on the trademark panther; also look for their interlocked rolling rings. **Boucheron** (⊠ 23 rue du Rhône, ☎ 022/3101311), a Paris-based jeweler, has a stunning selection of watches. **Bulgari** (⊠ 30 rue du Rhône, ☎ 022/3101500) has a series of striking, weighty rings with domed stones; some pieces are set with ancient coins.

L'Arcade (⊠ 20 rue de la Corraterie, ☎ 022/3111554) offers Edith Moldaschl's unique selection of "real" costume jewelry, both fine old pieces and unique new works. **Ludwig Muller** (⊠ 5 rue des Chaudronniers, ☎ 022/3102930) designs fine jewelry and gold pieces to order.

Linens

Frette (✉ 5–7 rue Céard, ☎ 022/3108523) carries luxurious household linens and gorgeous bathrobes. **Langenthal** (✉ 13 rue du Rhône, ☎ 022/3106510) sells pretty, practical Swiss goods.

Lingerie

Fogal (✉ 8 rue du Marché, ☎ 022/3115136) sells fine Swiss hosiery; they're often quite expensive, but there's a wider range of sizes than the usual small/medium/large, and there's a tempting selection of colors, textures, and fancy seaming. Look for the sale bins.

Watches

Of Geneva's myriad watchmakers, three are known for unparalleled excellence. **Piaget** (✉ 40 rue du Rhône, ☎ 022/3107388) has high prices to match its high-quality timepieces. **Vacheron-Constantin** (✉ 1 rue des Moulins, ☎ 022/3103227), opposite the Jardin Anglais, is a Geneva tradition. **Patek Philippe** (✉ 22 quai Général-Guisan, ☎ 022/7812448), on the Right Bank overlooking the place de l'Ile, has been based in Geneva for well more than 100 years; it created the first-known Swiss wristwatch. For a fun souvenir, look for Michael Jordi watches with their kitsch-hip Swiss themes; these are sold in many general timepiece stores.

GENEVA A TO Z

Arriving and Departing

By Bus

Bus tours generally arrive at and depart from the **Gare Routière de Genève** (bus station, ✉ pl. Dorcière just off rue du Mont-Blanc, ☎ 022/7320230), behind the English church in the city center.

By Car

Approaching Geneva by car is straightforward enough, as a major expressway (**A1**) enters from the north via Lake Geneva's northern shore, connecting through Lausanne by way of either Bern (**A12**) or Martigny in the Valais (**A9**). It's easy to enter from France, either from Grenoble to the south or Lyon to the southwest, as border controls are minimal. From the Valais, you also can approach Geneva from the scenic southern shore of Lake Geneva, via Évian-les-Bains. (You will, of course, need your passport and *vignette* [Swiss road-tax sticker] no matter how brief the foray.)

By Plane

Cointrin (✉ About 2 km//1 mi northwest of city center, ☎ 022/7913111), Geneva's airport and the second-largest international airport in Switzerland, is served by several airlines that fly directly to the city from New York City, Toronto, and London. **Swissair** (☎ 800/221–4750 in the U.S.; 0171/434–7300 in the U.K.) serves the airport most frequently. **Crossair** (☎ 0171/439–4144 in the U.K., 022/7980881 in Geneva), the domestic airline, connects Cointrin with Bern, Zürich, Lugano, and other Swiss cities—as well as to several European capitals.

BETWEEN THE AIRPORT AND THE CITY CENTER

By Bus. Regular bus service runs between the airport and Geneva center. The ride is about 20 minutes, the fare 2.20 SF. Some hotels have their own shuttle system.

By Limousine. Privilege (☎ 022/7383366) rents Mercedes and stretch Rolls. Chauffeured limos can be hired through **Globe** (☎ 022/7310750). Some luxury hotels either keep their own fleet or will arrange one through the concierge.

By Taxi. Taxis are plentiful but very expensive and charge at least 25 SF to the city center. Tips are expected for luggage only.

By Train. Cointrin has a direct rail link with **Cornavin** (✉ pl. de Cornavin, town center, ☎ 1572222), the city's main train station. Trains run about every 10 minutes, from 5:30 AM to midnight. The six-minute trip costs 5 SF.

By Train

Cornavin (✉ pl. de Cornavin, ☎ 022/1572222) is an important terminus for the Swiss Federal Railways, with direct expresses coming from most Swiss cities every hour.

Getting Around

By Boat

Compagnie Générale de Navigation (CGN) sur le Lake Geneva (✉ Jardin-Anglais, CH-1204 Genève, ☎ 022/3112521) offers steamer transportation among most lake ports, including those of France as well as Lausanne and Montreux. Holders of the Swiss Pass (☞ Train Travel *in* the Gold Guide) travel free. Those with a Swiss Boat Pass (☞ Boat Travel *in* the Gold Guide) receive a 50% discount.

Boat excursions onto the lake are offered by several smaller private firms, including **Mouettes Genevoises** (✉ 8 quai du Mont-Blanc, ☎ 022/7322944). **Swissboat** (✉ 4 quai du Mont-Blanc, ☎ 022/7324747) plies the lake as well.

By Taxi

Taxis (☎ 022/3314133) can be immaculate, and the drivers are polite, but do expect a 6.30 SF minimum, a 5 SF charge per passenger, plus 2.70 SF per kilometer (about ½ mi). There's a surcharge on evening and Sunday fares as well.

By Tram and Bus

Geneva has an excellent network of trams, buses, and trolley buses, extremely efficient and inexpensive. Every bus stop has a machine selling tickets, and for 2.20 SF you can use the system for one hour, changing as often as you like. A trip limited to three stops, with return within 30 minutes, costs 1.50 SF. If you plan to travel frequently, buy a *carte journalière,* a ticket covering unlimited travel within the city center all day for 5 SF; it's available at newsstands that display a TRANSPORTS PUBLICS GENEVOIS (TPG) sign near the stop. Holders of the Swiss Pass can travel free on Geneva's public transport system.

Contacts and Resources

Consulates

Canada (✉ 1 rue du Pré de la Bichette, ☎ 022/7339000). **United Kingdom** (✉ 37 rue de Vermont, ☎ 022/9182400). **United States Mission** (✉ Rte. de Pré-Bois 29, ☎ 022/7981615).

Emergencies

Police (☎ 117). **Ambulance** (☎ 144). **Hospital** (✉ Hôpital Cantonal, 24 rue Micheli-du-Crest, ☎ 022/3723311). **Doctor referral** (☎ 022/3202511); emergency house calls (☎ 022/3484950). **Pharmacies** (☎ 111).

English-Language Bookstores

Librairie Payot (✉ 5 rue Chantepoulet, ☎ 022/7318950; ✉ 5 rue de la Confédération, ☎ 022/3109266). **Elm** (✉ 3, rue Versonnex, ☎ 022/7360945).

Guided Tours

BOAT TOURS

Swissboat (⊠ 4 quai du Mont-Blanc, ☎ 022/7324747) offers guided excursions along the shores of Lake Geneva, with views of famous homes and châteaus. Departures are from the quai du Mont-Blanc; times vary with the season. **Mouettes Genevoises** tours (⊠ 8 quai du Mont-Blanc, ☎ 022/7322944) are not guided in person, but you're given a printed and numbered commentary with map to guide yourself on tours of the Geneva end of the lake.

ORIENTATION

Bus tours around Geneva are operated by **Key Tours** (☎ 022/7314140). They leave from Gare Routière de Genève (bus station; ⊠ pl. Dorcière just off rue du Mont-Blanc), behind the English church, daily at 2; during high season (May–October) there is also a tour departing at 10. The tours, at 29 SF, last approximately two hours and include an overview of the International Area and a walk through the Old Town; the commentary is in English. If you pay a slightly higher fare of 32 SF, you can complete your bus tour with a minitrain that connects at Place Neuve and carries you up the steep, narrow streets into the Old Town (May–October). Or you can take the minitrain tour independently, waiting at the base of the statue of General Dufour in front of the Grand Theatre on the place Neuve; it lasts about 30 minutes, costs 5.90 SF, and runs from March through October.

Key Tours also offers bus excursions into the countryside, the Jura, and Montreux/Chillon, as well as all-day trips to outlying attractions, including the Jungfraujoch and Chamonix, in the French Alps.

PERSONAL GUIDES

The **Geneva tourist office** (☞ Visitor Information, *below*) provides private guided tours by day or evening for fees starting at 35 SF for two hours (minimum two persons). Reserve in writing.

SPECIAL INTEREST

The **United Nations** organizes tours around the Palais des Nations. Enter by the Pregny Gate in the avenue de la Paix; if you take Bus 8 from Cornavin, don't get off at the Palais de Nations: Wait for the smaller Appia stop. Tours last about an hour and cost 8.50 SF; they're offered in English, but there are no set starting times.

WALKING

The tourist office will provide you with an audio-guided tour (in six languages, including English) of the Old Town that covers 26 points of interest, complete with map, cassette, and player. Rental is 10 SF, and a deposit of 50 SF is required.

Travel Agencies

American Express (⊠ 7 rue du Mont-Blanc, ☎ 022/7317600). **Thomas Cook** (⊠ 64 rue de Lausanne, ☎ 022/7324555). **Automobile Club Suisse** (⊠ 21 Fontenette, CH-1227 Carouge, ☎ 022/3422233). **Touring Club Suisse** (⊠ 9 rue Pierre Fatio, ☎ 022/7371212).

Visitor Information

The city has an excellent and well-organized tourist office, the **Office du Tourisme de Genève** (⊠ 3 rue du Mont-Blanc, ☎ 022/9097000, FAX 022/9097011). **Tourist information booths:** (⊠ pl. du Molard 4, Left Bank, ☎ 022/3119827; ⊠ Cornavin, ☎ 022/9097050). For information **by mail,** contact the administration (⊠ 10 Rte. de l'Aéroport, Case Postale 596, CH-1215, Genève 15, ☎ 022/9297000, FAX 022/9297011).

14 Portraits of Switzerland

Skiing Switzerland

Books and Videos

SKIING SWITZERLAND

TWO CABLE-CAR RIDES and thousands of feet above the resort village of Verbier, we sit in a mountain restaurant. On the table in front of us are one *café renversé,* two cups of hot chocolate, one tiny glass of bubbly white *Fendant* wine from Sion. Our legs tired from a long day of skiing, we catch our breath before the evening run, while the slopes and pistes below empty themselves of skiers and fill up with evening light. Outside, the sun hovers only inches above the horizon. Mont Blanc is an island of ice rising out of a sea of summits along the Franco-Swiss border. Peaks and passes stretch as far as the eye can see, an art director's Alpine fantasy in late light.

Verbier skiing is one reason I've returned to Switzerland in winter, faithfully, for the past 25 years. This is a giant of a ski area in a region of giant ski areas, perched high in the French-speaking, southwest corner of Switzerland, draped over four mountain valleys, embracing six villages, a labyrinth of interconnected lifts (more than 100), interlaced slopes (too many to count)—a ski area you can't explore in a week or even exhaust in a season.

For passionate skiers every trip to Switzerland is a homecoming. All our skiing archetypes originate here. White sawtooth horizons point to the sky, picture-postcard chalet roofs poke up under great white hats of snow, necklaces of lifts and cable cars drape themselves over the white shoulders of fairy-tale mountains, and runs go on forever.

These are big mountains, with vertical drops twice the length of those of the Rockies. In the Alps you can often drop four, five, or six thousand vertical feet in one run. Here runs are so long that halfway down you need a break—which you'll find at a little chalet restaurant in the middle of nowhere, where the views are as exhilarating as the schnapps that's so often the drink of choice.

These are pure white mountains, too, whiter than we're used to. In the Alps, the tree line is low, often only 1,000 m (3,000 ft) above sea level, and ski areas stretch upward from there. The skier's playing field is white on white; marked pistes are white rivers of groomed snow snaking down equally white but ungroomed flanks of Alpine peaks. There are more treeless bowls than you can count, than you can hope to ski in several skiers' lifetimes.

When European skiers tell you that the western Alps are higher and more glaciated, more likely to have good snow in a dry year, and that the eastern Alps are lower in elevation but full of charm, with more intimate, more richly decorated villages, they are usually referring to the difference between the French Alps and Austria. In fact, they could just as well be talking about the mountains and ski resorts of southwest Switzerland versus those of eastern Switzerland, Graubünden, and the Engadine; for Switzerland, with its many cantons, is a microcosm that mirrors the diversity of skiing all across the greater Alps. You can test your credit-card limits at the Palace Hotel in worldly Saint-Moritz, hear the Latin echoes of Romansh as you ride the cog railways of modest Kleine Scheidegg, or ponder the hearty existence of hearty mountain farmers among the peaks of French-speaking Valais—but always, the local mountain culture will be part of your ski experience.

As varied as the regions are the people who ski them. Depending on which canton you ski, you may hear the lilting singsong French of Vaud and the western Valais, the incomprehensible Swiss German of the Berner Oberland and eastern Wallis, or the haunting Latin echoes of Romansh in the high valleys of Graubünden. The ski pistes of Switzerland are the polyglot crossroads of Europe, where stylish Parisians in neon outfits rub elbows with Brits in navy blue, Munich businessmen in Bogner suits, and Swedish students with punk haircuts. And yet, when you're surrounded by mountains that will outlast fashions, lifetimes, and languages, such differences fade, and the mountains are all you can see.

We walk uphill through knee-deep powder toward the summit of the Allalinhorn—the friendliest of canton Wallis's many 4,000-m (13,120-ft) peaks. Early morning sunshine rakes the corniced ridges around us; the village of Saas-Fee still hides in shadow below. With climbing skins glued to the bottom of our skis, we've shuffled up the Feegletscher to earn a morning's bliss in deep untracked snow. This glacier highway is taking us above the domain of passes and ski lifts and groomed slopes, into a world of icy north walls, pure knife-edge ridges, undulating mile-long coverlets of fresh powder, summits of whipped meringue, and snow crystals sparkling at our feet. Munching cheese and chocolate as we climb, thinking that we must look like silhouettes in one of Herbert Matter's prewar Swiss travel posters, breathing deeply, climbing slowly, we daydream our way to the top. Our tracks, like zippers in the snow, stretch up to a vanishing point in the midnight-blue sky above.

IT'S A SOFT APRIL morning at Les Diablerets, a ski area on the frontier between francophone Vaud and the German canton of Bern. It's already 11 AM and the frozen corn snow is only now softening up on the wide glacier beneath the dark, thumblike peak of the Oldenhorn. From the topmost lift we can see west toward Lake Geneva, south toward the giant peaks of the Valais, and east toward the dark brooding peaks of the Berner Oberland. An observation deck on the roof of the Alps reveals mountains filling space to its farthest corners, to the hazy horizon, waves on a wind-tossed sea, frozen white, as far as one can see. On the deep valley flanks below Les Diablerets, winding west toward the Rhône Valley, another winter's worth of cow manure has performed its annual alchemy: The slopes are greening up with no respect for common-sense color—pastures of eye-dazzling kelly green under dark forests and crags. Only a few miles away, down the eastern German-speaking side of the mountains, the chic resort of Gstaad seems deserted; its jet-set winter guests have already hung up their skis and headed for the Mediterranean. The mountains are ours for a day.

At the top of the lift we break through the clouds. A sea of fog fills the Rhône Valley below us, a fluffy false plain, punctured only by snowy peaks, stretching to the horizon. Somewhere under these clouds is Lake Geneva, and far across, Les Dents du Midi ("The Teeth of Noon") rise out of the clouds like ice-sheathed knuckles. Villars-Gryon is a ski resort so small most American skiers have never heard of it, even though it's bigger than half the ski areas in Colorado. Alone, we ski along the edge of the piste, where the slope steepens and drops away in a succession of rocky ledges. Just over the border that separates the skier's world from the mountaineer's, we see a lone ibex, posing on a rock outcrop against the clouds, scimitar-shape horns swept back in wide twin arcs. We christie to a stop, stand in awe wishing we had cameras, and realize eventually that the ibex is not going to bolt. These are its Alps, its domain; we are the newcomers, birds of passage, intruders. It feels like a privilege to share the roof of Europe with this ibex, a privilege that our Swiss hosts have slowly earned over 700 years by farming basically unfarmable mountainsides, by making this land their domain. We push off, the cold winter snow squeaking under our skis. Behind our backs the ibex still stares off into the distance.

These images stay with me, indelible as the Alps themselves. Say the word *Switzerland* and I see the gentle slopes of the Plateau Rosa above Zermatt, perforated by the dotted lines of T-bars, peppered with tiny, bright-color skiers, slopes lapping in white waves against the base of the Matterhorn. Near Saint-Moritz, I see the blue-green crevasses of the Morteratsch Glacier, a frozen white-water rapid spilling down from the Diavolezza ski area: ice walls, blue ice caves, a labyrinth of ice. I see the three giants of the Berner Oberland, the Eiger, the Mönch, and the Jungfrau—the Ogre, the Monk, and the Virgin—shadowy 13,000-ft-high northern faces that loom above the toy skiers and runs of Grindelwald and Wengen.

That Switzerland has some of the best skiing in the world goes without saying. In the end, though, it's not the skiing I remember, or the runs, or the trails, or my turns. It's the mountains I remember. And so will you.

— Lito Tejada–Flores

Winter Activities at the Resorts

Resort	Lift-Ticket Cost (SF) * (one day/six day)	Elevation (m/ft)	Number of Lifts	Lift Capacity (number of riders per hour in thousands)	Maintained Trails (km/mi)	Snowmaking
Arosa	49/219	1,800–2,650 m 5,900–8,700 ft	16	21.7	70/43	❄
Crans-Montana	54/255	1,500–3,000 m 4,920–9,843 ft	42	41.0	160/100	❄
Davos-Klosters	52/259	1,560–2,844 m 5,118–9,330 ft	55	55.0	344/197	❄
Flims-Laax	56/280	1,160–3,292 m 3,808–10,798 ft	32	41.2	220/140	❄
Gstaad-Saanenland	50/233	1,100–3,000 m 3,600–9,843 ft	69	50.0	250/160	❄
La Vallée de Conches (cross-country)	n/a	1,300–1,450 m 4,265–4,757 ft	n/a	n/a	n/a	
Le Val d'Anniviers	38/200	1,350–3,000 m 4,430–9,843 ft	45	25.0	250/155	❄
Les Portes du Soleil (Champery and 14 linked Swiss and French areas)	48/219	1,000–2,500 m 3,280–8,200 ft	219	228.8	650/400	❄
Verbier (including 6 linked areas of Quatre-Vallées)	56/282	820–3,330 m 2,690–10,925 ft	100	72.7	400/248	❄
Saas-Fee	56/260	1,800–3,600 m 5,900–11,800 ft	26	26.4	100/50	❄
St. Moritz	54/258	1,856–3,060 m 6,100–10,000 ft	55	65.0	350/34	❄
Grindelwald-Wengen	52/232	1,300–3,450 m 4,265–11,330 ft	45	37.0	188/113	❄
Zermatt	60/296	1,260–3,820 m 4,132–12,530 ft	73	70.7	245/152	❄

* varies according to extent of areas selected to ski in
† depending on type and quality of snow, as well as grooming of slopes

Average Annual Snowfall (cm/in)	Difficulty of Terrain: % Beg/Int/Exp †	Cross-Country (km/mi of trails)	Glacier Skiing	Heli-Skiing	Para/Hang Gliding	Ice-Skating	Luge Runs	Skibob Runs	Ballooning	Accommodations (beds in hotels, chalets, and apartments)
692/272	31/57/12	26/16			❄	❄	❄		❄	8,000
518/204	38/50/12	48/31	❄	❄	❄	❄	❄	❄	❄	40,000
427/168	30/40/30	75/46			❄	❄	❄	❄		24,000
440/173	50/30/20	60/37	❄	❄	❄	❄	❄		❄	10,800
627/247	40/40/20	127/75	❄	❄	❄	❄	❄	❄	❄	12,500
522/206	n/a	180/53				❄				20,000
348/137	30/40/30	82/51		❄	❄	❄	❄	❄		20,000
619/244	25/40/35	250/155		❄	❄	❄				93,000
491/193	32/42/26	42/33	❄	❄	❄	❄	❄	❄		25,000
357/141	25/25/50	8/4	❄		❄	❄		❄		7,500
368/145	10/70/20	150/93	❄	❄	❄	❄	❄	❄	❄	12,000
389/153	30/50/20	17/10		❄	❄	❄	❄	❄		20,000
434/131	30/40/30	10/6	❄	❄	❄	❄				13,500

BOOKS AND VIDEOS

Books

Wilhelm Tell, by Friedrich von Schiller, is the definitive stage version of the dramatic legend. *The Prisoner of Chillon,* by Lord Byron, is an epic poem inspired by the sojourn of François Bonivard in the dungeon of Chillon. *A Tramp Abroad,* by Mark Twain, includes the author's personal impressions—and tall tales—derived from travels in Switzerland. *Arms and the Man,* by G. B. Shaw, was the source of Oscar Straus's Viennese operetta *The Chocolate Soldier;* both are about a Swiss mercenary with a sweet tooth. Novels set at least partially in Switzerland include *Heidi,* by Johanna Spyri (Maienfeld); *Daisy Miller,* by Henry James (Lac Léman, Chillon); *Tender Is the Night,* by F. Scott Fitzgerald; *A Farewell to Arms,* by Ernest Hemingway; and *Hotel du Lac,* by Anita Brookner (Vevey).

La Place de la Concorde Suisse, by John McPhee, was developed from a series of *New Yorker* pieces the author wrote after traveling with members of the Swiss army. *Heidi's Alp,* by Christine Hardyment, a first-person account of a family traveling in a camper-van in search of the Europe of fairy tales, includes an adventure with a latter-day alm-uncle in a cabin above Maienfeld. *Banner in the Sky,* by James Ramsey Ullman, is a powerful children's book about a boy's attempt to climb Switzerland's most challenging mountain. *A Guide to Zermatt and the Matterhorn,* Edward Whymper's memoirs of his disastrous climb up the Matterhorn, is now out of print, but it may be available in a library (excerpts appear in Chapter 11, Valais). Thomas Mann's *The Magic Mountain* is set in the ski resort town of Davos,

while *Terminal,* by Colin Forbes, is a murder-mystery tale containing fantastic descriptions of Swiss cities. There have been several books published on the recent findings of the Swiss banks' handling of Jewish and Nazi funds during and after World War II. Among these are *Nazi Gold: The Full Story of the Fifty-Year Swiss-Nazi Conspiracy to Steal Billions from Europe's Jews and Holocaust Survivors,* by Tom Bower, and *Hitler's Silent Partners: Swiss Banks, Nazi Gold, and the Pursuit of Justice,* by Isabel Vincent.

Videos

Heidi is undoubtedly the best-known film to be shot in Switzerland. Make sure you see the 1937 version directed by Allan Dulan, starring Shirley Temple. Swiss air must agree with James Bond; several films have Swiss scenes in them, including 1995's *GoldenEye* and *Goldfinger* (1964); *On Her Majesty's Secret Service* (1969) shows dazzling ski scenes of the Schilthorn in central Switzerland. You can also get glimpses of Swiss scenery in the 1994 version of *Frankenstein*. *Trois Couleurs Rouge (Three Colors Red),* the last in director Krzysztof Kieslowski's trilogy, and a big hit in Europe, is set in Geneva's Old Town, while Peter Greenaway's 1993 *Stairs* shows Geneva through the director's unique artistic vision. *The Unbearable Lightness of Being* follows a couple fleeing from the 1968 Russian invasion of Czechoslovakia. The moving *Reise der Hoffnung (Journey of Hope),* directed by Xavier Koller in 1990, centers on a Kurdish family fleeing Turkish persecution to seek sanctuary in Switzerland.

INDEX

You've read the book. Now book the trip.

For all the best deals on flights, hotels, rental cars, and vacation packages, book them online at www.previewtravel.com. Then click on our Destination Guides featuring content from Fodor's and more. You'll find hotels, restaurants, attractions, and things to do around the globe. There are even interactive maps, videos, and weather forecasts. You'll have everything you need to make your vacation exactly what you want it to be. All it takes is a trip online.

Travel on Your Terms™
www.previewtravel.com
aol keyword: previewtravel

preview travel SM

WHEREVER
YOU TRAVEL,
*H*ELP IS NEVER
FAR AWAY.

From planning your trip to providing travel assistance along the way, American Express® Travel Service Offices are always there to help you do more.

> ## *Switzerland*

BASEL
Reisebuero Wm Mueller & Co. Ltd.
Steinenvorstadt 33
41/61/2813380

LAUSANNE
American Express Travel Service
14 Avenue Mon-Repos
41/21/3101900

BERNE
Kehrli & Oeler
Bubenbergplatz 9
41/313110022

LUCERNE
American Express Travel Service
Schweizerhofquai 4
41/41/4100077

GENEVA
American Express Travel Service
7 Rue du Mont Blanc
41/22/7317600

LUGANO
VIP Travels SA
Via Al Forte 10
41/91/9238545/6/7

SION
Valais Incoming–Sion
Avenue De La Gare 4
41/27/3292424

Travel

www.americanexpress.com/travel

American Express Travel Service Offices are located throughout Switzerland.